The Millennial New World

The Millennial New World

Frank Graziano

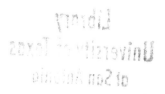

New York   Oxford

Oxford University Press

1999

Oxford University Press

Oxford   New York
Athens   Auckland   Bangkok   Bogotá   Buenos Aires   Calcutta
Cape Town   Chennai   Dar es Salaam   Delhi   Florence   Hong Kong   Istanbul
Karachi   Kuala Lumpur   Madrid   Melbourne   Mexico City   Mumbai
Nairobi   Paris   São Paulo   Singapore   Taipei   Tokyo   Toronto   Warsaw

and associated companies in
Berlin   Ibadan

Published by Oxford University Press, Inc.
198 Madison Avenue, New York, New York 10016

Oxford is a registered trademark of Oxford University Press, Inc.

Library of Congress Cataloging-in-Publication Data
Graziano, Frank, 1955–
The millennial New World / Frank Graziano.
p.   cm.
Includes index.
ISBN 0-19-512432-4
1. Millennialism—Latin America—History.   2. Latin America—
Religion.   I. Title.
BL2540.G73   1999
306'.1'098—dc21   98-36634

1 3 5 7 9 8 6 4 2
Printed in the United States of America
on acid-free paper

For Werner Herzog

The stars are a mess.

Acknowledgments

My greatest debt is to the hundreds of scholars whose fieldwork, archival research, and analyses provided the source material from which this survey was derived. I am particularly grateful to those scholars who commented on sections of the manuscript, including Alicia Barabas, Peter Bakewell, Gordon Brotherston, Michael F. Brown, Davíd Carrasco, Krishan Kumar, Richard Landes, Bernard McGinn, William L. Merrill, Steve J. Stern, and especially Rudolph Binion. The interlibrary loan service at Bender Library, American University, graciously accommodated my barrage of requests, and my student assistant, Maureen Contreni, expedited the research with admirable efficiency. American University's Department of Language and Foreign Studies funded this student assistance, and the College of Arts and Sciences funded travel that facilitated the research. The project was also significantly enhanced by a research fellowship at the Lilly Library, Indiana University, and by a residency at the Fundación Valparaíso in Mojácar, Spain. I express my sincere thanks to all. And finally, for my editor at Oxford University Press, Cynthia Read, I can only allude to a gratitude that remains ineffable.

Taylorstown, Virginia   F. G.
January 1999

Contents

The Millennial New World

Introduction

Ideologies and actions regarded variously as apocalyptic, messianic, millennial, and utopian have been prevalent in Latin America, as in much of the world, throughout the course of its history. Although the noted qualifiers tend to be used indiscriminately and, even when carefully applied, seem ambiguous, they nevertheless together designate a complex of cultural, social, religious, and political phenomena that hold identifiable attributes in common. My intent, following a succinct sorting of definitions, is to briefly catalog those attributes as an introduction to their illustration and analysis in the chapters that follow. It will become clear that the emphasis is on the syncretic post-conquest cases that predominate in the source material; that no individual case necessarily comprises all features of the generic composite; and that a certain suspension of nuance is necessary to collectively describe related but varied phenomena drawn from interacting African, American, and European cultures over a period of a thousand years. Such breadth likewise demands that the study as a whole make no claim to a comprehensive or exhaustive treatment. I intend an exposition more than an argument, pursuing the themes of millennialism across a range of representative cases and drawing conclusions only in passing. If overtly millennial ideologies and actions are considered beside those manifesting only nuanced suggestions, if nativist shamans, European kings, sect messiahs, and populists turn up with something in common, it is not to suggest that they are reducible to some secret essence, that they are equally important, or that their cultural and historical contexts are insignificant. The themes under discussion are dynamic precisely because the varied subject matter is permitted to speak through—not despite—the obvious differences.

That subject matter comes to us in texts that have the capacity to register millennial content regardless of their historical accuracy. The historian constructing a more or less objective representation of past events must sort through reliable and unreliable eye-witness accounts, competing oral and written histories, intentional and unwitting distortions, legend and myth, synthetic adaptations attempting to reconcile opposing paradigms, and political disinformation. All of these texts may evidence millennial thought, however, and they therefore together constitute this study's primary material. Myth and history, the apocryphal and the canonical, hearsay and hard data, distortion and the original that it bends to its purposes are in the present context all equally worthy of analysis, for it is indeed in the interplay of reliable and unreliable sources, in the forced reconciliation of opposing traditions, and in the defeat of implacable fact by the faith, hope, and deceptions elaborating it that the discourse of millennialism is generated. My primary concern is not the historicity of the events or the objective validity of the documents representing them, but rather how agreeing or competing versions register millennial thought in one culture, in another, or in the dialogical tension between the two.

The most fascinating Latin American cases are precisely those in which the millennial ideologies of opposing cultures came into contact and interacted. The Tupí-Guaraní, for example, migrated across the South American continent seeking the Land-without-Evil, a paradise promised by their prophets. Instead they found Spanish conquerors who were pursuing their own millennial myths and who, consequently, managed to hear in whatever the naked Indians uttered a confirmation that the fabulously rich El Dorado was located in the Amazon.[1] The instance is unique in that mutually alien peoples were guided by separate millennial traditions—one American, the other European—to this strange interchange outside of Chachapoyas, Peru. Each encountered only the other as both pursued their millennial dreams. Something of a hybrid composite was then actualized in the Jesuit reductions of Paraguay, populated by the Guaraní, in which culturally distinct meanings coalesced as both traditions (but under the purview of the priests) adapted to the new environment. For the Jesuits, Eden had triumphed over El Dorado. For the Guaraní, a land without forced labor may have seemed as good a Land-without-Evil as this world had to offer.

In other cases indigenous myths with millennial content were appropriated by the conquerors as part of a more general tendency to Christianize the remnants of native culture that survived deculturation and extirpation. Friars interpreting Aztec narratives of the returning hero Quetzalcóatl came to the fantastic conclusion that this legendary Toltec man-god was actually Christ's apostle Thomas, who was reputed to have evangelized "India." Once Quetzalcóatl had been absorbed by Saint Thomas, the Spaniards had new "evidence" applicable variously to explain the presence of crosses in the Americas, to claim that indigenous religions were nothing but a garbled Christianity, or to reinforce just-war arguments by appeal to the Christian responsibility to subjugate apostate natives who, as some believed, feigned ignorance and therefore made as much a mockery of the Spanish evangelization effort as they did earlier of Thomas's mission. An Aztec myth of messianic return was thereby strategically reinterpreted and deployed against its authors as a European empire expanded the domain of its own messiah.

A causal continuum of millennial thought and action likewise extended in the opposite direction, commencing with Spanish beliefs and terminating with adaptations that co-opted the Christian supernatural and redirected it to indigenous advantage. Motivated by Crusade ideology, medieval Last World Emperor traditions, and politico-religious interpretations of the New World, the imperial Spaniards viewed themselves as eschatological agents steering history toward its fixed conclusion in the millennial kingdom promised by John's Revelation. The natives on the receiving end of those ideals found in this colonial prelude to paradise not peace and plenty but rather a hellish subjugation that engendered a nativist response which drew from all sources—indigenous and imported—to construct a competing millennial ideal. Indigenous beliefs with pronounced millennial content inspired and sustained resistance efforts such as the War of Mixtón in Mexico, the Taqui Onqoy movement in the Andes, the Pueblo Revolt in what is now New Mexico, and the Caste War in the Yucatan, often borrowing strategically to redirect sacred Christian power (along with its indigenous counterpart) against the very Spanish invaders who introduced it. The salvation of one chosen people is the doom of another, but the latter maintains, as long as it can and by whatever means, the millennial dream of restoration. Meanings are volatile, identities are kept in circulation, and hierarchical relations are subject to inversion until the privileged position is secured by the rival who best manifests the power of the gods to establish forever, again, the beginning of a new era.

Definitions

The word *apocalypse* literally means "unveiling" or "revelation," implicitly of divine secrets regarding this world's destiny, and it counts among its primary meanings the literary genre in which such revelations are narrated. In this genre usage, for example, the Book of Daniel is referred to as an apocalypse. By trope and decree God reveals to the prophets his divine plan, which generally entails judgment, vindication, and redemption cataclysmically rendered.[2]

The adjective *apocalyptic* and its extension into the noun *apocalypticism*, however, have assumed distinct modern denotations pursuant to Judeo-Christian traditions epitomized by the concluding book of the Bible (known as both Apocalypse and Revelation). In this sense, apocalypticism stresses that the end, "however conceived, is imminent," with human history on the brink or in the midst of the last days.[3] Bernard McGinn has summarized apocalypticism, sometimes referred to as apocalyptic eschatology, as a "threefold pattern of crisis, judgment and salvation" and as "the conviction that the final division between good and evil, which is the goal of the divine plan for history, is in some way imminent."[4] If eschatology concerns the end of time and the final destiny of humanity, then its qualifier, *apocalyptic*, stresses the arrival of this end "in your own days, few and evil."[5]

The imminence is relative and the last days extend into centuries or millennia (perhaps because "one day with the Lord is as a thousand years, and a thousand years as one day"), but those adhering to apocalyptic beliefs nevertheless experience a sense of urgency.[6] While popular conceptions of apocalypse tend to gravitate toward doomsday imagery, apocalypticism can also be profoundly optimistic, with the focus on a heavenly hereafter or millennial kingdom envisioned beyond the conflagration.[7] Particularly in a multicultural context such as that of Latin America, "the apocalypse is ambivalent: condemnation of some and salvation of others, fear and hope, end and beginning."[8] Annihilation by cataclysm is uniformly forecast but not without providing that a righteous remnant will be spared and rewarded as lavishly as others will be punished. The apocalyptic hope or doomsday dread derive from each interpreter's expectation of "the great and terrible day of the Lord."[9]

The millennial kingdom developed in John's Revelation was preceded by the Old Testament prophets Ezekiel, Isaiah, and Daniel. In Isaiah's book, the past and present ages are viewed as defiled by sin, but an imminent new age promises total renovation through Yahweh's intervention in history. As worded in Isaiah 65:17–18, "I create new heavens and a new earth; and the former things shall not be remembered or come into mind." Isaiah's transformed world recovers something of the Eden lost in Genesis: "Then the wolf shall dwell with the lamb, and the leopard shall lie down with the kid; and the calf and the lion and the fatling together, and a little child shall lead them."[10] The blind shall see, the deaf shall hear, "then shall the lame leap like a deer, and the tongue of the dumb sing for joy."[11] Those unworthy of paradise, however, are slated for a separate fate in this decisive, divisive rebeginning. The warrior god Yahweh will destroy Israel's enemies along with "the wicked," "the lawless," and the "ungodly" Jews: "I will destine you to the sword, and all of you shall bow down to the slaughter; because, when I called, you did not answer."[12] Ezekiel 38–39 introduced the related idea, adapted by John in Revelation, that Israel's triumph in a cataclysmic war against Gog would inaugurate an age of peace, justice, and prosperity.

Military triumph as a prelude to an earthly paradise is also developed in the apocalypse of Daniel, where the Jews' "kingdom shall be an everlasting kingdom," because "it shall break in pieces" all other kingdoms "and bring them to an end."[13] When these ideas were later annexed by Christian tradition, emphasis was placed on a community of "holy ones" on earth—"people of the saints of the Most High"—who provided a this-worldly complement to the angelic "holy ones" in heaven.[14] Daniel prophesied four ages to be followed by a fifth, which features the Son of Man leading the armies of God to the final victory that precedes the everlasting kingdom. "The perfected state would be on earth, and the perfection of the people would be obtained not by their being transplanted to the sphere of Jehovah's abode, but by His coming down and dwelling among them."[15]

In the New Testament, John the Divine followed suit by announcing Christ's Second Coming to reign in glory over a terrestrial kingdom that would endure for a thousand years. According to a literal reading of Revelation 20–21, Satan would be bound in chains and sealed inside a bottomless pit to prepare the realm for the commencing blessed age. Christ would then realize the "first resurrection" of the martyrs whose steadfast faith merits the reward of exclusive residence in his kingdom. (Adepts of assorted millennial agendas "have equated the martyrs with the suffering faithful—themselves—and have expected the Second Coming in their lifetime.")[16] Once the thousand years had concluded, Satan would be freed from his imprisonment "for a short time," would resume his assault on God's kingdom with the auxiliary armies of Gog and Magog, and would be conquered by Christ once and for all as good definitively triumphed over evil. A second resurrection would summon forth "the dead, great and small" for the Last Judgment, and those "not found written in the book of life" would be sentenced to "the second death" and "cast into the lake of fire." The ordeal concludes felicitously for the righteous in "a new heaven and a new earth," a "new Jerusalem, coming down out of heaven from God," so that "the tabernacle of God is with men, and he will dwell with them, and they shall be his people, and God himself shall be with them, and be their God."[17]

Innumerable variations on this master plot have resulted from assorted exegeses of the cryptic tropes in Revelation, from simplified and secularized versions deployed for various religious and political purposes, from imperfect command of doctrine among the faithful, and from intermingling of the Revelation account with other apocalyptic and millennial traditions, all of these likewise "elaborated and reinterpreted and vulgarized."[18] Some interpreters classify these variations into two general tendencies, one "premillennial" and the other "postmillennial." Premillennialism follows the Revelation text most literally, holding that Christ's catastrophic Second Coming precedes and inaugurates the thousand-year reign; the role of humankind in this scenario is passive receipt of the divine plan, save the prudent preparation of one's soul. Postmillennialism, conversely, maintains that Christ returns after an earthly triumph by his vicars, who generally view themselves as living on the threshold of the Second Coming and charged with the awesome responsibility of preparing the world for their savior's reign. What remains constant in both cases are the major narrative components relating "a cataclysm from which the world is to emerge totally transformed and redeemed"; what varies is the degree of human agency.[19]

The term *millennialism*—also known as *millenarianism* and, in its Greek derivative, *chiliasm*—has detached from its thousand-year etymology (the Latin *mil* means "one thousand," and *annum* means "year"). Millennialism has come to signify any doctrine of salvation or redemption that is collective, total ("it is to utterly transform life"), and realized on this earth—in human history—rather than in a heavenly hereafter.[20] As Richard Landes has summarized it, millennialism is "a belief that these final events will usher in a reign of Peace, Justice and Plenty *here on earth* and that salvation for the Just will be collective and its rewards experienced while living in the flesh."[21]

The Judeo-Christian origin and connotations of *millennialism* make for clumsy application of the term to indigenous American cultures, to slave cultures, and, perhaps to a lesser degree, to secular political phenomena. My use of *millennialism* in such applications is a matter of convenience to avoid repetitive and cumbersome circumlocutions; where appropriate, the discussion is qualified by the adjective *nativist* to stress the explicit affirmation of indigenous culture in the means and goals of millennial programs. In these as in most instances of millennialism, the reference to a literal thousand-year kingdom presided over by Christ has been left in the etymological distance. The term *millennial* is applied far more broadly to religious, quasi-religious, and often secular phenomena that are motivated by a quest for salvation and by a deliberate effort to revitalize a society and culture, generally with the goal of inaugurating a golden age or accessing a paradise.[22] A conflagration with pronounced moral or religious content serves as the threshold event through which one troubled age is terminated and another glorious one is ushered in. The transformation occurs in human history, on earth rather than in a heavenly hereafter, and following the always promised but rarely realized triumph a messiah, or else his representative, presides over the chosen people who establish (or restore) the paradise that they exclusively inhabit and enjoy. Much millennial thought is also apocalyptic, which is to say imbued with a certain urgency exerted by the conviction that the end of time is imminent. Apocalyptic millennialism has a "politically dangerous quality" insofar as its quest for a communal, this-worldly redemption gains expression in violent struggles to restructure society.[23]

The power of millennialism among diverse peoples throughout history is partially the consequence of the dynamic, mutually reciprocating relation that it activates between religion and politics. Millennialism catalyzes postponed insurrections and provides holy-war legitimation for assaults against regimes perceived to be evil. It imbues the local dispute with cosmic importance, renders militancy—however bloody—a manifestation of divine will, rewards success in battle with eternal and universal sovereignty, and assuages defeat with the promise of heroic return or divine vindication. Exemplary among the Judeo-Christian antecedents of modern millennialism is Daniel's prophesy (written during the Maccabean Revolt, which resulted from persecution under Antiochus) that forecast the overthrow of the Greek empire and Israel's subsequent dominion of the world for all eternity. In the New Testament, John's Revelation (not to mention Jesus' crucifixion) was also politically conditioned, here by a "savage opposition to Rome."[24] Spanish millennialism was forged during centuries of warfare against Islam, with this crusading militancy later adapting to the New World theater where its imperial eschatology was refined. The insurrections of conquered American theocracies then emerged under the aegis of resuscitating deities calling for the revitalization of native cultures; these were followed in turn by wars of independence and by revolutions that in their respective ways found religious or quasi-religious impetus for economic, social, and political reform.

Although the distinction between internal and external factors that precipitate millennial movements is inapplicable in some cases and inexact in most, the classification of movements as "endogenous" or "exogenous" is provisionally useful in the New World context. Endogenous millennialism, such as that of the Spanish conquest and evangelization of the Americas, is self-propelled by the salvation agendas of nonoppressed and often imperial peoples who pursue an eschatology construed in the positive terms of a collaboration between God and his creation. Exogenous movements, such as nativist rebellions resisting colonial rule, emerge in response to external factors that threaten sociocultural survival. They demand efficacious action, usually violent, to eradicate the threat and revive an idealized version of their preconquest society.[25] "Because these movements are both popular and revolutionary, new and able to renew, because they are spurred by the urgent and vital needs of oppressed people and societies caught in a dilemma, they look to the future and to the regeneration of the world."[26] Whether millennial action is motivated from within, from without, or—as in many cases—from the dynamic relation of the two, "the very word 'movement' often implies something with far more coherence, more order, and more organization than the actual manifestation of collective behavior in reality possesses."[27]

The word *messiah* is derived from a Hebrew adjective meaning "anointed," used in the Old Testament primarily in reference to royal figures and high priests. Something of the politico-religious nature of modern *messianism* is suggested by the anointments carried in the etymology of the word, for these rituals were conducted on the occasion of a king's coronation or a priest's induction, conferring an elite, symbolic status upon their recipients. Messianism thereby emerged with two prototypes, the kingly and the priestly, with the dual identity of "the anointed one" often unified in a single politico-religious composite. As monotheism and the identity of the Israelites were consolidated, the model of Old Testament messianism evolved from the religion-based agency of priests and prophets to the military- and political-based agency of warrior kings. This new messiah was summoned to defeat Israel's enemies and to enthrone himself on Mount Zion, reigning—like David—as vicar of the mighty Yahweh, "terrible in glorious deeds," who himself consolidated political (warrior-king) and religious (deity) identities.[28] As Exodus 15:3 unambiguously expressed it, "The Lord is a man of war." The later extension of politico-religious messianism into Christianity and Christendom is clear enough in the warrior Christ of Revelation; in the teachings of the Vatican, following Augustine's realized eschatology, that the millennial kingdom of Christ is nothing other than the Catholic Church here and now; and in titles such as Holy Roman Emperor or Catholic Monarchs.[29] The messiah thinks religiously and acts politically, presiding over eschatological war, smiting the evil nations, delivering the chosen, restoring the empire, and reigning universally, absolutely, and vicariously for the deity he claims as his otherworldly ally.

Millennialism generally requires a messianic protagonist and terminates in what is sometimes described as a messianic kingdom, and consequently *millennialism* and *messianism*, along with their corresponding adjectives, have often been used interchangeably. In more careful usage, *messianism* is reserved to emphasize the centrality of a numinous leader as the agent of a salvation agenda, whereas *millennialism* is employed as the more comprehensive term, providing the context in which the messiah is meaningful and accentuating not individual action but the long view of eschatological transformation for the collective. While the term *messiah* is heavily freighted with religious and, particularly, Judeo-Christian connotations, its broader usage encompasses cultural heroes and charismatic leaders whose programs are characterized by salvation, delivery, or redemption of aggrieved communities disposed to but hitherto incapable of collective action against political or religious adversaries.[30] Oppressed peoples "anticipate the emergence of a hero who will restore their prosperity and prestige," and even secular leaders who appear amidst such anticipation are "imbued with religious fervour."[31]

A prophet is generally distinguished from a messiah in that the former announces or represents a savior, whereas the latter is regarded as that savior himself. The distinction seems contrived, however, in contexts where a coalescing of constructed identities blurs the difference between the one who announces the messiah and the one who incarnates him. When the message is appealing, particularly among uneducated or polytheistic communities, a prophet is frequently deified and received as a messiah, sometimes despite repeated efforts to defend the distinction and sometimes to the prophet's glee and greater glory as he or she maneuvers among a people predisposed to manipulation. A true prophet—distinguished now from the messiah—is a messenger announcing (but also interpreting) a revelation presumed to be of divine or semidivine origin. Prophets recruit, be it to prayer or to warfare, on the strength of popular conviction in their revelations, which frequently feature the imminence of or need for an eschatological cataclysm, the coming of a messiah or other agent of cosmic transformation, and the customary millennial kingdom awaiting the well-behaved who heed their call.

The word *utopia* was introduced by the publication of Sir Thomas More's book by the same title in 1516, but the concept of a golden age that informs More's *Utopia* was recorded early in antiquity.[32] Like *apocalypse*, *utopia* is sometimes used in reference to a literary genre, in the present case one born of "aesthetic discontent in view of squalor, corruption, disorder, and disharmony" to envision instead "an ideal society created by conscious human effort on this earth."[33] For Louis Marin, "Utopia is a critique of dominant ideology insofar as it is a reconstruction of contemporary society by means of a displacement and a projection of its structures into a fictional discourse."[34]

In the seventh century B.C.E. Hesiod was already lamenting the loss of a time when people "lived as if they were gods, their hearts free from all sorrow, and without hard work or pain" because "the fruitful earth yielded its abundant harvest to them of its own accord, and they lived in ease and peace."[35] Plato, Virgil, and Ovid followed suit, but the most celebrated utopian narrative resulted when the golden age was assimilated to Judeo-Christian tradition to produce the Genesis account of the Garden of Eden, a paradise lost as the Bible commences. Eden and the innumerable lost-paradise myths of indigenous American traditions attest to the perennial human longing to recover (even if the original was mythic) a squandered or elusive utopia. Hesiod's golden age is gone forever and "bitterly lamented," but Christianity made the necessary compensatory adjustment to provide a paradise that "lay not only in the past but also in the future," and not only in time but also in space.[36]

Like *messianism*, the term *utopianism* tends to be confused with *millennialism*, in this case because both utopias and the kingdoms with which millennial programs conclude are variations of terrestrial paradise. Although *utopia* is imbued with more secular and *millennial kingdom* with more religious connotations ("a utopia is indeed the City of Man and not a City of God," "free from the medieval entanglement with theological concerns"), differentiation of the concepts on that basis is unsatisfactory in a Latin American context in which, for example, viceroys were guided by the Bible and bishops consulted More's *Utopia* during their joint cross-and-sword colonization of a New World.[37] Another ready but ultimately useless distinction is provided etymologically, with *millennium* being essentially temporal and *utopia*—sliding between *ou-topos* (no place) and *eu-topos* (good place)—being spatial. This led Martin Buber to identify the search for "perfect time" on one hand and "perfect space" on the other, but in human, earthbound experience time comes only with space, delivering renditions of the elusive utopia as always here but not now, or now but not here.[38] As Northrop Frye put it, "Utopia, in fact and in etymology, is not a place; and when the society it seeks to transcend is everywhere, it can only fit into what is left," an imaginary space or a future time.[39]

Utopia and the millennium together occupy a past-future that recovers an imaginary ideal projected onto an inaccessible landscape. When space is sorted from time, the millennial promise is perpetually imminent but perpetually postponed, a deferred eschatology that is complemented in the spatial realm by utopias that always dissipate in the haze just beyond reach. The psychosocial and certainly political benefits of utopian and millennial thought are not in the realization of paradise on earth, for this never occurs, but rather in the amelioration of a painful present through its negation and projection—inverted, perfected—out of range. Utopianism and millennialism are inherently doomed to failure, but their benefits survive their postponed demise through a flight to the future that redeems the present. Collective hopelessness is defeated by the possibility, however slim, of the promise's fulfillment. A community in abeyance celebrates its ecstatic faith against the odds, balancing suffering with hope and helplessness with the efficacy of symbolic actions that challenge fatalistic despair.

The Attributes of Millennialism

A crisis, be it real or perceived, sudden or chronic, provides the context of instability, profound discontent, and often desperation within which a salvation agenda is introduced. The specific factors conducive to emergent millennial sentiments include "slavery, colonization, economic and social exploitation, political and social domination, migration, forced deculturation, racial segregation, simple cultural diversity, and the tension, malaise and socio-cultural disorganization which these factors cause in the traditional society or parts of it."[40]

The protagonist of salvation tends to be a charismatic male from outside the community, generally more privileged, educated, and experienced than his poor and naive followers.[41] This aura of superiority is sometimes acquired by an individual of humble origin who leaves the community and then returns empowered (after education, religious experience, or military service, for example), having assimilated aspects of the dominant culture. He merits special regard as an inside-outsider who in some sense has been chosen—but who also himself has chosen—to deploy his ingenuity, relative social superiority, and seemingly supernatural capacities on behalf of his underclass people. In all cases, the messianic leader's outsider status is particularly meaningful given the "liminality" ("any condition outside or on the peripheries of everyday life") within which he emerges.[42] He is often accompanied by a coterie of close and dedicated followers, sometimes referred to in religious terms as "disciples," "apostles," and "holy family" or, in the many cases in which this inner circle is female, as "virgins." The messianic leader may be racially distinct from the people who follow him, but he nevertheless exploits racial tensions. He is frequently perceived as the return of a previous cultural hero or deity—with this figurative death and rebirth paralleling that of the defeated social order being revitalized—and his claim to power is validated by the revitalization, adaptation, and selective emphasis of corroborating myths and prophesies of salvation. His radical message provides "a refuge from a world of decay, deprivation and increasing isolation," along with "a locus of stability, certainty, and confidence in times of bewildering and disruptive change, and a sense of vision and purpose for a future that otherwise appeared perilous and uncertain."[43] Those who follow him look backward as much as forward, seeking continuity in rupture, projecting a reconstructed traditional ideal, and recuperating a nostalgic past in an imaginary future. What they escape is the present.

A messiah is heroic insofar as his followers are dispossessed. The people most receptive to the messianic message are disenfranchised, marginalized, and defeated social groups that have had extended contact with a dominant culture. They are characterized by political voicelessness and chronic poverty, collective loss of dignity, disorientation, and destabilized confidence in imposed or traditional morals, values, and solutions. A "crisis of integration," often forced integration, favorably disposes them to the radical alternative offered by eschatological interpretations of injustice.[44] Communities prone to messianism are particularly volatile when their basic subsistence needs are jeopardized, when they lose benefits to which they once had access, when they are literally or figuratively overtaxed, or when chronic hardships and abuses are aggravated by augmented labor obligations, assaults against the sacrosanct, epidemics, or other traumatic surprises. Like the followers of Jesus in Galilee, they need not be pious or worthy to be received; "the fact that they were usually excluded was commendation enough."[45] In an entrapping circularity, they are chosen because they are members of an underclass and then they constitute a new, elite underclass— often perceived as a political threat—by virtue of having been chosen. If radical solutions appeal to them it is because "they have rarely been afforded the luxury of open, organized, political activity," and because attempts at licit sociopolitical action have proved "dangerous, if not suicidal."[46] Having exhausted or despaired of options within the system, they gravitate toward apocalyptic politics that seek "a sudden and total transformation of their physical, social and psychological environment."[47]

The messiah's charismatic force, often perceived to be indicative of his divine origin or election, is usually made manifest through an agitative oratory that mobilizes masses by tapping the reservoir of their collective, repressed needs. As the messiah expresses this prohibited discourse he transforms individual despair into collective hope, massive indignity into the collective glorification of a chosen people who, no longer helpless, can exercise their two basic options: retaliation channeled toward millennial ends or isolationist retreat into a peaceable kingdom. His interpretive and rhetorical skills lend a voice to the voiceless, articulating the latent aspirations of people who "feel their problems rather than know them," perhaps because they have lived, as Ambrose encouraged, by the "pious ignorance" that accepts rather than inquires.[48] The charismatic speaks back to the community its own unarticulated desires, but he at once demands submission to the dogmatism and absolute authority by which he benevolently reigns. He appeals to and often integrates a community's traditions, values, and belief systems into the alien message of salvation that he introduces, but his balancing act manipulates these, breaking down previous allegiances and animosities, reconfiguring social hierarchies, revising traditional beliefs and morals, and rearranging social reality and individual self-identity in conformity with the new paradigm that he introduces to reverse the existing social order. Tradition is at once exalted and jettisoned as a "charismatic bond" of mutual (if asymmetrical) interdependence forges the fate of the leader and his community.[49] The messiah is both son and father, the one born of the community and the one who lays down the law. His authority and worthiness of veneration are undisputed because they are advanced on credit, but the fate of his contingent, precarious reign is determined first by the masses who for better or worse assess his performance and then by the troops who are eventually dispatched to detain him.

The legitimacy of the messianic leader is generally grounded in little more than his charismatic presence and, in many cases, the mythic charge he accrues as the return of a previous deity or cultural hero. The greater the faith in the probability of a return, the greater the reception of a messiah. His strongest assets are his capacity to "accept" the identities superimposed on him—thereby drawing on reserves of traditional as well as charismatic legitimacy—and in all cases to be the embodiment, the resurrection of the moribund collective will of a people. He need not believe in the authenticity of his powers in order to represent them convincingly to his followers. A messianic leader initiates or enhances his claim to legitimacy with supernatural reinforcements such as prophesies, miracles, nonmedical cures, or, more generally, some authorizing doctrine or document. If the medieval messiahs appeared in villages with letters from Christ or the Virgin, modern messiahs are buttressed by oracular messages, commandments from heaven, royal mandates, ancestral callings, doctrines demystified for the uninitiated, and, perhaps most important, the authenticating folklore generated by the recipient communities themselves, which eventually precedes the messiah—now mythologized—to condition his reception among new constituencies. In many Latin American cases, a fusion of indigenous and Christian beliefs endows the messianic leader with a highly charged composite identity.

Insurrections instigated by such leaders sometimes have one meaning for their protagonist and quite another for the indigenous peoples enacting or witnessing them. The millennial content emerges in this nexus where actions engage dialectically with the multiple interpretations seeking to claim them.

Unification or reunification of a perceived fragmentation, particularly when imbued with a sense of morality or urgency, is also characteristically millennial. The messiah reassembles a world that is falling apart, and the pieces align in accord with the gravitational pull of the new paradigm installed to reconfigure them. Social reality is polarized to reduce complexity to duality, and a struggle reminiscent of that between archetypal good and evil positions the chosen people in opposition to all otherness. Paradise is the reward of those who follow the messiah; others, inimical by default, are consigned to an apocalypse often introduced by the armed hordes of the messiah's legions. When force is insufficient or inappropriate, withdrawal and ritually reinforced separatism isolate the chosen people from the polluted world that they abandon. Within sacred confines they are reborn through purification and initiation, possession states, rituals of undoing and redoing, return to tradition, common bellicose cause, and blood sacrifice. Adherence to the movement abruptly restructures their perceptions to privilege a "moral regeneration: the creation of a new man, the creation of new unities, the creation of a new society."[50]

And also the creation of a new age. Christian history is necessarily "universal, providential, apocalyptic, and periodized," but syncretic and nativist millennialism likewise play as "strongly periodized dramas."[51] The commencement of the new age coincides with the appearance of a messiah and the inception of a movement or, in more apocalyptic visions, with an era beyond some cataclysmic punctuation—flood, holocaust, earthquake, total war, change of suns—that stops the clock and restarts it. In this "eschatological dualism" enforced by some rigid temporal marker, the chosen people often view themselves as the protagonists who intervene in history to separate the past from the future.[52] On one side of the divide are decadence and woes plummeting toward cosmic catastrophe, and on the other side are regeneration, plenitude and joy. When the transition between ages entails a punitive conflagration, then an asylum (such as an ark, treetops, rapture, or an Edenic safe haven) shelters the saving remnant so that it may return to the purified earth and procreate the new humanity.

A hierarchical inversion of social roles, like that of carnival, is also patent in millennialism. Social outcasts become chosen people, the slaves become masters, and the poor become wealthy as the world is turned upside down. Once insurrectional, an oppressed people's earlier exaltation of equality and justice tends to yield to the vengeful violence that accompanies their (temporary) inversion of social roles. The mimetic nature of such violence is conspicuous—the perpetrator and the victim have merely exchanged roles. Mimesis also characterizes the movement's construction of its own identity in relation to the antithetical other that it seeks to depose and destroy, but also to become. The enemy is depicted in the absolutely negative terms characteristic of this polarized milieu, and the chosen community establishes its own identity dialectically as an inversion of the negative paradigm that it has constructed. The other's pure evil becomes the chosen people's pure goodness as negative attributes assigned to the other are inverted and retrieved in the construction of an idealized self-image. Despite their genocidal efforts to eliminate their enemies, the existence, meaning, and purpose of many millennial movements are ultimately dependent upon Manichean opposition.

Such symbolic targets as cruel and corrupt officials, members of a privileged class, representatives of the sacrosanct, or their hapless, more accessible surrogates are selected from outside the chosen community (executed insiders are first ostracized or otherwise symbolically distanced, sometimes through mock trials). The generation and ritual "sacrifice" of scapegoats provides that the negative attributes associated with them (oppression, greed, evil, guilt for the kill) flow away from the chosen community, while their positive attributes (power, wealth, dignity, status) flow toward it.[53] Such executions also function as foundation sacrifices insofar as the spilled blood bonds the community and founds its common destiny on a transgression that cannot be atoned. Millennial violence often begins as necessary and selective; progresses to a more indiscriminate, normalized violence; and then, by appeal to innovative arguments of morality, divine right, self-defense, or genocidal obligation, graduates to a celebratory violence reinforced by vindictiveness and rage.

In the last stage the violence is ritualized and graphic, with the fallen and sometimes dismembered body of the enemy serving as an emblem of the chosen people's victory and as a "speaking corpse" (the creation of a community formerly voiceless) emitting messages through its brutalized silence. The paradoxical discrepancy between the declared and actual beneficiaries of such violence is sometimes conspicuous, with the destruction falling back precisely upon the chosen people who are ostensibly being saved by the movement. This is particularly evident when the boundaries between the chosen and the other are not clearly delineated, when a messiah exploits ignorance to his political advantage, or when the authoritarian demand for absolute compliance generates "traitors." When the messiah himself dies or is killed, the active agenda that he inspired and maintained tends to relax into a latency charged with anticipation until it is reactivated by a new crisis or new charismatic leader.[54]

The violent death of most adherents to millennial movements is the result of attack by the armed forces of regimes eager to eliminate the manifest or potential threat of heresy, subversion, or insurrection. As the inverted hierarchy is restored to its "natural" order, the messiahs who had made promises—the stones would turn into allies, the dead would be spontaneously resurrected, the enemy's bullets would be transformed into water—are incapable of protecting their followers from the massacre that invariably awaits them precisely where they had expected their millennial kingdom. The messianic promise is always broken.[55] Having sought alleviation of despair in a radical program unacceptable to a dominant class or culture, the chosen people find themselves again with nowhere to turn except toward the fatal consequences of their salvation.

1
Crisis and Salvation

The kingdom of God is at hand.
—Mark 1:15

The Imminent End

An end is always imminent in millennialism; what varies is the way it is regarded. In cases sometimes referred to as "premillennial" a preoccupation with sinfulness results in an emphasis on judgment, with a vengeful deity punishing the wicked perhaps more than he rewards the righteous. A salvation agenda intervenes to prepare the chosen—meaning those recruited to that agenda—not so much for heavenly glory as for a gloomy, apocalyptic doomsday. The clock lingers at the last hour, and in the borrowed-time eschatology characteristic of Evangelical Protestants in Latin America today this reprieve is humanity's last chance. The dispatch of individual souls to hell will be generalized for the wretched collective, once and for all, through a deluge of fire and brimstone.

A "great fear, sprung from a dark diagnosis of the present," is generated and deployed as extra incentive for those not motivated by the beneficence of grace alone.[1] In the Catholic mission centuries earlier Luis de Granada unambiguously asserted that an emphasis on judgment and hell "contributes greatly to terrify the hearts of men" and consequently "disposes many hearts to accept the Faith."[2] Hernán Cortés had barely begun the conquest of Mexico when he informed the natives, Moctezuma among them, that their idolatry reserved for them a special place in hell, "where they would burn forever in living flames."[3] Bernardino de Sahagún elaborated the point in his sermons to the conquered natives, synthesizing an Atzec afterworld and the Christian hell to depict a locale "in darkness, in gloom" where sinners are tormented by fire, beatings, worms, stench, hunger, thirst, and fatigue at the will of human-eating monsters with metal teeth, tongues of flame, and molars like sacrificial stones.[4] Among a people who had no concept of postmortem punishment of sin but who held that human transgression could provoke cosmic destruction, the friars also found it expedient to associate individual or social sins with collective, end-of-the-world scourges, again rendered apocalyptically.[5]

The Christian concepts of sin and guilt were prominent among the abstract commodities exported to the Spanish colonies. The fear of punishment and damnation that expedited the conversion of conquered natives to Catholicism also generated the by-product of a new breed of prophets—now indigenous—who internalized, Indianized, and literalized the friars' message, setting out then to disseminate their innovative sad tidings among the people. In seventeenth-century Mexico, an Indian named Miguel Ximénez preached an apocalyptic homily with crucifix in hand, announcing the imminence of doomsday, the punishment of drunkards, and the damnation to hellfire of the incredulous. "If you do not believe what I say," Ximénez added, "when you leave the church you will drop dead."[6] The prophet of a 1711 movement among the highland Maya similarly extorted obedience by convincing his people that the Christian God would annihilate their unworthy corner of creation.[7]

The threatened apocalypse never materialized and the distant or indifferent deity seemed vengeful only through the agency of Spaniards, but edifying narratives nevertheless circulated to reinforce the promise that God is terrible, that sins are punished, and that the end is always imminent. Such was the moral of a tale concerning an indigenous prophet who, by his own claim, had been sent by the Christian God to redeem the Chiriguano people. The prophet warned that God was prepared to "destroy by His own hand" those who rejected the true faith. In flagrant disregard of the prophet's prohibition against cannibalism, however, a cacique had a slave boy cooked and died immediately following his feast.[8] The tale registers the interplay of the three basic options available to conquered Indians—active acceptance, passive compliance, and overt defiance—to echo the familiar message that backsliding into pre-Christian practices provokes the retaliation of God, not to mention that of the extirpators. More ominous was the fear that persistence in idolatry or apostasy would result in destruction of the entire unrepentant race. As the Christianized Andean chronicler Felipe Guaman Poma de Ayala expressed it from Peru in the early seventeenth century, God "will make the earth swallow us up as He made it swallow Sodom and He burned the three provinces with fire from the sky." He added, "You have another Sodom in Huamanga, Quito, Cuzco," and therefore "someday the punishment of God will come" bringing "judgment and justice."[9]

The Maya in particular were adamant in their adherence to adaptations of Christian apocalypticism. Amidst descriptions of the four-cornered Maya cosmos and a series of exclusively indigenous episodes, a passage in the *Chilam Balam* describes a flooded finale for humankind, followed by a sacrifice-laden Second Coming featuring Jesus Christ appearing beside Jerusalem, "where he redeemed us with his holy blood." "He shall descend in a great cloud to bear true testimony that he was once obliged to suffer stretched out on a cross of wood," and he will then "level off the world for the good and the bad, the conquerors and the captives."[10] The modern Yucatec Maya complement this version of the world's end with a customized apocalypse rendered in full detail. At the imminent end of time the sun will mercilessly scorch the earth for seven years, during which "not even an ant" will be born. Water will be stingily apportioned only to those who relinquish their infants to a mysterious wench in the ruins of Uxmal. The Maya will be nourished by prayer until the trumpets sound, Christ appears, and the dead are resurrected, at which time the Last Judgment, also in Uxmal, will bring a series of trials. One trial requires balancing on "the great living rope" that leads into the open mouth of a dragon; another torturous episode has the Antichrist extract the nails of fingers and toes in an attempt to coerce false witness. The heavenly gates are opened for those who persevere in the faith, the fingernails and toenails are restored, and the dreaded eternity of agony fades into oblivion as one is subsumed into everlasting grace and joy. The damned, however, eternally suffer the consequence of their iniquities in the horror chambers of a Mayanized inferno.[11]

Apocalyptic scenarios are plentiful among the prophets of doom whose churches proliferate throughout contemporary Latin America. Frequently repeated admonishments such as "time is running out" and "we are living in the last days" combine with literal readings of apocalyptic imagery—"the sun will be darkened," "stars will fall out of the sky"—to engender an existential fear that only the faith can alleviate.[12] One Pentecostal missionary believed that the end of the world was imminent in 1970 because nine conversions coincided with a bright light in the sky above Chetumal.[13] When the Puerto Rican Pentecostal preacher Yiye Avila visited Arequipa, Peru, in 1987, he set the tone of coercive enlistment by appealing to natural catastrophe as the instrument of God's punishment. Avila's booming oratory informed Arequipans gathered in the coliseum that they "rightly deserved God's wrath for their terribly sinful conduct." Arequipa was a city without faith (because of its traditionally strong Catholicism) and destined for oblivion unless it renounced its evil ways. Avila cited scripture to prophesy earthquakes and volcanic eruptions (the city has a history of both) along with other God-sent "rewards" to scourge this "pool of evil" that had so insolently provoked God with its audacious sinfulness. Once the sermon had reached its climax and Avila had maximized the collective mood of panic and dread, this ambience, as one observer put it, "served as a bridge to the next item on the agenda": conversion. Avila felt the presence of Jesus in the coliseum, called for converts "because time is running out," and then counted backward from ten as he mimed in miniature his eschatological message, warning that "everlasting death" would await whoever failed to respond to the call.[14]

In the distance traveled from the colonial Catholic Miguel Ximénez to the modern Pentecostal Yiye Avila the message and strategy have changed little, save for the refinement of the drama and props for the modern market and the shift of register that insulated Avila's "everlasting death" from tests of truth. Ximénez's skeptics who dared to reject the faith, disregarded the warning that they would "drop dead," and survived their insolent exit from the church had nothing to fear, for they exposed the empty threats of the (false) prophet by calling his bluff. Indeed, in a parallel Andean case during the 1781 Túpac Catari rebellion, a friar warned Indians in the church at Tiguina that they would be punished for their disrespect of the holy sacrament and for their audacious profanation of God's sanctuary. The Indians paused to consult, decided to sack the church anyway, and departed defiantly, but not without a lingering fear that God might strike them dead as they crossed the threshold. When the threatened punishment failed to materialize, they understood that the ersatz or absentee deity was no match for their armed apostasy. The rebel Indians reentered the church, slaughtering all the Spaniards there.[15]

Ximénez unwittingly defined the life span of an agenda that could not survive its own contentions, which set the stage for reciprocal empowerment of those, like the Túpac Catari rebels, who were willing to risk a test of its veracity. Avila, conversely, clouded the meaning of death and the imminent end in a halo of imprecision and tangency, his prophesy always sufficiently vague to absorb its failure to materialize and always sufficiently volatile to have its exigency renewed from without by apocalyptic oratory and from within by the guilt and fear generated by his audience's "sins."

The tendency of Christian apocalypticism to attach its indeterminate imminence to a specified date was initiated by Jesus himself, who erroneously maintained that the kingdom of God would be established before the death of his apostles.[16] The Pauline predicament "of an end-time that would not end, an ahistory that was itself becoming historical," has since constituted Christian apocalypticism's inherent paradox.[17] In Latin America the end of the world has been scheduled by innumerable disconfirmed prophesies, but once the dates come and go they are glossed over, revised with updated prophesies and visions, recalculated by sevens, and insulated in accommodating generalities as prudent prophets exploit the ambiguity of "soon." The magnetism of eschatological urgency can coexist with a measure of longevity only insofar as the concept of imminence is blurred. In the 1920s when a Seventh-Day Adventist named F. A. Stahl brought a doomsday message to the Peruvian jungle, an imminent end most literally interpreted made no such compromise in the minds of the Asháninka, who "expected Christ to appear today or tomorrow." A massive following of Asháninka congregated on the banks of the Perené to await the cataclysm in which "the dead would arise, all evil would be destroyed, and the believers and risen dead would be taken to the house of God in the sky where there would be no more sickness, death, or growing old."[18] For modern Tupí-Guaraní peoples, the world does not end at a specified time but rather when the sky, overladen with too many of these risen dead people, bursts open and collapses onto the earth.[19]

For others, the end of time is fixed by divine appointment on a date of particular significance, such as the end of the millennium in the year 2000. Pentecostal converts among the Chilean Mapuche share with many indigenous Christians the expectation that the world and the millennium end together.[20] Customized millennial expectations among the Pilagá of South America's Gran Chaco feature an angelic brass section announcing the Second Coming for the year 2000, with Christ returning in the company of the cultural hero Luciano.[21] For members of the Brotherhood of the Cross in the Amazon, the end of time "will be around the year 2000, when the Brotherhood will have spread all over the world."[22] An anthropological survey conducted in the Peruvian jungle in the late 1970s likewise documented the widely held belief that "the world is going to end in the year 2000," in part because "the world is tired."[23]

A stress on apocalypse tends to overshadow the encore promised as much by Jesus' resurrection as by John's Revelation, but the millennial kingdom beyond doomsday has not been forgotten. As an Ecuadorian Evangelical summarized it, "The world is going to end at the end of the century; but Christ, who will come on clouds, is going to form a new world" in which he will be "the King and only politician."[24] In 1969 a Christian Toba of the Argentine Chaco also revived the geriatric earth when he reemphasized the millennial provision for rejuvenation: "The world is old, everything is old and worn out," he conceded, but "Jesus Christ will change things and make them be born anew, as in the times of Noah's flood."[25] Other indigenous Christians find in the legend of Noah's ark an alternate route to salvation. Practical millennialists among the Shipibo and Conibo of the Peruvian Amazon have constructed floating wooden houses to survive the deluge and earthquake that will soon "liquidate" the earth.[26] In the Yucatec city of Campeche, similarly, the followers of a woman called María Regina began in 1980 to sell their properties in order to finance the construction of a new Noah's ark, upon which they too plan to navigate the coming flood.[27]

The tendency to literalize—Bible stories, salvation, even liquidation—combines with the tropes of physical and sociocultural weariness ("the world is tired") to represent a complex human drama of survival in all of its senses: corporal, cultural, metaphysical. But survival is not salvation, and those indoctrinated in the faith with greater depth and sophistication recognize that a houseboat is beside the point because it confuses the body in this world with the soul in the next. "The cross is similar to the ark of the patriarch Noah," relates a member of the Brotherhood of the Cross; "it is the only means to escape this terrible disaster."[28] One escapes doom not by bobbing about on a lifeboat but, like Christ, by standing up sin free to be counted, because the gain far exceeds the pain. That was the message that had the power to congregate the Asháninka on the riverbank: death undone by resurrection, death as life everlasting in paradise.

When the year 2000, like former predicted ends, comes and goes without cataclysm, the prophets of doom have recourse to any number of biblical passages to patch up their damaged credibility: "It is not for you to know the times or dates the Father has decided by his own authority," or again, "Of that day or that hour no one knows, not even the angels in heaven, nor the Son, but only the Father."[29] One can also argue that the linear or cyclical nature of human time is inapplicable to the eternal present of deity, a simultaneity shared by souls while bodies are sentenced to death in mundane temporality. In his *Book of Prophesies*, Christopher Columbus noted that "in the Holy Scriptures the verbs in the past tense are sometimes used for the future." Then he quoted Isidore of Seville on the point: "But why should future events be described as having already happened? It is because things that are still future to us, have already happened according to God's viewpoint in eternity."[30] Along these same lines, in recent years, the voice of God revealed to the Peruvian messiah Ezequiel

Ataucusi Gamonal that Ataucusi himself was the author of the Book of Ezekiel, one of the biblical texts most associated with apocalyptic and millennial ideologies. Ataucusi asked how this was possible, and the oracular reply revealed that the soul's eternal moment extends into the past as much as into the future: "Your body is from this age, but your spirit is very old."[31]

A preoccupation with dating but also postponing the end of the world has delivered a range of temporal schemes, early among them the Apocalypse of Weeks—"a consideration of ten weeks embracing the whole of human history"—developed in 1 Enoch.[32] Another reckoning is represented in an apocryphal account of the Garden of Eden, where Adam takes God's word literally and weeps because he believes that the world will end in five and a half days. The merciful God then clarifies that "these were 5,000 and 500 years," after which time the savior will appear and "then will I give thee the fruit of the Tree of Life, and thou shall eat, and live forever."[33] In the second century a similar "millennial week" was developed by Barnabas when he superimposed the thousand-year day in Psalm 90 onto the seven-day creation in Genesis. Thus human history is played out "in six days, that is in 6000 years," after which "the universe will be brought to its end." The seventh day of rest in Genesis and the thousand years Barnabas associated with it combined to deliver Christ's millennial kingdom. As Irenaeus put it later in the same century, "This 7th day is the 7th millennium, the kingdom of the just, where creation renewed will become incorruptible."[34] These and many subsequent reckonings, such as the dispensationalism popular among modern Evangelicals, are noteworthy not for the rigor of their logic nor for their ability to predict the end of time accurately, but rather for their capacity to cohere and mobilize masses that find consolation and meaning in an end that, like human death, is specified but "postponed." The speciousness of the doctrine and the intensity of the faith that it inspires tempt one to suspect a causal relation.

The faulty but insistent prediction of doomsdays seems ultimately to be an asset rather than a liability of apocalypticism, for the countless converts who subscribe to a prophet's doctrine of urgency wish not to be troubled by facts but rather to be enchanted by faith, to be delivered from their implacable daily reality into a redemptive realm with a logic more malleable, more accommodating than that of their wearied world. Such a faith in itself might be millennial kingdom enough, no matter how many times the predictions are botched. Anticipation of the imminent end becomes a way of life, with its ethics, its rituals, and its logic by which erroneous predictions can be disavowed and reintroduced in support of faith's subordination of science. As Frank Kermode understood this paradox, "When we refuse to be dejected by disconfirmed predictions we are only asserting a permanent need to live by the pattern rather than the fact, as indeed we must."[35] The imminent end is forever postponed, but the magnetic pull of apocalypticism overpowers false prophesy to focus the faithful on a vanishing point that gives all lines emanating from it their meaning. A retroactive end returns to transform the present, endowing each life with an intense, compensatory meaning that redeems the general meaninglessness, often brutalized and undignified, of everyday life in the tired world.

Messianic Imperialism

In other millennial ideologies, sometimes referred to as postmillennial, the stress falls less on an apocalyptic ending of the present age than it does on expediting a glorious new age beyond it, conceived as "the very apotheosis of history" and the "climax toward which the whole of history was moving."[36] Here history is theophany, the mood is constructive, and the actions are decisive, with human efficacy guided by divine will as the cosmic plan unfolds. God and his creation collaborate in the progression, perfection, and culmination of history; enterprise becomes eschatology. Calculations and date predictions are still prominent: Pope Innocent VIII informed Queen Isabella that the end was imminent in 1489, for example, and Columbus, following Alfonso the Wise and Pierre d'Ailly, believed that "our Lord is hastening things" because "the Gospel must now be proclaimed to so many lands" in the century and a half that remained before the end.[37] The tenor nevertheless tends to be positive, the eschatology open-ended rather than foreclosed, and the announced end more a new beginning in God's millennial kingdom than a manifestation of divine wrath.

Viewing itself as God's "holy nation" and still guided by "the medieval conception of the world as an homogenous Christendom with an infidel fringe," early modern Spain took the offensive on the dual fronts of mission and crusade.[38] Mission intended to evangelize pagans or gentiles (such as the New World's indigenous peoples, who were unfamiliar with the word of Christ), whereas crusade, having survived the Middle Ages, persisted in the extermination of infidels (notably Moslems, considered intrinsically unregenerate for knowing but rejecting the true faith). By these two means, mission and crusade, the friars and the soldiers of the Catholic (meaning "universal") Church prepared the world for Christ's return. If despite Spanish efforts the infidels and pagans seemed to multiply exponentially—Moslem, Jew, Protestant, idolater—and thereby to undermine the gains and frustrate the endeavor, this setback, from a certain angle, could also be construed positively. Traditions following Joachim of Fiore maintained that antichrists would increase as the last days approached, only then to consolidate into the great archetypal Antichrist, who would be definitively defeated by Christ himself. Matters would get worse before they got better, but the "abomination of desolation" would ultimately succumb to Christ's majesty.

Whatever the outcome of Spanish mission and crusade, the results could always be interpreted in such a way as to support the imperial designs that millennialism sustained. Among the most reliable (if perennial) signs of the approaching end of the world was precisely this shifting balance of power between the agents of Christ and of Antichrist as they engaged in earthly conflicts of cosmic significance. Ignatius Loyola, himself a Basque soldier before founding the Jesuit order, offered one characteristic representation of these dichotomous battle stations: he envisioned "a vast plain embracing the whole region of Jerusalem, where the supreme Captain-General of the good is Christ our Lord: and another plain, in the region of Babylon, where the chief of the enemy is Lucifer."[39] When the cosmic conflict was localized on the battlefield of the early

Reconquest, Moslem-occupied Iberia was accordingly biblicized as the land of Gog and Magog that would soon be restored by Christ's vicar, Alfonso III, to the millennial kingdom that God intended.[40]

That bellicose apocalyptic tropes and a religious reading of political events captivated the imagination of Reconquest Iberians comes as no surprise, nor is it unexpected that the representatives of Christ and Antichrist, Jerusalem and Babylon, and good and evil were assigned by all rivals to their own advantage and in the terms of the culture that their warfare defended. More surprising is the survival of these essentially medieval concepts in modern Latin American politics, sometimes as tired metaphors rejuvenated for speech making and other times as guiding paradigms that condition the interpretation of political conflicts and imbue the perpetrators of even the most barbarous atrocities with a sense of eschatological mission.

In the context of anti-imperialist nationalism of the 1920s, World War I was given an apocalyptic interpretation by Nicaragua's Augusto César Sandino and his inspirational ideologue, Joaquín Trincado. "One arrives at Armageddon," according to Trincado, because "all the kings and captains and armies of the earth (as told in the Apocalypse) have risen in arms, and there have been all sorts of plagues." Absent from the scenario was only "a great earthquake" that would "abolish borders and landmarks," and private property with them, in order to inaugurate the "redemptive commune."[41] In February 1931 this upbeat millennialism was boosted by the "Light and Truth" manifesto that Sandino presented to troops combatting the "blond beasts," meaning United States Marines, who were occupying Nicaragua.[42] "Many times you will have heard of a Last Judgment of the world," and by this "should be understood the destruction of injustice on the earth and the reign of the Spirit of Light and Truth, that is, Love." Sandino continued: "You also will have heard that this twentieth century, that is, the Century of Enlightenment, is the epoch for which the Last Judgment of the world is prophesied." "The trumpets that will be heard will be the bugles of war," true enough, but rather than subsequent doom and gloom, "the only thing that will be submerged for all time is injustice," because the oppressor will be defeated, "and Love, king of Perfection," will reign with "Divine Justice."[43] Trincado topped off the exaltation with a prophesy of his own, forecasting the year 2000 as "the date on which the whole earth may sing the Hymn of Victory."[44]

The apocalypticism of warfare went beyond rhetoric and grandiloquent imagery during the Argentine "dirty war" of the late 1970s, when reactionary Christianity sanctioned military solutions to social, economic, and political problems. In official publications and proclamations of the dictatorship and the Church hierarchy associated with it, the excessive and illegal force deployed against unarmed civilians was exempt from "moral or natural limits" and was realized in a register "that transcends the human level," precisely because its intent was to terminate "the brief reign of the Antichrist of Apocalypse." The enemies were "pagan agents of the Antichrist" and "forces of evil," whereas the military was "a profession of religiosity," a "holy order," and "a modern crusader for God and Freedom" comparable to the crusaders of the Iberian Reconquest. "What we are seeing," one general summarized, "is the 'present act' of that constant war between good and evil." In the neomedieval perspective of the armed forces, the enemy sought "to dominate the spirit" and to deprive Argentines of "entrance into the kingdom of Christ" by "implanting the Kingdom of the Antichrist and enslaving all men and all nations, separating us from our one Savior." In response the junta mobilized its Christian soldiers to deliver "a new natural order for renovation in Christ, which offers the inhabitants of the Fatherland an authentic opportunity for temporal perfection."[45]

The Argentine junta's superimposition of holy war over dirty war is one of innumerable instances in which perpetrators interpret their atrocity as theophany. Grotesque and excessive violence is religiously condoned, rewarded, and often sanctified because it is construed as benevolent severity detached from base human motives and realized, at great personal risk, as a lesser evil that preempts a greater one. Warfare becomes a loving abnegation as the suffering servants of God emulate Jesus and sacrifice their lives for the salvation of others. When this position is forced to its theocratic conclusions, as it was in the Spanish conquest of the New World, then warfare is legitimated as a dutiful compliance with divine will. It is not merely just to make war against natives, "but rather the Pope and the Crown of Castile are obligated to subject them, whether they want to or not." Miguel de Arcos, writing in the mid-sixteenth century, further observed: "We Christians are obligated to give the alms of light and doctrine to those who through their invincible ignorance sin mortally and live in a state of perpetual damnation."[46] The passage is exemplary not only in its comfortable arrogance but also in its demonstration of how theocratic empires—those native to the Americas included—formulate self-congratulatory theologies to justify expansionism. "Who can doubt," as Gonzalo Fernández de Oviedo inimitably expressed it, "that the gunpowder used against the infidels is incense for the Lord?"[47]

In Iberia and then again in the New World conquest, the supernatural reinforcements that facilitated victory in holy war included frequent apparitions of Santiago (Saint James), the apostle of Christ who became the patron saint of Spain. At decisive moments during the Reconquest campaigns, beginning with the legendary battle of Clavijo in the year 844, Santiago Matamoros (Saint James the Moor Killer) charged down from the heavens on a white horse to assist the defenders of Christianity in their battles against Islam. The adaptability of divine alliance to various ages, battlefields, and causes then facilitated Santiago's migration with the Spaniards across the Atlantic, where a makeover to suit the new campaign yielded Santiago Mataindios (Saint James the Indian Killer). Santiago intervened at least thirteen times during the conquest, four in South America and the remainder in New Spain.[48] Here, as in Iberia, Santiago descended from the sky at the decisive moment of battle, sometimes accompanied by other saints, angels, or the Virgin who fought daintily beside him. It would have been impossible for so few Christians to defeat such vast indigenous armies, as one Spaniard put it following an indigenous insurrection in New Galicia, "if it were not for the help of God, of Santiago and of the angels, who on such occasions remember their people."[49] Diego de Córdova y Salinas likewise expressed the widely held view that God reinforced the Spanish arsenal with miracles and defended soldiers "with celestial assistance" in order to "better introduce His law and Gospel." Juan Suárez de Peralta agreed categorically: "The war waged against the Indians was entirely a work of God."[50]

This concept of supernatural reinforcement in battle owed a debt to early Judaic apparitions of Yahweh's "heavenly army." The prayers of Judas Maccabaeus were answered, for example, when a divine warrior galloped out of the sky on a white horse to lead the troops, who then "advanced in battle order, having their heavenly ally, for the Lord had mercy on them."[51] The War Scroll from Qumran states, "A host of angels are among those mustered with us, the Mighty One is in our congregation, and the host of His spirits is with our steps."[52] A related antecedent is suggested in the Islamic concept of jihad or holy war, which motivated soldiers on the enemy side of the Crusades and Reconquest. As the *Poem of the Cid* has it, "The Moors call him Mohammed, the Christians Santiago." The transformation of Santiago from an apostolic paradigm of pacifism into a warrior—"a kind of Christian Mohammed"—may have emerged, in part, as a retaliatory construct responding in kind to the otherworldly forces deployed during the Moorish conquest of Iberia.[53] But precedents within Christianity itself are equally compelling, from the distant echoes of armed archangels and the dragon-slaying Saint George to the stylized warrior Christ of Revelation, who arrives with heavenly armies on white horses and "smites the nations" with the "sharp sword" in his mouth.[54] The consolidation of Santiago and Christ is reinforced by the popular belief that Santiago was Jesus' cousin (or brother) and by the iconographical representation of Santiago with facial features similar to those of Jesus.[55] The Spaniards' heavenly ally presents as Santiago but carries in the palimpsest of his identity the Judeo-Christian warrior god epitomized by the Christ of Revelation.

In retrospect it would seem that the enemies of God were serially reinvented to coincide with those of Spain and that this coincidence was contrived to petition divine endorsement of imperial expansion. The early modern view, however, was inverted by millennialism. As a Spanish soldier put it, "I am your sword, Lord, forgive me, I will continue fighting against your enemies who, being such, are my enemies too."[56] If Spain's enemies and God's enemies were one and the same, it was because Christian soldiers, guided and reinforced by otherworldly powers and pursuant to a gradually revealed eschatological plan, fought Christ's battles on earth. As Francisco López de Gómara understood it, "having completed the conquest of the Moors, which lasted more than eight hundred years, the conquest of the Indians began, so that Spaniards would always fight against infidels and enemies of the holy faith of Jesus Christ."[57]

The Crusade ideal of uniting and expanding a Christendom fragmented by the advances of Islam culminated in Iberia in 1492, when eight centuries of intermittent warfare ended with the Spaniards' successful completion of the Reconquest. Since 1344, expulsion of the Moors had been a low priority delegated to local nobles, but the effort was reinvigorated in the late fifteenth century by papal Crusade propaganda, by a general resurgence of Crusade sentiments following the fall of Constantinople, and by the union of Aragon and Castile.

The last Moorish stronghold, Granada, finally surrendered on January 2, 1492, "the most distinguished and blessed day there has ever been in Spain," according to an eye witness.[58] Catholic interpreters of the event reasoned that Spain, the "paradise of God" described by Isidore of Seville, had fallen into a sinfulness that resulted in destruction by the Moors, but the victory of Ferdinand and Isabella "redeemed Spain, indeed all Europe."[59] The Vatican duly celebrated the victory, hyperbolically rendering the reconquest of Granada an equitable compensation for the loss of Constantinople and a prelude to the "liberation" of North Africa. The invasion of Africa indeed began in 1497 with the taking of Melilla, followed by a series of beachhead conquests that were authorized by popes and that revived the ancient idea of accessing the Holy Land through Africa.[60] The defeat of Islam had as its ultimate goal the reconquest of Jerusalem, and regional Christian victories such as that of Granada accordingly derived their ultimate meaning and legitimacy from this great, final, unaccomplished recovery of the Christian world's symbolic center. As Hieronymus Münzer put it during a royal audience following the fall of Granada, "Nothing remains to Your Majesties except to add to your victories the reconquest of the Holy Sepulchre of Jerusalem."[61]

With the Iberian Reconquest concluded, the Catholic Monarchs (as Pope Alexander VI titled Ferdinand and Isabella) directed their attention to consolidating their emerging empire: "She with her prayers, / He with many armed men," as a period poem has it.[62] Programs of racial cleansing, homogenization of cultural diversity, and definition in Christian terms of what it would mean to be Spanish brought the Jews again under royal scrutiny. An edict signed at the newly taken Alhambra in Granada on the last day of March 1492 and promulgated a month later imposed upon Spanish Jews the options of conversion or expulsion. The edict argued that a "great harm is caused by intercourse of Christians with Jews," notably in "some bad Christians who follow Jewish ways and apostatize our Holy Catholic Faith." Since previous segregation edicts (in 1480 and 1483) did not appear to be efficacious, the edict stated "we banish all Jews and Jewesses dwelling within the confines of Our Kingdom, never to return," giving them three months to leave but also to leave behind "gold, silver, and minted coins or other objects that fall under existing prohibitions."[63] Between eighty and two hundred thousand Jews chose exile. Those who remained in Spanish Iberia were subject to the scrutiny of the Inquisition, revitalized to cull the crypto-Jews from the "New Christians" who maintained a sincere façade.

Antonio de Nebrija's celebrated dictum, also of 1492, signaled language as the perfect instrument of empire, but in Iberia as much as in the colonies the Catholic Monarchs and their successors privileged religion as the instrument of imperial cohesion. Religious purges consolidated and secured the territories of an expansionist Christianity with universal aspirations, attempting to deculturate Moor, Jew, and Indian through a process of imperial unification that would recast even the most savage subjects on the model of "Christian laborers in Castile."[64] At the same time, in governance of the old Christians themselves, the faith served paradoxically as both a stimulant and an opiate. It inspired some

Spaniards (rulers, soldiers, explorers, conquerors) to seemingly superhuman feats, while it subdued others (particularly those in lower social strata) to passive submission through religious fear, restrictive moral codes, and the fatalistic resignation encouraged by the clergy.

The most notorious event of 1492, the first Columbian voyage, was a fortuitous extension of the imperial events preceding it. The defeat of the Moors, the expulsion of the Jews, and the gradual unification of Spain had positioned the Catholic Monarchs on the threshold of the politico-religious potential that their papal title implied, with each imperial success resonating through Rome and beyond into a higher, eschatological register. God compensated the Catholic Monarchs' great deeds, as Pedro Sarmiento de Gamboa saw it, by "choosing them from among all the other kings in the world to carry the faith to America," and to carry home the corresponding riches.[65] When Columbus departed from Palos in early August, three days after the last ship of Jews had sailed from the same port ("legend has it that the seamen could see the sails of the exiles in the distance"), his voyage marked the symbolic "culmination of one series of conquests and the beginning of another."[66] The fragmented world was coming together under the aegis of triumphant Christendom.

Columbus himself, influenced by Franciscan apocalyptic traditions and with a patent mystical inclination of his own, gave a millennial interpretation to his discoveries. From the beginning, with documental evidence dating as early as 1489, he intended that the revenues generated by his enterprise be used to fund a new Crusade (maintaining the momentum of the Reconquest) that would accomplish the ultimate goal of liberating the Holy Sepulchre in Jerusalem.[67] For Columbus and his contemporaries, Jerusalem had not only the mundane worth that its complex religious history had earned it but also an intense, otherworldly, symbolic importance as "navel of the world" and as the paradigm Christian reliquary, even though its tomb was empty. In his diary entry of December 26, 1492, following the first Christmas in the New World, Columbus recorded his prayers to discover riches sufficient to fund the Crusade within three years. "I said to Your Highnesses that all of the profits of my enterprise would be spent on the conquest of Jerusalem," he recalled, and then recorded the royal response: "Your Highnesses laughed."[68]

Columbus himself took the new Crusade seriously. With his geography under the influence of biblical legends and religious cartography, he hoped to locate King Solomon's mines and thereby provide the Spanish monarchy with gold equal to the task.[69] He referred to the liberation of Jerusalem repeatedly in his writings; he lobbied for it in a February 1502 letter to Pope Alexander VI; he anthologized passages foretelling it in his *Book of Prophesies*; and he established a fund in his last will and testament of 1498 to finance it.[70] The plan itself was specified earlier in Columbus's letter of March 4, 1493, in which he announced his discovery to Ferdinand and Isabella and expressed his hope that through the grace of God "in seven years from today I will be able to pay Your Highnesses for five thousand cavalry and fifty thousand foot soldiers for the war and conquest of Jerusalem," with another allotment of the same size and for the same purpose to follow five years thereafter.[71]

The ultimate liberation of Jerusalem provided Columbus with interpretive context and transcendental meaning for his voyages, but particularly following the apocalyptic trials of the third voyage he tended to stress the providential origin of his mission. He began the letter relating his third voyage by stating, "The Holy Trinity moved Your Highnesses to this enterprise of the Indies and through its infinite goodness made me its messenger."[72] In his undispatched letter to the Catholic Monarchs that prefaced the *Book of Prophesies*, Columbus re-iterated that belief—he had been illuminated by the Holy Spirit's "rays of mar-velous clarity"—and added that he had made his discovery "not aided by intel-ligence, by mathematics or by maps" but rather because the Lord had guided him through the trans-Atlantic crossing in order to fulfill biblical prophesy.[73] In moments of desperation, Columbus was reassured by a divine voice that spoke the discourse of scripture—"Do not fear, have trust: all of these tribulations are written in marble and not without cause"—or by the tangible presence of the Lord: "He raised me with his right arm, saying: 'Oh man of little faith, rise, it is I, be not afraid.' "[74]

The divine interventions were indices of the comprehensive guidance that God had always offered to Columbus ("Since you were born He held you in his greatest care") because Columbus and his majesties were the protagonists of Christian eschatology. The oracular voice of the fourth voyage compared Co-lumbus to Moses and David, then added, "Of the gates of the Ocean Sea, which were closed with such great chains, He gave you the keys."[75] With the key of David, Columbus could redeem the idolatrous souls lost in darkness, access the mines that would fund the liberation of Jerusalem, and thereby complete the mission and crusade that would ready the world for Christ's return. As though this were insufficient, however, Columbus then redoubled the millennial impli-cations by equating the discovered lands with the New Jerusalem: "Of the new heaven and of the new earth, which Our Lord made, as St. John writes in the Apocalypse, after He had spoken of it by the mouth of Isaiah, He made me the messenger and He showed me where to find it."[76] The allusions are to Revelation 21:1–4 and 21:22–27, where Jerusalem is transformed into a "new heaven and new earth" as the celestial city descends, and to Isaiah 65:17–25, where the "new heaven and new earth" seem almost a fusion of Jerusalem and Eden.

The more the earthly Jerusalem was desecrated or denied to the Christians, the more it seemed to proliferate elsewhere in promised lands and paradises carrying its name. The deprivation is transcendentalized and then returns in-verted and perfected: "A new earth merges into the new heaven."[77] Columbus will have his Jerusalem one way or another, by force of arms in a new Crusade, by appeal to biblical New Jerusalem imagery superimposed on the Americas, or by the "discovery" of the Garden of Eden on his third voyage, through which his Jerusalem becomes, like Isaiah's, "a return to origins, to a paradise lost."[78] Columbus is "the apostolic link and providential instrument that connects this world to the other, the Old World to the New, the New World to the Next, and the Next World to his mission."[79]

But Columbus was not alone in viewing himself as the human agency through which divine will realized its designs. Jaime Ferrer, an adviser to the Catholic

Monarchs, referred to Columbus as "an apostle and ambassador of God."[80] For Hernán Pérez de Oliva in 1528, Columbus was "chosen by God to carry His holy law across the Ocean Sea to other peoples who had never known it or had already forgotten it."[81] Lope de Vega envisioned America as "the Promised Land" where Columbus, a Christ-like "light of the New World," enlightened his flock of sheeplike noble savages as a prelude to the redemptive transformation of the entire human race.[82] And Gerónimo de Mendieta followed Columbus himself in the belief that the discovery was made "not by human science, but by some divine revelation." Columbus was the "means and instrument" chosen by God "to discover and open the way to this New World," and he was accordingly followed by Hernán Cortés, the new Moses, as "instrument and means of the first conversion that was made in the Indies."[83]

Cortés was doubly suited as a counterforce "to remedy the great evil," once because his conquest of the Aztecs terminated a demonic orgy of idolatry and human sacrifice, and again because New World conversions in the wake of his conquest more than compensated for the European souls lost to Satan thanks to Martin Luther. Mendieta attributed this efficient retaliation to Providence by erroneously coinciding the year of Cortés's birth (1485) with the birth date of Martin Luther (1483), as well as with the dedication date of the Aztec's Templo Mayor (the exact date is unknown), during which some twenty thousand humans were sacrificed.[84]

Inspired hermeneutics led others, notably Bartolomé de Las Casas and Columbus's son Ferdinand, to detect the work of God in Columbus's very name. The name Christopher, from the Latin *Christum ferens*, means "carrier of Christ," the title that was conferred upon Saint Christopher for having carried "the weight of the world and him who created it." The legendary saint transported the Christ child across a river and was thus awarded the privilege, then exclusive, of carrying Christ's name in his own. Columbus, the new Christopher, now carried across the Sea of Darkness not the Christ child himself but his word, and thus Columbus "was the first to give notice of Christ and make him adored among these innumerable nations forgotten for so many centuries." The popular belief that God named or renamed his elect to reflect their divinely ordained vocations also exerted its influence on Columbus himself, who from 1501 until his death in 1506 concluded the cryptic symbols of his new signature with the words *Christum ferens*.[85]

Christ was the symbolic cargo transported from Europe to the New World, and in handy, neomedieval symmetry the preferred cargo for the return trip, gold, was also spiritualized. The religious interpretation of colonial exploitation began with the mentioned intent to channel New World revenues into holy war, with the express purpose of retaking Jerusalem in preparation for Christ's return. The crusade scheme died with Columbus, but the obligation to defend the faith gained momentum on a separate front as the colonization of America and the Reformation in Europe coincided. During the Hapsburg dynasty the "temporal riches and treasures" of the colonies were exploited not for the crass material ends of luxury and ostentation, but rather because New World wealth "would make all of Christendom stronger" so that "the enemies of our Holy Catholic

Faith," whoever they might be, would be subdued by the swords of Christ's soldiers.[86] The mines of the Indies had been providentially apportioned to Spain for this purpose, and divine intervention was discernible even in the geology of New World mountains concealing mineral deposits. "God was pleased to create them in such a form that their very appearance, being so strange, made it clear that they held something precious within them."[87] Postconquest legends relate that the Inca Huayna Capac began to mine at Potosí, but a mysterious voice commanded in Quechua, "Take no silver from this hill. It is destined for other owners."[88]

Beginning in 1545 the "mountain of silver" at Potosí became a symbol of New World wealth and its uses in defense of the faith. As expressed by Guaman Poma, it was thanks to the riches of Potosí—"heart of this kingdom" and "relief [socorro] of the people of the God of Jerusalem"—that Castile "is Castile, Rome is Rome, the Pope is the Pope, and the king is the monarch of the world."[89] Philip II himself expressed much the same in the motto he had inscribed on a shield sent to Potosí: "For the powerful Emperor, for the wise King, this lofty mountain of silver could conquer the whole world."[90] In a Franciscan chronicle from around 1630, Potosí was the scourge of the Turks, the envy of the Moors, the terror of England, and the "column and obelisk of the faith." This same note was still being sounded a century later by Bartolomé Arzáns de Orsúa, who then nostalgically remembered the exhausted mine as "a singular work of the power of God" because it funded "a paid army against the enemies of the faith" and provided the "money with which heaven is bought."[91] The enemies had changed across the centuries, but holy war still cleansed imperial enterprise with a redeeming loftiness of purpose.

New World riches were likewise spiritualized on the missionary front. Mendieta was characteristic in his claim that the exploitation of temporal silver mines was a prelude to that of "eternal and spiritual silver mines," by which he meant indigenous souls.[92] It was often argued that an absence of riches would have resulted in a corresponding absence of Spaniards, thereby depriving the natives of salvation and retarding the process of Christian world unity. God had paired the Indians and "the greatest abundance of mines that there ever was" in order to attract Christians to the New World, in the same way that a father endows his ugly daughter with a rich dowry, "so that in this way she finds somebody who will love her."[93] As Juan de Matienzo described the lopsided trade relation of faith and wealth in 1567, "We give them doctrine, teaching them how to live as men, and they give us silver, gold or things of value."[94]

Columbus's own "messianic veneration" of gold evidenced a greater purity and faithful naivete. During his brief governance of Hispaniola, he "did not allow the Christians to collect gold without first confessing and taking communion," as though to purify the miners ritually before they made contact with the sacred.[95] This quasi-reverential attitude toward mining is reminiscent of the medieval alchemical traditions that equated gold, the most noble, quintessential matter, with Christ, the most noble, quintessential spirit. As alchemists have it, "What is called the 'absolute,' the 'absolute perfection,' and the perfection of Nature [gold], are one and the same."[96] The metaphorical equation of Christ and precious metal—in this case silver—is also represented by iconography of the Virgin of the Hill at Potosí, in which the maternal body and the mountain of silver are one and the same. If in Andean perspective the fusion of the Virgin and the mountain suggests a syncretic Mary-Pachamama earth mother, in European perspective the mined silver accommodates a reading as Christ delivered from the Virgin-mine. The same was reinforced by human ontogeny tropes applied to mining: gold gestates "in the entrails of the earth" and is "born" (*nace*) as the earth "gives birth to it [*lo pare*] or pushes it out of itself."[97] In the words of a 1619 Augustinian chronicle, "Mary is the mountain out of which came that stone without feet or hands that is Christ." And again: "Christ is the cut stone from the divine mountain that is Mary."[98]

The symbolics of the "Columbian exchange" suggest a bilateral commerce in a single commodity, Christ, transacted in spiritual and material representations back and forth across the Atlantic. Christ is exported from Spain in the intangible form of the evangelical word and exported from the Americas as precious metal. The intricate associations of gold and Christ, gold and crusade, gold and mission, and gold and world unity together delivered Columbus's exclamation that "Gold is most excellent. Gold constitutes treasure, and he who possesses it may do what he will in the world, and may even cast souls into Paradise."[99]

The Last World Emperor

> *There shall be one flock, and one shepherd.*
> —John 10:16.

The Bible makes no mention of an emperor who arrives at the end of time to consolidate ecumenical Christianity and usher in the millennial kingdom. This heroic identity was indebted rather to the *Sibylline Oracles*, "with their prophesy of a great emperor who is to arise before the Second Coming, massacre all Moslems, establish a Golden Age of plenty and make his way to Jerusalem."[100] The emerging ideal of an eschatological emperor owed a debt to the sacred-king traditions of antiquity—in which dynasties aspired to "exercise authority like gods" and "rule the entire world" forever—but it was most advanced by the renovation of apocalyptic thought after the conversion of Constantine and the Christianization of the Roman Empire in the fourth century.[101] Following Eusebius, it became an orthodoxy in the early Christian empire that "Augustus had united the world under Roman rule, Christ under God's, and Constantine welded together the two unities in a Christian society which was, in principle, universal."[102] The once detested emperor thus became God's representative on earth, and the once beastly empire a terrestrial replica of the kingdom of heaven. By the end of the fourth century, "a potent new symbolic figure was in the making": the Last World Emperor who would annihilate Christ's enemies, "smashing them to bits like earthenware," and then "go to Jerusalem, lay down his crown and robe on Golgotha and surrender his rule and care of Christendom to God."[103] The Last World Emperor's accomplishment is the final human contribution to cosmic integration, to closing the distance between this world and the next as the two fuse into a single kingdom, on earth as it is in heaven, with Christ reigning from the throne vacated for him.

The Last World Emperor's abdication was predicated on the belief that Christ was Lord and landlord of the earth, and that temporal kings reigned in regency only until he returned. God sent his son to redeem humanity, and this work was continued by the pope, vicar of Christ in the lineage of Saint Peter, availing himself of monarchy and its armies to restore the original unity compromised by infidelity and sin. In the 1493 Bulls of Donation, Pope Alexander VI accordingly "donated, conceded and assigned" the non-Christian world in halves to Spain and Portugal "by the authority of Almighty God conferred upon us in blessed Peter and of the vicarship of Jesus Christ which we hold on earth."[104] The notorious document known as the Requirement, used in the field between 1513 and 1542, summarized the universal vicariate as a prelude to "asking and requiring" that without resistance the Indians "acknowledge the Church as the ruler and Superior of the whole world, and the high priest called Pope, and in his name the King and Queen . . . as superiors and lords and kings of these islands and this mainland." Peoples native to the Americas were trespassing on royal property because the world belonged to the "Vicars of Christ in the entire universe."[105] If Indians did not heed the Requirement, then according to the document's author, Palacios Rubios, "they may be invaded and conquered, reduced by force of arms, have their possessions seized, and their persons placed in slavery, because war on the part of the Christians is justified."[106]

As a popular medieval allegory depicted it, the pope's dominion over the spiritual and temporal realms was defended by his two swords, one of which, the temporal, was entrusted to secular rulers.[107] Holy war was contracted out to kings who engaged in the bloody business of conquest that made possible the King of Kings' eternal reign. In his New Year sermon of 1642, the Portuguese Jesuit António Vieira accordingly anticipated an end to intra-Iberian political struggles so that the Portuguese could also dedicate themselves to the tasks of world unity, bathing their swords in "the blood of heretics in Europe, and the blood of Muslims in Africa, the blood of heathens in Asia and in America, conquering and subjugating all the regions of the earth under one sole empire, so that they may all, under the aegis of one crown, be placed gloriously beneath the feet of the successor of Saint Peter."[108]

As royal revenues and crusade eschatology mutually enhanced one another in Spanish Iberia, "the discovery of the Indies, the conversion of all the Gentiles, and the deliverance of the Holy Sepulcher were considered to be the three climactic events which [would] foreshadow the end of the world."[109] The end was ever closer as the Catholic Monarchs accomplished the requisite deeds, expanding and consolidating Christendom even in lands unknown and strengthening the conviction that Ferdinand—with his sobriquets King of Jerusalem and the New David—was the monarch who would universalize God's kingdom. Ferdinand seemed to be the Last World Emperor announced in the prophesy (erroneously attributed to Joachim of Fiore) that "the restorer of the House of Mount Zion would come from Spain."[110] His wife Isabella, addressed in period poetry as Queen of Jerusalem, was sent by "the Omnipotent on high" to collaborate in that effort as though she and Ferdinand were "animated by a single spirit, for they rule with one mind."[111]

The end of the Catholic Monarchs came before the end of the world, but the identity of eschatological emperor readily gravitated toward Charles V, king of Spain and Holy Roman Emperor, who regarded his "divine mission" to be of universal magnitude and "was perceived as the individual towards whom the history of Revelation had been pointing for more than a millennium."[112] In 1528 a Benedictine chronicler expressed the common belief that Charles was "after God common father of all," the "lord of the world" who was guided "by God's hand" to acquire "universal monarchy."[113] Hernán Cortés addressed Charles as though a "monarch of the universe," "king of kings," and "emperor of the world," and in Peru the Dominican friar Vicente de Valverde described Charles in much the same way to the puzzled Atahualpa, who expressed interest in meeting the "Monarch of the World" but also protested that he, as Inca, "would not pay tribute to anyone."[114] Oviedo was particularly militant on the issue, noting that "the Universal monarchy of our Caesar" will bring all "under his scepter," and therefore "there shall be no kingdom, sect, nor race of false belief that shall not be humiliated and subjugated to his yoke and obedience."[115]

With Charles's 1556 abdication in favor of Philip II, who "regarded religious unity as the indispensable condition for political unity," the Spaniards were again envisioning the globalization of Christendom with "one Monarch, one Empire, and one Sword." Many Christians expected that Philip would reconquer Jerusalem and revive the title "emperor of the East," with all of the corresponding eschatology intact.[116] Slogans honoring Philip in the early 1580s captured the tone—"as if to the lord of the world" and "the world is not enough"—as did the canvases of Titian, representing the privileged relation between "the king of Heaven and the king of Spain."[117] Other images featured God himself crowning Philip and investing him with the imperial regalia, much the same as earlier royal iconography had depicted Daniel relating his dream of the four monarchies to a seated, astonished Charles V.[118] As Tommaso Campanella summarized these sentiments in the early seventeenth century, "This monarchy of Spain which embraces all nations and encircles the world is that of the Messiah, and thus shows itself to be the heir of the universe."[119] Colonial discourse followed in kind, with Mendieta, before he despaired of his king, referring to Philip II as "monarch of the world" (Guaman Poma referred to Philip III with the same words) and sharing in the belief that "the spiritual unity of mankind" would be "forged by the Spanish sword."[120]

Philip II was not up to the eschatological task that tradition had assigned him, particularly after the onset of illness in 1585. The resultant sociopolitical despair—compounded by constant warfare, crop failure, plague, rebellion in the Netherlands, disrupted trans-Atlantic trade, and bankruptcy—steered the ideology of messianic imperialism back toward a gloomy apocalypticism. It then seemed in Spain that "everything here will collapse at once."[121] A prominent Augustinian preached that the Armada would be defeated because "our sins are great"; and in Granada, in 1588, the discovery of lead boxes holding forged

Greek and Arabic documents revealed that the end of the world—but not the joyful end scripted for the Last World Emperor—was scheduled for "the years just short of 1600."[122] The seemingly incessant disasters visited upon Spain brought the fatalistic despair of a people who felt betrayed, "perhaps by a God who had inexplicably withdrawn His favor from His chosen people."[123] When Philip II returned to Madrid on New Year's Eve, 1592, the well-wishers "fell silent as their pale sovereign trundled past, slumped in the back of his carriage, looking almost dead."[124]

The Jerusalem crusade that these pretenders to world monarchy could not accomplish in fact gained compensatory theatrical representation in the American colonies in 1539, when the Tlaxcalans, under missionary supervision, presented a play entitled *The Conquest of Jerusalem*. Believed to have been written by the Franciscan known as Motolinía (Toribio de Benavente), the play represented the victorious siege of the holy city by the combined forces of Spain and New Spain.[125] The Great Sultan of the Turks made an unconditional surrender, acknowledged Charles V as God's Captain for all the world, and then in humility, deference, and gratitude accepted baptism by the pope. The subsequent theatrical baptism of lesser "Turks"—actually indigenous actors—inspired the duly moved, duly conquered Tlaxcalan audience to accept baptism in turn. The conquest of Jerusalem, accomplished in theater but not in history, was thus instrumental in the conversion of Indians and in the Franciscan propagation of the colony as a New Jerusalem.[126]

Crusade, one might say, had been superseded by mission. The mandate "Teach all nations," given to the apostles by the resurrected Jesus, was adopted by imperial missionaries who counterbalanced the crusade ideal and the ominous, end-of-the world prophesies (in, for example, Mark 13) with a positive emphasis on the collaboration of God and his creation to end this world in the new heaven and new earth "wherein dwelleth righteousness."[127] As the Third Catechism of Lima summarized it, following Matthew 24:14, "When the Gospel has been preached to all peoples of the world, then the end will come."[128] The enormity of the task—the peoples were many in the Americas alone—left some impatient Franciscans wondering, "When will this prophesy be fulfilled?"[129] At the same time, however, the impossibility of completing the task felicitously postponed the end ad infinitum, providing a measure of relief to those less anxious for death or obsolescence while the tallying of conversions by the thousands still documented a good-faith effort in the progressive closing of the distance between this world and the next.

In the meantime, many friars who were perplexed by the origin of New World peoples and grappling with a potential threat to orthodoxy found an expedient solution in the equation of Indians with the lost tribes of Israel. The reappearance of the "lost sheep of the house of Israel" in the New World was fortuitous, for it provided a biblical origin for the unknown peoples, satisfied the medieval belief that the Jews would be converted as the Advent approached, and fulfilled the prophesy in Revelation 7:4–9 (presuming the end was near) that the lost tribes would appear on the day of judgment.[130] The residual benefits were also appealing: the Indian-Jews, unlike their Old World counterparts, were innocent of Christ's crucifixion and therefore could be welcomed more graciously into the faith.[131]

Among the advocates of the Indians as Israelites was the Dominican Diego Durán, who introduced his late-sixteenth-century history of New Spain with the assertion, "These Indians are Jews and are descended from Jews."[132] In the 1607 *Origin of the Indians of the New World*, Gregorio García, also Dominican, developed this thesis, including among the evidence for his argument an adventurous etymology of the word *Mexico*, which he erroneously traced to the Hebrew *mexi*, meaning "leader" or "head."[133] (The same word under the analysis of Fray Servando de Mier—who in 1820 was still insisting that the Americas had been evangelized by Christ's apostle Thomas—meant "where Christ is or is adored, so that Mexicans are the same as Christians.")[134] In the third book of his treatise, García itemized the character traits—timidity, incredulity, ingratitude, lack of charity, idolatry—that he believed the Indians and Jews held in common. He also specified external similarities in dress, customs, speech patterns, and physiognomy, including reference to the Indians as the only people "who have Noses as big as the Jews'."[135] In 1650 the Portuguese Jew Menasseh Ben Israel was similarly of the opinion that the New World "was in ancient times inhabited by the ten Tribes, that from Tartaria passed through the Straight of Anian, or of China, and that even today live hidden by divine providence in the unknown parts of the said America."[136]

Others more generally reasoned that the Indians, if they were human, were necessarily descendants of either Ham, Japhet or Shem, the three sons of Noah. In his mid-seventeenth-century account of the Incas, Fernando Montesinos related that after the flood a grandson of Noah's settled in "Hamerica," with that curious spelling registering Montesinos's own ambitious etymological belief that the continent's name "is a mysterious anagram of *Hec Maria*, the Mother of Christ, and not derived from Amerigo."[137] The descendants-of-Noah theory was not without its difficulties, however, since it invited unorthodox observations such as that of Amerigo Vespucci, who on his voyages saw new animal species in such abundance that they "could not fit in Noah's ark."[138] The naked Indians who were mysteriously "unashamed of their shameful parts" in defiance of the Genesis account of expulsion from Eden could also pose problems, although ready—if inadequate—responses were found in the view of the Americas as prelapsarian.[139] Orthodoxy was further challenged by revelation of continental landmasses not accounted for by scripture, generating the retaliatory insistence on appending the New World to Asia.

Whoever the Indians were, their "discovery" renewed the enthusiasm of eschatological discourse and provided new horizons for revitalization of primitive Christianity. As López de Gómara put it in 1551, "The greatest thing since the creation of the world, save the incarnation and death of Him who created it, is the discovery of the Indies that are thus called the New World." This celebrated passage, in a dedication to Charles V and in homage to the themes of Last World Emperor, continued to explain that God had revealed the Indies in those particular times in order to confer upon the Spaniards the privilege of evangelization.[140] The belief that "the New World is the End of the World" generated, in

turn, abundant literature depicting precontact indigenous history as a prelude
to conquest, an extended preface to the true history under the cross where the
world would await "the hidden end of time."[141] This view was held by many
great colonial authors—José de Acosta, Bartolomé de Las Casas, the Inca Garcilaso de la Vega, Felipe Guaman Poma de Ayala—who in their respective ways
understood the pre-Columbian empires (like the Roman Empire earlier) as transitory pauses in the progression toward ecumenical unity. Las Casas described
the Inca empire as a social, political, and religious consolidation of disparate
primitive civilizations advancing toward monotheism, a gathering of the flock
in preparation for the arrival of the word of God and Christian salvation. For
Garcilaso, it pleased God that the first Inca appear as "a morning star to give
them in the dense darkness in which they dwelt some glimmerings of natural
law, civilization, and the respect men owe to one another."[142] Subsequent Incas
were then entrusted with the mission to "tame those savages and convert them
into men" who were "rendered more docile" to better welcome the Spanish
mission. Garcilaso emphasized "how much prompter and quicker to receive the
Gospel were the Indians subdued, governed, and taught by the Inca kings," while
others outside the empire "are still today as savage and brutish as before."[143]
World unity was served in the harmonious confluence of American and European imperial purposes, for Garcilaso "was able to attribute to Incas and Spaniards analogous roles in the march of all peoples toward Salvation, thus finally
uniting the history of the New World with that of the Old."[144] History was a
gradual progression from chaos to order, from paganism to Christianity, from
savage primitivism to Western civilization.

Recurring Ends

Despite the implacable finality implied by eschatology, the end endlessly announced in propaganda as much as in prophesy brings not the ultimate closure
of history but rather the termination of one age and the beginning of a new one,
with the corresponding overhaul of value, belief, and social systems. Whenever
a millennial kingdom is promised, the progression toward perfection stalls on
the threshold of a final age that never begins. The accent therefore falls on the
progressions and periodizations themselves, on the transformations realized en
route, on the recurring ends as opportunities within history to mime the grandeur of the renovation anticipated in the elusive climax beyond it.

In the Christian world, the new age and the new calendar began with the
birth of Christ, through whom "old things are passed away" and all things
become new.[145] The messiah's arrival punctuated the end of one era and the
beginning of another, but the schema remained open-ended because the messianic age inaugurated by Jesus was posited as the prelude to a greater one still
forthcoming. The Christian age will end and rebegin with the Second Coming,
and this recurring end is itself destined to be repeated, presumably with finality,
at the conclusion of the millennial kingdom. Recurring ends likewise characterize
the Old Testament tradition of four successive kingdoms that rise and fall before

culminating—as Daniel prophesied—in a fifth, messianic kingdom that never arrived. In Genesis itself God creates, bemoans, and destroys his creation, only to revive it through Noah and again, in the New Testament, through Jesus as the new Adam and new Noah. The very term "end of the days" used frequently in the Hebrew Bible suggests a flexible eschatology, for it "typically refers to some decisive change at a future time" without necessarily signifying the finality that is implied.[146]

In modern Latin America, the political exploitation of new ages has been extraordinary among leaders anxious to jettison troubled histories and to keep their wearied constituencies looking toward the promise of the future. Periodic regeneration offers the opportunity to alleviate social and political exhaustion, to overhaul and rejuvenate, to introduce new paradigms and their accompanying symbolic regalia, and to defuse social tensions by loading blame onto scapegoats, be they common enemies, leaders buried in the abandoned past, or internal groups ostracized from the emerging new society. The promises far exceed the accomplishments, of course, and the stress thus falls on the dazzling ostentation of the transition. The citizens' faith in the future is conditioned by their relief of being freed at last from the past.[147]

The periodization of history has been particularly conspicuous in the interrupted democracy of modern Argentina. The massive demonstrations that symbolically inaugurated Peronism in Buenos Aires on October 17, 1945, divided Argentine history into what Eva Perón characteristically described as "two perfectly defined epochs."[148] At the time of his 1966 coup (the fifth of six Argentine coups that century), General Juan Carlos Onganía similarly announced, "Argentina has completed a historical cycle" and thus would disengage from the "anonymous past" in order to "create a new nation."[149] The junta that deposed Isabel Perón in a 1976 coup then introduced its de facto regime as a Process of National Reorganization that would bring "the final closing of one historical cycle and the opening of a new one." The military had arisen "like a spontaneous reaction" to redeem the people from "corruption," from "deterioration," from "anguish and desperation," and from "the scourge of subversion," all of which constituted "an irreparable loss of greatness and faith," a "grave crisis" "capable of sinking us into anarchy and dissolution." The Argentine people would be delivered from this decadent past into a glorious future, however, because the junta assumed the "indispensable," "immense," and "rigorous task of eradicating, once and for all, the vices that afflict the nation." The "dirty war" sought a "final solution" (including the elimination of "future subversion" by executing "infiltrated" youth) so that new-age Argentina would be an "empire of virtue, well-being, and grandeur."[150]

The same tendency toward renovation and periodization is discernible in populist, revolutionary, and military governments throughout the region, be it the New State of Getúlio Vargas in Brazil until 1945, the New Nicaragua that Augusto César Sandino died for in 1934 and that the successful Sandinista revolution attempted to develop beginning in 1979, the Cuba of Fidel Castro after 1959, the renovation of Chile under Salvador Allende from 1970 to 1973, or the New Bolivia of Hugo Banzer in the 1970s. Peru's Víctor Raúl Haya de la

Torre lent his characteristic quasi-religious and continental vision to political renewal when he announced in 1936 that Latin America as a whole was approaching "spiritual autonomy in the dawn of a new day."[151]

The rhetoric and gestures of political recyclings are not always empty, however, and particularly in populist and revolutionary cases a faith in the ideals of a new state can have a profound influence on values and lifestyles. Peronism, Haya's American Revolutionary Popular Alliance (APRA), the revolutionary society of Cuba in the 1960s, and liberation theology are outstanding examples of sociopolitical programs that bring new beginnings—for better or worse—to their constituencies. In such cases binary periodization tends to divide history into a "before" and an "after" separated by a temporal marker of religious or political significance. Sometimes the long view suffices and the marker is primordial: the Waiwai of the Amazon (like many Judeo-Christians) refer to ages "before the flood" and "after the flood."[152] More representative of the political cases was a bipartite division in postrevolutionary Nicaragua: "Before, there were a lot of human rights abuses," but "now, all of that is different," and "things are better for the common people." By 1988, however, U.S. foreign policy had sabotaged socioeconomic stability in Nicaragua enough to engender disfavorable assessment of the Sandinistas. Praise then yielded to complaints, but the temporal marker remained fixed at 1979: "Before, there was more food, and in greater variety—meat, fish, eggs. Now, it's just beans and rice—and sometimes not even that."[153]

At the initiation of its armed phase in 1980, Peru's Sendero Luminoso (Shining Path) offered a separate version of the revolutionary rebeginning, pledging to write a "new history with the points of swords, with the light of fire, leveling iniquity, making the future be born." The movement's leader, Abimael Guzmán, offered multiple variations on the theme—"from the old the new will be born," "communism will be born forever" like a glorious phoenix—along with tropes of discontinuity. "Trumpets are beginning to sound" to announce that the comrades "are reconstituted" as the new humanity "whose millennium is beginning." After the "time of great rupture," Guzmán will deliver his people to the communist utopia on the far side of a "river of blood."[154] For devout Senderistas even the originality of Guzmán's thought constitutes a dividing line "that will mark all that came before and after him."[155]

In religious cases the rebeginnings assume multiple forms, including the internal overhaul of churches seeking to renovate their missions, the founding of splinter groups and new religious movements, the decidedly periodized world views of apocalyptic doctrines, and the social and ritual rebirths, such as baptism, experienced by the faithful. Renovation of the Catholic Church by the Second Vatican Council (known as Vatican II) had profound consequences in Latin America following the 1968 conference of bishops in Medellín, Colombia, bringing "a new historical era" that was "intimately linked to the history of salvation."[156] The resultant liberation theology movement organized base communities in which the poverty and oppression of parishioners was reinterpreted in light of biblical precedents. Through a process of *concientización* (consciousness raising), poor Catholics learned to abandon the fatalistic acquiescence that the colonial and neocolonial Church, ally of the oligarchy, had lauded as pious.[157] A new era in the history and identity of these peoples commenced as liberation theology guided them from defeatist apathy to social activism, advocation of their interests, and collective recuperation of dignity. The ancillary benefits, such as the educational experience of *basismo* developed by the Brazilian Paulo Freire, combined with the socioreligious gains for what many described as a "salvation." The new age made them a new people. As one Chilean woman put it with characteristic simplicity and humility, "Before I was a nobody," but "now I am a person."[158]

In other religious movements, particularly sects, the adherents tend to fix the divide of their before-and-after lives at the date of their spiritual rebirth. Members of the Brotherhood of the Cross are typical in their separation of an abandoned past "before Brother Francisco arrived" from a new age that began with his mission. The reference is to the wandering prophet Francisco da Cruz, who complemented this informal bipartition of individual histories with a recurring-end doctrine integral to his eschatology. Christ realized "the first universal reform of Christianity," Martin Luther realized the second, and the third was entrusted to Francisco, whose Brotherhood as a "temple of the living God" offers humanity's last chance for salvation.[159]

In these few cases and the many that they represent, a paradigm shift reconfigures history to the advantage of a new political or religious program, always with the intention of disowning a troubled past and reshaping social reality for a new era, a new citizen, a new deal. Portraits are reshuffled, walls are painted and repainted with competing slogans, flags go up and down the mast, Jesus is taken off the cross and put back on, land holdings are reformed and reconsolidated, place names are changed and changed back, and concepts of enmity are reconfigured with today's hero becoming tomorrow's villain as one recurring end yields to the next. The "irreversibility of events" in linear time preconditions an appeal to cyclicity ("the final closing of one historical cycle and the opening of a new one") or else impels corrective action and reaction into a future that is captured, by periodical foreclosure and rebeginning, before it is lost to an ominous eternity.[160]

In the pre-Columbian Americas, concepts of cyclical destruction and recreation made the recurrence of ends an inherent and central aspect of historical progression. Characteristic were "visions of worlds that are cyclically destroyed and regenerated, making way for the emergence of new peoples and golden ages or paradises of happiness and abundance."[161] Time became sacred as cyclicity rendered the primordial past recoverable and repeatable, and eschatology fused with cosmogony because the beginning and the end were variations of one and the same cosmic progression.[162]

For the Incas and many modern Andeans, *pachacuti* signifies the periodical cataclysms that come between ages or "suns" to turn the world upside down.[163] "At the end of each world the Sun disappears, all is overturned, and then a new world is born, under a new Sun, and the count begins again of the years accruing in the new cycle."[164] This process of cyclical regeneration has established a calendar of past ages similar to that of Daniel: "From the beginning of the world to the present there had been four suns, excepting this one that at present shines on us."[165] Guaman Poma also described four preceding ages in his Andean chronology, but he complemented that periodization with another five-aged biblical schema. A reconciliation that would preempt future pachacuti was then derived from two points held in common by the rival periodizations—the incarnation of Christ and the conquest—which led Guaman Poma to envision the confluence of Inca and Christian histories together flowing toward a syncretic, golden-age culmination.[166]

The indigenous past was annexed to the conquered present, and accordingly the roundabout detours of cyclicity flattened into linear time progressing dead ahead toward the end point fixed by Christianity. In modern Peru, a biblicized Andean periodization is central to the eschatology of the Israelites of the New Covenant. The Israelites believe that the present third age will be followed by tribulations, a millennium, more tribulations, and finally reintegration of the rogue planet earth into cosmic harmony, because "God wants to complete the hundred planets so that they are holy."[167] The Israelites' apocalyptic reading of natural disasters and social ills maintains the constant pressure of imminence, and the apparent crises are supplemented by calculations that have the sun "descending from its normal position since 1978."[168] The solar descent is exemplary in its detour through pseudoscience to arrive at a traditional Andean conclusion: pachacuti brings a change of suns.

Cyclical time predominated in Mesoamerica, where the *Florentine Codex* recorded that the past "will be again," that "things will be the same, some time, some place," and that "those who now live, will live again."[169] At the time of the conquest, myths held that the Mesoamerican world (like that of the Incas) had been destroyed four previous times, in this case by cataclysms resulting from rival gods' struggle for domination. A new order and the world's repopulation by new beings followed each destruction, but the Aztecs believed that existence under the fifth sun had reached its zenith, that the stages of creation had exhausted all possibilities, and that the forthcoming destruction would be the final one ending the world and humanity forever.[170] The Aztec sun stone calendar represents each of the four previous ages by the force that destroyed it, and shows the fifth age—that of the Aztecs, which is to be destroyed by earthquakes—with concentric circles closing around a face believed to be that of the underworld sun, its tongue a sacrificial knife.

The "fundamental religious preoccupation" of the pre-Columbian Maya was the ordering of time and history "in reference to temporal cycles inferred from astronomical observation."[171] Here again the world had evolved through a series of destructions and re-creations, including three previous human creations, until the interruption of conquest, described as "time gone mad," brought chaos. As the *Chilam Balam* has it, people of the ancestral past were good, wise, healthy, devout: "They walked with bodies erect." Once the "murderers of the world" arrived, however, "the beginning of suffering" followed, with discord, illness, tribute, enslavement, and crime.[172] A mood of "apocalyptic fatalism" resulted from the prophesy (a retrospective prophesy, written after the conquest) that foretold cataclysm and a new age reorganized by the conqueror's religion.[173]

Cyclicity is self-restoring, however, and the *Chilam Balam* anticipates restitution when the earth turns over again.

American myths of creation are replete with recurring ends occasioned by floods, fires, and other conflagrations by which angry gods retaliate against unworthy humans. The Andean Viracocha created, destroyed, and then re-created humanity, and coastal Peru's Pachacámac took his human creation through the cycle four times.[174] In the Brazilian jungle, Yanomami myths relate the fall of the sky, the creation of a new sun and moon, and a world inside out as much as it is upside down: "This earth where we stand today is nothing but the back of that first sky, which has been replaced by a new sky." The re-created cosmos is reiterated in the recycling of humans, as the smoke from a burned skeleton rises to the sky and "after the soul has been rejuvenated in a bloody lake on the moon it is sent back to the earth again." The collective depopulation and repopulation of the world is also expressed by the Yanomami, as by many peoples throughout the world, in flood myths featuring a few survivors who procreate the new humanity.[175]

The Sikuani of eastern Colombia likewise recount a flood unleashed by the wrath of deity, the water in this case infested with genocidal piranhas. Re-creation follows the flood, with some humans transformed into an alien otherness through a gesture reminiscent of fellatio. A worm, or elsewhere "a big cigar in the form of a worm," is covered with the deity's sperm, and "whoever smeared his mouth with the sperm or decided of his own free will to suck a bit of the sperm changed his language and spoke Spanish."[176] One is "reborn" of sperm that procreates in one's mouth the discourse of the dominant other.

Punitive floods and fires likewise periodically destroyed the Mataco, with one of the floods caused when "a menstruating woman was killed and eaten by the rainbow."[177] For the Toba, also of the Gran Chaco, a flood of fire destroyed the world before its re-creation, as did a great freeze, a great flood, and a great darkness due to a "clash of power" among the people.[178] In a separate series of Toba myths, a great fire resulted when the moon was attacked and wounded by jaguars that were spirits of the dead, and then "fragments of the moon fell down upon the earth and started a big fire."[179] In most of these cases and in mythic cycles of destruction and regeneration generally, the recurring ends are stages of an evolutionary progression toward an ideal of civilization and morality. The myths' authors assess their past from the privileged viewpoint of their present accomplishments. As the Sikuani put it, "Long ago people were like those of today, but not quite as perfect."[180]

Cyclical time, natural cycles, and solar and lunar deities together constitute a symbolic complex of death and regeneration. The Aztec case is most suggestive, for here the very survival of the deified sun was contingent upon human sacrifice. In order to re-create the cosmos, the Mesoamerican gods gathered at Teotihuacán and, after intricate penitential rituals, cast themselves into an enormous fire to restore the sun and the moon. The sacrifice of other gods was required to set these celestial bodies moving on their cyclical courses, thereby establishing the paradigm for reciprocal obligations between gods and humans. The blood of sacrificial victims (called "the divine dead") would repay the debt and restore the sun's power to burn, to cycle, and to defeat the forces of darkness.[181] A causal relation was established between the contrived imminent end and the necessity for ritual murder: "The threat of destruction never passes, and the demand for blood is unrelenting."[182] The end of the world, or collective death, is averted by the ritual, recurring death of scapegoats. This self-appointed mission and the political eschatology that it served rendered the Aztecs "the chosen people of the sun," conferring upon them the privilege of being lords of the world that they redeemed from destruction. "Only through endless warfare, conquest, and sacrifice could the Mexica [Aztecs] save the universe from daily threat of annihilation."[183] An apocalyptic end impelled the imperial military outward from the center of the universe, Tenochtitlán, counterbalancing the perpetual social disequilibrium of warfare with the harmony of cosmic order restored under a new sun daily.

Joachim of Fiore and the Americas

In twelfth-century Europe an influential variation on the motif of recurring ends was introduced into apocalyptic traditions by the Calabrian abbot Joachim of Fiore. Joachim "imparted a rhythm and expectation to the course of history" by devising three ages (or "states," *status*) corresponding to the three persons of the Christian Trinity. [184] The age of God the Father commenced with Adam and terminated with Jesus. The Son's age began with the incarnation and ended in 1260. And the age of the Holy Spirit, due since that date but late in appearing, would establish a millennial kingdom governed by friars and fashioned in the likeness of a monastery. In harmony, grace, piety, and ecstatic bliss, this third-age world reborn into the purified Catholic Church would dedicate itself to prayer and contemplation.

Joachim's writings were particularly espoused by the Spiritual Franciscans, who parted company with the Conventual Franciscans in order to interpret Saint Francis's vow of poverty literally and to dedicate themselves to contemplative asceticism. In 1524 the conqueror Hernán Cortés requested that Charles V send missionary friars to the New World, and the Franciscan "twelve apostles" who were dispatched in response brought with them the concept of trinitarian history and the dream of a millennial kingdom modeled on Joachim's third age. As the twelve departed Spain, the minister-general of the Franciscan order described their mission as "the beginning of the last preaching of the gospel on the eve of the end of the world."[185] Cortés himself anticipated that "there will, in a very short time, arise in these parts a new Church, where God, Our Lord, may be better served and worshipped than in all the rest of the world."[186] The age of the Holy Spirit, the return to primitive Christianity, the millennial kingdom promised in Revelation, and the restitution of Eden all coalesced to inspire a new Church worthy of its New World.

The Joachite superimposition of the Trinity onto history traveled with the Franciscans to the most remote frontiers of the colonies, where despite the incompatibilities of linearity and cyclicity Christian apocalypticism was assimilated to indigenous periodizations. In the Andes and parts of the Peruvian jungle, syncretic fusion was fostered by imperfect command of the catechism, the tendency to process out nuance or to reconcile rival doctrines by privileging similarities, and the difficulties of translating metaphysical concepts between Spanish and indigenous languages. One typical neo-Joachite periodization from the modern Andes associates Dios Yaya (God the Father) with the past, Dios Churi (Jesus Christ) with the present, and Dios Espíritu (Holy Spirit) with the future.[187] The three ages, like the three persons of the Trinity, are Andeanized: the age of the Father is considered the "gentile" era, before the Andeans received the true faith; the age of the Son is the present era that commenced with conquest, during which the Andeans endure sufferings associated with those of Christ; and the age of the Holy Spirit is the anticipated future era of restitution, when the Andeans recuperate their lands and cultural identity.[188]

According to a version from Urcos, "Other beings will inhabit the earth" during this last age charged with millennial expectations. An informant in Quinua pointed into the distance to add, "The city of the Holy Spirit will be on the peak of that mountain," and the angelic third agers will be winged (as is the Holy Spirit in dove imagery) to fly beyond the reaches of sin.[189] Another informant, from Ayacucho, echoed the Edenic vestiges of Joachite thought when he observed that "in the epoch of the Holy Spirit one need not dress nor eat. They will live by grace alone."[190] Until then, according to the Urcos version, Indians of the second age are dominated by white conquerors who are inherently superior because they were created after the Incas on an evolutionary continuum that, like the three ages themselves, progresses toward perfection. White people "do whatever they please and God puts up with their sins," but not for long. Apocalyptic signs will reveal that "this world is going to end in the year 2000," and the third age will then commence. The cataclysmic transition features motifs adapted from John's Revelation: "The wandering Jews will appear and will fly but will never reach the earth," and "the antichrists, who are the sons of priests, will also appear."[191] Interviews conducted in Quechua in the 1970s registered a similar consensus that "this age is going to end in the year 2000" at which time "the Judgment will arrive" and "the age of God the Spirit" will begin.[192] The messiah of the Israelites of the New Covenant counts among his identities one that is congruent with a quasi-Joachite mission: "Just as the son of God was incarnated in Jesus of Nazareth, the Holy Spirit has been incarnated in Ezequiel Ataucusi Gamonal."[193]

A quasi-Joachite messianism is also suggested outside of the Andes in Mexico's Spiritualism sect, which was established in 1866 by Roque Rojas. Tripartite history here culminates in a third age inaugurated by Rojas, characterized by communication of a Divine Spirit with humanity, and scheduled to endure two thousand years before the Last Judgment.[194] A threefold pattern of redemption is also central to the Mita sect, founded in Puerto Rico in 1940 and established since the 1960s in the Dominican Republic, Colombia, Venezuela, Mexico, and Haiti. The faithful hold that God has communicated to his creation through three revelations: that of the Old Testament; that of Jesus' preaching; and that of the sect's Pentecostal founder, Juanita García Peraza, known as Mita, which means "the 'Word of Life' that is bestowed upon the chosen." As the incarnation of the Holy Spirit, Mita's mission was to reestablish the primitive Church among the chosen people. She died in 1970 before that mission was accomplished, but the Holy Spirit then "entered the body of the new leader, Aaron, and is continuing to issue revelations to the whole world."[195]

The periodization of history is inherently subversive, for it implies the overthrow of an existing order by a projected future order, always superior, that is predestined to succeed and perfect it. The old is displaced by the new as paradigms are overhauled to revitalize social reality from within. The radical potential is implicit in Joachite doctrine's emphasis not as much on ages as on stages, on renovation and progression, and not as much on the end of the world as on the millennial kingdom that precedes it. The ideology of the early Spiritual Franciscans themselves was clearly subversive in its depiction of the Church as the Whore of Babylon and the pope as the Antichrist. The Spiritualists were condemned as heretics and expected "a saviour from their own ranks to mount the papal throne as the 'Angelic Pope' chosen by God to convert the whole world to a life of voluntary poverty."[196]

In the eighteenth century a redeeming angel of another ilk attracted a massive following of indigenous peoples for a syncretic Joachite salvation in the jungle. Among the complex, multicultural identities of the revolutionary Juan Santos Atahualpa was one as incarnation of the Holy Spirit and thus legitimate heir to the third-age kingdom.[197] In reference to Santos Atahualpa, a testimony observed "that in this world there are only three Kingdoms, Spain, Angola, and his Kingdom, and that he has not gone to steal anyone else's kingdom, and the Spaniards have come to steal his; but the Spaniards' age is now over and his age has arrived."[198] Tripartite space and time intermingle as Santos Atahualpa resynchronizes the indigenous age with its place by means of a Christianized pachacuti.

Signs

Prophesy and the religious meaning of events are predicated on the belief that God is "a personality who ceaselessly intervenes in history," manifesting his will and expressing his intentions through interpretable signs.[199] Human reality is a mystery revealed encoded to the chosen. Natural disasters, crop failure, apparitions, famines, comets, epidemics, abusive tyrants, wars, Antichrists, false prophets, iniquities, economic crises, and miserable social situations are all frequently cited as signals and symptoms of God's interaction with his creation. Such signs, like many biblical passages, are sufficiently ambiguous to accommodate whatever meaning a given interest wishes to derive from them, and they thereby lend themselves to self-serving random readings as much as to pro forma repetition of traditional readings that serve interests already institutionalized. "What is consistent is the implicit dispensational instruction to 'read history backward,' to interpret the significance of present events as 'signs' that tribulational prophecies are always already coming true, that future events are unfolding now."[200]

One simple example of an ambiguous signifier interpreted with bias is found in competing responses to an earthquake in Huaraz, Peru. A campesino understood the disaster as a sign announcing the imminent return of the indigenous cultural hero Inkarrí, whose messianic appearance would redeem the Andeans from five hundred years of oppression. A landowner dismissed that interpretation as ignorant and superstitious, offering instead the opinion that the earthquake was the second sign—the first being agrarian reform—which announced the "uncertain future" of the new age that could deprive him of his land holdings.[201] A similar conflict of interpretations occurred in a religious context following an earthquake in Ayacucho. All parties agreed that the earthquake was a "punishment from God," but the Catholics of the community blamed the scourge on God's displeasure with villagers who had abandoned the true faith and converted to Evangelical churches. The Evangelicals responded with precisely the opposite interpretation: the earthquake was punishment for the Catholics' failure to convert and for their persecution of God's chosen people.[202] As evidenced in both the Huaraz and Ayacucho cases, the inherent meaninglessness of the sign in itself renders any interpretation a tautology reinforcing the fears, hopes, and beliefs that generate it. The sign is empty and, as such, a ready receptacle that can be filled and refilled at will.

In other cases a prophesy from the past conditions, contextualizes, or restricts the interpretations of present events. A constant recirculation of biblical places and personalities provided a common currency by which ideas were traded in hispanic Christendom, and thus wherever there was a mine there was Ophir, wherever there was evil there was Antichrist or Satan. A tendency to biblicize reality, to forge a consonance between sacrosanct traditions defended by dogma and a chaotic New World that challenged European postulates, established the interpretive frame of reference that restricted the polyvalence of American signs to the imposition of alien meanings. Often the Spaniards reinforced their own erroneous presumptions by projecting European ideas into the Indians' discourse, retrieving these ideas in their "distorted" indigenous version, and then correcting that distortion so that it would conform—now as a mystery revealed—to the original projected idea. The Indians thereby served as something of an echoing wall from which the Spaniards retrieved a version of their own presumptions. To close the gap between the word *Cipango* (Japan) and the indigenous word *Cibao* that named an interior region of Hispaniola, for example, Columbus "simply indicated that the indigenous people did not know how to pronounce the name of their own island."[203] Evidence contrary to the original supposition (the indigenous name of the island, not to mention the nature of the landscape and people) was thereby metamorphosed (the "corrected" name) to serve as evidence in support of Columbus's erroneous belief that he had reached the Far East described by Marco Polo.

A similar maneuver is evident when American phenomena are read as signs restricted to signify the religious meanings, generally self-serving, imposed by Europeans. The epidemics that devastated indigenous populations in the sixteenth century were commonly interpreted by friars as a punishment for "vices and crimes and idolatries," and in more extreme reckonings as a divine genocide to exterminate the entire Satanic race.[204] These positions were concordant with the more general belief that God had delivered the Indies to Spanish tutelage because of "the great sins and abominations" committed there.[205] Responding to the two-year plague in Mexico beginning in 1575, Sahagún reasoned that the Indians were suffering the fate of the Jews as prophesied by Jeremiah: conquest and cataclysm to "destroy them and their gods."[206]

The inexplicability of the Spaniards' immunity to the diseases that devastated the Indians contributed to the seeming divinity of the conquerors, godlike in their own resistance to death and in their capacity to disseminate it among their adversaries. Common among Spaniard and native alike was the interpretation that the epidemics originated in the arsenal of a Christian god manifesting support for his soldiers. As the initial shock of conquest settled into colonization, many indigenous groups eventually revised their interpretation to conclude that death by disease was a by-product of baptism and conversion, as though Christianity itself were the contagion or, alternatively, as though their own gods had deployed the epidemics in punitive retaliation for having abandoned traditional religion.[207] Indigenous theories of humanly or divinely disseminated biological warfare endured for centuries—the church bells attract diseases, the spooky friars are emissaries of death—to include as late as 1837 a Guatemalan revolt precipitated by the belief that the government had deployed a cholera epidemic in order to exterminate natives.[208]

Las Casas was the outspoken advocate of a different and more apocalyptic reading of the demographic tragedy that followed conquest, arguing that legible in the Spanish destruction of the Indies was a sign that Spain itself would be destroyed in divine retribution for "such great sins" committed in the "unjust, iniquitous, and tyrannical" conquest and colonization.[209] The Spanish Christians, like the apostles in the Roman Empire, were to face martyrdom as they peaceably evangelized the American frontier, but the reality played out quite to the contrary because the Christians were "not like sheep or lambs among wolves, but rather like furious wolves among lambs and sheep."[210] Mendieta pursued a similar line of reasoning to its Franciscan conclusion by interpreting the epidemics as an instrument of a divine plan to reward the Indians and punish the Spaniards (by, in part, depriving colonists of free labor). He argued that the epidemics among natives were "not for their harm but for their benefit," because they occurred in such measure that only those died who had first prepared themselves by confession. The Indians succumb to the disease "in conformity with the number of priests they have." The climax of this orderly apocalypse followed the notion that judgment came after the accumulation of a predetermined number of saved souls: "undoubtedly our God is filling up the chairs in Heaven with Indians, so as to end the world."[211]

Earthquakes, like the one in Ayacucho, have been exploited by innumerable politico-religious agendas to document God's grumbling displeasure with human endeavors. The theophany that delivers earthquakes (along with lightning, thunder, and hail) in Revelation 6:12–14 and 11:19 is rendered more literally in indigenous American myths that associate tremors with movements of an earth-god. For the Aztecs, earthquakes were likened to uterine contractions and intrauterine fetal movement, with the earth taking back life it had bestowed while giving birth to chaos.[212] When the deity Pachacámac (He Who Shakes the Earth) stretches, the earth of coastal Peru trembles. He moves only when he is angry with his creation, for even the mere turning of his head causes an earthquake.[213] "If he were to turn over his whole body, the universe would end in an instant."[214] In related imagery, the Toba of the Gran Chaco regard earthquakes as an apocalyptic sign caused by the movement of giant underground armadillos. At the end of the world, "when the destruction begins" the armadillos will emerge to wander across the ruined earth, "and God will kill them with a falling star."[215]

In popular Christianity, anti-earthquake virgins, saints, and Christs, notably the Lord of Miracles in Lima, are carried from their churches on litters and paraded through the streets with pomp and veneration to placate the divine wrath that makes the earth tremble. The grizzly Lord of Earthquakes in Cuzco, reputed to have been a gift from Charles V, inaugurated its enduring fame in 1650 when an earthquake that had displayed stark indifference to the other cult objects that were carried from the cathedral miraculously ended when this Christ crossed the threshold to earn his title.[216] The association of the Lord of Earthquakes with Charles V is doubly suggestive, first because it is erroneous and then because, by extension through the miraculous image, it confers upon the Holy Roman Emperor a power greater than that of nature. If a religious emblem of Charles's power can still the forces of natural or supernatural wrath, then the inversion of that feat places natural and supernatural forces (like the epidemics) in the emperor's arsenal for deployment against enemies of the empire.

An appeal to royal omnipotence was made later when the earth under Caracas shook on Holy Thursday in 1812. In a "pathetic spectacle of religious frenzy" monks took to the streets, blessing the dead, taking confessions, and disseminating their interpretation of the tragedy as a scourge punishing disloyalty to the crown.[217] In the Plaza de San Jacinto an "excited monk" fueled the fear of a crowd inclined to believe that king, God, and nature had joined forces for this Holy Week offensive in retaliation for transgressions against theocracy. But Simón Bolívar, leader of the independence effort, violated the sacrosanct to provide in gesture a counterinterpretation of the earthquake. Bolívar drew his sword, leapt onto the improvised pulpit, pulled down the monk, and threatened him with death if he resisted.[218] "If nature opposes us," said Bolívar when it was suggested that nature had allied with the Spaniards, "we will fight against it and make it obey us."[219] The Liberator thereby challenged the religious interpretation of the earthquake by silencing the monk's prophetic harangue, by demonstrating an irreverent disbelief in the alleged royal theophany, and by claiming for independence the earth-shaking omnipotence that would now be redirected to subdue nature and god-king alike.

A less dramatic but no less suggestive response to tyranny also came to a critical juncture following the 1972 earthquake that devastated Managua. Corruption in the Anastasio Somoza regime impeded the flow of foreign aid to its proper recipients, resulting in "prophetic interpretations" by Catholic clergy and the consequent upscaled support of resistance to the dictatorship. If in the Bolívar case the earthquake and the Church impeded revolution, in the Nicaraguan case they catalyzed it. Relief services organized by Evangelicals, meanwhile, found in the same earthquake an opportunity to solidify a position in Nicaragua for their alternate route to salvation.[220] In Guatemala, similarly, the Church of the Word began its ministry in the aftermath of a 1976 earthquake, with one of the church's elders, General Efraín Ríos Montt, becoming de facto president in a 1982 coup.[221] According to one Evangelical, the rapidity with which the new churches are breaking down traditional structures is itself seismic: "The earthquake of '76 in Guatemala is nothing compared with what is happening now."[222]

The general depiction of revolutions as earthquakes or other natural cataclysms metaphorically allies the imposing and inexhaustible power of nature with the insurgents, just as it had earlier with theocracies. It also represents the revolutionary effort as an upheaval outside the laws of the state but within the laws of nature. Bolívar's revolution is thus "the flood-tide of a devastating torrent"; Sendero Luminoso is "a roaring armed hurricane"; and the God of liberation theology is an "erupting volcano."[223] Natural powers can also be recruited to a revolutionary cause when an inadequate arsenal, war chest, and muster of soldiers makes a magical, compensatory alliance with nature desirable. This was the case among rebelling Zapotecs in Oaxaca, Mexico, who in 1547 "no longer wanted to serve God but rather to be in their land as before." The natives had no need to make war against their oppressor, "because there would be eight days of earthquake and great darkness" in which all of the Spaniards would die.[224] In other cases, a collaboration between revolutionary and natural forces is suggested. Juan Santos Atahualpa was believed to have caused earthquakes—particularly those that shook Lima in 1746—as part of his more comprehensive military offensive "to expel the Spaniards."[225] A similar interpretation was made in Santiago, Chile, when in the midst of a 1647 earthquake a black slave proclaimed himself King of Guinea, recruited some four hundred followers, and rampaged with a vengeance until he was hanged by the neck. In the coincidence of the earthquake and the slave rebellion a bishop deciphered a message from God, "saying we have sinned against His Divine Majesty and against his humblest creatures, who are the Negroes of Angola."[226]

In modern liberation theology, chronic "signs of the times" have been distanced but not detached from their reference in Matthew 16:3 to events preceding the end of the world. The phrase now refers to conditions in human history, notably massive poverty and oppression of Latin American peoples, that call for an efficacious response to guarantee the love and justice that Christ intended for his creation. Sin and a "rejection of the Lord" have been institutionalized in the inequitable economic, social, and political structures of Latin America.[227] Because "it is in history that God reveals the secret of his person," the signs of the times are not only revelations conveying otherworldly messages but also "a call to commitment, a summons to make our own the demands of the kingdom."[228] The resulting social movements (interpreted by militarized states as signs of atheist "communist subversion") were in this perspective interpreted as "the coming of the Kingdom" because "the struggle for justice is also the struggle for the Kingdom of God."[229] As Gustavo Gutiérrez put it, "the eschatological vision becomes operative" when it attaches to social reality to deliver "political the-ology." By reading and then acting on the signs of the times, "the political is grafted onto the eternal."[230] And finally, "the sign of the coming of the messiah is the suppression of oppression: the messiah arrives when injustice is over-come."[231]

In other quarters, signs of the times are superfluous as calamities programmed for the last days (trees sweating blood, water burning, fish moaning, stars falling like fruit) combine with visions, dreams, revelations, biblical passages, prophe-sies (often retroactive or falsely attributed), and a religious reading of everyday life to generate divine messages in abundance.[232] Signs speak back to a com-munity the message with which they are invested. A prodigious example oc-curred in the court of King Sebastian of Portugal when Cardinal Henrique was served a dinner of swordfish that revealed on one side a cross and on the other the numbers "1578," indicating the year that Sebastian would be—and was—killed. The king's death, which inaugurated the messianic tradition of Sebas-tianism that endures in Brazil today, was itself the consequence of crusade am-bitions that were catalyzed in part by another sign, the November 1577 comet (*cometa*) that whipped its tail from Portugal to Africa as a call for attack (*acom-eta*) against Islam.[233] In 1649 omnipresent deity was also found everywhere by Hernando Avendaño, who reminded New World missionaries that "God put his mark and his sign on all creatures, so that we would know that all beings are the work of God." Examples of this hallmark followed: the Southern Cross, the condor that flies in the form of a cross. And "have you not also seen that when you cut a *lucina* at the top, there appears there a brown cross? And in bananas, if you cut them in half, you also see the same cross, and in the passion flower and in the *puche puche*, one also sees the sign of Jesus Christ's pas-sion."[234]

If prophesy "shapes a future to confirm it," the future may also return to shape the prophesy, particularly when feigned foreknowledge assists a society in processing, understanding, overcoming, or undoing a catastrophe.[235] As Na-than Wachtel put it, "Retrospective prophecy is evidence of the need to root in the past an event too extraordinary to contain its own meaning."[236] After the fall of Tenochtitlán, it seemed that the ominous approach of conquest had been insistently foretold by signs that had begun to appear a decade earlier. A comet described as a bleeding "wound in the sky," a fire in the temple of Huitzilo-pochtli, unusual winds, lightning strikes, lake water that appeared to be "boil-ing," two-headed people, a woman wailing in the darkness ("O my children, we are about to go forever"), a strange bird with "a mirror in its head" that held the image of foreign warriors, and other harbingers foretold "some imminent, unparalleled catastrophe."[237] The retroactive invention or interpretation of signs softened the indignity of unforeseen conquest by providing mythologically for its anticipation. In other cases, the reading of signs served to offer a mythopoetic explanation for the inexplicable and to justify retaliatory actions for actual or perceived offensives. A simple example is found in late-eighteenth-century Alto Peru, now Bolivia, when rebels under Túpac Catari executed a priest who they believed had said a "mass of damnation" that resulted in their defeat on the battlefield.[238] The sign is the defeat, the interpretation searches retroactively for its meaning, and the murder neutralizes the defeat through retaliation against its imaginary cause. The rebels' reading of the sign, despite the obvious error, coincided with the truth: the priest was the enemy and would rally whatever forces he could muster—military and supernatural—to defeat the native insurgency.

The Perpetual Threshold

In *The Sense of an Ending*, Frank Kermode followed Joachite studies to underscore how present historical moments are often perceived as transitional, as threshold eras, as turning points in human destiny.[239] This "peculiarity of our imagination, that it chooses always to be at the end of an era," is nowhere more patent than it is in apocalypticism (we are living at "the ends of the ages" according to Paul), be it that of doomsday sects, of military dictatorships, or of great imperial powers endowing their conquests with politico-religious import.[240] The concept of threshold is also implicit in the empires that are held in regency for a returning god (the Last World Emperor abdicates to Christ, Moctezuma to Quetzalcóatl), registering the belief that humans can bring history to the brink of culmination but must reserve the grand finale for a returning deity.

Life on the threshold gains continuous religious expression as a hypothetical future exerts its pressure on present interpretations. One outstanding example is the Andean Christ of Huanca, whose image was painted on a rock to commemorate two seventeenth-century visions (a third followed in the eighteenth century) of a bound Jesus stripped and bleeding during flagellation. The contemporary cult, numbering some fifteen thousand, has assumed millennial traits derived from interpretations of the image's gradual fading. "A woman pasturing her flocks in the vicinity is said to have been visited by angels, who told her that the image of Christ and his torturers would eventually disappear and that when this happens, the Day of Judgment will have arrived."[241] These poetics of disappearance are polyvalent: in one reading the gradual fading of the image represents and accelerates the gradual ending of the world, with the chosen community of Huanca and its local deity ushering in a day of judgment that is optimistically anticipated. At the same time, the erasure of the image by divine or natural forces implies an end to suffering, that of Christ under the whip and of his faithful under the burden of their poverty and oppression. The latter reading is enhanced by Christ's identity as shepherd, which he shares with the woman who had the vision, and by his symbolic presence duplicated within the flock through his iconography as a lamb. The faithful of Huanca are positioned in a transitional period between the apparitions themselves and the disappearance of the image representing them. A vision projects forward to endow the image's ultimate disappearance with eschatological importance, and that unrealized future event then works retroactively to establish the threshold from which the community interprets the image today. The future absence of the image lends its meaning to the present abjection of the community, perhaps in part because the community itself is disappearing.

"We project ourselves—a small, humble elect, perhaps—past the End, so as to see the structure whole, a thing we cannot do from our spot of time in the middle."[242] If each religious subject is posed between the golden age of childhood and the heavenly hereafter that defeats death, then in millennialism the collective repairs to a prelapsarian past and anticipates an Edenic future in order to ameliorate the hardships of the present. The significance of human action is jeopardized without perceptions returning from beyond the end to endorse the conviction "that time is related to eternity, that the history of man has a discernible structure and meaning in relation to its End, and that this End is the product not of chance, but of divine plan."[243] Once the redeeming long view is instituted, meaning can be discerned "where the uninitiated sees only chaos or catastrophe."[244]

Contemplating the union of New Granada and Venezuela in the midst of postliberation instability, Simón Bolívar concluded his 1819 Angostura address with his soul ascending "to the heights necessary to view the mighty panorama." His imagination traveled through future ages, and, he said, "observing from that vantagepoint, with admiration and awe, the prosperity, the splendor, the life that this vast region has received, I feel enraptured and believe that I already see it as the heart of the universe" and as "the bond, the center, and the emporium of the human race."[245] Bolívar was preceded in that vision by his Spanish enemy (aroused by "a future felt to be already present"), but most conspicuous is the passage's utopian flight from a troubled today to an idealized tomorrow, where the freed colony is "crowned by glory, seated upon the throne of liberty with the scepter of Justice in her hand, disclosing to the Old World the majesty of the New."[246] The wars of independence and the postliberation consolidation are endowed with global and transcendental importance because their anarchy is disavowed and they are viewed through accomplishments that they have not yet realized. As Karl Marx put it, "The social revolution of the nineteenth century cannot draw its poetry from the past, but only from the future."[247]

Without anticipation of victory and the eventual consolidation of gains, all of the bloodshed becomes meaningless and abandons one in the expanse between an infinite, dead past divested of its worth and an infinite, cold future promising nothing. Millennial thought calls rather for "a concord of imaginatively recorded past and imaginatively predicted future."[248] It accentuates the tendency to make "considerable imaginative investments in coherent patterns which, by the provision of an end, make possible a satisfying consonance with the origins."[249] It is the product of opposing perspectives that negotiate a conciliation in order to recover and perfect the lost past in the imaginary future. The present is always its enemy. The future is its place as much as its time, and the righteous who have suffered unduly can view themselves—here, now—from that distant world as glorious as this one is penitential.

Collective Death

Millennial agendas tend to be sympathetically received not by privileged and secure peoples but rather by the disoriented, exploited, poor, and oppressed. Their receptivity to radical solutions rises in proportion to their exhaustion of options within the system. Once a predisposition to challenge previously uncontested givens is catalyzed, it generally activates a corresponding shift into a higher register of expectation and demand. If previously a shorter workday, a lower bus fare, another tortilla, or lower taxes were the goal, now nothing short of total expulsion of the oppressor and "restoration" of an idealized age of peace and plenty is acceptable. If previously resistance consisted, as E. J. Hobsbawm put it, of working the system to their minimum disadvantage, they now endeavor to work it to their maximum advantage.[250] If previously the villagers were traditional, conservative in their values, and resistant to change, now, "with an anger born of hope," they defend to the death radical programs that are incapable of delivering the redemption that is promised.[251] The shift of register likewise inflates the value of local hardships and sorrows by representing them as symptoms of a greater, often eschatological crisis. The village perspective becomes national, global, cosmic as "they assess their dismal station in terms that are sacred to them."[252] The old, enduring problems, borne with resignation for decades or centuries, become imbued with a moral urgency.

If in early Christianity the combat myth of Revelation functioned "to reinforce resistance to Rome and to inspire willingness for martyrdom," then modern variations on the theme pose the new oppressed against the new oppressor, the forces of righteousness against those of evil in a grand eschatological struggle that subordinates the life of the individual to the eternal cause.[253] The victorious warrior Christ of Revelation alternates with the martyred Christ sacrificially slaughtered as each Christian group assesses its fate and negotiates its identity. Ideologies processing the incomprehensibility of a chosen people's collective, violent death stress Christ's triumph not through his military prowess but through his defeat, torture, and execution. Each martyred Christian is another "lamb to the slaughter" who shares in the resurrection because he or she shared in Christ's Passion.[254] As liberation theologists expressed it to the brutalized poor, Jesus "embraces his lot, he forgives, he suffers for the multitudes, and he dies in absolute surrender to the persons who killed him." In this manner "to die is to gain," because "death is embraced in a project that reaches beyond this life; thus it is overcome and integrated."[255] Eulogizing the four American church women murdered by the Salvadoran military on December 2, 1980, the Jesuit Jon Sobrino lauded "the Christian resolve to keep on, shoulder to shoulder with a massacred people, even if it meant that the church must march once more to the cross."[256]

A preoccupation with eschatology is ultimately inseparable from the urge to transform senseless suffering and death—or even senseless joy and life—into meaningful experience that survives individual mortality and is validated by its contribution to some enduring social or supernatural design. Collective salvation intervenes where the individual death seems as meaningless as it is inevitable.

The medieval pope Boniface VIII missed the point when he scornfully remarked, "Why are these fools waiting for the end of the world? The world ends for each man when he dies."[257] The fools were awaiting the end of the world precisely because the world ended with their deaths and because the stark irreversibility of their individual destiny was redeemed by the collective salvation promised by Boniface's Church, if not here then hereafter. The millennial kingdoms, the promised lands, the fountains of youth, the new calendars, the revitalized cultures, and the reborn selves all ultimately emerge as creative responses of suffering humans searching for an escape more amenable than that of their inevitable death.

If in some cases millennialism inspires insurrections that challenge fatalistic despair, in others it serves quite to the contrary as a strategy of adaptation to social situations that are grim, chronic, and inescapable. Following a vision in which Jesus ordered him to preach to peoples everywhere, Francisco da Cruz journeyed through Brazil, Argentina, Uruguay, Paraguay, Colombia, and Peru, bringing the word of God, curing the sick, founding churches, and raising the wooden, Christless crosses that have come to symbolize his Brotherhood of the Cross movement. The majority of his followers are illiterate indigenous peoples who believe that they are poor because of "luck, fate, or the will of God" and that this irremediable condition will endure until all inequities are smitten at the end of time, with corresponding punishment for their guilty oppressors.[258] Members of the Brotherhood abandon their homes and repair to isolated communities, and "what most motivates the people, as they leave to search for the Holy Land, is the idea of the proximity of the end of the world."[259] A life of despair seemed inevitable, but the movement offered the attractive alternatives of the end of the world and, in the indeterminate interim, a life of withdrawal that rehearsed the promised eternity of grace.

The defiant cultural revitalization that is made manifest by colonial rebellions and modern nativist movements is in the present context displaced, or benumbed, by paralyzing demoralization, cultural despair, loss of identity, a sense of eschatological abandonment, and self-depreciatory sentiments of inherent inferiority. The last of these is lamentably explicit in a modern myth from the Paraguayan Chaco, in which the Chamacoco relate that they were created from excrement, precisely that of a primeval chief who "wiped his rump" with a dog's collar that he then threw away. In another myth, the Chamacoco are again disposable, now because the creator conceived them as an afterthought: "He made them badly, hurriedly, and then threw them aside." The text concludes by recapitulating that "the Chamacoco sometimes think that perhaps because they were created in a hurry they are always so stupid and slow to learn."[260] The Toba, also of the Gran Chaco, relate how a miscalculation in creation resulted in the ugliness of the primeval woman lowered from the sky. "This woman married the only man left on earth, and that was the origin of the Indians today." Had the error not been made, "she would have been beautiful, and then all the Indians would be white and handsome."[261]

Crisis itself becomes salvation by default when a culture capitulates that it is "necessary for people to die because God will only accept mankind after all die."[262] Fatalistic resignation yielded to despair for the Guaraní who inhabited an exhausted world longing to ease into the peace of oblivion. They described the earth as being old and tired, crying out to its creator "that it was weary and awaited its end." The tribe's people, too, were diminishing, and those who remained "expressed their wish to see the dead."[263] The trope of the tired world is common among exhausted cultures of the modern Americas, and its precedents in colonialism were reinforced by catechisms that likewise maintained that the world "is already old and shows signs of wanting to end."[264] Christian apocalypticism could thus engage dialectically with the demoralization of conquered cultures to deliver an eschatology of an appeal as great as its duration was short. The Guaraní also suffered the consequences of ancestral searches for the Land-without-Evil that ended only in death and destruction, with this failed eschatology compounded by epidemics, progressive encroachment, deculturation, and social collapse that eventuated "the morbid manifestations of fascination with death and suicide."[265]

Among the modern Cuna of the San Blas Islands, such manifestations were sufficiently prevalent to render a diagnostic category—"the illness of suicide"—with corresponding rituals seeking a cure.[266] In the mid-sixteenth century among the Quimbaya in what is now Colombia, a wandering messiah itemized mistreatment under Spanish subjugation and concluded that "it would be better for all to die than to serve the Christians." The Indians responded in kind, "Let's all die, because it's better than hauling trunks and giving boys for the doctrina, or men for the mine, or women to serve the Christians."[267] When facing encroaching colonization in 1545, Indians living under the imperial protection of Las Casas's Vera Paz experiment in Guatemala seemed to be of the same mind when they remarked sardonically, "We want no more privileges; we prefer to die."[268] A group of rebelling Indians in Mexico who were offered the opportunity of returning "to peace and to work in the mines" likewise "preferred to die of hunger enjoying their freedom" than to live as colonial subjects.[269]

The preference for death often resulted in mass escapist suicide that accumulated in quotas the collective death of an apocalyptic doomsday. Trapped in a tautology, the conquered people die because their world has ended, and their world ends because they die. Early chronicles report the autogenocidal efforts of natives who poisoned themselves, "hanged themselves for little reason," and induced abortions "to avoid having children who were going to serve the foreigners."[270] According to Inca Garcilaso de la Vega, natives of early colonial Cuba committed suicide in such haste and quantities that entire villages—men, women, and children—met their tragic fate overnight, leaving behind only the macabre sight of corpses dangling from trees.[271] In his 1565 account, Girolamo Benzoni related that epidemic suicide among natives in the Caribbean was brought under control only when the Spaniards threatened to likewise commit suicide, to pursue the natives into the next world, and to enslave them there for all eternity.[272] The same logic was deployed in defiance of Spanish authority when the Hispaniola cacique Hatuey boldly rejected baptism and took his pagan chances after learning that Spaniards populated the heaven awaiting him beyond his imminent execution.[273] Defiance also characterized the frequent suicide of black slaves, who accomplished in one and the same desperate gesture an exit from servitude, an act of sabotage against the master's property and means of production, and—in some beliefs—a journey of the soul back to Africa.[274]

Indian suicides were also a consequence of defeat in battle. One chronicle related that in the 1530s a mortally wounded Yucatec Maya avoided this-worldly shame and perhaps otherworldly complications when he distanced himself from the enemy and "in view of his people hanged himself with a vine."[275] The Tupís reputedly starved themselves to death when captured, and massive group suicide—soldiers and civilians alike—followed the fall of Mixtón, New Galicia, in 1541, and the fall of the Acoma Pueblo on the northern frontier in 1599.[276] For the Aztecs, who considered themselves the chosen people of a warrior deity, defeat was a collective trauma with cosmic consequences: "Let us die, then, / Let us perish then, / For our gods are already dead."[277] A sense of eschatological abandonment also overcame the Maya, who were willing to concede that "the first gods were perishable gods" but not without the grim recognition that "with the true God came the beginning of our misery."[278]

When literal suicide is not at issue, collective death is suggested by revolutionary movements whose slogans—Free Country or Death, Victory or Death, Power or Death, Revolution or Death, Religion or Death, Peronism or Death, All or Nothing, War to the Death—make it clear that there is no turning back. The cadres are usually young, poor, and driven by various combinations of indoctrination, idealism, leader worship, desperation, vengeance, fatalism, machismo, orphanhood, and coercion. The romantic, bookish ideals of the educated revolutionary vanguard contrast conspicuously with the necessity that drives the destitute rank and file into battles from which it rarely benefits. The white or mestizo leadership from the middle and upper classes experiences popular revolution with something of a defiant adrenaline magnificence—"it is like being in ecstasy"—while the lowest-class campesino followers sign on with fatalistic resignation because there is "nothing left to do but to go all the way."[279]

"All the way" is usually their fate, leader and troops alike, as the victims of hope are massacred or executed by the superior forces of the state. This is particularly evident in the anticolonial nativist insurrections, which were predisposed by imminent cultural collapse and religiously conditioned to a fanatical, all-or-nothing determination. A slow, undignified demise in subjugation inclined these rebellions to place everything at stake because death was not the worst of the options. Thousands of Indians charged the artillery with sticks, spears, bows, and slingshots to die together the certain death that from the outside may seem senseless but that for them held the supreme sense of defending the single vision that gave their lives dignity, hope, and purpose. As the young Colombian Jorge Eliécer Gaitán later put it, those who rise in rebellion are perhaps members of "a society that produces monsters, only to destroy them."[280] Sendero Luminoso's second in command, Osmán Morote, captured the essence more chillingly from an inside perspective: "A frightening thirst for vengeance devours me."[281]

When Gaitán, now leader of the Liberal Party and probable presidential candidate, was himself assassinated in 1948, the distress among his followers was so intense that it triggered the massive two-day riot known as the Bogotazo.

One Gaitanista who was struggling with his apocalyptic despair "seriously proposed poisoning the city's water supply so that the whole population would go the way of the leader." There was no turning back. Chaos reigned, bonfires raged, the world's end was rehearsed in miniature. At one fire the rioters burning treasures looted from a museum were interrupted when a boy, taking advantage of the confusion, made off with a pillow. An old woman who took her task to heart pursued him, overcame him, and grabbed the pillow from his hands with the scorn that his insolence merited. "We have come here to destroy, to end everything," she screamed, "not to steal." She then threw the pillow into the fire.[282]

2
The Chosen People

And they shall be my people, and I will be their God.
—Ezekiel 11:20

Symbolic Inversion

In 1963 a Canela woman working manioc fields on the savannahs of Brazil began to receive messages from the fetus in her womb. Dry Woman, as the fetus came to be known, foretold the return of a Canela cultural hero, Awkhêê, who would reverse the social order in favor of the oppressed natives. The Canela would move to the cities from whence they would govern, driving trucks and flying airplanes, while the *civilizados* (nonindigenous backlanders) would assume the subordinate social station, roaming through the brush to hunt scarce game with bows and arrows. Dry Woman's prophesy intervened to overturn not only a social hierarchy that disfavored the natives but also a Canela myth that emerged in the nineteenth century to provide a rationale for indigenous subordination. In a primordial but not so distant past, Awkhêê, assimilated to Emperor Dom Pedro II of Brazil, parceled out shotguns to the Christians but only bows and arrows to the Canela, who feared firearms. The imbalance of power and its consequences in racial hierarchy were thereby established, and the myth served de facto to condition Canela acquiescence. The scheduled reappearance of Awkhêê, assimilated now to Dry Woman rather than to a symbol of imperial authority, would neutralize past myths detrimental to the millennial aspirations of the community and would enact a hierarchical inversion to reverse social stations. With the birth of Dry Woman, the Canela would be reborn.[1]

The meanings and interrelations of above and below, center and periphery, good and evil, pure and impure, sacred and profane, rich and poor, legitimate and illegitimate, and many similar pairs of opposites are inverted by the millennial community as it constructs a world reordered in accord with its ideals.

Symbolic inversions and the attending discourse and rituals of reversal enact a radical, usually rapid overhaul of a community's identity, violating routine codes of deference and profaning the sacrosanct, ungrounded givens upon which inferiority is predicated.[2] As implied by the Andean concept of the *mundo al revés*, referred to in English as the "world upside down," the reversals in millennial ideology tend to be total and absolute, with everything that was once above now below, and vice versa, as the world turns over.

The pachacuti-like Sendero Luminoso of Peru was exemplary in its revolutionary quest to "turn the country upside down."[3] In a separate manner, the Huichol of north-central Mexico were explicit in their conception of inversion, anticipating an age when "all will be different, the opposite of what it is now." Inversion is rehearsed in the interim during peyote rituals in which "everything is backwards": "good morning" is said at evening and "goodbye" is said instead of "hello," for example, so as to "change everything, all the meanings" and remake the world "as it was in ancient times, so that all can be united."[4] The Huichol ritual is typical in its through-the-looking-glass inversions proper to a future conceived as the restoration of a defiled past, but it is also atypical in that it lacks the usual stress on role reversal between protagonist and antagonist. More characteristic in this regard are the nostalgic "king times" remembered by a Miskito woman in contemporary Nicaragua, during which Creoles "didn't count." "If a Miskitu walked into a bar and Creoles or Spaniards were there drinking, they all had to leave."[5] The idealized past stigmatizes the unaccommodating present as much as it rationalizes it, predisposing action, often revolutionary, for a "restoration" in the future.

The prominent pattern of inversion in nativist millennialism is mimetic: "The Indians had been subjected by the Spaniards, and now the Spaniards would be by the Indians."[6] The myth of Adaneva among modern Andeans remedies earthly injustices in a heaven where "Indians turn into *mistis* [mestizos, here the dominant class] and make those who in this world were *mistis* work by force, even whipping them."[7] In a narrative from Cuzco, the hierarchical reversal of the relation between *gamonal* (landowner of the provincial aristocracy) and *pongo* (native domestic servant) affords retribution and a kind of summary justice, with the inverted domination again remaining constant. A Spanish master is condemned to lick excrement off the body of his servant forever, while the once demeaned Indian, now exalted, licks honey off the master's body.[8] Both the Adaneva myth and the pongo's dream convey the message that the next world reverses the hierarchies of this one, but not without registering a lingering deference. In Adaneva a subaltern uncertainty is betrayed by the word "even" ("even whipping them"), as though the narrator cannot believe his luck. In the pongo's dream, a more insistent counterdiscourse is carried by the imagery's perpetuation of inequity: the Indian is covered in excrement for all eternity, while the master is clothed in honey like a gilded, gleaming El Dorado.

Myth and prophesy provide escape from a demeaning social station and access to the privileged position monopolized by an oppressor. The former superiors are relegated to the inferior position, and a reinterpretation of social roles, usually hyperbolic, legitimates and accentuates the majesty of the new masters along with the corresponding lowliness of their slaves. The positive attributes that were assigned previously to the oppressor (power, wealth, status, dignity) are now claimed, redoubled, by the new chosen people, and the negative attributes that those who were previously oppressed had once suffered (poverty, ethnic inferiority, subjugation, dehumanization) are projected onto the fallen oppressor, who at once absorbs all that is vile, evil, and worthy of punishment. Pilagá millennialists forecast the apocalypse for the year 2000, when on the re-created earth "the whites will be metamorphosed into animals."[9] The struggle for dominance among human groups becomes moot as the white antagonists are collectively relegated to a status beyond—or beneath—the pale. During a Mocoví rebellion in 1905, a prophesy that white people would turn into pigs was followed by sightings of colonists with squiggly little tails.[10] This visionary dehumanization seeks restitution by projecting and literalizing a trope: *they treated us like animals* becomes *they are animals*. The same holds true for the pongo who once "ate shit," with that degradation repaid in the demetaphorized culinary exotica that becomes the gamonal's eternal fate.

Once myth, prophesy, or insurrection bring the ambitious objectives of millennialism into range, the egalitarianism championed earlier is jettisoned as the hope for a fair share yields to a gamble for all or nothing. Such a progression was evident in a 1761 nativist rebellion in Mexico, which began with the assertion that "the world is a cake that must be shared among all" and ended with a call for genocide, so that the natives could monopolize the goods and privileges once coveted by the Spaniards.[11] The meek's inheritance of the earth is usually absolutist, perhaps because the adherents to millennial movements harbor the unacknowledged, ineffable realization that their predicament is insurmountable, that their goals are impossible to achieve, and that their fantasy is entitled to all because reality allots them nothing. They thus remain meek even in their absolutism, for their covetous usurpation is an extension of their humility, as though their collective dream had gotten snagged in the machinery of reality before they knew what had happened. They take up arms because nothing ever came to them without a struggle, and they ride the swell of their fleeting empowerment because its promise, however specious, is a better bet than the quotidian alternative.

Role identities and their values are kept in circulation, with one or another privileged to suit a particular occasion. In the sixteenth and seventeenth centuries the Indians were fashioned as descendants of the lost tribes of Israel to suit the demands of orthodoxy and noble savagery, but by the eighteenth century the regard for these recycled Israelites was overhauled in response to rebellion. On New Spain's northern frontier in 1751, a colonist justified the beating of his native slave by saying, "God has given me life so that I might do to these Jews what they did to Our Holiest Lord."[12] In the Andes, at the end of the century, a respected priest was consulted for his opinion concerning the Túpac Amaru and subsequent uprisings; in response he cited Gregorio García's *Origin of the Indians of the New World* to establish the Andeans as descendants of Christ killers, with whom they held in common "ingratitude, brutality, and idolatry."[13]

Many eighteenth-century natives nevertheless regarded themselves as the true Christians and the colonial authorities as hypocritical bastardizers of the faith. When their syncretic Christian images were being "killed" and their manner of worship obstructed, the rebelling Maya projected the Christ-killing identity back to their hispanic enemies, now referring to them as Jews.[14] During the 1712 Tzeltal Rebellion in the Yucatan, a Maya prophet and his coterie of "true" (which is to say native and unordained) priests went to war to dislodge this "Church of the Jews" that corrupted the Catholic faith.[15] Inversion was the rule in the Tzeltals' rebel center at Cancuc, where Indian men were called Spaniards and Indian women Ladinas, while true Spaniards were called Indians (as well as Jews). As the center of power was co-opted and incorporated into the native domain, Cancuc itself came to be called Ciudad Real (Royal City), the name of the regional Spanish capital, and the actual Ciudad Real, home of the "Jews," was referred to mockingly as Jerusalem.[16] In Passion plays among the contemporary Maya in Chiapas and Guatemala, Judas, who is referred to as "the Jew," is "unequivocally identified with Ladinos" and hung from the bell tower "to show the world that he killed Christ."[17] A similar assessment of hispanic Catholicism was made in the Andes, as illustrated by a mid-eighteenth-century mestizo painting in the church of San Cristóbal de Rapaz that depicts Christ being whipped and tortured by Jews dressed as Spaniards.[18] During the rebellions in the 1780s, the qualifiers changed but the point remained the same: Spaniards were called "heretics," "apostates," "devils," and "Lutherans."[19] The respective Catholic adversaries, hispanic and indigenous, both accorded an inherent superiority to their faith, devalued the other in stereotypes predominantly of biblical origin, and found in their religious indignation a rationale for warfare.

When they had the occasion, rebelling natives often actualized role inversion and reciprocated forced acculturation. White men captured by the rebels during the Tzeltal Rebellion were forced to dress as Indians, and abducted white women—reversing the Spanish use of native concubines—were assigned to Indian men and obliged to dress and behave according to Maya customs.[20] The rebels who took the Bolivian town of Oruro in 1781 similarly forced non-native inhabitants to dress as Indians and engage in the native practice of chewing coca leaves. Reculturation was enforced during another Bolivian uprising a century later, when rebels imposed indigenous dress on those "wearing trousers."[21]

The Spaniards' earlier perception of the New World as in some sense upside down was indebted to medieval geography of the Antipodes, an "other world opposite to our own" that after 1492 was often equated with the Americas.[22] In 1552 Francisco López de Gómara surveyed the literature on the Antipodes to conclude that the world is divided into two hemispheres, an upper and a lower: "Asia, Africa and Europe form the one part, and the Indies the other, in which are found those called Antipodeans."[23] These people who walk upside down on the other side of the globe—"foot against foot" with Europeans, as John Mandeville put it—provided a simple model of antithetical otherness.[24] Medievals who deemed belief in the Antipodeans heretical solved their problem by introducing other inversions faithful to the etymology (from the Greek, "with the feet opposite") to again envision a people in some sense inverted, here because their feet were turned backward. These backward people with their backward feet were among the many humanoid monsters—headless, dog-headed, sciapod—that were imagined to inhabit "India" and conditioned interpretations of the New World natives during the sixteenth century.[25]

Colonial Spaniards who maintained that everything in the New World "is the reverse of what it is in Castile," or that "the things of this world can be truly perceived only by looking at them backwards," became the protagonists of a realignment that adjusted the backward or upside-down world to conform to Iberian notions of order.[26] The interpretive struggle en route to such conclusions is preserved in oxymorons that register the clash of Old World paradigms against the New World realities that challenged them. Exemplary was Columbus's description of the "beautiful deformity" of palm trees.[27] An oxymoron used later by López de Gómara captured the Spaniards' more aggressive inversion of indigenous religion: "the principal god" in Hispaniola "is the devil."[28] For natives on the receiving end of these perceptions and the colonial apparatus that instituted them by force, the imposed paradigm constituted not a corrective adjustment of an upside-down world but rather the turning of a world upside down. The up and down sides are culturally relative, and nativist responses to conquest intended a counterinversion that would correct the imposed aberration. If in Spanish perspective apostasy and insurrection were the brutish undoing of the natural order introduced to a savage continent, then in native perspective a variation of the same held true in reverse, with order lost to chaos in the wake of a ruthless invasion. Nativist rebellion undoes the oxymorons, restoring the divinity of the gods and repairing the deformity of the trees. The idea was captured precisely by the Taqui Onqoy movement's image of traitors walking on their heads, left upside down when the world turned over.

Reduction and Polarization

Inherent to symbolic inversion is the reduction of complexities to simplified dualities that are polarized in diametrical opposition. When its mission is conceived in the extreme, a chosen people squares off against all otherness as it divides the moral universe into the absolutist dichotomy of a struggle between good and evil. The envisioned end is not in resolution or harmonious coexistence between the polarized rivals, but rather in total war that completes the process of reduction by eliminating one of the poles and reducing the once multiple, then dichotomized field to an ultimate homogeneity. Each of the adversaries views itself as the righteous protagonist whose violence, no matter how indiscriminate or grotesque, is defensive, while the antithetical counterpart is viewed as an evil antagonist whose violence, no matter how reluctant or measured, is aggressive. The self-identity of each is defined by viewing its inverted condition in the mirror of the inimical other. Construction of the other's identity with hyperbolically negative attributes reciprocates inversely to reload its counterpart with hyperbolically positive attributes. Every earthly messiah, like every mythic hero, is defined and guaranteed by rivalry, and this model extends, generalized, to the collective identity of a chosen people.

The predominant binary oppositions defining struggles in Latin America have included conqueror and conquered; master and slave; hispanic and indigenous; European and Creole; civilization and barbarity; tradition and change; domestic and foreign; urban and rural; coast and highlands; civil and military; communism and democracy; and liberal and conservative. This last pairing is characteristic in its hyperbolic polarization of the field and its transcendentalization of politico-economic concerns. Particularly when the Church is party to conservation of an elite status quo, the liberal cause is construed apocalyptically as a "war against God, against Christ, and against his Vicar," and, what is more, against liberty, justice, law, morality, prosperity, family, country, and society.[29] In 1915 an equally indignant bishop of Ayacucho made clear the diametrical oppositions at the base of constructed enmity: "Nobody can be a Catholic and a liberal at the same time. These are mutually exclusive terms, such as truth and error, good and evil, or light and darkness."[30]

Categorical polarization lends itself to cheers and slogans but also to inversions that reallocate the negative and positive attributes. The "Holy Federation" of the Argentine caudillo Juan Manuel de Rosas was exalted in dichotomous relation to the "Savage Unitarians," but once Rosas fell out of favor the campaign against him was in turn "holy and glorious."[31] The reshuffling of heroic and antiheroic identities was more recently apparent in Peruvian campesinos' reception of Sendero Luminoso. When it made its Robin Hood debut in 1980, Sendero was perceived as a messianic redeemer reminiscent of Inkarrí, a mythological hero who emerges from defeat for a rematch with the Christian conqueror. By the late 1980s, however, the displaced, brutalized campesinos had switched myths to regard Senderistas as *pishtacos*, the monstrous foreigners who dissect natives. That autochthonous assessment was compounded by antiheroic qualifiers introduced by Evangelicals—"diabolical," "Antichrist," "worse than a devil," "on the path of evil."[32] In this as in many cases, yesterday's savior becomes today's predatory, demonized beast as volatile identities flop between poles.

No praise is equal to the grandeur of a chosen people, and no depreciative scorn is equal to the lowliness of its rival. The adversaries are "enemies of humanity and religion," a "sinister plague," "a savage horde" responsible for every ghoulish atrocity and lavishly rendered in the tropes of subhumanity, disease, evil, and putrefaction.[33] The faces of the enemy change from conflict to conflict and from culture to culture, but the inimical attributes remain constant. The Huaorani of the Ecuadorian Amazon refer to outsiders as *cowode*, which denotes "nonhuman cannibals" or "those who cut all to pieces," like the Andean pishtacos. The term is applied as much to the Huaorani's indigenous enemies as to Christian missionaries (some were speared to death upon first contact in 1956), thereby indexing a world divided between the tribe and a comprehensive, subhuman otherness.[34] During the Yucatec Caste War, the Cruzob, or People of the Cross, referred to themselves as the true Christians and true Maya, thereby representing their inimical stance before the white enemy as well as before all Maya outside of the movement.[35] The modern Tarahumara more typically polarize adversity across race lines, considering themselves the children of God and non-Indians the children of the devil.[36]

Alliances are often reconfigured in conformity with external pressures that oblige a community to reorganize its identity or priorities. The Spaniards skillfully manipulated indigenous rivalries to gain allies among peoples who were more likely to be their enemies, notably during the conquests of Mexico and Peru. On the eve of their 1680 revolt, the Pueblos responded in kind by allying with their traditional enemies, the Apaches, in order to expel the colonists, while the Spaniards, facing the threat, patched up Church-state rivalries in order to present a united front of defense. In one version of the Andean myth of Inkarrí, the Spanish king orders Juan Pizarro to escort the Inca to Spain for an audience. The Inca refuses, the conqueror decapitates him and returns with the head, and the king repays the transgression with the retaliatory decapitation of Pizarro.[37] The same is dramatized in *The Tragedy of Atahualpa's End*, a colonial play still performed in Andean folk theater. When Pizarro delivers the Inca's head, the angered king exclaims, "How could you have done this! / This face that you have brought me / is my own face."[38] The Inca is the mirror of the king. The admonishment of Pizarro implies that the two monarchs' rival claims to power are reconciled, unified, and realigned to indigenous advantage in order to defeat conquerors—if only in myth and theater—who desecrate the sacrosanct.

The eighteenth-century rebel Juan Santos Atahualpa was a master at reorganizing alliances, cohering sometimes mutually hostile peoples in the common cause of decolonization.[39] The Franciscan missionaries had classified Indians as converts, neophytes, or infidels, but Santos Atahualpa forked a new path to salvation with a clean dichotomy. He regarded those who followed him as redeemed without clerical hocus pocus and those who did not as doomed to the precarious salvation offered by the Church that was being expelled.[40] Relations were thereby reorganized horizontally between political groups and vertically between the respective groups and their concepts of deity.[41] The traditional identities and social relations, already destabilized by missionary deculturation, were metamorphosed by the paradigm of revolt.

In modern Latin American struggles the lines of adversity are likewise redrawn in accord with shifting paradigms. For some liberation theologists, "the division is no longer between those who have faith and those who do not have faith. It is a line between those who are on the side of the interests of the poor and those who defend the privileges of the rich and the oppressors."[42] The theoretical incompatibility of Christianity and militancy was reconciled during the Sandinista Revolution, in which one could be a revolutionary and a Christian— "and there is no contradiction between the two"—because revolution was a Christian response to injustice. This politico-religious fusion was condensed in the slogan that welcomed Pope John Paul II to Nicaragua, "Thanks to God and the Revolution."[43] On the opposing side of the postrevolutionary struggle, however, Contra propaganda of the mid-1980s likewise claimed, "God is on our side" and "The Pope is with us."[44] That message was warmly received by, among others, the Moravian Church on Nicaragua's Atlantic coast, which encouraged the Miskitos to join the Contra cause as a holy war against the enemies of God. Where a Nicaraguan stood in relation to this beleaguered concept of Catholicism depended as much on class and politics as on profession of the faith. The adversaries made competing claims to the authenticity of their nationalism and their Catholicism, and friend could be sorted from foe only by redefinition of identities on both sides of the battle line.

A simplified world view schematized into an expedient dualism was patent in U.S. foreign policy toward Latin America during the Cold War, when popular revolutions disfavorable to U.S. interests, Nicaragua's among them, were regarded as pawns of a world communist conspiracy and were penalized accordingly. An ethnocentric self-perception as a chosen people with a global mission contributed to such policies, as it did earlier to Manifest Destiny and the Roosevelt Corollary to the Monroe Doctrine. The "giddy dreams of the day" in the mid-nineteenth century included "a destiny to perform, a 'manifest destiny' over all Mexico, over South America, over the West Indies and Canada." By taking the "larger view," the United States seemed "no longer bounded by the limits of the confederacy" and set its sights "abroad upon the whole earth."[45] The statesman Albert J. Beveridge gave the message a more messianic tone in the early twentieth century, when he announced to the U.S. Senate, "God has not been preparing the English-speaking and Teutonic peoples for a thousand years for nothing but vain and idle self-contemplation and self-admiration. No. He made us master organizers of the world to establish system where chaos reigned." Following praise of the "spirit of progress" and governing skills that bring "savage and senile peoples" into the fold and prevent "relapse into barbarism and night," Beveridge concluded, "He has marked the American people as His chosen nation to finally lead in the redemption of the world."[46]

The idea of a "redeemer nation" is at least as old as the book of Exodus, where God chose his people—"you shall be to me a kingdom of priests and a holy nation"—for politico-religious conquest of the world.[47] In U.S. foreign policy, imperial mission inspired by specious precepts of redemption were renewed during the Ronald Reagan administration beginning in 1980. Like the advocates of Cold War who preceded and accompanied him, Reagan operated under the presumption that the United States was threatened by an "evil empire," "a Russian-inspired, Moscow-dominated, anti-American, quasi-military conspiracy against our government, our ideals and our freedom." According to Reagan, the world was a polarized Armageddon, "half slave and half free," with a corresponding conflict between "totalitarianism and freedom." The time for action had arrived: "It is late in the afternoon of the day of decision," or again, "You and I have a rendezvous with destiny. We'll preserve for our children this, the last best hope of man on earth, or we'll sentence them to take the last step into a thousand years of darkness."[48] The middle ground was disavowed as much in the pick-one eschatological options—millennial joy or apocalyptic doom—as it was in the absolutist depiction of the adversary.

The apocalyptic mood in Cold War Latin America was enhanced by the coincidence of military and religious interests in "counterinsurgency" against an enemy regarded as anti-Christian. Xenophobic nationalism, entrenched ethnocentrism, intolerance of heterodoxy, and terror of huge, racially distinct underclasses generated the constant fear that traditions espoused by the oligarchy would be subverted by "exotic" ideologies. *Communist* became the expedient qualifier that stigmatized any opposition to the status quo, affording the fringe benefits of U.S. defense dollars and benedictions from the conservative Church. *Communist* was applied indiscriminately—to campesinos in Central America, to intellectuals in the Southern Cone, to unionized workers, to Jesuits considered atheists or Antichrists—in order to represent any expression of social discontent as an instrument of Soviet or Cuban aggression.

Among Latin American revolutions the solipsistic Sendero Luminoso was extreme in its reduction and polarization of social reality, eliminating all otherness until nothing remained in the field but the movement and its inverted reflection. The revolution, "a purging mechanism for the attainment of absolute purity, perfection, and truth," enacted Abimael Guzmán's conviction that the only solution to historical antagonisms in a polarized Peru was "eradication of one of the poles."[49] Total war was waged without allies because Sendero dismissed the Peruvian and international left as "Fascists" and "revisionists," rejected other Latin American revolutions as "puppets" of "foreign masters" (with Che Guevara dubbed a "choir girl"), and directed its antagonism as much toward the Soviet Union and China (for "betraying" Mao Tse-tung) as toward the United States.[50] All social reality was divided into sharply contrasting absolutes of good and evil represented by "the soul of two flags," a black one that would be destroyed and a red one that would prevail. The armed struggle played like a "cosmological battle" for "the transformation of our people," with Sendero upholding "the purest principles" while its enemies were "rotten." A choice was forced because "there is no room for intermediate positions": "Either you side with the people and its struggle or you side with the reaction and its repressive apparatus."[51] Those who chose the latter, as Guzmán put it following Friedrich Engels, constituted a "colossal heap of garbage" that must be "swept away little by little."[52]

Sendero intended to transform Peruvian society through a purging violence that would annihilate by force of arms whoever fell into the movement's broad concept of enmity, including a healthy "quota" of campesinos. In Guzmán's speech to the cadres entitled "We Are the Initiators," he described the people rising up, arming themselves, grabbing imperialists and reactionaries by the throat to strangle them, to rip them apart, to tear them to shreds, and to bury, burn, and scatter the remains, "so that nothing is left but the sinister memory of what must never return."[53] That rhetoric of rage translated in the field to atrocity facilitated by dehumanization: "Everything that opposes this revolution will simply be crushed like one more insect," and "We crush the enemies of the people like rats, like insects."[54] In one type of execution the victim was made to kneel "like a pig" and was then beheaded, with the head sometimes crushed "like a frog with a stone."[55] Despite these inhumane means implemented en route, Sendero promised "a single, irreplaceable new society, without exploited or exploiters, without oppressed or oppressors, without classes, without state, without parties, without democracy, without arms, without wars."[56] The polarized duality yields to a millennial new society of "great harmony" when nothing exists but the party.[57]

Sendero sought to polarize the field precisely because a heavily populated middle ground obstructed the objectives of a "people's war" conceived in the university and not necessarily supported by the people. After emergency zones were declared by President Fernando Belaúnde Terry in December 1982, the campesinos of Ayacucho found themselves caught in the cross fire of an insurgency and counterinsurgency, both of which demanded absolute compliance. Neutrality was as criminal as enmity. If, in Mao's trope, the people are the water in which the revolutionaries move, then, in the counterinsurgency's counter-trope, the sea must be drained. As explained by the Peruvian minister of defense, "If we kill a hundred people and among them there was one subversive, then doing it was worth the effort."[58] The people are "saved" by Sendero and then by the military, but the salvation always results in their destruction.

The scorched-earth policies of the Guatemalan military since 1954 evidence a more sustained genocidal strategy to eradicate one of the poles. Troops converging upon a Guatemalan village in 1982 were typical in their belief that all of the campesinos were guerrillas, "even the women and children."[59] This ideological annihilation of civilian neutrality was then actualized in massacre. As a soldier explained the operation to a reporter, "The order is to attack everybody alike" because "practically all of them are guerrillas."[60] The "practically" concedes that some of the campesinos were not guerrillas but at once disavows that recognition as insignificant. Reduction and polarization of Guatemalan natives was formalized by the government's "beans and bullets" policy, which despite its clumsy application in the field ostensibly intended to sort the guilty from the innocent, again by eliminating neutrality. As an army officer explained the program to campesinos in El Quiché, "If you are with us, we'll feed you; if not, we'll kill you."[61]

The context and enemy were quite different during the Argentine "dirty war" a few years earlier, but a genocidal violence pursuant to polarization remains constant. Ambiguity was felonious; anyone not actively manifesting support for the counterinsurgency was as guilty as an armed insurgent. In the words of the governor of Buenos Aires province during the "dirty war," "First, we are going to kill all of the subversives; then their collaborators; then their sympathizers; then the indifferent; and, finally, the timid."[62] The last categories were populated by "useful idiots" and "automatons" who participated in the revolution by default through their susceptibility to manipulation.[63]

The guerrilla in the Andes and Guatemala and the "ideological enemy" in Argentina disappeared indistinguishably into the population, necessitating polarization to clarify the target of counterinsurgency. Slogans such as "Separate the wheat from the chaff" used frequently by populists Juan Perón and Víctor Raúl Haya de la Torre, or Fidel Castro's slogan "Within the Revolution, everything; against it, nothing" index a political parallel to the military and para-military exploitation of divisive rivalry. Polarization facilitates purges, and in some cases, such as that of Paraguay under José Gaspar Rodríguez de Francia, it can be followed by national isolation that seals the purified realm from the corrupting incursions of otherness.

Separatism is more commonly the hallmark of religious sects that polarize society as they found their identity in opposition to institutionalized sin. In the late nineteenth century, such Brazilian messiahs as Antônio Conselheiro congregated dispersed peoples into isolationist holy cities where their lives were structured, disciplined, and integrated into God's eschatological plan. Congregation and segregation facilitated the paradigm change that transformed individual sinners into a unified messianic community. The distant, prostituted society became an antithetical construct against which the chosen people measured their sanctity. When urban sects must live in close proximity to the world that they reject, codes of behavior and rituals of exclusion intervene to enforce the isolationist purism. The Luz del Mundo (Light of the World) sect, which began in Guadalajara, Mexico, during the Cristero Rebellion of the late 1920s, is particularly vehement in its enforcement of dissociation. A wall separates the community from the exterior world, and extramural outings are monitored by ministers to prevent "contamination with sin."[64]

During conquest and the earlier years of colonization the identification of an antithetical other was simple enough insofar as race was concerned, for the distinction between Indian, European, and, later, African was absolute and the middle ground of mixed races was still insignificant. The polarization of native and Spaniard was further induced by the generic misnomer "Indian," which awkwardly collapsed into a single category some 350 major tribal groups and more than 160 linguistic stocks, from the Taínos "naked as their mothers bore them" and the Tupí-Guaranís *sin fe, sin ley, sin rey* (without faith, without law, without king) to the highly developed empires of Mesoamerica and Peru.[65] The distinctions became less clear after centuries of race mixing, with a notable exception caused and perpetuated by slavery. In a series of rebellions by black Moslems in Bahia between 1807 and 1835, stark contrasts of race, class, and faith defined the agenda: to exterminate white people, take power, and abolish Christianity in the name of Allah.[66] In 1826 fugitive slaves in the *quilombo* (maroon society) of Urubú similarly hoped to "kill all whites they found in order to obtain their freedom," and a decade later, again in Bahia, a captured rebel confessed "the goal of killing all whites, mulattos and creoles."[67]

By the time nativist insurrection returned in earnest at the end of the eighteenth century, the processes of race mixing, acculturation, and syncretism had intermingled the antithetical counterparts of a once polarized field. Even many of those who led race wars—Túpac Amaru II is the paradigm—had half of their genes in the enemy camp. Under these circumstances calls for genocidal annihilation of the adversary were more an incendiary battle cry than an enterprise that could be defined, much less accomplished. Creoles could ally as Americans with natives in insurrections directed against Spaniards, or, conversely, they could ally as whites with Spaniards against natives. Malleable identities among the mixed races could be formed by choices—from within and without—as individuals and groups were redefined along the contours of a particular cause. Mestizos in particular, "defined only by negation" as neither white nor Indian, could register a political choice through dress, lifestyle, language, and religion in order to stress one side or the other of their volatile identity.[68] In the manifestos of modern nativism, the mestizo is sometimes regarded as "a de-indianized Indian" and therefore as "recuperable."[69] In all cases, the imprecision of racial, cultural, and political indicators required that each struggle reconstruct its inimical archetype.

The tendency in colonial nativism was to adhere to the imprecise agenda of exterminating white people, identified as much by class and lifestyle as by race. The independence wars that followed then constructed an enemy congruent with the separatist agenda, posing Caucasians born in America (Creoles) against those born in Spain (known as Chapetones in South America and as Gachupines in Mexico). During the struggle for Mexican independence José María Morelos, himself a mestizo, characteristically situated Europeans on one side of the divide and all Americans on the other, dissolving the colonial structures of caste and slavery in order to unite an alliance of "everyone generally American."[70] Accessible Spanish-born colonists became the scapegoats blamed and punished for centuries of exploitation. On All Saints Day in 1810, indigenous villagers of Atlacomulco, Mexico, attacked a Gachupín merchant, wrecked and sacked his store, brutally murdered him, and disfigured his body beyond recognition. In a separate instance, a Gachupín on a country road was murdered instantly by a lance thrust, but then his assailants "bashed in his head with stones and stabbed him several times for good measure."[71] The excess and the encore attest to the passion with which the crimes were perpetrated, not so much against the individual as against the "Spaniard" as inimical archetype. Hereditary guilt conditioned the kill, and rage, revenge, and triumphant defiance were celebrated on the corpse.

Polarization of Europeans and Americans was exemplary under the command of Simón Bolívar as he confronted massive New World populations that were indifferent or opposed to liberation. In the words of his aide-de-camp, "Most of the Spanish forces were, in fact, made up of Venezuelans, which grieved Bolívar more than a little," and "some of America's native sons were the most stubborn enemies of independence."[72] In an effort to remedy the troubling situation of South Americans resisting their own liberation, Bolívar proclaimed a War to the Death and signed the corresponding decree on June 15, 1813. This "terrible measure to which Bolívar had to resort" intended to reconfigure previous patterns of alliance and to clearly define the battle as one between royalists and republicans.[73] Spaniards could expect death unless they allied with the cause of liberation, in which case they would be "treated as Americans." Conversely, Americans who had gone astray from the "path of justice" by fighting along with Spanish troops were invited to reverse their allegiance and accept an absolute amnesty. The decree concluded with these words: "Spaniards and Canarians, count on death, even being indifferent, if you do not actively work to achieve the liberation of America. Americans, count on life, even when you are guilty."[74]

The New Humanity

The periodic annihilation of the gods' unworthy or exhausted creations is a recurring motif of mythologies throughout the world. The universal flood survived by Noah's entourage in Genesis and the promise in Revelation of a post-apocalypse millennial kingdom for the just are prominent Judeo-Christian instances of the regeneration of a purified race on the far side of eschatological cataclysm.[75] Christ becomes the new Noah emerging from baptismal waters and the new Adam dying "once for all" to give humanity a "new birth" beyond sin.[76] As worded in 1 Corinthians 15:22, "For just as in Adam all die, so too in Christ shall all be brought to life."

Evangelicals hold that Christ's chosen people will be spared the tribulations visited upon creation during the transition to the millennial kingdom. The Second Coming occurs in two stages, first "rapture," in which Christ secretly returns to raise the faithful, and then the Advent proper with its fire and brimstone. The basis for rapture is in 1 Thessalonians 4:15–17, where the returning Lord resurrects the "dead in Christ" and then raises the living chosen people to the clouds, where they together "meet the Lord in the air." The scripture is taken quite literally by Latin American Christians who anticipate their imminent ascension: "Any day now one will read in all the newspapers of the world: 'Thousands of Evangelicals have disappeared.' "[77]

In sect Christianity, too, a variety of means are provided for the postapocalypse repopulation of the earth. Followers of the messianic Cícero José de Farias in the Brazilian Northeast awaited "an authentic repetition of Noah's case," but with an updated method of destruction. Around the year 2100 the detonation of atomic bombs will be complemented by stones falling from the sky. The chosen "will be guarded from the catastrophe" in order to "form a new generation," and Brazil will become "the cradle of the future generation of the Third Millennium." God will install a president, "by force if necessary," who will pay the national debt and reign eternally. Engineers will arrive from abroad and "from other planets by means of flying saucers," the New Jerusalem will be constructed on sites revealed through the collaboration of prophesy and science, and the earth, bathed in "its own light," will rotate peaceably in a new orbit.[78]

Extraterrestrial assistance for Brazil was also the "pleasant surprise" received by Dino Kraspedon, who opened his front door one Sunday expecting the tirade of another Evangelical only to realize that his interlocutor was "the captain of a flying saucer." Discussion with the preacher-extraterrestrial revealed that cosmic upheaval would result in a "new sky," a "new Earth," and a new humanity: "The Earth will begin its new millennium with a new source of light to illuminate it. Many people will vanish forever from the face of the Earth but a small community, obedient to the laws of God, will remain, and present suffering will cease. There will be peace and abundance, justice and compassion. The unjust souls will get the punishment they deserve, and the just will get their recompense." The extraterrestrial also observed that "the Earth is not the center of the planetary system, as was previously believed, but the center of evil."[79]

Repopulation of a new-age world by a saving remnant is also widely represented in native traditions. The Araweté, a Tupí-Guaraní people of the Brazilian Amazon, typically relate that a past world was destroyed by flood and devouring beasts but that two men and a woman saved themselves by climbing a bacaba palm to become the ancestors of current humanity.[80] Tupí-Cocama converts to the Brotherhood of the Cross equate such a tree with the huge crucifixes erected in their villages; taking up the cross promises eternal salvation, but climbing up it assures this-worldly survival.[81] In some cases, the chosen people themselves are both the instigators of the cataclysm and the saving remnant that populates the new world beyond it. According to the reckonings of the Colombian prophet Manuel Quintín Lame in 1939, if one God redeemed all humankind from evil, then a few natives would suffice for redemption from the white man's "evil administration of justice." "The day shall come when a handful of Indians shall form a column to reclaim their rights as God reclaimed humanity."[82]

A similar design was central to a messianic movement that began in 1972 among the Chinantecs in Oaxaca, Mexico. The scheduled construction of a hydroelectric dam on the Santo Domingo River would result in flooding and forced dislocation of twenty thousand natives, and the Chinantecs found themselves helpless before the political bureaucracy that dismissed their protests. It was then that the Great God Engineer, reinforced by the Virgin of Guadalupe, appeared to Andrés Felipe and revealed the mission that would reverse matters to indigenous advantage. Massive pilgrimages converged upon a cave as shrine and cult center, the Chinantecs prepared for exodus to a highland retreat indicated by the Great God Engineer, and the elders instructed the shamans to send "rays" to kill the president of Mexico, Luis Echeverría. The Chinantecs intended to temporarily relocate to the "promised land" of Potrero Viejo, a safehaven where they would await destruction of the dam and the consequent flood that would wash away their enemies. As the sole survivors of the cataclysm, they would then return to the ancestral lands in the valley to live in peace as the gods intended.[83] Through intercession of the Great God Engineer, believed to be more powerful than the engineers of the dam, the Chinantecs thus strategically borrowed the harnessed power reserved for the electricity of others and turned it against its source. Rather than flooding ancestral lands and dispossessing the Chinantecs, the inundation would purify the indigenous milieu by purging it of contaminating encroachments, thereby providing a promised land apropos of a chosen people returning from exile.

The establishment of a new society is often preceded by inner transformation of the chosen people themselves, either to assume an identity worthy of the kingdom they anticipate or to re-create society proactively as the composite product of their individual transformations. Outstanding among the latter cases was the discourse on the New Man propagated during the Cuban Revolution.

Fidel Castro hoped to telescope the stages of Marxist historical development in order to arrive quickly to the communist society, in which each person would receive according to his or her need and all would give according to their capacity. The model for the New Man was provided by the revolutionaries themselves, the "vanguard of the vanguard," with Che Guevara as paradigm. The Cuban Revolution's official morality was a normalization and extension into everyday life of the virtues exemplified by the guerrillas in the Sierra Maestra, including austerity, discipline, abnegation, and comradeship.[84] If the mountains where revolutionaries were trained was a "School for the New Man," then to cultivate the consciousness of the new humanity "society as a whole must become a huge school."[85]

As described by Guevara, the qualities of the revolutionary New Man include physical and moral courage, willingness to die for the cause, and a balanced combination of initiative, discipline, and loyalty.[86] In leadership and warfare, the New Man is "guided by strong feelings of love" but at once "must combine an impassioned spirit with a cold mind and make painful decisions without flinching."[87] The personal sacrifice is formidable, but "the reward is the new society, where human beings will have different characteristics."[88] As the revolutionary agenda is internalized and socialized, the comrades, driven by what Castro described as a "moral compulsion," apply themselves diligently to the common cause. The emerging new society would have to "compete fiercely" with the patterns of a corrupt past, but new generations would be born "free of 'original sin.'"[89] Guevara referred to the transformation as "a change in consciousness" and "complete spiritual recreation," "without direct pressure of the social environment but bound to it by new habits."[90] The Cuban Revolution would create a "new human being" motivated by "moral incentives" rather than material gain, a "man freed from alienation" who would achieve "complete spiritual recreation in the presence of his own work."[91]

In Latin America the concept of a New Man is most associated with Che Guevara and the Cuban Revolution, but its variations have also played a central role in other programs of social reform. Juan Perón hoped to "reconstruct the Argentine man, destroyed by long years of economic, political, and social submission."[92] According to Eva Perón, the reborn workers, once an "element of human exploitation," became "synonymous with national victory" and the incarnation of "progress, national unity, and collective well-being."[93] In the 1940s a "spiritual socialism" guided reformist president Juan José Arévalo Bermejo in his quest for the "moral integrity" of Guatemalans, and in Nicaragua Augusto César Sandino regarded revolution as "synonymous with purification" that readies the realm for a new society.[94]

Liberation theology later accommodated the Marxist new humanity in the Christian millennial kingdom, reconciling the incompatibilities in order to stress common cause in redemption of the poor. The Nicaraguan poet, priest, and later politician Ernesto Cardenal characteristically commented, "I was not drawn to Marxism by reading Marx, but by reading the gospel," and "I am a Marxist who believes in God, follows Christ, and is a revolutionary for the sake of his kingdom."[95] After the Sandinistas came to power in 1979, Catholic priests were appointed to several senior posts, including foreign minister, minister of culture, and ambassador to the Organization of American States, and priests were later elected to the Sandinista Assembly. According to Cardenal, the goal of the revolutionary government was to create a "new race," and all government programs were implemented "with the intention of creating such a new being."[96]

The Sandinistas' ideals were more generally espoused throughout Latin America by liberation theology's call for "structural changes" and a "new society" that would accommodate the disenfranchised masses.[97] As Leonardo Boff put it before the Vatican ordered him to obedient silence in 1985, liberation theology sought a "reinvention of the Church" following Paul's concept of a "new creation" in Christ.[98] In more social terms reminiscent of Marx and Che Guevara, Gustavo Gutiérrez explained that Christians participate in liberation to "create a new man," "a new kind of man in a qualitatively different society."[99] More bold in its blending of soft Marxism and militant Christianity was a 1972 proclamation from the Movement of Priests for the Third World, which asserted that from "a struggle and confrontation" would emerge "the new man and new society, of which Christ, the New Man par excellence, is both prototype and guarantee."[100] The manifestos of indigenous movements influenced by liberation theology, most recently the Zapatista rebellion in Chiapas, Mexico, also evidence the reconciliation of Christianity and radical social action. In 1980 the Guatemalan Declaration of Iximché embedded Christianity in the essentially Marxist call "that all of the discriminated and exploited indigenous peoples of the world, that all the workers of the world, that all the authentic Christians of the world, join in solidarity with the struggle of the indigenous people and other exploited peoples of Guatemala."[101]

Outstanding among the millennial attributes of liberation theology is its focus on collective, terrestrial salvation rather than on traditional Catholicism's individual and often fatalistic preparation for salvation of the soul hereafter. The Christian poor forged grassroots communities pursuant to Vatican II's promise that an emerging "new human family" would foreshadow the "new age," and the base communities' social rather than spiritual reading of the Bible found in scriptural precedents a model for interpreting oppression and for legitimating activism in response.[102] "We compare all that was lived in those times with what we also live in our community," a Guatemalan catechist explained, with a predilection for the persecuted Jesus and for Moses' deliverance of the chosen people from slavery.[103] Liberation theology interpreted the repressive and inequitable structures of Latin American society as institutionalized "social sin," and redemption therefore required social action to purge that defilement of God's creation and to realize on earth the kingdom that Christ intended.[104] A liberation theologist in Guatemala explained that the Bible opens with "the chaos before creation" and concludes with the New Jerusalem, and therefore the task of the Christian in the middle is to "make a new society out of chaos."[105] According to Paulo Freire, "We have to earn our heaven here and now, we ourselves. We have to build our heaven, to fashion it during our lifetime, right now."[106]

Far from a model for passive suffering, Christ of the social gospel is the "Defender of the Poor" who by example "taught us to demand justice."[107] The historical Jesus wandered about "inciting the people to revolt," was arrested and executed for sedition, and required that each of the faithful "take up his cross" to pursue the difficult, risky, subversive path of the messiah.[108] The benumbed acquiescence of traditional Christianity was abandoned as this radical Jesus returned to the faithful demanding efficacious and even revolutionary action. When asked why God permits poverty, the great majority (46 percent) of the poor Peruvians surveyed in the early 1980s responded, "because he wants men to be the ones who put things in order." The majority likewise believed that God was not pleased with the inequitable socioeconomic situation: "He is by no means happy. If he were he wouldn't be God." Most also agreed that being Christian required social action pursuant to the example of Jesus' "solidarity with the poor, fighting for justice and equality." While 36 percent chose the sacramental option of confessing sins and receiving communion as the proper means of professing the faith, 40 percent maintained that God was better served through impoverished peoples' struggle for justice.[109] A girl from the urban middle class in Guatemala argued to the same effect to justify her participation in the popular revolution: "I was obeying Christ's mandate to create his kingdom on earth."[110]

The incorporation of liberation ideology into traditional liturgy gained prominence as the gospel became increasingly social. During a procession of Our Lady of Aparecida in São Jorge, Brazil, a crowd of some three thousand Catholics responded to the calls of a customized Lord's Prayer: "From police violence and death squads, deliver us, O Lord"; and the crowd responded, "Deliver us, O Lord." The pattern continued: "from unjust and oppressive laws"; "from the lack of health, diet, and literacy for our children"; "from the foreign debt, the IMF [International Monetary Fund], multinational corporations." During the mass that followed, the priest raised the eucharist and proclaimed, "With this sacrament, we affirm our commitment to struggle for the people's liberation."[111]

The social action catalyzed by liberation theology generally met with augmented military repression, and this reactionary violence fostered, in turn, the growing conviction that armed insurrection was the only viable alternative for the poor. The priests who had organized, indoctrinated, and mobilized the masses were consequently faced with the paradox of a pacifist Church arming itself as social action evolved toward revolution. Each priest committed to the movement faced the dilemma of abandoning the guerrillas, violating his vows to take up arms, or negotiating some compromise position. The consequences of all the options were often unpleasant. "You pushed us into insurrection," indigenous Guatemalans told a popular Church assembly in 1984, "and when the difficult moment came you left. You use us, what we are and what we do, for ends that are not ours."[112]

The Colombian Camilo Torres was among the priests who joined the armed struggle and, in this case, died in it. In his 1965 "Message to the Christians," Torres argued that "the Revolution is not just permitted but rather obligatory for those Christians who see it as the only ample and efficacious means to achieve love for all."[113] In Guatemala during the early 1980s, Donald McKenna, an Irish priest, fought with the Guerrilla Army of the Poor because "counterviolence" (a lesser evil to prevent the greater evil of genocide against natives) was "the only possible solution for Guatemala."[114] McKenna took up arms because "the responsibility of a priest is to be beside his people," and because "the violence of the poor is not violence, it is justice."[115] This last point was pursued into social millennialism by a Nicaraguan priest, who argued from the premise that the Somoza regime "is a sin": "To free ourselves from oppression is to free ourselves from sin, and with a rifle in my hand, full of love for the Nicaraguan people, I must fight until my last breath for the advent of the kingdom of justice in our country, that kingdom of justice that the Messiah announced under the light of the star of Bethlehem."[116]

Representation of the poor as the suffering just and "the natural bearers of the utopia of God's Kingdom" constitutes another of liberation theology's millennial attributes.[117] The traditional Church had defended the interest of the elite, but liberation theology reinterpreted the Christian mission with "a preferential option for the poor": "We are called to build a Church from below, from the poor, from the exploited classes, from the marginalized races, from the depreciated cultures."[118] This "messianic inversion" is predicated on such scriptural dicta as "the meek shall inherit the earth," which explicitly privilege the humble and relegate the rich to "the very bottom of the abyss."[119] For Gustavo Gutiérrez, the reversal of the first and the last in Matthew 20:16 "is not a frivolous and manipulative political slogan"; rather it "sets before us a radical demand" to defend the interests of "those who today are marginalized and oppressed by political structures and laws that are of benefit to, and defend, the privileges of the 'first' of society."[120] The voiceless poor are the "messianic people," "a people journeying through history and continually bringing about the messianic reversal—'the last shall be first'—that is a key element in every truly liberating process."[121]

The overturning of a jealously defended order, even if only in homilies, was not without its consequences for the clergy and parishioners associated with liberation theology. In the years around 1980, the persecution of the Church in El Salvador, summarized by the slogan "Be a patriot, kill a priest," included the murder of clergy, lay workers, prominent Jesuits, and Archbishop Oscar Arnulfo Romero. In neighboring Guatemala, the less-publicized but no-less-severe repression resulted in the murder of twelve priests and several hundred lay catechists. Army persecution of Catholics was so severe in El Quiché that the bishop there, following an attempt on his own life, closed the diocese and withdrew his personnel for a "forced absence" in "protest against the authorities."[122] The catechists who filled the gap then became the martyrs of persecution, in some cases suffering crucifixion as a punishment that fit the crime.[123] The Bible had become, as Rigoberta Menchú put it, the "main weapon" of indigenous Catholics, and even the mere possession of a Bible or hymnal was sufficient cause for torture and disappearance.[124] The repression of Catholicism was so severe in November 1980 that a priest hid eucharists inside tortillas so that a village catechist could smuggle them past the army and the secret police.[125] Catholicism became an underground "Church of the Catacombs" like that of the first Christians among Romans: "Their cause is our cause and for that we are persecuted just as they were persecuted."[126] Multitudes of indigenous Guatemalans sought refuge by conversion to Evangelical churches, and in some villages, such as the Mayan village of Ri bey, entire populations converted at once.[127] Under Lucas García and again under born-again dictator Efraín Ríos Montt, the pace of conversion escalated because "Protestantism was simply safer than Catholicism."[128]

In absence of such extenuating circumstances, most Latin Americans convert to Evangelical churches less for asylum than for religious reasons conditioned by poverty. The great majority are attracted to Pentecostalism, in which baptism in the Holy Spirit is a crisis experience that affords even God's lowliest servants a rebirth into the new humanity: "We are the chosen people, the saved people, the holy nation."[129] In the fourth century, Saint John Chrysostom literalized the metaphor of baptismal rebirth by explaining that "when we plunge our heads into the water as into a sepulcher, the old man is immersed, buried wholly; when we come out of the water, the new man appears at the same time," and therefore baptism "represents death and burial, life and resurrection."[130] The ritual water dissolves former identities and washes away sin, and the chosen people "dead to sin" become a "new creation" with a share in Christ's resurrection.[131]

Pentecostalism distinguishes itself from other Protestant denominations by actively pursuing gifts of the Holy Spirit, including speaking in tongues, prophesy, and faith healing. The scriptural basis is in 1 Corinthians 14, where the faithful are instructed to "eagerly desire spiritual gifts," and in Acts 2:1–4, where during Pentecost a violent wind from heaven brought "tongues of fire" that settled on the heads of the apostles. "All of them were filled with the Holy Spirit and began to speak in other tongues as the Spirit enabled them."[132] The intent was to make these multilingual emissaries of the Gospel intelligible to foreigners, but modern Pentecostals stress instead the joyful noise of glossolalia that results from possession.[133] The mood is captured in Acts 4:29–31: "When they prayed, the place in which they were gathered together was shaken; and they were all filled with the Holy Spirit and spoke the word of God with boldness."

The body is overtaken when it is possessed by spirits, and as much in Christianity as in native, African, and syncretic religions the resultant physical expressions include crying and shouting, convulsions, ecstatic dance, dissociative states, and other demonstrations that corporal control, like personal will, has been relinquished to a supernatural power. This disjuncture of the individual from the group, which is encouraged and reinforced by the congregation that ultimately benefits from it, replicates in miniature the social dissociation of the chosen people collectively from the profane world around them. The prominence and similarity of possession states in disparate cultural contexts suggests that the forfeiture of autonomy—"you are not your own," as 1 Corinthians 6:19 has it—is an expedient to the mutually reinforcing relations between the possessed individual, the group, and the god. Speaking in tongues provides an ideal index, for "it has a very distinct pattern that does not vary from language to language: persons speaking various English dialects, Portuguese, Spanish, or Maya, all display the same pattern in this vocalization."[134] The result, by default, conforms to the apostolic communication intended by the gift of tongues: an international language that, though unintelligible, speaks from the soul to a multilingual congregation.

When it seems to those outside of the chosen community that the spasmodic ecstasy is more a sign of madness than of divine possession, more the sign of a lost creation than of a new humanity, then Christians respond, "If we are out of our minds, it is for God."[135] The persecution of Christianity deemed aberrant is as old as the faith itself, and in the Spanish empire it was institutionalized by the Inquisition. Before he was burned at the stake in colonial Lima, the Dominican friar Francisco de la Cruz cited scripture to defend his "mad" singing and dancing as perfectly biblical, like that of "the sons of the prophets praising God." Citing Saul's attempted murder of David as example, Fray Francisco called the categories of profane sanity and sacred madness into question. Those who "sang and danced and praised God" had relinquished their volition to divine inspiration, and thus they were "neither sane nor totally out of their minds."[136]

Divine Alliance

If a "a motley bunch of Spanish adventurers" could defeat the great imperial armies of the Americas, then for conqueror and conquered alike it seemed reasonable to presume that a mighty god had manifested his will through his soldiers.[137] Power is enhanced as it recycles between the God and his chosen people, each mutually re-creating and reinforcing the other while the invincibility of their alliance is tested on the battlefield. Even the tropes of evangelism—"spiritual calvary," "conquering souls"—attest to the untroubled crossovers between sacred and profane and to a bellicose model for the American mission. The 1523 document instructing the "twelve apostles" dispatched to Mexico explained that the natives were held captive by Satan and that the Franciscans would liberate them "armed with the shield of faith, with the armor of justice, with the sword of the divine word, with the helmet of health, and with the lance of perseverance."[138] The endurance of militarized religious tropes into the present is evidenced in such movements as Argentina's Catholic Nationalism, which styled itself a "grand offensive" in the "total war" where "Christ is King."[139] Many Latin American Pentecostals view themselves as "Warriors of Prayer" waging "spiritual warfare" with divine reinforcement: "He [God] is calling us to the battlefield, and has promised to give us all of his resources for this battle."[140]

On occasion the Warriors of Prayer must trespass on literal battlefields more precarious than those of their rhetoric. When Sendero Luminoso and Evangelical churches competed for the same souls in Apurímac, Peru, and when prayers for divine intervention brought no results, the Evangelicals were forced into "holy war" against the "sons of Abimael."[141] This clash of two peoples regarding themselves as chosen resulted in crisis when the Senderistas demanded universal compliance with the people's revolution. A Protestant in one village responded, "I am an Evangelical. I only believe in God, and I refuse to accept your doctrines." The man was shot on the spot, and other Christians attending services were shot or burned alive.[142] The grim situation readily accommodated apocalyptic interpretations, and some Evangelicals equated Abimael Guzmán's claim to be the "fourth sword" of world communism with the fourth horseman of the Apocalypse, who "was named Death" and "given power over a fourth of the earth to kill by the sword."[143] "I was no longer a simple fighter," remarked one Christian soldier confronting such evil, "but a fighter for God, under God's protection." In one of the many legends of divine intervention, the apparition of "heavenly armies" frightened off Senderistas who were closing in on an Evangelical in Anchihuay.[144]

However demonic his mission and atheistic his vision, Guzmán himself occasionally pontificated in Christian rhetoric. In a 1979 speech anticipating the armed struggle that the "holy family" would begin a year later, Guzmán opened with the words, "Many are called but few are chosen" and later applied Pauline theological virtues to the task at hand: "Our love, our faith, our hope are collective; they are realizable, they are three in one flag."[145] More explicit than this trinitarian metaphor was a 1981 Sendero booklet: "War is holy, its institution is divine and one of the sacred laws of the world."[146] Guzmán's spiritual inclinations were partially indebted to José Carlos Mariátegui, for whom "Communism is essentially religious" but "the religious motives have shifted from heaven to earth."[147] The name Sendero Luminoso (Shining Path) is itself derived from the motto "By the Shining Path of José Carlos Mariátegui," predisposing Guzmán's rhetoric and mission to an "essentially religious" aggrandizement as "the most luminous and grandiose mission delivered to any generation."[148] The father of a high-ranking Senderista suggested that anyone who could not understand the violent rebellion of oppressed classes reread Matthew 21:12–13 (Jesus casting the money changers from the temple), where "one will find the millennial explanation of a wrath that many men of the world judge as holy."[149] A Sendero commander was more explicit in his allusions to Guzmán's messianic mission when he forced villagers to replace the common exclamation "Oh, Jesus" with "Oh, Gonzalo" (Guzmán's nom de guerre).[150]

The belief that God was on the side of his holy warriors was less a political expedient than an earnest conviction of Augusto César Sandino in Nicaragua. Following studies of Seventh-Day Adventism and Theosophy, Sandino, a "Spiritual Communist," was deeply influenced by the ideology of nothing less than the Magnetic-Spiritual School of the Universal Commune. In his "Light and Truth" manifesto of February 1931, Sandino explained that "a divine impulse has animated and protected our army from the start," and that therefore the soldiers deploy a force superior to them "and to all the forces of the universe." The creation of the universe was "a great desire To Be on the part of that which was not, and which is known to us by the name of Love." Love is the beginning of all things, "the only Daughter of Love is Divine Justice," and Sandino's army had been "chosen by Divine Justice to begin the prosecution of injustice on earth."[151]

The threat of communist revolution, its priestliness notwithstanding, has brought retaliatory divine forces to the aid of conservative chosen peoples. As liberal Christianity gained prominence in the 1960s, the Tradition, Family and Property sect, "sentinel of the West," spread from Brazil to hispanic South America to combat "the penetration of Marxism into the Catholic Church." The sect was characterized by such cultish practices as initiation rites that included the signing of a document in blood; the practice of celibacy reinforced by explicit misogyny; and a "totally military regimen" in its indoctrination camps. "Those monks are a mixture of soldiers and priests," one former member reported from Argentina.[152] The movement maintained that agrarian reform was a "collective mortal sin" and advocated a return "to monarchy in order to constitute a medieval and harmonious Latin America."[153] Anticommunism is also central to the Unification Church of Reverend Sun Myung Moon, which recruits Latin Americans attracted to the doctrine that the new messiah will not establish his kingdom on earth "until communism, which is the contemporary incarnation of Satan, has completely disappeared."[154]

The armed forces have also made appeals to the medieval orders of crusading monk-knights and at every opportunity describe their mandate as holy. In the 1960s an Ecuadorian lieutenant observed that "the soldier's abnegation is a cross heavier than that of the martyr; let us carry it with resignation, for only the greatest of men earn both cross and Calvary."[155] In Cuba under Fulgencio Batista, the soldier was "the priest of that religion called patriotism," while in Bolivia of the 1950s the army was to the nation "what the priest is to the temple."[156] Paraguayan officers were instructed in 1983 to inform their soldiers of certain analogies between military and Christian life: the helmet was a crown of thorns, the shouldered rifle was a cross, and their forced marches were Christ's itinerant preachings in the Holy Land.[157] This Christianization of warfare was complemented in iconography by the militarization of Jesus, not only by representing the God of love with firearms, swords, and military uniforms but also by adorning statues and paintings with military decorations.[158]

In Argentina at the time of the 1966 coup, General Juan Carlos Onganía referred to the military's "profound spiritual constitution" that "confirms the dominance of moral values over material ones."[159] Onganía's "desire to perfect a moral order" was refined through his active participation in the Cursillos de Cristiandad, whose weekly meetings imbued in officers a "mystical messianism." These courses provided "moral armament" for soldiers who would transform the world into a New Christendom.[160] That uncompleted mission then extended into the Process of National Reorganization after the 1976 coup because, as a member of the governing junta put it, "God has decided that we [the junta] should have the responsibility of designing the future."[161]

In the Chilean armed forces, Catholicism was inspired by biblical holy war and devotion to the Virgin of Carmen represented as a general. Chilean officers regard their conservative faith as inherently superior to the slack, "infiltrated," undisciplined Christianity of the masses.[162] They perceive themselves to be the Christian elite entrusted with defense of the Church even against the waywardness of fellow Christians (liberation theologists, adherents to popular Catholicism, converts to Protestantism, even the pope) who stray from their path of righteousness. "The military *incarnates* the fundamental values of Chile and can be relied on to maintain constant vigilance for the 'purity of faith.' "[163]

On September 9, 1973, the reactionary Church hierarchy in Chile prayed for a "miracle of peace." The prayers were answered two days later when General Augusto Pinochet, with the help of God and the U.S. Central Intelligence Agency, staged the coup in which Salvador Allende died. If Allende's first name (Savior) had a certain resonance for his followers, the supporters of the coup saw Pinochet as the "blessed soldier" of the Lord unsheathing his sword to free Chile from the satanic bonds of socialism. As one monsignor explained it as late as 1985, "Mary performed the miracle. It was the second independence of Chile."[164] A militarized theology was also evident in the discourse of Pinochet himself, who in the 1970s remarked that Chileans overwhelmed by evil "prayed for their salvation" until "the hand of God" came to their rescue. The coup, he summarized, "was the response of God to the prayer of all believers who see in Marxism the satanic force of darkness in its maximal expression." In 1984 Pinochet revealed the reason for his regime's endurance: "I am a man who fights for a just cause; the struggle between Christianity and spiritualism, on the one hand, and Marxism and materialism on the other. I get my power from God."[165]

Also empowered by God was the born-again General Efraín Ríos Montt, referred to as "Dios Montt" by more irreverent Guatemalans.[166] In 1974 Ríos Montt, a candidate for president, lost the fraudulent election and went to Spain as a minor diplomat; he returned to Guatemala in 1978. Ríos Montt renounced Catholicism and became a member of the Church of the Complete Word, known as El Verbo, or the Word Church, which had been established in Guatemala by Gospel Outreach of California in 1976. Shortly after taking power in a coup by junior officers in March 1982, Ríos Montt removed the other two members of the junta, declared a state of siege, suspended the constitution, and ruled by decree. He claimed to have ended the death squads prevalent under his predecessor, but according to Amnesty International the atrocities continued on a grand scale, augmented by a selective assassination program of "preventative terror."[167]

The Word Church provided two elders as official aides and "spiritual advisers" to Ríos Montt and coordinated a relief effort supported from the United States by International Love Lift. Love, as Ríos Montt explained to the *New York Times*, was "the only solution" to the civil conflict in Guatemala. When the reporter pressed on the issue of human rights, including the murder of unarmed women and children, Ríos Montt responded "It is war, a permanent war." A few months later he explained, "We declared a state of siege so we could kill legally," but also "We defend ourselves not by the army or its sword, but by the Holy Spirit."[168] Those close to Ríos Montt held similar views: his private secretary, for example, stated that the Holy Spirit was the driving force behind the special and paramilitary troops responsible for the massacre of Indians.[169] In December 1982 when a pastor of the Word Church was asked why natives were being attacked, he responded, "The army does not kill Indians, it massacres devils, because the Indians are communists, possessed by the devil."[170]

Ríos Montt repeatedly declared that God had sent him to save Guatemala and that "the one in charge is Jesus Christ."[171] Members of the Word Church, who referred to his "anointment" as president, elaborated: "Like king David of the Old Testament, he is the king of the New Testament."[172] Ríos Montt as messianic king reciprocated in kind to his subjects—"Guatemalans are the chosen people of the New Testament"—but the privilege turned out to be costly.[173] The biblical foundation for dictatorship in Romans 13:1–2 also provided a basis for divinely sanctioned oppression: "The authorities that exist have been established by God. Consequently, he who rebels against the authority is rebelling against what God has instituted, and those who do so will bring judgment on themselves."[174]

An Evangelical dictator provided the opportunity for an efficient assault against Indians, Catholicism, and communism, all of which had been collapsed into a single, expedient stereotype. As one Gospel Outreach publicist wrote, the rise of "Brother Efraín" to power presented "an extraordinary opportunity" amidst "the turbulent darkness of Latin America," "a vibrant alternative to the rising tide of Marxism-Leninism in that region, and a glorious testimony to the reality and truth of Jesus Christ."[175] Fundraising literature lauded Ríos Montt's regime as "God's miracle in Guatemala," and contributions to Gospel Outreach would "show the world that when a nation turns to God, and God's people unite, His marvelous plan is fulfilled."[176] After God's marvelous plan was deposed by a counter-coup in 1983, Brother Efraín, a "hero of the Faith," spoke before the Word Church: "Heroes generally return covered with medals and decorations. I only want to be covered with the Blood of Christ."[177]

The New Morality

The identity of a chosen people is forged in opposition to the hopelessly corrupt society that surrounds it, and the community therefore accentuates differentiation as it consolidates its unique self-image. The inner transformation of the chosen is often accompanied by outward demonstrations that signal adherence to a new doctrine and allegiance to an alternative community. Codes of dress and hair style are common overt signs that contribute to uniformity within the messianic community and to the community's segregation from society at large. Adherents to the sixteenth-century Taqui Onqoy movement returned to indigenous dress because "what the body wears must correspond to what the body as a social and religious sign signifies and contains."[178] The same was true of innumerable nativist movements, with the rejection of Spanish clothing registering both an end to forced acculturation and a new ostracism of those who opted to keep their trousers. Modern Guatemalan natives relate that when the Spaniards arrived with "mirrors, ear rings, and razors" they cleaned up and groomed one of the Indians. The man experienced "a great change in his personality" to the degree that "he felt like a Spaniard," but this resulted only in the scorn of his people and a dressed-up subordination: "he was forced to work alone for the Spaniards."[179]

In modern religious movements, dress and hair codes serve to identify, and sometimes stigmatize, a chosen community. The messiahs of Brazil fashioned themselves after biblical images of mendicant piety, sporting sackcloths, sandals, walking sticks, and long hair and beards, thereby conforming to a paradigm held in popular imagination.[180] The consonance of their appearance and their message lent them an authenticity lacking in the hypocritical worldliness of the Catholic clergy. More recently in Brazil the "counterimage" of the Catholic priest was projected by the prophet Francisco da Cruz, who unlike his clerical antithesis was disinterested in the material world, accepted no fees, dressed simply, and slept on the floor.[181] Members of his Brotherhood of the Cross follow the way and the will of their prophet by wearing simple, body-covering attire adorned by a cross that is inscribed with the anagram for *salva tu alma* (save your soul). In daily life the cross distinguishes members of the Brotherhood from the general population, and on the day of reckoning, amidst the confusion of tribulations, it will identify them to God as the saving remnant.[182] The visual cues of individual appearance also extend into the collective when it goes public on missionary outings. The brothers and sisters travel by boat along the rivers of the Amazon, wearing the cross over white clothing, singing religious hymns, and flying the movement's white flag at full mast.[183]

Visual identification is yet more conspicuous among the Israelites of the New Covenant in Peru, who follow the "vow of the Nazirite" in Numbers 6 "to separate themselves unto the Lord." Because Numbers mandates that "no razor shall come upon his head," Israelite men wear their hair and beards in the style of the Old Testament prophets.[184] From without, the uncut hair is an identifier of Israelite membership; and from within, it is "a kind of antenna" through which God transmits knowledge, strength, and health to his chosen people.[185] The hair styles are complemented by matching accouterments: men wear blue, white, or red robes, and women wear white dresses with rope belts and cloth kerchiefs that cover the hair.

Accompanying these outward signs of individual and communal transformation are new moral and social codes that differentiate the chosen community from the world it rejects. Coherence of the group is often predicated on severing or at least distancing previous social and familial bonds. The several roles that each convert once assumed in society must be abandoned to accommodate the all-encompassing demands of the messianic community. Patterns of interaction are discontinued, participation in village traditions ceases, norms of deference are overhauled, gender roles are modified, and the hierarchy of relations is reconfigured. As the recruiting Christ put it in Luke 14:26, "If anyone comes to me without hating his father and mother, wife and children, brothers and sisters, and even his own life, he cannot be my disciple." The frequent reference to the new community as a family and the co-adepts as brothers and sisters underscores the primacy of the commitment and the dissolution of previous bonds. An Evangelical characteristically asserted that "the people of the Church are my family," just as a female guerrilla of Sendero Luminoso protested that she no longer

belonged to her family because "the people" were her family."[186] Some take up
the cross and others the gun, but all restructure their social milieu to privilege
the movement and its ideals.

Among modern Evangelicals, as among the first Christians, asceticism and
purity "symbolised the separateness of the eschatological community, its fitness
and readiness to enter into the kingdom at any moment."[187] Characteristic are
puritanical ethical and sexual mores and a wide variety of abstinences. Converts to Pentecostalism leave behind drinking, gambling, adultery, rowdiness,
dances, movies, jewelry, makeup, provocative clothing, and anything else that
"awakens one's carnal appetites."[188] They also boycott the "pagan" Catholic
celebrations (with their drinking, adultery, rowdiness) that are central to village
life.[189] For some Pentecostals in the Peruvian jungle, personal purity is extended
into high standards of cleanliness, because God is an invisible guest in one's
home.[190] The behavioral restrictions and the consequence of violations are yet
more rigorous in such sects as that of Pau de Colher in Brazil, which required
its members to cancel all debts, abstain from vices, lead a family life in strict
adherence to Catholic dogma, and avoid any sign of vanity. Death was the penalty for backsliders who "turned into beasts" by resorting to the world's sinful
ways.[191] Israelites of the New Covenant also advocate capital punishment for
adulterers, homosexuals, liars, thieves, idolaters, and "all who commit unjust
acts."[192]

In some cases the new morality is reduced to symbolic gestures that cohere
the chosen community but fail to achieve the spiritual transformation befitting
a baptismal rebirth. Natives in parts of the Peruvian Amazon are divided into
Protestants, who do not drink the alcoholic beverage *masato*, and Catholics,
who do, and this is "practically the only difference."[193] In other cases, the new
morality genuinely results in transformation of the social milieu constructed by
separatist communities, even if at times the morality must be dogmatically enforced. In the Luz del Mundo colony in Guadalajara, "there is peace, security,
and unity among the people and the social vices so common in Mexican cities
are practically non-existent."[194] Evangelicals living in the outside world, such as
Ecuadorian Quichuas who have converted from Catholicism, feel as though the
members of their new faith "can be trusted," "act like real brothers," "are willing to share," "are more honest," "work harder," "don't drink and are more
reliable."[195] The conversion of agricultural workers brought down the wrath of
one Catholic latifundista on a parish priest, but when the landowner realized
the benefits of the new faith—including the Evangelicals' avoidance of unions
and campesino activism—he changed course, asserting, "The Protestant Indians
are more rational, more worthy of trust."[196] The indigenous Evangelical is indoctrinated to be "disciplined, dedicated, obedient, and anti-communist," leading many to observe that one intent of Protestant missions in Latin America is
"to establish and legitimate a capitalist counter-culture camouflaged by religion."[197] That contention is reinforced by the U.S. origin of the missions and by
the capacity of many Evangelical churches to control the vote of their congregations.

In another perspective, Evangelicals "may be 'model citizens,' but their religious identity carries with it a subtext of noncompliance."[198] The Evangelicals' dispossession of entrenched Catholicism and the traditional society that extends from it, including patron saint festivals and the cargo system of shared civil and religious (but Catholic) responsibilities, has had profound social consequences.[199] Hierarchy is virtually collapsed in Pentecostalism because the Holy Spirit possesses all believers, equalizing all as instruments of God—"all one in Christ Jesus"—and, as a by-product, broadening the faith's attractiveness to the lower classes.[200] This leveling effect disturbs the castelike society in which it proliferates, and even more so the rigid hierarchy and vertical command of the armed forces. Equality within the Evangelical churches themselves is symbolized by the open pulpit. Rather than being reserved for the word of a sacred elite as it is in traditional Catholicism, the pulpit is accessible to all who were previously voiceless.[201]

New moralities are also central to secular efforts, like the Cuban Revolution, that seek the "rebirth" of a population. Envisioning "salvation" of Peru as the composite result of individual transformation, the American Revolutionary Popular Alliance (APRA) coached its members on the ideals of strength, abnegation, and freedom from vice and ignorance.[202] A party publication from 1934 was typical: "Aprista: become cultured, educate yourself, prepare yourself, improve yourself. The work of our Party must emerge all-powerful in order to save this country."[203] Later in Peruvian history a new morality was introduced and enforced, often brutally, by Sendero Luminoso. In the earlier years the crimes and punishments were limited to those of Andean tradition, such as whipping and hair cutting as penalty for cattle rustling and adultery.[204] The punishments then became more severe—usually capital and always public—to chastise theft, corruption, wife beating, unsatisfactory work in communal projects, participation in fiestas and rituals, and buying or selling at local markets. Sendero also closed discotheques, exiled prostitutes, and executed homosexuals. A similarly rigorous moral program of unlikely origin was undertaken by the Colombian drug cartels, whose death squads purged their respective realms—notably Cali and Medellín—of thieves, prostitutes, homosexuals, and others whom they deemed undesirable.[205]

What presents as a new morality is most frequently a return to a moral order lost in an idealized past. The chosen people isolate themselves from the bastardizers of approved human conduct with the intent of first restoring it among themselves (sometimes with libertine innovations) and then among those who survive the cataclysm (war, Last Judgment) that shifts the paradigm. On occasion the restoration of a lost order is explicit, as when Juan Manuel de Rosas was considered Restorer of the Laws in a context perceived to be anarchical and iniquitous. The same title was used by the Venezuelan caudillo José Antonio Páez in the 1840s, and the concept was popular among caudillos, conservatives, and military governments even when the sobriquet was absent.[206] Mexican caudillo Antonio López de Santa Anna endeavored to bring order to what he called "the empire of anarchy" and "to break the triple yoke of ignorance, tyranny and vice." The reactionary response to social change perceived as perverse always intends to redeem "the conservative principles."[207]

Conspicuous in many new moralities are provisions for indulgence in the forbidden. Among some sects an intermingling of piety and sexuality extend Christian love into a celebration of the joy that God intended for his creation. Inquisition records document a range of cases, from the sex cults consolidated by the visions of a beata to the exotic penance performed on the bodies of priests in confession booths.[208] Native clergy during the Tzeltal Rebellion explained in homilies that the Virgin would be pleased if women did not deny their husbands' "sensual appetite."[209] In 1761 the Mexican messiah Antonio Pérez preached that "sleeping with women was not a sin" provided that the women were blessed before penetration. Pérez himself partook of a married woman ("all three slept on the same mat") so that "the Son of God would be born."[210]

The frontiers of religious eroticism were explored more brazenly by California's Children of God movement, founded by David Brandt Berg during the late 1960s when it was "prohibited to prohibit." Adepts of the Niños de Dios, as the sect is known in Latin America, are required to sever all ties with their former lives—work, school, family, friends, possessions—in order to submit absolutely to "new authorities chosen by God." Once a member of "the Family," an Argentine convert related, "I felt like I was one of the Lord's chosen," and at the same time, "I began to hate the world, my parents, the Catholic Church, and everything that was outside of 'the Family.' "[211] This dissociation of the chosen people from all otherness was complemented by a characteristic, but here literalized emphasis on rebirth. One of the chants introduced by the movement's leader—known as "Mo," for Moses—was "I want to become a baby, baby, baby."

The Children of God based their faith on Christian love that encompassed not merely charity and mystical union but also orgiastic love, hetero- and homosexual, among members of the family. Even the movement's apocalypticism carried the erotic message: "Enjoy yourself! It's later than you think." The writings of Mo mandated sexual freedom and included explicit instructions on how, for example, to deflower a virgin.[212] One publication represented the Holy Spirit as a seductive woman in a translucent tunic, her arm hooked into that of God the Father.[213] Beginning in 1974, members of the Children of God, particularly women, were encouraged and then required to tend to the ministry of sexual love, picking up partners in bars and hotels to disseminate the Lord's grace with their bodies.[214]

Though less explicit in its flaunting of broken taboos, an Argentine sect led by José Luis Cobo, known as Silo, also emerged in the 1960s with a hippy ideology endeavoring to "humanize" the planet.[215] Many nineteenth-century utopians likewise advocated libertine sexuality, but in practice—as Giovanni Rossi explained from the 1890–93 Cecilia Colony in Brazil—the residents were ultimately disinclined to indulge because of the husbands' jealousy, the wives' reputations, the disruption of domestic customs, and the consequence of abandoned women and children.[216]

Licentiousness in the realm of violence is also legitimated by appeal to religious and moral doctrines. The pompous religiosity of dictatorships is exemplary in its conception of atrocity as a benevolent service to humanity, but civilian cases are also prevalent. José López Rega, an adviser to Juan and Isabel Perón and leader of the Argentine Anti-Communist Alliance responsible for two thousand political assassinations between 1973 and 1977, was insistent in his use of dictums such as "Above all one must do good."[217] A century earlier, the sanction of well-meaning atrocity characterized caudillo struggles including the "religious crusade" that brought José Rafael Carrera to the Guatemalan presidency. When Carrera attacked Guatemala City in 1838, some four thousand "drunken and excited guerrillas armed with machetes, staves, and rusty muskets, draped in crucifixes and rosary beads" screamed, "Long live religion and death to the foreigners." Pausing from the massacre, the crusaders "all knelt down in the square and sang the '*Sanctus Deus*' and '*Ave Maria.*' "[218]

Holy war again flourished in the Cristero Rebellion as marauding Catholics defended the faith against an "aggressively secular" Mexican state.[219] Under the battlecry "Long Live Christ the King," the Cristeros murdered teachers and bombed a train full of civilians, but their magnum opus was conspired under the spiritual guidance of a nun known as Madre Conchita. The originally "mystical" pursuits of Conchita's circle became increasing militant and concluded finally with the 1928 assassination of president-elect Alvaro Obregón. The divinely inspired mission was entrusted to a young artist, José de León Toral, who welcomed the opportunity to eliminate the "Antichrist Obregón" and then face the fate of the early Christian martyrs.[220]

In Colombia during the 1950s, Christ the King also inspired the conservative goon squads that regarded Protestants, particularly Pentecostals, as "Communist subversives." In the region of La Morena, a Pentecostal preacher was dismissing his congregation with prayer when an assailant stabbed him in the chest shouting, "Long Live Christ the King!"[221] More genocidal was the theorizing of a group of Brazilian beatos in the mid-1930s, who reckoned that the murder of nonbelievers was a "communal good, not a heinous crime" and who also stabbed to death any disobedient members of their own community.[222]

Punitive and ritual murders are common in authoritarian personality cults that condition a willingness to kill and be killed in defense of a spiritualized ideal. On occasion the syncretic elaboration of apocalyptic Christianity is impetus enough for a latent fury, as when a Jehovah's Witness in Oaxaca, Mexico, "sacrificed" ten Indians in 1985.[223] In provincial Argentina some twenty Mapuches fasted, sang, and prayed for several days in order to save the soul of a woman of their congregation who had been "possessed by the devil." On August 26, 1978, in a state of collective trance and amidst voices announcing the end of the world, the woman was beaten to death by her fellow adepts, ostensibly in an effort to exorcise her demons. Like many adherents to millennial movements, she would be saved even if it killed her. The frenzied prayers and rituals continued, and by the time they concluded her two children and a two-year-old niece had also been murdered.[224]

A Practical Faith

"All religions are good," a Brazilian remarked in 1977, "but each one has its occasion. For someone who has no problems in life, the best religion is Catholicism. One has the saints, one goes to church when he wants to, and no one bothers him. For someone who has financial difficulties, the best religion is that of the *crentes* [Pentecostals], because they help you as brothers; the only thing is that one can't smoke, drink, dance, or anything. Now, for someone who suffers from headaches, the best religion is that of the Spiritists. It's demanding, one can't miss any sessions, but it really cures. If God wills it, when I am totally cured I'll return to Catholicism."[225]

This migration among religions is common throughout Latin America and evidences a search for specific gains—material as well as spiritual—from services offered in a competitive market. The majority of Indians in a Chiapas village had become Jehovah's Witnesses, Seventh-Day Adventists, or members of the Evangelical Presbyterian Church, but when the volcano Chichonal erupted in 1979 they surreptitiously returned to prayer for the intercession of Catholic saints.[226] Much the same had occurred among the Yucatec Maya centuries earlier, in 1560, when a hurricane devastated the peninsula. Because the disaster was interpreted as a punishment from the gods abandoned by conversion, the Maya apostatized to resume the indigenous cult. Traditional rituals before an "altar of idols" were supplemented by human sacrifices performed inside the Catholic churches, as though a simultaneous appeal to all deities could terminate the scourge.[227] The desire to reap the benefits of competing religions without attracting the wrath of any is also evident in a modern Peruvian Evangelical's assertion, "I believe that God is one, who is Jesus Christ," followed by, "and I also venerate Pachamama, mother earth, asking for her blessing."[228] In folk healing throughout Latin America curanderos similarly combine Christianity with African or native rituals for a syncretic experience that, as one curandero described it, "is like going to Church."[229]

If Pentecostalism draws its adepts predominantly from the lowest classes, it is perhaps because the Holy Spirit provides compensatory rewards to those deprived the gifts of this world. The lack of one such gift, health, is a primary inducement to conversion as a quest for the miraculous salvation of body as much as soul. An emphasis on faith healing in Brazil has resulted in "healing halls," often situated near state clinics, which feature miraculous cures at the climax of services. In Managua, Nicaragua, where "the movie theaters are almost all churches now," the seats are filled by busing in converts from the barrios for theatrical displays of the Holy Spirit's powers. These megachurches tend to lack the dedicated following of the smaller, more personal Pentecostal groups, attracting instead those who show up once or twice "looking for something specific in the religion market." "They want healing, or they've got economic problems, so they go there and buy the amulet, look for the holy water brought from Israel," and then continue the pilgrimage from church to church as the miracle they seek eludes them.[230]

Chilean Pentecostals relate that their congregations attract "the poorest of the poor," who through the faith alleviate the weight of their poverty: "We let go of ourselves, we unburden ourselves, we turn our problems over to the Lord who is the life of the world." If earlier the Pentecostal churches had "separated the spiritual and the material," now they acknowledge that humans "are holistic beings and that spiritual things are closely joined with the concrete problems of hunger and poverty." Christ brought the message that satisfies spiritual appetites, but, as in the Sermon on the Mount, he "also wanted to satisfy the people's hunger."[231] In the Beatitudes he went even further, parceling out the kingdom of heaven. The millennial promise of a status reversal often stresses such material gains, even through the conception of a Last Judgment in which the property of the rich is distributed among the poor.[232] The promise of spiritualized enrichment attracts impoverished peoples to the congregation, but its fulfillment might ultimately result in deconversion. When an Andean was asked by a minister which side wins in the constant battle between his body and soul, he responded, "Whichever one I feed better."[233] A Guatemalan native was more explicit: "If we are poor, we remember God and we have necessities that make us go to God. If we are rich, we do not [remember] because we only have the ambition to have more."[234]

After a long drought on the Argentine Chaco in 1933, the devastated Indians roaming hopelessly received word that the prominent Toba shaman Natochí (also known as Evaristo Asencio) was summoning natives to El Zapallar, where a new "era of happiness and abundance" was beginning. Natochí claimed to be the son of lightning and thunder, announced the imminent end of white domination, and ordered the boycott of habitual activities and Christianity. Those who wished to be counted among the elect were required to buy one of the *bastones de poder* (walking staffs symbolizing power) sold by the shaman; when everyone had one, the ancestors would return, the whites would be exterminated, and the natives would assume the wealth and governance of the region. Contact with white people was to be avoided, save to confiscate whatever possessions the natives desired, because "everything belonged to them legitimately."[235]

The movement was broken up by the authorities, but many of those possessing the staffs charged with ancestral power regrouped in Pampa del Indio. New leadership by the young Tapenaik sought fulfillment of prophetic dreams that foretold an era of prosperity. Tapenaik consolidated the group into a cargo cult based on the belief that airplanes would arrive from Buenos Aires (the source of the goods enjoyed by white people) to deliver loads of merchandise for the natives. Old clothing was to be burned and traditional foods avoided because "both clothes and food would come from the sky, brought by airplanes." Rejection and destruction of everything associated with the onerous past made way for the future age of plenty. The movement suspended all activities, established a cult center for ritual song and dance, and set to the task of building a landing strip to receive the aircraft. Dreams, ecstatic trance, and renewed prophesies maintained the ambience of festivity and anticipation, but the police arrived in lieu of the cargo.[236]

Rather than await manna from heaven, Evangelicals transcendentalize mundane well-being with a "health and wealth" gospel and a "theology of prosperity." Converts improve their lot in this world through industriousness and abandonment of costly vice, which in turn improves their odds in the next world.[237] Guatemalans who converted to Protestantism in the 1970s described their transformed lives as *del suelo al cielo* (from the ground to the sky/heaven), with their sinful, money-squandering destitution soaring into holy prosperity and toward greater rewards awaiting them on high.[238] Even the most sacred discourse, that of spirit possession, sometimes reveals a pragmatic faith that prefers a full plate to esoteric mysteries. Trance states are considered a kind of death among the Pentecostal Toba, and those who return from the other world bear witness to what they have seen. "One young married Toba male reported that his vision involved a command to learn to farm and to appreciate vegetables rather than to continue to depend exclusively upon fish and wild meat for sustenance."[239]

A practical message from the spirits is also evident in the discourse of religious ceremonies that emerged from an 1858 revolt in Venezuela. Venancio Kamiko, the leader of the revolt in response to hunger, deprivation, and abuse, was later mythologized as a messianic cultural hero assimilated to Christ. Ritual advice given during male initiation among the Wakuénai is attributed to a new perspective introduced by Venancio: "The White men are thieves who buy our wares cheap and sell their merchandise to us at high prices. That is why they are rich and we are poor. Know that the Whites are your enemies. Hide your hatred because it is strong and treat the Whites with distrust because they are traitors."[240] Venancio's messianic promise waned, but his message was adapted to the practicalities of enduring injustice in a world that remains unredeemed.

Campesinos and the urban poor often adhere to alternative religions and messianic movements more to pursue social, economic, cultural, and psychological security rather than to manifest their allegiance to doctrines that, in most cases, they do not fully understand. The liturgy and attending obligations serve to organize and legitimate their faith, but many sign on because the movement promises tangible gains. The tropes that have been taken literally—kingdoms of peace and plenty, role reversal of rich and poor—speak in hyperbole to the perennial human quest for fulfillment of such basic needs as security, dignity, and justice, of which the great majority of Latin Americans are deprived. The millennial ideals are in this perspective a compensatory inflation of the humble hope that matters show some modest improvement or, that failing, that they at least not get any worse. After an apology for her incomplete understanding of doctrine, a Nicaraguan convert to Pentecostalism stated that Christ "is going to save his church and it will be taken to a place that he has where there will be no sadness or pain; that is the hope that we have."[241] The simplicity of the faith and the naive beauty of its promise are themselves the impetus for conversion, providing refuge for a community beleaguered both spiritually and temporally. "They take up a collection that is not obligatory," a Peruvian woman explained, and "you get a cup of tea and a cookie."[242]

3
Nativist Rebellions

The Extirpation of Christianity

On November 8 and 9, 1546—5*Cimi* 19*Xul*, Death and the End, in the Maya calendar—the *chilam* (priest) Anbal summoned seven Yucatan provinces to rebellion. Spaniards were killed in conformity with preconquest rituals, including the roasting of children over fires smoking with copal, and bodies were dismembered and distributed to nonrevolting provinces as proof that the godlike conquerors were defeatable. The "end of an era" prescribed by the Maya dates required even literal extirpation: "Spanish trees, Spanish plants, were ripped out of the ground; Indians who had served the Spaniards save under duress were slaughtered; even the cats and dogs were hunted down and killed."[1] The indigenous milieu defiled by conquest must be resacralized, and in its thorough manifestations the purge of foreign contaminants supplements genocide with the destruction of all foreign agriculture and material culture, the prohibition of foreign language and customs, and the execution of natives failing to comply.

Four hundred years later, in the Peruvian Andes of 1947, the persistence of a pan-indigenous will to annihilate the conqueror was registered in a village near Cuzco when a schoolboy informed his teacher that "the only way to reform and reorganize the empire is by exterminating all of the whites." Even white dogs would have to be killed, because they were "the spirit or soul of the Spaniards."[2] The restoration of a prehispanic world in the mid-twentieth century was more an ideal than a possibility, and the means were more rhetorical than bellicose, but what obtains through the centuries framed by the two examples is the quest for a nativist revitalization that would reverse deculturation and reciprocate conquest by extirpating all vestiges of the conqueror.

A predilection for religious targets was natural among revolts that sought revitalization of the defeated gods and their cults. The missionaries were likely recipients of nativist violence owing to their assault on traditional religion, their complicity with the conquering deity and his soldiers, their association with epidemics, their vulnerability as an unarmed vanguard, their willingness for martyrdom, and their imposition and enforcement of alien ethics and customs (burial, monogamy, sacraments) that were rigorously contested by the natives. A sense of betrayal also contributed to animosity as the glad tidings that promised salvation brought devastation instead. The protest of one converted cacique is noteworthy in both its expectation and its disappointment: "You gave me the cross as a defense against my enemies, and with that very cross you tried to destroy me."[3]

Typical of the resultant apostasy was a scenario in Baja California in 1735, where ten years after having more or less graciously accepted the faith natives were killing friars, desecrating churches, and razing mission towns.[4] The leader of a 1632 rebellion in Nueva Vizcaya spoke for many when he argued, "Let's kill this deceiver who prohibits us from having many wives and makes us go to church. Let's kill the other one who came from far away to do the same, so that no more priests will come to our land. What do we need priests for?"[5] Tepehuan apostates of the same period illustrated that missionaries were often murdered as symbols, not for who they were but rather for what they represented: "We are not killing you because you have done us harm, but rather because you are a priest."[6] The symbolic nature of the guilt did not necessarily translate into a humane execution, however, and in subsequent Tepehuan revolts the Jesuits, with "rosaries upraised in their hands, knelt to receive showers of thousands of arrows in their bodies." The corpses were then dragged to a nearby log, "where their heads were crushed by blows from Indian macanas, and their bodies further mutilated with thrusts from enemy knives."[7]

Apostate violence seeking to extirpate the missions often had this ritual quality of excess beyond any pragmatic need. Defilement of the sacrosanct manifested a defiant joy and carnivalesque mockery, a victory dance of triumph and relief celebrated on and amidst the remains of the impotent, dead God and his defeated priests. Tepehuans rebelling in 1616 stabbed and shot arrows into the crucified Christ, stomped on the eucharist, knocked down crosses, used the chalices "for their filthy drunkenness," whipped an image of the virgin, and "put the dress of Our Lady on an Indian named Magdalena," who they then paraded on the Virgin's litter to mock Christian worship.[8] Spaniards who had gathered in the village church at Zape to celebrate the arrival of a Virgin statue from the capital were taken unawares by the rampaging Tepehuans and were slaughtered. When the Spanish troops arrived "on a night of bright moonlight, they found themselves surrounded by corpses, all stripped of their clothing and dreadfully mutilated."[9]

The military architecture of frontier churches provided a fortlike edifice to shelter colonists and converted natives when the power of God failed to ward off pagans. If rebelling natives managed to gain entry, as in Zape, the consequences were lamentable. In 1777 a Christian kneeling before the eucharist petitioned a miraculous salvation as rebelling Ecuadorian natives busted into the church where the community had taken refuge. The natives mocked that supplication—the eucharist "was nothing but a piece of bread"—and went about an orgiastic slaughter that included song, dance, the covering of the monstrance with blood, and torturous execution: "They dragged them from the tails of horses, they took out their brains, they ate their hearts and drank their blood."[10] In Guamote and Columbe, Ecuador, in 1803, the eucharist representing an omnipotent deity was again of little effect in subduing apostates intent upon exterminating Christians. When the holy sacrament was paraded in an attempt to pacify the rebels, they mocked the divine pretensions with such exclamations as "That is not God but only a tortilla made by the Sacristan." The ordeal concluded with the dismemberment of the victims' corpses and the conspicuous display of the parts, with written inscriptions attached to them. The leader of the uprising, Julián Quito from Columbe, gave long speeches "with his open hands toward the sun," creating a state of "great expectation" that the enemy would be eliminated and the stolen land returned to the Indians.[11]

In other regions and periods the same excessive violence characterized assaults against the missions. When the pioneering Jesuit Gonzalo de Tapia was killed in 1594 by natives in Sinaloa, Mexico, "these savages severed his head and an arm from his body, drinking his blood."[12] In 1601, Acaxée rebels made a surprise attack on Spaniards and Christian natives sleeping in a church and then "chopped the bodies to pieces and distributed the parts throughout the land." During a 1648 Tarahumara revolt, "the Indians tied a rope around the father's neck and dragged him toward the church, shooting him full of arrows and clubbing him all the while." Another priest was wounded with darts and clubs, until "they finally killed him by hanging him from one arm of the cross."[13]

The examples could be multiplied ad nauseam, but these few suffice to suggest that the death itself was merely the culmination of a more complex symbolic drama. Unlike massacres that rapidly and efficiently eliminated as many Spaniards (and converted Indians) as possible, these slow, torturous executions evidence a discrepancy between the violence needed and the violence deployed, with their assault directed at the victim's body rather than at the simple termination of a life.[14] The kill appears on the surface to be inefficient but replays in symbolic registers as extremely efficient because it satisfies at once the multiple determinants that condition it. Excess and mutilation index an intent to kill the missionaries with a finality beyond any doubt, beyond resurrection, dead forever, and then to celebrate victory over the corpses. The demise extends to the God incapable of protecting his vicars, and this "death" of Christianity—rehearsed on the statues of saints, Virgins, and crucified Christs—revalidates the indigenous warrior deities under whose aegis the victory is accomplished. In this dramatization of the dissymmetry between the omnipotent rebels and the helpless missionaries, often accompanied by a script of explanatory jeers, the natives also mime in reverse their history since conquest, switching the roles of cruel master and pitiful slave while celebrating the inversion with carnivalesque jubilation. The kill is protracted to lend the natives' triumph and the Christians' agony a measure of longevity in this telescoped undoing of the conquest. Extirpation, hierarchical inversion, reempowerment, revenge, and the mocking joy of triumph over a seemingly invincible (and sometimes supernatural) adversary together condition religious executions and church desecrations.

Hostilities directed toward the Church were often formidable even when a rebellion was ostensibly pro-Catholic. Once the marauding masses were unleashed, a rebel leader's personal religious convictions or compromises to political expediency were insufficient to contain spontaneous outbursts of popular wrath. Despite Túpac Amaru II's repeated insistence that his revolt was "not in the least way against Our Sacred Catholic Religion," natives rebelling in Cochabamba in what is now Bolivia declared themselves soldiers of the cause and rampaged, killing priests and profaning churches.[15] The revolt spread quickly throughout the province, and when the rebels entered Tapacarí during celebration of mass they killed four hundred Christians inside and around the church and buried Spanish women alive.[16] At Palca, the priest was executed with the eucharist in his hands as a prelude to the massacre of hundreds of parishioners. A 1781 letter reported that an old woman among the rebels picked up the monstrance and spit at the God who was supposedly inside it, "saying that it was a lie and that God was not in it, because it was nothing but filthy flour that she herself had carried up from the valley."[17] This recurring motif of disbelief in transubstantiation was complemented by the also frequent modus operandi of spilling consecrated eucharists on the floor, trampling them, and drinking fermented corn beverage (*chicha*) from the emptied chalice. In another episode from the same rebellion, for which Túpac Amaru had declared Our Lady of Mount Carmel as patron, a massacre of Spaniards concluded with the rebels' stripping an image of the Virgin and piercing its body with pins.[18]

The ambivalent position of the rebel Túpac Catari toward the Church incited yet greater liberties among his followers. Although he prohibited Catholic worship, Túpac Catari, a former sacristan, himself attended mass and spared priests during massacres. That mixed message brought mixed results, as evidenced in March 1781, when Tomás Calisaya appeared in a village near La Paz with a rope around his neck, like Christ of the Passion. Calisaya claimed that he had orders to hang by that rope all those who failed to tell the truth. He assembled the natives and informed them that "the sovereign Inca King [Túpac Catari] orders me to put to the knife all corregidores, their ministers, caciques, collectors, and other dependents," along with "every person who may be or seem to be Spanish, or at least is dressed in imitation of such Spaniards," without regard for age or gender. That was essentially the party line of Túpac Catari's revolt, but Calisaya then improvised a provision that modified the boycott of Catholicism to include execution of the clergy: "The priests shall be put to the knife and the churches burned."[19] All of the Spaniards in the village were then slaughtered, along with a hundred natives reluctant to join the rebels.

In these instances from the Túpac Amaru and Túpac Catari rebellions, popular hostility toward the Church was expressed even when the rebel leaders claimed to be Christian (Túpac Amaru) or at least discourage assaults at the clergy (Túpac Catari). The renegade excesses of an ostensibly pro-Church or tolerant policy evidenced much the same pattern that was repeated as a matter of course during the rebellions whose apostasy was unambiguous: violation of the church as sanctuary; murder of clergy; burlesque profanation and desecration of the eucharist, sacred images, and religious objects; and the more general massacre of white Christian men, women ("after having performed on them their clumsy desires"), and children, along with natives adhering to the faith.[20] The ordeal generally terminated in a fire that razed the church and monastery together with the rest of the village, eliminating every trace of the conquerors. In the blazing light of one mission torched during the 1690s, Tarahumara apostates exclaimed, "Here is a pleasant sight to see! This is more interesting than hearing Mass, being baptized, and listening to the fathers while they say strange things."[21]

Genocidal violence is often accompanied or followed by a symbolic purification that disinfects the indigenous milieu of foreign contaminants. This was particularly conspicuous when epidemics were present, with floods and fires prophesied to purge the disease and debris of colonization. Such mythic remedies provided a complement to the decontamination effected by apostates who boycotted the Church, refused sacraments, and destroyed religious objects (or sometimes all foreign objects) because they were believed to be contagions.[22] The natives' strong association of disease and conversion had many determinants, most of which emerged from the coincidence of a belief (diseases are of supernatural origin); a fact (diseases arrived with the Spaniards); and a practice (congregated Indians fled infected missions, causing the contagion to radiate outward from its source). The Tarahumara believed that church bells summoned the diseases and that baptism caused illness and death.[23] An apostate in northern Mexico spoke for many when he pointed to the ground where epidemic victims were interred and said that their souls were buried there with them, that the church was the source of the epidemic, and that the priest had disseminated illness and hunger with his catechism. By accepting Christianity, the natives had unwittingly called upon themselves the sickness and hunger that was destroying them.[24]

The very nature of the friars themselves may have contributed to the conviction that epidemics were disseminated by the Church. Some indigenous testimonies in Mexico described the friars as "poor and ill" people to be pitied for preferring "sadness and solitude" to "pleasure and contentment," or alternatively as "dead men" whose habits were "like shrouds" and who "fell apart" at night to descend into the underworld, "where they kept their mistresses."[25] These spooky brokers of contagions were to be avoided lest the word of life everlasting result in more death, both literal and figurative. As an Asháninka cacique put it before he murdered a Franciscan, "You and yours are killing us every day with your sermons and doctrines."[26]

The natives' religious interpretation of conquest and colonization rendered the Church ultimately guilty of all secular affronts (defeat, tribute, forced labor, demographic collapse) and thus multiply worthy of extirpation. The secular nature of grievances that provoked attacks against the Church became most explicit in the eighteenth century, even to the degree that one complaint of a 1765 uprising in Ecuador was that "the Catholic Religion is very expensive."[27] Sermons addressed to the natives encouraged complacence and construed insubordination as a sacrilegious offense against "both majesties," the King of Kings and the king of Spain.[28] Use of the pulpit to announce unpopular edicts likewise evidenced the Church as an instrument of colonization, defending the interests of the empire before those of the native congregation. Many indigenous peoples recognized the hypocrisy and rose as Indians and as Christians to defend themselves, and sometimes the faith, against the repressive alliance of cross and sword. In 1777 when a Mercedarian priest in Cotacachi, Ecuador, attempted to read a royal edict concerning the levying of new taxes, a group of women known as the *cacicas* blocked his passage to the pulpit, catalyzing an antitax but also anticlerical rebellion. The rebels' position in this and innumerable other uprisings was grounded in an earned disgust and distrust of the entire church-state hierarchy: "From the king down they were all thieves."[29]

The Church was therefore a preferred but not the exclusive target of rebellions with social, political, and economic grievances. In the eighteenth-century Andes secular animosity naturally gravitated toward the *corregidores* (district governors), who were notoriously and unscrupulously corrupt in their exercise of virtually absolute powers. Guaman Poma described them as lords more absolute than the king, who "do not fear God or justice" as they "cruelly destroy, steal and punish."[30] Túpac Amaru II concurred, referring to them as "diabolical and perverse," and others made similar reference to the corregidores' "infernal avarice" and "insatiable greed" in "a system so perverse" that "one cannot imagine a more tyrannical infliction."[31] Among the most incendiary means of exploitation was the *repartimiento* of merchandise, by which the corregidores obliged Indians to purchase overpriced, inferior, and unwanted goods. In some cases, "they were compelled to purchase razors when they had no beards, silk stockings, books, mirrors, ribbons, velvet, silk, cambric and blue powder for their hair," as well as, more generally, "damaged goods, sick and dying mules, [and] inferior merchandise at double or triple the price of sound items."[32] The financial burden of the repartimiento was aggravated by tribute (with many corregidores keeping double books in order to skim a profit), taxes, fines imposed under specious pretenses, fixed low prices for native goods, and church tithes and fees. The permanent imbalance disfavoring natives forced them out of the village, into the colonial economy, and, in turn, into rebellion when then found that there was no escape from the mounting burdens imposed on them.[33]

Like the *encomendero* (grantee of native labor) earlier and the gamonal later, the corregidor was despised as an abusive official and greedy individual but also as the synecdoche of an entire exploitive race that merited genocide for its collusion in the abuse of natives. These representatives of secular authority, like clergy representing the Church, were penalized accordingly, once as those responsible and again as symbols. The common protocol of executing corregidores as a prelude to more comprehensive slaughter was outlined in 1776, when Juan de Dios Tupa Orcoguaranca announced that the following year, the "year of three sevens," would bring revolution: "For all of the Indians in this kingdom are going to rise up against the Spaniards, and they are going to kill them, beginning with the corregidores and mayors and [then] the rest of those with white faces and light-colored hair."[34]

A symbolic kill epitomizes and inaugurates the genocide, often setting the tone with its excess. In a 1750 uprising in Huarochirí, rebels topped off their murder of the corregidor and those accompanying him by mutilating the corpses and then eating the tongues. In revolts near La Paz some thirty years later, the live and dead bodies of Spanish victims were decapitated and dismembered, while natives "danced around the cadavers."[35] And as late as 1927, well beyond the age of the corregidor, Andeans rebelling near Potosí directed the symbolic kill toward a hacienda owner, eating parts of his body and sacrificing the rest to a mountain-deity.[36] The insistent postmortem rituals of mutilation and cannibalism are particularly suggestive as reciprocations: the oppressors had dismembered and devoured the indigenous social body to feed their greed, and now, the roles reversed, the natives dismember and incorporate the oppressor's body to feed their revitalization. When the trope of cannibalism is pursued to its conclusions, the indigenous social body is nourished by the symbolic body that it digests, and the balance is expelled as excrement.[37]

Strategic Borrowing

An alien, imposed paradigm had reorganized the indigenous world, and within that context the natives negotiated to their advantage a "selective synthesis" of autochthonous and imported resources.[38] Global rejection of the conquerors did not preclude emulation and expropriation of select aspects of Spanish culture, while at the same time nativism revived and emphasized select aspects of indigenous culture to define, authorize, and mobilize decolonization.[39] Both the selective borrowings and the privileged indigenous traditions acquired new meanings within the nativism that summoned them forth. The elements borrowed from the conquerors were integrated, disengaging from their source and shedding their foreign associations as they became components of indigenous culture, itself transformed in the process. The complementary internal selections privileged those myths, rituals, and tutelary deities that endorsed the nativist agenda, and these too were reformed or adapted under the pressures of colonization and liberation.

Through contact and conflict the internal and external elements are reconditioned and recombined in a process of mutual, synthetic mutation.[40] The ultimate nativist objective is to consolidate powers—whatever their source, and what better source than the almighty conqueror—in order to deploy them in the struggle for autonomy. Selective borrowing becomes strategic when appropriated external elements, often religious, are turned against the very conqueror who introduced them. Sacred power is severed from its European origin, otherworldly alliances are reconfigured to indigenous advantage, and the Christian supernatural, now with "alternate and decolonizing meanings," enters the nativist arsenal.[41] Acculturation itself is thereby redirected as "an instrument in the service of revolt."[42]

The pragmatic adoption of select elements from Spanish culture included many borrowings that had multiple uses, only some of which served resistance.

The antihispanic agenda of Manco Inca's exiled state at Vilcabamba did not preclude the welcome of select Spanish imports—horses, firearms, food, clothing—that benefited daily life as much as the resistance.[43] The same was true of both the Chichimecas who attacked Spanish supply trains and the runaway slaves who borrowed liberally from Spanish culture even as they lived in isolation and revived African traditions. King Benkos, of an early-seventeenth-century Colombian *palenque* (maroon society), enhanced his regal image with Spanish clothes, a sword, and a golden dagger while he led assaults against agricultural settlements.[44] Most explicit in the adaptation of enemy resources and technology was a "liberator and apostle" of apostate Tepehuans, who in 1616 informed his people that "they would be the absolute lords of the land," but with a bonus: "they would take advantage of the livestock introduced by the Spaniards." Having learned to farm and to mine, "they would live joyful, happy, free, with all of the comforts that they desired."[45] New weapons were always welcome en route to that millennial end, including "steel drills taken from the mines, and even a few harquebuses."[46]

The bicultural orientation of many nativist leaders also contributed substantially to selective and strategic borrowing. Most prominent rebels had strong religious backgrounds, some through education in monasteries (Juan Chocne, Juan Santos Atahualpa, Túpac Amaru II) and others through close Church contact in various capacities, including service as sacristan (Túpac Catari) or—in independence struggles with nativist dimensions—as clergy (Miguel Hidalgo, José María Morelos). Much to the friars' dismay, renegade students could redirect the practical skills and the salvationist ideology that they had acquired in the monastery toward enterprises not pleasing to God or king. The mestizo or creole lifestyle of some eighteenth-century insurgent leaders likewise attested to the adaptation of education and privilege to new meanings on the far side of race and class lines. There was much to be learned from the "double knowledge" of contact culture, including the means to subvert it from within.[47]

Strategies of evangelization used by the friars predisposed syncretic fusions that could also be used to indigenous advantage. The earliest contribution of enduring consequence was the tendency to Christianize native holy sites by replacing idols with crosses and Virgins. The results were uneven, for the practice provided a basis "to join, to confuse, to mix," as Jacinto La Serna put it in 1656, and to incorporate these new Christian "idols" into the native pantheon.[48] As the Franciscan Motolinía cynically remarked in Mexico, "They had a hundred gods and wanted to have a hundred and one."[49] Conquerors and friars had already been displacing idols with Christian images for half a century when the First Lima Council formally mandated "that the huacas be demolished, and in the same place, if it is decent, churches be built or a cross be placed."[50]

The construction of Christian religious edifices over those of the natives augmented the practice and the consequences of simple image displacement. Churches and monasteries were constructed on sacred grounds or ruins, often with recycled materials from the wrecked indigenous temples. The Inca temple of the sun, Coricancha, was converted into a Dominican monastery; and even before completion of the cathedral in Cuzco mass was celebrated in a temporary

structure built over the former Inca temple of Viracocha, with a mural of Santiago Mataindios driving home the message of conquest.[51] In Mexico, recycling
demolished religious structures included adornment of the cathedral with columns featuring hieroglyphs that alluded to precolumbian deities. The stones
from a wrecked shrine to Huitzilopochtli were similarly used to build a church
in Tlatelolco named for Santiago.[52] All of these displacements illustrated that
the Christian God had deposed the indigenous deities and reigned in their stead,
but the coincidence of sites and the recycling of materials also provided that the
traditional faith could be perpetuated within or "under" Christianity. An architectural palimpsest thereby stood as monument to the syncretism and cryptopaganism that would proliferate in the culture around it.

Another expedient of evangelization, the appeal to similarities between Christianity and indigenous religions, also brought short-term gains with long-term
consequences. The practice had ample precedent in early Christianity, whose
theologians argued that pagan religion and philosophy were a kind of Christianity in the rough that could be tapped to facilitate conversion.[53] In both the
Old and New Worlds, Christians—who viewed conversion the way they viewed
history, as part of a gradual, ecumenical awakening of the true faith latent in
all peoples—hoped that potential converts would discover in their own beliefs
a basis for understanding and accepting the gospel.

In Mexico the similarities between Christianity and Aztec religion were many,
including sacrifice, communion with a deified body, virgins, floods, crosses, processions, concepts of the hereafter, clerical hierarchy, military-monastic orders,
and rites resembling baptism, to mention just the outstanding.[54] The Aztecs also
practiced a confession ritual known as "straightening one's heart," which restored internal order through absolution. The friars' use of the Nahuatl term to
designate Christian penitence made the sacrament more familiar in native frames
of reference, but it also predisposed its adaptation and the survival, under cover,
of its prehispanic parallel.[55] Whenever an appeal to native religion was the basis
for instruction, the mixed result had the catechism, cryptopaganism, and syncretism advancing in tandem.

The native subjects of forced conversion became adept at persevering in traditional worship under the façade of Christianity, "making it seem as though
they adored the cross while they adored the devil."[56] Idols were hidden beneath
crosses, inside statues, in foundations and cornerstones of churches, "in the hollow niches of the saints in front of the holy altar, and others below the altar,
placed there by the sacristan."[57] Hiding idols on the litters of Corpus Christi
processions was a notorious practice among Andeans. In 1590 José de Acosta
complained that the natives—suffering from "a hereditary idolatrous sickness"—
were feigning participation in the Christian festivities while surreptitiously celebrating their own Inti Raimi (Dance or Fiesta of the Sun), which also occurred
in June.[58] The same was revealed in Chinchacocha, when the "dissimulation and
boldness" of the Indians was such that during the feast of Corpus Christi they
had "slyly hidden a small huaca on the very platform of the monstrance of the
Holy Sacrament."[59] The qualifiers for such slyness tended toward the demonic
and the punishments were severe, but more sensitive Spanish observers recog-

nized that the natives were often seeking continuity in rupture: "They want to seem Christians being idolaters, believing that the one and the other can exist together."[60]

The ritual of human sacrifice was common to Christianity and many indigenous religions, particularly in Mesoamerica, and after contact it became the locus of a struggle between its literal and commemorative expressions. In Catholic belief, the consecrated host (from *hostia*, a "sacrificial victim") is not a representation of Christ's body but rather is metamorphosed into that body itself. As dogmatized by the Council of Trent, it is "the same Christ contained and immolated in an unbloody manner, who, on the altar of the Cross, offered himself once in a bloody manner."[61] The regularly celebrated sacrificial ritual of Catholicism, the mass, hovers between the vehicle and tenor of its central trope of transubstantiation—not exactly a repetition of the crucifixion but not a mere symbolic reenactment either. For the friars in Mexico, theological finesse was required to neutralize the awkward semblance between, on one hand, Christ's sacrifice and the congregation's eating of the transubstantiated eucharist and, on the other hand, Aztec human sacrifice and the ritual eating of deified victims. Both were based on the divinely mandated repetition of the deities' death in sacrifice (as established in the Bible and in Aztec mythology), with the crucial difference being that the Aztecs fulfilled the mandate literally and the Catholics figuratively, or almost so, through the ritually demetaphorized eucharist. As an Augustinian explained it in 1541, "God does not demand, as your idols do, the lives and hearts of men. It is He Himself who descends to the altar to pour out His graces upon His servants."[62]

The grizzly baroque images of a scourged, bleeding, crucified Christ may have provided entries into the alien supernatural world introduced by the conquerors, once through appeal to the prohibited rituals of sacrifice and again through the abused natives' identification with "endlessly proliferated representation of a tortured and murdered god of love."[63] If instruction by didactic images was generally useful, then the horrific had a special capacity to fix images and their messages—sacrifice, suffering, martyrdom, resurrection—in the minds of indigenous neophytes. As a modern Mexican priest explained it, "The more horrible the sight of the scourged Christ, nailed to the cross, his blood gushing out, the more strongly Christ's sacrifice makes an impact on the Indians."[64] It is perhaps for this reason that many of the most miraculous images of Christ—the Christ of Great Power, the Lord of Earthquakes—are also the most gruesome.

The crucified Christ gave meaning to the suffering of indigenous Christians who identified with their martyred savior. Many Catholics in modern Latin America biblicize the chronic abuses they suffer, regarding themselves as "sheep to the slaughter" who have learned from Christ "how to suffer with patience" and "how to die."[65] A Uru of Bolivia was typical in describing his incarceration as being "martyred like Christ," adding, "They tortured me the way Christ was tortured."[66] Persecution of Catholics in Guatemala during the 1980s likewise had "the same characteristics as the death of Christ," with "the same causes, the same murderers, the same circumstances."[67] In El Salvador, where "every day is Good Friday," announcements made at the stations of the cross associated

Jesus' crucifixion with the suffering of persecuted Catholics. At the first station, Jesus is condemned to death: "In our day the people of El Salvador are condemned to death by the Pentagon, [Roberto] D'Aubuissón, and [José Napoleón] Duarte, and the war they wage against our people." At the tenth station, Jesus is stripped of his garments: "We, too, have been stripped of the fruit of our labor, our land, our work, our dignity, our children, and our martyrs like Archbishop [Oscar] Romero." Identification ultimately yields to fusion as the mystical body of the faithful reactualizes Christ's Passion: "Today, as Salvadorans, we can say that Jesus bears the cross and is murdered in our crucified people."[68] Christ's martyrdom is perpetually rehearsed in his people's, thereby endowing agony with purpose and providing for triumph in defeat: "The resurrection of Jesus is the proof that we are going to have a day of resurrection."[69]

The image of natives as crucified peoples is also registered in syncretic iconography that depicts Christ with indigenous facial features and regional clothing.[70] The same metamorphosis occurs in individual religious experience, as indexed by an indigenous Chilean who reports that the God of his mystical visions has "the face of a Mapuche."[71] In popular theater Christ is indianized through reenactments of the Passion, most explicitly during Holy Week in San Pedro Paracho, Michoacán, where a Tarascan Christ is escorted to his doom on Good Friday with his "face, shoulders and body bathed in blood."[72] A more nuanced drama of symbolic identification occurs during Holy Week dramas among the Maya in Guatemala. The effigy of a Judas Iscariot figure known as Maximón is treated in accord with multiple determinants, some of which elicit homage and others which elicit derision or abuse. During the course of the carnivalesque celebration the Maya transpose the villainous traitor of Christ into "an icon of their own oppressor, the Christian Ladino" in order to "subversively act out their incorporation of Ladino power and their triumph over the source."[73] The Maya implicitly assume the role of the betrayed Christ sentenced to death, but the defeat is provisional, like the messiah's, because it holds in reserve an ultimate triumph over death and oppression.

Reenactment of the Passion among the Maya had more gruesome, literal antecedents beginning in 1546, when some sacrificial victims, among them captured Spaniards, were crucified.[74] In one case, two Spaniards were immobilized on crosses, and "shooting little by little at the two crucified boys, being the target of their indignation, they covered them with arrows." The dead bodies were lowered from their crosses, the decapitated heads were put on poles, and the dismembered bodies were distributed.[75] Lacandones rebelling in Chiapas from 1553 to 1556 "sacrificed [Spanish] children on the altar and pulled out their hearts and with the blood smeared the images that were in the church." Others were sacrificed at the foot of the cross, and as the apostates burned down the Church they yelled, "Christians, tell your God to defend you."[76]

Sacrifice also took a more syncretic turn as the Maya struggled to accommodate Christianity within indigenous frames of reference. During innovative Holy Week exercises in 1557, a native priest tied two Maya girls to crosses, saying, "Let these girls placed on the cross die as Jesus Christ died, who they say was Our Lord, only we don't know if he was." Following this mock crucifixion the girls were sacrificed in Mesoamerican fashion, by heart excision. On another occasion, in 1562, two boys were nailed to crosses to suffer a mock–Christian Passion that concluded with the removal of their hearts.[77] These early efforts to consolidate aspects of native and Christian sacrifice culminated centuries later when a Chamulan boy was crucified in an effort to produce a Maya Christ.

The events began in December 1867, when a young shepherd named Augustina Gómez Checheb saw three rocks fall from the sky. Pedro Díaz Cuscat, a sacristan sent to investigate, took the stones home and kept them in a box. The stones made such a racket, "knocking at the door to get out," that they awakened Díaz Cuscat with the divine and apparently urgent message that he and Augustina then interpreted together. The parish priest confiscated the oracular stones, but the cult went underground and replaced them with surrogate relics including three clay figurines that emerged from the womb of Augustina, now referred to as the Mother of God. A chapel was constructed for "God and mother Augustina," along with the venerated objects. In the ensuing weekly meetings, Díaz Cuscat preached that "the time had arrived to expel all people who were not of their blood" and to replace the white God with a Maya Christ who would be created by crucifixion. The Passion was staged in the plaza of Tzajalhemel on Good Friday of 1868, when Augustina's ten-year-old brother was nailed to a cross through the hands and feet "while the faithful worshiped him with incense and aguardiente."[78]

The intent to produce a racially consonant deity on the Christian model may also have motivated a domestic cult originated by a mulatta in Guatemala. In 1694 the Inquisition began investigating Sebastiana de la Cruz, who along with a small group of devotees worshiped her thirteen-year-old son as the son of God. The boy was adored with incense, displayed in a wall niche as though he were a statue, and dressed in biblical garb according to the mood, sometimes as the Child of Bethlehem and others as the crucified Christ, with a crown of thorns.[79] Assumptions of Christian identities were also explicit in Tierradentro of the Colombian Andes in 1833, when a supernatural apparition instructed the community to destroy all Catholic statues, crosses, and symbols. The natives dutifully obeyed and then, of their own volition, stepped into the void they had created: women adorned themselves with altar cloths and church ornaments; the chalice was used to drink *guarapo* (fermented cane juice); and the niches vacated by the saints were filled with villagers. Where the Virgin had been, they put a beautiful fifteen-year-old girl, and two boys replaced Saint Anthony and Saint Michael. The transference of sanctity was ritualized and "everybody worshipped" these children as they were paraded across the countryside on litters "decorated with lights and with flowers from the fields."[80]

When they were not displaced by surrogates, Christian saints, persons of the Trinity, and Virgins were often coupled with indigenous deities. In the early Mexican mission, such associations were "tolerated and even encouraged" because they seemed to serve evangelical objectives. The coupling of the Virgin with Tonantzin and with Xochiquetzalli yielded the Virgin of Guadalupe and the Virgin of Ocotlán, respectively, and the friars regarded these composites as

Christian triumphs—the syncretism notwithstanding—because the Virgin seemed to predominate. For the Franciscan Martín Sarmiento de Hojacastro, it mattered little whether the Indians saw the Virgin or the indigenous goddess, as long as the ultimate effect was veneration of the mother of God.[81] Much the same held true in the Andes, where prehispanic religion intermingled with Christianity to produce such composites as the Virgin of Copacabana. This miraculous sculpture of madonna, child, and postpartum purification symbols was enshrined at an Inca sanctuary on Lake Titicaca, once a center for child sacrifice attended by Virgins of the Sun. [82]

In parts of Mexico, Saint John the Apostle was identified with the youthful Tezcatlipoca, and Saint Anne, mother of the Virgin Mary, was identified with the maternal grandmother goddess Toci.[83] In the latter case, Toci's sanctuary in Tlaxcala was converted by the Spaniards into a church dedicated to Saint Anne.[84] Water served as the medium for linking John the Baptist with the rain god Tlaloc, and thunder and lighting served to link the Inca's Illapa with Santiago. The high Maya deity Hunab-Ku was reinterpreted as the Christian God the Father, and the lunar goddess Ixchel (along with other indigenous lunar deities) fused with the Virgin Mary. Such coupling was also characteristic of black slave acculturation to Christianity. In modern Brazil, the *orisha* are reinterpreted as Catholic saints, the concept of the Trinity is used to invoke the unity of diverse African deities, and the symbol of the Holy Spirit commonly hovers above the altars of these deities.[85] The pairing of African gods with Christian saints in Haitian Voodoo includes Legba with Saint Anthony and sometimes Saint Peter, and Damballa with Saint Patrick. Similar couplings are common in Santería, Candomblé, Shango, and other African-American religions.[86] Variation by region is conspicuous: in Brazil, for example, Ogun is paired variously with Saint George, Saint Jerome, and Saint Anthony, whereas in Cuba he is paired with Saint Peter.[87]

Saints and Virgins were recruited to authorize and empower nativist and, later, independence offensives, the conqueror's otherworldly allies being coopted for the purposes of decolonization. Along with their claims to have royal decrees authorizing elimination of the "bad government," popular insurrections of the eighteenth-century Andes repeatedly announced Saint Rose of Lima's apocryphal prophesy of the Inca empire's return to its "legitimate owners."[88] In 1776 it was "common knowledge in the Indian community" that a general nativist uprising would occur in "the year of three sevens" to fulfill Saint Rose's prophesy, now bolstered with a prophesy by Saint Francis Solano. Such was also the message of an old Andean named Joseph Gran Quispe Tupa Inga, a former mine worker dedicated to wandering, who claimed descent from Inca royalty and anticipated his own coronation in 1777 as fulfillment of the saints' prophesies. According to a version by Juan de Dios Tupa Orcoguaranca, the prophesies would be fulfilled by a general uprising, extermination of the whites, and return to an indigenous kingdom, but Catholicism would remain because "the intent was to change not religion but sovereignty and government in order to live in freedom."[89] Túpac Amaru II himself reportedly commented, "The time for the prophecies of Saint Rose of Lima to be fulfilled is upon us, the time when it will be necessary to return the kingdom to its former rulers."[90] After the execution of Túpac Amaru II it was also the time to recruit more otherworldly reinforcements to the cause, and Saint Toribio de Mogrovejo was added to the roster of prophets when Felipe Velasco took the rebellion to Huarochirí.[91]

The most prevalent co-optation of Christian saintly power occurred in indigenous adaptations of Santiago (Saint James the Great), whose invocations as Matamoros (the Moor Killer) and Mataindios (the Indian Killer) attest to his enduring status as the symbol of supernatural alliance in Spanish conquests. While some natives succumbed to defeat and identified with the crucified Christ or with the Moors trampled under the hooves of Santiago Matamoros/Mataindios, others Indianized the warrior saint and recruited him to their cause. In the Andes the process began with the assimilation of Santiago to Illapa, the god of lightning and thunder. The thunderous beating of horse hooves, the harquebuses' explosion of light and sound (which the Andeans also called Illapa), and their accompaniment by the Spanish war cry "Santiago" all contributed to the to the syncretic fusion.[92] When an Andeanized Santiago arrived to rescue the conquerors beseiged in Cuzco in 1536, he descended "with great thunder, like lighting falling from the sky."[93] According to Garcilaso de la Vega, the Incas who saw Santiago wondered, "Who is that Viracocha [Spaniard], who has lightning [illapa] in his hand?" Later syncretic iconography of Cuzco-school paintings carried the same image, with Santiago brandishing a sword in the form of a lightning bolt.[94] Quechua-speaking campesinos still refer to lighting as "Santiago Apu Illapa" and to people who have survived lightning strikes as "sons of Santiago."[95]

Christian and pagan European antecedents may also have contributed to the link between Santiago and Illapa. In Mark 3:17, Jesus bestows upon James (Santiago) and John the honorific title Boanerges, which means "Sons of Thunder." Américo Castro has identified a Roman parallel or precedent for the title in Castor and Pollux, who were offspring of Jupiter (the thunderer) and therefore Sons of Thunder. Castor and Pollux—both venerated in Roman Iberia—conform to the prototype as they charge down from the heavens on white horses to slay their people's enemies in battle. A 1648 Spanish description clearly situates Santiago Matamoros within this tradition by referring to the saint as "that divine lightning, son of thunder."[96] With Illapa on one side and European supernatural warriors on the other, the American Santiago emerged as a new expression of the crosscultural effort to militarize the heavenly power made manifest in thunderstorms.

The Andeans' strategic borrowing of the saint was suggested early in the colonial period, in 1573, when the Chiriguanos informed Viceroy Francisco de Toledo that a man called Santiago had been sent to them by Jesus. Dressed as an Indian but accompanied by a cross "which precedes him wherever he goes without his lifting or carrying it," Santiago cured the ill, performed miracles ("he enters this church through the roof as if the top were open"), and persuaded the Indians "to be Christian and to live by natural law and to stop eating human flesh."[97] The message in this case was contrary to the nativist call for apostasy

and decolonization, but cautious vestiges of co-optation were nevertheless registered in the native dress, the privileging of the indigenous community for the
apparition, and the association of this Santiago with thunder and lightning.
Throughout the Andes, natives began taking the name Santiago or giving it to
their offspring, as though the saint's magical powers could be transferred by
denomination. The extirpator Pablo José Arriaga mandated in 1621 that no
Indian "shall be called by the name of lightning"—including Santiago—but indigenous uses of the saint could not be contained.[98]

In 1656 an Indian in the province of Vilcas took the name Santiago, prophesied imminent destruction, and convinced an entire village to apostatize and
return to the mountains for sacrificial offerings.[99] Centuries later in Lircay, in
the province of Huancavelica, Peru, authorities were startled when a group of
Indians arrived after midnight, playing drums and bells and asking that the
church be opened. Their leader, Pedro Alanya, was regarded as the prophet or,
in some versions, the incarnation of Santiago, and he "wanted to preach at the
main altar."[100] This Santiago was revered as a fertility god who exercised his
power through regional deities. Had the authorities not impeded it, the celebration of mass would have been the culminating act of a series of syncretic rituals
seeking restoration of a more bountiful past. During the group's previous services, the candlelight was extinguished and the voice of Santiago spoke to them:
"Now I return so that you will return to previous times; you will no longer
suffer from hunger."[101]

Santiago also had a prodigious and more militant history in Mexico, beginning with the Tlaxcalans who emulated the conquerors by reciprocally crying
"Santiago" as they charged into battle.[102] The saint was also adapted to indigenous purposes through multiple Mexican variations of the *Dance of Moors and
Christians*, which represented triumph in Iberian Reconquest campaigns thanks
to Santiago's apparitions. In one version, the roles were rescripted for "mock
engagements between mounted Indian townspeople and impersonators of wild,
heathen Chichimecs," the former to be victorious with Santiago's aid and the
latter filling the role once held by the vanquished Moors. One such performance
was recorded in 1590 by the Franciscan Alonso Ponce, who raised his eyebrows
when he was welcomed into a Michoacán village by some twenty mounted Indian guards who were dressed as Spaniards and armed with wooden swords,
mock lances, and a harquebus. Their leader bid the friar welcome, informing
him that this entourage had come to guard his safe passage into the village
because there were Chichimecas in the vicinity. The Indians then patrolled the
area screaming "Santiago, Santiago" until a dozen of their counterparts, on foot
and dressed as Chichimecas, with the corresponding bows and arrows, engaged
them in a mock skirmish. Once the group reached town, a drama on the order
of *Moors and Christians* ensued, with the mounted natives repeatedly "saying
'Santiago, Santiago,' and those on foot dancing around one on a horse with a
white mane," like Santiago's horse, until the performance concluded at night-
fall.[103] Identification with Santiago in this case does not result in antagonism
toward the Spaniards, but the natives have nevertheless assimilated the saint's

military power, along with Spanish horses and firearms, and consequently claim their superiority to native adversaries. Their self-appointment as the friar's escort likewise attests to the presumption of status and power.

Another indigenous drama rehearsed an attempt to neutralize Santiago's power as much as to co-opt it. In 1815 a villager in the district of San Pedro Tlaquepaque rode through the plaza dressed as Santiago, striking Indians with his sword. The performance ended when the Indians pulled this Santiago off his horse for retaliatory abuse that included "the many obscenities that they mutter both in Spanish and Nahuatl, and also their indecent actions once they turn to 'stripping the skin' from the one who acts as Santiago." As William B. Taylor observed, the conclusion of the spectacle was doubly suggestive: first because it inverted the original scenario of an untouchable Santiago arriving at the decisive moment to assure victory; and then because it echoed precolumbian rituals such as the festival of Toxcatl, "which ended with the deity impersonator (*ixiptla*) of Tezcatlipoca being assaulted and stripped of his mask and regalia and then sacrificed."[104] Santiago as paradigm of sacrosanct Christian power is defeated as though he were a sacrificial victim, thereby nativizing the source of the sacred power, providing the rituals to access it, and neutralizing its inimical origin in the process. Santiago as an impersonator (which is to say displacer) of deity must ultimately face the sacrifice that revitalizes the native gods and bestows upon the community the powers released in bloodletting.

The final stage in this progressive theatrical co-optation of Santiago is represented with great explicitness but also refined subtlety in a Jalisco version of *Moors and Christians* known as *Los Tastoanes*. During celebrations on or around his saint's day, the warrior Santiago "who has done us much harm" is killed, flayed, and disemboweled. The job begun in the earlier examples is thereby completed with a heavy hand. Indeed, in the village of Jocotán one of the Tastoan kings (his identity overdetermined by his name, Herod) "pretends to cut up the body as if he were slicing beef."[105] Santiago is then resurrected, however, to become a saintly *curandero* (healer) administering to a cue of natives who await "healing blows from the flat of his sword."[106] Once Santiago is defeated, murdered, and mutilated, the foe is reborn a friend and his malevolent power becomes beneficent. The inversion extends to Santiago's sword, once bathed in native blood and now a wand of magical cures that, during the drama, even resurrects the Tastoanes fallen in battle. Santiago is disassembled and reassembled to indigenous advantage, with his Spanish prototype reconfigured, like the face of Jesus, to the contours of indigenous needs. This transference of identities through fragmentation and reconstitution is also represented in the Andean context, where "Santiago, killer of the Indians, becomes his antithesis, Santiago Inkarrí, liberator of the Indians."[107]

In late-sixteenth-century Oaxaca, an Indian named Mateo Pérez, governor of the town of Santiago de Atitlán, engaged in the apostate practice of sacrificing hens and puppies, mixing their blood with pulque and maize, and offering them to deities. Pérez conducted these rituals on the feast day of Santiago (with the saint's name echoed again in that of the town and church), invoking both the Christian God and the indigenous god of thunder. In justifying his rituals to the Mexican Inquisition, Pérez explained that "the devil" had appeared to him in a dream, mandating the sacrifices lest the devil "cause thunder to strike the church."[108] The allusion to Santiago's thunder attribute is noteworthy in comparison to its more prevalent expression in the Andes, but most compelling is the propitiatory function offered in explanation for the sacrifices. Pérez's ritual accessed the conglomerated powers of Santiago, the Christian God, and the god of thunder, but it did so by order of "the devil." The term "devil" is an expedient used in Inquisition discourse for any force that disrupts Christianity, but in the present context of supernatural power co-optation its presence registers a characteristic inversion. According to the dream in which he appears, this "devil" instigates Pérez's pagan rituals in order to safeguard the church. The heroes and villains circulate as the Inquisition intervenes to prohibit the ritual and thereby subject the church to the thunderstorm attack that Pérez warded off so dutifully. The church is safe insofar as Pérez (the natives, the "devil") is free. If Pérez and syncretic worship are prohibited, however, then the powers of God-Santiago-thunder are unleashed and directed against the church, now as sanctum of the oppressor. To that degree Santiago might conclude his career, at least in theater, myth, and ritual, under the invocation Santiago Mataespañoles (Spaniard Killer).

Christian religious power was also channeled into nativist resistance through the assumption of clerical titles and sacerdotal prerogatives. In some cases a mimetic co-optation sought only to nativize the faith; in others the usurped titles and privileges were instruments of deconversion or decolonization. Instances of the first type frequently seem the consequences of poorly catechized natives struggling to accommodate an alien doctrine within indigenous frames of reference. Their intent was not to subvert Christianity but rather to participate in it as best they knew how. In the earliest stages of contact, the first Christian statues given to the Taínos were considered fertility idols and treated accordingly. The Indians meant no disrespect—on the contrary, they were manifesting their faith—when they buried the statues in the yucca fields and irrigated them with a shower of urine, but their rituals nevertheless met with friarly scorn.[109] Also exemplary of a well-meaning, heterodox naivete was a 1618 case reported by the Jesuits in Paraguay. An indigenous shaman, accompanied by a man and woman, announced that because he was God he could destroy and re-create all things with his breath. The messiah congregated the masses by the riverside, donned a garment of feathers, "and shaking a sort of rattle made of a goat's skull, cried in a mad manner, proclaiming himself absolute lord of death, seed, and harvest." The encore was an exegesis on the Trinity, in which the shaman explained that with his two companions he "was three in persons but one God." He continued, "I begot my companion with the splendor of my face, and this young woman proceeded from us both, whom we equally love, making use of her by turns."[110]

In some regions the disappearance of priests after they nominally converted the natives created a vacuum that could be filled by whoever rose to the occasion. Among the Pueblos in the mid-seventeenth century, a Hopi took advantage of the local priest's absence to summon the natives to church, don the ritual vestments, cense the altar, chant the *Salve*, and sprinkle holy water "in the manner

priests do it."[111] This tendency may have been further predisposed in some remote areas of Mexico by the natives' celebration of "dry mass" (mass without
consecration of the eucharist) when the scarce or indolent clergy failed to show
up on feast days.[112] Also common, and explicitly co-optative, was the creation
of a sacerdotal absence only to fill the void with indigenous vicars. In 1628 a
group of rebelling Guaranís executed the three Jesuits among them, and then a
cacique-shaman dressed himself in a priestly costume, placed an ersatz eucharist
and chalice on an improvised altar, and raised the bread and wine while mum-
bling in imitation of the priests.[113]

Many shamans contested the missionaries' monopoly of supernatural powers
by continuing to exercise a native-officiated religion, even though the gods and
rituals had changed. Rather than convert themselves to the faith, they converted
the faith to themselves. Native clergy surrogates proliferated among the always
innovative Maya, "using maize tortillas for the Host and gruel for wine."[114] In
1610 one Maya called himself "pope" and another "bishop" as together they
"deceived the ignorant" by administering sacraments while venerating idols on
the altar.[115] A century later, Tarahumaras who had abandoned the missions
improvised ritual utensils for celebration of the eucharist—a clay cup as a chalice, a round box top for the paten, a stone inside a metal mortar as a bell—and
celebrated mass in their manner. They heard confessions, performed baptisms,
and "created their own sacraments, which they considered to have the same
effect as those used by the Christians."[116]

A more enduring syncretic faith administered by natives was maintained by
the mid-seventeenth-century movement in Bahia known as Santidade. The founder was a Jesuit-educated Indian named Antonio, who escaped to the jungle
with an entourage including various "saints" as well as the ubiquitous Mary.
Antonio himself was both pope and Tupanasú (an indigenous deity), and among
the legends accruing to him was his escape of the universal flood by climbing to
the top of a palm tree. The millennial message pivoted on the common promise
of hierarchical inversion: God had sent Antonio to announce the imminent reversal of roles between Indians and Europeans. Henceforth the whites would
work the land, and those who refused would be transformed into stones or trees.
God had also ordered that the Catholic faith, which was full of errors, be corrected by Antonio. A church was built, a baptismal font and an idol were installed, and offerings were made as Antonio pretended to read from tablets that
formed the semblance of a Bible. Trance was induced with dance, song, and
tobacco, but the joyful noise continued only until the troops intervened to resume forced labor on the sugarcane plantation.[117]

In each of these cases, the natives co-opt clerical privileges for celebration of
an Indo-Christian, native-administered religion. The rituals evidence mimetic
strategic borrowing, religious empowerment, reparation of displaced elite status,
and experimentation with mysteries once monopolized by Spaniards, but generally without overt insurrection. In other instances Christianity was more audaciously redirected into deconversion or decolonization, as when the title
"bishop" was adopted by a rebelling Mexican cacique in 1536 for the patently
secular purpose of expelling the conqueror.[118] A Dominican in late-sixteenth-

century Chiapas indexed another characteristic model in his report of natives who "call themselves the Twelve Apostles" but at once hold meetings "plotting against our Christian religion."[119] In 1603 an Acaxée of the Sierra Madre Occidental convinced his people "that he was God the Holy Spirit who had come down from heaven," and "that he was a bishop and had come to teach them how to be saved." The messiah preached that the catechism brought by the Jesuits was false "and that he would teach them another and better doctrine." Accompanied by his disciples, named Santiago and Saint Peter, he said mass, taught the natives prayers "other than Christian ones," "rebaptized the Indians already baptized by the priests," and annulled Christian marriages, remarrying the former couples to new partners of their choice.[120] All was done to effect a nativist, but syncretic, return to the past, with the policy on decolonization made manifest in the destruction of some forty churches.[121]

Undoing Christian sacraments, notably baptism and matrimony, was a common demonstration of the acquisition of powers once exclusive to the Spanish clergy. Between 1635 and 1637 a Paraguayan cacique named Yaguacaporo "told whoever would listen to him that he was a reincarnated deity." His messianic movement cohered a powerful alliance of resistance to Jesuit incursions. Indigenous "bishops," "vicars," and other entitled personnel attended to their jurisdictions, while "apostles" entered the jungle to preach, build temples, and deconvert natives. The unambiguous purpose of rebaptism was captured in liturgy: "I baptize you in order to take away baptism." Each deconverted native then received a new name to replace the Christian name conferred with baptism by the Jesuits.[122] In the same region another advocate of apostasy congregated his followers, reinstated ritual dance, and "tried to undo the spell that through baptism the Priests had put them under." He informed the natives that they need not obey the Jesuits because "the faith of the Christians was pure fiction" and "heaven did not hold the joys that they preached."[123]

For Juan Tetón, the leader of a nativist cult in sixteenth-century Mexico, the "spell" of baptism had apocalyptic consequences. Tetón reckoned that with the ending Nahua calendric cycle, known as the "tying of the years," a complete darkness "will descend, will eat us and there will be a transformation." Thus, "he who eats the meat of cow, will be transformed into one; he who eats the meat of pig, will be transformed into one," and so on, just as those who converted to Christianity had been transformed into Spanish capes and hats. Tetón incited his followers to wash the stain of baptism off their heads, lest they suffer an uncomely metamorphosis.[124]

The longevity of messianic and deconversion movements is determined by that of their leaders, who are generally eliminated in short order by the authorities. On occasion patterns of heroic return provided for the replication of a messianic prototype in a series of successors, thereby affording a measure of continuity or periodical revitalization. This was the case beginning in the mid-nineteenth century when Venancio Kamiko appeared in the Upper Río Negro region among Tukanoan and Arawakan peoples "disoriented and demoralized" by the encroachment of soldiers, missionaries, and traders. Venancio proclaimed himself Christ, surrounded himself with a coterie of elderly ministers given the names of saints, and offered a syncretic Christianity loaded heavily with, among other elements, indigenous myths of world destruction and renewal. He claimed to have gone to heaven, spoken with God, and returned as harbinger of the apocalyptic conflagration scheduled for Saint John's Day in 1858. The movement was dispersed by military campaigns, and Venancio Christo fled with an exodus of some five hundred of the faithful who abandoned and burned their villages, but Venancio left behind the hope of messianic return that was fulfilled in short order by three other "Christos."[125]

One of these, Vincent, directed his Christian power to the common nativist objective when he prophesied hierarchical inversion of the social order and the extermination of any white people who mistreated natives.[126] Another, the mestizo Alexandre Christo, covered the territory disseminating his nativist gospel and declaring himself the only god of the Indian nation. He performed sacraments, made prophesies, coerced absolute obedience, and had the faithful kiss the large cross hanging from his neck. Before repairing with his followers to their holy city in the jungle, Alexandre preached a rebellious doctrine that included the pro forma millennial inversions: "Indians would be transformed into whites" to enjoy "the same powers and riches."[127]

Venancio Christo and his successors, like innumerable nativist messiahs on the Christian model, bypass the mere usurpation of sacerdotal or prophetic privileges in order to incarnate the deity themselves. Many such messiahs are accompanied by Virgins, not always chaste, or are married to saints epitomized by the ill-reputed Magdalene.[128] Reports of a 1660 Arecayá rebellion in Paraguay typically noted that the natives "adore an Indian named Rodrigo as God" and "as Our Lady the Virgin, an Indian woman, his wife."[129] In the 1761 case of a Mexican curandero-turned-messiah, a more ambitious assumption of Christian identities combined with other innovations for a comprehensive millennial extravaganza. Antonio Pérez declared that the Church was hell, the laws evil, the archbishop Lucifer, and God and the saints "just a lie." He was unambiguous about his own divinity—"I am God"—and his faithful adepts followed suit: "I believed that Antonio was God and that I was one of the saints." Antonio heard confessions, baptized children, wore altar cloths, and advocated a libertarian sexuality. A rapid path to sanctity passed through his bed, with one postcoital partner becoming the Virgin of the Seven Sorrows (perhaps reflecting on Antonio's performance) and her mother becoming Saint Anne.

In this procreation of an indigenous Christian pantheon, Antonio believed that the new messiah would be fruit of the womb of "a young girl called María, from the barrio of San Juan." He accordingly made a cigar of grilled-corn and other powders, "whose smoke María took in by mouth to conceive the Son of God." The corn was particularly significant in light of Antonio's Nahua-Christian theology: "My god is the Ear of Corn, and the Three Corns are the Holy Trinity." Antonio found it expedient to back up María's impregnation by smoke with "indecent relations," which were performed before an audience of the faithful "reciting the Credo on their knees." This holy community would be spared an apocalypse in which "the earth will begin to boil," and one of the "saints" would be king until the saving remnant could "unearth holy Christ, who had been buried for a thousand years."[130]

Perhaps the essence of strategic borrowing is captured nowhere as efficiently as in the curing ritual of a Toba prophet who appeared around 1950 on the Argentine Chaco. Mateo Quintana denounced the Pentecostal missionaries and white people generally, preaching that henceforth the word of God should come "directly to the Toba" without foreign intermediaries. His teachings conformed to the Toba tendency to fuse traditional religion with Pentecostal Christianity, but his curandero rituals more radically represented the nativist agenda by annihilating the imported faith as elements of it were extracted to benefit the community.[131] Quintana tore pages from a bible and burned them as his patients inhaled the curative smoke. The power of the Word was thereby internalized by the Toba, while the text itself, and its white source, were gradually reduced to ashes.

The War of Mixtón

In 1539 Francisco Vásquez de Coronado, preparing a large expedition in search of the fabled Seven Cities of Cíbola, recruited among Spaniards of New Galicia, leaving the frontier sparsely populated and insecure. The colony's vulnerability had already been predisposed by a growing mood of apostasy and rebellion evidenced by the natives' abandonment of Spanish settlements and escape to the highlands. The hostilities that would evolve into the War of Mixtón began in 1540, when the murder of one encomendero was followed in rapid succession by assaults on others and on friars in Xalpa, Tlaltenango, and Juchipila. The strategy was guerrilla: attacking isolated ranches and small Spanish villages, killing the inhabitants, burning down the buildings, and then retreating to the strategic mountain enclaves where forces were consolidating for the major offensive to come. The leaders of the movement—Tenamaxtle, also known as Diego el Zacateco, and Francisco Aguilar, the cacique of Nochistlán—eventually led a coalition of seventy thousand rebels in an explicitly genocidal insurrection.[132]

Mixtón, near the Pacific coast in New Galicia, became the strongest rebel position and was the last to fall. The war that bears its name was a Tarascan prophetic rebellion catalyzed by the imminent return of a warrior deity who would annihilate the invaders and implement a nativist recuperation of preconquest religion and culture. The prophets of the movement announced themselves as messengers of the god Tecoroli (or Tlatol):

> Accompanied by his ancestors, whom he has revived, he is coming to seek you. . . . He will make you believe in him, not in [the Christian] God, on pain of never seeing the light again and of being devoured by beasts. Those who believe in him and renounce the teachings of the friars and follow him will never die, but will become young again and have several wives, not merely one, as the monks order, and, however old they may be, will beget children. Whoever takes only one wife will be killed.[133]

The god would then travel to "wherever there are Christians from Spain" in order to "slaughter them all." With this accomplished, "he will go home, and you will live happy with your ancestors, suffering no more hardships or pain."[134]

The religious nature of the nativism made Christianity a preferred target. The Indians murdered friars; burned down churches, monasteries, and crosses; defiled Christian symbols; performed sacrifices on altars; and enacted a certain tragicomic parody of sacrosanct Christian rituals by, for example, feigning celebration of the eucharist by mockingly worshiping a tortilla. Initiation into the movement was by de-Christianization through rituals of undoing and purification. The obligatory washing of the head removed the "stain" of baptism, and penance neutralized the time one had spent as a Christian.[135]

The massive indigenous armies, the impregnable mountain bases, and the natives' holy-war determination made the insurrection seem invincible. Two Spanish pacification expeditions failed, and the natives, emboldened, took the offensive to seize several garrisons. Some fifty thousand Indians advanced as far as Guadalajara, which they besieged until troops under Cristóbal de Oñate, reinforced by an apparition of Santiago, managed to push them back. A third assault against the rebel stronghold—led by Governor Juan de Alvarado and comprising two hundred Spanish soldiers and five thousand indigenous auxiliaries—also failed grimly, leaving its commander mortally wounded. Mexico City was sufficiently threatened to inspire an expedition headed by Viceroy Antonio de Mendoza himself, and the campaign's early mixed success ultimately ended in complete victory. Mixtón was bombarded and its temple, idols, and prophetic cult were destroyed to finalize what would grandiloquently be dubbed the "second Conquest of Mexico."[136] The natives of New Galicia were never completely docile, however, and the decades of war with the Chichimecas later in the century were in many ways a continuation of the revitalization effort begun in 1540.

The War of Mixtón is exemplary in its representation of the major motifs of nativist millennialism. The incidental revolts in response to forced labor, forced conversion, and deculturation were cohered into a movement by virtue of a prophesy that endowed the struggle with a supernatural ally and with a sacred purpose, meaning, and objective. The prophetic message polarized social reality, with the divisive line drawn not only between native and Spaniard but also between those Indians who would abandon Christianity and those who would not. Each individual's fate was determined by his or her position in relation to the prophetic message: those who heeded the call were rewarded with fecundity, procreation, cultural survival, life everlasting, and prosperity, whereas those who rejected the recuperation of tradition were sentenced to darkness, devouring beasts, and execution. Gestures of ritual undoing (washing off the stain of baptism) and overt acts of reviving preconquest customs (taking many wives) demonstrated allegiance to the movement, and millennial promises then combined with coercion to exact the principle manifestation of one's collaboration: warfare.

As in all prophetic rebellions, the promised life everlasting came to none and early death on the battlefield to many. The prophets of Mixtón spoke for a deity with an absolutist policy toward the conqueror, not content merely to expel the Spaniards and resume preconquest life but rather determined to slaughter Spanish Christians everywhere. The prophets represented this total war as a feat of supernatural omnipotence, but the always imminent, never actualized return of the deity leaves the implementation to the earthly agents. The people's will (to eliminate the Spaniards, to return to tradition) is rerouted by the prophets and returns transcendentalized, hyperbolic, and oracular. Once that roundabout authorization is accomplished, and once the claim is made that the deity will accomplish the mission with supernatural intervention, then the people go to war. The deity serves as a means to objectify, sanction, legitimate, consolidate, and empower the will of the people. The ancestral, pain-free paradise anticipated beyond victory is likewise conditioned by this doubled monologue that echoes between community and deity.

Taqui Onqoy

The region of Huamanga (Ayacucho) had barely been colonized twenty years in the early 1560s when the "sickness" of the Taqui Onqoy movement spread through the Andes like a contagion. In the chaotic postconquest ambience and at "a critical juncture of disillusion, resistance, and reassessment in once cooperative native societies," Taqui Onqoy's influence reached as far as Lima, Cuzco, Arequipa, and La Paz.[137] The leaders of the movement, referred to as "taquiongos" and probably headed by a Christianized *curaca* (cacique) named Juan Chocne, prophesied a pachacuti in which an ensemble of resuscitating *huacas* (local deities, here associated primarily with lakes and mountain peaks) would "recreate another world and other men." The taquiongos claimed to be "the messengers of the huacas" that were making war (or, in some versions, planning to make war) against the Christian God, who "would be conquered soon."[138] The natives "should not recognize any other god except their huacas" because "everything that the Christians teach is false." As the natives' position was registered by Cristóbal de Molina: "now the world is turning around" and consequently "God and the Spaniards will be defeated this time, and all of the Spaniards [will be] dead."[139]

As the taquiongos (but also the Spaniards) understood the conquest, the fate of warring peoples on earth is determined by the will and power of their deities on high. The Spaniards' victory against the Andeans was the consequence in the lower world of Christ's victory against the huacas in the upper world. The Andean gods had ill served their people, perhaps because their people had ill served their gods, with colonial subjugation and deculturation as the consequence. The relation of the Christian victor and the Andean vanquished would now be reversed, however, because the huacas had resuscitated and allied their forces to reengage Christ in battle. In the world below, meanwhile, the taquiongos complemented those otherworldly struggles by clearing the field through a peaceful (not armed) sociocultural resistance that would prepare and facilitate restitution of the huacas' domain. Taqui Onqoy called for an absolute extermination of

Spaniards and hispanicized natives, but it left the violence to the deities, operating instead through passive resistance and separatist reculturation.

If one approaches Taqui Onqoy with the nontheistic presumption that the true consolidation of forces occurred not in the world above but rather in the traumatized indigenous milieu of the postconquest Andes, then Taqui Onqoy is revealed as a socioreligious movement that, as in Mixtón, understood itself as the earthly agency of a cosmic battle but that in fact preceded the metaphysics that ostensibly called it forth. From within the movement, resuscitating deities and cyclical eschatology conditioned a revisionist interpretation that foretold reversal of the cataclysmic conquest; from without, the huacas seem a transcendentalized projection returning to its human source as the quasi-causal paradigm of revolt. The huacas' imminent return served as a means to authorize and empower the struggle for cultural survival, and it provided a model for the recuperation of deposed supernatural meanings inherent to Andean cosmovision. Humans created the otherworldly scenario that reflected and remedied their crisis; then they enacted its agenda in this world. The depiction of a unification above (the huacas joining forces against a common enemy, Christ) served as the model for unification below (the Andeans joining forces against a common enemy, the Spaniards). Fragmentation was unifying horizontally and vertically: the gods above, the people below, and these two spheres reintegrated in their reciprocal, hierarchical relations as the Andeans returned to traditional worship.

The name Taqui Onqoy, meaning "sickness that dances" or "dancing sickness," referred to the ecstatic trance state experienced by taquiongos who were possessed by huacas. Like possession by the Holy Spirit in modern Pentecostal Christianity, ecstatic trance signaled transformation under the force of supernatural powers, a ritual rebirth into an elite defined by its privileged union with deity. The taquiongos became man-gods bespoken by deity because the huacas "now entered the bodies of the Indians and made them talk."[140] Spanish sources recorded the corporal manifestations of huaca possession, but not without a depreciatory assessment: "They trembled and rolled about on the floor," making strange faces and gestures "like idiots and people who had lost their reason."[141]

It was precisely this possession by huacas that grounded Taqui Onqoy in a terrestrial, millennial agenda, that "lowered" the upper world and joined it to the earth through intermediary messianic agency. The distinction between prophet and messiah, between taquiongo and huaca, blurred as these possessed, composite messengers engaged in the divinely instigated transformation of their polity. From its origin in relatively few initiators the movement spread rapidly by virtue of possession, for each new walking huaca became an activated advocate of the movement and a tangible object of veneration.[142] The natives worshiped the possessed taquiongos "as the huaca or idol that they said had entered the body," making sacrifices to them, lavishing food and gifts upon them, and keeping village houses orderly in the event that a taquiongo wished to spend the night.[143]

Purification rituals also contributed to Taqui Onqoy's program of reculturation. Under the tutelage and sometimes intimidation of the taquiongos, the Andeans were to revitalize their uncontaminated past by abandoning the Christian God and his commandments, rejecting Christian images, boycotting churches, relinquishing Christian names, confessing to taquiongos rather than to Catholic priests, and purging from their lives all material culture, including food and clothing, associated with the conqueror. Bodily purification complemented the cultural cleansing through fasts and avoidance of *ají*, salt, corn, alcohol, and sexual relations.[144] At the same time, the huacas (in this case, sacred objects) that had been destroyed by the extirpators were restored as the wandering taquiongos requested their remains, ritually cleansed them, and returned them to their preconquest sites of worship.[145] Atonement, propitiation, and purification thereby combined to resacralize a cosmos profaned by conquest and to resume disrupted reciprocity relations with the gods whose favor was solicited.

The taquiongos prophesied that the Spaniards would be destroyed and their cities washed away by the flooding ocean, so that the new age, inhabited by ritually purified people, would be cleansed of all foreign contaminants. Other purges realized through natural and supernatural cooperation would protect the posthispanic kingdom from the corrupting vestiges of enmity, because the huacas "had planted many fields of worms, to put them into the hearts of Spaniards, their livestock from Spain and the horses, and also in the hearts of the Indians who remained Christian." The world was turning over, and hispanicized Indians remaining in the upside-down past would accordingly "die and walk with their heads on the ground and their feet above." Those faithful to the movement, conversely, "would do well in all of their endeavors and they and their children would be healthy and their harvest would be large."[146]

The volatile tropes of sickness and cure claimed both negative and positive attributes as they migrated between their divine sources and their earthly interpreters. In one common indigenous view, the huacas, "withered and dying of hunger" for want of the offerings that nourished them, took revenge on the Christianized Indians by sending the epidemics.[147] This explanation in itself constituted a nativist reclamation through its inversion of the friars' claim that disease was the Christian God's punishment for idolatry. Taqui Onqoy transposed the epidemics from Christian to Andean origin, thereby neutralizing a weapon in the Christian arsenal by bringing the power of disease under native control. The "sickness" of Taqui Onqoy's dance then functioned as a cure, because its revitalization of huaca worship placated and sustained the vengeful deities. Once the huacas were no longer "withered and dying," then presumably they would withdraw the punitive epidemics to restore Andean well-being.

As though fighting fire with fire, the sickness dance thereby attempted "to cure the disease of invasion," a malady represented beyond the epidemics in the chaotic, pathogenic nature of the upside-down colony as a whole.[148] The myth of the *pishtaco*, or *ñaqa*, believed to have originated during Taqui Onqoy, represented the Spaniards as monstrous aliens who slaughtered Indians to extract their fat for purposes that have evolved with the ages—to build churches, to make bells, to pay the foreign debt, to lubricate space ships.[149] Cristóbal de Molina reported that according to native sources the purpose of fat extraction in 1561 was to cure a disease that had broken out in Spain. The sick Indians, once dead, became a cure for Spanish disease. That transcultural relation of illness and health had an antecedent in the conquerors' occasional dissection of native corpses to extract fat as a dressing for battle wounds.[150] In the pishtaco myth of Taqui Onqoy, it was not the disease that killed but the cure—being the cure, being dismembered as a body and a social body for the well-being of a conqueror who spared nothing, not even fat. If the Spaniards were expelled to tend to their own wounds and diseases ("I and my companions suffer from a disease of the heart which can be cured only with gold," as Hernán Cortés put it in Mexico), then the natives could turn their curative properties inward, patch up relations with their epidemic-sending deities, and thrive in restored health and peace.[151] The Spaniards, conversely, deprived of their "cure," would be destined to the demographic collapse once suffered by the natives. By these co-optations and the inversion of the injurious and the curative, Taqui Onqoy provided a symbolic means not only to control disease but also to deploy it against the conquerors: "The Spaniards in this land would soon be finished because the huacas sent sicknesses to kill them."[152] The Spaniards, for their part, were in unwitting poetic collusion when they referred to spreading insurrections as "epidemics."[153]

The concept of sickness was yet more integral to the ideology of a movement known as Muru Onqoy (Sickness of the Spots), which emerged in response to a major smallpox epidemic around 1590. The natives again interpreted the illness as a scourge sent by the abandoned huacas to punish conversion to Christianity. Some prophets announced that they had seen "the plague" in person, others that the Inca had appeared to them, and all that the time had come to eliminate the Spaniards and return to ancestral religion.[154] The church was boycotted; Christian marriages were undone; and all religious paraphernalia and other Spanish manufactured goods were discarded. One prophet of the huaca Picti mobilized a pilgrimage to the sacred mountains, where offerings, including the sacrifice of a female convert to Christianity, were made to propitiate the wrathful deity.[155]

The military alliance of huacas in Taqui Onqoy directly parallels the Old Testament combat myth, which entails "the attempt of one god or group of gods to usurp the kingship or power of another god or group of gods."[156] A passage from Saint Augustine excerpted by Columbus in his *Book of Prophesies* exemplifies this cosmic conflict's extension into Christianity, where it also produced the warrior Christ of Revelation, Santiago, and the hosts of crusaders who emulated them in holy war. Just as Taqui Onqoy forecast the imminent triumph of the huacas over Christ, Augustine described Christ at war against pagan deities, and "the Lord shall win the victory against them and destroy all the gods of the nations of the earth."[157] Columbus anthologized the passage not for monastic contemplation but rather, just as the taquiongos used the huaca myth, to authorize and mobilize a politico-religious consolidation mandated by a tutelary deity.

The huacas' unified front in Taqui Onqoy suggests an appeal to the implied advantage of monotheism—one all-powerful god—as opposed to the distribution of power and the potential for divisive rivalry in polytheism. The Judeo-

Christian parallel is again conspicuous, as polytheism was "widespread at every level of Israelite society" until Yahweh, the "jealous" god, prevailed as "a great King over all gods," absorbing lesser dieties into his monotheistic, conquering majesty.[158] Unification into a single, omnipotent deity is also suggested by the Christian Trinity—three separate identities but one being—and by the informal, subordinated pantheon of saints. In Christianity a multiplicity is provisionally permitted insofar as an ultimate monotheistic unity is recognized, whereas in Taqui Onqoy polytheism is the norm, with the unification of huacas an exceptional expedient in response to the crisis of conquest. The federation of huacas against a common rival suggests a monotheistic consolidation, if only informal and transitory, to retaliate with sufficient muster against a monotheistic conqueror. In one report this consolidation is particularly conspicuous because it accomplishes its unification in stages. The huacas "had risen to life again and were drawn up on two sides, the one side with the huaca Pachacamac and the other with the huaca Titicaca." The many had been reduced to a characteristic Andean duality (not unlike the Christian Trinity), which then forged the final, unified front as these "two greatest" huacas "joined forces to give battle against God Our Lord."[159]

Christian influence is suggested by Taqui Onqoy's possession states, warrior gods, and perhaps confession rituals, but the influence is explicit in the assumption of biblical identities by members of the movement's leadership. Juan Chocne, who had studied under friars, was accompanied by two women who were known as the Virgin Mary, Mary Magdalene, "and other names of Saints that among them they had taken so that they would be revered as Saints."[160] Polytheism is generally prone to the incorporation of powerful foreign deities into its pantheon, and nominally Christian Andeans may have understood the saints as "hispanic huacas," but the paradox nevertheless obtains because the nativist agenda and the polarized religious field required comprehensive rejection of Christianity.[161] If the Christian identities were not assumed merely in carnivalesque mockery, then they can be understood as an expedient co-optation of religious symbols by peoples sorting through the chaos of an undermined past, an unfinished conquest, and a superficial evangelization. The inherent contradiction was dissolved, dismissed, processed syncretically, or deemed irrelevant in native frames of reference. The taquiongos posed as the agents of both Andean and Christian huacas until the latter—already co-opted, already Indianized—could be assimilated or cleared from the field following defeat of the god who empowered them.

The Pueblo Revolt

Spanish colonists along the upper Rio Grande inhabited by the Pueblos were always few and, consequently, always vulnerable. Juan de Oñate took formal possession of the region for Spain in 1598, tending thereafter to the cross-and-sword mandate given him by Philip II: "Your main purpose shall be the service of God Our Lord, the spreading of His holy Catholic faith, and the reduction and pacification of the natives of the said provinces."[162] Franciscans had been on the vanguard since 1581, saving souls and suffering the consequences. One revolt among many occurred in February 1632, when converted Zuñis responded to Fray Francisco Letrado's call to mass by "smashing his head with their clubs in order to prevent him from preaching the word of God to them any longer." Letrado's successor was also killed, and the Zuñi mission was suspended for more than a decade.[163]

In the 1660s an organized prelude to the Pueblo Revolt began to concretize under the direction of an Indian named Esteban Clemente. If the conspiracy had not been discovered and Clemente had not been hanged, the Pueblos would have rebelled on Holy Thursday with the intent of not sparing "a single religious or Spaniard."[164] In a 1672 revolt at the Abó Pueblo, the local friar was stripped, flogged, and then beaten to death with tomahawks; his dead body was displayed hugging a crucifix and an image of the Virgin. Three dead lambs, lambs of God, were left at his feet, as though this botched literalization of Christian imagery symbolized death of the Trinity along with its priest.[165] A similar message may have been intended in the Santo Domingo Pueblo, where three priests were killed in the monastery, dragged to the church, and piled in front of the altar.[166]

For a decade before the 1680 Pueblo Revolt, the gods seemed to be conspiring against the natives. Drought, crop failure, and famine characterized the years from 1667 to 1672. Food was so scarce in 1670 that nearly half of New Mexico's population, native and Spanish alike, escaped starvation only by eating hides and leather cart straps, "soaking and washing them and roasting them in the fire with maize, and boiling them with herbs and roots."[167] These hardships were redoubled by epidemics and by increased Apache and Navajo attacks in retaliation for slave raids conducted by the Spaniards.[168]

The Pueblos were "not unwilling to accept the externals of the new faith," but they expected in return that the Christian God serve their needs at least as competently as had the traditional deities deposed by the friars.[169] By 1673 the dominant indigenous interpretations of starvation and disease vacillated between the Christian God's impotence and the traditional deities' punishment of betrayal. Relations between Spaniards and Pueblos became strained because "it began to appear that the Christian deity was no better at preventing epidemics than providing good weather," and consequently "bewilderment soon turned into resentment, and resentment into a resurgence of loyalty to the traditional norms of folk-culture."[170] Revitalization of the indigenous cult, which was regarded by the Spaniards as a backslide into "sorcery," was rigorously punished under the governor Juan Francisco de Treviño. The most significant incident occurred in 1675, when three Pueblo shamans were hanged and forty-some others, one among them named Popé, were publicly flogged and destined for slavery until the belligerent Tewa forced their liberation.

Based first at San Juan and then at the more remote Taos Pueblo, Popé began to conspire the 1680 rebellion upon his release from custody. His plan called for the sudden and simultaneous uprising of all pueblos in the region to rapidly slaughter as many colonists as possible. Firearms would be seized, roads would be closed, and Santa Fe would be isolated from the more populated Spanish settlement at Río Abajo. The plan's secrecy was guarded so rigorously that Popé murdered his son-in-law, the Indian governor of San Juan Pueblo, when it was suspected that he might inform Spanish authorities of the impending insurrection. Indians unwilling to participate were also killed, and the threat to destroy entire communities extorted the compliance of pueblos reluctant to revolt.[171]

Popé's recruitment effort nevertheless relied more on millennial promise than it did on purge and coercion. "He told the disaffected, the hungry, and the displaced that their ancient gods would not return bearing gifts of happiness and prosperity until the Christians and their God were dead."[172] As reported by a native and recorded by Spaniards after the revolt, Popé convinced the Pueblos

> that the father of all the Indians, their great captain, who had been such since the world had been flooded, had ordered the said Popé to tell all the pueblos to rebel and to swear that they would do so; that no religious or Spanish person must remain; and that after this they would live as in ancient times, regaled like the religious and the Spaniards, and would gather a great many provisions and everything they needed.[173]

Another testimony, taken in January 1682, suggested the causal relation between the nativist insurrection and the millennial reward. Popé

> made them kill priests and Spaniards, together with their women and children, and burn images and churches, and cease living with the wives to whom they were married, leaving them and taking others, and he caused them to wash their heads in order to take away the water of baptism, so that they might be as they had been in ancient times; and he told them that they would gather large crops of grain, maize with large and thick ears, many bundles of cotton, many calabashes and watermelons, and everything else in proportion.[174]

Within weeks after the inception of the Pueblo Revolt on August 10, 1680, some four hundred of the twenty-five hundred Spaniards north of El Paso had been killed. The decisive battle began on August 15, when the Pueblos besieged the colonial capital at Santa Fe with "boldness and barbarous atrocity" and attempted "to destroy the whole kingdom completely."[175] Antonio de Otermín, governor and captain general of New Mexico at the time of the revolt, reported that the Spaniards were most grieved by "the dreadful flames from the church and the scoffing and ridicule which the wretched and miserable Indian rebels made of the sacred things, intoning the *alabado* and the other prayers of the church with jeers."[176] One of those jeers was patently revitalist, protesting that the indigenous gods had never died but "now the God of the Spaniards, who was their father, is dead," as were the Virgin Mary, "who was their mother," and the saints, who were "pieces of rotten wood."[177] Ridicule yielded to strategic borrowing in the accouterments worn by the Indian commander of the siege, who boasted "a sash of red taffeta which was recognized as being from the missal of the convent of Galisteo," along with "harquebus, sword, dagger, leather jacket, and all the arms of the Spaniards."[178]

Having refused an offer to withdraw from the region peaceably, Otermín decided that an honorable death in battle was preferable to a slow demise from thirst and starvation. On August 20, invoking the protection of the Virgin, Spaniards attacked and drove back the natives, ending the five-day siege. Santa Fe was abandoned the following day, with the entire Spanish population evacuated to the south. (The convergence of these refugees onto El Paso precipitated the Suma revolt of 1684, with similar consequences: "The sacred vessels have been profaned, the holy vestments have been trampled, and Our Lord has been again crucified by a new breed of barbarians.")[179] An attempted reconquest of the Pueblos in 1681–82 was unsuccessful, yielding only reports that the natives were "course and intractable, as full of idolatry as their ancestors," and that they had been more "Christians by force than Indians converted to the holy faith."[180]

The Pueblos remained free of Spanish domination for twelve years, during which Spanish religion, customs, and language were prohibited, agriculture was returned to traditional crops, and the desecrated kivas were resacralized.[181] The resumed autonomy concluded in 1692 when Diego de Vargas led a "bloodless reconquest" (a bloody one followed, along with recolonization, the next year) under the banner of a Virgin known as the Conqueror. The Pueblos rebelled again in June 1696—burning churches, killing friars and settlers, abandoning villages—but their determination in this round was unequal to the strength and entrenchment of the colonists.

Conspicuous during the 1680 revolt and its aftermath was a sustained effort to extirpate all vestiges of Christianity. Otermín reported that the Pueblos "profaned the holy temples, burning them and the images from their altars, mocking at the things belonging to divine worship, wearing the priestly vestments in their idolatrous dances, and making trophies of them, as well as of the sacred vessels."[182] Another Spanish report from October 1680 was more graphic:

> Their hatred and barbarous ferocity went to such extremes that in the pueblo of Sandía images of saints were found among excrement, two chalices were found concealed in a basket of manure, and there was a carved crucifix with the paint and varnish taken off by lashes. There was also excrement at the place of the holy communion table at the main altar, and a sculpted image of Saint Francis with the arms hacked off by an axe.[183]

After fulfilling Popé's order "to burn the churches, convents, holy crosses, and every object pertaining to Christianity," some Pueblos retrofitted Christian ruins to suit the restored indigenous cult. As reported by a reconnaissance mission during the attempted reconquest in 1681–82, the remains of a monastery had been "made into a seminary of idolatry" and furnished with the corresponding paraphernalia.[184] This reversal of the Spanish practice of adapting indigenous temples to Christian purposes was complemented by the use of building materials salvaged from churches for the construction of new kivas.[185]

Deconversion also required the neutralization of Christian sacraments that exerted an influence on native culture even in the absence of friars. Pueblo men were ordered to separate from the wives taken in Christian marriage and to recouple with spouses of their choice. In some accounts the entitlement to polygamy accrued in quotas proportionate to one's accomplishments in battle: "Who shall kill a Spaniard will get an Indian woman for a wife, and he who kills four will get four women, and he who kills ten or more will have a like number of women."[186] The dissolution of Christian marriage was complemented by the undoing of baptism to cleanse the "wet-heads"—as the Pueblos called baptized Indians—of Christian contamination: "In order to take away their baptismal names, the water, and the holy oils, they were to plunge into the rivers and wash themselves."[187] In stark contrast to the promised rebirth into life everlasting, baptism left on the Pueblos the insignia of deaths that accompanied their induction into Christendom—death by disease, death by labor, death by deculturation.[188]

The Pueblos persevered as reluctant converts to Catholicism even after the 1692 reconquest. A missionary report almost a century later was still lamenting how the Pueblos preferred their native names, "and when we call them by their saints' names they usually have their joke among themselves, repeating the saint's name to each other as if in ridicule." What is more, "their repugnance and resistance to most Christian acts is evident, for they perform the duties pertaining to the Church under compulsion, and there are usually many omissions."[189] The friar Francisco Atanasio Domínguez distinguished Picurís and Taos Pueblos as those who "outdo all the rest" in their disdain for Christianity. If the natives there see a priest, "they are as terrified as if they were to see Lucifer himself and they would like to make themselves invisible. They flee from him like the devil from the cross, and the children even cry, running as if from their cruelest enemy."[190] Another friar similarly reported from Senecú that the Pueblos were "totally lost, without faith, without law, and without devotion to the church." In Isleta a Franciscan unable to restrain the Indians from performing their traditional dances "went through the pueblo with a cross upon his shoulder, a crown of thorns, and a rope about his neck, beating his naked body, in order that they might stop the dance."[191] The effort, however, was in vain.

The Pueblo Revolt is exceptional among nativist insurrections for its success, even if transitory, in accomplishing the always stated but rarely realized goal of expelling the conqueror. No rebellion can deliver on its millennial promise, just as no religion can regulate its gods' dispensation of illness or rain, but in this-worldly terms the Pueblos' victory was an unqualified success. The revolt is also exceptional in the rigor and almost burlesque nature of its assault against the Christian sacrosanct. It seems as though the Pueblos were more convinced than were most natives—perhaps because they were less indoctrinated—that the Christian deity was "dead" and that they could therefore mockingly profane his symbols with impunity. Once the friars were dead too, the churches burned, and the wet-heads dried, a new horizon opened for the Pueblos. Because all troubles had arrived with the Christians, it seemed reasonable to presume that all would disappear as the colonists retreated downriver.

The Tzeltal Rebellion

By the early eighteenth century several Virgin cults were emerging among the Maya, forging a heterodox popular faith that, once repressed by the clergy, became the basis for millennial insurrection. The origins of a 1708 cult were typical: a prophetic hermit preached from the hollow of an oak tree that the Virgin had appeared to save the Maya, asking in return that a shrine be built for her veneration. The priest of Chamula had the tree chopped down and the prophet incarcerated in Ciudad Real's Franciscan monastery, but two years later the prophet reappeared to enshrine another Virgin who likewise became the focal point of cult worship and pilgrimage.

In a similar occurrence, a native-made image of the Virgin spoke to a girl: "She told me she was a poor woman named Mary, who had come from heaven to help the Indians." The Catholic authorities, having attempted in vain to suppress the emerging cult by confiscating the image, resorted to the deception that the Virgin's proper home was the cathedral. After two thousand of the faithful accompanied the Virgin on her journey, the image was confiscated upon arrival and locked away in the episcopal palace.[192] In the Maya perspective the same story kept repeating itself, attesting to the conqueror's obstruction of grace that the Virgin wished to bestow directly upon indigenous Christians. Whenever the Church authorities intervened, apparitions became disappearances.

The Virgin was not easily dissuaded, however, and her insistent predilection for the Maya resulted in the Tzeltal Rebellion (also referred to as the Zendal Revolt and the Cancuc Revolt) of 1712. In this instance the Virgin instructed a Tzeltal girl, María López, daughter of the village sacristan, to build a chapel for a cross that had miraculously appeared on the outskirts of Cancuc in Chiapas. When the authorities intervened the girl—now known as María de la Candelaria—retracted her story under coercion, but it was already too late.[193] The parish priest who attempted to suppress the cult was threatened with death and was run out of town by "men, women, and children with sticks and stones saying in unison: 'death to the Father.' "[194] Death had also been wished, if less explicitly, on other officials, among them a bishop driven by "limitless greed" and a governor who was likewise "blinded by his greed and ambition."[195] Avarice and exploitation provided a social context conducive to millennialism, but the Church's refusal to recognize the authenticity of the apparition precipitated the revolt. The Christian supernatural split into rival factions divided by race and class, with the syncretic cult on one side and the colonial Church on the other.

Letters signed "The Blessed Virgin María de la Cruz" (Mary of the Cross)—the new name assumed by María López—were sent to the leaders of the Indian towns in the district to summon them to Cancuc "because there is no longer God or King." The villagers were ordered to bring "all of the silver" and other objects of value from their churches, along with "all the books and funds of the confraternities." Further inducement was provided by warnings (dissenters would grow devilish horns and tails) and by apocalyptic forebodings of a great flood that would end the world.[196] The Indians had to come to Cancuc lest "the

Most Holy Virgin die on the Cross on which her Son Jesus died," because the authorities were conspiring to destroy her. Only native intervention could save the Virgin and the world she promised, where "there is no longer tribute, nor King, nor President, nor Bishop."[197] The time had come to "shake off the yoke of the Spaniards and restore freedom in their lands." While the Tzeltals were tending to that divine mission rather than to their chores, "angels would come to plant and care for their milpas."[198]

Twenty-one villages responded to the call, and on August 10 a new proclamation was announced to the rebellious multitudes who celebrated the feast of the Virgin. The premises were first reasserted: "there was no longer God or King and they [the natives] must only adore and obey the Virgin who will descend from the sky to the village of Cancuc with the objective of protecting and governing the Indians." A more explicit mandate followed: they were to "kill all fathers and priests, as well as Spaniards, mestizos, blacks, and mulattos, so that only the Indians remain."[199] Over the next three months religious, civil, and military mandates from the Virgin governed what one native priest described as "the beginning of a new world."[200] The community eventually encompassed some twenty thousand Tzeltals and Tzotzils, defended by five thousand "soldiers of the Virgin."

Unlike most indigenous revolts of the colonial era, the struggle in Cancuc was not to restore a prehispanic ideal but rather to practice the Catholic faith in a manner consonant with indigenous traditions. An initial quest for inculturation became extremist because it met with an authoritarian, repressive response from the clergy. Once the cult was prohibited and ostracized, its adherents took the offensive to safeguard their faith and to find in the Virgin's silent discourse an articulation of their millennial aspirations.

The ideological force behind the movement, Sebastián Gómez de la Gloria, claimed to have been transported to heaven, where he consulted with the Trinity, the Virgin, and Saint Peter; was named general vicar; and was empowered to ordain native priests and bishops. As they went into battle the troops were blessed by Maya priests dressed in Dominican habits, but the soldiers of the Virgin were nevertheless unequal to the professional military of their adversary and Cancuc fell after suffering some thousand native casualties. The leaders of the cult escaped, splinter groups continued the struggle into 1713, and the Most Holy Virgin María de la Cruz died in childbirth three years later.[201] New uprisings, such as one among Zoques and Tzeltals in 1727, were inspired by the belief that "the Virgin is still alive," with corresponding apparitions in the sky, in images, and in incarnations.[202] The tireless Virgin was not alone in perturbing the authorities, however, because a "venerable old man"—probably Gómez de la Gloria, who had never been apprehended—was "claiming to be St. Peter in some places and in others the Redeemer."[203]

The Caste War

In 1761 a wandering beggar named Jacinto Uc de los Santos, known as Jacinto Canek, appeared in a central Yucatan village claiming to be the returning king prophesied by the Bible. Canek, a Maya who had studied with the Franciscans, later clarified that he was Christ the King and subsequently compounded this identity with another as Moctezuma. Following initial disbelief, the people of Cisteil coronated their new messiah, who for the occasion dressed himself in the crown and blue mantle of the Virgin of the Conception and assumed the title King Jacinto Uc de los Santos Canek Chichan Moctezuma. The coronation, theocratic investiture, and litany of titles consolidated in the person of Canek (a name borrowed from the Itza Maya ruler deposed by conquest) a potent composite of indigenous and Christian symbols. The new king held court in the church, drank wine from the chalice, was paraded on a litter and incensed with copal, and took the Virgin as his wife, "being, as he was, King of the Earth." The governor would pay him homage, he announced, or would suffer the supernatural consequences. One captured Spanish soldier was made to kiss the "royal and not very clean" feet. Canek took control of the town, distributed titles to his accomplices, and ordained an indigenous clergy to administer the sacraments. The nativist agenda aspired to fulfill the *Chilam Balam* prophesy of an end to foreign domination, but Canek's reign ended first when the promise of invincibility failed the test of Spanish troops assaulting the village. The deposed king met his grizzly destiny in December 1761, when he was sentenced to be torn apart by pincers "until he dies naturally."[204]

In the same eastern region (now Quintana Roo) where Canek's revolt had occurred, Mayanized Christianity later provided the ideological and spiritual motivation for the protracted attempt at decolonization known as the Caste War. The rebellion was directed by shamans, Maya priests, and regional political leaders including Jacinto Pat, Cecilio Chi, and the popular Manuel Antonio Ay. Signatories of the first rebel proclamation were Ay and the deceased Jacinto Canek, who made a mythic return from the grave to continue with his vicars the revolution begun in 1761. The proclamation cited the *Chilam Balam* to argue that the Maya had lived in peace until the deceptive foreigners ("the Lord Jesus Christ no longer exists in their words") arrived and began to kill them.[205] By the time the Caste War began in 1847, the foreigners had compensated for their loss of Jesus with the appropriation of Maya communal lands.

Absolutist intentions, or at least rhetoric, characterized both sides of the conflict. A mestizo rebel officer, José María Barrera, wrote in April 1850 that the insurgents would not rest until all of their demands had been met: "We will kill all of them, or all of us will be killed."[206] The opposing view was expressed in a Mérida newspaper in November 1848: "That [indigenous] race must be subjugated and even thrown out of the country, if that were possible." The natives' ferocity had exhausted all indulgences and they now "must be repressed by a strong hand. Humanity and civilization thus demand it."[207] Ay was killed early on, and Pat and Chi followed in 1849, but the protracted military confrontations resulted only in stalemate until 1850, when the Talking Cross spoke up to shift the balance of power in Maya favor.

Having been driven from Kampocolche, the wearied troops under Barrera repaired to the sacred confines of a cenote in the forest, a place that came to be known as Chan Santa Cruz (Little Holy Cross). A wooden cross was erected, the bewildered rebels addressed to it their supplications, and, "the ventriloquist Manuel Nahuat being among them, God answered."[208] The Talking Cross had precedents in the oracular deities of precolumbian temples who spoke to the Maya—as in this case—through an intercessor and in postconquest stones, statues, and other objects that likewise communicated through interpreters.[209] The cross at Chan Santa Cruz instructed the Maya to resist their white enemy; to have no fear of bullets, for God would protect them; and to launch a new attack against Kampocolche. The oracular word reversed the mounting demoralization and revitalized the mission of a chosen people fighting for its just and holy cause: "This war originates with God and only he will be able to end it."[210] Thus the emboldened soldiers returned to battle, commended to the care of their Lord.

On the night of January 3, 1851, Maya troops, armed with machetes and believing themselves to be bulletproof, attacked Kampocolche as ordered by the Cross. Their reckless bravery nearly won them victory, but the counterattack of a well-armed adversary ultimately resulted in massacre. The authorities coerced information from captured rebels and made a surprise attack on the shrine in March. The Cross was confiscated and the chilam who had received its messages, Manuel Nahuat, was killed. Barrera survived, however, and provided for uninterrupted communications from the Cross, now in writing, through his secretary, Juan de la Cruz Puc. A trinitarian multiplication of the Cross also seems to have occurred at this time, perhaps "because not One but Three mysterious personages will take command of the situation."[211]

The new messages of the oracle, signed with three crosses but also by Juan de la Cruz (John of the Cross) as intercessor, stated that "because of the sacrilegious murder of Nahuat, the Crosses will never speak again, except to the Seraphim and the Apostles." The Maya as "true Christians" must "rise and take vengeance for the spilt blood," destroying their hypocritical enemy and recuperating Maya lands.[212] Barrera enshrined the crosses in a thatched church with an inner sanctum accessible only to a theocratic elite. The congregation worshiped in the main, outer room, at a distance that fostered a sense of religious mystery and facilitated ventriloquism. "A pit was dug behind the altar, and there crouched a hidden spokesman who used a wooden cask as an echo chamber to amplify, project, and give resonance to his voice."[213]

Barrera died in 1852, and under the direction of Juan de la Cruz Puc—also known as Juan de la Cruz Tres Personas (John of the Cross Three Persons)—the cult became increasingly messianic. Juan de la Cruz continued circulating letters signed either with the three crosses and his own name, with "Lord Jesus Christ, Creator of Christians," or with "Son of God."[214] The discourse of the Cross remained essentially the same—mandating caste war, promising invincibility and triumph, providing social norms, consoling the community—-but with the added feature now of propagating Juan de la Cruz as a messianic figure, a Maya Christ.[215] The Cross spoke as though it were the deity, Juan de la Cruz as signatory stood in for the absent God, and the identities of Juan de la Cruz, the Cross, and the deity intermingled in ambiguous circulation. This was facilitated by the colonial Maya's fusion of the cross and the crucified Christ into a single entity, "the cross losing the Christian significance of the instrument of

God's self-sacrifice and becoming the God himself."[216] The absent God and the mute, sequestered God-Cross left extant only Juan de la Cruz's Three Persons, in whom all the godliness of this trinitarian arrangement consolidated. There was only one voice echoing in the confines of the tautology that empowered it: the Cross bespoken by Juan and Juan bespoken by the Cross. The discourse is proper to the God-Cross, but the first-person pronoun is assigned to its signatory (Juan de la Cruz), thereby conferring upon him an identity as Christ: "Because it was I who caused you to be created; I it was who redeemed you; I it was who shed my precious blood on your behalf."[217] Juan de la Cruz came to be viewed not as a mouthpiece for the Cross but rather as a messiah sent by God for salvation of the Yucatec Maya.[218]

A complicated military history with no victories filled the subsequent years, during which the people of the Cross developed an identity as the Cruzob, a name composed of the Maya plural suffix appended to the Spanish word for cross. The Cruzob developed a highly stratified military theocracy and after 1855 had so consolidated their position that the conflict seemed "not a rebellion or Caste War, but rather a struggle between two sovereign powers, Mexico and Chan Santa Cruz."[219] Until it was conquered by federal troops in 1901, Chan Santa Cruz functioned as a sacred society in a state of perpetual warfare, with its social and political orders jointly defined by the Cross's divine mandates and the pragmatics of military governance.[220] The Maya of Quintana Roo still hold "that holy war is essential, and that it must occur so that the chosen people become again the owners of their territory."[221] Folklore from the 1970s had Juan de la Cruz return in the person of Felipe Yama, a leader of the war in the 1890s. Yama died but resurrected after three days and then fused with the Wonderful True God, saying, "I am Juan de la Cruz" and "there isn't anyone else."[222] The message is perennial because it is millennial; the Cross, still talking as late as 1904, repeats itself endlessly with a revised message adapted to the ages. As a Maya guide informed a historian in 1959, someday the English will provide the firearms with which the Maya will overthrow their oppressors. One will know that this day—"the end of the world"—is imminent "when money disappears from the hands, Mexican money."[223]

Andean Rebellions

After a two-year alliance with the Spaniards against the Quito faction in the Inca civil war, Manco Inca had a change of heart. In 1536 he besieged Cuzco to initiate the resistance that would last, under his successors, until 1572. The end of the neo-Inca state exiled in Vilcabamba came when the last Inca, Túpac Amaru, was defeated and then executed by order of Viceroy Francisco de Toledo. The Inca as a symbol of resistance and messianic hope survived through the centuries, however, as did the anticipation that the conquered Andeans would be redeemed from subjugation.

To many it seemed as though the time of redemption had arrived in 1780 when the curaca of Tungasuca, José Gabriel Condorcanqui, took the name Túpac Amaru and rose in revolt against colonial abuse of the Indians. Túpac Amaru II claimed direct descent from Juana Pilcorvaco, daughter of the Túpac Amaru who had been executed in 1572, and viceregal authorities recognized this claim. In nativist perspective he held a hereditary claim to legitimate reign, but Inca nobility had mutated over centuries of colonial rule and by 1780 was more hispanic than indigenous in its lifestyle. The new Túpac Amaru, a mestizo born in 1740, had considerable wealth and education, lived ostentatiously, and was married to a Creole. The corregidor considered him a "fraudulent Indian."[224] Whatever nativism Túpac Amaru II might manifest would be derived from his proximity to the suffering natives and from the race mixing and syncretism at the source of his contact culture. As a curaca reporting to and collecting tribute for the Spanish authorities, he was intimately familiar with the impact that the colonial economy had on the Andeans. He necessarily viewed their misery through his luxury, but he was intent on using his privileged position—first by juridical and then by military means—to alleviate the exploitation that was destroying them.

The repartimiento of merchandise had the Andeans in "a deplorable state of death with its immense excess," but the most egregious socio-economic abuse was the *mita*, a system of forced draft labor in Spanish mines and textile mills.[225] The silver mine at Potosí became a symbol of cruel exploitation, a "mouth of Hell" that devoured natives or "a kind of monster that absorbs bodies into the depths of the earth."[226] A Spanish assessor later observed that if a hundred Indians leave for mita service, "barely twenty return."[227] If an Indian did survive his tour, he generally found himself indebted at its conclusion, because the meager salary that he earned was no match for the tribute and fines deducted from it.[228] He was therefore required to continue forced labor at the mine, trapped in a vicious circle with little hope of repaying the ever-increasing debt. In 1777 when Túpac Amaru II petitioned the viceroy, to no avail, for the abolition of the mita, he stressed the "imponderable hardships" suffered by the Indians to fulfill the obligation (such as the three-month walk to reach Potosí), the mines' deplorable work conditions, the merciless length of the workday, and the insufficient pay. Because of the mita, Túpac Amaru argued, "there are no Indians left." The depopulated villages would soon be nothing but "a pitiful monument."[229]

It was against these economic abuses and their social consequences that Túpac Amaru II, having exhausted legal remedies in Tinta, Cuzco, and Lima, rebelled in 1780. Viceroy Agustín de Jáuregui well itemized the causes of the revolt as excessive repartimiento, forced labor, infringement on privileges conceded to the Indians, lack of legal recourse for injustices, as well as "the venerated memory of the Incas, and the hopes that Túpac Amaru had awakened in the credulous masses."[230] In a 1780 letter, Túpac Amaru made explicit his intent to eliminate the repartimiento, the mita, the taxes, and the tributes, but the inimical rage gravitated most readily toward the corregidores who symbolized colonial exploitation, corruption, and tyranny.[231] The insurrection accordingly made its November 1780 debut in Tungasuca with the arrest and execution of Antonio de Arriaga, detested corregidor of the province of Tinta. The execution was prefaced, in Quechua and Spanish, with the legitimating but false claim that Túpac Amaru II had been mandated by royal decree to eliminate the bad government: "The king our lord orders that the life of this man be taken."[232] The same was reemphasized insistently: "I have royal orders"; "I have superior orders to exterminate corregidores"; "The King has ordered me to proceed extraordinarily against several corregidores."[233]

That claim, beyond its formulaic appeal to the mythic benevolence of royalty, is reminiscent of the versions of the myth of Inkarrí in which permission is required from Spanish royalty or Christian deity before Inkarrí can return and accomplish his mission. As a cultural hero on the model of Inkarrí, Túpac Amaru II enacts an essentially nativist response to colonial oppression, but he dares to do so initially only under the aegis, which is to say under the false pretense, of royal authorization. In a paradoxical web of deference and defiance, he purports to be empowered by the paradigm Spanish colonizer—the king himself—in order to legitimate his nativist insurrection against colonizers. At the same time, he turns royalty against viceroyalty, defending the king's moral intentions against their corrupt manifestation in bad government, but always to the advantage of the natives. Positioned between subordination to the crown and Church on one side and his agonizing people on the other, and between regal benevolence and its viceregal corruption, Túpac Amaru must wage his war within the oxymoron of destroying the colony in order to save it. He is in the predicament of the middleman, the mestizo between cultures, struggling for an integrationist compromise that will eliminate the abuses but preserve the racial and cultural components integral to his own identity and that of his society.

Túpac Amaru II was thus eager to clarify that his rebellion was "not against God nor against the King" and "not in the least way against Our Sacred Catholic Religion," but rather against the bad government, elements of the Church included, that covetously interpreted and executed the benevolent intentions of theocracy.[234] In his letter of March 5, 1781, to the *visitador* (inspector), José Antonio de Areche, Túpac Amaru affirmed that he was not of a "cruel heart" like the tyrannical corregidores; rather he was a "very Catholic Christian," firm in the faith that "our mother the Church and her sacred ministers teach and preach to us."[235] The king, himself acting on behalf of divine providence, had recruited the very Catholic Túpac Amaru to terminate colonial iniquities, to purify the system of the aberrations corrupting it from within, and to defend the integrity of sacrosanct power.

Túpac Amaru had barely commenced that mission when it clashed with the interests of his intended beneficiaries, Indians, thereby putting his insurrection in the peculiar position of having to subvert the authorities that it purported to uphold. Once the rebellion had been instigated, the nativist agenda gained a momentum of its own far in excess of the regal, Catholic, and Creole-friendly façade that characterized its debut. The native rank and file, some fifty thousand strong, demonstrated this in the selection of its targets and the celebratory nature of its violence. The moral imperative of their Inca was not feigned, however, and like earlier nativist Catholics he regarded his Christianity as superior to the ostentatious but morally vacant faith of the Spaniards.

The response of Church hierarchy to the rebellion was itself indication enough that the Catholicism defended by Túpac Amaru and the institutionalized Catholicism of the viceroyalty were not one and the same, just as the king defended by Túpac Amaru and the king in Castile coincided only in name. The bishop of Cuzco, Juan Manuel Moscoso, greeted the rebellion by excommunicating Túpac Amaru as a "Traitor to the King" and "usurper of Royal Rights," thereby undermining Túpac Amaru's politico-religious pretensions and causing uneasiness and defection among his troops.[236] The political basis of the excommunication, with God and king teaming up to defeat the rebel who claimed to represent them, was followed by Moscoso's more pragmatic defense of colonial prerogatives: "I became a soldier, without ceasing to be a bishop; and likewise when this conflict was most serious I armed the secular and regular clergy."[237]

The Church reaction, like the anticipated creole and mestizo support that never materialized, were partially consequences of the terror that native insurrection evoked in the nonindigenous elite. The patently nativist tone that the rebellion could assume in the rank and file, with a genocidal rage intent on "finishing off the Spaniards," was more moderately conceived by Túpac Amaru, but the privileged class nevertheless ran for cover. Some testimonies claimed that Túpac Amaru ordered the death of all Spaniards or that he planned to incarcerate them in Cuzco, where "they must remain until death."[238] More likely was his hope to forge a new state that would integrate select aspects of Andean and colonial orders, a state like himself. Privileges would be restored for natives and slaves, but everyone would be welcome to remain, "under the condition that they recognize the power of the Inca."[239]

When Túpac Amaru began to refer to himself as Inca—as he did, for example, in a December 23, 1780, document signed, "The Señor Don José Gabriel Túpac Amaru Inca, descendant of the Natural King of this Kingdom of Peru, and its principle and only Lord"—he made explicit a nativist discourse that was incompatible with the deferential vassalage expressed elsewhere.[240] Popular regard of Túpac Amaru as the messiah of Andean redemption was registered in a litany of sobriquets, including Liberator; Giver of the Earthly Order; Redeeming King, and Proprietary Lord of the Kingdoms of Peru; and Liberator of the Kingdom, Restorer of Dignity, Common Father of all Who Wept Under the Yoke of Spanish Servitude. Such status demanded not defense of the Spanish king's interests but rather the pachacuti of denaturalization, with the world turned upside down and the quasi-divine Inca reigning again where once there had been royalty imposed by conquest.[241]

By March 1781, the "faithful vassal of the King, Our Lord" was asserting a rival claim to sovereignty by divine right.[242] In the Edict of Chumbivilcas, Túpac Amaru referred to himself with the exhaustive title of "Don José the First, by the Grace of God Inca King of Peru, Duke of the Most High, Lord of the Césars and Amazons and over the realm of Gran Paitití. Commissary Officer and Distributor of Divine Piety as Public Treasurer without Equal."[243] He had come to regard himself as an agent of divine will (at first through the less ambitious detour of royal will) who had been summoned to his mission because "the clamoring for justice on the part of Peruvians has reached heaven." The spiritual and material gains to be lavished upon the natives would be outdone only by the divine wrath—exerted through the agency of Túpac Amaru—scourging the wicked Spaniards who had desecrated moral order and abandoned the "True God of Heaven and Earth."[244] Túpac Amaru ultimately "regarded himself as antithetical to Jesus, for Jesus was, as it were, a competing son of God," the Son allied with the Spaniards.[245] As Inca-King he deposed the Christian king whom he ostensibly represented, and then as Inca-Jesus he subsumed the deity whose moral order the insurrection defended. When he entered Livitaca in November 1780, the natives greeted him accordingly: "You are our god and lord."[246]

Barely five months after the rebellion began, on April 6, 1781, the body of Túpac Amaru was mutilated with a thoroughness reminiscent of the extirpators' smashing, burning, and scattering of idols, as though the messianic symbol embodied by the Inca were being demolished forever. All vestiges of the Inca were assaulted in the purge that followed, which included burning genealogies; confiscating and destroying paintings that depicted Incas; making some one hundred arrests on false or specious charges; and instituting prohibitions against mourning dead Incas, performing popular theater commemorating Incas, wearing Inca clothing and crowns, and even using the sobriquet Inca, because "it is a title that anyone can take, but that makes an infinite impression on those of his class."[247] Also prohibited was Garcilaso's *Royal Commentaries of the Incas*, avidly read by Túpac Amaru, because its nostalgic depiction of a lost Inca age was regarded by the Spaniards as incendiary. In 1782 the king ordered quiet confiscation of the book, from which "these natives have learned many injurious things."[248] The preferred procedure was surreptitious, "having copies of these Works bought by third Persons in all confidence and secret," with funds from the royal treasury, so that "these Natives no longer have this motive to revive their bad customs with such documents."[249]

Túpac Amaru's execution and the wave of oppressive deculturation that came in its wake were countered by a reinvigorated continuation of the rebellion. The nature of the violence indexed a shift of register from the initial defense of moral ideals to an outburst of vengeful rage. When the besieged Puno fell in August 1781, the rebels under Andrés Túpac Amaru massacred some ten thousand people, sparing only the clergy.[250] More congruent with the aspirations of the executed Inca were the inclinations of his cousin, the curaca Felipe Velasco, who took the rebellion to Huarochirí under the name Túpac Inca Yupanqui. Túpac Amaru II had earlier claimed sovereignty over Paititi, a mythological haven for Incas who survive their defeat, and now Velasco boosted his own insurrection with a millennial charge by announcing that Túpac Amaru, far from dead, was "on the imperial throne as absolute Inca" of Paititi.[251] Velasco went the way of the Inca a mere month after his rebellion began—tortured, executed, and quartered under viceregal orders on July 7, 1783.[252]

Nativist rebels concurrent with or preceding Túpac Amaru similarly catalyzed messianic insurrection in Alto Peru. Noteworthy was Tomás Catari, who like Túpac Amaru began his struggle with litigation before graduating to an armed offensive against a system that mocked his good intentions. Catari also held in common with Túpac Amaru a quasi-divine status among his followers. According to a report by the corregidor Manuel de la Bodega, the submission of native troops to Catari exceeded all military expediency to become "superstition and idolatry."[253] Catari was regarded as King, Sovereign, "and even other Divine names because they look at him as though at the Redeemer of his People from the tributes and other obligations."[254] The passage is noteworthy because it captures the effortless shift back and forth between political and religious registers, along with the less explicit shift between cultures. Catari's rebellion, like the others of the eighteenth-century Andes, originated in politico-economic grievances; was cohered, inspired, and maintained by the nativist exaltation of a quasi-divine Inca; and integrated European theocratic precepts (such as the benevolent despot and the warrior god of love) into the construct of Inca. The multiple determinants were then collapsed into the composite that unified them: the returning Inca redeems with all of the splendor of Jesus but from "the tributes and other obligations."

Following Tomás Catari's execution, his brothers Dámaso and Nicolás, both executed in 1781, led some seven thousand natives on a rampaging encore to the rebellion. As in the aftermath of Túpac Amaru's revolt, the Catari brothers' insurrection brought myths of messianic return (Tomás would soon resurrect to resume command) along with excessive, genocidal violence, "the Indians taking revenge for all they had suffered until that moment."[255] Both of these traits likewise extended into the subsequent insurrection of Julián Apasa, a "sacristan, forced laborer, and baker" who took up arms in the region of what is now La Paz, Bolivia. Apasa made his debut with an appeal to heroic return by assuming the name Túpac Catari (consolidating the identities of Túpac Amaru and Tomás Catari), complementing that potent composite with the title Viceroy borrowed from the enemy. His forty thousand soldiers were conditioned by "insignias of power," esotericism, and terror, and they obeyed him as though he were "a true deity."[256]

The apotheosis of Túpac Catari, along with the conflicting demands of his past as sacristan and his future as Inca, amounted to an ambivalent policy toward the Church. Túpac Catari enforced a boycott of the eucharist, holy water, and prayers, but at the same time he attended the mass celebrated daily in his camp, executed two rebels who failed to show respect for the Virgin of Copacabana, and generally spared priests during massacres (which induced some clever laymen to disguise themselves as clergy).[257] The revolutionary program nevertheless endeavored to eradicate all aspects of foreign domination, the Church included, through a genocidal violence of a grotesque, cultlike nature. During the siege of La Paz, the rebels decapitated and castrated fifty Spaniards, in one case embellishing the standard procedure by amputating the hands and legs and excising the heart. In other battles they drank blood ("saying Spanish blood tasted good") or painted their faces with the blood of fallen enemies, and they sometimes ate parts of the mutilated bodies. Túpac Catari himself received the heads of dead Spaniards and removed the eyes.[258] When troops from Buenos Aires finally caught up with him, the colonial authorities indulged, in turn, in the perverse luxury of dismemberment. On November 13, 1781, a judge im-

posed a sentence that he believed would be "pleasing to God and to the King."
Like Túpac Amaru II before him, Túpac Catari was quartered and decapitated,
with the various body parts distributed to towns of symbolic importance in the
rebellion.[259]

The ritual, reciprocal, and perhaps retaliatory dismemberment of the enemy's
body alternates between adversaries in accord with their hierarchical relation.
When they had the opportunity, nativist rebels tended to celebrate their victory
on any or every fallen body in multiple, indiscriminate mutilations. The Spaniards used penal mutilations to terrorize natives, but in executions they more
formally concentrated dismemberment on select, symbolic bodies, manifesting
restitution of the law and closure to their absolute victory by mutilating the
symbol along with the victim that embodied it. The same alternation of privilege
extended into extirpation of the adversary's culture. As long as nativist insurrection could be sustained, a purge of unwanted hispanic and Christian elements
served as the prelude to more comprehensive reculturation. When the Spaniards
maintained control of their colony, conversely, a general, concerted program of
deculturation was boosted and targeted as special occasions demanded, in one
age to extirpate idols at the center of nativist cults and in another to obliterate
the Inca as symbol.

In a report following his audience with Túpac Catari, the friar Matías Borda
recorded an instance of nativist reculturation. Having greeted the Inca in Spanish, Borda reported, "He reprimanded me, ordering me to speak no language
other than Aymará, which he had imposed as law under pain of death."[260] The
friar also reported that the rebel intended to "totally separate himself from all
Customs of the Spaniards."[261] As indicated by Túpac Catari's Catholic worship—however exotic—and by his signature "I, the Viceroy Túpac-Catari," that
separatist ideal would have to strike a compromise with those aspects of enemy
culture that had been internalized during centuries of contact. Once the Spaniards were eliminated and nativism resumed its course of self-determination, any
cultural purge would necessarily be confined to the internal dialectics of syncretism.

Natives absorbed more elements of hispanicism than Spaniards did of nativism, but on occasion sympathetic idealists from the dominant culture emerged
to advocate an indigenous cause. Noteworthy was the unlikely rebellion of two
middle-class Creoles who sought not the independent republic soon to be envisioned but rather a return to Tahuantinsuyo. Gabriel Aguilar and Manuel
Ubalde at first considered that Aguilar could be crowned as Inca, but then it
occurred to them "that to be Inca it is necessary to descend from one." They
consequently "searched diligently through the streets of Cuzco for an Inca" who
would serve as sovereign. The two rebels were hanged in Cuzco in 1805, leaving
behind only Aguilar's apocalyptic hope for justice beyond "that tremendous
judgment where everyone will tremble."[262]

Social action on behalf of natives often suffices to attract the title Inca regardless of lineage or race, as evidenced by popular regard for Juan Bustamante
Dueñas, founder of the Friends of the Indian Society in Puno around 1867, and
for the campesino leader Hugo Blanco a century later.[263] A crossover from the

dominant culture to the indigenous cause became more explicit and militant in 1913 when a mestizo army officer named Teodomiro Gutiérrez Cuevas was sent to Puno to investigate native protests resulting from the massacre of three hundred campesinos. The gamonales' obstruction of justice and the inefficacy of bureaucratic solutions frustrated Gutiérrez's efforts for an equitable remedy within the system, finally resulting—as in the cases of Túpac Amaru II and Tomás Catari—in more radical action. In 1915 Gutiérrez took the name Rumi Maqui (Hand of Stone), proclaimed himself "Restorer of the Empire of Tahuantinsuyo," and led a native insurgency. As Rumi Maqui described his program, the rule of "liberty, law, and justice" would be established by destroying "the sinister and brutalizing power of the gamonales" in order to found, once and for all, "the most important, richest, noblest and most Christian alliance in America."[264]

It is because that dream remains unrealized and inexhaustible that the Inca recycles in perpetual return. Each of these cases, from the Túpac Amaru II rebellion to the reception of modern indigenous heroes as Inca or Inkarrí, commences when a prototype messiah revives the diminishing hope that an oppressive regime can be overturned. Deification of the messianic protagonist is conspicuous in all of the eighteenth-century cases, and it occurs within the more global interpretation of socioeconomic abuse as a moral aberration requiring the remedial intervention of deity. The polarization of social reality, the genocidal and ritual violence, the strategic borrowing from the enemy's religious and secular power symbols, the upside-down world of reversed roles, and the promised end in peace and plenty all relate these late colonial rebellions to their antecedents in postcontact nativism.

4

The Promise of Paradise

It is not in vain but rather with much cause and reason
that the world here is called "New World,"
not because it was newly found but
rather because it is, in its peoples
and in almost everything, like the world
of the first golden age.
—Vasco de Quiroga

The Dissipating Image

The utopian map represents a territory that it precedes, that it engenders without empirical reference.[1] Elusive paradises dissipating in the mist are "closely related to the ancient theme of the Golden Age, which so many travelers had longed to find in some part of the world."[2] The quest of those travelers was doubly doomed a priori, first because an age is not a place and then because paradise can claim a location only insofar as its geography is imaginary. Space and time must be variously stressed to safeguard the no-place out of range. Inaccessibility became the hallmark of European paradises, with descriptions of the lost, impenetrable, elusive realms paying poetic homage to the inaccessible peace, harmony, leisure, and plenty that they represented. Islands protected by unexplored or unnavigable seas provided an ideal locale, and on some *mappamundi* (world maps), such as the late-eighth-century Hereford map, Eden itself was depicted as an island.[3] Insular utopias were described by Hesiod, Homer, Pindar, Plutarch, Diodoros of Sicily, and Tommaso Campanella, among many others, and the modern prototype was provided in 1516 when Thomas More located his Utopia on an island in the New World.[4]

Medieval traditions held that after angelic visions Saint Brendan sailed westward from Ireland, survived marvelous trials, and arrived finally at a "Promised Land of Saints." The mythic Saint Brendan's Isle appeared on most medieval maps (including those of Fra Mauro in 1460 and Paulo del Pozzo Toscanelli in 1484) and on Gerard Mercator's map in 1569, and it was searched for by Spanish expeditions as late as 1721.[5] The mysterious Atlantic was also believed to conceal Antilia, a mythical island of early medieval origin that found a New World location in the Caribbean "Antilles."[6] Early modern Europeans also believed that the Americas encompassed the mythical Atlantis described by Plato, and in 1627 this tradition was updated by Sir Francis Bacon's utopia, *New Atlantis*.[7] Many modern utopias have likewise been insular, as exemplified by Domingo Faustino Sarmiento's *Argirópolis*, written in 1850 on the eve of Juan Manuel de Rosas's fall, which had its capital on an island.[8] Insular myths and utopias were also complemented by newly discovered mainlands—Yucatan, Florida, California—that entered cartography as islands.

The inaccessibility of mythical realms on islands, unexplored frontiers, and mountain peaks made utopianism exempt from tests of truth. The unfulfilled promise remained a failure of human industry or a sign of providential postponement rather than a demonstration of the realm's nonexistence. As suggested by the etymology of the word *paradise*, which derives from an ancient Persian root denoting a walled enclosure, utopia is an enclave protected from encroachment. Genesis was characteristic in its guarantee that Eden was on earth but also that humanity was locked out. The intramural location and the flaming sword that defends Eden in Genesis 3:24 were consolidated by Isidore of Seville to depict an impenetrable realm surrounded more formidably by "a long wall of flame" whose "fire reached almost to the sky."[9] John Mandeville later provided a comprehensive image of inaccessibility, save "through the special grace of God," because paradise was situated at the highest point on earth, enclosed by a wall, surrounded by darkness and wild beasts, and protected by the four rivers that washed away approaching navigators.[10]

No sooner was one frontier explored to no avail than paradise was projected into the next. Belief in the progressive revelation of providential designs offered a comforting rationale for the elusiveness. The New World as a whole was revealed to Christ's vicars on the eve of his Advent, so it seemed logical that the lesser mysteries would be unsealed in turn as God apportioned his "secret and hidden" wisdom.[11] At the end of time "there will be nothing hidden in the world that will not be revealed," but until then the essence of apocalypticism is disclosure.[12] A paradise revealed would be a paradise undone, normalized by access and degenerated like the world surrounding it.

Lost islands and fabulous kingdoms exerted a magnetic pull that enacted myth as history. A chimera of the promised paradise, a faint mirage, sustained the explorers' outward momentum toward discoveries that sometimes bore an uncanny resemblance to the myths that served as impetus. A legend of Brazilian origin contended that the river now called La Plata (Silver) led to the Sierra de la Plata where a White King reigned covered in silver. This king existed only in a mythic complex that also generated the gilded king known as El Dorado, but explorations in search of the White King led to the "mountain of silver" at Potosí. Much the same occurred in Mexico, where the search for a mythic Mountain of Silver "to the north" helped push back the frontier to the discoveries in and beyond Zacatecas.[13] The myth of El Dorado resulted in exploration of the Amazon; the quest for a fountain of youth led to the discovery of Florida;

efforts to contact the legendary Prester John culminated in Vasco da Gama's discovery of a sea route to India; and expeditions to Quivira and the Seven Cities of Cíbola brought New Mexico into the empire.

The search for the Seven Cities of Cíbola had begun earlier in the Caribbean, where the myth of seven bishops fleeing Iberia during the eighth-century Moorish invasion intermingled with the myth of Antilia. Around 1528 the Seven Cities were projected to the expansive terra incognita of the northern frontier and were accommodated there by a fortuitous numerical coincidence with the seven caves, also to the north, in Aztec myths of origin.[14] Active searches for the Seven Cities of Cíbola were stimulated in March 1536, when Spanish slave raiders in Sinaloa encountered the survivors of a shipwrecked expedition that had intended to colonize Florida. Alvar Núñez Cabeza de Vaca and his three companions had traveled eight years through regions unexplored by Spaniards, and their mythopoetic reports reinforced the inclination to believe that the Seven Cities were beyond the frontier.

A reconnaissance party led by the Franciscan friar Marcos de Niza left Mexico's northernmost outpost in March 1539, guided by the black slave Estevanico, who had traversed the territory with Núñez Cabeza de Vaca. Estevanico traveled ahead of the party and reported the magnitude of his discoveries by posting crosses of a corresponding size. As Fray Marcos advanced he encountered progressively larger crosses, until at one day's distance from what he assumed to be Cíbola (actually Hawikuh, the southwesternmost of six Zuñi pueblos) he learned that Estevanico had been killed.

Based upon a distant glimpse of Hawikuh, Fray Marcos made a journal entry describing the pueblo as "a very beautiful city" and "bigger than the city of Mexico."[15] By September 1539, back in New Spain, his descriptions were decidedly hyperbolic and promised "seven great cities" beyond the splendor of both Mexico and Peru.[16] A more substantial expedition was dispatched under the command of Francisco Vásquez de Coronado, but the myth was deflated in June 1540, when the explorers arrived to Zuñi pueblos and discovered that Fray Marcos (now dubbed The Lying Monk) "had not told the truth in a single thing."[17] Coronado's two-year expedition traveled through Arizona, New Mexico, and parts of Texas, Oklahoma, and Kansas, but instead of gilded cities and fabulous empires it found only modest Indian settlements. The quest to find "another Mexico" under one mythic guise or another endured, however, with the contrary evidence accumulated by exploration always subordinate to the mythic force that revised it. As he embarked for New Mexico in 1599, Juan de Oñate struck the common chord in a missive to the king: "I trust in God that I shall give your majesty a new world, greater than New Spain."[18]

As exploration and conquest continued, mythological cities of American origin began to compete with those generated by the transculturation of European myths. Paitití, a fabulous Inca city located in the Amazon, was typical in its absorption of elements from gilded utopias that preceded it. When friars near Puno asked the meaning of the word *Paitití* in the seventeenth century, natives responded that it referred to a river beside which exiled Incas founded "a huge settlement."[19] The White House or White Palace of Paitití was believed to be the "magnificent and opulent Court of a powerful Kingdom," but its whereabouts were unknown until an itinerant Franciscan claimed to have been inside. A 1670 expedition was dispatched pursuant to the friar's report that in the palace "there was nothing more ordinary nor more abundant than gold," but when the discoveries were again limited to "so many tribes of poor Indians" the friar's claims were attributed to visions.[20] God may reveal his secrets to the prophets, but to have a vision is not to have seen. The visionary's map hovers above its discoveries and leads only back to its source.

Modern Andean traditions hold that the Incas fled to Paitití during conquest, founding there a kind of mythic Vilcabamba in which the Inca regime was preserved. In Paitití everything of use is made of gold, the only work is to extract it, and the residents live immortally. Andeans subscribing to a trinitarian periodization of history relate that the Incas in Paitití will emerge when the age of the Holy Spirit commences.[21] Israelites of the New Covenant, themselves awaiting the millennium in Amazon retreats, claim to know such Incas hidden in the jungle.[22] At the end of time, the Israelites and the Incas of Paitití will together be transported on "flying chariots of fire" to a valley irrigated by a "foamy river of milk."[23]

Among the many efforts to locate Paitití were the adventures of the "Inca" Pedro Bohorques. In 1659 this Spanish soldier claimed descent from Manco Capac, took the name Inca Huallpa, and reigned among the Calchaquíes near Tucumán. Having heard of treasures hidden by Manco Capac in Paitití, Bohorques, "carried on the shoulders of the Indians, like the old Incas of Peru," set out in search of the kingdom. He "only found the miserable nation of the Pelados" and established his monarchy among these people who "obeyed and adored" him, partially because he kept out the Jesuits. Bohorques remained among the Pelados for more than two years as he searched for Paitití, but his effort failed and his reign concluded grimly with his arrest and decapitation in Lima.[24]

Also prominent among the lost kingdoms of American origin is the enchanted City of the Césars, which emerged in sixteenth-century traditions and is preserved in modern Chilean folklore. In 1524 Sebastian Cabot left Spain in command of a fleet to the Pacific, but his plans were changed when storms obliged a delay in southern Brazil. Shipwrecked sailors stranded on the coast related tales of the White King and his Mountain of Silver, now at the end of the Paraná River, and Cabot led an expedition to locate them. He returned in 1529 without success, but under the command of captain Francisco César he sent fourteen men farther inland "to discover the mines of gold and silver and other riches."[25] Six or seven of them survived to submit the pro forma reports "of gold and of silver and precious stones and other things" equally wondrous.[26]

Rumor held that the soldiers who never returned from the expedition either founded the City of the Césars or were welcomed into a community of sophisticated natives "very rich in silver and gold."[27] The city, named after Francisco César, then experienced a demographic explosion as the census of folklore populated it with Europeans shipwrecked in the Strait of Magellan; exiled Incas, like those of Paitití; and a new and mysterious civilization formed by the intermarriage of these peoples. Spaniards in the city had forgotten their mother tongue over the years, but they persevered in their allegiance to pope and king.[28]

Various eighteenth-century accounts added embellishments worthy of Marco Polo. Some claimed that the City of the Césars was fortified, that it was accessed by a drawbridge across a mote, and that its immortal residents sat on gold and silver chairs. The buildings were incomparable, silver was so plentiful that even shovels were made of it, and the streets were paved in bars of gold and silver. Others described "a mountain of gold and another of diamonds" situated "in the middle of a great lagoon," where the residents were "white and blond people who do not speak Spanish." A 1707 account added that the weather was so temperate and illness so rare "that the people die of pure old age." More ambitious chroniclers maintained that the contemporary inhabitants were identical to those who founded the utopia, because "in the City of the Césars no one is born and no one dies." All that lacked to perfect the realm were more colonists eager to "extract so much wealth."[29]

On Good Friday, the "spatio-temporal point in which life becomes death in order to emerge as superior life," one can see glowing in the distance the gilded skyline of the enchanted City of the Césars.[30] In exemplary homage to the poetics of the dissipating image, however, explorers and travelers remain unaware of the city even when they have stumbled upon it. A thick fog shrouds perceptions and seals in a mystery that will not be violated. No one can discover the city even when trespassing within its boundaries, and whoever does somehow enter loses memory of the route that led there. A protective amnesia also reconditions the residents, who forget their past upon arrival to the city, "and if they someday leave it, they forget what they have seen." Dissociation safeguards the sacrosanct realm from incursions that would undermine it. When the enchantment of the City of the Césars is violated, "it will be the last day of the world."[31]

In both Paitití and the City of the Césars, an inaccessible utopia becomes the repository of deaths, failures, and defeats that are denied by inverting them into their antitheses. The inhabitants of both cities, all dead or doomed in the historical accounts, are resurrected to receive in myth a princely compensation. They inhabit a paradise beyond mortality, enjoy a wealth beyond exhaustion, and live in unprecedented (sometimes interracial) harmony because they live in the beyond, out of range of both corruption and verification. Like heaven hereafter, these utopias grant an eternity of grace, with the excessively material nature of the gains attesting to the poverty from which they are conceived. Both myths blend European traditions regenerated by contact with indigenous traditions of messianic return. The Césars myth seems to absorb Paitití as the realm of exiled Incas, and its hybrid utopianism is reinforced by the intermarriage of the two saving remnants—Spanish survivors and escaped Incas—who create the new humanity. Race mixing is permitted insofar as the genetics breed the quintessential Caucasian ("white and blond"), and cultural syncretism is lauded insofar as the symbols that guarantee Western civilization—pope and king—remain intact.

A Roaming Locus

The Aztecs held that their ancestors migrated from Aztlán, suffered unbearable hardships as they searched for their sacred homeland, and concluded their quest with the founding of Tenochtitlán on an island in Lake Texcoco. The ritual that imbued this epicenter of emerging theocracy with significance was also registered in myth by the heart of a sacrificed enemy thrown into the center of the lake, the "heart of the altar," where the sacrificial cult that venerated Huitzilopochtli would be based. The migrating Aztecs knew that their journey had ended when they saw an eagle nesting on a great nopal cactus growing out of stone. An image in the *Códice Azcatitlán* united the predominant themes by rooting the nopal, on which Huitzilopochtli is represented, in the body of a sacrificial victim. The homeland is integrally related to the divine mission that will be carried out there, with the people, the place, and the gods interacting to imbue one another with eschatological importance. The promised land was not so much located as created, and migration thereby became a rite of passage from a nomadic anonymity to an entitled identity as a nation of priests and warriors.[32]

Centuries later, Aztlán reappeared as a symbolic construct among Chicanos on the border between cultures in the southwestern United States. The concept was introduced at the First Chicano National Conference in 1969, where a "Spiritual Plan of Aztlán" asserted, "We are a nation, we are a union of people, we are *Aztlán*." Geographically Aztlán represented the region of Mexico ceded to the United States in the 1848 Treaty of Guadalupe Hidalgo, but mythologically it evoked "a paradisiacal region where injustice, evil, sickness, old age, poverty, and misery do not exist." The ostensible political objective of Chicano nationalism was to recover the Southwest lost to Manifest Destiny, but the unlikely realization of that mission has accentuated the millennial and "spiritual" meanings of Aztlán as a promised land and unifying principle. The geographical locale becomes the "spiritual homeland" of Chicanos, a nontopical ideal, an inner place of "spiritual union."[33]

Sacred place provides a fixed center from which a people orients itself "in the chaos of homogeneity," deriving privileged uniqueness from amorphous sameness and "founding the world" anew.[34] The egocentric universe of the individual extends into the ethnocentric universe of a culture. The Aztecs "manipulated segments of the cosmological and historical tradition in order to place themselves and their deity Huitzilopochtli at the center of universal space and time."[35] Tenochtitlán became "the foundation of heaven" and "the root, the navel and the heart" of the world.[36] The Incas similarly established their capital, Cuzco, as the center of the world revealed to ancestors by deity. A modern Andean myth elaborated on the designation of body parts, with Lake Titicaca as the vulviform canal from which Peru was born, Cuzco as the palpitating heart, Lima—locus of discourse and devouring power—as the mouth, and conquering Spain as the right hand.[37]

In Judeo-Christian tradition the sacred center, Jerusalem, was also founded theocratically. Under David and Solomon, Jerusalem became the holy dwelling of Yahweh, establishing the pre-Christian city as "the center and foundation" of "a divinely appointed order that had ceaselessly to be defended against the agents of chaos."[38] When Jesus made Jerusalem illustrious by his coming, beautified by his presence, consecrated by his suffering, redeemed by his death, and glorified by his burial, as Pope Urban II put it in 1095, it then became "the navel of the world" and the "royal city at the center of the world."[39] Jerusalem was accordingly situated at the center of the medieval mappamundi, while other traditions disregarded the aridity to exalt Jerusalem in Edenic terms as "the land fruitful above all others, like another paradise of delights."[40]

Jerusalem later became a roaming prototype for a variety of holy and promised lands in the New World. The New Jerusalems established by religious movements metaphorically regained the holy city twice, first as replicas of the symbolically laden historical Jerusalem and again as earthly rehearsals for the perpetually imminent celestial city. The New World as the end of the world made it the opportune landing pad for the New Jerusalem's descent from the sky. Meditating on the conquered Tenochtitlán, Motolinía wrote, "You were once Babylon, full of confusion and evil; now you are another Jerusalem, the mother of provinces and kingdoms."[41] Elaboration of the Indians as descendants of the lost tribes of Israel reinforced the link between the New World and the New Jerusalem, notably in the ponderings of Agustín de Betancur at the end of the seventeenth century. Following a tally of twelve religious "families" in Mexico, Betancur mixed metaphors to celebrate his noble city as "a new Jerusalem with twelve gates through which to enter the Jerusalem of triumph." The "twelve tribes of Israel" are "twelve precious stones" that "shine like stars in the crown of the woman of Apocalypse."[42] Symbolic architecture also made a contribution, with the decorative columns and capitals of at least one Franciscan church in Mexico apparently modeled on those of the Temple of Jerusalem.[43] Retaliatory New Jerusalems then emerged in syncretic nativism, as for example a Zoque cult in Chiapas used the name to describe the inner sanctum of a cave where the apostates' gods were worshiped.[44]

Modern sects tend to ground their apocalyptic Christianity in towns construed as New Jerusalems and surrounded, on occasion, by environs biblicized to match. In late-nineteenth-century Brazil, the messianic Cícero Romão Batista "transformed" Joazeiro into the Holy Land, renaming places with such laden signifiers as Mount of Olives, Calvary, and Garden of the Holy Sepulcher.[45] Pilgrims arrived by the thousands for "the imminence of a new Redemption," because from Joazeiro "new Apostles will march" as they did from the first Jerusalem following Jesus.[46] In the 1960s, another Brazilian sect believed that the New Jerusalem would "be raised up from nothing by a new Noah."[47] The same connection was central to a Mexican sect, known as both the New Jerusalem and the New Ark of Salvation, founded in Michoacán in 1973 when the Virgin of the Rosary announced the end of the world to a campesina. Creation would be consumed by flames, but the Virgin intended to spare the sect and its holy city by lifting them into heaven. This ascension inverted the customary descent of New Jerusalem from the sky, which in the interim was represented by the sect's holy center as "a piece of heaven on earth."[48] Cities here and hereafter have also intermingled in such politico-religious programs as Guatemala's sixteen-month "march toward the New Jerusalem" behind the dictator Efraín Ríos Montt.[49]

The Amazon has been particularly rich in holy towns conceived as New Jerusalems. The predominantly indigenous residents dislocate from an alien and demeaning national context to reestablish themselves at the no-place where they live by their millennial ideals.[50] The Brazilian sect known as the Doctrina del Santo Daime accesses a sacred inner "place" as prelude to entry into its New Jerusalem geographically conceived. Ingestion of the hallucinogenic Daime (ayahuasca), which is referred to as "taking communion" and includes a ritual "decontamination," fosters visions of the Virgin of the Conception and revelations concerning the salvation of humanity.[51] Holy towns, such as Céu do Mapiá, were founded pursuant to divine mandates, and therein the material "world of illusion" dissolved as the faithful entered the invisible world of spirituality, guided by doctrine and psychotropic visions. In the Doctrina del Santo Daime, New Jerusalem referred not only to the holy city of Revelation concretized on earth by the community but also to the "spiritual state" and "superior self" in which the sect members likewise found paradise.[52]

The New Jerusalem is also integral to the message of Ezequiel Ataucusi Gamonal, a "New Moses" followed by "Israelites." One of the principle Israelite hymns, "Privileged Peru," summarizes the sect's belief that Peru became the New Jerusalem when the messiah, Ataucusi, appeared there to introduce the new covenant: "Scripture says Christ will return / All is fulfilled, Christ is already here."[53] Many Israelites withdraw to holy towns in the jungle to rehearse the life anticipated beyond the apocalypse, but in the broader view of Ataucusi's mystical nationalism. Privileged Peru in its entirety is a holy land. A sacred place grounds the relations by which humanity and deity reciprocally re-create one another, and the place itself is transformed by those relations. As the paradigm shifts, the center of the universe moves with it.

Peoples that do not invest their homelands with religious meanings often make pilgrimages to place themselves in contact with the sacred. Presence at the holy site transfers supernatural graces to the pilgrims, and this exchange is enhanced by touching or ingesting spiritually charged objects and liquids. In some cases, such as the Andean pilgrimages to mountain peaks, the ambience itself is divinized; in others, a representation or manifestation of deity—images, miracles, apparitions—sanctifies the site. Santiago de Compostela in the Old World and the shrine of the Virgin of Guadalupe in the New are outstanding examples, the former housing Santiago's remains and the latter commemorating the Virgin's apparition. As time passes, the sites are sanctified not by the historical validity of their claims but by the very pilgrimages they generate. The process begins with spontaneous responses to the discovery of relics, the visions of shepherds, the blood of martyrs, the preaching of hermits. Espinazo, an inconsequential Mexican village, became a holy land and site of international pilgrimage when Niño Fidencio performed miraculous cures there.

When the New Jerusalem is slow in descending, Old Testament persecutions and promised lands provide alternative biblical models for interpreting oppression. Religious suffering is an experience of pain but also a protest against it, and senseless agony becomes purposeful once integrated into God's plan for redemption.[54] Franciscans in Mexico compared the conquered natives to Israelites oppressed in Egypt under the pharaoh, and Guaman Poma discerned the same parallel in Peru, inviting Andeans to plead for deliverance as the Israelites had in Egypt. When deliverance arrived in 1780, Túpac Amaru II compared himself to Moses and David, Peru to Israel, and the empire to an Egypt where the Andeans suffered under "many Pharaohs."[55] With a stick and a sling a humble young shepherd, David, "liberated the unfortunate people of Israel from Goliath and the Pharaoh," and Túpac Amaru, dwarfed by his rival, intended to do the same.[56] The protagonists of the 1781 Comunero Revolution also saw themselves as "the instrument of Divine Providence's will" to castigate the guilty and "to lead the suffering people of New Granada from the oppression of Pharaoh to the Promised Land."[57]

In modern Latin America, Nicaraguan revolutionaries of the 1930s subscribed to Joaquín Trincado's musings on the hispanic people as new Israelites and America as the promised land that Moses consigned to his successor, Amerigo Vespucci.[58] The Exodus narrative of Moses leading his people from oppression was later one of the popular didactic models used in liberation theology's base communities. A Salvadoran campesino characteristically compared his plight to that of the Israelites, because "Moses had to struggle to take them out of Egypt to the Promised Land." He summarized the resemblance of his people's hardships with those recounted in Exodus and concluded, "Our struggle is the same: Moses and his people had to cross the desert as we are crossing one right now; and for me, I find that we are crossing a desert full of a thousand hardships, of hunger, of misery and of exploitation."[59] With "deliverance" by the Sandinistas in 1979, Nicaraguans passed "through the Red Sea, leaving slavery behind in order to walk to the Promised Land."[60]

Relocation of the sacred center is expedient in the foundation of new polities seeking autonomy and legitimacy. As Francisco de la Cruz explained to the Inquisition in 1578, "Rome has been the head of the Catholic Church up to now, so from now on Lima will be."[61] The Church must be returned to the people of Israel, meaning the peoples of the Indies, and Fray Francisco as king, pope, and archbishop would be "the first head of this new Church of Israel."[62] Fray Francisco was the "figure of our Lord Jesus Christ, of his death and resurrection in glory, as was David before the coming of Christ," and accordingly he would die, resurrect "in imitation of our Lord," and assume responsibility for "the reduction of the people of Israel to the faith."[63]

This precocious separatism came of age in nineteenth-century independence discourse that envisioned an American utopia free of all European domination, including that of the Vatican. A voluminous treatise by the Peruvian priest Francisco de Paula González Vigil defended American civil and religious authorities from the "pretensions" of the Roman curia.[64] The ideal of an American Church purified of European vice similarly appealed to the clerical leadership of the 1810 struggle for independence in Mexico.[65] Liberation theologians continue this tradition into the present when they unambiguously assert that "Europe is no longer the center of Christian history. Latin America is."[66]

The "recuperated" New World was romanticized as a promised land in a flurry of benedictions, from José Martí's "our America" (and its extension into the Cuban Revolution) to José Vasconcelos's explicit description of America as "the true Christian promised land."[67] The Chilean Jesuit Manuel Lacunza intermingled familiar Edenic and millennial ideals to envision a Christ-governed, thousand-year kingdom in which the righteous of South America would "inhabit a city of delights as rich and splendid as that described by St. John in the Apocalypse."[68] For Rubén Darío, America was "the future of the world," and in the more explicitly messianic assertion of Francisco Pí y Margall, America was "called to save the world."[69] Simón Rodríguez believed that More's "Utopia will be, in reality, America," and Pedro Henríquez Ureña argued that "true freedom" will lead, "at last, toward our utopia." Modern humanity inherited from the Greeks "the restlessness of constantly perfecting ourselves," and the American contribution would "return to utopia its essentially human and spiritual characteristics." Once the "absurd economic organization in which we are prisoners" is escaped, humanity will be "open to the four winds of the spirit."[70]

Utopianism acquired messianic attributes as immigrants bailed out of the degenerate Old World and forged a conception of the Americas consonant with the redemption that they anticipated. A new people founded itself at a new political center, staking its claim to terrain, grounding its mission, divesting itself of the past, and aspiring to a world worthy of its ideals. The utopian ambitions of immigrants to Latin America were registered in place names—Puerto Alegre, Ciudad Paraíso, Puerto Eden, Jauja, Valparaíso, New World—but when that dream faltered their descendants began an updated exodus to the north, surrounded by scores of campesinos.[71] The impoverished immigrants and refugees who made it across the border then discovered a rude reality incapable of accommodating the myth of "el Norte" as a promised land. The land had already been promised to someone else, reducing new allotments of the American dream to precarious footholds on the margins.

Utopia and Subversion

In the golden age, as Hesiod described it, people "lived like gods, without sorrow of heart, remote and free from toil and grief; miserable age rested not on them; but, with legs and arms never failing, they made merry with feasting, beyond the reach of all evils."[72] The Romans adapted the golden age to Saturn's reign over the new creation, and humans again "enjoyed a leisurely and peaceful existence," while fields "untouched by the hoe, unfurrowed by any share, produced all things spontaneously."[73] Eden similarly offered a life that was "entirely happy" and "carried on without any labor," with the leisure and luxury enhanced by perpetual springtime, the bounty of "every tree that is pleasant to the sight, and good for food," and rivers that, according to the pseudo-Paul, flow with wine, milk, oil, and honey.[74] Later embellishments endowed Eden with attributes from Isaiah's peaceable kingdom and with generous allotments of this-worldly treasures.

After 1492, Edenic and golden-age ideals were projected onto the pristine landscape and noble savages of the Americas, particularly in the tropics. Some chronicles, such as that of an Augustinian describing Mexico, privileged the biblical model: "Just as in Paradise He created the plants in growth and the fruits all ripened, so in the gardens of this new Paradise He did not delay in ordering the imperfect to the perfect."[75] In 1514 Peter Martyr favored the Greek model when he observed that the natives of Hispaniola "go naked and know neither weights nor measures, nor that source of all misfortune, money: living in a golden age, without laws, without lying judges, without books." Everything among them was common property and all happily shared the abundance because there was no sense of "mine and thine."[76] The longevity and natural law that were frequently attributed to noble savages were combined in the caption of a 1505 German woodcut: they "live to be one-hundred and fifty years old and they have no government."[77] The inhabitants of the prelapsarian New World enjoyed perpetual youth and effortless harvest of the earth's bounty, exempt from the "sweat of the brow" that came with Adam's life sentence to hard labor.

This indigenous idyll of toil-free luxury was necessarily disrupted by colonists seeking free labor. Slavery and *encomiendas* (grants of native labor) transferred the work-free plenty to Europeans, and the profits were redoubled by myths of "money growing trees" and riches that, having awaited centuries to be "discovered," offered themselves in gratitude and relief.[78] Such was a dream come true for the seventeenth-century Spanish *pícaro* (rogue), whose slogan was "We want to eat without working."[79] Even before the great empires handed over their treasures and the mountains of silver revealed themselves, placer gold deposits in Hispaniola made the coveted metal almost miraculously accessible "without having to dig for it." If Spaniards were "in a state of Grace," then God "would give them more freely the temporal and spiritual goods they sought."[80] This Edenic entitlement to effortless bounty later extended into the "delightful city" of modern Chilean folk poetry, where the chickens are walking cold cuts; the rivers run with brandy, milk, chicha, and wine; and "the pigs made ham / wander in the pasture / each with its sign / that says, 'Carve me up, sir.' "[81]

Work-free paradises are also prominent in indigenous traditions that prophesy the restoration of primordial fecundity and prosperity. The Maya's *Popol Vuh* characteristically related that a mattock stuck into the ground tends to cultivation, while the axe "cut into the tree by itself."[82] Prophets of a sixteenth-century rebellion in Mexico assured that even "pines would bear squash and corn," and others similarly promised that hungry Indians worked to death would be the recipients of effortless abundance.[83] Crops ripen spontaneously, fish jump out of the water into nets, and game presents itself humbly for the banquet.

"It would be dangerous to ignore it," Pope Paul VI argued, "the invocation of utopia is frequently a comfortable pretext of those who wish to evade concrete tasks in order to take refuge in an imaginary world."[84] The infallibility of ex cathedra pontification here coincides with a viable position, but the invocation of utopia lends itself just as readily to decisive, subversive action to replace an inadequate order with an envisioned one that improves or supersedes it. The urge for utopia is "a necessary condition of historical change," "the power which changes reality," and "the tension which thrusts humanity beyond every calm and security into new insecurity and unrest."[85] Utopia renders the present necessarily inferior to the idealized future against which it is measured. It is predicated on rejection of a dominant model that it escapes antithetically by perfecting its inverted complement. Many early modern utopias—beginning with Thomas More's—were "a sort of anti-Europe" devised through corrective renovation, and they therefore found their fortuitous locale in a New World viewed as pristine.[86] The same was true in indigenous American cases exemplified by the Land-without-Evil, which was conceived as the "counter-order" of a society itself regarded as evil.[87]

In the new Christianity fostered by liberation theology, utopianism is the "driving force of history" that fosters a "radical transformation." As Gustavo Gutiérrez summarized his position, "faith and political action will not enter into a correct and fruitful relationship except through the effort to create a new type of person in a different society, that is, except through utopia."[88] Leonardo Boff argued similarly that hope and grace catalyze "historical efforts at dissent, transformation, and the construction of utopian models of reality." Unlike Paul VI, however, Boff hastened to add that "these models are not escape mechanisms. They are forces stimulating people to make alterations that will bring their forms of life ever closer to utopia."[89] (Gutiérrez concurred: "Far from making the political struggler a dreamer," utopia "radicalizes his commitment.")[90] The once oppressed, now glorified Jesus is the realization of the utopian promise, "the sign that our struggles and hopes for total liberation are not condemned to fade into the distance of some unrealized utopia. No, the Christian utopia becomes radiant, brimming *topos*. It acquires a local habitation and a Name."[91] Christ's resurrection guarantees that "the humiliated, the rejected, have a future," and therefore "suddenly utopia is real."[92]

Utopians regarded social discord as a consequence of the privatization of wealth long before Pierre-Joseph Proudhon popularized the slogan "Property is theft," and consequently they envisioned new societies without the divisive distinctions of mine and thine. Elimination of private property as the root of evil—materialism, greed, envy, inequality, crime—was essential to Plato's *Republic*, More's *Utopia*, and Campanella's *City of the Sun*, to mention only a few of the classics.[93] Early Christianity likewise required forfeiture or common ownership of possessions, and the communal harmony forged by disregard for materialism later became the model for monastic orders.[94] The New Jerusalem at the end of history also promises a classless, egalitarian society, as did the "profoundly subversive" age of the Holy Spirit introduced by Joachim of Fiore.[95] ("Where grace is," Joachim maintained, "law is abolished.")[96] In the indigenous Americas, such communal land holdings as the *ayllu* of "Incan communism" were complemented by the more informal socialism and communal property of nonimperial peoples.

Despite its basis in capitalism, modern democracy also has an essential "utopian dimension" in its promise of freedom, equality, and justice for all.[97] In stark contrast to the socialism emphasized in classical utopias, however, the dominant cultures of the late twentieth century (like those of the sixteenth) have pursued the myth of progress into a materialist utopia that privileges select aspects of utopianism—luxury and abundance, for example—while deemphasizing or dismissing the abolition of private property, the subordination of individual interests to the common good, and the centrality of value and moral codes. Early suggestions that this manufactured utopia ultimately self-destructs included the Cuban missile crisis (interpreted apocalyptically in religious quarters) and, more generally, the chronic social and environmental symptoms of a carcinogenic environment that corrodes itself from within. The fetishistic adoration of technology has created a virtual utopia that profoundly alters human interests, values, perceptions, and identity. Postmodern capitalism as "the pretension to construct a perfect, heavenly world on earth" might thus "produce its opposite, the most frightening hell" as it empties its past into disposable receptacles fashioned by trends of the market.[98] The disenfranchised indigenous masses who have converged upon Latin American cities contribute to that countereffect as they seek integration into an outdated dream that their very presence subverts. They have no more a share in the capitalist utopia than they do in the democracy that purports to represent them, but from the fringes their own utopian ideal vacillates between entering and overturning the society that excludes them.

In the nineteenth century, Latin American intellectuals contested bourgeois materialism to propose the loftier ideals of a spiritual, cultural, enlightened world driven by human aspirations more noble than consumption. Pursuant to European trends they envisioned a new humanity that would overhaul society to create "a moral commonwealth where the individual will harmonizes perfectly with the general will." Utopian theory was founded on the premise that "there is nothing in man, nature or society that cannot be so ordered as to bring about a more or less permanent state of material plenty, social harmony and individual fulfillment." Robert Owen's 1813 *A New View of Society* was characteristic in its conviction that "humanity is perfectible."[99] A debt to Christianity was later acknowledged when Owen equated the "Great Advent of the World" and the "second coming of Christ" with the spread of his social philosophy, "for Truth and Christ are one and the same." "I therefore now proclaim to the world the commencement, on this day, of the promised millennium, founded on rational principles and consistent practice."[100]

While serving as Mexican ambassador to London in 1828, Vicente Rocafuerte received a letter from Robert Owen, who had just returned from the United States after the failure of his New Harmony colony in Indiana. Owen requested that Mexico cede the province of Texas y Coahuila to carry out a new experiment that would, as he put it, cause "a radical change in human nature." In his report to the Mexican government Rocafuerte commended the theory but rejected the project as impractical and unrealizable, "although it is very beautiful, very plausible, and very philanthropic on paper."[101] Owen argued that the creation of the new humanity was impossible under previous gubernatorial and social systems, and that therefore "a new region is needed in which the known laws, institutions and preoccupations do not exist, in order to found this new state of society." The relatively undeveloped border region of Texas would be the "most appropriate point on the globe" to commence "the regeneration of the human race's way of being." The new society would end political and commercial rivalry and the wars they generate, putting into practice the dictum "Peace on earth and good will toward men."[102]

At the end of the century, Albert Kinsey Owen, an engineer from the United States, similarly envisioned a Mexican utopia, in this case the "Socialist Metropolis of the West" that he would establish on the Gulf of California in Topolobampo. The Metropolis would be "an ideal community—with an ideal people that would forever struggle for the ideal life, the ideal religion, the ideal home," and, in short, "the ideal of perfection." The first three hundred residents arrived from New York in 1886, but nine years later economic collapse and epidemics brought the experiment to an end.[103]

Under the influence of Robert Owen, Claude-Henri de Saint-Simon, Charles Fourier, Mikhail Bakunin, Karl Marx, and Friedrich Engels, immigrants to Latin America applied utopian theory to socialist, anarchist, and communal projects. The New World was still viewed as a virginal expanse more conducive to utopianism than was decadent Europe, and in this regard the nineteenth-century utopians revived in secular guise the social experiments conducted earlier by missionaries. The primary difference, excepting those resulting from the respective religious and secular intentions, was demographic: the utopian communities were almost exclusively populated by immigrants segregated from local people and affairs, whereas the missions were founded and governed by Europeans but populated by natives. Foreign utopians arrived even from Australia, establishing in Paraguay the communist Cosme Colony of the mid-1890s.[104] Paraguay was also the site of New Germania, a short-lived Aryan colony founded in 1886.[105]

Among the most prominent commune experiments was the Cecilia Colony in Paraná, Brazil, founded in 1892 by a group of Italian anarchists under the direction of Giovanni Rossi. The lands and support for this colony were donated by Brazil's emperor Pedro II, who, following Rossi's failed attempt near Cremona, suggested that "what is difficult in Italy is realizable in Brazil." The colony was established in remote desert terrain at Palmeira and Genoese residents began arriving in 1890, but by 1893 the project ended in economic failure. Rossi cited limited capital, inexperienced farmers, and isolation as the reasons. "We enjoyed freedom in our internal relations, but we lacked material well-being, and man esteems and desires something more than what he possesses."[106]

Other utopian projects were conducted by various designs and in diverse regions, but the conclusion in failure was consistent. Early efforts in Mexico included Francisco Severo Maldonado's blueprint for a utopia seeking "economic equality" and the 1825 attempt by José María Alpudre, a priest and senator, to found a socialist community among Freemasons.[107] Victor Considérant lost the family fortune on a phalanx in the border region of Texas in 1854, and utopian agricultural communities were organized in Peru in 1884. More common than these intents to put theory into practice was the parlor utopianism that flourished among Europeans with Latin American ties (such as Flora Tristán) and Latin Americans who returned from Europe entranced by utopian socialism (such as Esteban Echeverría). In 1855 the Brazilian "general of the masses," José Ignacio de Abreu e Lima, formerly a soldier under Simón Bolívar, published *Socialism*, the most extensive utopian treatise of the period. The general maintained that socialism is not a science, a doctrine, a religion, or a sect, but rather "the design of Providence" for the human race to become "a single and immense family."[108]

Also outstanding in the genre was the *Socialist Primer*, published in 1861, in which the Greco-Mexican Plotino C. Rhodakanaty advocated a Christianized Fourierist socialism. Rhodakanaty opened his work, presented as a "catechism," with the premise that socialism was the doctrine of Jesus and that the socialist "dream of the visionaries" was now "taking on the form of reality."[109] The theory was applied in a center for socialist studies, a "humanitarian society," workers unions and movements, and, in Chalco, a socialist school complemented by an attempted agricultural commune. The Chalco activities also engendered a brief 1869 insurrection headed by Julio César Chávez to free "all of the oppressed and poor peoples of Mexico and the Universe." Chávez took his dream to the grave, screaming, "Long live socialism" as he was shot by a firing squad.[110]

"The philosophers have only *interpreted* the world, in various ways," Marx asserted in the "Theses on Feuerbach"; "the point, however, is to *change* it."[111] Utopian efforts toward that end were "necessarily doomed to failure" according to Marx and Engels, because utopians were both impatient and disinclined to revolution. Utopian theorists erroneously expected that "historical action is to yield to their personal inventive action, historically created conditions to emancipation of fantastic ones, and the gradual, spontaneous class-organisation of the proletariat to the organisation of society specially contrived by these inventors." Although the founders of utopian movements are in some sense revolutionary, the isolationist nature of the communes results in "mere reactionary sects" that comprise disciples who follow the sacrosanct doctrine of their master "in opposition to the progressive historical development of the proletariat."[112] Marx thus dismissed as "pure fantasy" the ambitions of such prophetic utopians as Saint-Simon, Fourier, and Robert Owen, who as "alchemists of revolution" tried to institute socialism before the necessary historical conditions were present. While utopians were envisioning ideal societies, Marx and Engels were discovering the "law of motion" by which history itself would deliver utopia as its final accomplishment.[113]

Return to the Future

Utopia is generated by the tension between a present reality, a past ideal, and a future paradigm of perfection.[114] The myths of a golden age or paradise that many traditions situate at the beginning and end of time render history a process of recovery, a detoured return to "the perfect and pure world of the 'Beginning,' when it had just been finished by the Creator."[115] The lost past inexhaustibly replicates itself until the elusive kingdom comes, imbuing linear eschatology with a sense of cyclicity. Judaism left behind cyclical time when Yahweh insinuated himself into history, but Christianity recuperated the past in the future, Eden in New Jerusalem, with Christ and the Virgin as the new Adam and Eve.[116]

Recuperation of the past is at once reactionary and radical, at once a rearview retrieval of a defiled ideal and a revolutionary commitment to renovation. Millennial movements enact reform as restoration, appealing to a "purposeful past" not so much temporal as ideological, a fabricated precedent that legitimates, a "refuge of prohibited desires."[117] Like the discourse of the dead (ancestors, mummies, saints) interpreted by the living, the past speaks a malleable message adaptable to diverse purposes.

One of the most sustained endeavors of recuperation among native peoples has been the quest to restore a mythologized Tahuantinsuyo. According to the indigenist writer Virgilio Roel Pineda, time is cyclical and also cumulative, because "the past continues to exercise an influence on the present" and "the present holds the seed of the future." The restoration of Tahuantinsuyo is guaranteed by temporal cycles: "just as there was a time of invasion and conquest, so also there will be a time of liberation and reconquest." Pachacuti and "the law of eternal return" will deliver a "Second Tahuantinsuyo," but in both colonial and modern nativism "Tahuantinsuyo" refers more to a preconquest, primordial ideal than to the historical reign of the Incas.[118] It is not the empire that is recovered, but rather the autonomy, status, and prosperity that it represents.

In the 1920s, millennial anticipation radicalized Andean campesinos when the Tahuantinsuyo Committee for Indigenous Rights announced the restoration of a just government "similar to that of the Inca epoch."[119] One of the movement's delegates was the driving force behind revolts on cattle ranches, where his intent was reportedly "to destroy everything and restore the empire of Tahuantinsuyo and the cult of the sun."[120] The leader of a related uprising would modernize imperial sovereignty after liberation by proclaiming himself "President of the Inca Republic."[121] That failing, a compromise solution was later offered by the APRA party, promoting itself as a resumption of "the truncated project of the Incas" and a return to "the Social Justice of Tahuantinsuyo."[122] Something of the same mood characterized the cooperative, utopian Tahuantinsuyo proposed in the early 1960s by the Cuzco labor leader Emiliano Huamantica, who envisioned harmonious union of all races and classes "as in the time of our Inca forefathers."[123] A "second Tahuantinsuyo" was also on the agenda of the Peruvian Indian Movement, whose "Inca-inspired socialism" would redeem indigenous peoples from the subjugation and destitution of neocolonialism.[124]

In other quarters, a return to the future was rendered poetically by fountains of youth that anticipated in miniature the corporal immortality afforded by paradise. Each individual who drank of or bathed in these baptismal-like waters entered a new age of agelessness, a "victory of eternity over time."[125] The future (old age) was displaced to the past (youth), where it hovered in perpetuity. In the absence of such waters, utopian medicine intervened for the residents of Campanella's City of the Sun, who knew a secret for rejuvenating life after seventy. The first edition of Francis Bacon's *New Atlantis* included an appendix cataloguing the benefits of science, with the list headed by "the prolongation of life," "the restitution of youth in some degree," and "the retardation of age."[126] The desire for perpetual youth in modern times has made lucrative not only formal medicine (including cosmetic surgery) but also the trade in potions, aerosols, soaps, salves, and other hocus-pocus paraphernalia that claim to postpone the inevitable. One such rejuvenating elixir was marketed in Brazil in 1967 by José López Rega, an adviser to Juan and Isabel Perón. The label featured an image of the robust Juan Perón captioned by the slogan, "He stays young because he drinks this medicine."[127]

The first extant mention of the Fountain of Youth was in the twelfth-century letter attributed to Prester John, which reported that anyone who drank from a spring near Paradise would "always be as a man thirty two years old, however long he may live."[128] From his armchair journeys John Mandeville similarly described a "noble and beautiful well," known as the Well of Youth, whose water originated in Eden. Anyone who drinks of the well three times on an empty stomach "will be healed of whatever malady he has. And therefore those who live near that well drink of it very often, and so they are never ill but always seem young."[129] In other medieval versions the old, the infirm, the lame are brought to an idyllic pool and "naked, bathing in the regenerative water, they emerge healed, young, happy, and ready for dances, feasting, and love."[130] The restored virility was also duly noted in Peter Martyr's 1587 *Decades of the New World*, which gave the first account of Juan Ponce de León's expeditions. The "marvelous virtue" of these waters "makes old men young again," and in one case an islander "grievously oppressed with old age" was restored to such strength that he engaged in "manly exercises": "he married again and begat children."[131]

The rejuvenating properties of the Fountain of Youth are particularly suggestive given the source of the miraculous waters in Eden. The four rivers of Paradise are traditionally believed to originate beneath the Tree of Life, whose fruit grants immortality to whoever eats it. As explained in Genesis 3:22–24, Adam and Eve were locked out of Paradise precisely to prevent them from eating of this tree—as they had of the Tree of Knowledge—and from thereby gaining the immortality reserved for deity. The medievals reckoned that the waters flowing from Paradise carried its blessings, including rejuvenation, and distributed them throughout fallen creation.[132] Edenic waters were linked symbolically with those of baptism, which rejuvenated through rebirth in Christ, and this equation was reinforced when the apocryphal *The First Book of Adam and Eve* granted waters near Eden the capacity to cleanse sin.[133] The divine properties of Edenic waters were also enhanced by God as "the fountain of living waters," and by Jesus' reference to himself as a spring: "if anyone thirst, let him come to me and drink."[134] The fountain as the source of the four rivers in Eden, the refreshing fountain in the Renaissance courtyard, and the fountain of the baptismal font all contributed to the composite image of a fountain of "living waters" that restored youth.[135] As water from the Tree of Life slipped past the cherubim guarding Eden and flowed into the Fountain of Youth, immortality escaped its confinement to Paradise and nature became, as Peter Martyr put it, almost as powerful as God.[136]

The intermingling of these European traditions with native myths of the regenerative land of Bimini led Ponce de León on the two expeditions (1513 and 1521) that resulted in the discovery of Florida. Rejuvenating waters, lands, and trees were also prevalent in native traditions elsewhere in the Americas. In the Orinoco region the moriche palm was venerated as "the tree of life," and its fruit was the raw material from which the new humanity was created after destruction of the earth by flood. Other indigenous groups revered similar "trees of immortality" that imparted their life-sustaining forces to the rivers that flowed past or beneath them, as in Eden. According to some accounts, natives from Cuba migrated in search of a river with rejuvenating waters where "old men become young."[137] Revitalization was both corporal and cultural when after conquest an apostate native in northern Mexico told skeptics, "Look at me now in this figure of an old man; because tomorrow, having bathed myself in the river, you will see me as a young man. The same will happen to you." According to a Jesuit report, the apostate delivered on his "fiction" and "fraud," "appearing before them in the likeness of a twenty-year-old."[138] Christian baptism was slow in delivering spiritual rebirth, but apostasy literalized it quickly on the body.

Fragmentation and Unity

The medieval and early modern quest for universal monarchy was predicated on the belief that a once unified creation had been fragmented by malevolent forces. Between the thirteenth and fifteenth centuries European Christians hoped to secure an alliance with Oriental rulers in order to consolidate ecumenical Catholicism by mounting a two-fronted assault against Islam. The crusade with an eastern front never materialized, but compensatory legends provided the desired ally in Prester John, the Christian king somewhere in "Ethiopia" or India. Amidst failed crusades and uncertain preparations for a renewed effort, forged letters from Prester John were received around 1165 by emperors and the pope. As worded in the letter to the Byzantine emperor Manuel, "I, Presbyter John, the lord of lords, surpass all others walking beneath the heavens in virtue, wealth and power."[139] The imagined existence of Prester John made the Christian world seem not so much fragmented as divided into eastern and western kingdoms by the insertion of an infidel wedge. The search for this ready, wealthy, and powerful ally endured at least until the end of the fifteenth century, when Vasco da Gama embarked on his famous voyage carrying a letter of credence for Prester John. Mercator's *Atlas* (1569) explained that the elusive monarch "is believed, down to the present time, to be reigning in Asia."[140]

The medieval march toward world unity ran into an unanticipated obstacle when the Columbian and subsequent voyages revealed enormous deficiencies in the European concept of what constituted the whole. Christian scholarship dedicated itself to integration of the missing piece, the "new" world, into traditional geography and cosmology. Chaotic parts were pulled into orbit by the force of dogma, and the obedient interpretation of new data confirmed what tradition had suspected. The slightest "evidence" sufficed to extrapolate fantastic conclusions, as when, for example, a coin found in Tierra Firme led a sixteenth-century historian to conclude that America once belonged to the Roman Empire.[141] Erudite, baroque calculations reformed the new landscape in conformity with old paradigms, rendering Hispaniola both Cipango (Japan) and Ophir, Indies and Antilles, as oriental, biblical, and mythological interpretations competed, confused, and finally synthesized under the rubric of a conceptual reorganization serving orthodoxy, homogeneity, and unity.[142] The guiding principle, as Hernán Pérez de Oliva explained in 1528, was "to unite the world and give to those strange lands the shape of our own."[143]

Christian world unity had been fragmented long before Islam and the discovery of the New World troubled the ecumenical ideal. The dispersion of unified humanity began when Adam and Eve were banished from Paradise, and it was accelerated when God intervened at Babel. According to Genesis 11, "The whole earth was of one language" until God broke up the union to handicap unbecoming collaborations. The united people aspired to godlike enterprises, and consequently "the Lord scattered them abroad from thence upon the face of the earth," giving them mutually incomprehensible languages.

Primordial union followed by separation is also prevalent in indigenous and syncretic traditions. A characteristic myth of origin from the Mataco of the Gran Chaco relates that Christians and natives were originally one and the same, living together in a house that lacked nothing. One sad day, however, the covetous ancestors of modern Christians "took the axes, tools, horses, cattle, and beautiful clothes for the women and went away with them, leaving only clay pots, dogs, and other inferior things for the Mataco."[144] Material wealth and race are also the basis for division in a neo-Joachite myth from the Guatemala highlands. History is periodized in an age of the Father, an age of Jesus Christ, and a post-crucifixion age, and in the first of these "there was no difference in race because only one class of person existed." During the age of Christ, "God permitted the races to differentiate," and consequently "the rich"—here a signifier of race as well as class—began to roam and colonize until eventually a mestizo race emerged as "a mixture of foreigner and native."[145] The ending is happy insofar as the race mixing bodes a modified recuperation of primordial sameness, in conformity with the harmonious reunification of Joachim's third age.

Recovery of the unity lost to sin in Eden became one of the missions of the crucified Christ, and a vigorous mythopoetic cleanup worked retroactively to assure consonance and continuity between the old Adam who doomed humanity and the new Adam who redeemed it. The third-century *Legend of Seth* featured Eden's Tree of Life producing three clones that are felled, hewn, and assembled to make the cross on which Christ was crucified. Variations on the theme have the cross made of the Tree of Knowledge or of a new tree growing from Adam's buried body.[146] One of two sixth-century guidebooks to the Holy Land, the

Breviarius, sought the same unity by transposing the sacred nexus from Eden to Golgotha, where Christ was crucified: "There Adam was formed out of clay; there Abraham offered his own son Isaac in the very place where our Lord Jesus Christ was crucified."[147] In the seventeenth century, many versions converged in Antonio de León Pinelo's *Paradise in the New World*, where Adam's son Seth, at the gate of Paradise by permission of the cherubim guarding it, gathered a few seeds from the tree where his father sinned. Seth planted the seeds in the deceased Adam's mouth, a tree grew with a kind of trinitarian trunk of cedar, cypress, and palm, and the cross of Christ's Passion was later made from this wood.[148] This insistent relation of Adam's sin and Christ's redemptive crucifixion provides metaphorically that the old Adam die on the cross while the new Adam is reborn to renew the covenant and restore primordial union.

World Christian unity, referred to in the Church as ecumenicalism, is based on such biblical passages as John 17:21, where Jesus prays that humanity "may all be one," united in the faith. Ecumenicalism was a priority of Vatican II, and Pope John Paul II likewise emphasized "the restoration of union between all Christians."[149] The Latin American bishops' conference in Puebla conceded that "what is not assumed is not redeemed," but the concept of inculturation—introduced in 1977 and adopted by John Paul in 1979—recognized the multicultural composition of Christendom and sought unity of faith while maintaining cultural diversity.[150] In his address to the natives of Oaxaca and Chiapas, John Paul cited Galatians 3:27–29 to emphasize baptism as the great equalizer: "There is neither Greek nor Jew, slave nor free, male nor female, for you are all one in Jesus Christ."[151]

The political convictions dividing Catholics in Nicaragua brought citation of the same passage during the pope's 1983 "Unity of the Church" sermon in Managua, because "a divided church cannot fulfill its mission." John Paul deemphasized the divisive this-worldly issues to stress "the unity of the church, of the people of God, of the 'flock' of the one shepherd." Pausing occasionally in annoyance to silence a crowd calling for peace, the pope referred to himself as the "foundation of visible unity" and drove home the message of "one Lord, one faith, one baptism" and one God "who is over all and through all and in all."[152]

In the secular conception of José Vasconcelos, humanity evolves toward harmonious unity as the result of racial and cultural blending. The white race established in Latin America "the material and moral bases for the union of all men in a fifth, universal race" that supersedes and is intrinsically superior to all races that preceded it. Cultural syncretism and race mixing will yield "the first synthesis race on the globe," "a race made with the treasure of all those previous to it, the final race, the cosmic race."[153] Early twentieth-century intellectuals in Peru also viewed race mixing as the means to unify the diverse cultures of a fragmented society, and a century earlier the same opinion was expressed by Simón Bolívar: "The blood of our citizens is varied; let it be mixed for the sake of unity."[154] For Pedro Henríquez Ureña, evolution toward such a "universal man" in a "world of utopia" did not necessitate the loss of diversity, because cultural differences would be "conserved and perfected" in the harmonious "voices of the peoples."[155]

Another model for postconquest unity borrowed and recombined the best that indigenous and European cultures had to offer. Were he successful in his 1536–37 resistance, Manco Inca's alleged intent was to drive the Spaniards back to their ships, to reconstitute the Inca state, "and through the Spanish women remaining in Peru, to create a new generation combining the virtues of the two races."[156] One of the Incas at Vilcabamba, Titu Cusi Yupanqui, later converted to Christianity, leading some Cuzco mestizos to envision a new Tahuantinsuyo that would integrate the advantages of European culture.[157] Schemes of improvement by combination were again prevalent as independence began to recuperate, at least in rhetoric, the discounted indigenous past. Francisco de Miranda envisioned independent South America as an Inca empire renovated and improved by "the institutional structures of a constitutional monarchy."[158]

Unity was most readily forged when a common enemy strengthened loose alliances or created new ones. Miguel Hidalgo's message to Mexico—"we only need to unite" to achieve independence—spoke for insurrections and social movements throughout the Americas.[159] In a 1958 "Unity Manifesto" and subsequent statements, Fidel Castro emphasized the unity of disparate interest groups as prerequisite to the military and political success of the revolution. Rival insurgencies elsewhere in Latin America often patched up their differences to make common cause against the state, as in El Salvador and Guatemala in the early 1980s and in Argentina a decade earlier. The transcendentalization of such alliances brought parallel unification of deities in earlier struggles, as epitomized by the federation of huacas in Taqui Onqoy during the 1560s.[160]

Unity as "one of the leit-motifs of Latin American utopian discourse" was most prevalent during the consolidation of republics following independence.[161] Its most notorious advocate was Simón Bolívar, who in conformity with a common messianic pattern first fragmented the unity of a status quo and then served as the agent of a modified reunification. Bolívar argued that rupture must precede union, and accordingly he undermined imperial monarchy and then attempted to restore political stability by establishing a federation of American states.[162] Bolívar's Gran Colombia would comprise Venezuela, New Granada, and Ecuador and would subsequently unite with an Andean Federation (Peru and Bolivia) and, ultimately, a pan-American league of nations. Unity would eliminate domestic anarchy and local caudillo rule, and the federation would command greater international presence than the respective republics could individually. In his 1818 letter to Juan Martín Pueyrredón, Bolívar argued for an "American pact" and the formation of "a body politic comprising all our republics," and he concluded that a united America "could truly style herself the Queen of Nations and the Mother of Republics."[163] In his celebrated Angostura address the following year, Bolívar reiterated the motif for the Venezuelan National Congress: "Unity, Unity, Unity—that must be our motto in all things."[164] Upon retirement from his political career he implored Colombians—"I ask you, I beg you, to remain united so that you will not be the murderers of the fatherland and your own executioners"—and on the eve of his death he was still cautioning, "Union, Union, or anarchy will devour you."[165]

Nationalism rather than continental federation won the day in Latin America, but the quest for unity had a varied roster of advocates. Vicente Solano, José Gervasio Artigas, Andrés Bello, Domingo Faustino Sarmiento, Eugenio María de Hostos, and José Martí all had their say in a discourse on unity that began immediately after the battle of Ayacucho.[166] For Benigno Malo in 1866, it was "time to wake up" and adopt union as "the only resolution capable of warding off danger of such magnitude." Latin America was "mutilating itself, breaking up, fractionizing," but in his "New Map of America" Malo proposed four regional confederations that would realize the "golden dreams" of independence.[167] Unity was also implicit in Americanist literature propounding consolidation of regional identity, culture, and pride. José Enrique Rodó's *Ariel*, published in 1900, challenged the tendency to depreciate and disregard Latin American culture while exalting and imitating that of foreigners. Similarly Americanist were José Ingenieros, Manuel Ugarte, and other authors of anti-imperial discourse that responded to the Spanish-American War of 1898.[168]

At the conclusion of *The Communist Manifesto*, Marx and Engels asserted that "the proletarians have nothing to lose but their chains. They have the world to win." This was followed by the slogan that would make "the ruling classes tremble": "Working men of all countries, unite!"[169] In the 1930s and 1940s, Leon Trotsky believed that Latin American nations could not liberate themselves from backwardness and dependency without unifying into a "Socialist United States of Central and South America."[170] With the "export" of revolution after the Cuban Revolution in 1959, Che Guevara sought "a spiritual union of all our countries" and "a war that would be continental." The scope went global in his "Message to the 'Tricontinental' "—this being an "Organization of Solidarity of the Peoples of Africa, Asia, and Latin America"—because in 1967 the time had come "to settle our discrepancies and place everything we have at the service of the struggle." The great strategic objective was "the total destruction of imperialism," which necessitated "the people's unity against the great enemy of mankind: the United States of America."[171]

The dream of continental unity was more explicitly Bolivarian in the discourse of the Nicaraguan revolutionary Augusto César Sandino. In 1929 he wrote a "Plan for the Realization of Bolívar's Highest Dream," which included "the establishment of one nationality, to be called the Latin American nationality."[172] Sandino found quasi-mystical reinforcement for his goal in the Magnetic-Spiritual School's Declaration of Principles: "The universe in solidarity. The whole world communized. The law is one. Substance is one. One is the principle. One is the end. Spiritual magnetism is everywhere." The Hispano-American Oceanic Union that was instrumental to Sandino's envisioned unity was organized on Columbus Day in 1920, because in the New World "rebels would be strengthened" and "the voice of a unified mankind" would emerge.[173] Less spiritual unification plans for the region included the United Provinces of Central America established in 1823 under the guiding influence of the Honduran Francisco Morazán, whose efforts were repaid in 1842 by execution during a conservative reaction. Juan José Arévalo Bermejo also advocated the creation of a Central American union during his Guatemalan presidency in the 1940s.

Bolívar's dream of continental unity received another otherworldly gloss when the cause was assumed by Víctor Raúl Haya de la Torre and his Popular Revolutionary Alliance of America, known as APRA. Between 1930 and 1945, APRA-inspired parties emerged in Peru, Bolivia, Ecuador, Venezuela, Costa Rica, and Cuba, demonstrating an "extraregional transcendence as an anti-imperialistic movement of Latin American unity."[174] "If Bolívar was the Liberator," Haya announced, "I am the Unifier."[175] APRA would be "the realization of Bolívar's great principle," but the envisioned unity was now "spiritual."[176]

Haya viewed the countries of Indo-America as "inseparable, like parts of a great whole" whose unity was preserved despite imposed political boundaries.[177] "I maintain that the force of American unity lies not in the European elements that envelop us," he exclaimed, "but in the Indian elements in which we are rooted."[178] Coexisting in modern Indo-America were two rhythms in a "historical fourth dimension," a slower one of the indigenous cultures and a more rapid one of the industrial culture imported from Europe and the United States. APRA would synchronize these through a "gear mechanism" to achieve a "regeneration through the harmonious blending of disparate entities."[179] These conclusions resulted from Haya's meditation on esoteric truths, including "rhythmic planetary emanations from a pristine spiritual unity."[180]

The Land-without-Evil

Tupí-Guaraní peoples of the Amazon held that a Land-without-Evil was accessible beyond the bounds of society. This terrestrial enclave of perpetual well-being was initially the realm of creator gods and primordial ancestors, but the evolving myths gradually opened it first to the privileged dead—such as shamans and warriors—and then, particularly as conquest made life unbearable, to all natives who showed "courage and constancy."[181] Migrations in search of the Land-without-Evil were accordingly complemented by quests for purification and self-perfection, notably through ritual dance that made the body sleek for its passage into paradise. The Land-without-Evil would be found by those fit to enter it, as though it were located where the corporal, geographical, and spiritual dimensions of human reality intersected and were mutually perfected. Much the same beliefs are held in regions of the modern Amazon converted to Evangelical and sect Christianity, save that the religious exercises have shifted from body to soul. "Those who have a too material idea of the Land-without-Evil, considering it only a place, will fail in their search."[182] The Land-without-Evil can be located outwardly only by those who have first found it inside themselves.

Like the paradises of many cultures, the Land-without-Evil is a primordial realm that provides bounty without toil for its immortal inhabitants. Arrows hunt on their own, fields plant themselves, unattended crops ripen spontaneously, and the people spared their workaday chores dedicate life to ritual drink and dance. Taboos are relaxed as society yields to the freedom of utopian ideals that at once undermine and perfect it. The same dismantling of constraints guarantees immortality, "as if the correspondence between the social order of rules (which implies matrimonial exchange, labor, etc.) and the natural order of generation (which implies birth and death) were such that it sufficed to abolish the first to be free of the second."[183] The sentence to hard labor and death in the temporal world is commuted to an eternal present of luxury in the Land-without-Evil.

Authority in Tupí-Guaraní society was balanced between elders known as *paí*, who manifested some shamanic and prophetic attributes but were primarily defenders of tradition and order; and *karaí*, who were feared and revered shamans living on the fringes of society. From their liminal positions, the karaí exerted a supernatural counterforce that opposed established society, prophesied its cataclysmic destruction, and emptied it by mobilizing migrations in search of the Land-without-Evil. "The absence of evil—the Land-without-Evil—is the counter-order" liberated from the laborious rigidity of institutions. This counterorder was rehearsed in the free zone of transition beyond society, where norms of work, authority, and matrimony were altered or suspended during migrations.[184]

After conquest the religious attributes of the Land-without-Evil invited its comparison to the Christian heaven, but the Jesuits ran for cover when they realized that "all is permitted" and "transgression is the rule" in the Tupí-Guaraní paradise.[185] Indeed, it was through incest that the mythological hero Karaí Jeupie (The One Who Had Risen in an Abnormal Manner) discovered the Land-without-Evil and became the first of its man-gods.[186] Particularly after the founding of Jesuit reductions in Paraguay beginning in 1610, many Tupí-Guaraní peoples themselves began to adapt the Land-without-Evil to the paradigms of Christianity. The mestizo karaí of a huge migration from Pernambuco proclaimed that "he was not a man born of a father or mother" but rather "had come from the mouth of God the Father." This messianic word-made-flesh controlled the weather, the harvest, and all forces serving the natives' sustenance and well-being, while he himself "was fed by God with a certain fluid which came from Heaven."[187]

For the converted Guaraní in Paraguay, residence in the Jesuit reductions combined the practical advantages of sedentary life (now more structured than ever) with the task of constructing a Land-without-Evil rather than migrating in perpetual search of it. For those who learned their catechism, the Jesuits provided both a compromised fulfillment (reductions) and a deferred fulfillment (millennial kingdom, heaven) of the karaí's broken promise. Colonial society, with its slave raiders and encomenderos, was a Land-with-Evil that the Guaraní could escape by migrating to the counterorder of Jesuit reductions.[188]

In more recent years, the Land-without-Evil has been assimilated to Francisco da Cruz's Holy City on the Juí River, referred to among the Tupí-Cocama as the Holy Land, New Jerusalem, and Earthly Paradise.[189] The Brotherhood of the Cross constructs and resides in isolationist villas that like the Jesuit reductions are founded on a utopian counterorder reminiscent of the Land-without-Evil, but beyond these enclaves the Brotherhood regards the Juí River site as the ultimate destination of humanity's migration through history. This hybrid composite of the Land-without-Evil and the Christian millennial kingdom is first a refuge where the Brotherhood will be spared doomsday and then, when the clock restarts, becomes a new Eden-Jerusalem where "the land is blessed" and procreation of the new humanity commences.[190] As in the earlier Tupí-Guaraní migrations, the Tupí-Cocama abandon society pursuant to the eschatological message of quasi-divine prophets (Francisco da Cruz and his emissaries) who ritually prepare the community for treks that are as much away from corrupted society as toward an elusive ideal.[191] In earlier centuries the migrations and then the Jesuit reductions protected the natives from forced labor, and currently migration to the Brotherhood's holy towns withdraws Tupí-Cocama labor from lumber, rubber, and fish industries eager to perpetuate neocolonial exploitation.[192] As Christianized Lands-without-Evil the holy towns have no need for law or authority: "We all live without sin" and "among us there is no evil or injustice."[193]

The Tupí-Guaraní migrations of earlier centuries lacked any semblance of that happy conclusion. In a migration from 1539 to 1549, more than ten thousand Tupinambá abandoned agricultural communities in coastal Brazil and paddled across the breadth of the continent, upriver, until three hundred survivors arrived at the Amazon headwaters. Pulled by their myths and pushed by Portuguese encroachment, the Tupinambá found at the end of the journey only what they had fled: forced labor, now aggravated by dispersion throughout Peru to prevent their escape in subsequent migrations. A single karaí later led some forty to sixty thousand people in a 1609 search that covered more than a thousand miles, and nearly three centuries later an Apapocuvá-Guaraní led a migration eastward until the Atlantic Ocean blocked its passage. An alternative tradition located the Land-without-Evil at the center of the world rather than on the eastern periphery, so the karaí regrouped and rerouted the wearied natives back toward the interior from whence they had come. Only two migrants survived the journey, but the karaí returned to Mato Grosso, assembled a new migration, and set out until—after thirty-five years of searching for the Land-without-Evil—he himself died en route in 1905.[194]

When the three hundred survivors of the Tupinambá migration arrived at Chachapoyas in November 1549, they were captured and debriefed by colonists eager for information on unexplored regions of the jungle. Francisco de Orellana's failed Amazon expedition of 1542 had generated reports that El Dorado was located among the Omaguas, and the Tupinambá migrants, having traversed the unknown territories, provided the opportunity for corroboration. The corregidor of Chachapoyas interrogated the natives about what they had encountered during the ten-year journey, and in the dialogical construction of their response they described the peerless "grandeur of the Omagua." The Indians "told of the fertility of that province, the abundance of its people, the inestimable value of its riches," and other "marvelous things" in excess, including "very long streets inhabited by people whose sole occupation was to work with gold and precious stones."[195] The Pedro de Ursúa expedition of 1560 resulted, but it discovered in the Amazon only what the Tupinambá themselves had encountered: an inhospitality friendly only to myths.

Eden and El Dorado

In 1256 the Venetian merchants Nicolo Polo and Maffeo Polo departed on a journey that led them eventually to the Tartar khans' capital in Peking. Nicolo's son, Marco, accompanied the brothers on a second trip in 1271, and some seven years later, while a prisoner of war in Genoa, he co-authored the book *Travels* that bears his name. Marco Polo had enormous influence on the seaborne Iberians who took literally his fanciful descriptions of Oriental wealth "almost beyond computation." The luxury in Cipango was epitomized by a royal palace "roofed with fine gold" and boasting coordinating floors "paved with gold to a depth of more than two fingers' breadth."[196]

The far reaches of "Asia" explored in 1492 instead featured huts of thatch and mud, but traces of gold on the coast kept alive the hope that gilded utopias would be discovered farther inland. The abundant riches of Mexico made Marco Polo's descriptions seem a prophesy fulfilled, and the loftiness of purpose claimed for gold elsewhere was belied by covetous greed. The uncouth conquerors, "like monkeys," grabbed gold away from Aztec nobility because Spaniards "were gluttonous for it, starved for it, pigishly wanting it."[197] The myths of fabulous Oriental wealth were overhauled and localized, initiating quests for "another Mexico" that paid off with the conquest of the Incas in 1533. Centuries of discourse on gilded kingdoms handing over their riches were actualized when Atahualpa offered a princely ransom after his capture in Cajamarca. The conquerors under Francisco Pizarro melted down more than eleven tons of gold objects to produce nearly seven tons of twenty-two-carat gold, along with an additional thirteen tons of pure silver.[198] The wealth pillaged from Cuzco following its fall in November was even greater, and most conquerors "thought of nothing other than to extort as much gold as possible from the Indians and their chiefs."[199] Pizarro himself was unambiguous: "I have come to take their gold away from them."[200]

Throughout conquest and early colonization, the mythologized search for gold as a commodity tended to intermingle with the quest for restoration of a golden age.[201] Evangelization, millennial eschatology, and the amassing of incalculable wealth became dimensions of one and the same agenda emerging from the polysemous signifier *gold*. Peter Martyr characteristically attributed the natives' "living in a golden age" to their unashamed nudity, their natural communism, and their peaceful society without laws.[202] Romantics reckoned from a distance that the noble savages and their pristine garden had "all the pictures with which poetry has bedecked the golden age."[203] This indigenous golden age was constructed only to exploit it, however, to mine and undermine it, with the gold of the age demetaphorized as bullion. The natives' golden age ended when they were enslaved to extract the gold from within it, and the golden attributes were transferred to the empire. Marco Polo's Cipango, the romanticized Aztec and Inca empires, mythic realms such as the Seven Cities of Cíbola, and even, in turn, the fallen Jesuit reductions became "utopias of pillage": "The perfect city was searched for in order to sack it."[204]

The paradigm utopia of pillage was the elusive El Dorado, a fabulous realm named for the mythic, gilded monarch who corporalized the trope of a kingdom made of gold. The sixteenth-century traditions of a gilded king were mytho-poetically extrapolated from reports on the Chibcha, whose caciques were covered in gold dust during rituals of accession. In what is now highland Colombia, Chibcha caciques made offerings of gold and emeralds by throwing them into a lake, where they then washed off the dust that gilded their bodies.[205] Chibcha lands were plentiful in salt, not gold, which was imported for the ceremony, but the myth of El Dorado found in the images of these ceremonies—the golden body, the disposable wealth, the sedimentary accumulations in the lake—a synecdoche of kingdoms reminiscent of Marco Polo. The original myth situated El Dorado in unexplored Guyana, but the fabulous realm then roamed southward through the Peruvian Amazon until fruitless searches there finally resulted in its projection to the northern frontier. A 1632 description of California paid homage to the central motifs, reporting "a great lagoon surrounded by many villages that have a king who wears a crown, and from this lagoon they extract great quantities of gold."[206]

While conquests and plunder were fueling the myth of El Dorado, the tropical landscapes, the noble savages in their prelapsarian simplicity and innocence, and the general regard of the New World as pristine were constructing the counter-image of the Americas as Edenic. Bartolomé de Las Casas described Nicaragua as "a paradise of the Lord, a place of delights and joy for the whole human race."[207] The friar Diego de Córdova y Salinas observed that Eden and the Americas held in common abundant, crystalline waters running through "sands of gold and precious stones," which led to the popular belief that "Earthly Paradise was in this fourth part of the world." Other natural attributes—"the mildness and gentleness of the winds, the freshness, verdure, and beauty of the trees," "the graceful and cheerful disposition of the lands"—reinforced this belief, as did a roster of authorities who maintained that Eden was not only in the East (America) but also on the equator.[208] Columbus was convinced that Paradise was located on the northern coast of South America, and the spectacular natural beauty there led even the more level-headed Amerigo Vespucci to the same conclusion.[209] In 1650 León Pinelo published two volumes of baroque erudition to prove that the shores of either the Marañón or Amazon River were the site of "Paradise, the Home of Adam, and of his first Descendants, and of the Departure of Noah in the Ark."[210] The evidence included the "eternal summer and perpetual spring," the four great rivers (Amazon, Orinoco, Cauca or Magdalena, and Plate) presumed to flow from the source in Eden, and the great architectural monuments of Mesoamerica and Peru, constructed by the early descendants of Adam prior to the flood.[211]

The name Eden in Genesis was derived from a Sumerian word that the Israelites associated with the native Hebrew *eden*, which meant "luxury" and "delight."[212] Through the gradual assimilation of these worldly qualities, paradise evolved from God's garden to a garden of earthly delights, a lush idyll whose plenty was mildly sensualized by unashamed nakedness and enhanced by the precious metals and stones added during the Middle Ages. The belief that Eden, King Solomon's mines, and El Dorado were all located in the New World made them overlapping, when not coterminous, realms. In a sixteenth-century treatise one of Eden's primary attributes, the source of the world's four rivers, was transposed to El Dorado as "a silver fountain, which spouted through four golden pipes."[213] The description remained essentially unchanged, but the fountain detached from Eden to reappear, embellished, as an attribute of a gilded paradise. The transposition occurred in reverse in León Pinelo's treatise, now by locating the Garden of Eden in the Peruvian Amazon, precisely where earlier myths had situated El Dorado.[214] America was "the paradise and mine of the world," offering inexhaustible, luxurious delights that were decidedly material but always spiritualized by an Edenic gloss.[215]

The Columbian Discovery of Paradise

No one, so far as I know, has ever written a history of discovery as an esthetic pleasure; if one were to do so . . . one would have to regard discovery as a kind of esthetic blank that is filled in differently in accordance with the nature of both individuals and of historic periods.

—Wolfgang Iser

On May 30, 1498, Christopher Columbus departed on his third voyage, heading southwest past the Cape Verde Islands and onward to the latitude of Sierra Leone, where the first Portuguese gold discoveries had been made in the 1460s. He then steered a course due west along that parallel en route to the new colony in Hispaniola. Subscribing to the traditional, erroneous belief that gold, precious stones, and spices were most abundant in the "torrid zone," Columbus pursued this southern route hoping to discover the riches upon which his credibility depended.[216] The events, however, turned out otherwise.

In mid-July the fleet was becalmed for eight days in heat so intense that it seemed all would burst into flames. The casks exploded, the wheat burned, and the meat roasted.[217] This earthly inferno was not without consequences for the African population, which appeared to become progressively negroid as Columbus ventured deeper into the torrid zone. On the coast of north Africa, Columbus observed, "the people are black and the land very burned"; as one continues southward to the Cape Verde Islands, "the people are much blacker"; until finally, at Sierra Leone, "the people are black to an extreme degree."[218]

When the winds again began to blow, the immobilized fleet resumed its course due westward. Columbus's experience had taught him that "immediately after passing a hundred leagues to the west of the Azores, there was a very great change in the sky and in the stars and in the temperature of the air and in the

waters of the sea."[219] The same occurred on this voyage: "As soon as I came to
be directly on this line, immediately I found the temperature very mild, and as
I went further forward, so it became more mild, but I did not find the stars
corresponding with this."[220] The line to which Columbus was referring had special significance after 1493, when the Bulls of Donation fixed the border between
the Spanish and Portuguese hemispheres at one hundred leagues west of the
Azores. The Portuguese realm and its dark continent were torrid, but when one
entered the Spanish domain an "immediate" change signaled the increasing beneficence to come.

Such was the official story dispatched to the Catholic Monarchs in October
1498, but in his earlier diary entry Columbus complained off the record that
the heat was intense on both sides of the line. The contrived contrast, along
with the discourse on skin pigmentation, provided the first evidential install-
ments to support Columbus's belief that he had located the Garden of Eden.
Throughout the journey, conditioned perceptions and narrative smoothing contributed to the construction of an ambience worthy of Paradise. Columbus had
dedicated the third voyage to the third person of the Trinity, and when three
mountains appeared on the horizon on July 31 the Christian paradigm commenced its metamorphosis of the landscape through denomination of the island
as "Trinidad" (Trinity). In Eden, Adam names and in Paradise Columbus re-
names as the first gesture of possession.[221] Such denominations as Tierra de
Gracia (Land of Grace) and Jardines (Gardens) prepared the Paria peninsula for
the Paradise that its lush foliage would conceal.[222] The land was "the greenest
and most beautiful and populated" in the world, "the most beautiful thing that
eyes have ever seen."[223]

Columbus likewise found the natives in Paria to be exceptionally suited to
the thesis that Eden was in the vicinity. While their African counterparts at the
same latitude were "black to an extreme degree," these noble savages were "all
in the prime of life, well-proportioned and not negroes, but whiter than the
others who have been seen in the Indies, and very graceful and with handsome
bodies, and hair long and smooth, cut in the manner of Castile."[224] These were
the descendants of the primordial Judeo-Christians, and Columbus's retroactive
ethnic cleansing rendered them accordingly in the likeness of Europeans who
inherited Adam's legacy through Christ. By the time Columbus had finished,
these anti-Indians were "as white as we are."[225] The natives of Paria were taller,
braver, more attractive, more intelligent, and more conversant than were other
indigenous peoples.[226] Their Edenic attributes included even their unashamed
nudity, although this too appears to have been contrived.[227]

This circumstantial evidence accumulating in support of Columbus's conviction that he was in the vicinity of Eden was grounded by two pieces of mythic
hard data: the fleet's position at "the end of the east," where tradition located
Eden; and the presence of inexplicable quantities of fresh water, which evoked
Eden as the source of the world's four rivers. Before it gained a symbolic charge,
fresh water was a precious commodity during the fleet's two months of Atlantic
crossing in the scorching heat. Land was nowhere in sight, only one full cask of
water remained on the flagship, and the threat of dehydration was imposing.

When fresh water finally did appear, it gushed into the Gulf of Paria with such voluminous force that it created a "very great roaring," with corresponding turbulence that almost capsized the fleet.[228] The Orinoco delta emptied huge continental rivers into the resisting salt water of the Atlantic, raising the ships to the top of waves as high as hills.[229] Columbus gave the name Boca de la Sierpe (Mouth of the Serpent) to the inlet where he suffered these trials, and Boca del Dragón (Mouth of the Dragon) to the corresponding inlet on the other side of Trinidad. In the latter, the fleet was saved from what Columbus called a "battle" of opposing forces because "the fresh water was always victorious." He elaborated, "The same fresh water, defeating the salt water, cast the ships out imperceptibly, and thus they were delivered to safety."[230] Columbus was thereby twice saved by "the water of Paradise," once from dying of thirst and again from shipwreck in the apocalyptic Mouth of the Dragon.[231]

Interpretation of the same water would also save his mission. The powerful thrust of fresh water into the Gulf of Paria perplexed Columbus, for such force could only be exerted by an enormous river, which, in turn, would require a continental landmass to produce it. Under the influence of Ptolemy's *Geography*—which dated back to the second century but was reintroduced in a 1410 Latin translation—Columbus understood the earth's surface as a single, continuous landmass, an Orbis Terrarum (Island of the Earth) that wrapped the northern girth of the globe and was surrounded by water. Despite the evidence that his own voyages had accumulated to disprove Ptolomean geography, Columbus held faithfully to the medieval worldview and was therefore caught in a hermeneutic predicament when the reality before him challenged the theory. Acknowledgment of the South American continent would constitute not merely a dismissal of centuries of erudition but also a heretical revision of a cosmovision defended by dogma.[232] For Columbus on the shores of northern South America in 1498, Ptolomean geography was a reactionary force that restricted interpretation. The excessive fresh water would have to be explained without admission that an unknown continent had produced it.

Reasoning back and forth between the empirical data before him and the religious erudition behind him, Columbus arrived finally at a solution: "I have never read or heard of so great a quantity of fresh water so coming into and near the salt," save that "Holy Scripture testifies that Our Lord made the earthly paradise and in it placed the tree of life, and from it issues a fountain from which flow the four principal rivers of the world."[233] The Edenic origin of the water was reinforced by the common belief, recorded by John Mandeville, that Paradise was protected by unnavigable turbulence: "Those rivers flow with so strong a current, with such a rush and such waves that no boat can sail against them."[234] If the fresh water "does not come from there, from paradise," Columbus reckoned, "it seems to be a still greater marvel, for I do not believe that there is known in the world a river so great and deep."[235] Columbus noted in his diary that the fresh water was inexplicable "unless this is a mainland," but this conclusion demanded by the evidence was dismissed as a "greater marvel" to permit the retreat to orthodoxy.[236] "I say that if it is not from the earthly paradise that this river comes, it originates from an infinite land, lying to the south, which hitherto was unknown. But I am much more convinced in my own mind that there, where I said, is the earthly paradise."[237]

Columbus's theory of the fresh water's origin in Paradise afforded the immediate benefit of neutralizing the perplexing evidence before him, but ultimately he would have to acknowledge the new discovery as continental. The narrative of the third voyage was dispatched from Santo Domingo in October 1498, and by 1500 Columbus was referring to the once denied continent as "another world" and "a new heaven and a new earth, which until then had been hidden."[238] The heterodoxy of the deferred recognition was defused because the southern landmass was doubly biblicized, first as Eden and then as the New Jerusalem. The discovery was then acceptable as a "very large" or "infinite" mainland and might necessarily have been so: had Adam not sinned, Las Casas explained, all humanity would have been accommodated in Eden.[239] The inadmissible argument (continent) and the fabulous argument (Paradise) fuse into a composite that is content with its internal contradictions. As Edmundo O'Gorman observed, Columbus "must end by postulating a vast mainland, the very consequence that he wished to avoid."[240]

Also essential to Columbus's Paradise theory was his belief that he had reached the "end of the east," which is to say the farthest reaches of Asia that wrapped the globe and were separated from the western coast of Europe only by the Atlantic.[241] The location was crucial because according to Genesis 2:8, God planted his garden "in Eden, in the east." *The First Book of Adam and Eve* provided details agreeable to Columbus's calculations: "God planted the garden in the east of the earth, on the border of the world eastward, beyond which, towards the sun rising, one finds nothing but water."[242] In the fourth century Isidore of Seville defined Paradise as "a land situated somewhere in the East," in the twelfth century Hugh of Saint Victor spoke of Eden as though it were a province of Asia, and the anonymous *Relation of Enoch and Elias* of the same century asserted unequivocally that Eden was in India.[243] One of the texts most studied by Columbus, Pierre d'Ailly's *Imago Mundo* (1410), situated Paradise precisely where Columbus discovered it in 1498: at the far eastern point of the Orbis Terrarum, where the sun rose on the day of creation. In a marginal note beside d'Ailly's description of mountains in Asia, Columbus wrote, "The Terrestrial Paradise is there."[244]

Eden's location at the eastern extremes was recorded on medieval mappamundi that situated the east where today the north would be. Paradise, at "the end of the east," was accordingly in the uppermost position of the map, just beneath heaven. At the same time, topographically, Paradise was believed to be located at the summit of the earth, on a mountain so high that it "touches the sphere of the moon."[245] These heights accorded with Eden's transitional position between heaven and earth and protected it from encroachments, including the universal flood.[246] Negotiating the multiple demands of dimension restricted by the flatness of the page, the mappamundi synthesized the "end of the east" with the loftiest peak on earth by situating Eden at the highest point on the map. As Las Casas consolidated the geography and topography that follow Thomas

Aquinas, Paradise "is situated at the highest place on earth, and this is the East."[247]

Paradise as the "point of epiphany" between heaven and earth was important for Columbus's discovery because the altitude could account for the sudden change in climate and skin color.[248] By comparing inaccurate Polaris readings with other readings (also inaccurate) that he made on earlier voyages, Columbus concluded that once he passed the line of demarcation, "the ships went rising gently toward the sky" in a "continuous ascent."[249] The mild climate of Paria and the whiteness of the people were consequences of "the fact that the land is highest in the world, nearest to the sky."[250] On one side of the line of demarcation there was an earthly inferno and on the other side an earthly paradise.

By considering the tropical landscape, the temperate climate and "people as white as we are," the presence of enormous quantities of fresh water, the "continuous ascent" to the highest point on earth, and the fleet's position at the "end of the east," Columbus concluded that he had located Eden. If earlier he was reluctant to breach the postulates of religious science, now Christian cosmography was jettisoned as he argued daringly in support of his theory. The earth was not spherical as Ptolemy and other authorities had supposed on the basis of insufficient data, but was rather, Columbus submitted, "the shape of a pear."[251] During the uphill sail, his fleet had risen from the wide base and ascended the narrower part of the pear that concealed Eden at its summit. In an alternate image, Columbus explained to their majesties that the earth "is like a very round ball, and on one part of it is placed something like a woman's breast, and that the part where the nipple is found is highest and nearest to the sky, and it is beneath the equinoctial line [on the equator] and in this Ocean sea, at the end of the East."[252] Las Casas summarized the conclusion: "On that nipple he believed that terrestrial Paradise could be located."[253]

The image of a breast-shaped world with Eden as its nipple suggests the return to primeval Paradise as a recuperation of the paradise of infancy, where maternity provides all in peace and plenty, warmth and comfort, during an eternity afforded by incognizance of time and mortality. The thirsty Columbus revitalized by a primal nutrient font is anticipated in a passage from Judges 5: 25: "He asked for water and she gave him milk." With Paradise as a point of contact between heaven and earth, the breast image also accommodates a vision of Mother Earth nourishing the son-deity, Christ, in symbiotic bliss as he bestows grace upon his prelapsarian or atoned creation. The people in this Land of Grace, as Columbus named it, would also receive showers of the breast's lactations, not unlike the sinners in purgatory who are nourished and comforted by milk that the Virgin squirts from her breast.[254] The breast is the fountain at the source of the world's great rivers, distributing the essence of maternity, nourishment, and procreation until "the hills flow with milk" as in the promised land.[255] Maternal waters were similarly represented in the iconography of Jesus offering the wound in his side as though it were a breast, generally to female mystics nourished on spiritualized liquids.[256] The twelfth-century Psalter mappamundi provided an interesting variation in its depiction of Christ's navel as the source of Eden's rivers.[257] The waters of life flow out of Christ and into Paradise, where they are channeled to the four rivers for distribution throughout the world. In Isaiah, milk is the water of life when Jerusalem is represented as a mother whose children come to "suck and be satisfied with her consoling breasts."[258] No less should be expected of Columbus's Eden as the New Jerusalem, particularly since in Revelation 21:2 the celestial city descends in more youthful feminine guise as "a bride adorned for her husband."

Columbus never returned to his theory of Paradise, Peter Martyr dismissed it, and Las Casas apologized for it, but the presumed discovery of Paradise provides an exemplary expression of the dynamics between Eden, New Jerusalem, and El Dorado. Gold, as Columbus later put it, casts souls into Paradise, but few souls would be hurled with the bullion returning on his ships, and the Catholic Monarchs were running short of patience. The lack of gold on Columbus's first voyage fostered a rhetorical compensation in his diary: "Signs of the presence of gold must appear on every page."[259] By the conclusion of the third voyage of 1498–1500, however, rhetoric was insufficient. Columbus could not deliver on his promise of gold, but since gold was merely the means to a greater objective, Paradise, he could perhaps fulfill his promise more directly. "Although ships, laden with gold, have not been sent back," Columbus wrote, he had brought into the empire "these lands which I have newly discovered, in which, I am assured in my heart, there is the earthly paradise."[260] Eden was delivered in lieu of El Dorado, making the Catholic Monarchs "the legitimate kings of the earthly paradise."[261]

Millennial Missions

> On earth, as it is in heaven.

It occurred to the Franciscans at the inception of the American mission that the Lord would best be served if Indians were segregated from Spaniards. Franciscan documents of the period called for "two nations" or "independent republics," one of natives and the other of colonists, in order to quarantine the prelapsarian Indians from the epidemic of sin that would contaminate their precontact purity.[262] Already in 1529 Juan de Zumárraga, bishop and later archbishop of Mexico, recommended to the king that Spaniards be prohibited from remaining among the natives for more than a day.[263] In his *Doctrina breve* and *Doctrina cristiana*, works directly influenced by Thomas More's *Utopia*, Zumárraga proposed a theocratic, Indo-Christian republic parallel to Spanish settlements but governed by Franciscans who would report directly to the viceroy.[264]

These aspirations, which resulted in missionary experiments by Dominicans and Jesuits as well as Franciscans, were grounded in perceptions of the natives as innocent, childlike, and impressionable. The natives were Christianity's perfect raw material, the "most blessed peoples in the world if only they knew God."[265] They were humble, obedient, ascetic, "meek as sheep," "more patient than Job," "without arrogance, without greed, without ambition," and "of such simplicity and purity of soul that they do not know how to sin."[266] This assessment was made by several prominent observers—Columbus, Motolinía, Mendieta, Las Casas, Vasco de Quiroga—and was often accompanied by emphasis on the natives' susceptibility to Spanish influences. "These are not ordinary souls," Mendieta argued, "but they are souls as tender and as delicate as soft wax upon which the stamp of any doctrine (Catholic or heretical) or any customs (good or bad) can be imprinted, depending upon what they are taught."[267] Motolinía similarly maintained that once the Indians were "humble, calm, and broken" by conquest, they were "as inclined and ready as soft wax to receive the imprint of all virtue."[268]

It therefore seemed imperative that friars assume responsibility for the New World natives, sculpting their soft wax as God's hands had formed Adam in Eden. The Indians were "purely children," and God would be best served if the king made friars the "fathers of this poor nation, commending them to us like sons and small children so that as such (which they are) we would raise and teach and protect and correct them."[269] Justice would be administered by the same token, since "fathers and teachers have the divine and human natural right to raise, teach, and punish their sons and disciples."[270] Mendieta concluded that the natives were created "to be not teachers but disciples, not prelates but subordinates, of which they are the best in the world."[271]

In their respective manners, the Franciscans, Dominicans, and Jesuits viewed the New World as an opportunity to recuperate the primitive Church that had been corrupted in Europe. The apostolic Church of the Old World ended with the conversion of Constantine, but it could be renewed in a "Primitive Church for the Indians."[272] Much of the discourse on the millennial kingdom, the New Jerusalem, the restoration of the golden age, the construction of a Christian utopia, and the recuperation of Eden emerged from this effort to return Christianity to the fundamental teachings of Jesus—love, peace, charity, equality, pacifism—that had somehow been turned around to justify conquest, plunder, and exploitation. Old World Christians, as Desiderius Erasmus put it, "twist divine Scripture until it conforms to the customs of the times," rather than "correcting the customs and straightening them to conform to the rule of the Scriptures."[273]

Recuperation of the lost ideal was the impetus behind such utopian projects as those of Vasco de Quiroga, who envisioned a "primitive, new, and renascent Church in this New World," with a corresponding congregation of new Christians.[274] Mendieta held that the Church of the Americas, liberated from the errors of the past, would develop "the most perfect and healthy Christianity that the world has ever known."[275] The natives would practice a faith so pure that it would seem "as if the whole province were a monastery," because "they would live virtuously and peacefully serving God, as in a terrestrial paradise."[276] The New World would become, like Joachim of Fiore's third age, Tommaso Campanella's City of the Sun, and modern holy towns, a monkish prelude to the millennial kingdom.

Frustrating that ideal was the more dominant interest in turning a profit on the colonies. If the Indians were in church, they were not in the mines; if they were at prayer, they were not at work; and if they were in isolated missions, they were not in encomiendas. The troublesome "double purpose of the crown to make profits and at the same time Christianize the Indians" made for tension between friars and the colonial elite.[277] The New World was Ophir and El Dorado as much as it was Eden and New Jerusalem, and the competing interests made competing claims.[278] The millennial-minded friars also held the minority view on the appropriate means of making contact with natives. They favored peaceful, religious contact with little or no armed escort, whereas the majority—including many clergymen—held that "the innate brutality and utterly barbarous customs of these Indians demand in justice that they should first be ruled, disciplined, and subjugated." A Jesuit writing in the eighteenth century rendered the same argument more poetically: "These barbarous peoples do not listen to the voices of the Gospel preachers unless they have first heard the sound of gunpowder."[279]

In 1531 even the humanitarian Vasco de Quiroga endorsed armed conquest as a means of colonial and missionary expansion, but by 1535 he repudiated the practice and advocated peaceful expansion "as Christ came to us."[280] Zumárraga, a close associate of Quiroga, similarly argued for nonviolent evangelization in place of armed "butchery": "good war and conquest would be that of souls," sending friars instead of soldiers "as Christ sent his apostles."[281] The Indians would respond positively to the good news just as they had in *Utopia*, where "through the mysterious inspiration of God, or because Christianity is very like the religion already prevailing among them, they were very well disposed toward it from the start."[282] Even when the faith was graciously received, however, the later arrival of colonists to exploit native labor often resulted in lamentable consequences. As a chronicler put it after Indian trust was breached by slave raids, "Without much delay the Dominicans purged with martyrdom the sins of their compatriots."[283]

In his 1536 *De Unico Vocationis Modo*, Las Casas argued that divine providence had established gentle, reasonable persuasion as "the one and only means of teaching men the true religion."[284] The friars should enter the unconquered frontier like "angels among men," peaceful "as rain and snow fall from heaven, not impetuously, not violently, not suddenly like a heavy shower, but gradually, with suavity and gentleness, saturating the earth as it falls." Patiently and persistently they would "induce, persuade, plead with, supplicate, follow, attract, and lead by the hand those individuals who are to embrace the faith."[285] The mission would be accomplished as much by deed as by word, with the friars as exemplars of "the apostolic life of the primitive Church, given to prayer, to continuous vigils, fasts, and other pious deeds, so that, for those who saw and heard them, they were worthy of being heard, believed, and also loved."[286] In this way, Las Casas concluded, "they will render Your Majesty great service, for together with the bishops they will pacify the Indians and bring them to serve God and Your Majesty, unlike the soldiers who scandalize and slaughter them."[287]

Las Casas arrived to the New World in 1502, had an encomienda in Hispaniola, renounced it in 1514, and a year later began his defense of the Indians, which lasted until his death in 1566. Between 1516 and 1519 he devised a series of plans for agricultural communities that entailed pairing Indians with select Spaniards. The principles of farming and the manners of Christian, European civilization would be assimilated through this "unification of good policy and good company," as Vasco de Quiroga put it in a separate context.[288] Through interaction and intermarriage an ideal, Christian, mestizo community would gradually emerge, making the natives a "noble and civilized people" who "know how to live by themselves."[289]

In 1521 the plans were put into action on the coast of Paria in Tierra Firme, where some twenty years earlier Columbus thought he had discovered Paradise. As would occur in many subsequent utopian endeavors, an auspicious beginning ended in "complete and humiliating failure," here because soldiers escorting the missionaries, ostensibly to protect them, provoked a revolt by slave raiding.[290] Las Casas repaired to the Dominican monastery in Santo Domingo, entered the order a year later, and separated himself from the affairs of the world for nearly ten years.

The most substantial experiment in peaceful colonization was conducted by Las Casas and his Dominican associates in northeastern Guatemala between 1537 and 1550. The region chosen was the indomitable Tezulutlán, dubbed the Land of War because it had resisted three attempted conquests. Prior to commencing evangelization, Las Casas proposed two conditions to the governor: that the pacified Indians be direct vassals of the crown (to whose treasury they would pay a modest tribute) and that no Spaniards other than approved Dominicans be permitted to enter the province for five years. In May 1537, the requests were approved, with subsequent confirmation by the viceroy and king. The jurisdiction and powers of the caciques as "natural lords" were maintained in the region.

Las Casas and his associates—Rodrigo de Andrada, Pedro de Angulo, and Luis Cáncer—made their initial contact through the intermediary of Christianized Indians who traded in Tezulutlán. These Indians were taught ballads "that were virtually a history of Christianity," and they were trained to sing these "in a pleasing manner." With the baggage of trinkets for gifts, the emissaries set out in August 1537, mesmerizing audiences with their artistically rendered performances. "When the Indians wanted to know more, they were told that only the friars could instruct them." The description of the friars itself augmented the appeal, for they were unlike other Spaniards in their appearance, their celibacy, their disinterest in gold, and their repertoire of mysterious words and images.

Fray Luis Cáncer returned with the native merchants and received a warm welcome, most importantly by the cacique of the region who "was particularly impressed by the friar's vestments and cleanliness, for his own priests went about in filthy clothes, their hair matted with blood, and their temples were no more than sooty, dirty hovels." After receiving assurances that armed Spanish incursion would not follow, the cacique converted to Christianity and urged his people to do the same. The Land of War was renamed the land of Vera Paz (True Peace) in celebration of the transformation.

The church, the chapter house, and community buildings were built around a central plaza, from which residential streets "extended in straight lines." Native buildings were destroyed ("to make the Indians' return to their former ways more difficult") as were indigenous places of worship.[291] The initial success of the experiment and the effective diplomacy of Las Casas in Spain resulted in a flurry of royal decrees supporting Vera Paz and endorsing conversion elsewhere by peaceful means.[292] Word of the experiment was also disseminated regionally, and as late as 1606, when the Maya of Tzuctoc petitioned for autonomous administration under missionary tutelage, they cited Vera Paz as a precedent.[293] The Vera Paz experiment nevertheless had a tragic conclusion in 1550 when, for reasons unknown, the apostate natives murdered the friars, sacrificing some before idols.[294]

A similar evangelical model was proposed to the Council of Indies by Vasco de Quiroga shortly after his arrival in Mexico as an *oidor* (judge) in 1531. Quiroga made the familiar argument that the Indians had an innate humility, obedience, docility, and disregard for worldly goods, and that in order to become "true and perfect Christians" they lacked "nothing but the faith, and knowing the things of Christian instruction."[295] A trace of the lost ideal of primitive Christianity was discernible even in the Indians' appearance, with bare feet and hair styles "like those used by the apostles."[296] Here, as in the other millennial missions, benevolent treatment of the Indians was predicated on dismissing their culture and emptying their subjectivity in order to emphasize their receptivity to imposed doctrine: "so soft the wax and so blank the slate and so new the vessel on and into which nothing has been imprinted or drawn or poured until now."[297] The perfection of Christianity "is more proper, easy, and natural" for Indians, and therefore one could best recuperate "Christian doctrine and life and its holy simplicity, meekness, humility, piety, and charity in this renascent Church, in this golden age, among these natives."[298]

Such worthy raw material remained underdeveloped, however, because the Indians live "like irrational animals" in disorderly dispersion across the countryside. They are "idolatrous and get drunk and do whatever they want," but only until abducted by colonists who "depopulate the villages and populate the mines."[299] The solution proposed by Quiroga was to gather the flock into structured missionary villages where through proper instruction, they would cease to be "barbarous, tyrannical, rude, and savage people."[300] Zumárraga similarly maintained that evangelization was hindered by the dispersion of Indians "like wild beasts," and that the Spaniards should concentrate them in planned, structured, and regulated communities "with streets and plazas," "as in Castile."[301] The villages would civilize the Indians, save their souls, rescue them from forced labor ("they live dying and die living in despair"), and spare them the demographic collapse suffered by Caribbean peoples.[302] Both temporal and spiritual affairs would fall under the jurisdiction of friars in simultaneous "service to God and to his Majesty on this earth," with this missionary governance facilitating the harmonious synchronization of indigenous virtues and primitive Christianity.[303]

In the period between 1531 and 1535, while awaiting a response to his royal petition, Quiroga donated his own funds to establish a hospital-village outside of Mexico City. The word *hospital* encompassed its current meaning and the broader sense derived from its Latin root, *hospes*: a "shelter" or "home" that provides "hospitality" to those in need of it, as did medieval hospitals.[304] Quiroga's hospital-village, named Santa Fe, was reminiscent of the Las Casas project and of More's *Utopia* in its conception of the community "as if it were a single family."[305] Royal endorsement of the experiment came in 1534, ordering that natives in Michoacán "be gathered in order to be better instructed."[306] Establishment of the first Michoacán village, also called Santa Fe, was followed by others in 1537 when Quiroga became the first bishop of the region.

Quiroga's greatest accomplishment was in actualizing utopian theory, in creating "a rare political atmosphere where the world of ideas embraced and intermixed with reality."[307] The debt to Thomas More was significant and explicit: in 1535 Quiroga proposed "that the life of the communities of Indians in the New World be organized in accord with the rules of the island of Utopia, conceived by the famous English humanist."[308] Quiroga's *Ordenanzas* systematized the model of Utopia, following More's text closely in codifying governance of the missionary villages.[309] A related influence came from the revitalized golden age described in the second-century "Saturnalian Letters" by Lucian of Samosata. For Quiroga, the natives of Mexico compared favorably with Lucian's golden age people, whereas the Spaniards—deprived of "simplicity and good will," lost in vice, greed, and war—had degenerated to the lowly iron age.[310] The golden age could be recuperated, Quiroga concluded, "in our times, although not among us."[311]

The most sustained accomplishment of millennial missions in Latin America began when the Company of Jesus entered Paraguay in 1585, working beside Franciscans who had arrived a decade earlier. The first Jesuit reduction, San Ignacio Guazú, was founded in 1610 by the Italian priest Marcello Lorenzana. As described by Antonio Ruiz de Montoya in his 1639 *Spiritual Conquest*, "These people were unconquerable by arms; this man conquered them with only the Gospel, charity, and the patience of Christ."[312] Others who ventured unaccompanied into Guaraní territories met a less fortunate end, and most supplemented Christian charity with more tangible gifts that placated the caciques' wrath.[313] Once peaceful contact was consolidated and evangelization advanced, the missions were populated by natives attracted to the combined appeal of life in Christ and exemption to encomienda. Given their natural inclination toward Christian demeanor, the Guaraní "become apostles almost at the same time as their conversion."[314] Between 1622 and 1629 eleven reductions were founded by Ruiz de Montoya himself, and at the height of the "Kingdom of God on Earth," in 1732, there were thirty reductions inhabited by some hundred thousand Guaranís.

The transformation that came with conversion was exemplified by pacification of the hostile cacique Guirabera. When the Jesuits settled among his people, Ruiz de Montoya related, they found "a den of wild beasts, where no one had ever seen anything but drunkenness, dishonesty, enmities, death, [and] eating each other, like followers of the devil." The Jesuits turned that around, however, and "now that land has been made a Paradise" where mass is celebrated, prayers are heard, neophytes assiduously prepare for baptism, and "instead of sharpening human bones for their arrows they make Crosses to wear around their necks."[315]

The term *reduction* implied the concentration of dispersed natives into missionary villages where relatively few Jesuits could teach and enforce a Christian way of life. In a highly structured regimen the converted Guaranís dedicated themselves to agriculture, crafts, and worship. The Jesuits were granted exclusive jurisdiction over the "unconquerable" regions that they managed to pacify, and entry by Spaniards was prohibited except when the Jesuits extended an invitation for some special purpose, such as to train natives in a particular skill. Unlike the Franciscan missions, which made natives available to encomiendas, the intent in the Jesuit reductions was precisely to isolate the natives from exploitation and the corrupting influences of the colonists.

Between 1628 and 1641, the reductions were plagued by *bandeirantes* (slave raiders) from São Paulo. Tens of thousands of the Guaranís were abducted during excessively violent raids that included massacre, rape, and the burning down of missions. The severity of the marauding finally warranted the 1631–32 evacuation of fifteen missions in Guayrá and Iguazú. In a migration reminiscent of the earlier quests for the Land-without-Evil, some twelve thousand natives followed Jesuits three hundred miles southwest to Yaveirí (now Missiones, Argentina) in a four-month journey during which half of the pilgrims perished.

The bandeirante raids continued after resettlement, however, and in response the Jesuits began to arm the natives. Having been frustrated by the unaccommodating authorities of Asunción, who represented a more genteel version of the bandeirante's enterprise in free labor, Ruiz de Montoya traveled to Madrid, pleaded the Jesuits' case, and returned with royal permission to establish a Guaraní militia. Unification of Spanish and Portuguese monarchy ceased in 1640, and a year later the Guaraní troops were at the disposition of the governors in Asunción and Buenos Aires for campaigns against Portuguese incursions into the unstable border region. Such military expeditions violated the principles of isolationism, and upon return to the reductions the troops sometimes manifested a worldliness incompatible with primitive Christianity and Jesuit authority.[316] The militias also seemed to substantiate the impression that the reductions were a state within a state, thereby contributing to the Jesuits' eventual expulsion.

The reductions' most enduring and ultimately most detrimental problem was antagonism by lay colonists in the region. The large force of cooperative native labor in the reductions produced agricultural surpluses that the Jesuits shipped to Buenos Aires and then exported to Europe. The colonial elite objected, arguing that the reductions provided unfair competition and that the Jesuits (instead of the secular elite) were enriching and empowering themselves through exploitation of native labor exempt from encomiendas. Tension was particularly strong between 1642 and 1668, when the efficiency of the reductions and distribution through established religious networks gave the Jesuits an advantage in the yerba maté market.[317] Paraguayan encomenderos ultimately advocated elimination of the reductions, and nearly a century later, between 1721 and 1735, aggrieved *comuneros* (participants in popular revolt) likewise sought to rid themselves of Jesuits.

The fall of this beleaguered paradise began when the 1750 Treaty of Madrid relinquished to Portugal a territory in which the Jesuits had seven reductions. Evacuation was ordered and refused, and the ensuing dispute resulted in the Guaraní War of 1754–56. In the decisive battle of February 1756, the native resistance was assaulted by a well-armed expedition of combined Spanish and Portuguese forces. The inequality of the adversaries was registered in the disproportion of their casualties: fifteen hundred Indians and five Europeans.[318] The Portuguese expelled the Jesuits in 1759 and Spain followed suit in 1767, banishing them from Iberia and its colonies for having "usurped the authority of the King."[319] The Guaranís were subsequently vulnerable to exploitation and slavery, and within a decade the reductions were in ruins.

Like many missions that preceded them, the Jesuit reductions in Paraguay were ultimately undermined by the incompatibility of utopian Christianity and profit-oriented colonization. The ideals of a restored primitive Church and a liturgically organized world were often more amenable to the natives upon whom they were imposed than to the Spaniards who regarded them as a romantic squander of free labor. The Jesuits, Las Casas, and Quiroga, all beleaguered by the hostility of encomenderos and civil authorities, offered a viable but unwanted option to violent conquest followed by encomienda. Their noble ideal drew only the applause that drowned it out.

Utopias throughout Latin American history, be they missionary reductions, isolationist holy towns, or enclaves of nativist revival, are always regarded as subversive and attacked accordingly. Utopianism, however, is itself a response to subversion, an attempt to recuperate the subverted principles upon which a society was founded. Created by negation, utopia is an antisociety governed by antiauthorities for disenfranchised peoples in liminal regions. It is the unflattering reflection in which society must view its inversions: the Land-without-Evil replaces evil institutions, the Land of War becomes the Land of True Peace, and savages exchange roles with Christians. Utopia is subversive because it founds itself as restitution of a previous subversion; it overturns an upside-down world.

5

Return of the Cultural Hero

In the late eleventh century rumor held that Charlemagne, "the heroic champion of Christ, the tireless defender of Christendom," had returned from the tomb to lead the first Crusade against Islam. According to popular traditions, Charlemagne, a new David, had once campaigned to Jerusalem and "won the world" for Christ, so it seemed fitting that he should do so again. The possibility of Charlemagne's return was facilitated by the ancillary belief that he had never actually died but was rather hibernating in a deep sleep, "either in his vault at Aachen or inside some mountain," awaiting the opportune moment to resume his messianic mission.[1]

Charlemagne never showed up, but throughout the middle ages the anticipated return of a sleeping, exiled, or incognito hero migrated from one dead emperor to the next. Baldwin of Flanders became emperor of Constantinople in 1204 and was killed a year later by Bulgarians, but he survived his death in legends that assured he was quite alive and would soon return disguised as a hermetic beggar. Such messianic anticipation provided fortuitous and irresistible opportunities for actual beggars adept at manipulating circumstances to their advantage. A noteworthy instance occurred in 1225, when a wanderer believed to be the dead Baldwin was received in Valenciennes with ecstatic cheers of jubilation. A month later this pseudo-Baldwin was crowned Count of Flanders and Hainaut and Emperor of Constantinople and Thessalonica: "Clad in imperial purple, borne in a litter or mounted on a noble palfry, surrounded by the banners of his domains in the East and West and preceded by the cross which traditionally preceded the successors of Constantine—yet still wearing the long beard of a holy hermit and carrying the white wand of benevolence instead of a metal scepter, he must indeed have seemed the messianic Emperor, come at last to fulfil the old Sibylline prophecies." The imposter's reign ended within a year, when he was hanged in the marketplace at Lille, but the hope for fulfillment of the prophesy lived on to raise countless phantom kings from their graves.[2]

In Iberia, one such resuscitation occurred in the late sixteenth century when Gabriel de Espinosa, a Spanish pastry maker, was received in Portugal as the returning King Sebastian. The context for this ersatz messianic return had been established earlier in the century by the popular *Trovas* of Gonçalo Anes Bandarra, which prophesied a Portuguese eschatological emperor who would conquer Africa and the "promised land," convert all pagans and infidels to the true faith, and deliver his people to happiness and glory.[3] Sebastian himself was received in that mood of messianic anticipation, departed at a tender age to lead a crusade in North Africa, and died without heir in the battle of Alcazarquivir on August 4, 1578, predisposing Portugal to occupation by Philip II of Spain. The fulfillment of the prophesy, now undermined, could be salvaged only by negation of Sebastian's death, and rumor held accordingly that the king had escaped from the battlefield and had returned to Portugal under cover. The messianic image of the young warrior king, the precarious sociopolitical situation that preceded and followed his reign, and the official acceptance of his death interacting with its popular denial together engendered the potent, death-defying myth of Sebastian's return—an eternal, unfulfilled return that endured in Portugal and flourished in its Brazilian colony for centuries. "All the ills which befell the unfortunate nation were traced back to the mutilated body of the young king found on the battlefield," and so it seemed that all the ills could be remedied if that body were resurrected. "Martyrdom and misfortune gave the young king a saintly aura befitting one who was predestined to be the savior of his people."[4]

Sebastian returned not only in Gabriel de Espinosa and the three other impostors who stepped into the void of the king's anticipated reappearance but also in the subsequent leaders (João V, Alfonso VI, Dom Pedro) who were to varying degrees interpreted in terms of Sebastian's mythologized prototype. In Pernambuco, Brazil, the manifestations of Sebastianism were yet more radical. Sylvestre José Dos Santos announced in 1817 that when the number of faithful reached one thousand Sebastian would return from the Isla de las Brumas, would liberate Jerusalem, and would establish a paradise in which the poor would be rich. Until the troops intervened, destroying the community and massacring most of its inhabitants, Dos Santos and his four hundred followers awaited the savior and practiced innovative religious rites in their City of Terrestrial Paradise.[5]

Passive anticipation of Sebastian's return was not the agenda in the Enchanted Kingdom of Vila-Bela of Pedra Bonita, Pernambuco, some twenty years later. According to the prophet João Ferreira, the demonstration of absolute faith was necessary to effect the return of King Sebastian and, with it, a reversal of the worldly order. The prophet established his community beside two enormous rocks that formed the entryway to the Enchanted Kingdom, where mulattoes and blacks would become white, the old would become young, the ugly would become beautiful, and all would become rich, powerful, and immortal.[6] Smearing these boulders with blood was the means of inducing Sebastian's return, but the prophet assured that those who gave their lives would later be resurrected to enjoy the paradise made possible by their sacrifice. On May 11, 1838, Ferreira's father was the first victim. Thirty children, twelve men, eleven women, and fourteen dogs followed three days later. The Enchanted Kingdom ended not with the return of Sebastian but with the arrival of the police, who contributed to the body count twenty-two additional martyrs dying in dutiful compliance with the belief that their sacrifice would expedite the messiah's return.[7]

The Sebastian of Vila-Bela, like most returning messiahs in Christendom, made an appeal to the paradigm provided by Christ himself, returning from the dead before ascending to heaven and then promising a second return to establish his millennial kingdom. The date of the savior's advent is unspecified and consequently, for the faithful, perpetually imminent, with the messianic anticipation tending to intensify at moments when hardships on earth make a heavenly deliverance most appealing. As evident in Sebastianism, the messianic identity migrates from one hero to the next in a repeating pattern of fall and redemption, always reverting to the paradigm, itself evolving, as it adapts to a new hero or new circumstances. The identities of heroes accumulate in layers, and the original King Sebastian thus becomes a mere point of departure for the palimpsest of identities venerated in such communities as Vila-Bela.

The great majority of religious, quasi-religious, and secular cults of return emerge in the aftermath of a charged historical or mythical event, usually a defeat that must be undone. Christ's crucifixion, undone by resurrection, triumph, judgment, and reign in glory, provides a model not only for the suffering faithful and their serial, Jesus-like messiahs but also for lay revolutionaries who find in Christian eschatology a recipe for redeeming defeat. Elevation of the defeated leaders to the status of deity makes possible their heroic return. The specious but common claim that sacrificial victims or fallen soldiers will be resuscitated is in this context a microcosmic representation of the more comprehensive promise that the defeated revolution will return "from the dead" for vengeance and victory.[8] Defeat, even total defeat, is inverted and reintroduced as the commencement of a final, triumphant offensive that never comes.

Political exploitation of the Second Coming took a more theatrical turn following the Cuban Revolution, when an ersatz Christ was concocted to redeem the kingdom defiled by Fidel Castro. According to Senate Select Committee hearings in 1975, a plan proposed by Ian Fleming provided for the dissemination in Cuba of rumors to the effect that the messiah would soon return to denounce Castro as the Antichrist. Once an apocalyptic mood had been established among the populace, a bearded Central Intelligence Agency frogman would appear on a beach claiming to be Jesus, while a U.S. submarine would cover the sky with star shells to lend the Advent a pyrotechnic otherworldliness.[9]

More sincere, if not authentic, Christs have appeared in Latin America throughout the course of its history. In the village of Tacobamba in what is now Bolivia, an Indian named Miguel Acarapi claimed to be Christ in 1602. He was accompanied by twelve apostles and various female saints, conducted rituals using chicha (referred to as the "Blood of Christ") and the hallucinogenic drug known as San Pedro, and stated he had come to redeem the world. A century

later, during the intensified exploitation of native labor under the Marquis of
Castelfuerte (1724–36), natives in the Puno region received with devotion another indigenous Jesus of Nazareth. The messiah walked barefooted, wore a
crown of thorns and a rope around his neck, carried a cross, and blended a
potent anti-Hispanic message into his gospel until the corregidor had him hanged.[10] The later debut of a Tlaxcalan named Mariano was more political than
religious, and Mariano expected to be coronated in early January 1800 to the
fanfare of a mounted guard, banners of the Virgin of Guadalupe, and assorted
civil ostentations. He declined a crown of gold or silver, however, preferring the
crown of the crucified Jesus in a local church because, like Jesus, he had come
"to suffer in order to liberate his sons."[11] Such suffering was not on the agenda
of a messiah in modern Nicaragua who channeled his divinity into miraculous
cures. A former mechanic and Sandinista officer named Marco Antonio Arauz
Bonilla, known as Jesus of the Poor, was unambiguous in his claim to be "Jesus,
son of God." He added for clarity, "I am the very same one who was crucified
almost two thousand years ago, but this time I won't die on the cross."[12]

The hermetic wandering, mystery, and selective didactic contact with the
faithful that were common in medieval messianism also characterize the many
Latin American Christs and kings conforming to the model of El Deseado (Desired—but elusive—One) or El Encubierto (literally, Covered One, implying a
disguised or hidden identity). The phantom presence of these messiahs pays homage to their literal absence, mysteriously crossing the landscape to leave in their
wake the legendary impact of their passage. Indians captured by loyalist troops
in 1810 reported that the King of Spain, traveling through the Mexican countryside in a dark coach, had ordered them to join the independence revolt headed
by Miguel Hidalgo. The strategic borrowing of royal legitimation is yet more
patent in other reports that have Hidalgo traveling in the company of the king,
who concealed his identity by wearing a silver mask.[13] Amazon myths less pom-
pously relate that Christ once "roamed around the forest as a ragged and worn-
out old man," rewarding those who graciously received him and punishing those
who turned him away. The disappearance of that mythic messiah left behind a
model of ministry that predisposed reception of his vicars: "In ancient times
Christ roamed about" performing miracles, but now "He goes around in the
figure of Brother Francisco [da Cruz], curing the sick and announcing the end
of the world." Once Brother Francisco was called to his maker, death-defying
legends in turn generated his phantom appearances as a Christ-like wanderer.
One rumor holds that Francisco "travels around Europe preaching his message
among scholars and sages."[14] If the messiah, immune to mortality, is late in
appearing, it is because a greater destiny detours his return.

In secular cases, too, a means must be found to recycle the messianic hero in
perpetuity. As Che Guevara put it in reference to fallen revolutionaries, "Their
life does not end so long as the people do not will it."[15] Such was certainly the
case with the ubiquitous Guevara himself, immortal as an icon of revolutionaries, idealists, and, more recently, pop culture, with his image gracing products
from wristwatches to skis. Earlier in Cuban history, the fallen soldiers of independence also returned "all over the place," in this case as spirits or ghosts.[16]

The same occurred with particular insistence in the popular response to the death of Mexican revolutionary Emiliano Zapata, who was killed in a 1919 ambush. Some claimed that Zapata was in Puebla, in Hungary, in Arabia, "and the Arabs loved him like a god." Others compared him to Moses, having left his people temporarily to receive the Tablets of the Law in the Holy Land; to Quetzalcóatl, because he will return from the east; and to the prototype of El Encubierto, "disguised as an earthenware salesman." When the poetics of absence and surreptitious return yielded to apotheosis, Zapata was spotted as a celestial warrior—on a white horse, donning a sombrero, his sword shining in the moonlight—and those who saw him through binoculars "did not know if it was Zapata or Santiago." The Christian messianism culminated finally in the equation of the hero and the God—"he died like Jesus Christ" so that "everyone else will be saved"—thereby providing for a second coming: "Zapata will return."[17]

The traumatic death of the messiah is unacceptable and therefore impossible, so the death is undone through resurrection, reconstitution, reawakening, mistaken or assumed identity, exile or hiding, ascension into heaven, mysterious disappearance-reappearance, or any number of other representations that acknowledge absence but deny death. The messianic hero's identity migrates between the mundane and the divine, between the historical personage and the construct that emerges from its mythopoetic elaboration. A man departs, and a man-god returns. The messiah as a cultural hero creates order out of chaos, culture out of primitivism, justice out of exploitation, plenty out of nothing, and good out of evil. When he disappears, his return is keenly anticipated because his sacred accomplishments have been desecrated and his people oppressed, thereby creating the need for restitution and salvation that like a vacuum draws him back from the grave.

In a myth told among Aymará-speaking llama herders in Bolivia, a syncretic Christ arrives as a powerful stranger, twice emerges from the tomb in which his local opponents lock him, and then rises to become the sun, destroying the savage society that rejected him and creating the new society enjoyed by those who tell the myth.[18] In its simplicity the myth evokes most of the major themes: the cultural hero oscillating between god and man, the antithetical force that disrupts his kingdom, the (multiple) resurrection and return, the triumph over evil and savagery, the new age, and the reign in glory among his chosen people.

The happy ending is often postponed because the hero's return is prevented, projected into an indefinite future, or left hovering in perpetual imminence. Postconquest legends from many cultures relate the flight of cultural heroes to lakes, mountains, jungles, the sky, or hidden cities where they hold in reserve the offensive that will expel the conqueror. Communities are cohered and peoples "saved" not because these heroes actually return from the dead, but rather because the messianic promise preserves their potential in suspension between life and death, between history that subjugates and myth that redeems.

Movements such as Taqui Onqoy could thus mobilize masses on the strength of the huacas' imminent revival, and the later Moro Onqoy was similarly cohered in anticipation of an Inca who would "liberate the Indians from death."[19] The myth of Inkarrí, discussed later in this chapter, is exemplary in its anticipation of a messianic hero who conspires a return to undo conquest. The modern Asháninka also treat the motif of obstructed heroic return in a myth that relates the fate of an indigenous genius kidnapped by the enemy. The genius is forced to reveal his scientific secrets, and as a result the white people who hold him captive acquire the technological advantage by which they oppress the Indians. When this Asháninka genius escapes and returns to his people, the balance of power will shift in indigenous favor and the era of oppression will end.[20] Fulfillment of the messianic promise must be postponed until the hero overcomes the obstacles impeding the completion of his mission, but in the meantime the myth recuperates cultural pride by depicting technomilitary supremacy not as an attribute intrinsic to the Western world but as another piece of stolen Indian property. The kidnapped Asháninka genius may never realize the anticipated return, but his "existence" in incarcerated custody—the trope of an indentured, sequestered culture—itself restores a measure of hope, if not salvation, to his people.

The myth thus defends the interests of its authors as they confront adverse events. In other cases myth and theater aggressively return to unacceptable events in order to undo or reverse them. The theatrical *Dance of the Feathers* in Mexico defused the trauma of conquest by switching the scripts of the players. At the drama's conclusion Moctezuma, finally face-to-face with Hernán Cortés, asks the conqueror his purpose. Cortés states that he has come to offer baptism, to which Moctezuma responds, "Do you claim that my gods are false? To what length will your insolence go?" Battle ensues, Cortés is defeated and begs for death, Moctezuma spares him, and Cortés pleads for forgiveness in gratitude. The defeat, plea for death, and pardon mime in reverse the scenario between Cuauhtémoc (replaced in the play by the more symbolically significant Moctezuma) and Cortés, but most important is the play's greater reversal, its rehearsal of the conquest undone.[21] The inversion defies history in order to liberate and redeem the conquered people, once chosen and now vanquished. The myth speaks for its authors because the events do not.

When the conqueror returns to history, conversely, the intent is not to reverse the conclusion but rather to reenact it. The *Dance of the Moors and Christians* and its theatrical adaptations to the conquest of Mexico dramatized Spanish supremacy before native audiences that often bowed for mass baptism as the curtain closed.[22] The theater of conquest also tended to spill off the stage into the military expeditions themselves. Francisco Pizarro's emulations of Cortés demonstrated that successful strategies of the past could be repeated, but the theatrical mimesis of a "new Cortés" rose to singular heights in 1595 when Juan de Oñate set out to conquer New Spain's northern frontier. Oñate presumed that the Pueblos were familiar with the conquest of the Aztecs and choreographed his invasion accordingly. The props, all borrowed from Cortés, included a banner of Our Lady of Remedies, Tlaxcalan allies, and an Indian mistress and interpreter—kidnapped from New Mexico earlier—who would serve as "a second Malinche." Twelve Franciscan "apostles" also accompanied Oñate, and in imitation of Cortés's famous 1524 gesture Oñate knelt before them, kissed their hands and their hems, and then invited the Pueblos to do the same.[23]

In modern times, the desire to be the new version of an idolized hero has gone beyond mere theatrics to rituals of metempsychosis. Argentine president Carlos Saúl Menem, an avid reader of Domingo Faustino Sarmiento's *Facundo*, was edified in his earlier years by transformative identification with the dead military hero. Some of those close to Menem in La Rioja reported, "He used to go out on the patio screaming, and he raised up his arms asking that the spirit of Facundo enter his body." Menem also went on all-night vigils in search of the spirit of Facundo Quiroga and, as a believer in reincarnation, practiced rituals to better make himself "the 'dwelling' of the Caudillo's spirit."[24] Juan Perón was reportedly "in direct contact" with José de San Martín through seances, and in the 1950s the Colombian dictator Gustavo Rojas Pinilla believed himself to be the reincarnation of Simón Bolívar.[25] Guatemalan presidents José Rafael Carrera in the mid-nineteenth century and General Jorge Ubico Castañeda in the 1930s both fanatically identified with Napoleon, and Ubico surrounded himself with busts and portraits of the hero to better emulate his demeanor.[26]

When a hero himself does not return, adaptations (often bastardizations) of his cause are championed by surrogates who for better or worse draw upon his surplus numinousness. In several modern cases stolen relics, including bodies and body parts, have been fetishistically exploited to transfer identity, power, and legitimacy to those who maneuver in the void of a dead hero's absence. Exemplary was the corpse of Eva Perón, first embalmed for "absolute corporal permanence" and then sequestered from tomb to tomb pursuant to the myth that whoever possessed the corpse would govern Argentina. The immortality symbolized by the body's triumph over putrefaction was then transcendentalized to fortify the sanctity of the popular Saint Evita, nurturing madonna of the workers, who on occasion appeared in the sky. An attempt to corporalize Evita's return to her needy people was made when the "witch doctor" José López Rega sought to transfer her spirit into the body of Juan Perón's third wife, known as Isabel, who in the 1970s served as vice president and then president of Argentina.[27] All of these returns—in the incorruptible flesh, in the hearts of the workers, in the popular pantheon, in the ersatz surrogates—were reinforced by political exploitation of Evita's last will: "I want to live eternally with Perón and with my People."[28]

The transference of symbolic power concentrated in a relic was suggested a century earlier when Mexican caudillo and president Antonio López de Santa Anna had his amputated, mummified leg exhumed, transported to Mexico City, and ceremoniously enshrined. The leg, which had been shattered by a French cannonball during Santa Anna's heroic resistance, was offered to the fatherland in speeches, poems, and songs, all politely applauded by the cabinet, congress, and diplomatic corp. Once Santa Anna fell from grace, however, the leg came to no good end as "a gang of hooligans had disinterred and paraded it insultingly through the streets," chanting, "Death to the cripple."[29] The symbolic significance of body parts was similarly volatile following the 1967 execution of

Che Guevara. Guevara's hands were amputated from his corpse as a trophy to document his demise, but later the hands were received in Cuba as semisacred political relics. Panegyric eulogies by Fidel Castro—"the hands in which he carried his weapons of freedom, with which he wrote down his brilliant ideas, with which he worked in the cane fields"—were followed by enshrinement.[30]

Most appeals to a past hero's identity content themselves with less gruesome mementos. The Ecuadorian independence hero Eloy Alfaro doubly returned to the 1980s movement Alfaro Vive, Carajo (Alfaro Is Alive, Damn It), once in name and again when the insurrection introduced itself by stealing the sword and a sculpted bust of its namesake. In January 1974, the Colombian M-19 movement made a similar debut by stealing the sword and spurs of Simón Bolívar, whose innumerable returns (registered even in graffiti: "Wake up, Bolívar, your people need you") are perhaps matched only by those of Che Guevara (with corresponding graffiti: "In every youth there is a Che").[31]

The taking of the forebear's name, as in the Eloy Alfaro example, intends to legitimate a new movement by representing it as the resumption of a fallen hero's mission. The Zapatistas in Chiapas make that appeal to Emiliano Zapata, the Sandinistas in Nicaragua to Augusto César Sandino, and the Farabundo Martí National Liberation Front of El Salvador to Agustín Farabundo Martí. In earlier history, José Gabriel Condorcanqui documented his lineage from the rebellious Inca Túpac Amaru and then led his 1780 insurrection under this name. The two rebel Incas, compounded into the now polysemous signifier Túpac Amaru, resulted in the name's later reference not so much to one or the other as to a composite heroic symbol of resistance. In modern times the name has been assumed by such struggles as the urban Tupamaro insurgency in Uruguay and the Túpac Amaru Revolutionary Movement in Peru.

In Alto Peru, Julián Apasa chose Túpac Catari as his nom de guerre as he resumed the missions of Túpac Amaru and Tomás Catari.[32] At the time of his own execution Túpac Catari made a prophesy—"Tomorrow I will return and will be millions"—that had partial fulfillment a century later when Pablo Zárate Willca, the general of a rebel Indian army until his death in 1899, was regarded as Túpac Catari's reincarnation. Zárate Willca himself made innumerable postmortem appearances that culminated thirty years later when legend held that his body had been transported on a litter to La Paz, where he presided over the "restoration of the throne of the Incas."[33] A more enduring response to Túpac Catari's prophesy came in 1978, when an indigenous movement declared, "Today we are those Túpac Cataris and there are millions of us."[34] The name, now synonymous with Bolivian indigenous causes, reappears in the many movements that aspire to the rebel's ideals: Túpac Katari Campesino Confederation, Tupaj Katari Indian Movement, Tupac Katari Revolutionary Movement.

Contrived resuscitations can also tap the eternal life beyond death of fallen heroes and channel it into insurrection. Leaders of the Yucatec Caste War of 1847 included Jacinto Canek among the signatories of their first communiqué, despite the fact that this leader of a 1761 Maya rebellion had been executed more than eighty years prior.[35] Canek himself made an appeal to the indigenous past "by taking the Peten Itza ruler's name of Can Ek," to which he added

"Chichan [Little] Moctezuma."[36] Several versions of a written call to participate in the 1712 Tzeltal Rebellion in Chiapas similarly included the promise that Moctezuma would be resurrected to assist the Maya in defeating the Spaniards.[37] Both Canek and Moctezuma are defeated leaders who nevertheless return as empowered symbols of triumph.

A recurring return of another sort was perpetuated in the precolumbian Americas by the intermingling identities of priests, rulers, deities, and deified ancestors. Unlike the abstract and anticipated Christian God, whose most compelling colonial presence was in a proliferation of miraculous images, the indigenous deities of imperial cultures claimed a certain tangible presence through human representation on earth. Andean gods enjoyed earthly perpetuity in their royal namesakes, as for example Viracocha was the name of both the creator god and a fourteenth-century Inca. After death Inca royalty was in turn deified and perpetuated in the form of venerated mummies known as *mallquis*.[38] In Mesoamerica, such divine names as Quetzalcóatl signified first a deity and then the priests who venerated and represented that deity, serving as god bearers marked with the deity's insignia and carrying his "sacred bundle" of objects. When these priests died and one or more of them were themselves mythologized into the status of deified ancestors, a new divine layer was superimposed onto the original Quetzalcóatl. And so the process continued as the centuries passed, with the original deity always seen through the palimpsest of those who embodied him and now, to no small degree, constitute his identity.

Quetzalcóatl and Saint Thomas

At about the time of the collapse of Teotihuacán (circa 650–750), a new Toltec ceremonial center began to emerge in Tula for veneration of the god Quetzalcóatl.[39] In the Toltec pantheon the Plumed Serpent was configured in opposition to the rival Tezcatlipoca (Smoking Mirror), these "polarized deities" being together venerated as the creator gods but with the myths apportioning the positive attributes in greater measure to Quetzalcóatl.[40] Tula also produced a legendary priest, named Quetzalcóatl after the deity, who was "committed to maintaining the purity of the traditional cult," opposed to human sacrifice, and beleaguered by the politico-religious adversity of Tezcatlipoca's priests.[41] This human Quetzalcóatl was elevated to the status of a Toltec priest-king and exalted for his virtuous promotion of civilization, culture, wisdom, and the proper exercise of priesthood. His adversaries never tired of conspiring against him—"the sorcerers often tried to trick him, / so that he would perform human sacrifices," for example—and they ultimately achieved their goal of deposing him.[42] Quetzalcóatl was persuaded to drink pulque and, in the consequent intoxication, succumbed to incestuous relations with his sister. He abandoned Tula in guilt and humiliation, heading east "to the interior of the sea, toward the land of the red color, there he disappeared."[43] His flight occasioned the dispersion of his people and left behind the messianic anticipation of his return. Tula fell in 1168 to nomadic invaders from the north, and a century later the Aztecs entered the valley of

Mexico, also from the north, battling their way to an island in Lake Texcoco to establish Tenochtitlán in 1325 as the base for imperial expansion.

The one name Quetzalcóatl used in reference to both the mythological deity (also called Ehécatl Quetzalcóatl) and the historical priest-king (also called To-piltzin Quetzalcóatl) has resulted in a volatile interaction of identities, sometimes by intent and other times by confusion. For the Mesoamericans, the fusion of the human and divine identities was by design: The priests of Quetzalcóatl carried his name, his emblems, and his "fire" as they to some degree became the god whom they venerated, became man-gods who corporalized the absent deity's presence and constituted a permeation of the absolute boundary between human and divine realms.[44] The constant circulation of identities between gods, priests who assumed gods' identities, and deified ancestors kept the dynamics of theocracy in motion. After conquest the man-god composite acquired novel resonances because the polysemous Quetzalcóatl was readily susceptible to manipulation by Christian, indigenous, and syncretic interpretations inclined to draw upon whichever aspect of the composite—the god, the man, the man-god—best served a particular politico-religious interest. The concept of man-god also evoked Christ as a returning deity incarnate, thereby generating a new and often syncretic line of associations, images, and identities.

The Aztecs, Nahuatl-speaking like the Toltecs, included the creator gods Quetzalcóatl and Tezcatlipoca in their pantheon, but these were subordinated to the supreme deity, Huitzilopochtli, a war god associated with the sun and commensurate with the Aztecs' emerging identity as a chosen people with an imperial mission. Following Toltec tradition, however, the Tenochtitlán nobility anticipated the return of a deified royal ancestor whose arrival would "shake the foundation of heaven."[45] The strange apparition of the Spanish conquerors—with their unimaginable ships, beards, horses, armor, and firearms—was inexplicable in Mesoamerican frames of reference until the mystery was processed by Quetzalcóatl mythopoetics and began to assume meaning as a prophesy fulfilled. A series of coincidences seemed to corroborate. Hernán Cortés entered Mexico in 1519, precisely the year of the cyclical Aztec calendar—ce ácatl, or 1 reed—that was associated with the god Quetzalcóatl, that gave him his calendric name, and that was said to be the birth and death year of Quetzalcóatl the priest-king. Cortés arrived by sea and entered Mexico from the east, and the latter—of particular importance in the mythology of Quetzalcóatl's return—resonated through ce ácatl's designation of the eastern region.[46] The ships and their sails may also have evoked Quetzalcóatl's identity as the god of wind, "bearing his temples [ships] on his shoulders." Quetzalcóatl is the precursor who "sweeps the road" for the approaching storm of other gods (or Spaniards), just as the wind announces and opens the way for rain.[47]

Positioned between an incomprehensible apparition on one side and the Quetzalcóatl myth on the other, the Aztec emperor Moctezuma arrived reluctantly at the logical, erroneous conclusion that Cortés must be, in some sense, the deified priest-king Quetzalcóatl, returning to resume sovereignty of his domain. Bernardino de Sahagún's informants in the Florentine Codex are explicit: Moctezuma "thought and believed that it was Topiltzin Quetzalcóatl who had landed. For they were of the opinion that he would return, that he would appear, that he would come back to his seat of authority, because he had gone in that direction [eastward] when he left."[48]

Were Cortés actually the returning Quetzalcóatl, Moctezuma would be obliged to defer to the man-god's higher authority and to abdicate in favor of the ancestor returning to a throne held for him in regency. Moctezuma's military response to the Spanish invasion was therefore burdened not merely with uncertainty regarding the nature and intentions of the alien newcomers but also with a hesitancy and, finally, a reverential deference that gave Cortés the strategic advantage. "You have arrived in Mexico, your home," the messengers told Cortés, and under Moctezuma's instructions they dressed him in the bejeweled image of Quetzalcóatl as the man underwent (and accepted) ritual transformation into the man-god.[49] Upon their return to Tenochtitlán, the messengers were ritually cleansed with sacrificial blood to neutralize their contact with the deities. A feast for the Spaniards was likewise drizzled with sacrificial blood because Moctezuma "took them for gods, considered them gods, worshiped them as god." When Cortés-Quetzalcóatl was formally received in November 1519, Moctezuma acknowledged him as the returning ancestor, welcomed him home to Mexico, and offered him the throne held in his absence by the Aztec royalty. "Be doubly welcomed, enter the land, go to enjoy your palace; rest your body. May our lords be arrived in the land."[50] By the time Moctezuma realized his error he was already in irons.

The messianic expectation of a returning cultural hero thereby predisposed the Aztec empire to conquest by a European empire, itself motivated by a messianic agenda. The Quetzalcóatl myth turned against its authors, it would seem, but at the same time the imposition of Spanish paradigms and the circulation of ideas between cultures during the early colonial era calls the authorship of the myth into question. The post-conquest source material on which understanding of Quetzalcóatl is based—notably the *Florentine Codex*, derived from Christianized native accounts—makes it difficult to determine what predated conquest, what was generated by the invasion itself as its incomprehensibility was mythopoetically processed, and what was revised syncretically in retrospect to bestow upon European-American history a measure of meaning, coherence, closure, and adaptation to the new guiding paradigms. A myth that is thus overdetermined may also suggest the strategic redirection of nativist discourse back toward its source, "so that Indians appeared to themselves as active participants in their own victimization."[51]

One indication of retroactive mythopoetic cleanup seems apparent in the interpretation of signs that, according to the *Florentine Codex* and the *Historia de Tlaxcala*, began announcing the conquest some ten years prior to Cortés's arrival.[52] More than preceding and foreboding the cataclysm, the signs, or at least their interpretation, may have emerged after the fact and then "returned" to contextualize an event "too extraordinary to contain its own meaning."[53] The reinterpretation or invention of unusual natural phenomena softens the blow of the surprise attack by retroactively announcing its predictability, and it ameliorates the damaged cultural pride of having been duped by an unforeseen imposter. The defeat is inexorably fixed in the subjugation of colonialism, but mythopoesis—even when guided, surveilled, or syncretized—can recuperate the past, revising history and resisting deculturation to render an excruciating present more tolerable.

The redirection of events toward specific political purposes was far more patent on the European side of the conquest, notably in the earliest extant account of Quetzalcóatl, that of Cortés. In his shrewd second letter to Charles V, Cortés utilized discourse attributed to Moctezuma to imply indigenous grounds (the European grounds had been established earlier, by the 1493 Bulls of Donation and pursuant documents) for Charles's legitimate title to Mexico. Far from the man-god of the *Florentine Codex*, Cortés's Quetzalcóatl is humanized and depicted politically as Moctezuma refers to a "chieftain" of whom the Aztecs "were all vassals." The descendants of this chieftain had sent soldiers, led by Cortés, to reconquer Mexico. Cortés-Quetzalcóatl is represented not as a returning god or deified cultural hero, but only as the commander of a military expedition dispatched by the heirs of an emperor who had been deprived of his domain and returned now vicariously to claim it. The military reconquest was just, according to the Moctezuma speech related by Cortés, because the exiled chieftain had previously attempted to resume his reign, only to be driven off by force of arms. Thus, Moctezuma continued, "We have always held that those who descended from him would come and conquer this land and take us as their vassals."[54] In the indigenous accounts, Quetzalcóatl's return, however cataclysmic, is imbued with godliness and messianic anticipation. In Cortés's account, conversely, Quetzalcóatl is three or four times removed from the origin (god, priest-king, descendants, military emissaries), and the promised return, far from messianic, is recast as a threat of retaliation, conquest, and subjugation.

The stylized Moctezuma of Cortés's letter defers not to an ancestral deity but rather to a distant emperor whose emissaries demand the throne from vassals who have usurped it. This emperor's entitlement is further enhanced because the "indigenous" people themselves turn out to be intruders. In words attributed to Moctezuma, "Neither I, nor any of those who dwell in this land, are natives of it, but foreigners who came from very distant parts."[55] The meaning of that statement within the regional, Mesoamerican context was subject to manipulation when recontextualized in global terms, implying here that the two "foreign" conquerors—Moctezuma and Charles—both had claims to Mexico but that Charles's claim was privileged by precedence because he had ruled earlier (as Quetzalcóatl) and now "returned." Moctezuma, speaking as though coached by just-war theorists, submitted finally to the greater authority that had presented itself: "We believe and are certain that he [Charles V] is our natural lord." The proper deference was then extended to Cortés when Moctezuma assured him, "We shall obey you and hold you as our lord in place of that great sovereign of whom you speak."[56]

The letter's coauthored discourse—part speech attributed to Moctezuma, part its appropriation and adaptation to the Spanish political milieu—transferred the lordly reception and imperial entitlements that may have been lavished upon Cortés-Quetzalcóatl to His Majesty Charles V, evidencing a deference that behooved a loyal Spanish subject on an (illegal) expedition. Cortés's strategy, as he worded it in the letter, was to make Moctezuma "believe that Your Majesty was he whom they were expecting."[57] If on the battlefield Cortés maneuvered Quetzalcóatl mythology to his military advantage, he ultimately had to step out of the myth and the deity's accouterments to be, as he was, a conqueror in service of the crown. That exit must have been as shocking to Moctezuma as the entrance into Quetzalcóatl's identity had been to Cortés. The Lord worked in strange ways, "sweeping the road" with Quetzalcóatl to open the path by which Cortés (and even Charles) made a detoured "return."

A measure of divinity was later restored to Quetzalcóatl by the friars, but it disavowed the indigenous origin to co-opt the man-god for Christianity. In this nexus of messianic myths from opposing cultures, many friars reckoned that Quetzalcóatl was actually Saint Thomas, the apostle of Christ, whose identity had been Indianized and distorted over the centuries.[58] The transformation of Quetzalcóatl into Saint Thomas required a retroactive physical metamorphosis that endowed the Aztec hero with Caucasian features, including a long, bearded face. Accompanying the superimposed apostolic appearance was a growing litany of "Christian" virtues that were attributed to the priest-king Quetzalcóatl. He was born of a virgin and dedicated to the messianic task of redeeming a sinful people. He was opposed to human sacrifice but promoted asceticism and self-sacrificial rituals.[59] He led an exemplary moral life, was chaste (though in Aztec accounts he has the incestuous relation with his sister), worked miracles, promoted monotheism, was betrayed, was persecuted, and disappeared promising return. The *Ramírez Codex* is most explicit in its Christian attributes, endowing Quetzalcóatl-Thomas with a Bible that he leaves with the natives as he bids them farewell.[60] In the long view this Quetzalcóatl composite—from its virgin birth to its messianic promise—alludes through Thomas to Jesus himself, who according to Matthew will return from the east.[61] Just as Quetzalcóatl the priest-king stands in for Quetzalcóatl the god, so Thomas is specified but Jesus is invoked.

Once the friars began looking, evidence linking Quetzalcóatl and Saint Thomas seemed to turn up everywhere. Even philology contributed to the theory: the Nahuatl *cóatl* (as in Quetzal*cóatl*) and the Greek *Thomé* both mean "twin," with the one hero doubling the other.[62] The chroniclers also cited as evidence the progression toward monotheism in the imperial indigenous societies, as well as similarities between native rituals and the Christian sacraments of baptism and communion, all of which seemed to suggest prehispanic evangelization. A single identity for Quetzalcóatl and Thomas was so compelling to the Dominican Servando Teresa de Mier that as late as 1813 he was asking, "What was the religion of the Mexicans but a Christianity confused by time and the equivocal nature of the hieroglyphs?" The Indians had jumbled things up with their strange inscriptions, but the gospel was nevertheless discernible. In separatist arguments implying that the Americas owed not even the faith to Spain, Mier pointed out that in their semiotic clumsiness the conquerors "destroyed the same religion that they professed, and put back the same images that they burned because they were under different symbols."[63]

This line of reasoning had found its symbolic climax earlier, on December 12, 1794, when Mier startled the viceroy, archbishop, and others who had gathered at Tepeyac to pay homage to the patron of New Spain. Four propositions made Mier's position clear: that the image of the Virgin of Guadalupe was imprinted not on the tilma of Juan Diego but rather on that of Saint Thomas, "apostle of the kingdom," known to the natives as Quetzalcóatl; that Saint Thomas had built a temple for veneration of the image some 1,750 years before in Tenayuca, and the natives there venerated Mary as the Mother of God; that when the Indians apostatized Saint Thomas hid the image, which remained undiscovered until the Virgin revealed its whereabouts to Juan Diego; and that the image dated from the first century, miraculously imprinted for Thomas by the Virgin Mary herself.[64] The syncretic Tonantzin-Mary and the patently hispanic Virgin of Guadalupe were thereby displaced by a composite counterimage— Quetzalcóatl-Thomas—that was as devoid of native content (Quetzalcóatl is a misnomer for Thomas, Tonantzin and Juan Diego are demoted, the natives are unreliable Christians) as it was of Spanish content (American Christianity predates the Iberian mission). The creole future thus opened unencumbered.

As recorded in the apocryphal *Acta Thomae*, Saint Thomas was the apostle popularly accredited with evangelization "beyond the Ganges" (India is America), and this belief was widely held by Iberians of the sixteenth century.[65] In graphic representation, the region of Thomas's ministry was registered in the mappamundi illustrating the 1203 *Beato of Burgo de Osma*, one of a series of illuminated manuscripts following the *Comentarios al Apocalipsis* written in 776 by the Beato of Liébana. On this map the frontiers of Christendom are indicated by positioning the apostles' tombs in the regions that they are believed to have evangelized. Thomas is situated in the uppermost position on the map (east on the mappamundi is located where north is located on modern maps), precisely— to use Columbus's biblical phrase for the Americas—at "the end of the east."[66] The same is registered in an 1165 forged letter dispatched to the pope and European emperors, in which Prester John boasted that his lands extended into the far reaches of India, "where the body of the holy apostle Thomas lies."[67] In a letter of 1495, Jaime Ferrer reminded Columbus that Saint Thomas, going overland to the East, had carried Christianity to the peoples of India and that in 1492 Columbus had renewed Thomas's mission by sailing in the opposite direction, westward, to the East.[68] Such beliefs constituted part of the broader tendency of imperial Christians to view themselves as returning with entitlement to lands previously held (Crusades, Reconquest), visited (Marco Polo, John Mandeville, explorers), or evangelized (Thomas and other apostles, Prester John) by their ancestors and allies, however legendary or distant.

The presence of crosses in Mexico contributed substantially to the Thomas-Quetzalcóatl equation, for the crosses seemed to be indisputable, tangible proof that the natives had once been Christianized. According to Peter Martyr, Spanish explorers found crosses on the Yucatan coast in 1517. When they inquired as to the origin of one cross, the Indians replied "that a certain, most beautiful man had left them the said relic as a souvenir. Others said that on it a man more radiant than the Sun had died."[69] Whatever the natives may have actually said, the Spaniards were inclined to overlook the cross's non-Christian meanings (as representation of the rain god or four cardinal points, for example) and to steer indigenous discourse toward a priori European assumptions. A certain inquisitive objectivity was feigned—Diego Velázquez, the governor of Cuba, included among his instructions to Cortés that the significance of Mexican crosses be ascertained—but true investigation was preempted by resort to conclusions that were congruent with Christian paradigms. As the Franciscan Diego López Cogolludo summed it up in 1688, indigenous crosses were in themselves sufficient basis for the Spaniards "to presume an evangelization of the Indies by the apostles."[70]

Thomas's evangelization of the New World included South America as well as Mexico, with popular accounts holding that the apostle began his mission in Brazil and Paraguay and then crossed the Andes to Peru. In 1508 Portuguese sailors learned of Thomas's mission in Brazil, and friars found hard proof of the same in footprints discovered on a riverbank.[71] Antonio Ruiz de Montoya, a founder of early Jesuit reductions, discussed Thomas at length in his 1639 *Spiritual Conquest* and believed that the Jesuits' success was indebted to the "divine mysteries" that Thomas had revealed to the natives earlier.[72] Certain "capricious euphonic semblances" also led Jesuits in Paraguay to equate the Guaraní Paí Zumé with the apostle Padre Tomé.[73] A more sustained fusion of the apostle with an indigenous hero occurred in Peru, where traditions told of a white, bearded sage called Tunupa who left as monument of his mission the great stone cross at Carabuco. As it was explained by Francisco de Avila in a 1646 sermon to Peruvian natives, Tunupa, "which means St. Thomas," had come to teach the ten commandments but was bound, sentenced to death, and escaped across the waters of Lake Titicaca, leaving behind the indestructible cross.[74]

The Christianized indigenous account of Pachacuti Yamqui has Saint Thomas in the Andes immediately before the region's imperial consolidation by the Incas, helping out here on the road to monotheism as he did in Mexico in the guise of Quetzalcóatl. This white-haired sage in flowing robes, again called Tunupa, appeared shortly after Jesus' birth, bringing the true faith, healing the sick with his touch, preaching in all languages, performing miracles among his "sons and daughters," and then disappearing over the sea.[75] Pachacuti Yamqui dramatized the sixteenth-century "return" of Christianity to Peru through a scene in which Pizarro, the friar Vicente de Valverde, a defeated Inca, and "the holy Gospel of Jesus Christ, Our Lord" together crossed the threshold of the Coricancha temple, "with great royal splendor and pomp of great majesty." There, "at last, the law of God and his long-awaited holy Gospel entered to take possession of the new vineyard," and there Valverde "preached like another Saint Thomas the apostle, patron of this kingdom."[76] The apostolic mission and the Carabuco cross also appeared in the work of Guaman Poma, with the apostle in this case not Thomas but Bartholomew, and not coming for the first time but following up on work initiated by a son of Noah, "all of which arrived in this kingdom before the Spaniards."[77]

The Tunupa-Thomas legend was often reinforced by artefacts and testimony that lent it authenticity. Thomas's footprints and knee prints in stone were popular, and in one noteworthy Peruvian case, after a failed attempt to move one of the knee-imprinted rocks, the archbishop Toribio Alfonso de Mogrovejo enshrined it in situ with a chapel. Mogrovejo also heard a report from elderly Indians concerning a tall, blue-eyed, long-bearded man dressed in the fashion of prophets, who "preached and did not sleep." The newly explored Amazon was the unlikely site of a separate discovery when one of Lope de Aguirre's soldiers reported having found a statue "with a long beard and foreign dress and with a book in one hand."[78] Juan de Betanzos, the Inca Garcilaso de la Vega, and others believed that a statue in the Inca temple of Viracocha also evidenced the former presence of an apostle, for it seemed that "the individual it represented had worn an ankle-length white tunic, had held an object resembling a priest's breviary in his hands, and had his hair cut in the priestly tonsure."[79]

Like the myths and crosses interpreted and used differently by opposing cultures, Quetzalcóatl had one meaning for the prehispanic Aztecs, another meaning for the Spaniards who distorted the myth to conform to the European myth of Saint Thomas's evangelization of India, and a third meaning in the contact culture of the Christianized natives, with each of these meanings evolving as the years passed. What the multiple versions in the Quetzalcóatl-Thomas complex hold in common is the insistence of a return that brings salvation or transformation. Quetzalcóatl promises his return, Cortés returns as Quetzalcóatl, Thomas returns as Quetzalcóatl, Jesus returns in Thomas, the Christians return to lands believed to have been previously Christianized, and the mission of Thomas and these Christians prepares the world for the return of Christ, who plays a messianic role in Christendom not unlike that of Quetzalcóatl in Aztec mythology.

The conquered people's myth was ultimately absorbed into the conqueror's mythology and metamorphosed accordingly to satisfy Christian millennialism, but in the process of this assimilation the separate indigenous, hispanic, and syncretic interpretations of Quetzalcóatl provided an interpretive continuum— also millennial—by which "Indians and Spaniards believed that they belonged to one and the same historicity," whether they liked it or not.[80] What may have seemed like rupture to the uninitiated was actually continuity on the march toward world unity. The cosmos was on course, had meaning, and evidenced divine guidance toward an (imposed) Christian destiny that would accept Cortés as Quetzalcóatl and insist upon Thomas as Quetzalcóatl because these two errors—one indigenous, one European—supported the same conclusion.

If in most instances the Quetzalcóatl myth seems to have turned against its authors, in nativist rebellions a Quetzalcóatl prototype resurfaced with a vengeance to generate heroes whose messianic return empowered multiple insurrections. "It was time to shake off the Spanish yoke" for the Zapotecs of Oaxaca in 1550 because an assimilated Quetzalcóatl, "having disappeared, promised to return in later centuries to liberate his nation from its enemies." The rebellion's leaders maneuvered the return efficaciously, recruiting "the youth to take up arms, announcing that the divine caudillo had arrived and that he would free them from the slavery in which they suffered."[81] The Mixes, like the Zapotecs and also the Chontales, were in the same years inspired by the return of a messianic hero, in this case the mythological Cong Hoy. When the Spaniards arrived Cong Hoy hid in a lake, promising to return and liberate his people. The moment came in 1660, when chronic abuse was aggravated by the whipping to death of a cacique. With the inspiration of Cong Hoy's imminent appearance (along with that of his Zapotec and Chontal counterparts), a massive rebellion challenged colonial authority in Oaxaca.[82] Later in the seventeenth century, similarly, rebelling Tarahumaras and Tepehuans of northern Mexico expected "that a powerful man would come from the east and would liberate them from the Spanish devil."[83] The 1847 Caste War likewise had the Yucatec Maya anticipating the return of a cultural hero who would "arrive from the east to be crowned as King of the Yucatan."[84] All of these rebellions were initiated and sustained not by the cultural hero himself (who as a mythological construct never arrives), but by the promise of return, the possibility of messianic redemption, the power that the imminent return imbues in the leaders who "reincarnate" the myth. As a contemporary Nahua poet put it, the awaited messianic hero "will never arrive/because he is in ourselves./He has been asleep,/but now he is awakening."[85]

The Myth of Inkarrí

The myth of Inkarrí probably began to circulate in the early seventeenth century, was of great currency in the eighteenth century (sometimes referred to as "the century of Inkarrí"), and is still prominent in the Andes today.[86] Against a complex backdrop of history and legend, the myth synthesizes the two most symbolic executions of the Spanish conquest of the Incas—the garroting of Atahualpa in 1533 and the decapitation of Túpac Amaru in 1572—into the death of a single mythological hero, Inkarrí, who has become powerless because his head is separated from his body. Once his head and body are reunited, Inkarrí will defeat Christ and the Andeans will "recuperate their history," ending the age of "disorder, confusion, and darkness" that was initiated by conquest.[87]

In versions with more literal tendencies, one or the other of the executed Incas is specified, as illustrated by the following passage's allusion to the ransom of Atahualpa: "The conqueror Pizarro arrived. The Inca offered him a room full of silver. Pizarro's ambition cannot be satisfied, so he kills Inkarrí."[88] The transition from Inca to Inkarrí in this modern narrative is natural and untroubled, as though the one were the other. Beginning in 1533, however, a causal relation is suggested: "The death of Atahualpa cast the universe into chaos," and this absence and trauma engendered the messianic longing that gradually mythologized the dead Inca into the resurrectable Inkarrí.[89]

The execution of Túpac Amaru thirty-nine years later had the greatest mythopoetic force, for the beheading of the last Inca vicariously repeated Atahualpa's death, punctuated the definitive defeat of the Incas, and was staged as a gruesome spectacle in the central plaza of Cuzco, once capital of the empire and navel of the Inca cosmos. The executioner "severed the head with a cutlass at one blow, and held it high for all to see" as the cathedral bells tolled and several thousand indigenous witnesses "deafened the skies, making them reverberate with their cries and wailing." Viceroy Francisco de Toledo ordered display of the head on a pole, but because—in Toledo's words—"no punishment could have sufficed to [prevent] the adoration they [the Andeans] made towards it," the head was removed and buried with the body, which had been interred the day after the execution.[90]

The severance, display, and then disappearance of the dead Inca's head provided focus and momentum for the myth of Inkarrí's central motif. When the cult of the royal head was denied the object of its veneration, rumors gradually consolidated into myths that filled in the hollows of the absence. Some versions held that Túpac Amaru's head defied putrefaction and became progressively more beautiful after death. This defiant reversal of the execution—with denied death emerging as triumphant survival—later registered an enhancement not of beauty but of power, of potency held in reserve, of potential. The head had been irretrievably confiscated by the Spanish executioners, but the very display and then abrupt disappearance of the head, the construction of a reliquary only to vacate it, enhanced the mournful emptiness that was seeking consolation in the hope of a messianic return. Out of these circumstances Inkarrí's twofold mission was born: he would reintegrate his fragmented body and, thus empowered, would return from the (denied) death to redeem the Andean people.

The reconstitution of Inkarrí's head and body is represented in many variations. Frequently the head is imprisoned—in Cuzco, Lima, or Madrid—and has no access to its buried corpse, so Inkarrí must grow a new body, from the head downward, to realize his resurrection.[91] The difficulty of that task and the rewards of its successful completion are stressed in a 1972 Quechua version from the community of Auquilla. The myth introduces the traditional motif—the Spaniards have decapitated the Inca and have stolen his head—and then embellishes it with innovations indebted to technology, politics, and Christian apocalypticism. The head is growing a new body, "but the said regeneration is not easy because [the head] is imprisoned in shackles and chains." The head has four eyes, just "as the world above has four eyes" and "our world has four parts." The cosmology of quarters and the rigor of imprisonment dictate that four thousand years will be required for Inkarrí's return, at which time "four suns will come out" and "will completely burn all of the *mistis*, all of the Peruvians, all of the Spaniards, all of the white thieves." These suns' punishing rays will forgive no one—"not the police, not the president, not [reformist dictator General Juan] Velasco Alvarado, in short, no one"—except the saving remnant of Inkarrí's people: "he will send us to another part of the world" where "we will have to wait until the end of the holocaust." The millennial kingdom following the cataclysm provides for "reencountering our ancestors" and for the "pardon of all of our faults." "When our Inca King [Inkarrí] returns, when the son of the sun comes back, then there will be no hunger, no wars, no atomic bomb."[92]

In other versions that follow the Túpac Amaru historical account more closely, the head and/or body are buried (rather than imprisoned) and from underground conspire reintegration. This subterranean effort, beyond its modern appeal to the metaphor of a political "underground," echoes a syncretic colonial configuration of a two-tiered cosmos. As described by Pachacuti Yamqui, Spanish conquest turned the Andean world upside down, so that the sacred above-ground world—now profaned and destroyed—"was sent to the subterranean world that protects and conserves it."[93] A subterranean preservation is also evident in the traditions maintaining that the Incas "are still alive beneath the city of Cuzco," waiting to reemerge with the new age, as well as in the burial of huacas, often beneath crosses, to protect them from colonial extirpators.[94] The buried Inkarrí repairs to the womb of Pachamama (Earth Mother) to be reconstituted, regenerated, and reborn in triumph over chaos and darkness. Deposed in the heavens as the Inca-Sun, he becomes the subterranean Inkarrí who, like the sun cycling through the underworld, returns in a new dawn.[95] The pachacuti of Inkarrí's return will realign the above and the below to restore their Andean order, and the infernal colonial world imposed by the Spaniards will then be relegated to an underground that evokes graves and hell more than safekeeping.

The myth of Inkarrí was originally, and radically, anti-Christian and anti-Hispanic, but the syncretism suggested in all versions and patent in many tends toward consolidation of the opposing Christian and Andean cosmovisions. The name Inkarrí itself is a composite of the signifiers designating the supreme Andean leader, Inca, with the supreme Spanish leader, *rey* (king). Guaman Poma anticipated such a universal monarch who would consolidate Inca and king in a composite sufficiently potent to catalyze the final pachacuti that restores harmony. The same urge for reconciliation is expressed in theatrical representations of the conquest: The capture of an Atahualpa surrogate as dramatized in the village of Chiquián concludes with the Inca and Pizarro embracing, dancing together, and presiding jointly over the next day's bullfight.[96]

Consolidation of Inca and king also found expression by continuity in several series of paintings produced during the eighteenth and nineteenth centuries. The twelve Incas and the Spanish monarchs who supplanted them are depicted together in portraits that seem to represent an uninterrupted succession, as though the conquest were a stormy transition between dynasties rather than the end of an autonomous Andean regime and the beginning of an imposed foreign empire.[97] At least one of these series pursues an alternative lineage by following the last Inca not with Spanish monarchs but with the Liberator, Simón Bolívar. As the idea was dramatized in period poetry, Huayna Capac crowns Bolívar as legitimate successor of the Incas and says, "From here begins/The new age of the promised Inca/Of liberty, of peace, and of grandeur."[98] In 1825 an indigenous priest expressed the same sentiments, now clearly Christianized, to Simón Bolívar himself: "God wanted to unite the savages into an empire, and He created Manco Capac. His race sinned and God sent Pizarro. After three centuries of expiation He took pity on America and created you. You are, thus, the man of a providential design."[99]

The interaction of Christian and Andean religious beliefs often resulted in bicultural composites that included, and sometimes metamorphosed, attributes from both of their sources. The original combat myth of the deified Inkarrí resurrecting to defeat Christ was condemned to a slow death as centuries of colonization, neocolonization, and institutionalized Christianity redirected the hope for indigenous redemption into the compromise of Christ and Inkarrí returning together. A version of the myth that is extreme in its absorption of Christianity features Inkarrí as the vicar of Christ, an intermediary situated between the indigenous people and the white God. The central motif of conflict between Inkarrí and Christ dissolves into an alliance—hierarchical, to be sure—of the opposing forces: "Inkarrí does on earth what Jesus Christ orders and we obey what Inkarrí orders."[100] This intermediary, Christianized Inkarrí is not unlike the indigenous messiahs who appear as sons of "Father Jesus," as though they were second-generation surrogates, sons of the Son, serving as liaisons between an alienated people and an absentee, patriarchal deity.[101]

The reconciliation of opposing divine forces in folk syncretism is also expressed by the Lord of Chalhuanca, a composite deity from Apurímac, Peru, whose history is reminiscent of Inkarrí. The people of Chalhuanca venerate a wooden head of Christ that, like the head of Túpac Amaru severed in 1572, showed signs of life beyond death when it was found in an agricultural field. According to reports from the fieldwork of Luis Millones and Hiroyasu Tomoeda, the faithful of Chalhuanca are gradually rebuilding the absent body with wooden parts, as if to assist in the corporal restitution that Inkarrí never accomplished on his own.[102] The god is fleshed out by his church, and in Chalhuanca miraculous consequences are anticipated when the body and the head (like Inkarrí and Christ) are integrated. The head in this case—enshrined rather than imprisoned, Christ's rather than Inkarrí's—indicates not battle between rival deities but rather, as in the Christianized myth and the continuum of portraits, a compromised peace, an attempt to accommodate the conquered past in the enduring present. Túpac Amaru's disappeared head is finally put back into its reliquary, but as the head of Jesus.

Andean cosmology is conducive to messianism, but it was the body of Christ that activated messianic return by providing a corporal prototype for resurrection. The brutalized, resurrected Christ taught the brutalized, conquered Indians that death was reversible, that the fragmented body could be reconstituted, that a dead body could signify empowerment and salvation.[103] Just as Inkarrí and earlier gods of death and regeneration (Osiris, Asar) are fragmented and reintegrated, so Christ of the Passion is metaphorically equated with the broken bread of the Last Supper, reconstituted first by resurrection and then by unity of the mystical body: "we who are many are one body, for we all partake of the one bread."[104]

The distant echo of early Christians among Romans is discernible insofar as Inkarrí serves as the vehicle of salvation for his persecuted people, as the trope of the "dead" Andeans seeking reconstitution in a resurrection that triumphs over death. In European legends paralleling those of the Andean Inkarrí, the apostle Santiago (Saint James) was decapitated by Herod and thrown to the dogs. Christians retrieved the fragmented body, embalmed it, buried it temporarily, and upon disinterring it were astonished to discover that the head had reattached to its corpse. When the meek apostle trained to turn the other cheek later reappeared as the warrior-saint Santiago Matamoros during the Reconquest of Iberia, he himself then vengefully beheaded his enemies, leaving Moorish heads, "turbaned and bloody, scattered at the feet of his raging steed."[105] In the traditions of Santiago and Inkarrí the protagonists and cultural context change but the narrative components remain essentially the same, with a defeated hero's corporal reconstitution serving as trope of a people's triumphant resurrection, empowerment, and vindication. Whether or not the Santiago legend contributed to shaping the motifs of Inkarrí, the narrative similarities of the two texts are patent and supernatural powers are adapted in both to a bellicose agenda of liberation.

In Andean tradition, the detached head may be partially the consequence of an effort to understand the alien concept of the Christian soul that was introduced by the friars. Modern Andean folk beliefs hold that flying heads leave their bodies and carry out missions independently, with these powers complemented by the capacity to construct new bodies. Several South American tribes with wide regional distribution likewise have myths featuring a rolling (but still living) head or skull.[106] As Henrique-Oswaldo Urbano understands it, "The flying head is animated with life and seems to possess some characteristics of immortality," like the Christian soul.[107] The trope of Inkarrí's head may therefore count among its readings an Andean adaptation of the Christian soul departing from its dead body, with the reunion of body and head, of body and soul, bringing the renewed life promised as much by pachacuti as by Revelation. This is certainly suggested by a version from Paruro, in which the Christian God defeats Inkarrí but cannot kill him because Inkarrí's soul has escaped to the mythological Paititi in order to one day return.[108]

Among the many extant versions—all modern—of the myth of Inkarrí is the following from the Quechua-speaking community of Q'ero:

> The first god is Inkarrí. He was son of the sun by a savage woman. He made everything that exists on earth. He tied up the Sun at the top of Osgonta mountain and locked up the wind in order to finish his work of creation. . . . Inkarrí was imprisoned by the Spanish king; he was tortured [*martirizado*] and decapitated. The head of god was taken to Cuzco. The head of Inkarrí is alive and the body of god is reconstructing itself deep inside the earth. But because he no longer has any power, his laws are not obeyed and his will is not respected. When the body of Inkarrí is whole, he will return, and that will be the day of the Last Judgment.[109]

As a mythological hero Inkarrí shifts registers between the divine and the mundane, sometimes a god ("the first god"), sometimes a man-god (of divine father and earthly mother), and sometimes a man (captured and decapitated by

the Spaniards). The divine father (sun) channels his procreation through a
mother who contributes human form but not human culture, because the latter
is yet to be developed (or improved) by the civilizing hero. The son effectively
subjugates the father (sun) and other forces (wind) in order to conclude his
civilizing mission on earth, but he is no match for the Spanish king. In the
context of the conquest out of which it emerged, the myth suggests that the
"creation" of civilization undertaken by the Incas (represented by Inkarrí) was
interrupted by the Spaniards, and that the severance of the head (and Inca as
head of state) from the body (and social body) has resulted in a disruption of
Andean development. This state of affairs would be remedied by the reconstitution and return of Inkarrí, an event here described in terms of a Last Judgment.
If in Revelation Christ binds Satan so that the messiah can finish his business
on earth, here Inkarrí binds the forces opposing him (sun/father, with the distant
echo of the Christian God the Father) so that he may carry out his mission.
While Christian tradition presumes that Christ will deliver on his messianic
promise, Inkarrí's plans are frustrated and the realization of his millennial kingdom is foreclosed by conquest. In that predicament Inkarrí readily represents
the Andeans as a collective social body imprisoned, subjugated, martyred, and
decapitated while the conquerors finish the "creation" in accord with their own
culture and volition.

Like Christ, the Inkarrí of the Q'ero version is the incarnate son of deity who
comes to earth with a mission, develops an identity distinct from the Father's
(even though they may ultimately be one), is captured and martyred, in some
sense "survives" death, creates people who do not obey his law, and returns in
judgment at the end of the world. Unlike Christ, however, Inkarrí has no terrestrial mission of redemption through his vicarious suffering and death. Inkarrí's execution interrupts his essentially creative mission (proper to God the
Father in Genesis), which would perhaps include reigning over his happy kingdom upon its completion. Also distinct in the biblical and Andean accounts is
the balance of power between son and father: in Christianity God the Father
incarnates his only begotten son for the express purpose of having him crucified,
whereas Inkarrí—far from passively submitting to the Father's will—turns his
apparently greater force against the sun and binds it in independent pursuit of
his own designs. Christ holds his omnipotence in reserve so that the Father's
will may be done (although Christ's earthly enemies and death itself are ultimately defeated by the resurrection). Inkarrí, conversely, and despite his prowess
in the sky, is powerless at the hands of his enemies on earth (because they are
agents of a mightier god), but on the strength of his record he conspires reintegration and an almighty return.

In the most common versions of the myth, that return has a purpose other
than the Last Judgment. Inkarrí is recorporalized as a deified cultural hero to
initiate the offensive that will redeem Andeans from subjugation. Religious and
political enmity are alternately stressed as the identity of Inkarrí's rival vacillates
between Christ and Españarrí (Spain-king). The following is from a version recorded in Quinua, a Quechua- and Spanish-speaking village near Ayacucho.

It was [the Catholic] God who ordered the troops of the king-state to capture and decapitate Inkarrí. It wasn't the Spanish king who defeated him and had his head cut off. Between the two gods there was a previous exchange of mutually incomprehensible messages. Inkarrí's head is in the [presidential] Palace of Lima and is still alive. But it has no power because it is separated from its body. . . . If god's head is freed and reintegrates with its body it will be able to confront the Catholic god and compete with him again. But, if he does not manage to reconstitute himself and recover his supernatural power, we [the Indians] will perhaps all die.[110]

This version decidedly establishes the divine nature of Inkarrí and the impossibility of his subjugation by mere men. (A version from Andamarca is insistent on the point, with Christ nailing Inkarrí to the ground before decapitating him.)[111] The narrative's most moving line underscores the rival deities' mutual incomprehension and, consequently, the breakdown of communication on earth between the respective cultures representing them. One is reminded of the encounter in Cajamarca of Pizarro and Atahualpa, with its inadequate interpretations by the Indian Felipe ("instead of saying three Gods in one, he said three Gods plus one make four"), its Bible that would not audibly speak the word of God to the incredulous Inca, and its battle justified on the pretext of what was lost in translation.[112] Even when crashed by the syncretism apparent in these myths, the barriers blocking intercultural understanding seem as implacable as the gods.

In this Quinua version, as in the huaca alliance of Taqui Onqoy, a fragmented divinity must reconsolidate its forces in order to engage Christ in a rematch. If Inkarrí were to emerge victorious, the sociopolitical situation turned upside down by the conquest would be turned back again to inaugurate a new indigenous order. According to one version, after Inkarrí's victory the Indians would be rich and the Spaniards would eat excrement. A 1965 version from Vicos has Inkarrí's decapitated head "turn into money" and continues, "If he were still alive among us, if he had defeated the President, we would be rich—the biggest potatoes, the biggest choclos. We wouldn't be poor like we are now."[113]

In Quinua, Inkarrí's return—let alone his triumph—is not predicted but rather posited as an option contingent upon the will of his captors. Unlike many other versions, in which it is only a matter of time before Inkarrí bursts out of captivity, here the defeated hero seems almost to await a turnkey who might unwittingly collude with the paroled head's subversive intentions. The same political subordination is transcendentalized in a version from Puquio, where Inkarrí's return awaits the Christian God's permission, even though the fragmented body has already been reintegrated.[114] Equally pessimistic (or, one might say, realistic) is the Quinua version's transfer of the head from Cuzco (center of the Inca world) to the symbolic center of the viceroyalty and of republican Peru, the presidential palace in Lima.

In other versions, such as one from Chacaray, the head is sequestered in the yet more distant royal palace of Madrid. The Quechua-speaking informant related that Inkarrí had been summoned to Spain and was building a golden bridge in response to the call. Pizarro, taking advantage of superior weapons, killed

Inkarrí before he could finish the bridge, and the head, still alive, was sent to Spain. Once Inkarrí's death was reported to the powerful Christ, who "has the world in his hand like an orange," he gloatingly descended from heaven but wanted "nothing to do with Inkarrí" or his Andean people: "Christ remains apart, he doesn't mix with us."[115] The mixing, however, seems to have gained surrepticious expression in an innovative detail central to the Chacaray version: the imprisoned head is shaven once a month to prevent it from growing a beard. The presence of facial hair suggests a syncretic Inkarrí, with Christ-like, mestizo, or Spanish physiognomy. The shaving in that perspective reinforces the discourse on segregation, for it prevents Inkarrí from resembling those presumed to be his superiors. The image further provides a variation on the common motif of fragmentation and disempowerment; Inkarrí is not permitted to grow a beard in the same way that he is not permitted to grow a body. He is cut back to prevent or retard his reconstitution.

The head-body poetics central to the myth of Inkarrí have a long history in the Christian traditions that were disseminated in the Americas during evangelization.[116] Following Paul's resurrected-body tropes developed in Colossians, 1 Corinthians, Ephesians, and Romans, the medievals viewed the Christian faithful as a social body cohered and headed by Christ: "To the one and only Son of God and Son of Man, as if to its head, all members of the body are joined."[117] Thomas Aquinas elaborated, "Just as the whole Church is styled one mystical body for its similarity to man's natural body and for the diversity of actions corresponding to the diversity of limbs, so Christ is called the 'head' of the Church."[118] In the bull that dogmatized the doctrine in 1302, Pope Boniface VIII made the trope difficult in visual terms but illustrative of a two-tiered (or two-headed) cosmos, with Christ as the point of transition: the Church "represents one mystical body, the head of which is Christ, and the head of Christ is God."[119] According to a 1584 catechism, when asked to define the Church indigenous neophytes were to respond, "The congregation of all the Christian faithful, whose head is Jesus Christ, and his Vicar on earth the holy Pope of Rome."[120]

Progressive secularization of the mystical body concept extended its application to the bodies of kings, providing a European parallel to Inkarrí's alternating nature as god and man as well as a basis for the fragmentation that extends metaphorically from a king's (or Inkarrí's) body to the social body that it represents.[121] In this republic conceived in corporal terms, each limb and organ had a function upon which the whole depended. As Jacinto de la Serna observed in 1656, even the lowliest, most subjugated and exploited native subjects were essential: "Nothing can be done without them, not the mines, the fields, the factories, the buildings, because they are the blood of the mystical body of the Monarchy."[122] In this view European rulers by divine right had, like Christ, "two bodies," one natural and the other mystical, with the latter designation bringing "to the secular polity, as it were, a whiff of incense from another world."[123]

The decapitation of a two-bodied king can thus be figurative (separating the head of state from his people, as in the capture of Moctezuma or Atahualpa), literal (the actual removal of the head, as in the execution of Túpac Amaru), or both (the king is executed by decapitation and the social body is consequently deprived of its head). These options tended to intermingle as historical events were reinterpreted under the pressure of an emerging mythological paradigm. The most compelling example is the execution by garroting of Atahualpa, which has been insistently represented—by Guaman Poma, for example—as a decapitation.[124] The same concession to the myth of Inkarrí is evident in the colonial Quechua play *Tragedy of the Death of Inca Atahualpa*, still performed in many Andean villages, in which Atahualpa is likewise beheaded and promises to return. Such mutations of the historical account contribute to the consolidation of multiple executed Incas into one indomitable Inkarrí. In the myth both the literal and the figurative meanings of beheading are operative, and their interrelation, the ultimate inseparability of the king's human and social (or "mystical") bodies, is enforced by the myth's central premise: once Inkarrí puts the physical head back on his body, the head of state will have returned to the social body that thereby recuperates its vitality. Inkarrí is the "defeated god of an unconquerable people."[125] The corporal body can return because the mystical body keeps it alive.

It appeared to many Andeans that something of that nature was occurring when in 1780 the curaca of Tungasuca, José Gabriel Condorcanqui, rose in rebellion against the Spaniards as Túpac Amaru II. The climate of messianic anticipation greatly enhanced the reception of this new Túpac Amaru as the quasi-divine hero who would restore Andean order to the world upside down. Among other assorted messianic sobriquets the Andeans called him King Inca [Rey Inca] Túpac Amaru, and his own signature had many variations, including "Don José I by the grace of God Inca King [Inca Rey] of Peru."[126] His descent from Inca royalty, his name that "resurrected" a hero whose tragic death called for vengeance and mythopoetic undoing, his struggle against the conqueror on behalf of the Andeans, and his grandiose discourse and actions all seemed to indicate that the long-awaited messiah had arrived, that "the head of the Inca had grown a body."[127]

If Túpac Amaru II was Inkarrí, however, then the down side of the myth held in store for him a tragic death. The day came on May 18, 1781. Túpac Amaru II was sentenced to witness the execution of his wife, his sons, and other principal leaders of the rebellion, after which his tongue would be cut out, his body quartered, the trunk burned, and the ashes scattered in the wind. A monument as reminder of his crimes and death would be erected in Picchu ("where he dared to come to intimidate, besiege, and ask that that city surrender to him"), and his body parts would be distributed: the head to Tinta, the arms to Tungasuca and Carabaya, and the legs to Livitaca and Santa Rosa. The documents concerning Túpac Amaru II's descent from Inca royalty would then be burned in a public ceremony in Lima to eliminate the last vestiges of the claim that empowered him.

As an eyewitness reported it, ropes were tied at one end to Túpac Amaru's limbs and at the other to four horses positioned to pull in opposing directions. The horses were unequal to the task of pulling apart the body, however, and thus the Inca remained suspended "in the air, in a state that resembled a spider." The presiding royal authority, "moved by compassion" in witnessing the absurd and interminable agony, ordered that Túpac Amaru's head be chopped off. The feet and arms were then cut off for distribution as proscribed, and the body was burned in Picchu, along with that of his wife.[128]

If myths emerged to soften the trauma of the first Túpac Amaru's public execution, then they were redoubled when history seemed to repeat itself in progressively higher registers of cruelty, despair, and hopelessness. Three heavily freighted deaths, those of Atahualpa and the two Túpac Amarus, now sought refuge in the myth of Inkarrí. Recycling back into the myth were the body's heroic resistance to quartering, the "return" of Túpac Amaru II in other revolutionaries who continued the struggle in his name, and the storm that blew in to end a drought precisely while Túpac Amaru II was being executed, thereby providing sufficient cause "for the Indians to say that the sky and the elements lamented the death of the Inca whom the inhumane and impious Spaniards were killing with such cruelty."[129] If earlier the soldiers of Túpac Amaru II believed that those killed in battle would be raised from the dead by their Christ-like Inca, then after defeat the broken promise of those individual resurrections was collectively rerouted back to its source, the dead Inca himself, dead for them, dead again, which seemed sufficient proof that resurrection again was worthy of hope.

The penal methods devised by Spaniards in reaction to indigenous resistance contributed decisively to the myth of Inkarrí. Whether by design or by default, the Inca's body was subjected to a progressive fragmentation: Atahualpa was executed but remained corporally intact; Túpac Amaru was decapitated; and Túpac Amaru II was decapitated, quartered, distributed, burned, and scattered. When viewed in the perspective of the myth of Inkarrí, this progression emits an unmistakable message: the body is being rendered unresurrectable.[130] If the return of Inkarrí requires reassembly of the fragmented pieces, then the body (and by extension the social body it represents) must be mutilated and dispersed to such a degree that its reintegration becomes inconceivable. Insofar as dismemberment is a trope for disempowerment, Túpac Amaru II's resistance to quartering assumes mythic dimensions.

The frequent execution of rebels in Latin America by decapitation and, often, quartering enacts on the leader's body a dismemberment that extends metaphorically to his movement or to his people as a whole. When the "head" of a movement or a state is severed from its social body, the functions of that body are shocked into paralysis. Quartering of this corpse or moribund trunk then enacts in miniature, and graphically, the greater social dismantling that the leader's execution symbolized and that may extend into perceptions of cosmic destruction when the executed leader is considered to be in some sense divine.

The human body perceived and destroyed in quarters also underscores the corporal model that structures polities divided into quadrants. The Inca's Tahuantinsuyo (Land of Four Quarters) and the Aztec's Tenochtitlán are the outstanding examples, both designed in quadrants emerging from a center conceived as the navel of the earth. Guaman Poma represented the Indies as four cities with a fifth, Cuzco, in the center, and he represented Spain in the same fourfold configuration, with Castile occupying the privileged central position. In his mappamundi, Castile (having displaced Cuzco) is in the center, surrounded by quadrants representing Rome, Guinea, Turkey, and the Indies.

For the imperial Spaniards themselves, the medieval tripartite world—Africa, Asia, Europe—found its fourth quarter in America, this missing piece foreseen early on by, among others, Saint Isidore of Seville: "Besides the three continents originally known, there must also be a fourth one" on "the other side of the Ocean." Martin Waldseemüller's *Cosmographiae Introductio* gave the missing quadrant its debut as an island, but by 1585 Diogo Homem's map unambiguously labeled South America the "fourth part of the world."[131] Didactic religious art anticipated the cartographer's conclusions, as for example at a church constructed in 1534 in Juli, Puno, that exhibits a painting of the wise kings adoring the infant Jesus, with the standard threesome augmented by a fourth king, the Inca, to represent the newfound realm in Christendom.[132] The four cardinal points—along with the "four corners of the earth" in Isaiah 11:12 and the "four winds" in Matthew 24:31—suggest a universe formatted by human limbs, as do anthropomorphic deities such as the Aztec's fourfold Tezcatlipoca or, more graphically, Christ stretched out on his cross.[133] Medieval cartography superimposed the crucifix on its image of the world, and at least one mappamundi, the Ebstorf map of circa 1235, indicated the four directions with Christ's disembodied head, hands, and feet.[134] An anthropomorphic universe is yet more explicit in a codex image that depicts a man's naked figure surrounded by the twenty Aztec day signs, each connected to its corresponding body part.[135]

The fragmented and reconstituted body as well as the dead and resurrected body serve as loaded tropes of a collective death defeated by revitalization, redemption, and cyclical return that encompass the anthropomorphic universe's death and rebirth in new ages. When Inkarrí's body is pulled apart along the four *ceques* that converge at the sacred center in Cuzco, an age and a world are destroyed and the cosmos is cast into chaos as the stunned, headless body lumbers on its stumps through the darkness. But myth always reassembles the shattered, conquered world with whatever pieces remain, indigenous and imported, in whatever configuration works, until the hero returns to restore proper order. As an Inkarrí-like myth of the Guatemalan Maya has it in reference to a syncretic Christ: "He formed the world. He began thus when the others, the Jews, came, and they took Him, and they killed Him completely, they made pieces of Him, only the head remained. But He was not dead. When the people left, the pieces joined themselves and there He made Himself, and He was again."[136]

Son of the Sun

The supreme deity of the imperial Incas was the sun-god Inti, the royal dynasty was believed to have descended from him, and the temple of the sun, Coricancha, was accorded the most privileged position at the epicenter of the empire. At the beginning of the imperial period, in 1438, the Incas faced devastation as the invading Chancas beseiged Cuzco. Anticipating imminent defeat, the reigning Inca and his designated heir fled, leaving the command to Cusi Inca Yupanqui.

In a series of dreams and visions the young leader, who would soon earn the title Pachacuti (here, He Who Turns Around [or Transforms] the World), was visited by a deity who identified himself as "the Sun, your father." The sun-god reassured Pachacuti that he would be victorious and prevail as a great emperor if only he worshiped as the god prescribed. Pachacuti successfully defended Cuzco, became de facto Inca, and then after solemn sacrifices and ceremonies had his rule legitimated by the Sun, who spoke through an oracle, as well as by his father, Viracocha, who acknowledged him as "Son of the Sun."[137] The centrality of solar worship endured under a succession of Incas and, after conquest, was revitalized in Manco Inca's state in exile, situated at a sanctuary of the Virgins of the Sun in Vilcabamba. There a temple was built for the golden image of the sun god, which itself contained ashes of the hearts of mummified Incas, and the Son of the Sun cult was restored as the basis of Inca theocracy.[138]

The title Son of the Sun has subsequently disengaged from its original referent to assume more general usage in designation of men, usually outsiders, who propagate a message of transformation or redemption and are perceived to be in some sense godlike. Native anticipation or at least reception of sun-related man-gods has also been widely recorded outside of the Andean region, with reference to the Inca distant in all cases and nonexistent in most. Some of these Sons of the Sun have true attributes of the messianic hero; others, the majority, are impostors exploiting myth to their advantage. The 1541–42 expedition of Francisco de Orellana in the Amazon was showered with tribute (when not with arrows) because some caciques accepted Orellana's claim that the Spaniards were Sons of the Sun.[139] During their eight-year journey across what is now Texas and the southwestern United States, Alvar Núñez Cabeza de Vaca and his companions were likewise received as Sons of the Sun by some indigenous groups and were presumed accordingly to have the power of giving and taking life.[140] In Hispaniola, in the Aztec empire, on the northern frontier, and in multiple South American locations, Iberians making first or early contact with natives were likewise considered Sons of the Sun.

As in the case of Quetzalcóatl and Cortés, indigenous interpretations of the Europeans as divine or semidivine unwittingly conferred upon the conquerors a power that could be, and was, exploited to facilitate invasion. In July 1540, Pedro de Alarcón pointed to the sun and told the Pueblos in what is now New Mexico, "I came from the sun," and "I am its son." He backed up his claim with the harquebuses "that the sun had given" to the Spaniards and that "spat fire." The Pueblos, after receiving Alarcón's satisfactory replies to their interrogations, concluded, "You are a child of the sun, we all want you for our lord and want to serve you always," and they made him a sacrificial offering.[141] Friars in the same region followed suit, calling themselves Sons of the Sun and scourging their bodies mercilessly to demonstrate that Christ was the most ferocious of war gods.[142]

The friars' posture as Sons of the Sun could claim a measure of unintended legitimacy insofar as the Christian deity, like the principal deity of the Incas (Inti) and Aztecs (Huitzilopochtli), was solar. The many Christian tropes constructing a solar deity, from God-the-Father's emanation of heavenly rays to representation of Christ as the sun that never sets, have antecedents in ancient Egypt. The pharaoh, like the Inca, was believed to be son of a sun god. The Egyptian *Potter's Oracle*, from around the second century B.C.E., is unambiguous: kings are "sons of the Sun." That concept entered Judeo-Christian tradition partially through the Jewish *Sibylline Oracles*, composed in Egypt around the same period, which announced that "God will send a king from the sun."[143] A clear contribution to the consolidation of sun and king was also made by the pagan Romans, as evidenced for example by the rays of the sun-god that sometimes embellished the diadems of sacred emperors. Augustus Caesar cultivated his own image to suit that of the Roman sun god, Apollo, and referred to himself as a "rising sun."[144] Even Constantine was a disciple of the solar cult, and after his conversion to Christianity he established Sunday (Day of the Sun) as a holiday that would appeal to both Christians and pagans.[145] With a debt to these Egyptian, Roman, and Judeo-Christian traditions, Christ of the New Testament became "the light of the world" whose "face shone like the sun." The world "has no need of sun or moon to shine on it, for the glory of God is its light, and its lamp is the Lamb."[146]

The interaction of biblical imagery and indigenous traditions resulted in syncretic composites that endured for centuries. Unorthodox iconography in New Mexico was still depicting God the Father with a sun on his chest well into the nineteenth century.[147] Some modern Maya use "our father-sun" in reference to a syncretic paternal deity, the Aymara of Oruro and Potosí couple God the Father with the sun, and the fusion of Inti and Christian deity among other Andeans yields the untroubled admission that "Jesus Christ and the sun are the same thing."[148] The eucharist displayed and paraded in the sunlike monstrance, sometimes called the *sol* (sun) in Spanish, likewise evokes Inti among modern Andeans.[149] After conquest aspects of Inti Raimi (Festival of the Sun) were assimilated to the Christian celebration of Corpus Christi, with the mystical body of the quasi-solar Christ now processed where once the mummified Sons of the Sun had been.[150] While frowning upon the crypto-paganism prominent in Corpus Christi processions, the Church was not adverse to the solar associations that facilitated it. In the words of a papal bull issued by Paul IV, "Let the days that the Indians by their ancient rites dedicated to the Sun, and to their idols, be reduced in honor of the true Sun [*sic*: Sol] Jesus Christ."[151]

In modern times, particularly in the Amazon, a range of outsiders with varying intentions have been received as Sons of the Sun. In the 1890s the rubber baron Carlos Fitzcarrald, popularized by the Werner Herzog film *Fitzcarraldo*, was perceived by some natives to be a Son of the Sun, as was later a black guerrilla, Guillermo Lobatón, of the Movement of the Revolutionary Left (MIR).[152] Until his death in battle in November, 1965, Lobatón commanded the MIR's ill-fated central Peruvian front, the name of which—Guerrilla Túpac Amaru—itself carried the themes of heroic return. As one Asháninka recalled, "They worshipped the guerrilla. They said he was Itomi Pavá [Son of the Sun], that he had come to shower us with riches, with everything."[153] What the Asháninka received, however, was a shower of gunfire for their collusion in the doomed revolution, along with a clear sense of having been defrauded. Protes-

tant missionaries with an apocalyptic message were also regarded as Sons of the
Sun on at least two occasions, the first in the 1920s and the second in the late
1950s.[154] Israelites of the New Covenant in contemporary Peru have Andeanized
their messiah, Ezequiel Ataucusi Gamonal, and during theatrical ceremonies they
present him with the insignias of command as the new Son of the Sun.[155]

In urban Peru during the 1940s, the politician Víctor Raúl Haya de la Torre
was also "like one of the great sons of the Sun of the Andes," the Aprista Inca
who "brings the dawn in his arms," and awakens Indo-America from centuries
of postconquest slumber.[156] An appeal to such identities was again exploited
after the 1968 coup, with the propaganda of an unprecedented, seemingly pro-
campesino revolutionary dictatorship constructing the image of General Juan
Velasco Alvarado as a new Inca or Inkarrí who had arisen to save Tahuantinsuyo.[157] Politicization of indigenous messianism has more recently facilitated the
popular reception of Abimael Guzmán, a hybrid Son of the Sun illuminated on
his Shining Path.[158] Much of the charismatic authority that Guzmán commanded
among his Andean cadres was derived from party mythopoesis, including sobriquets such as Puka Inti (Red Sun) that alluded to the pachacuti-like powers
attributed to the seemingly invincible rebel. The chronic poverty, race tensions,
exhaustion of hope, and Andean millennial traditions out of which the movement emerged conditioned the elaboration of a hero—red with communism,
with blood, with dawn—and his radical, world-upside-down solution. Guzmán's
ability to evade capture for more than ten years found explanation in his capacity to transform into a bird, a snake, or a stone, or to vanish at will into a
spirit.[159] He made manifest the magical, Inkarrí-like powers of defiance and perpetuity against the odds: he was dead but had resurrected; he was dead, underground, or in exile but would return to redeem his broken people.

The bottom fell out of all speculations in September 1992, when Guzmán's
return took the form of a demythologizing arrest. The Peruvian government
endeavored to reverse the elevation of Guzmán into the semidivine Chairman
Gonzalo by propagating the counterimage of an overweight, psoriatic philosophy professor with a penchant for whiskey. Before the arrest a tipsy Guzmán
dancing like Zorba the Greek was broadcast on national networks, and afterward viewers watched the corpulent fallen deity meekly obeying orders to get
dressed. Some three hundred reporters were later summoned to the courtyard of
a police building, where after more than an hour of preparatory ceremony a
zoo-like cage was unveiled to reveal Guzmán in a striped prison suit reminiscent
of those in Alcatraz movies. The pathetic figure of the captured Inkarrí undermined the beliefs in magical transformation, disappearance and reappearance,
and death and resurrection that safeguarded the invincibility, immortality, and
eternal return of the cultural hero. Even the counterinsurgency effort made unintended poetic allusion to disempowering Inkarrí, as the apprehension of Guzmán sought to "decapitate the movement."[160] If generally Inkarrí's imprisoned
head conspires its recorporalization, escape, and empowered return, in some
versions of the myth, including perhaps the present one, the beheading of Inkarrí
kills the sun.[161] Guzmán's case well illustrates that the myth is always stronger
than the man and the hero's power always greatest in absentia.

The most explicit convergence of revolutionary and Son of the Sun identities occurred much earlier in Peruvian history with the appearance of Juan Santos Atahualpa. Dressed in a painted *cushma* (cotton poncho) or the regalia of Inca royalty, chewing coca leaves, wearing a crucifix, speaking Latin as well as native tongues, and preaching an innovative gospel, Santos Atahualpa, "the invincible," rocked the viceroyalty with revolution from 1742 to 1755. The movement spread rapidly from its Amazon base near Tarma to the Andean highlands as indigenous peoples manifested an enthusiastic interest in eradicating colonial rule and its Franciscan missions. As a 1742 document put it with clear allusion to the myth of Inkarrí, Santos Atahualpa endeavored to "recuperate the crown that Pizarro and the other Spaniards took from him, killing his father (that is what he called the Inca) and sending his head to Spain."[162]

In the earliest report of the insurrection, made in June 1742, this claimed descendant of deposed Inca royalty was already called Juan Santos Atahualpa Apu-Inca Huayna Capac.[163] Huayna Capac (Powerful Young One) was the last Inca governing before the arrival of the Spaniards; by taking his name, Santos Atahualpa resumed what the conquest interrupted and also emulated the Inca practice of assuming a royal name upon accession to status as Son of the Sun.[164] The deified aura that had accumulated around Santos Atahualpa was also apparent in the title Apu (God, Principal Lord), as it was again in the testimony of three captured rebels who revealed with reverential deference that "no one can touch the Inca's food, nor step on his footprints, and they must address him with the title 'Capac Inca Son of God.' "[165] The composite interrelation of the Christian Son of God and the indigenous Son of the Sun was also evidenced in Asháninka titles for the rebel, which included Son of the Sun but also Juan Santos-Kesha-Chamán (Juan Santos Messenger of the Catholic God).[166] The Asháninka had a strong messianic tradition that predisposed their acceptance of the rebel, and Santos Atahualpa also found a warm reception among the Amuesha, whose principal god, Yompor Ror, corresponded to the sun.[167]

The Christian Son of God superimposed on the indigenous Son of the Sun consolidated in Santos Atahualpa a powerful alliance of otherworldly forces. The name Santos was interpreted as a sign of the rebel's incarnation of the Holy Spirit (*Espíritu Santo*), and when compounded with Atahualpa "the roles of the biblical messiah and his Andean counterpart, Inkarrí, combined," as did "the vision of apocalypse and its indigenous version, pachacuti."[168] Santos Atahualpa announced that he had been sent by Jesus and the Virgin Mary, "as Christ and acting in the manner of Christ." The rebellion had been planned for many years (beginning around 1730) and Santos Atahualpa had hoped to begin it sooner, but he reportedly told missionaries that "God had not given him permission until that time."[169]

Particularly after 1752, however, Christ was more displaced than obeyed by Santos Atahualpa. In explanation he related that his "father," Huayna Capac, had been created by God after the Passion as a substitute for Christ, who had sinned. As this genealogy extended from mythology to history, and in a world whose center was shifting from Jerusalem, Rome, or Castile to Cuzco, Santos Atahualpa could refer to himself as "lord of all these lands, and son of the true

God." When a disbeliever took refuge in supplications to the Virgin Mary, Santos Atahualpa responded that the Virgin was in distant Spain, whose age had ended, and that the people should only believe in him, because he was "the omnipotent God, absolute lord of creation" whose time had come "to restore the empire of our Inca."[170] Proof was in the extraordinary powers attributed to him, drawn from both pachacuti and biblical poetics: he can stop the sun, he can turn stone into gold, he can make the earth tremble, he can raze the mountains, he can unleash a cataclysmic fire, and, perhaps most convincingly, he can sustain an insurrection against the conqueror.[171]

If Jesus resurrected to reign at the right hand of the Father, and if the dead Inca of prehispanic times enjoyed some otherworldly existence "with his father the Sun," then it was to be presumed that the messianic hero consolidating these man-gods would likewise survive his death and make a claim to patriarchal power.[172] For some Asháninka, Juan Santos never died; "his body disappeared giving off smoke."[173] In legends collected along the Huallaga and Ucayali Rivers in the late 1930s, nearly two hundred years after Santos Atahualpa's insurrection, indigenous peoples recounted how in the presence of several united tribes Santos Atahualpa ascended into heaven surrounded by clouds, "and they still await his return."[174] Other traditions maintain that "the creator and father of humanity" entered the jungle near Tarma (the region associated with the insurrection), again anticipating that he will reappear.[175] Inexhaustible and all-powerful but also cyclical—absent as much as it is present, dark as much as it is light—the sun provides a model for cultural heroes who come and go but nevertheless remain perpetually present.

The case of Juan Santos Atahualpa in the eighteenth century, like that of Guillermo Lobatón or Abimael Guzmán in the twentieth, evidences the fortuitous convergence of a messianic political agenda with the aspirations of peoples whose oral traditions and social stations predispose them to deify the messengers of radical solutions. The conflation of indigenous beliefs and alien revolutionary objectives allowed the Asháninka to impose "their own meaning on the message of Juan Santos, a meaning that overlapped sufficiently with that of the messiah for them to make common cause against the Spanish."[176] In the rebelling region the Franciscans held under their (precarious) control thirty-two mission towns with some three hundred Indians in each. The overlapping meanings were thereby infused with a friarly stress on guilt, judgment, punishment, and redemption, holding in reserve the grand payoff in a millennial kingdom. Santos Atahualpa enacted the Franciscan apocalyptic discourse and redirected it against the Spaniards themselves. As it was worded in a 1747 testimony, God was determined to "reduce the sinners to ashes" and chose for this mission Santos Atahualpa, the Inkarrí-Christ, the Son of the Sun and Son of God, "so that by crowning himself King of this World of Peru, he would be the restorer of the Divine Law, already lost by the Spaniards, and especially by the Corregidores."[177]

6
The Messiah

Supernatural Advantage

The relations between humanity and deity are strained when a presumptuous creation aspires to its own apotheosis. God is unambiguous in *The First Book of Adam and Eve* when he chastises his fig-leafed, disobedient children for having broken the covenant through "desire for divinity, greatness, and an exalted state, such as I have." The penalties included exile to "this land, rough and full of trouble," as well as retraction of the "bright nature" with which humans, now stupid, were once endowed.[1]

Judeo-Christian tradition is replete with messiahs despite the injunction, beginning with messianic kings like David and the "Son of David," the latter synonymous with the New Testament messiah.[2] In Psalm 45, the king is addressed as "God" and in Psalm 2 as the "son of God," with these unequivocal sobriquets reinforced by heavenly stations on "the throne of glory," often at God's right hand.[3] The human hero is then divinized and the god humanized in Christ, who is "the actualization of the most radical and daring utopia of the human heart: the longing to be 'like gods.'"[4]

The Spanish *Fuero Juzgo* (Book of Laws), in force from the seventh century to the mid-thirteenth century, recognized God as the first cause "who can do all things," followed immediately by his earthly vicar, the king.[5] Beginning in the seventh century, Spanish kings—like ancient kings in Babylonia, Egypt, and Israel—were consecrated with a "royal unction" that inducted them into a quasi-religious order. The monarch became an "anointed one of the Lord" and, in the popular formula endorsed by Thomas Aquinas, "king by the grace of God." He was the "supreme lay pontiff," the "Vicar of God" in temporal affairs.[6]

This vicarious administration of the Lord's worldly concerns brought not merely rivalry of papacy and monarchy but also confusion of God and king. Medieval and early modern monarchs in Iberia were "God on earth" or "human deities" belonging to "the family of God," and royalty merited "divine respect" and "adoration."[7] Erasmus held that the king was the "tangible and living image of deity," and Philip II himself evidenced this conviction when he remarked to one of his commanders, "You are engaged in God's service and in mine—which is the same thing."[8] The Spanish king is the point of contact between divinity and humanity, "the last of the gods and the first of men."[9]

When emissaries of theocratic European monarchy appeared suddenly among American empires, also theocratic, the representations of man-gods proliferated. To dispel a lingering perplexity, the Franciscan "twelve apostles" clarified for the lords of Mexico, "Do not believe that we are gods. Fear not, we are men as you are."[10] In Peru, the unimaginable and therefore godlike aliens were named after the Inca creator god, Viracocha. Titu Cusi described the perceived godliness as a consequence of differences in appearance (beards, dress), of horses, of the harquebuses thought to release bolts of lightning and thunder, and of the capacity to communicate silently (in writing) "by means of pieces of white cloth."[11] Arrival of the Spaniards during Inca civil war, immediately after Huascar had been captured by Atahualpa, also afforded the conquerors a transitory reception as divinely dispatched auxiliaries to Huascar's cause.[12]

During early contact, natives who were considering an offensive in Puerto Rico thought it prudent to first test the widely held hypothesis that the conquerors were immortal. A Spaniard was overpowered, held under water for a few minutes, and then laid out on the riverbank. The Indians watched the dead body "until it began to smell." The anticipated resuscitation never occurred, Spanish mortality was correctly deduced, and the natives then went to war, reassured that their enemy was human.[13] The dead-forever corpse was in this case a welcome demonstration of ungodliness. In more recent vigils, however, religious communities have been traumatized when their messiahs, presumed to be immortal, have failed to return from the dead. Followers of the Brazilian beato Antônio Conselheiro postponed his burial until the odor became unbearable, expecting that he "would be resurrected after three days in flesh and blood and that thousands of archangels would fill the sky with flaming arrows."[14] A disappointed deathwatch also occurred when Mexico's Niño Fidencio died in 1938, and again when Willy Nolasco Cubillas, a young prophet outside of Lima, died during the cholera epidemic of 1991.[15]

Aztec and Inca royalty were also imbued with divine attributes, as were priests of deities in the pantheon. Some names, such as Quetzalcóatl in Mexico and Viracocha in Peru, referred first to deities and then to the humans who served and represented them in theocracy.[16] Particularly among the Aztecs, a mutually enhancing circulation of identities between humans and gods created a powerful divine presence in the community. The Aztec man-gods were the cover of deity, holding divine energy in their hearts and serving as *ixiptla* (the "skin" of a god).[17] A divine power "penetrated the man, possessed him, transformed him into a faithful replica of god," and the people received him as "the very authority he adored."[18] Sacrifice also transformed some victims into "the divine dead," and when priests descended from the pyramids dressed in the flayed skins of victims the people screamed, "Our gods are coming now!"[19]

Mexican man-gods sometimes responded to forced conversion by directing their otherworldly powers into apostasy and resistance. In 1537 Andrés Mixcóatl declared himself a god and dismissed the friars' sermons as "good for nothing" as he advocated a return to sacrifice.[20] For the man-god Martín Ocelotl "apocalyptic anticlericalism" afforded reempowerment, and for others the practice of Christianity "was no longer a question of believing in new forces, but of incarnating them." One announced that he "was becoming St. Paul or St. John," thereby leaving "the fringes of paganism to settle, without knowing it, in those of heresy."[21] An Indian named Gregorio Juan aspired to a comprehensive apotheosis, "using his voice dramatically like the friars who preach" to announce himself as "God the creator of Heaven and Earth" and also the "Son of God."[22]

Syncretic messiahs could also "destroy the world and create it again" in Paraguay.[23] Exemplary was the Guaraní cacique Oberá (Resplendent One), who made the customary messianic promises and was adored as quasi-divine during a 1579 attempt at decolonization. Oberá identified with the sun, was God's son born of the Virgin, and was married to Our Great Mother. He had been educated by friars but escaped as "messenger of God" and "liberator of the Guaraní people," rebaptizing converts and building an insurrectional alliance. The comet he caught and stored was ultimately unequal to the Christian arsenal, however, and Oberá was abandoned by most of his allies when bullets penetrated their bodies rather than bouncing off as promised.[24]

Syncretic messianism forged a unique composite in 1866 when Roque Rojas founded the Mexican Patriarchal Church of Elijah and proclaimed himself the new messiah. Rojas was believed to have descended from a Sephardic Rabbi and an Otomí priest of the Temple of the Sun, both from strongly messianic traditions. His charisma, prophesy, and faith healing conformed to the standard of Judeo-Christian sect messiahs, as did his claim that Mexico was the "chosen Nation, the resuscitated New Jerusalem." The poor would be redeemed because Rojas as God incarnate arrived to found their millennial kingdom.[25]

The messianic community must discover a god within it, must lower a god to human level just as the celestial city is lowered from heaven to earth. Messiahs are "saturated with power" because they have the audacity to incarnate the people's will for a human deity among them.[26] Visions, dreams, epiphanies, or possession experiences recruit messiahs to their special destinies, choosing them as the vanguard of the chosen. Messiahs generally begin as prophets of a deity, but their affinity with the supernatural—bolstered by charisma, coercion, and mythopoesis—blurs the distinction between message and messenger until the god is subsumed by his priest.

Ecstatic transport to heaven, which was once the "dominant medium of revelation" in Christian apocalypses, was on occasion the basis for a modern claim to prophetic or messianic authority.[27] A Spanish prophet named Inés attracted a small following after her deceased mother assisted in transporting her to heaven, where she saw people "on golden chairs, in glory." Back on earth, Inés announced that the messiah would return and take *conversos* (converted Jews) to their promised land, "where they would eat off golden plates."[28] Contemporary Pentecostals similarly claim visionary ascent to heaven, and during an audience on high the Peruvian messiah Ezequiel Ataucusi Gamonal was presented the "New Covenant" between God and humanity.[29] Indigenous visionaries of the colonial era often returned from their otherworldly incursions authorized to turn the word of God against his Church. In 1565 a Yucatec Maya named Pablo Be learned in heaven "that the Holy Catholic Faith was nothing and that Christian Baptism is not valid."[30] The shaman of a 1584 Maya uprising also "travelled to the world of the gods to pick up his messages and orders," and a nativist prophet in Paraguay coerced his people into apostasy by threatening to rise into heaven to turn their world upside down.[31]

More common than round-trips to heaven are visions of deities, saints, Virgins, or other supernatural personalities who illuminate what the uninitiated see only through a glass darkly. Before the Lima Inquisition intervened in 1578, the Dominican friar Francisco de la Cruz was visited repeatedly by God, who inquired, "Would you like me to make you as holy as the Virgin Mary? Would you like me to receive you into the union of my divinity as I received the holy humanity of Jesus Christ, my son?" A "perfect light" made Fray Francisco "the best man before God that there is in the world today," thereby entitling him to escalating messianic identities, including "Pope and King of this land."[32]

Some visions, such as those of Martin Luther or Joseph Smith (founder of the Mormons), result in the establishment of splinter sects or new religions that have profound and enduring impact; others, the majority, serve as impetus only for transitory messianic encounters of small communities. The latter type was epitomized by a visionary Brazilian butcher whose mission was revealed to him after migrating to Rio de Janeiro. The prophet was instructed to write a book and to tattoo children with an anagram representing the message that God is alive. He duly complied with the discursive mandate, but his mission was interrupted by arrest as he "stalked the deserted streets searching for little children to tattoo."[33] In the 1950s and 1960s another Brazilian, Cícero José de Farias, received telepathic messages from God that had little impact beyond his Celestial Court on Earth, which comprised some twenty followers. With the assistance of his brother, who corrected the grammar of the divine communiqués, Cícero sent "a very loving" but unheeded message to leaders throughout the world: "Heaven shall be joined with Earth under one government and one Judge, who shall be God among men."[34]

More substantial were the consequences of visions experienced by the black prophet João de Camargo, also in Brazil. Camargo was visited by the spirit of a dead boy who said to him, "João, you have been reborn, and since you are poor I will protect you." The Virgin, the Christ child, and a saint later appeared to Camargo; he built a chapel on the site as instructed; and soon a church, then a village, and finally an African-Christian sect were born. The otherworldly cast appearing before Camargo culminated with a vision of God himself, but in short order the deity was displaced by an apotheosis that endowed the deified Camargo even with a mystical body: "The Church comes to dwell in the body of the prophet."[35]

Luz del Mundo is another of many movements that was founded pursuant to visionary mandates. During the Cristero Rebellion in 1926, Christ appeared to a Mexican and said, "Aaron shall be your name; arise, be baptized, and preach." Brother Aaron got right to work, and by 1991 the movement had four million adherents. The doctrine is an amalgam of Judaism, primitive Christianity, Pentecostalism, and nationalism, but it was conceived like many in antithetical response to Catholicism.[36] Prophets from Luther to Ataucusi Gamonal can challenge the imposing hierarchy of Catholicism because their heterodoxy is authorized on high by a God displeased with his institutionalized vicars. Nativist Christianity was similarly legitimated, often by Virgins who sanctioned adaptations of the faith to indigenous cultures and causes.[37] In modern Popayán, Colombia, the imprisoned indigenous leader Manuel Quintín Lame exemplified how legitimating visions can redeem the identities of prophets who are denigrated or dismissed by a dominant culture. Quintín Lame fell into a rapture "with a faith higher than that of Moses," during which it was revealed that he "was destined to overcome those men who had studied fifteen or twenty years, and make them bow their heads."[38] What Quintín Lame "hides under his hair is a mystery" from the outside, but from within, as he relates, "the mysterious shadow of Jehovah was transformed into a ray of light to point out to me the fountain produced by the breaking of the sardonix rock." Consequently, "savagery and ineptitude" ceased to exist and Quintín Lame, no longer a "wild ass," was empowered to discover where "the mystery of human life is hidden."[39]

Along the Río Negro in the mid-nineteenth century, nativist messianism accessed that mystery through the cataleptic seizures that gave Venancio Kamiko access to the supernatural. The natives watched Kamiko's racked body convulse, marveling "when he successfully emerged from the trance-like paralysis" to relate his visions and give instructions.[40] In colonial Mexico, similarly, a black slave named Lucas Olola gained a certain prominence among the Huaxteca through frenzied dancing followed by collapse into unconsciousness, "frothing at the mouth," until he rose again dramatically because "his spirit had come to him." Supernatural interpretation of this extraordinary performance gave Olola the power over life, death, and "any Indian girl of whom he wants to take advantage."[41]

In other indigenous cases, such as the War of Mixtón, prophetic visions channeled the power of native deities and deified ancestors into resistance and deconversion. In 1677 a mestizo confessed that an Indian woman had directed him to a cave "in which Moctezuma himself, sitting on a golden chair, had ordered him to take off his rosary and his relics."[42] Centuries later, in 1941, a Tukuna boy in Brazil had several visions of the tribe's creator, who instructed him to unite the Tukuna, make a clearing in the jungle, and build a temple for ritual dance. A great flood was supposed to have spared the Tukuna while eradicating their oppressor, but instead the authorities threatened an air strike, preempting construction of the temple and forcing the natives back to work.[43]

Complementing visions as a means to access the supernatural were oracles, talking idols, and other prophetic devices whose silent discourse was bespoken or interpreted by shamans. According to a Jesuit memoir, Tepehuans revolting in 1616 "erected a shrine in a remote spot to which they would come, as to an oracle, to ask for prophesies as to future successes in battle."[44] A prophet of the same revolt carried a stone idol which "was said to have the ability to speak to each Nation in its own tongue," as could also "a mirror-like crystal attached to his bare abdomen." The words from the mirror so impressed the natives that "they felt compelled to obey the mandates of this false prophet."[45] Another shaman in northern Mexico consulted and was counseled by "a head that moans and talks from within an olla."[46]

A Jesuit in Paraguay described a ceremony presided over by Tupí "sorcerers who pass themselves off as saints." One prophet "retires into a dark hut, sets down a calabash in the shape of a human head in a place most favorable to his trickeries; then changing voice into a child's voice, he addresses the Indians," informing them that "they should not bother working anymore," that "the harvest will grow alone," that "the Indians will kill many enemies," and that "old women will become young again." The prophet is empowered because "something sacred and divine in the calabash" transmits through his agency a message that coincides with the desires of a bewildered community.[47]

The oracle is always wrong and the consequences are generally grave, but the oracular word nevertheless maintains its imposing authority. Because it never speaks for itself, the oracle affords the wide interpretive leeway in which disconfirmed prophesy mutates to suit the occasion. In January 1963, a millennial movement emerged in Brazil when a Canela woman named Maria began to receive prophetic messages from the fetus in her womb. The unarticulated prophesy of Dry Woman, as the fetus was called, announced a hierarchical inversion of native and white people for May 15, 1963, when the return of a Canela cultural hero would coincide with birth of the fetus. The messianic community went into shock two days earlier, however, when instead of Dry Woman Maria delivered a deformed, stillborn male, nearly dying herself during childbirth. As is common in such instances, the prophesy was rapidly overhauled, the date clause removed, and the blame for failure projected back onto the community.[48]

A Maya tradition of talking idols predated conquest, and afterwards its adaptations ranged from clandestine oracles advocating deconversion to articulations from Mayanized Christian symbols. In a 1597 uprising Andrés Chi, a shaman from Sotuta, borrowed the voice of the Holy Spirit to announce himself as Moses while calling for deconversion, but only until the Holy Spirit was "dragged out of his hiding place in the thatch of Chi's hut."[49] During the Caste War centuries later, a Talking Cross gave the Maya struggle a supernatural, Christian sanction that, along with British firearms, enabled the Cruzob to resist reconquest for more than fifty years. The Talking Cross that initially inspired the battle-weary Maya was confiscated and the ventriloquist Manuel Nahuat was killed, but beginning in 1851 the silenced word of the Cross became yet more insistent through written communiqués "transcribed" by Juan de la Cruz. The locus of discourse ultimately shifted from the silent oracle to the human scribe who actualized it for the community, and Juan de la Cruz was accordingly deified. A variation of the same was repeated in the theocratic, military Patrons of the Cross, who were called Tatich (Father) or Nohooch Tata (Great Father), and whose "power comes from God and not man."[50]

Oracular discourse articulated by humans but attributed to otherworldly sources had an Inca complement in the cult of ancestors preserved as mummies. The royal mallquis, as the mummies were known, resided in Cuzco's Temple of the Sun, and many rural communities likewise preserved and ritually attended their dead. The mallquis were consulted for advice and petitioned for approval as though they were alive, and their malleable "response" was interpreted by the heirs who articulated the speechlessness. The mummy remained "aloof and dignified, the perfect image of lordliness," while those communicating for and with it found their own interests expressed and legitimated from the beyond.[51] Following conquest, a visionary complement was suggested by the mallquis-like basket that flew invisibly in the air beside Taqui Onqoy leader Juan Chocne, advising him on the proper course of action. Insofar as he heeded these mummified directives, Chocne spoke not his own word but that of the invisible deity who accompanied him, just as he and the other taquiongos were simultaneously bespoken and empowered when possessed by huacas.[52]

Authorization by ecstatic transport, visions, and oracles has a more tangible complement in the otherworldly documents of credence that legitimate messianic missions, particularly among the illiterate. Wandering messiahs like Peter the Hermit or the Master of Hungary introduced themselves in medieval European villages with letters received from Christ and the Virgin.[53] Heavenly letters and their variations—such as the letters of the Talking Cross or the New Covenant received in heaven by Ataucusi Gamonal—have survived the ages, but the authorizing document of preference for Latin American insurrection has been the ersatz royal decree.[54] The Liberator Cacique and Governor of the Universe who led an 1803 nativist rebellion near Quito cohered his following on the strength of his claim that both papal and royal edicts had mandated his mission. He presented printed Bulls of Crusade that, though beside the point and expired, duly substantiated his claim.[55] A 1749 Venezuelan revolt was catalyzed when Juan Francisco de León announced that the slaves had been emancipated by royal decree but that the corrupt Creoles had hidden the document to perpetuate slavery. According to captured rebels, a hero's spirit rose from the grave and traveled to Spain on a white horse to retrieve the decree. In 1770 one Cocofío likewise propagated the existence of an emancipation decree, and this claim became the ideological foundation of a 1795 rebellion in Coro.[56]

Phantom royal decrees provided textual reinforcement for the common eighteenth-century revolutionary slogan "Long live the king, and death to the bad government," which was used by native, mestizo, and creole peoples alike to endow sedition with a façade of legitimacy. The always unauthorized rebellions in name of the king provided a halfway-house shelter for movements hesitant to take on his majesty directly, and they allowed, in theory, for overhaul of viceregal administration while leaving the infrastructure of royal theocracy intact. Corregidores could thus be attacked as irremediably corrupt, while the king "remained shielded behind the assumption of benevolence."[57] The divinely ordered empire was not merely spared but defended as the people rose in arms to annihilate its aberrant manifestations. Contrived royal endorsement made insurrection seem a just if not holy war, but always with the unstated, often unacknowledged purpose of decolonization. By 1810 in Mexico, "the monarch, the archetypal figure of intrusive and oppressive colonial authority, was being venerated with messianic fervor while European-born colonists were being slaughtered with an almost ritualistic enthusiasm."[58]

In the Andes, Túpac Amaru II, the Catari brothers, Túpac Catari, and Felipe Velasco all claimed that the king had recruited them to eradicate rogue elements of the viceroyalty.[59] A lampoon that circulated in Cuzco in January 1781 characteristically depicted a benevolent king hoodwinked by "the Corregidores, the Visitador and the other inventors of tyranny." If Charles III knew how his subordinates mistreated the natives, then he "would unsheathe the Sword Against those who are the cause of this perdition."[60] The king remained unaware (or indifferent), however, so the people took up the task on his behalf. As a South American priest advocating independence in the early nineteenth century explained, "We are told that kings, intendants and other authorities are placed over us by God. True. But just as we get rid of certain forms of creation such as disease and illness and are expected to cure ourselves of these, so also we are obliged to throw off the yoke of tyranny, oppression, abuse, and despotism."[61]

The targets and objectives of the rebellions revealed the contrived allegiance to the crown as a political expedient, an unauthorized tap into royal power, prerogative, and protection. As a late-eighteenth-century trial transcript worded it, "Although they yell: 'Long live the king and death to the bad government,' " the rebelling natives in Peru "directed their conspiracy against the sovereignty of our Catholic monarch" and, upon victory, intended to crown a native "king of Cuzco." The true agenda became more explicit as movements gained identity and audacity: "Long live the Inca king and death to the king of Spain."[62] That message had precocious expression in Ecuador during the 1760s, when rebels appointed an Inca, rose under the slogan "Death to the king," and aspired to reestablish an indigenous state at the Spanish capital in Riobamba. All white people would be killed, save women who agreed to perpetual servitude and priests who, after castration, would minister to the natives.[63]

Once they were supernaturally empowered, the messiahs of nativist rebellions turned enemies into stones and stones into allies, destroyed creation with their breath, resurrected the dead, neutralized firearms, and controlled an arsenal of storms and earthquakes.[64] The priests and friars manifesting a competing claim to godliness retaliated by curing the ill, raising the dead, bringing the rain, calming the storms, and multiplying the loaves.[65] In Paraguay an Indian boy was spontaneously cured upon baptism, and victory in battle was attributed less to the prowess of soldiers than to Jesuit prayers.[66] Martín de Valencia, one of the "twelve apostles" in Mexico, counted to his credit the resurrection of a dead Indian boy and "some ducks."[67] The same miraculous powers have been attributed to modern sect messiahs like Francisco da Cruz, who according to the faithful turned water into wine, multiplied chicken and flour to feed the poor, walked on mud without sinking, talked to fish, cured the sick, darkened the sky, controlled storms, and had the power of ubiquity.[68]

The most prominent manifestation of divine power in modern messianism is miraculous cure. The messiah's salvation of the collective is replicated in miniature on each body redeemed by the empowered hand. Andean traditions attribute curative powers to popular leaders and extend the powers of curanderos into sociopolitics, as though curing the body and curing the social body were the same gesture in different registers.[69] Through the power of God, "the blind see, the lame walk, the lepers are cleansed, the deaf hear, the dead are raised," and the miracle workers, like Jesus, accumulate their followings in the wake of cures.[70] Pentecostal missionaries among the Toba in the 1930s owed much of their success to the coincidence of Christian and traditional healing. If faith healing was an index of divine power, however, then failed cures or illness of the healer were symptoms of its depletion and sometimes resulted in abandonment of the church. Following a Christian Toba's death, the Pentecostal ministry could be blamed for its curative impotence or its unsatisfactory intercession on behalf of the faithful.[71] The Jesuits in colonial Mexico were similarly attributed the power to heal, and the consequences were unbecoming when the Tarahumara realized they had confused the remedy with the contagion.[72]

Faith healing has contributed substantially to the reception of Pentecostalism throughout Latin America. A brochure advertising one Pentecostal meeting in Peru typically boasted, "Christ saves and heals—bring in the sick and expect a miracle."[73] A common pattern among indigenous converts entails illness, travel to a church directed by a foreign ministry, faith healing and baptism, and return to the village to witness or, on occasion, to establish congregations.[74] Pentecostals have no monopoly on faith healing, however, and the popularity of sect messiahs and alternative faiths is also contingent upon their reputations for miraculous cure. The Nicaraguan Jesus of the Poor spoke for many: "I have cured invalids; I have made the blind see and the mute talk; I can cure AIDS, cancer, and even cholera."[75] The Spiritists (also called Kardecists) in Brazil integrate healing into a doctrine that synthesizes science, philosophy, and aspects of Christianity.[76] The cult of María Lionza in Venezuela offers not only relief from physical and psychological ailments but also curative and protective measures against injuries caused by spells, the evil eye, and accidents. The cult's syncretic faith also incorporates the "gods of the Old Testament" and the star of David into the curandero's therapeutic ensemble.[77]

By serving as disseminators of divine graces and as points of contact between the community and the deity, messiahs from Jesus of Nazareth to Jesus of the Poor are themselves empowered and divinized. God may ultimately be responsible for the cure, but it occurs through the hands of a human. The god and the healer thereby become inextricably united as dimensions of one and the same supernatural power. An indigenous Mexican curandera named Catalina underscored human replication of the divine source when she reported that Christ "crucified her, nailing her hands to a cross; and it was while she was nailed to the cross that she was taught the art of healing" with her tongue.[78] Catalina was remade in the image of the God who empowered her, a metamorphosis that, if followed by successful cures, can eventually result in displacement of Christ by a second generation of Christ-like surrogates. After a plethora of miraculous cures, Niño Fidencio of northern Mexico "was really Jesus" insofar as his patients were concerned, and contemporary curanderos who continue Fidencio's work are empowered to heal when possessed by Fidencio, not by God.[79] The curanderas in the Venezuelan cult of José Gregorio Hernández, once a famous Christian surgeon and now a folk saint, are similarly empowered by invoking Hernández's spirit while in a trance.[80]

Mere humans become the gods of their communities when identification ultimately subsumes its divine prototype. Antônio Conselheiro maintained that "only God is great" and defended his human status among a huge following of Brazilian backlanders inclined to deify him, but the people of Canudos nevertheless called him "the Good Jesus" and, according to a police report, "adored him as if he were a living God."[81] In the 1920s some Asháninkas mistook the Seventh-Day Adventist F. A. Stahl for the doomsday God whose kingdom he announced, and in the 1940s the Pentecostal John Lagar was regarded as God by the Toba.[82] In the contemporary Amazon, Francisco da Cruz is "the Son of God," "Jesus of Nazareth," and "Christ himself," though he made no explicit claim to be so, and legend holds that the pope hoped to pay homage to this incarnation of deity but was obstructed by envious priests.[83]

Secular messiahs are less reluctant recipients of folk apotheosis, and their identities as divine or semidivine are often conditioned by the inflated images that they, their parties, or their devotees propagate among amenable constituencies. José de San Martín is a "Saint of the Sword"; Eloy Alfaro is a "messianic caudillo"; José María Morelos is adored "to the point of idolatry"; Lázaro Cárdenas is "something of a latter-day Jesus"; and Victor Raúl Haya de la Torre is "almost worshipped by workers."[84] Postindependence and postwar anarchy were particularly conducive to the deification and worship of caudillos who reconquered ungodly chaos.[85] Most of the Argentine clergy participated in secular veneration of the semidivine Juan Manuel de Rosas, parading his portrait through the streets, adorning it on altars, and closing the gap between the deity who created order and the hero who regained it: "If it is right to love God Our Lord, so it is right to love, obey and respect our Governor and Restorer of the Laws."[86] Apotheosis was even more insistent following the victory of the nineteenth-century Guatemalan caudillo and later president José Rafael Carrera, who "saw himself as a savior of the Guatemalan people." In 1839 a Guatemalan archbishop concurred—"It appears that God has destined you to redeem the Guatemalan people from their oppression"—and the campesinos followed generously in kind by referring to Carrera as "Angel," "Son of God," and "Our Lord."[87]

Essential to the construction of a messianic identity was the caudillo's own "propensity to exalt and magnify his personality beyond all limits" through "the theatrical gesture, the sumptuous uniform, the impressive monument, the spectacular performance." Ritual ostentation reinforced the "transcendental and exceptional character" of the caudillo and engraved "the ideal of a superman" in the minds of impressionable masses. Exemplary was the spectacle pomp of Mexico's Antonio López de Santa Anna, who in the first half of the nineteenth century held the office of president at least nine times. In addition to occasional theatrics, such as the solemn burial of his leg after it was shot off by a cannonball, Santa Anna was prone to a showy etiquette of majesty: "His ministers had the obligation to travel in yellow coaches with valets in green livery, while His Most Serene Highness—himself—was escorted by lancers in red uniforms and plumed hats."[88] His titles included "Savior of the Country," and "Grand Master of the National and Distinguished Order of Guadalupe," and the twelve hundred soldiers comprising his guard were "Lancers of the Supreme Power."[89]

When Marxism later emerged as a "new religion" or a "secularized version of messianism," social revolutionaries with utopian ideals became the priests and deities of a faith grounded on earth and in humanity.[90] As José Carlos Mariátegui saw it in 1925, "The power of revolutionaries is not in their science, but in their faith, their passion, their will. It is a religious, mystical, spiritual power."[91] Che Guevara preached that exemplary "moral conduct" and asceticism make the guerrilla a "true priest" and a "guiding angel" of revolution.[92] The doctrines of cultlike revolutions epitomized by Sendero Luminoso resemble gospel in their prophetic infallibility, and idealogues like Abimael Guzmán are revered as "without a doubt among the most brilliant personalities in the history of America."[93] Triumphant Sendero would necessarily assume control of Peru by 1987, because "Chairman Gonzalo [Guzmán] has stated this, and what he says must be fulfilled."[94] This blind faith was the payoff of an "almost hagiographical" image of Guzmán propagated by the party and defended by the demand for absolute compliance.[95] A letter to Sendero's central committee opened with the requisite deference by acknowledging "full and unconditional submission to the greatest living Marxist-Leninist-Maoist on earth: our beloved and respected Chairman Gonzalo, chief and guide of the Peruvian revolution and the world proletarian revolution, teacher of Communists and party unifier."[96]

"If God really existed," in the dictum of anarchist Mikhail Bakunin, "it would be necessary to abolish him."[97] God blocks the path of free will, takes the credit for human accomplishment, and humbles all creation to a subaltern deference. His very existence founds humanity outside of itself, in an alien essence whose totality—omniscient, omnipotent—demeans human reality and devoids it of intrinsic meaning. José Martí was consequently a "religious man without religion," but as the phrase suggests he was always locked in the paradox of a messianic identity derived from a disclaimed deity: "the Christ of America," "the Cuban Messiah."[98] A nontheistic, anthropocentric adaptation of the Christian mystical body is suggested in Martí's use of religious premises to undermine them: "There is a God: man; there is a divine force: all men."[99] Secular eucharistic devotion characterized a cult of admirers who congregated periodically in the 1920s to break bread in memory of Martí: "Let us eat his flesh to make ourselves stronger, drink his blood to make ourselves worthier"; "Let us receive the sacrament of his creative thought to make ourselves better."[100]

Che Guevara was also deified in folk Christianity after his death in martyrdom, and his superhuman image was redoubled by an ancillary identity as a folk saint. In Vallegrande, Bolivia, where Guevara was buried until his remains were disinterred in 1997, villagers associated the seminaked, bearded, wounded corpse with that of the crucified Jesus. Candles were lit and secret masses celebrated in his honor because he was "a great man—a god," with the leap from one to the other made naturally and without hesitation. "Saint Ernesto" is the patron of Vallegrande and believed to be as miraculous as any saint in the canon.[101] In La Higuera, where Guevara was killed, a traditional verse reads, "St. Che Guevara / Patron of La Higuera / Pray for my Country / Which always awaits you."[102]

Dialogical Power

Messianic leaders operate from a liminal position annexed to but autonomous from that of the community. Their place on the fringe of society becomes centric among peoples more marginal than they are, and their community's peripheral position shifts, in turn, as they institute a new center. At once within and outside, among and above, messianic protagonists are integral to but ritually distanced from the community. Their position is precarious and their stand is perpetually off balance as it renegotiates shifting allegiances.

Max Weber's classic but incomplete definition described the charismatic as a leader "set apart from ordinary men and treated as endowed with supernatural, superhuman, or at least specifically exceptional powers or qualities" that "are regarded as of divine origin or as exemplary."[103] Numinousness separated the karaí from Tupí-Guaraní society, and this distance was twice reiterated by his life "on the perimeter of Tupí communities, both physically and in terms of prevailing social and political norms."[104] In other cases, outsider status accrues to members of a community who depart, acquire their special powers through worldly experiences, and then return in fact, in myth, or as symbols to lead or represent their people. The rise to power from humble origins redoubles the mystique of such charismatic leaders as Eva Perón, Jorge Eliécer Gaitán, Benito Juárez, José Rafael Carrera, and Luis M. Sánchez Cerro ("he's a *cholo* like us").[105]

The great majority of messianic protagonists are alien to their communities owing to combinations of race, class, education, ethnic identity, region of origin, and worldliness. The extreme end of the spectrum is populated by outsiders like the Frenchman Orelie Antoine de Tounens, who hoped to reign in a kingdom of Araucania and Patagonia and received a messianic welcome from the natives there in 1861. Among the many messiahs in nineteenth- and twentieth-century Brazil, only one was black, even though the community was predominantly black and mulatto. Some of the messiahs were immigrants, and most dismissed indigenous and African elements to develop cultures that were "profoundly and exclusively European."[106] Juan Santos Atahualpa was a Cuzco native who based his insurgency among jungle tribes; Túpac Amaru II was a mestizo living like a Creole; the scholarly Miguel Hidalgo, also a Creole, was a priest; and the protagonists of sixteenth-century slave rebellions in Mexico were hispanicized blacks who had earlier rebel experience in the Caribbean.[107]

The leaders of popular revolutions in modern Latin America are predominantly educated whites and mestizos from the urban middle and upper classes.[108] Abimael Guzmán, a philosophy professor from Arequipa, Peru, was readily distinguishable from his Quechua-speaking constituencies, and a hierarchical racial pyramid is suggested by the middle ranks of Sendero Luminoso, which comprised youth drawn from the provincial lower-middle classes, "the majority holding university degrees and racially characterized as mestizos."[109] Some indigenous Andeans sarcastically referred to Sendero cadres as *los universitarios* (the university students).[110] Even the exalted hero of the early movement in Ayacucho, Edith Lagos, was a mestiza from a wealthy family.

Sendero's ideology was not particularly indigenist, and many of its policies—such as the prohibition of traditional markets or the displacement of kinship hierarchies by party committees—were patently anti-indigenist. Once elaborated by campesino interpretations that were reinforced and conditioned by propaganda, however, Sendero appeared to be a nativist movement resuming a struggle as old as the conquest. This was particularly true in the early years, when the peasant reception of Sendero was patiently conditioned by Quechua-speaking students trained by Guzmán at the University of Huamanga. The image of a pachacuti-like people's war was also facilitated by the movement's base in an impoverished, isolated region virtually devoid of federal programs; by its exploitation of chronic race and class tensions; and by its populist gestures, such as the execution of public enemies, the cancellation of debts, and the distribution of merchants' goods and landowners' livestock. Cadres epitomized by Edith Lagos became messianic heroes with extraordinary popular appeal, and Guzmán, the mysteriously absent supreme commander, assumed a mythic image congruent with that of rank-and-file heroes but in a higher, almost divine, register.

Liminality in the relation between messiah and community is complemented geographically by the regions in which many messiahs maneuver. The terrain of messianism is on the margins—jungle, sierra, backland, shantytown. Its frequent appearance in border regions or transitional historical periods replicates the relation between the messiah and the community and between the community and society at large. Essential to the nature and history of Jesuit reductions in Paraguay, for example, was their location on the frontier between Spanish and Portuguese empires. Brazilian messiahs proliferated in the "anxious transition from monarchy to republic," sometimes in contested regions, and in Spanish America nativist insurrection flourished on the fringes first during the transition between autonomy and colony and then in the transition to independence.[111] The messiah "maneuvers amidst disputes, dissensions, local rivalries," and crumbling polities to found a kingdom on the ruins.[112]

In 1866 an Andean sect submissively adored and obeyed a Bolivian woman who called herself the Virgin of the Rosary. The worship in itself seemed innocent enough, but the location in Puno, a border region destabilized by uprisings, predisposed interpretations of the sect as seditious. The "pernicious idea" that most worried Peruvian authorities was annexation of Puno to Bolivia in order to escape exploitation, and this motif was indeed a driving force in secular messianism fifty years later when a mestizo military officer, absent without leave, took the name Rumi Maqui to lead an indigenous insurrection.[113] More recently, the Palma Sola sect, founded in the Dominican Republic in the early 1960s, was inspired by the anticipated return of Liborio Mateo, a healer believed to be God's messenger on earth. The community attracted some five thousand people who practiced Voodoo-Christian rituals and sang hymns composed by Liborio, but its location in a volatile region near the Haitian border resulted in political unease and finally massacre by Dominican forces.[114]

Sect religion and border politics were also fatefully confused along the Mexican-United States border. In late 1891 campesinos of Tomochic, a village in northwestern Mexico, responded to the inequitable modernization imposed by Porfirio Díaz with the slogan, "We will obey no one but God." The uprising was inspired by faith in a regional folk saint, Teresa Urrea, whose home at Cabora had become a popular pilgrimage site. Teresa's explicit complicity in the uprising is doubtful, but following a rebel attack on Navojoa in May 1892, "the Saint of Cabora" was arrested and exiled across the border to Arizona. The cult and conflict then became international, bringing the accusation that Teresa violated U.S. neutrality laws by leading a "horde of fanatics in a religious war" to overthrow the Mexican government. On October, 20, 1892, federal troops besieged Tomochic, and nine days later the commanding general reported "the enemy eliminated to the last man."[115]

Such images as Jesus the shepherd followed by sheepish hordes imply a passive role for the masses in collective redemption, but in fact the messiah and the community engage in perpetual, mutual reinvention.[116] The charismatic messiah is an intermediary between the community and some higher religious or secular power, governed by bilateral obligations while fostering a "close dialectical unity."[117] The revolutionary cadre, as Che Guevara put it, must "be able to interpret the general directives issued by the central power, to assimilate them, and to transmit them as ideas to the masses," but must also fulfill "the people's wishes and deepest motivations."[118]

Be it the Holy Spirit, mythological heroes, deified ancestors, or the other-worldly mystique of doctrine, a power source once inaccessible becomes the vital force that reconfigures the universe until the community discovers itself, reborn, at the sacred center. Charismatics speak to and for the experience of their followers, empowering impotent rage and founding new identities on an eschatology that guarantees the supremacy of their communities. They offer their followers "a social myth most perfectly adapted to their needs," and in return the followers oblige the charismatics' dogmatism and absolutism by accepting without challenge the doctrines that, however specious or mysterious, underwrite their authority.[119] Charismatics remain outsiders even in relation to their doctrines, for in one direction the doctrines belong to the higher power that authorizes charisma and in the other to the communities that activate the doctrines with their acceptance. "It is as if the prophet did not have the power of inaugurating the discourse in which, on the contrary, he seems to be trapped, a discourse of which he can be only the echo without ever being its master."[120]

Marx described the collective's "mystical consciousness" as a "consciousness which is unclear to itself, whether it appears in religious or political form." If the charismatic can retrieve and clarify what has been buried under oppression, "then it will transpire that the world has long been dreaming of something that it can acquire if only it becomes conscious of it."[121] The messianic message originates with the people, is rerouted through the charismatic who imbues it with transcendental authority, and then returns to its source as a novel doctrine that—once decoded—suits the community as precisely as a tautology. The messiah gives the community back its own voice authorized.

The conviction to messianism is passionate against the evidence and the odds, but the paradox of unwavering faith in untenable doctrine is defused insofar as the appeal is emotive rather than rational. The charismatic messiah is as much coercive as persuasive, a soft coercion that obliges a community to take the leap from its demeaned existence on the margins to its wildest dreams as a chosen people.[122] Charisma is derived from and thrives on the crisis that it alleviates (against better judgment) with an impossible solution.[123] The agenda is insulated by vagueness, ambiguity, and an oracular mystique reducible to mantra-like slogans. It must be all things to all people, an accommodating receptacle that presents as an assertion. The messianic message must be simple enough to be easily misunderstood.

When he was inaugurated as president of Argentina on June 4, 1946, Juan Domingo Perón epitomized the ambiguous message with this scripturelike but empty rhetoric: "Those who want to hear, hear; those who want to follow, follow. My enterprise is high and what I stand for is clear; my cause is the cause of the people; my guide is the flag of the Fatherland."[124] Peronism was later defended to the death as much by Montonero guerrillas as by right-wing paramilitary goons, each believing themselves the true heirs to a flexible, shifting doctrine that catered to them both.

Often the message emitted by the charismatic engages dialogically with its interpretations to generate composite and syncretic meanings. Guillermo Lobatón among the Asháninkas and Abimael Guzmán or Che Guevara among central and southern Andeans had Marx on their mind, but their constituencies received them archetypally as Inkarrí, Son of the Sun, or Jesus Christ. The same occurred earlier, with the corresponding theories of the times, when Juan Santos Atahualpa and Túpac Amaru II were received by villagers. Each of these charismatics engages the gear of his agenda with that of its interpretation by the community, and the two together grind out the insurrection. The charismatic manipulates their mythology to his advantage, and they reciprocate by co-opting his revolution for their myth. It is partially for this reason, as Emiliano Zapata put it regarding his campesino followers, that "once the battle begins, there is no god that can restrain them."[125] In the eighteenth-century Andean revolts the masses likewise used the libertine environment created by insurrection to express hostilities and seek benefits not necessarily congruent with the plan of their commander. Once the people "are drawn from their repose," as Manuel González Prada put it, they "put into play their latent forces," often to the dismay of the idealogues who unleashed them.[126] Grievances endured in resignation become suddenly intolerable when the charismatic introduces the possibility of redress, and the masses effect a remedy in their manner.[127]

In the final analysis, the messianic community is the source of charismatic power, coauthor of its doctrine, and guarantor of its claim to authority. The charismatic is nothing without his people, and as illustrated by the tropes of a mystical or social body he is incorporated as the synecdoche of their cause. "We are all [Subcomandante] Marcos," chanted Chiapas Zapatistas beginning in 1994, just as earlier Simón Bolívar was said to have "burned with our own desire for freedom" and to have spoken "with the voice of our own natures."[128] Haya de la Torre cited Bolívar to assert that the people are "the only sovereign"; Jorge Eliécer Gaitán claimed, "I am not a man, I am a people"; and Evita described Juan Perón as "the incarnation of Argentine reality."[129] The people construct a messiah who exercises the power with which he is invested, and when the detour is followed back to the source it reveals a faith in themselves that they dared not activate until the messiah accommodated it in a reordered world. He is their messiah and they are his people, the two re-creating their universe through mutually reciprocating reinforcements. The messiah extrapolates his mission from their condition and they recover their initiative through his audacity.

As voice of the voiceless, the charismatic "externalizes and articulates" what others "can as yet only feel, strive towards and imagine but cannot put into words or translate explicitly into action."[130] Perón regarded himself as "the faithful reflection" of what Argentines felt and the interpreter "of the revolutionary will of the Argentine people."[131] In Colombia, Gaitán similarly regarded himself the "deep interpreter" of "the agitated depths of the collective soul."[132] Interpretation provides for certain liberties, however, and the charismatic "always knows exactly how to play the right social chords and to produce the sounds which he wants."[133] He is a "vehicle for the articulation of grievances," but also an "issue entrepreneur" who "obeys the laws of political expediency while being driven by irrational, at times even mystical, impulses."[134] He exploits confusion, catalyzes and manipulates social tensions, stresses some aspects of public will while repressing others, and reinterprets history to make his interest group, and above all himself, its hero and beneficiary.

The dialogical relation between the charismatic and the community is epitomized by oratory. Gaitán was "fundamentally transformed" in "an intoxication without limits" when he addressed the masses, and this "theatricality" was "indispensable to also mobilize the fantasy" of the people.[135] Perón had "hypnotic powers" over his audience, while he himself "seemed in a trance," could "divine what they were feeling and what they wanted," and "was like a medium" expressing their unarticulated thoughts.[136] He tended, in his own words, to "dialogue with the people in my speeches," a practice literalized by actual discursive interaction in response to questions screamed from the crowd.[137]

Preparation was at times unnecessary for Haya de la Torre, because the message was "dictated" to him by "this grand, magnificent, mass presence of a great people." Haya experienced something like "mystical ecstasy" as he translated the longings of the masses into "words of magical power," and the masses "responded ecstatically" in communal catharsis as their voicelessness gained expression. During rallies, Haya and his Apristas experienced a dialogical symbiosis in which they "vibrated" together, with the didactic content of the oratory always subordinate to its emotive and agitational power. During his famous address in Trujillo following the massacre of Apristas there in 1932, the weeping Haya produced a "deliriously cheering audience" in "religious ecstacy."[138]

The dialogical orator's capacity to articulate the will of the people was also characteristic of Fidel Castro. The Cuban masses attend rallies not to passively applaud speech making but rather to "manifest an attitude, a decisiveness, a state of mind" until—continuing in Castro's words—"sometimes one does not know who is speaking, whether it is oneself or the people."[139] Che Guevara described the relation between the early Castro and his audience as "something like the dialogue of two tuning forks whose vibrations summon forth new vibrations each in the other. Fidel and the mass begin to vibrate in a dialogue of growing intensity which reaches its culminating point in an abrupt ending crowned by our victorious battle cry." Between 1959 and 1989, Castro made a speech every four days, the length of each varying from an hour to half a day.[140] Guevara cautiously endorsed the personality cult sustained by Castro's oratory, "insofar as it incarnates the highest virtues and aspirations of the people."[141]

Religious leaders also become the voice of the voiceless, and the Salvadoran archbishop Oscar Romero explicitly identified himself as such. Some liberation theologists argue that the Latin American poor are aphonic and utopic—without voice and without place—but that the Bible guarantees them a fair hearing as much as a promised land.[142] In earlier sect Christianity the oratory skills of Antônio Conselheiro had the faithful feeling "as if they were flying up to the clouds."[143] Something of the impact was registered even in the mocking prose of Euclides da Cunha, for whom Conselheiro, a "buffoon enraptured in a vision from Apocalypse," performed only one miracle: "not seeming ridiculous." "Sparing of gestures, he would speak at length, his eyes fixed on the floor," stressing select phrases by punctuating them with silence. Conselheiro would then raise his head and suddenly reveal his eyes, "black and alive," to create a presence that "no one dared to look at." The faithful would "succumb, lower their eyes, fascinated under the strange hypnotism of that terrible madness."[144] Conselheiro captivated the backland masses not because he dominated them, but rather because he himself "was dominated by popular aberrations."[145]

Charisma advocates nonrecognition of other forms of authority, subordinating tradition and law as it establishes its absolutist claim. It is powerful insofar as its agent is present and numinous, but once the charismatic is arrested, dead, or otherwise absented the community becomes destabilized, usually beyond recovery. Surrogates sometimes emerge as "reincarnations" of a past charismatic, attempting to transfer or institutionalize an authority disembodied by the hero's passing. In lieu of such reduplication in heirs, populists like Castro or Perón seek the routinization of charisma in highly indoctrinated social bodies expected to perpetuate the sacred mission. Charismatic leadership is then "the formation of all souls" into a unified "collective soul" that has the capacity to act independently, but only on behalf of the messiah.[146]

The Broken Promise

One of the distinguishing characteristics of millennialism is the consistency with which it fails. Not a single messiah returned from the dead; no crops offered themselves for laborless harvest; the poor never exchanged places with the rich; and the kingdom never came. As Alicia Barabas summarized it, "The viability of millennial utopia must not be sought in its concretion," which never occurs, "but rather in the maintenance of hope that provides men with new meanings and mobilizes them in pursuit of a better world."[147] Even in the rare instances when millennial insurrections are successful, the outcome is necessarily dwarfed in relation to the fantastic rewards that are promised. Messianic leaders "eternally create kingdoms from which they find themselves no less eternally exiled, whether they succeed or fail."[148] The Pueblo Revolt of 1680 managed to expel the Spaniards, but it could hardly deliver the utopia that its leader, Popé, promised as inducement. Drought, small harvests, and continuing hardships of survival after the revolt led many Pueblos to believe that Popé had deceived them, and finally he was deposed "because of his excessive demands for women, grain, and livestock."[149]

Messianic leaders evidence a need to dramatically rescue lost ideals, and they detour these personal quests through collectives whose unfortunate social stations predispose them to recruitment. The masses are "the instrument of action within politics," exploited to implement and aggrandize a personal mission.[150] Charisma in this perspective becomes "the creative clash and embrace of inner fantasy and political reality," and abnegation becomes opportunism.[151] There also seems to be an element of unconscious revenge in messianism, because the leader engages masses in quixotries whose beautiful conclusions are foreclosed almost without exception by traumatic failure and usually by slaughter.[152] In some few cases, such as the mass suicides in the People's Temple compound at Jonestown, the leader's suicide is generalized to encompass the community; in the overwhelming majority, the messiah's botched mission ends in execution and massacre that indirectly distribute suicide, or suicidal recklessness, among the victims of hope. Balanced on the threshold where the fairytale meets the nightmare, the community is worthy of the messiah's scorn because it is not worthy of his ideal. The messiah walks a *via crucis* and fulfills the prophesy of his death for the cause, dying within the myth that he lived and taking with him a quota of followers.[153]

The greatest feat of many charismatics is to transform the poverty and powerlessness of others into their own wealth and power. Flagrantly exploitive are the autocracies of caudillos, dictators, and presidents whose programs for salvation include large-scale embezzlement that destabilizes troubled economies from within. These messiahs gamble against the odds, borrowing their high stakes from the public trust that they always eventually deplete. Self-interested supremacy was more refined but no less extreme among royalty of European and indigenous theocracies that claimed entitlement to tribute, opulence, and the power of life and death over their subjects.

Some religious messiahs are also eventually revealed as scoundrels exploiting ignorance and desperation to their this-worldly advantage. In the late 1940s a converted cacique named Pedro Martínez founded the Pentecostal Church of God in several Toba settlements, ordering that converts send him offerings that he would deliver to God in person.[154] Samuel Aaron, the "anointed one" who succeeded his father as leader of Mexico's Luz del Mundo movement, was more ambitious in his accumulations, taking frequent trips abroad and often returning with a new automobile. On one occasion "he made his entrance into the colony riding in a large white convertible, and all the people turned out to greet him waving palm branches and shouting, 'Blessed is he who comes in the name of the Lord.' "[155]

Most messianic leaders are driven not by financial gain (although, along with fame, it is an attractive perquisite) but rather by an idealist brinkmanship that, in turn, is expected of their followers. Perón believed that the great leader obeys an inner "superior force," borne of "faith in oneself," that impels one to daring feats. He is willing to gamble all on a single card because "great successes are obtained only by great risks."[156] In times of crisis, one must draw upon one's "spiritual forces" and "sacred fire" to risk even "dying gloriously."[157] The messiah ostensibly protects his followers with this "spirit of sacrifice," but in practice the willingness to die for the cause is reciprocally expected of faithful adherents. If the charismatic bond is to be forged and the messianic mission accomplished, each must defend the other. Evita Perón urged the *descamisados* (shirtless ones) to "offer their lives to Perón," and they obediently responded with the chant "My life for Perón."[158] "Men die," as Fidel Castro put it in Cuba, "but the Party is immortal."[159] When the messiah literalizes his own sacrifice, as did Getúlio Vargas in 1954, his martyrdom obliges the reciprocal dedication of his followers. As worded in Vargas's suicide letter to the Brazilian poor, "My sacrifice will keep you united and my name will be your battle standard. Each drop of my blood will be an immortal call to your conscience and will uphold the sacred will to resist."[160] The messiah saves the masses through his "sacrifice," and the masses reciprocate by offering their lives to safeguard the ideal he symbolizes.

Individual lives become expendable "casualties" consecrated to the lost cause. A captured Senderista, having learned how "fear can be overcome with ideology," typically commented that "the individual's life is worth nothing." Of paradigmatic importance were "the masses, led by the Party," and the party led by the charismatic. "We love life, but because we love it we are willing to give it up. Take Chairman Gonzalo, he is the greatest expression of life's affirmation over death."[161] The movement's messiah is represented as the quintessential dedication to which his subordinates aspire. He donates his "totality" to the cause, and in return the cadres gratefully risk a "glorious belligerent death."[162] As a Sendero manuscript confiscated in the Lurigancho prison worded it, "Your life does not belong to you, it belongs to the Party."[163]

The burden of salvation in religious cases also extends from the messiah to the community. Fearing assassination, the Brazilian messiah Cícero José de Farias, known as Israel, confounded his enemies by requiring that his followers likewise call themselves Israel, because "to persecute one, all must be persecuted."[164] Rather than sacrificing himself to save his people, dying "once for all," the people become a human shield or a mystical body in which this messiah dissolves to evade his fate. But even Jesus himself was uncompromising: "Whoever wishes to come after me must deny himself, take up his cross, and follow me. For whoever wishes to save his life will lose it, but whoever loses his life for my sake and that of the gospel will save it."[165] Revelation offers baptismal rebirth in the blood of the Lamb, reserving the first resurrection and the millennial kingdom exclusively for Christian martyrs. Friars in New Mexico were instructed in 1696, "Scorn your corporal lives," and they were taught to accept—if not seek—martyrdom, because "if it should happen that in your work you should lose your corporal life, you would be assuring the eternal life of your soul."[166] Martyrdom was the "greatest prize" among Jesuits in Paraguay, and many friars entering the American mission resigned themselves to the strong possibility that they would go the way of their savior. In a letter to his parents an Italian Jesuit departing for the New World wrote, "Consider me dead, without further hope," and asked, "Am I to end my life in bed, and Christ on the Cross?"[167] The murder of Christians in modern Latin America, among them many Jesuits, is likewise perceived as martyrdom that replicates the messiah's death in an endless accumulation of corpses for the kingdom.

These tragedies, like the gloomy cataclysms of John's Revelation, are assuaged by their deferred reversal in triumph, with the slain witnesses rising from the dead, the stained robes made "white in the blood of the Lamb," and the martyrs rewarded in a heavenly beyond where "God shall wipe away all tears from their eyes."[168] If that promise remains unfulfilled, however, then the spilled blood serves no purpose other than to edify the beautiful opera of the mass and a lovely fiction that is dangerous when mistaken for the truth. The martyrs who die for causes too good to be true are defrauded by their messiahs but also by themselves as, in a weary resignation conditioned by despair, they relinquish their claim to their lives. Whether denying themselves in order to take up the cross ("it is no longer I who live, but it is Christ who lives in me") or the rifle ("your life does not belong to you, it belongs to the Party"), the adherents to messianism abandon themselves, unload a burden onto the messiah, and forfeit the anarchy of freedom in order to defend to the death their own more amenable subordination.[169]

Death for the cause is further predisposed by the frequent claim that soldiers will be invulnerable to the enemy's always superior weaponry or, that failing, will be resurrected if killed on the battlefield. The powerful magic promised in these unequal contests is never a match for the oppressors' efficacious mobilization of force, but it usually suffices to get the troops into battle. Passages of the Koran stuffed in the pockets of slaves revolting in Bahia; a "very fat Indian woman" believed to be a goddess of rebels in colonial Chiapas; and messages from the Great God Engineer promising the Virgin of Guadalupe's protection to the Chinantecs in modern Oaxaca provide poetic variations on the common theme that the messianic community is bulletproof.[170]

The Mataco relate that the hero Tawkxwax took a fort single-handedly with no weapon other than a stick with a red flag that he waved to attract the soldiers' fire. He was shot, resurrected, and afterward the bullets broke against his body "like clay pellets" until finally, as Tawkxwax approached the fort to plunder it, "the bullets would not leave the barrels of their guns."[171] During the 1712 Tzel-tal Rebellion, the natives were assured that Spanish firearms "would shoot not bullets but water," and shortly after, in the 1761 rebellion of Jacinto Canek (who later suffered an atrocious execution), communiqués calling the Maya to war argued, "You can come without any fear" because "the Spanish arms no longer have power against us."[172]

More recently, in 1906, Santiago appeared to Guatemalan soldiers from Mo-mostenango, guaranteeing victory by making them immune to the enemy's bul-lets.[173] In the movement of Luciano Córdoba among the Pilagá in the 1940s, possession by traditional spirits and biblical figures during ecstatic trance was believed to make the natives bulletproof.[174] Colombian campesinos similarly be-lieved that the leaders of a revolutionary movement of the mid-1960s had "magic powers which made them invulnerable," and even in the 1990s Ataucusi Gamonal assured his Israelites that Jehovah would make them invisible and invulnerable to attacks by the rich, the powerful, and the Catholic Church.[175] When the more tangible danger of Sendero Luminoso approached, Israelites believed, "No bullets will enter our bodies. We will hold our hands before us and the bullets will be repelled by the palms of our hands."[176]

Once a few bullets penetrate the spiritual shield, however, the discourse on invulnerability must gracefully yield to the promise of resurrection. Tepehuans rebelling in northern Mexico in 1616 hurled themselves at Spanish swords and fortifications because they had been assured that they "would resuscitate within a few days" and that dying in battle gave entry to "a better and happier life."[177] Seven indigenous nations rebelling in Chihuahua in 1644 likewise had no fear of dying because "they would resuscitate on the third day."[178] According to a Catholic report from Cuzco, the followers of Túpac Amaru II "threw themselves into battle" blindly and "without fear of death" because they too were promised third-day resurrection.[179] Túpac Catari renovated the same claim and comple-mented it with the attempted resurrection of dead natives wherever he found them, screaming above their graves, "The time has come, return to the world to help me."[180] Some colonial Europeans may have similarly believed in the messianic power to revive fallen soldiers, as evidenced by negation in a statement made by the rebel Lope de Aguirre. Supposedly "the King resuscitates those loyal to him, although up to now we have not seen anyone resuscitated, because the King neither gives life nor heals wounds."[181]

Around 1870 a Bolivian known as Solares arrived to the emerging city of Tandil, populated by gauchos and surrounded by expansive pampas. Trading on the fame he had acquired through prophesies and cures, and reinforced by myths that he raised the dead and controlled the rain, Solares declared himself the redeemer of humanity and became known as Tata Dios (Father God). The time for redemption came in 1872, when encroachment by Spanish and Italian settlers cohered a messianic community in opposition. Solares prophesied that a marvelous city would rise once the evil had been eliminated, and the soldiers of the cause, guaranteed immunity to bullets, stormed Tandil, murdering the for-eigners that crossed their path. The local garrison then launched its counterattack, the bullets defied the magic that should have repelled them, and Solares was hanged by the neck.[182]

Much the same story characterized a series of rebellions between 1905 and 1933 among the Toba and Mocoví of the Argentine Chaco, a region where many indigenous groups gathered as colonial expansion displaced them from traditional homelands. In early 1905 the first of a series of Tata Dioses began to appear among the Mocoví, prophesying an apocalyptic cataclysm in which all white people would be destroyed. God had commanded that the land be returned to the natives, who should attack the enemy without fear of firearms because the bullets would be transformed into water and mud. The resultant offensives against settlements and missions were formidable but always resulted in massacre of the poorly armed natives, with follow-up punitive expeditions indiscriminately continuing the slaughter.[183] In one of these uprisings—the Napalpí movement among the Toba and Mocoví in 1924—the "god" Dionisio Gómez announced as part of a comprehensive millennial program that he was going to resurrect natives killed by white people. Requests were made for the resurrection of specific loved ones, "and their faith was such that the poor people occupied themselves in preparing clothes for those resurrected." Gómez also made the customary promises that bullets would bounce off the natives and that those who died in battle would be spontaneously resuscitated. El Aguará, where the movement was based, is now known as La Matanza (The Slaughter).[184]

Lope de Aguirre

There were more Spaniards than opportunity in mid-sixteenth-century Peru, and part of the intent in authorizing new expeditions was to alleviate the social pressure caused by thousands of soldiers unoccupied after the civil wars of the 1550s. Drunk, restless, and rowdy, the soldiers were particularly dangerous because "their dissatisfaction frequently led them to join seditious movements in the hope of being better rewarded."[185] Among this "rabble of Peru" was Lope de Aguirre, a malcontent Basque soldier who had participated in diverse New World campaigns and felt inadequately compensated for his loyal service.[186] Along with some three hundred Spaniards—soldiers, monks, mistresses, entire families—and thousands of Indians, Aguirre participated in the 1560 expedition to colonize "Omagua and Dorado" under the command of Pedro de Ursúa.

In early 1559 Ursúa had been named governor of Omagua and Dorado as a reward for defeating the slave revolt known as the Bayano War (1553–58).[187] His inept leadership on the Amazon expedition was aggravated by broken and rotted brigantines, harsh jungle conditions, the absence of El Dorado, and Ursúa's predilection for his mistress Inés de Atienza, "the most beautiful lady that there was in Peru."[188] General discontent and demoralization predisposed mutiny, and Lope de Aguirre orchestrated it at Machifaro.

The new age commenced on the first day of January 1561, when the rebels murdered Ursúa in his hammock. The deed was celebrated with the customary disclaimer, "Long live the King, the tyrant is dead," but Aguirre held in reserve a more radical objective. With a potent amalgam of rhetoric and terror he addressed the ragtag assembly of his co-conspirators, representing the murder as an act of redemption, convincing them that El Dorado was a myth, and protesting that the viceroy had sent them to their deaths in an uninhabitable land. He audaciously asserted that Philip II abused his loyal subjects, manipulating their destitution to exploit them under false pretenses. As the rebels worded it later, the New World had been conquered "with our persons and effort, spilling our blood, and [at] our expense," but the reward was "to exile us with deception and falsehood."[189]

According to Custodio Hernández, one of Aguirre's followers, all were initially "content with Aguirre" and "loved him and held him in esteem because he argued well in favor of war."[190] Persuasion was also facilitated by Aguirre's reminder that after the murder of the governor there was no turning back. Aguirre later asked his Marañones, as the group came to be named after the river, to sign a document that he prepared for the occasion, but all were shocked and refused when he undermined the loyalist pretenses by signing the document "Lope de Aguirre, traitor."[191] A series of murders purged dissent, and the other Marañones fell in line for inauguration of what is sometimes described as the first act of American emancipation.[192]

The rituals of denaturalization occurred on March 23, 1651, when a declaration of independence drafted by Aguirre was signed by 186 Marañones. Aguirre made the introduction:

> Gentlemen, I call upon those who are my friends to do as I do, and in order that this enterprise come to more and that our enemies fear us, it is fitting that our Don Fernando be our prince, and from here I say that I denaturalize from Spain and I want no King other than Don Fernando, and whoever also wants it thus, follow me and do as I do.[193]

With his followers behind him, Aguirre entered the lodgings of Don Fernando "and knelt down and said: give me your hands Your Excellency so that I may kiss them as those of my prince and lord, and I do not want any lord but Your Excellency." Don Fernando complied "as though astonished" and expressed his gratitude. "The others did what Aguirre had done," cuing up before their sovereign.[194]

Fernando de Guzmán, a nobleman of about twenty-five years of age, was thus made prince of the denaturalized Marañones, and Aguirre anticipated, "When we get to Peru we will crown him King."[195] Trumpets and drums were played as the prince made proclamations, signing them "Don Fernando de Guzmán, by the grace of God Prince of Tierra Firme and Peru and Governor of Chile." The outrages of uncompensated dedication were remedied by the prince, who parceled out titles, landholdings, and the coveted wives of others to his loyal Marañones. The benevolent despot came to an end as abrupt as his beginning, however, when he was murdered as Aguirre consolidated absolute, autocratic rule. According to the Marañon Alvaro de Acuña, Aguirre intended to become "king and lord of Peru, since he and his soldiers deserved it."[196] By June 1561, Aguirre had convinced his mostly coerced (though some called him Father) squadron of some two hundred "indomitable Marañones" to support him in a declaration of war against the king of Spain.

In his October 1561 letter to the king, Aguirre aired the grievances of exemplary soldiers treated unjustly, one of whom did more for "discoveries in this kingdom than the explorers of Moses in the desert." The perfected Christianity of the Marañones ("although sinners in this life") was contrasted with the evils of viceregal administration, of friars whose lives Aguirre ironically described as "rough and laborious, because each one of them for penance has a dozen girls in their kitchen," and of the king himself, an incarnation of evil, whose "promises have less credit than the books of Martin Luther." "Only a few kings go to hell," Aguirre summarized, "because kings are few."[197] The "cruel and ungrateful" king was more bloodthirsty than Lucifer, and if he did not attend to the injustices of his colony he would be visited by the "punishment of heaven," meaning Lope de Aguirre as "the wrath of God" fulfilling an "avenging destiny in the New World."[198] Aguirre signed off as "son of faithful vassals" but "rebellious until death for your ingratitude," and then, "Lope de Aguirre the Pilgrim."

The Marañones built two brigantines (significantly named Santiago and Victoria, Aguirre on the former) and began their journey out of the jungle.[199] Aguirre's paranoia, authenticated by brewing dissent, resulted in oppressive terror. He restricted movement on the brigantines under penalty of death and ordered "that no one talk in secret."[200] Once the Marañones reached the coast, the plan was to capture the port at Nombre de Dios (Panama) and travel to Peru by fleet, or else to cross the Andes, entering from the east. An army would be recruited from among disenfranchised colonists and slaves whom Aguirre would emancipate for this purpose.[201] According to Juan Gil, Aguirre's plans called for "the general slaughter of not only government personnel but also bishops, priests, and friars."[202]

In July 1561, the Marañones sailed into the Atlantic and landed at the island of Margarita, where the governor and some fifty others were summarily executed. Royal forces were apprised of the rebellion, and when representatives of the crown approached Margarita, Aguirre attempted to co-opt their spokesman, the friar Francisco de Montesinos, by promising to make him pope once the rebels conquered Peru.[203] Carnage and scorched earth marked the trail of Aguirre's advance, but the rampage ended in late October at Barquisimeto on the mainland. With royal forces approaching, his men deserting, and Aguirre suffering from a mounting "persecutory mania," he placed a crucifix in the hands of his fifteen-year-old mestiza daughter, Elvira, telling her to commend her soul to God.[204] Elvira responded by embracing Aguirre and saying, "Don't kill me father, the devil is deceiving you." To prevent her from becoming the "whore" and "mattress" of the royal soldiers, however, Aguirre "stabbed her three times screaming 'my daughter.' "[205] Aguirre was killed immediately after by his Marañones, and the governor then ordered that the body be posthumously decapitated and quartered.[206]

The attributes of millennialism are patent throughout the episodes of Lope de Aguirre, beginning with the disenfranchised soldiers manipulated by myth into a crisis mismanaged by Ursúa as a symbol of corrupt authority. Aguirre emerged in this seemingly exitless, jungle-bound hopelessness as the messianic agent whose mission would transform the decadent colony into a new, nostalgic empire of virtue.[207] The not-quite-charismatic Lope de Aguirre, his persuasiveness too dependent upon a reign of terror, displaced the El Dorado myth with a countermyth of restitution. Like many anticolonial rebels (Juan Santos Atahualpa, Túpac Amaru II), he understood and represented himself as an instrument of divine punishment, a guardian of purity seeking "spiritual restoration" of a defiled kingdom.[208]

Perhaps most compelling is the degree of deviation between Aguirre's self-perception as a lone ranger crusading against evil and the perception that most others—even most of his Marañones—held of him. No sooner was his quartered corpse hung at town gates than unequivocal assessments rendered Aguirre a "monster," "butcher," and "perverse tyrant" who "killed his own daughter when he had no one else to kill." He was "blasphemous, atheist, cruel, out of control"; his life was "a tapestry of unheard of atrocities" and there was "no vice that cannot be found in his person."[209] Lope de Aguirre was "the most evil man since Judas," and finally "he was not a man, but a desperate devil against God."[210] These perceptions are based partially on the carnage, "one wild orgy of madness and blood"; partially on his unprecedented audacity in sedition against the king; and partially on the somewhat grotesque presence of this tiny, vicious man with a lame leg and wild eyes, "boiling in his skull, especially when he was mad."[211] In Margarita, terror and panic overtook the superstitious locals who "thought they saw in the tyrant not a human being but rather an agent from hell."[212] When the assessments gravitated toward doomsday sentiments, Aguirre was "a kind of apocalyptic being," "the incarnation of the Antichrist," and "the true living sign of the final judgment."[213]

Aguirre as the "wrath of God" nevertheless understood his violence as a lesser evil neutralizing a greater evil, and many of his acts as heir apparent to the throne—distribution of lands, emancipation of slaves, elimination of corrupt officials, protection of the abused—evidenced a benevolent populism. Upon arriving at Margarita, Aguirre's first actions (after killing the governor) included destruction of the penal *rollo* that symbolized royal power.[214] It was this aspect of Lope de Aguirre, epitomized by his precocious declaration of denaturalization, that centuries later attracted the admiration of the Liberator, Simón Bolívar. Aguirre was mad, but his delusion coincided with the truth. As one chronicle put it, he "was a man in his right mind, although he used it badly."[215]

Simón Bolívar

Simón Bolívar devalued the demonic accusations in order to retrieve Lope de Aguirre as the first protagonist of South American independence. The starkly contrasting historical assessments of Aguirre and Bolívar underscore the degree to which history is a contingency of actions engaging with interpretations. Aguirre's plan to cross the Andes for a surprise attack was dismissed as insane, but Bolívar's accomplishment of the same was lauded as strategically ingenious. Bolívar departed with twenty-five hundred troops on May 27, 1819, and after nearly three months of Andean crossing, he descended for the victory at Boyacá (in what is now Colombia) that made a decisive contribution to liberation. The inadequately dressed and underfed soldiers, plagued by altitude sickness and the death of most of their horses, climbed through impossible terrain, torrential rains, and brutal cold that seemed strangely inferior to the determination of their commander. "Not even God will take victory away from me," Bolívar exclaimed.[216] Nature and God were challenged earlier, following the 1812 Holy Week earthquakes in Caracas, which were interpreted by many revolutionaries as a scourge for disloyalty to theocracy. While other republicans were begging for the "mercy and pardon of both the king and God," Bolívar confronted natural and supernatural adversity unflinchingly: "If nature opposes us we will fight against it and make it obey us."[217]

Bolívar's megalomania is distinct from that of Aguirre primarily because it was channeled into accomplishments that merited a retroactive romanticization. When the horses of Aguirre's men slid in the mud while ascending the foothills of the Andes, Aguirre, like Bolívar, faced the crisis by challenging the supernatural: "Does God think that, because it is raining, I am not going to reach Peru and destroy the world? Then he does not know me!"[218] Aguirre's outburst was "mad," owing in part to its apocalyptic tone, whereas Bolívar's similar exclamations invited comparison with the God he challenged. As romanticized by José Martí, Bolívar "was surrounded by a glory that inflamed him and stirred him into action. Is it not a sign of divinity to have conquered? He conquered men, swollen rivers, volcanoes, centuries, Nature!"[219] The political messiah is revered with the same awe that had Jesus' apostles wondering, "What sort of man is this, that even the winds and the sea obey him?"[220]

The degree to which Aguirre's insanity was constructed by the enemies who wrote his history is difficult to determine, but some level of dementia indeed constitutes a fundamental difference between his messianism and that of Bolívar. The means and goals of the respective insurrections would also appear to distinguish one from the other, but ultimately they hold much in common. Aguirre intended to eliminate all imperial government and establish himself as absolute ruler, and Bolívar accomplished the former and then accepted the paradoxical role of Liberator-Dictator. The excessive carnage that ostensibly distances the diabolical Aguirre from the deified Bolívar also fares poorly when revisited. After significant accomplishments most revolutionaries were willing to cease the campaigns and consolidate the gains, but Bolívar always insisted on continuing the wars of independence until, as his aide-de-camp put it, he had the "whole territory converted into a vast charnel house in which the victims sacrificed in the name of liberty and loyalty would be heaped."[221] In retaliation for the atrocities committed by loyalist Venezuelans under Tomás Boves, Bolívar ordered the execution in a single day of eight hundred Spanish soldiers imprisoned at Puerto Cabello, including those in the hospital.[222] Like Aguirre, he seems to have thrived as a protagonist of cataclysm: "I fear peace more than war."[223] When his doctor explained to him that he needed danger in order to stay sane, Bolívar responded that "upon creating me God permitted this tempestuous revolution, so that I could live occupied in my special destiny."[224] Aguirre's inclination to bloodshed led to demonization and posthumous quartering, but Bolívar's led to "knocking on the gates of glory with the golden hilt of his saber."[225]

Messianism is assessed in accord with evolving perceptions of what constitutes salvation and what means are acceptable to secure it. Transgressions committed en route to welcome ends are generally reconsidered in relation to the perceived value of the gains, with atrocity dismissed in retrospect as an unfortunate necessity or a sanctioned counteroffensive to neutralize a greater evil. Popular and historical assessments are partially governed by messianic protagonists' ability to make their destabilization of a dominant paradigm seem desirable, meaningful, and feasible, and by representation of their program—no matter how firmly rooted in their personal psychology and ambitions—as self-sacrifice on behalf of worthy beneficiaries. It was on these scores that Aguirre failed and Bolívar triumphed.

Bolívar recognized that one's reception as a messianic hero or as a scoundrel or buffoon was also conditioned by the chance configuration of chaotic events. One of his many statements to the effect carried a counterdiscourse that belied its self-deprecation: "The three great fools of humanity have been Jesus Christ, Don Quixote, and me."[226] At some moments, Bolívar dispelled the popular perception that "Providence has sent or destined me to redeem Colombia," citing instead his ambition, vision, and perseverance; and at other moments, such as the 1814 Assembly of Caracas (which met in a Franciscan monastery), he asserted to the contrary that "Providence, and not my heroism, has produced the wonders that you admire."[227]

Ultimately Bolívar's only religion was "the realization of his utopian dream," but recognition of the Liberator as quasi-divine was insistently expressed by beneficiaries of the promised utopia.[228] Bolívar was often referred to as Father and Savior, and his Christian attributes included a crown of thorns.[229] His final mistress, referring to him as a saint, summarized popular sentiments when she remarked, "The Liberator is immortal" and "now that he his dead I worship him."[230] In popular traditions Bolívar's white horse was assimilated to that of Santiago, affording the Liberator magical properties—he could fly, pass through mountains, disappear into white smoke—that made him invincible.[231] A bulletproof body was particularly useful to a messiah who saved the people from themselves: "Venezuelans! I march toward you to put myself between your gunshots and your chests."[232] This image of the self-sacrificing martyr was also captured in a variation of the apostles' creed composed by the Guatemalan Nobel laureate Miguel Angel Asturias: "I believe in Liberty, Mother of America, creator of sweet seas upon earth, and in Bolívar, her son, Our Lord. . . ."[233] When Bolívar made his triumphant entry into Potosí in October 1825, he was ceremoniously awarded the golden key to the Temple of Victory, "constructed expressly for that event in the Greek style." As an inspired historian described the occasion, "An ambience impregnated with aromas" and "the angelic echo of a chorus of nymphs" filled the air as "the immortal arm of Bolívar planted the banner of freedom on the lofty summit of the great Potosí." A "distinguished and beautiful lady" who headed the nymphs recited a poem with lyrics that referred to Bolívar as a "messenger," "celestial traveller crowned in beautiful splendor," "our mystical emblem," and a "sun that shines but never blinds."[234]

Bolívar dedicated his life as a soldier and a statesman to constructing a republic worthy of his utopian vision, but the social and political reality that followed liberation obstructed the realization of his ideal. He ended his career in despair, lamenting that he had plowed the sea because "America is ungovernable." "If it were possible for one part of the world to return to primitive chaos," Bolívar concluded, "this would be the final period of America."[235] Rather than progress toward the golden age as Bolívar had envisioned, postliberation South America degenerated into an iron age of bestial anarchy: "When I cease to exist, these demagogues will devour one another, as wolves do, and the edifice that I constructed with superhuman effort will crumble into the mud of revolutions."[236] Freedom was the sacred cause to which Bolívar had dedicated himself with the "heroic spirit of self-sacrifice," but he died disillusioned by the mess that his successors had made of the kingdom.[237] His was the image of the suffering messiah who redeemed an unworthy creation. Words of his boyhood mentor, Simón Rodríguez, could well have been spoken by Bolívar: "I, who wanted to make the world into a paradise for all, have made it into a hell for myself."[238]

Víctor Raúl Haya de la Torre

Secular religion grounded in the cult of a messianic personality was exemplary in Peru's American Revolutionary Popular Alliance (APRA), which Víctor Raúl Haya de la Torre founded in 1924 while exiled in Mexico. Haya, who had been educated in a seminary school in Trujillo, vacillated between the priesthood and politics, finally opting for the latter with quasi-religious conviction: "My conscience told me: this greatness calls you."[239] Latin America's problems, Haya maintained, were not only economical and political but also "moral and spiritual." The party would give politics a "cosmic interpretation" by consolidating temporal and spiritual needs and by "introducing man to the eternal."[240]

APRA thus forged its identity as "a religion of justice, with a creed of liberty" and with a substantial debt to Christianity.[241] Its actions accrued an eschatological resonance through constant reference to the cross, Calvary, baptism, faith, redemption, and martyrdom. Haya's mandate "Make of your party a religion" was echoed in Aprista hymn lyrics ("Peruvians, embrace the new religion") and in party literature, including an "Aprista Examination of Conscience," a "meditation," an act of contrition, an "Aprista Litany," and an "Aprista prayer."[242] Haya consolidated the party around the image of himself as a Christ-like redeemer and of his people as a martyred, mystical body, the two "joined by a messianic faith and engaged in the sacred mission of purifying the nation."[243]

In 1919, while still a student, Haya began to take upon himself the "noble and just" struggle of the workers.[244] When troops surrounded a meeting of strikers and threatened to open fire, he confronted the guns defiantly, and the following day he led the student delegation as a human shield, exclaiming, "Let them open fire; we will die arm-to-arm with the workers."[245] The decisive confrontation between Haya and the administration of Augusto B. Leguía occurred on May 23, 1923, when Haya led five thousand demonstrators to oppose Leguía's consecration of Peru to the Sacred Heart of Jesus. The troops were called, the blood of "martyrs" was spilled in the "baptism by fire" of a party soon to emerge, and Haya was arrested and exiled.

The religious press retaliated against APRA's seeming displacement of Catholicism by alleging that Haya "advocated the burning of churches, the rape of nuns, and the execution of priests."[246] The apocalyptic mood in Huaraz had clergymen displaying posters depicting APRA as a sign of the imminent Last Judgment.[247] APRA maintained the secular nature of the religion of justice in the slogan gracing the wall of the party's Lima headquarters—"Only God will save my soul. Only Aprismo will save Peru"—but in practice the deity tended to fall out of the schema as body and soul, politics and religion, were consolidated in APRA's comprehensive salvation.[248] A parish priest in Arequipa reported that Haya blasphemously asserted, "APRA yes, Christ no."[249]

In the Sacred Heart events, martyrdom and messianism commenced the mutually reinforcing relation that characterized the entire career of Haya and his party. In a statement smuggled out of prison before his exile to Mexico, Haya promised a messianic return "when the hour of the great transformation has arrived."[250] Protest songs praised the absent hero's "glorious deeds" and lamented how the villainous Leguía unjustly exiled "the Apostle of the new humanity" because "his only crime was to show the people / the path of Light and Truth." The void of the messiah's absence was filled by a genre of imaginary dialogues in which Haya consoled the workers: "Do not tire, continue onward: fear not the darkness in which you live because soon the day of eternal light will arrive." The same themes of illumination, compensatory presences that undo absence, and messianic return were echoed in a 1924 testimony: "Haya lives among us in spirit, his teaching is the beacon that guides us, his fighting words vibrate in our lives, bringing the promise of hope for the future."[251] Following his return from exile, Haya concluded the inaugural speech of APRA's first National Congress in 1931 with a call "to work, to struggle, and if necessary to die. Because only by giving ourselves entirely to this sacred Aprista cause from which comes 'the great transformation' can we realize the second revolution of the independence of Peru and America."[252]

Peruvian politics in 1930–31 were dominated by the competing populist forces of Haya and Luis M. Sánchez Cerro until the latter won the presidential election. The discontent of Apristas and the mounting assault against them by Sánchez Cerro culminated in a July 1932 insurrection in Trujillo, a region that strongly supported APRA. The insurgents took the city, the army garrison, and some fifty hostages, including military and police personnel, who were eventually executed and mutilated. The armed forces retaliated with the summary execution of a thousand Trujillo residents, and this in turn fostered the April 1933 assassination of Sánchez Cerro by an Aprista. The massacre in Trujillo had special meaning to a party founded on messianic martyrdom, because "Aprismo is a religion that grows with persecution and with the blood of its martyrs."[253] Slain Apristas were compared with the martyrs of apostolic Christianity, and Haya frequently seized the opportunity to observe, "We wash ourselves with the blood of our blood" and "this Party is made sacred by the memory of the dead that it carries within it."[254]

When Haya spoke in Trujillo in December 1933, he followed a eulogy to the martyrs with a call to action: "The hour of struggle has arrived. The hour of Calvary has arrived, of sweating blood. Our Golgotha is here." The messianic mission was collective—"we all bear this cross of redemption"—but it was condensed into the synecdoche of Haya as the Christ-like messiah who transformed the people's defeat into a glorified triumph: "My wound bleeds always, because it is the wound of the sorrow of a people, sorrow that is power, sorrow that is creation, sorrow that is hope, sorrow that is impulse, sorrow that will be victory."[255] The bond between the martyrs, the people, and the martyred messiah provided "immortality" for all because "Aprismo never dies."[256] It is like "a spirit wrapped in glory, a glory that is never lost because it continues to live in the midst of death."[257]

Haya founded the party, as he put it, "to redeem my people," but the messianic burden became collective as all Apristas were expected to "deliver themselves totally to the work of redeeming and of bringing salvation to our brothers."[258] Party literature urged Apristas to educate and prepare themselves and to transcend their former limitations so that the party would be equal to its redemptive mission.[259] The personal qualities required for participation in this collective salvation were "honesty, sincerity, and a firm commitment to sacrifice."[260] Apristas were the chosen people bonded by blood and fulfilling a destiny far beyond anything "merely human," and they accordingly would "forge a new conscience" on the vanguard of the great transformation.[261]

Haya was "the message so long awaited," the incarnate Word who through martyrdom transfused his mission into the party as a mystical body.[262] He compared his inheritance of a "bleeding and oppressed" Peru to "Christ receiving Lazarus, already dead, in order to resurrect him."[263] The wounded body would be revived by the touch of a messianic hand itself destined to the wounds of martyrdom. As a poem written by an imprisoned Aprista has it, "Christ, the invincible revolutionary, will not / Return to Heaven / Without first making men happy on Earth, / Thus says the new Religion."[264]

Juan and Evita Perón

The political messianism of Juan and Evita Perón altered the course of modern Argentine history beginning in 1945. Juan Perón came to power through his ability to mobilize disparate and generally neglected social and political groups, notably the disenfranchised workers known as descamisados. As an Argentine described these masses converging upon the Plaza de Mayo in 1945, "It seemed an invasion by people of another country, speaking another language, dressed in exotic clothing, but nevertheless they were part of the Argentine population." Perón astutely brought this "tremendous and aggressive force" to the surface, maneuvering it to his advantage and always propagating the message that he and the descamisados were "inextricably united for the glory of the Nation."[265]

The messianic codependence of Perón and the descamisados predisposed the development of Peronism into a secular religion. According to Evita, Peronism was "conviction," "faith," and "brotherly love" that were forged into a party by Perón's introduction of the "hope that was lacking in the Fatherland."[266] For Juan Perón, "ethical principles" and "moral values" were of the highest order, and Peronism accordingly "is telling the truth, is defending love among all, is making spiritual values prevail over material values, is speaking of justice and guaranteeing it" and, in short, is "doing good everywhere."[267] The party doctrine would be "a true mysticism" "for which we are prepared to sacrifice everything" because "the triumph of that mysticism is the triumph of our nationality."[268]

The official Peronist doctrine, Justicialismo (Justicialism), was instituted in 1949 as a third-way alternative to capitalism and communism but also, at first informally, to Catholicism and atheism. Peronism offered a "practical, Justicialist Christianity" that veered from the path of Vatican ritual and dogma to achieve a "real and honorable" faith.[269] This position was derived from Perón's own religious identity as an anticlerical Catholic who accepted the doctrine of Christ but not the vicarship of the Church. He regarded himself "a pure Catholic" because "one act of the Doctrine" is more valuable than the endless empty ceremony of sacerdotal Christianity. Evita was the paradigm of this purity in action, manifesting more Christianity in a single day of her work for the poor "than all of the priests in the Argentine Republic in their entire lives." Peronist anticlericalism was consonant with the more general, centralizing tendencies of autocratic populists: "We who fought against all intermediaries (economic, political, union . . .)," Perón argued, "did not want intermediaries in religious matters either."[270]

Perón had promoted Catholicism in the early years of his administration, reintegrating it into a society that was becoming increasing secular. By 1954, however, he had withdrawn his support from the Church and launched an assault to dislodge it from the privileged position that he himself had provided. (This pattern was later repeated in his treatment of the Montoneros.) Perón's efforts to separate Church and state included the prohibition of such holy day celebrations as Epiphany, Corpus Christi, Assumption, All Saints Day, and the Immaculate Conception, while such quasi-religious Peronist holidays as Loyalty Day (October 17) and the commemoration of Evita's death (July 26) were emphasized.[271] As in the case of APRA under Haya de la Torre, institutionalized Catholicism was undermined but also displaced as the party repackaged it for secular messianism. Perón's attack on the Church ultimately served to consolidate the mounting opposition against him, and in 1955 he was deposed by the military. In a pastoral letter following the coup, Argentine bishops referred to Perón's presidency as a "totalitarian regime" that "persecuted the church by attempting to replace it."[272]

Both before and after the martyrdom that Perón suffered in exile for eighteen years, military, oligarchic, and clerical opposition tended to strengthen faith in Juan and Evita Perón as underdog messiahs who struggled, like their people, against the odds. Deification was often expressed unequivocally: Perón "is God for us, so much so that we cannot conceive of heaven without Perón." Evita provided the precedent echoed there—"I cannot conceive of heaven without Perón"—along with a model for "faith in Perón" and acceptance of Peronism as one's only religion.[273] Speeches at the labor union confederation maintained that Perón ruled by divine right, and that "God himself" preached "Perón's doctrine before Perón."[274] Peronism accrued the graces disencumbered by the assault on the Church, and some "considered Argentine devotion to Christ and the Virgin Mary to have been superseded by Perón and Eva."[275]

The messianic relation between Perón and the workers had been forged first by inversion—the community saving its messiah—after he was arrested as a young colonel heading the labor ministry in an effort by authorities to curtail his prolabor populism. On October 17, 1945, between a quarter- and half-million workers converged upon the Plaza de Mayo to demand Perón's release. As reported by a correspondent for the London *Times*, a crowd "hysterical with impatience" and "not preoccupied with ideologies or doctrines of programs" wanted nothing more or less than Perón. The befuddled authorities complied, and when Perón appeared for the great symbolic inauguration of his movement the masses reached a "frenzied climax." "The crowd felt an almost religious emotion for Colonel Perón and not satisfied with having him as president, wanted to canonize him as well. On the walls was chalked, 'Saint Perón, President of Argentina.' "[276] Perón later described his folk canonization as a spontaneous manifestation of popular sentiment to which he informally acquiesced. The first anniversary of the October 17 event fell on a Friday, and after Perón's speech the crown pleaded that the next day be declared a "Saint Perón" holiday. "Well, all right, I said. Since tomorrow is Saturday and only half a work day, not much is lost. Yes, let it be 'Saint Perón.' "[277] The sanctity is thereby constructed in the dialogical relation between the charismatic who gains from it politically and the followers who seek an otherworldly messianic salvation, not to mention the day off from work. Perón announced his presidential candidacy on February 12, 1946, as a response to the workers' "longing for social redemption" and to "the resonant echo of a single collective will."[278]

The party was more actively involved in the glorification of "Saint Evita." "Eva Perón is an instrument of my creation," Perón asserted, insofar as "a leader must imitate nature, or God." The faithful would soon lose respect for God if he were to appear among them frequently; "for that reason, God works through Providence. That was the role which Eva filled: that of Providence."[279] God's work was facilitated in 1947 by Evita's purchase of the newspaper *Democracia*, through which she propagated her identity as "First Worker," "First Samaritan," "Queen of Labor," "Lady of Hope" and "Spiritual Mother of All Argentine Children."[280] In due time, as described by Perón, every Peronist household had "an altar dedicated to Evita," and thus "there is no saint in the Catholic Church that has as many devotees in Argentina as Evita."[281]

Immediately following the publication of her "autohagiography," *La razón de mi vida*, in 1951, an Evita debilitated by cancer and propped up by her husband's arm appeared before the masses for the annual October 17 celebration.[282] The next day's Saint Perón celebration, transmuted by popular demand in honor of the moribund first lady, became Saint Evita Day, thus registering a shift in the locus of power from Perón to the "creation" that began to supersede him. In May 1952, congress declared Evita the Spiritual Leader of the Nation; her autobiography, which depicted her with a halo, was made a school text; and her confessor led the nation in prayers for her recovery, declaring her a martyr sent by God as a model of self-sacrifice and faith.[283] The image of saintly abnegation had been enhanced shortly before when the military prohibited Evita from running as Perón's vice presidential candidate. Her decline to accept the candidacy, referred to in quasi-religious terms as The Renunciation, was regarded as "an exalted and altruistic passion to reach the height of martyrdom."[284] Evita, although she had no choice, renounced ambition and status in order to return to anonymity among the descamisados: "I have wanted to be for you only 'Evita.' "[285]

On the day of her death in July 1952, the front page of *Democracia* noted that "the image of Eva Perón is and always will be an object of intimate devotion."[286] Peronist literature and union devotional pamphlets reinforced her identity as a saint or Virgin—including the Madonna of America—who excelled in purity, intercession, sacrifice, and martyrdom.[287] Argentine unions petitioned the Vatican to canonize Evita as patron of American workers, public and private altars proliferated, and the party erected special mailboxes for communicating with Evita in the hereafter. Prayers followed ("Evita, our love who art in Heaven, may your Goodness always accompany us"); images of Evita began performing miracles; and within a few years Peronist women formed a Congregation of Our Lady Eva Duarte de Perón to serve their Virgin and their party wearing nuns' habits.[288]

Peronism's great success among Argentine workers resulted in part from the strategic distribution of messianic attributes between Juan and Evita Perón. Their complementary political roles, with Perón as the undisputed source of doctrine and Evita as its sanctified incarnation, was captured in the slogan of the early years: *Perón cumple, Evita dignifica.*[289] In her autobiography Evita summarized this division of labor apropos of 1950s gender roles by noting that Perón operated "with the intelligence; I, with the heart," and therefore "he knowing well what he wanted to do; I only feeling it."[290] In the last analysis her emotive image had greater charismatic appeal than did Perón's paternal intelligence, particularly because the masses "do not think, they feel."[291] When the Peronist left later armed itself, its objective was "to bring back Perón" but it fought "because of Evita—and for her."[292]

Evita, of humble origins in Chivilcoy, struggled and suffered as one of the people but from her privileged position as Perón's wife. "Evita was the perfect manifestation of Perón," but also of the masses, and she became the point of contact between them.[293] Publicly she was always between Perón and the people, and when she was alone with Perón the people were "always present and always consulted."[294] As the intermediary "bridge of love," she provided for open exchange; and as intercessor, she pleaded the people's case before Perón and Perón's case before the people.[295] Just as she had been retrieved from poverty and exalted for her goodness and dedication to Perón, so too would the descamisados who remained faithful to their messiah. Evita provided the model for messianic veneration of Perón, demonstrating at once her own bilateral conviction to the people and their leader by sacrificing herself on the altar of their common cause.[296]

The age of two-edged messianism ended with Evita's death, but the party made every effort to capture the disembodied, dissipating numinousness and channel it toward Perón. This charismatic transfer was most ambitiously expedited in Evita's last will and testament, which was read by Perón to the multitudes gathered in the Plaza de Mayo on October 17, 1952. Evita wanted the masses to understand that Perón's love for the people was greater than her own. Her "flesh and soul and blood" of humble origin necessarily integrated her into the workers' cause, but Perón, from a privileged family, came to "understand and love" the workers by his own volition and initiative.[297] The people's loyalty to Perón, through Evita's death as through her life, would constitute loyalty to her ideals, to Argentina, and ultimately to themselves.[298] Party propaganda finalized the charismatic transfer by equation: "Eva Perón is also Juan Perón, and Juan Perón is also Eva Perón."[299]

Throughout his career Perón had fostered a populist image as a laborer through reference to himself as "this humble man who speaks to you" or a "simple citizen mixed in this sweaty mass."[300] The message was always that Evita, Perón, and the masses were dimensions of one and the same messianic mission. Perón was "burning up his life to illuminate the Peronist century," Evita "literally burned herself up" for the cause, and by these fires the two were melded together with one another and the workers.[301] The slogan "One's life for Perón" indexed the reciprocal loyalty that Evita exemplified in relation to both Perón and the masses. "I put my soul beside the soul of the people," she told them, because together they would "realize the dreams of General Perón."[302] "Let us think that we are in a paradise," Evita counseled, "and that with the patriotism, with the love, and with the abnegation" exemplified by Perón "we will obtain the well-being and the happiness that he desires for his people."[303]

The Messiahs of Brazil

The backlands of the arid Brazilian Northeast "yielded, in times of drought, visions of the Last Judgment," and drought was the rule between 1888 and 1892.[304] The same period coincided with the transition from monarchy to republic following the coup that exiled Dom Pedro II in November 1889, and the ensuing dictatorship brought a stalled economy that aggravated chronic poverty. A "sense of helplessness" predominated among backlanders, some recently emancipated following abolition of slavery, who were dominated and exploited by a landowning elite.[305] The liminal location, the transitional period, the destitution compounded by drought, and the sociopolitical deprivation together provided an ideal ambience for the proliferation of messianism.

It was in this context that Antônio Vicente Mendes Maciel, known as Antônio Conselheiro, attracted his massive following. Conselheiro first appeared in 1867 among other wandering beatos who brought apocalyptic messianism to the backlands.[306] Dressed in a coarse tunic and living by an austerity that complemented the landscape, Conselheiro wandered for twenty years to preach, tend to rural churches and cemeteries in disrepair, and provide a model of mendicant piety.[307] "First making a courtesy call to the local priest, if there was one, the emaciated missionary set himself up in the public square, doing repair work by day, taking small meals when offered, preaching at night, but mostly reposing in silence."[308] The relative absence of clergy in the region and, when present, its opposition to popular Catholicism fostered the backlanders' belief that "only their penitents, their beatos, their messiahs" practiced the true faith.[309] Backlanders "sanctioned an apocalyptic view of life" and "tended to blend everyday stoicism and resignation with messianic hopes."[310]

Conselheiro was born in 1830 in the backlands of Ceará. His home life was characterized by his father's declining economic status, bouts of drunken aggression, and general lack of affection toward him and by his mother's "harsh religiosity practiced as a kind of penitence."[311] One of his contemporaries later observed that Conselheiro had the expression of indefiniteness "characteristic of mystics and dreamers."[312] A priest who visited Canudos described him as dressed in a blue tunic, with unkempt hair and beard, a long face "with corpse-like pallor," a grave demeanor, and the "air of a penitent."[313] Conselheiro resisted his followers' tendency to elevate his status from beato to messiah, but nevertheless they regarded him as in some sense divine and expected that he would resurrect after death.[314]

In 1873 Conselheiro founded his first community, Bom Jesus, at Bahia. "Apostles" served as department heads or ministers (of police, of agriculture, of exterior relations), and a priest entered on occasion to administer the sacraments.[315] Bom Jesus was more or less tolerated until the newly proclaimed republic was regarded by Conselheiro as "supreme indicator of the ephemeral triumph of the Antichrist," thereby redoubling political cause for adversity.[316] Popular verses reinterpreted Conselheiro's mission in antithetical relation to the new evil: "The Antichrist has arrived / To govern Brazil, / But Conselheiro is there / To free us from him."[317] This politicization of the apocalypse also complicated strained relations with the Church, and in an 1882 letter sent by the archbishop of Bahia to all of his parishes, Conselheiro was accused of preaching "superstitious doctrines and an excessively rigid morality." The archbishop "absolutely prohibited" parishioners from hearing Conselheiro's sermons, but nevertheless a later document attested, "They listen to him and follow his orders in preference to those of the parish priest."[318] In 1887 the archbishop requested state intervention, because through "subversive doctrines" Conselheiro was "distracting the people from their obligations." The archbishop also claimed that Conselheiro was "trying to convince them that he was the Holy Spirit."[319]

Following an attack by the Bahian state police in early 1893, Conselheiro began to advocate repair to a holy city isolated from the evils of this world.

Bom Jesus was abandoned later that year as Conselheiro guided his disciples to the Empire of Bello Monte, better known as Canudos, which was founded on a remote and abandoned ranch in the Bahian backlands. Thousands were entranced by Conselheiro's "charismatic madness," and within two years Canudos became the second largest city in Bahia.[320]

For Conselheiro and his closest followers, "Canudos represented an earthy ·vale of tears,' a transitory passage awaiting the final judgment and the coming of the end of the world."[321] Da Cunha's less accommodating assessment described masses "immersed in a religious dream," indifferent to this life, preoccupied with the next, and living in "an exaggerated form of collectivism."[322] Conselheiro's message was a repetition of "the same extravagant millennialism, the same dread of the Antichrist, the same imminent end of the world."[323] A series of prophesies recorded in Conselheiro's notebooks offered variations on such common themes as status reversal (in 1896 "the backlands will become beaches and the beaches backlands") and Christian world unity (in 1897 there will be "one shepherd and one flock"). Other prophesies compensated in poetry for what they lacked in clarity: "In 1898 there will be many hats but few heads." The most developed notebook entries registered the apocalypticism that was predominant in Conselheiro's vision and that provided the ideological basis for his holy towns. After the seas turn to blood in 1899, "there will be a great rain of stars," and then "in 1900 the lights will go out."[324]

Conselheiro's isolationist sect Christianity was essentially religious and apolitical, but the apocalyptic gloss on republicanism and the disruption of the prevailing social order made Canudos antagonistic to those outside of it. As viewed by the ruling class, the Canudos residents were "madmen, criminals, exslaves, and, most of all, religious fanatics," "without a single one who is a human being."[325] Deprived of its cheap and docile labor force, the landowning elite felt that Conselheiro was "either insane or criminal," an "absolute monarch" who was "imposing his own laws, raising an army of soldiers," and "exercising more power now than the first Napoleon."[326]

To remedy this "bizarre" situation the landowners demanded military intervention, partially under the pretense that the community was a refuge for monarchists.[327] Four military expeditions were sent in 1896 and 1897, and in the last of these the Brazilian army besieged and bombarded Canudos with heavy artillery. "On the morning after the final assault, soldiers smashed, leveled, and burned all 5,200 houses in the settlement."[328] Prisoners were executed, and fire and dynamite left behind only scorched earth. The dead numbered some fifteen thousand.

Conselheiro, who had died two weeks prior, was exhumed and decapitated, and the head was taken to Salvador for display on a pike that led the military parade.[329] His skull was later presented to a professor of forensic medicine who studied the physical traits of criminals and "had gained prominence through his theories about the degenerative effects of miscegenation and the links between mental illness and 'messianic contagion.' "[330] During the siege and for those who survived it, that contagion safeguarded Conselheiro's messianism by recontextualizing it within the older tradition of Sebastianism. Conselheiro would return from the grave, escorted by King Sebastian and his armies, to vindicate his people, annihilate the impious, and usher in the end of the ages.[331]

The demise of monarchy was also apocalyptically interpreted by the messianic movement that culminated in the Contestado Rebellion between 1912 and 1916. Decades earlier João Maria Agostini had appeared near São Paulo as a wandering preacher who intermittently withdrew to caves for penitential exercises. Though a layman, he was referred to as a "friar" and "venerated as a saint."[332] Social, economic, and political instability later combined with messianic legends to create an anticipation of João Maria's return, and in 1912 a deserting soldier and curandero took the name José Maria to associate himself with the anticipated holy man.[333] José Maria cured the sick, read aloud nightly from *The History of Charlemagne*, conducted prayer and preaching sessions, and, like Antônio Conselheiro, convinced his three hundred homeless followers to reject the republic and retreat to an isolated refuge "where they would wait for evil to consume the rest of the world."[334]

The chosen people took refuge in a holy city founded by José Maria, but the evil came to consume their settlement rather than the iniquitous world outside. José Maria was killed in the attack, and the community, eventually encompassing several thousand, was reorganized under the new leadership of José Euzébio Ferreira dos Santos, who established the remote Holy City of Taquaraçu to await José Maria's return with heavenly armies. Officials interpreted the settlement as a disguised effort to occupy disputed Paraná lands, and troops were again dispatched. The massacre of more than three thousand people resulted in March 1914, when "men, women, and children defended themselves against machine-gun fire by draping themselves in a large green and white flag, convinced of their immunity to the army's weapons."[335]

This monotonous conclusion—conditioned from within by the broken messianic promise and from without by intolerance of anomaly, labor diversion, and political dissent—was successfully avoided by Padre Cícero Romão Batista. In 1870 Cícero, the only clergyman among these Brazilian messiahs, dreamed that a scene reminiscent of Leonardo da Vinci's *Last Supper* was being enacted before his eyes. As Christ rose to address his twelve disciples the room became crowded with peasants dressed in rags. Christ lamented the miserable condition of his creation and threatened to destroy it, but he pledged to make one last effort to "save the world." At that moment he turned to the unsuspecting young priest and, pointing at the peasants, commanded, "Padre Cícero, take charge of them."[336]

Cícero arrived to the village of Joazeiro the same year and was well established there when the serious droughts came at the end of the 1870s. His appearance was not unlike that of the lay beatos, with a threadbare cassock, tangled hair, a long beard, and a pilgrim's walking stick.[337] A community was founded and grew rapidly in tandem with Cícero's reputation as a benevolent patron of the poor, but the messianic movement was cohered and began exponential expansion following a miracle in 1889, the same year as the fall of Brazilian monarchy. On March 1, Cícero was administering communion to the beata Maria de Araújo when suddenly the eucharist in her mouth transformed into the blood of Christ. This "great marvel that merits to be spread throughout the entire world" merited for Araújo veneration as a living saint.[338] Along with the beatas who proliferated in her image, Araújo later enhanced the movement's apocalyptic message, counting among the signs of the last days the overthrow of monarchy and the new republic's disestablishment of the Church.[339]

More skeptical observers held that blood from the beata's mouth had stained the eucharist. After an initial hesitation the local Church hierarchy contested the miracle and in 1892 suspended Cícero from holy orders. The Vatican concurred two years later, ruling the miracle a hoax and upholding Cícero's suspension. In 1898 Cícero traveled to Rome to plead his cause and was conditionally reinstated, only to have his privileges again revoked by the bishop upon his return.[340] Cícero was ordered to abandon Joazeiro and refused, a confrontation ensued, and the Church acquiesced in order to preempt a potentially disastrous uprising of his followers. The clerical attitude toward Cícero was indexed by the unambiguous opening of a homily delivered in 1909 by a priest in the bishop's entourage: "I beg your permission to speak about the filthy rabble of Juazeiro who live guided by Satan."[341]

Cícero ranked among the most important political figures of the Brazilian Northeast, and "his movement, once religious, became eminently political."[342] He presided over social and political as well as religious matters of his community—which had come to be called the New Jerusalem—and eventually exerted his influence over the broader sphere of backland politics. In 1911 he assumed public office at the local level, in 1912 at the state level, and in 1926 he was elected to the Brazilian national congress.[343] In 1914, however, Cícero's political adversaries gained control of the region and mounted a concerted effort to destroy the messianic community.

Cícero responded with both rhetorical and armed counteroffensives. In the "holy war" of 1914 the provincial government was the Antichrist, and therefore, "God wanted it overthrown so the land of perfect happiness could be established."[344] The poorly armed but multitudinous faithful—who had been guaranteed by the Virgin, through Cícero, immunity to the enemy's bullets—engaged the troops dispatched to besiege Joazeiro. The city was defended, partially by military means and partially because Cícero had influential political allies, one of whom successfully appealed to the president for withdrawal of federal troops. The faithful of Joazeiro held that their final victory would coincide with the reestablishment of monarchy, which was government by God's appointed vicar. This did not occur, but divine will triumphed locally and Cícero maintained political control of the region until his death in 1934.[345]

Cícero's death brought folk canonization, effigies warding off evil in backland homes, myths assuring messianic return, and a bronze statue that still brings pilgrims to their knees in the holy land of Joazeiro. Multiple surrogates also perpetuated Cícero's legacy vicariously, among them a black penitent and former aide named José Lourenço, who founded a New Joazeiro to await the Padre's return.[346]

An unrelated Cícero of a new-age variety surfaced in the same region during the 1930s. Cícero José de Farias, who was called New Israel or Israel Farias because he would establish the second Israel, "abandoned shoemaking" in 1932 in order to "look for treasure."[347] He wandered about in boots and an engineer's hat searching for lands rich in minerals, until one night he saw a star "different from the others" that grew before his eyes and approached him. As his secretary—who was "in second place under Cícero in the Supreme Order"—later worded it, "The star transformed itself perfectly into Jesus, and the night became like day." Jesus telepathically communicated with Cícero and "showed him where the New Zion was to be, where the celestial court would be set up on earth, in a place in Arcoverde." For sometime afterward the prophet was "in an ecstatic state, and was not himself," but he could channel supernatural powers by curing the ill with his touch.[348]

Little is known about Cícero's activities for the next twenty years, but he resurfaced in Teixeira, eighty miles northwest of Arcoverde, in 1952. There he built two concentric fences, with the epicenter occupied by the hut and cave in which he lived and transcribed the mandates received from God telepathically. His secretary reported that "God ordered him to organize a group of men, lovers of God, that would set up a tabernacle of God on earth," but the all-too-human flock revolted when "God began to apply the laws—no smoking, no drinking" because "people are used to doing these things."[349] The police, summoned by Church authorities, arrested Cícero and shipped him back to Arcoverde as a madman.

In the late 1950s Cícero was working on a farm in Paraíba and continuing his search for minerals, along with "enchanted treasures and remnants of past civilizations to use in the founding of his New Jerusalem."[350] The "mines and treasures," which were protected from other exploitation by an electromagnetic belt, would finance Cícero's millennial kingdom.[351] Pursuant to continuing telepathic communications from God, the treasure hunt was complemented by a quest to contact extraterrestrials residing incognito in caves marked by "hieroglyphics" and others who would arrive from outer space in flying saucers.[352] In 1959 Cícero went to Joazeiro, attempting to arrange the donation of lands previously associated with Padre Cícero Romão Batista in order to construct there the Temple of Redemption in the form of a pyramid.[353] This and subsequent efforts failed, but between 1960 and 1965 the indefatigable Cícero dispatched his "Letters of the Second Advent" to officials in Brazil and to the heads of state in three hundred countries. The letters announced that Cícero, the "promised Comforter," had been informed telepathically of the "coming of Jesus as King of Brazil and governor of the world." Jesus would reign over a new humanity after the last days, which were already unfolding.[354]

The unrelenting failures and an attempt on Cícero's life eventually lent a more paranoid and apocalyptic tone to the messiah's tidings. God announced through Cícero that he was "going to destroy the capital, Recife, and disband the congregation because there was an attempt to murder Israel." Cícero began to evade public exposure "so that he would not be crucified," and some traitorous members of the inner circle were sentenced to death because they allegedly conspired "to destroy Jerusalem and Israel."[355] One adherent to the movement, herself sentenced to death, observed that a joyless God was responsible for the move-ment's failure. Cícero and his close associates created "a God for themselves and no one likes this God," loveless and cold, who gave to the earth "this atomic bomb which is destroying the people."[356]

Ezequiel Ataucusi Gamonal

Ezequiel Ataucusi Gamonal, one of fourteen children of a Spanish-and Quechua-speaking family, was born in 1918 in Cotahuasi, located in the highlands of Arequipa, Peru. His mother instilled in him the idea that he would be a "priest and prophet," sometimes as a consolation after he had been beaten by other boys. At the age of six he reproached his mother for venerating a crucifix instead of the living God in heaven; at twelve his room was permeated by an other-worldly light; at fourteen an apparition resembling God the Father revealed to him that saints were a fabrication of Catholic priests; and at eighteen he was miraculously saved from drowning by an enormous fish. These singular events of youth punctuated the mundane routine of poverty and economic survival until 1956, when Ataucusi, now a shoemaker in Tarma, began "to understand God's message."[357]

After fifteen years as an Adventist, Ataucusi had a mystical experience during which he was entrusted with a special mission. As he was being transported to the "third heaven" for an audience with the Holy Trinity, on the stairway head-ing upward he had a chance encounter with Ellen G. White (mid-nineteenth-century leader of the Seventh-Day Adventists) and Joseph Smith (founder of the Mormons, who in 1823 discovered a new covenant of his own in the woods of central New York). The three persons of the Trinity were seated at a table, and the Holy Spirit ordered Ataucusi to copy the New Covenant that was written on a blackboard and to make it known throughout the world. Ataucusi was thirty-eight years old at the time. The first congregation of the Evangelical As-sociation of the Israelite Mission of the New Universal Covenant was established in 1958, and the sect received official government recognition eleven years later. By the early 1990s there were some twenty thousand Israelites and eight hundred temples distributed throughout Peru, with considerable growth also in Bolivia.[358]

Ataucusi's messianic identities among his people are many, including First-Born of God, Son of Man, the New Moses, the New Inca, Great and Only General Missionary, Israel, and Christ of the West.[359] In reference to the last title, the biblical Jesus is called the Eastern Christ "because he was born in Palestine. And his spirit has reincarnated in Ezequiel Ataucusi, who is called the Western Christ."[360] God chose "Privileged Peru" as the site of the new advent, and Ataucusi, as the Son of Man and incarnation of the Holy Spirit, will preside there over the third Judgment at the imminent end of time.[361] According to an Israelite preaching in Lima's Plaza San Martín, the apocalypse will bring "a great affliction, something terrible, something incomparable to the two previous judg-ments," featuring hunger, earthquakes, pestilence, war, and "many calamities that have not been written."[362] Until then the Israelites sing hymns with such titles as "The End Is Approaching," heeding Ataucusi's solemn reminders that "there is not much time left."[363]

Ataucusi's followers are drawn primarily from Andean campesinos who have migrated from the highlands to the coastal cities. The seventy Israelite temples in Lima's shantytowns attract these displaced, uneducated indigenous villagers who suffer a marginal existence and sense of social inferiority but have been urbanized to the degree that they identify themselves as mestizos.[364] Ataucusi's New Covenant offers a third way between the dejected native culture and the dominant culture that includes Andeans only insofar as it exploits them. It is a radical option, but it offers rupture a measure of continuity because it adapts traditional Andean messianism to the new knowledge, experiences, and problems of migrants redefining themselves in marginal urban settlements.[365] Ataucusi reaccommodated Christianity in an Old Testament context less associated with the Church of the conqueror and ruling class, blending into it elements of native cosmology and rituals. Andean concepts of messianic cyclicity, the influence of traditional music on hymns, the similarity of Israelite "holocaust" to llama sacrifice still practiced in parts of the Andes, the recognition of Manco Capac as the first prophet of Peru, the use of the rainbow (associated with Tahuantinsuyo) as logo, and a certain neo-Inca nationalism all contribute to the indigenous appeal. Some view the New Covenant received by Ataucusi as a completion of the Inca law *ama sua, ama quella, ama llulla* (don't be idle, don't steal, don't lie).[366]

When migrants become Israelites their identity is transformed from deculturated natives demeaned by a system that excludes them to chosen people on the vanguard of messianic destiny. The status reversal repairs devastated cultural pride and grants these previous outcasts the privileged centric position (though the center has shifted), affording them a certain sense of superiority and defiant disdain for all others, including socially dominant whites, who are not among the saving remnant. Indeed, the dominant classes in particular are responsible for the degeneration that occasioned the advent of the new messiah and the emergence of a new chosen people. As one Israelite put it, Ataucusi "chose the simplest and most humble people, the forgotten, the despised, and the illiterate," in order to "shame the wise and the rich."[367] A corresponding shift of center occurred geographically, from the eastern Holy Land to "Privileged Peru."

The Israelites' immediate task is to "cleanse the dirtiness of the world" and restore the purity lost to selfishness, envy, materialism, hate, and vengeance that "have dehumanized us" and "turned us into robots, without human conscience."[368] Members of the messianic community are separated visually from society at large by their prophetic, Old Testament appearance; ideologically by their dogmatic morality, their chosen-people identity, and their eschatological doctrine; and pragmatically by strictly enforced religious obligations that preclude most activities outside of the movement, including any employment whose hours conflict with religious services. Being a member of this sect, like any other, reinforces marginal status rather than facilitating integration, but it reconceives marginality as exclusivity and renders it a privilege.[369]

As in most cases, the Israelites' exalted self-image is counterbalanced by its antithesis in the perspective of outsiders. When they are not dismissed as crackpots, the Israelites are often depicted as sinister, criminal cultists. The magazine *Vistazo* responded to the Israelites' spread into Ecuador with an article describing a "murdering sect" accused of capital crimes and bigamy in Peru. Ataucusi was depicted as a "short, fat, and bearded" retired shoemaker who "thinks he is the new Messiah."[370] Local newspapers in Peru have run similar stories with such headlines as "Sect of the Damned," and many highland campesinos blame the Israelites for divine scourges ranging from hail and drought to terrorism.[371]

Ataucusi's millennial community is antisocial but not apolitical, as indicated for example by placement of the Peruvian national anthem at the opening of the sect's hymnal.[372] More ambitious of Israelite nationalism was the establishment of a political party, the Popular Agricultural Front, as the venue for Ataucusi's presidential candidacy in 1990. The platform called for a nationalist, theocratic, and revolutionary Tahuantinsuyo. Thousands of the faithful appeared at rallies waving paper fish that represented temporal as much as spiritual salvation, a combination that characterizes the sect and contributes to its success among the poor. With two fish and five loaves Jesus fed a crowd of thousands, and elsewhere in Matthew the kingdom of heaven "is like a net thrown into the sea."[373] The apostles of Christ were "fishers of men," and this mission was resumed by Ataucusi as the new messiah—himself once miraculously saved by a fish—who called upon the Peruvian electorate to endorse his millennial reign.[374]

Among the faithful it seemed that Ataucusi's authenticity was verified on March 19, 1990, when during the presidential campaign a "miracle" coincided with the patron saint festival in the fishing village of San José, near Chiclayo. The villagers' preparations for the fiesta were interrupted when fish began to appear on the beaches, amassing within hours to hundreds of thousands of tons stretching down the coast for five miles. The local priest blessed the heap as a "gift from heaven," and all activities were deferred as the harvest was reaped, but Ataucusi made a counterclaim to the bounty:

> God wants to help me because I am his instrument, and, for that reason, he helps me by sending me millions of tons of fish. And he will do this not only in the north, but also along the coast of the whole country. If he were asked, he could even send me sacks of silver and gold to help the poor and pay off the national debt. Abundance, wealth, and the multiplication of foods would then begin. The fish is a biblical symbol; that is why we chose it. With what happened in Chiclayo, God is giving us his blessing.

Since Peru's crises were consequences of "divine punishment," Ataucusi believed that his presidency in Privileged Peru would bring God's graces rather than scourges. "I will ask for abundance, wealth, peace, and love."[375]

In developing the religious doctrine of the Israelites of the New Covenant, Ataucusi retained much of the Adventist emphasis on Old Testament mandates, including dietary laws and observance of the Saturday sabbath. The sect's beliefs, codes of behavior, and protocol—including hair and dress styles, abstinences, separation of genders at rituals, and sexual conduct—are derived primarily from Ataucusi's literal interpretation of biblical passages and from divine mandates revealed to him in dreams.[376] Rituals of biblical origin include presentation of the newborn in the temple, baptism, purification in conformity with Leviticus 15, sacrificial offerings as described in Numbers 28 and 29, expiation, and an initiative and curative anointment called "circumcision of the heart."[377] Full-day Saturday services include prayer, singing, and brief readings from the Bible. Women sit on the left, men sit on the right, and guards policing the aisle between them punish with sticks those slow or remiss in locating the Bible passage being read.[378] This dogmatism yields to greater freedom in the ecstatic dimensions of the faith, as most Israelites dance, cry, and speak in tongues during possession states. Israelites also report visions, prophetic dreams, levitation, revelations, and conversations with God.[379]

The most central and solemn Israelite ritual is the holocaust, or burnt offering, performed in an ambience of "intense mysticism."[380] The sacrifice of lambs, calves, doves and other animals is considered the quintessential ritual that renovates the New Covenant between God and his people, and it is accordingly preceded by purifying rituals of abstinence.[381] On Easter Sunday, thousands of Quechua-speaking migrants gather at the principal Israelite temple in Cieneguilla, outside Lima, for celebration of the holocaust. The slaughtered and ritually prepared sacrificial offering and its pyre are encircled by the gender-sorted assembly. "Praises of the Congregation of Israel" are sung for a half-hour, during which some of the faithful are possessed by the spirit and begin to speak in tongues, their heads and bodies shaking. Ataucusi kneels before the altar in all solemnity and holds his arms to the sky as he addresses a brief supplication to Jehovah. The holocaust then bursts into flame, the second song begins, and the level of awe, emotion, and religious mystery rise with the smoke into a higher register.[382]

Beginning in the late 1960s the Israelites organized migrations to agricultural colonies in the Peruvian jungle, where communal subsistence, apocalypticism, and sect rituals characterize daily life. As Ataucusi put it, "It is the fusion of a religious concept and a solution for economic problems."[383] That comprehensive salvation has also resulted in the Israelites' establishment of cooperative enterprises, schools, markets, and public cafeterias.[384] In the jungle settlements, some ten thousand families live in six communities situated in the departments of Pasco, Huánuco, and Ucayali. The relative prosperity of the communities is the result of the low cost of living, a strict work ethic sometimes violently enforced, and several thousand hectares of cooperative farmland whose fruits are distributed in a manner reminiscent of Inca tripartition, with one-third each for family, community, and Israelite Mission.[385]

The holy towns are the prelude to the millennial kingdom that Ataucusi will found, like Christ, in an advent following his death and resurrection. Sinful humanity will be exterminated in the transformative cataclysms, and the sky will darken not later than the year 2000, but those who follow the messiah will be guided through the labyrinth to their just rewards, with the jungle foliage closing in behind them.

Notes

Introduction

1. The word *Indian* has fallen into ill repute, but English lacks the one viable alternative—*indígena*—available in Spanish. Unless a particular context dictates otherwise, I use *native* as the preferred term—particularly in reference to indigenous peoples of modern Latin America—and *Indian* alternatively when reference is to the inhabitants of the "Indies" during the early-contact and colonial periods.

2. On the genre, see John J. Collins, *The Apocalyptic Imagination: An Introduction to the Jewish Matrix of Christianity* (New York: Crossroad, 1984) 1–32. For discussions of the terms treated in this and the following paragraphs, see also Bernard McGinn, *Visions of the End: Apocalyptic Traditions in the Middle Ages* (New York: Columbia University Press, 1979) 1–11; Norman Cohn, *The Pursuit of the Millennium* (New York: Oxford University Press, 1970) unnumbered opening pages of the introduction; and Richard K. Emmerson and Bernard McGinn, eds., *The Apocalypse in the Middle Ages* (Ithaca: Cornell University Press, 1992) 3–11.

3. Richard Landes, "Lest the Millennium Be Fulfilled," in Werner Verbeke et al., eds., *The Use and Abuse of Eschatology in the Middle Ages* (Louvain, Belgium: Louvain University Press, 1988) 205.

4. McGinn's first quoted passage is from McGinn, *Visions*, 6; and his second is from Bernard McGinn, "The Meanings of the Millennium," a lecture at the Inter-American Development Bank, Washington, D.C., January 17, 1996.

5. Quoted in Bernard McGinn, ed. and trans., *Apocalyptic Spirituality* (New York: Paulist Press, 1978) 117.

6. The quoted passage is from 2 Peter 3:8, following Psalms 90:4. Old Testament citations throughout this study are from the Revised Standard Version, with occasional minor revisions. New Testament citations are from John R. Kohlenberger II, ed., *The Precise Parallel New Testament* (New York: Oxford University Press, 1995). The specific translation used is determined by context;

for example, the New International Version and the New American Standard Bible are preferred when discussing Evangelicals.

7. Bernard McGinn's introduction to Emmerson and McGinn, *Apocalypse*, 8–9. See also, in the same volume, Paula Fredriksen, "Tyconius and Augustine on the Apocalypse," 20 n. 1.

8. Alberto Flores Galindo, "Los sueños de Gabriel Aguilar," *Debates en sociología* 11 (1986) 172.

9. Malachi 4:5.

10. Isaiah 11:6–9.

11. Ibid. 35:5–6.

12. The quoted passage is from ibid., 1 65:12. See also Norman Cohn, *Cosmos, Chaos and the World to Come: The Ancient Roots of Apocalyptic Faith* (New Haven: Yale University Press, 1993) 158–162.

13. The quoted passages are from Daniel 7:27 and 2:44.

14. The quoted phrase is from Daniel 7:27. See also Cohn, *Cosmos*, 173.

15. Krishan Kumar, *Utopia and Anti-Utopia in Modern Times* (Oxford: Basil Blackwell, 1987) 14.

16. The quoted passage is from Norman Cohn, "Medieval Millenarism: Its Bearing on the Comparative Study of Millenarian Movements," in Sylvia L. Thrupp, ed., *Millennial Dreams in Action* (New York: Schocken Books, 1970) 31. The same text is included in the unnumbered first pages of Cohn's *The Pursuit of the Millennium*.

17. The quoted passages are from Revelation 21:1–3.

18. The quoted passage is from Cohn, *Pursuit*, 281.

19. The quoted passage is from ibid. See also George Shepperson, "The Comparative Study of Millenarian Movements," in Thrupp, *Millennial Dreams*, 44–45; Timothy P. Weber, *Living in the Shadow of the Second Coming* (New York: Oxford University Press, 1979) 9–12; and Susan Harding, "Imagining the Last Days," in Martin E. Marty and R. Scott Appleby, eds., *Accounting for Fundamentalisms: The Dynamic Character of Movements* (Chicago: University of Chicago Press, 1994) 57–78.

20. Cohn, *Pursuit*, unnumbered introductory pages.

21. Landes, "Lest the Millennium," 206.

22. See Anthony F. C. Wallace, "Revitalization Movements," *American Anthropologist* 58 (1956) 265; and see Landes, "Lest the Millennium," 206, for millennialism as "a variable *band of time* during which Heaven descends to earth."

23. Landes, "Lest the Millennium," 207.

24. The quoted phrase is from McGinn's introduction to Emmerson and McGinn, *Apocalypse*, 13.

25. See Vittorio Lanternari, *The Religions of the Oppressed: A Study of Modern Messianic Cults*, trans. Lisa Sergio (New York: Alfred A. Knopf, 1963) 306–313.

26. Ibid., 22. See also Henri Baudet, *Paradise on Earth: Some Thoughts on European Images of Non-European Man*, trans. Elizabeth Wentholt (New Haven: Yale University Press, 1965) 34.

27. Bryan R. Wilson, *Magic and the Millennium: A Sociological Study of Religious Movements of Protest Among Tribal and Third-World Peoples* (London: Heinemann, 1973) 4.

28. The quoted phrase is in Patrick D. Miller Jr., *The Divine Warrior in Early Israel* (Cambridge: Harvard University Press, 1973) 113. The word *Christ* is the Greek equivalent of the Hebrew *messiah*, meaning "the anointed one."

29. This position following Augustine is sometimes referred to as "amillennialism."

30. In most general terms, messiahs are "eschatological figures" who have "important roles in the future hope of the people"; see John J. Collins, *The Scepter and the Star: The Messiahs of the Dead Sea Scrolls and Other Ancient Literature* (New York: Doubleday, 1995) 12.

31. Kenelm Burridge, *New Heaven, New Earth: A Study of Millenarian Activities* (New York: Schocken Books, 1969) 3.

32. Sir Thomas More, *Utopia*, ed. and trans. Robert M. Adams (New York: W. W. Norton, 1975). The word *utopia* was "fabricated by More as a Latin neologism from a fictitious Greek word"; see Louis Marin, "The Frontiers of Utopia," in Krishan Kumar and Stephen Bann, *Utopias and the Millennium* (London: Reaktion Books, 1993) 8.

33. The quoted passages are from Miriam Eliav-Feldon, *Realistic Utopias: The Ideal Imaginary Societies of the Renaissance* (Oxford: Clarendon Press, 1982) 2.

34. See Louis Marin, *Utopics: Spatial Play*, trans. Robert A. Vollrath (Atlantic Highlands, N.J.: Humanities Press, 1984) 195–200.

35. Kumar, *Utopia*, 3.

36. Ibid.; and Krishan Kumar, *Utopianism* (Minneapolis: University of Minnesota Press, 1991) 4–5.

37. The quoted passages are from Eliav-Feldon, *Realistic Utopias*, 8 and 132. Thomas More was tardily beatified in 1886 and canonized—four hundred years after his execution—in 1935.

38. See Kumar, *Utopianism*, 3.

39. Northrop Frye, "Varieties of Literary Utopias," in Frank E. Manuel, ed., *Utopias and Utopian Thought* (Boston: Houghton Mifflin, 1966) 49.

40. Vittorio Lanternari, "Nativistic and Socio-Religious Movements," *Comparative Studies in Society and History* 16 (1974) 483. The catalog of attributes that follows in the text conforms to the primarily exogenous nature of Latin American millennialism. The exception of imperial Spain is treated in the next chapter.

41. Given the strong predominance of male protagonists, the masculine pronoun will be used in discussions of messianism throughout this study. Exceptions will be made as specific contexts require.

42. The quoted passage is from Victor Turner, *Dramas, Fields, and Metaphors: Symbolic Action in Human Society* (Ithaca: Cornell University Press, 1974) 47.

43. Michael Adas, *Prophets of Rebellion: Millenarian Protest Movements Against the European Colonial Order* (Chapel Hill: University of North Carolina Press, 1979) 113.

44. The quoted phrase is in Oscar Agüero, "Milenarismo y utopía entre los Tupí-Cocama de la Amazonía peruana," in Alicia Barabas, ed., *Religiosidad y resistencia indígenas hacia el fin del milenio* (Quito: Abya-Yala, 1994) 134.

45. Cohn, *Cosmos*, 200.

46. James C. Scott, *Weapons of the Weak: Everyday Forms of Peasant Resistance* (New Haven: Yale University Press, 1985) xv.

47. Lanternari, "Nativistic and Socio-Religious Movements," 483.

48. The first quoted phrase is from Kenelm Burridge, *Mambu: A Melanesian Millennium* (London: Methuen, 1960) xx. Regarding Ambrose, see Don Cameron Allen, *The Legend of Noah* (Urbana: University of Illinois Press, 1963) 4.

49. I borrow the quoted phrase from Douglas Madsen and Peter G. Snow, *The Charismatic Bond: Political Behavior in Time of Crisis* (Cambridge: Harvard University Press, 1991).

50. The quoted passage is from Burridge, *Mambu*, 247.

51. The first quoted passage is from R. G. Collingwood, *The Idea of History*

(Oxford: Clarendon, Press, 1946) 49 (see also 46–52); and the second is from Theodore Olson, *Millennialism, Utopianism, and Progress* (Toronto: University of Toronto Press, 1982) 7.

52. The quoted phrase is in McGinn, *Visions*, 8.

53. For a short introduction to the concept of scapegoating, see René Girard, "Generative Scapegoating," in Robert G. Hamerton-Kelly, ed., *Violent Origins: Walter Burkert, René Girard, and Jonathan Z. Smith on Ritual Killing and Cultural Formation* (Stanford: Stanford University Press, 1987).

54. See Alicia M. Barabas, "Utopías indias: esperanza al futuro," in Oscar Agüero and Horacio Cerutti Guldberg, eds., *Utopía y nuestra América* (Quito: Abya-Yala, 1996) 73.

55. See Robert D. Stolorow and George E. Atwood, "Messianic Projects and Early Object-Relations," *American Journal of Psychoanalysis* 33 (1973) 213–215.

Chapter 1

1. The quoted phrase is from Jean Delumeau, *Sin and Fear: The Emergence of a Western Guilt Culture, Thirteenth–Eighteenth Centuries*, trans. Eric Nicholson (New York: St. Martin's Press, 1990) 524.

2. Quoted in Robert Ricard, *The Spiritual Conquest of Mexico: An Essay on the Apostolate and the Evangelical Methods of the Mendicant Orders in New Spain, 1523–1572*, trans. Lesley Byrd Simpson (Berkeley and Los Angeles: University of California Press, 1966) 202.

3. Quoted in Luis Weckmann, *La herencia medieval de México* (Mexico City: Colegio de México, 1984) 1/378.

4. See Luis Villoro, *Los grandes momentos del indigenismo en México* (Mexico City: Colegio de México, 1950) 30–31; and Louise M. Burkhart, *The Slippery Earth: Nahua-Christian Moral Dialogue in Sixteenth-Century Mexico* (Tucson: University of Arizona Press, 1989) 54–55.

5. See Burkhart, *Slippery Earth*, 79.

6. Quoted in Serge Gruzinski, *The Conquest of Mexico: The Incorporation of Indian Societies into the Western World, Sixteenth–Eighteenth Centuries*, trans. Eileen Corrigan (Cambridge, U.K.: Polity Press, 1993) 223. Translation modified.

7. Alicia M. Barabas, *Utopías indias: movimientos sociorreligiosos en México* (Mexico City: Grijalbo, 1989) 175.

8. Jack Autry Dabbs, "A Messiah Among the Chiriguanos," *Southwestern Journal of Anthropology* 9 (1953) 51–52. For a similar modern example from Mexico, see Manuel Gutiérrez Estévez, "The Christian Era of the Yucatec Maya," in Gary H. Gossen, ed., *South and Meso-American Native Spirituality: From the Cult of the Feathered Serpent to the Theology of Liberation* (New York: Crossroad, 1993) 264.

9. Quoted in Nathan Wachtel, *Sociedad e ideología: ensayos de historia y antropología andinas* (Lima: Instituto de Estudios Peruanos, 1973) 221–222. See Genesis 19.

10. Quoted in Inga Clendinnen, *Ambivalent Conquests: Maya and Spaniard in Yucatan, 1517–1570* (Cambridge: Cambridge University Press, 1987) 191.

11. Gutiérrez, "Christian Era," 275.

12. The apocalyptic images are from Mark 13:24–25. See also Matthew 24:29; Isaiah 13:10; Ezekiel 32:7; Joel 2:10; and Revelation 6:13.

13. Felicitas D. Goodman, "Apostolics of Yucatán," in Erika Bourguignon, ed., *Religion, Altered States of Consciousness, and Social Change* (Columbus: Ohio State University Press, 1973) 206.

14. Frans Kamsteeg, "The Message and the People," in Susanna Rostas and

André Droogers, eds., *The Popular Use of Popular Religion in Latin America* (Amsterdam: CEDLA Publications, 1993) 135–136. For another example of Avila's preaching, see María Albán Estrada and Juan Pablo Muñoz, *Con Dios todo se puede: la invasión de las sectas al Ecuador* (Quito: Editorial Planeta, 1987) 65–68. See also Alfredo Silleta, *Las sectas invaden la Argentina* (Buenos Aires: Puntosur, 1991) 59.

15. See Lillian Estelle Fisher, *The Last Inca Revolt* (Norman: University of Oklahoma Press, 1966) 246.

16. See Mark 9:1 and 13:30.

17. Djelal Kadir, *Columbus and the Ends of the Earth: Europe's Prophetic Rhetoric as Conquering Ideology* (Berkeley and Los Angeles: University of California Press, 1992) 10 (see also 13). In 1 Corinthians 11:26, the calendar is kept open "until he comes."

18. Michael F. Brown and Eduardo Fernández, *War of Shadows: The Struggle for Utopia in the Peruvian Amazon* (Berkeley and Los Angeles: University of California Press, 1991) 75–76.

19. Eduardo Viveiros de Castro, *From the Enemy's Point of View: Humanity and Divinity in an Amazonian Society*, trans. Catherine V. Howard (Chicago: University of Chicago Press, 1992) 63.

20. Roger Y. Kellner, "Christian Gods and Mapuche Witches," in Rostas and Droogers, *Popular Use*, 163.

21. Anatilde Idoyaga Molina, "Una esperanza milenarista entre los Pilagá," in Alicia M. Barabas, ed., *Religiosidad y resistencia indígenas hacia el fin del milenio* (Quito: Abya-Yala, 1994) 67.

22. Quoted in Oscar Alfredo Agüero, *The Millennium Among the Tupí-Cocama: A Case of Religious Ethno-Dynamism in the Peruvian Amazon* (Uppsala, Sweden: Uppsala Research Reports in Cultural Anthropology, 1992) 95. See also Jean-Pierre Chaumeil, *Historia y migraciones de los Yagua*, trans. María del Carmen Urbano (Lima: CAAP, 1981) 114.

23. Jaime Regan, *Hacia la tierra sin mal: estudio sobre la religiosidad del pueblo en la Amazonía* (Iquitos, Peru: CETA, 1983) 1/143.

24. Quoted in Albán and Muñoz, *Con Dios*, 27.

25. Edgardo Jorge Cordeu and Alejandra Siffredi, *De la algarroba al algodón: movimiento mesiánico de los guaycurú* (Buenos Aires: Juárez Editor, 1971) 146. See also José Antonio Maravall, *Utopía y reformismo en la España de los Austrias* (Mexico City: Siglo Ventiuno, 1982) 203 and 205, where New World fertility replaces Old World exhaustion.

26. Regan, *Hacia la tierra*, 2/132.

27. Gutiérrez, "Christian Era," 274.

28. Quoted in Regan, *Hacia la tierra*, 2/154. See also Agüero, *Millennium*, 80, 83, and 108.

29. Acts 1:7; and Mark 13:32. See also Matthew 24:36.

30. Christopher Columbus, *The Libro de las profecías of Christopher Columbus*, trans. Delno C. West and August Kling (Gainesville: University of Florida Press, 1991) 103.

31. See Manuel M. Marzal, *Los caminos religiosos de los inmigrantes en la gran Lima: el caso de El Agustino* (Lima: Pontificia Universidad Católica del Perú, 1989) 348.

32. Bernard McGinn, "Symbolism in the Thought of Joachim of Fiore," in Ann Williams, ed., *Prophesy and Millenarianism: Essays in Honor of Marjorie Reeves* (Essex; England: Longman, 1980) 148. See also John J. Collins, *The Apocalyptic Imagination: An Introduction to the Jewish Matrix of Christianity* (New York: Crossroad, 1984) 49–52.

33. Rutherford H. Platt Jr., *The Forgotten Books of Eden: Lost Books of the Old Testament* (New York: Gramercy Books, 1980) 6 and 26.

34. Quoted in Richard Landes, "Lest the Millennium Be Fulfilled," in Werner Verbeke et al., eds., *The Use and Abuse of Eschatology in the Middle Ages* (Louvain, Belgium: Louvain University Press, 1988) 142–143. On "apocalyptic arithmetic" as related to Columbus, see Kadir, *Columbus*, 22–23.

35. Frank Kermode, *The Sense of an Ending: Studies in the Theory of Fiction* (New York: Oxford University Press, 1967) 11.

36. Marjorie Reeves, *The Influence of Prophecy in the Later Middle Ages: A Study in Joachimism* (Oxford: Clarendon Press, 1969) 295. The title of this text section, "Messianic Imperialism," is borrowed from Marcel Bataillon, *Erasmo y España: estudios sobre la historia espiritual del siglo XVI* (Mexico City: Fondo de Cultura Económica, 1950) 226.

37. The quoted passages are from Columbus, *Libro*, 109 and 111. See also Alain Milhou, *Colón y su mentalidad mesiánica en el ambiente franciscanista medieval* (Valladolid, Spain: Casa-Museo de Colón, 1983) 469.

38. The first quoted passage is from Exodus 19:6; and the second is from J. H. Parry, *The Spanish Theory of Empire in the Sixteenth Century* (New York: Octagon Books, 1974) 13.

39. Quoted in D. A. Brading, *The First America: The Spanish Monarchy, Creole Patriots, and the Liberal State, 1492–1867* (Cambridge: Cambridge University Press, 1991) 182.

40. See Peggy K. Liss, *Isabel the Queen: Life and Times* (New York: Oxford University Press, 1992) 34. For a modern adaptation of similar ideas, see Vicente Solano, "Bosquejo de la Europa y de la América en 1900," in Arturo Andrés Roig, ed., *La utopía en el Ecuador* (Quito: Banco Central del Ecuador and Corporación Editora Nacional, 1987) 315–351.

41. Quoted in Donald Hodges, *Sandino's Communism: Spiritual Politics for the Twenty-first Century* (Austin: University of Texas Press, 1992) 123.

42. The quoted phrase is in Fernando Mires, *La rebelión permanente: las revoluciones sociales en América Latina* (Mexico City: Siglo Veintiuno, 1988) 386.

43. Sergio Ramírez and Robert Edgar Conrad, eds., *Sandino: The Testimony of a Nicaraguan Patriot, 1921–1934*, trans. Robert Edgar Conrad (Princeton: Princeton University Press, 1990) 361–362.

44. Quoted in Hodges, *Sandino's Communism*, 120.

45. See Frank Graziano, *Divine Violence: Spectacle, Psychosexuality, and Radical Christianity in the Argentine "Dirty War"* (Boulder: Westview Press, 1992) 13 and 123–128.

46. Lewis Hanke et al., eds., *Cuerpo de documentos del siglo XVI: sobre los derechos de España en las Indias y Filipinas* (Mexico City: Fondo de Cultura Económica, 1977) 3.

47. Quoted in Lewis Hanke, introduction to Bartolomé de Las Casas, *Del único modo de traer a todos los pueblos a la verdadera religión* (Mexico City: Fondo de Cultura Económica, 1942) 28.

48. See Joan Myers et al., *Santiago: Saint of Two Worlds* (Albuquerque: University of New Mexico Press, 1991) 17. For Santiago's reemergence in 1862 to assist the mestizo Mexican army against the French troops invading Tabasco, see 19. See also Weckmann, *Herencia*, 1/149–152 and 1/199–205. A Spanish Military Order of Santiago was founded in 1170 to fight the Moors.

49. Quoted in María Teresa Huerta and Patricia Palacios, *Rebeliones indígenas de la época colonial* (Mexico City: Instituto Nacional de Antropología e Historia, 1976) 232. Priests were still making this argument in the late eighteenth century, now to rebelling Indians, with the hope of pacifying them; see Segundo E. Moreno Yánez, *Sublevaciones indígenas en la audiencia de Quito: desde comienzos del siglo XVII hasta finales de la colonia* (Quito: Ediciones de la Universidad Católica, 1985) 97.

50. Quoted in Emilio Choy, *Antropología e historia* (Lima: Universidad Nacional Mayor de San Marcos, 1979) 1/425; and in Pedro Borges, "El sentido trascendente del descubrimiento y conversión de Indias," *Missionalia hispánica* 13/37 (1956) 159.

51. Quoted in Patrick D. Miller Jr., *The Divine Warrior in Early Israel* (Cambridge: Harvard University Press, 1973) 142–143.

52. Quoted in ibid., 144.

53. See Américo Castro, *Santiago de España* (Buenos Aires: Emecé Editores, 1958) 22–25; and Choy, *Antropología*, 1/432.

54. The quoted passages are from Revelation 19:16, which echoes Deuteronomy 33: 26–29. For an early image of Christ as warrior, see Robert Markus, "From Rome to the Barbarian Kingdoms," in John McManners, ed., *The Oxford Illustrated History of Christianity* (Oxford: Oxford University Press, 1990) 88.

55. See Castro, *Santiago*, 38–41. Regarding the relation of Santiago to Jesus, see "James, Son of Zebedee" and "James, Brother of Jesus," in Ronald Brownrigg, *Who's Who in the New Testament* (New York: Oxford University Press, 1993) 93–94. Among the Pueblo of New Mexico, Christ and Santiago were coupled with the Twin War Gods, resulting in dances performed on Christmas morning "to honor the newly born war god, Jesus Christ"; see Ramón A. Gutiérrez, *When Jesus Came, the Corn Mothers Went Away: Marriage, Sexuality, and Power in New Mexico, 1500–1846* (Stanford: Stanford University Press, 1991) 85.

56. Quoted in Claudio Sánchez Albornoz, *La edad media española y la empresa de América* (Madrid: Instituto de Cooperación Iberoamericana, 1983) 80.

57. Francisco López de Gómara, *Historia general de las Indias y vida de Hernán Cortés* (Caracas: Biblioteca Ayacucho, 1979) 31. For an exemplary statement on holy war, see Paulo Suess, *La nueva evangelización: desafíos históricos y pautas culturales*, trans. María Victoria C. de Vela (Quito: Abya-Yala, 1991) 44.

58. Quoted in Felipe Fernández-Armesto, *Ferdinand and Isabella* (New York: Taplinger Publishing, 1975) 89.

59. See Milhou, *Colón*, 351; and Fernández-Armesto, *Ferdinand*, 90.

60. See Jonathan Riley-Smith, *The Crusades: A Short History* (New Haven: Yale University Press, 1987) 237–238.

61. Quoted in Liss, *Isabel*, 240.

62. Quoted in Fernández-Armesto, *Ferdinand*, 96.

63. Lewis A. Tambs, "Expulsion of the Jewish Community from the Spains, 1492," in Bryan F. LeBeau and Menachem Mor, eds., *Religion in the Age of Exploration: The Case of Spain and New Spain* (Omaha: Creighton University Press, 1996) 49–50. Peter Martyr d'Anghera saw the Jews as "obscene, detestable, vile, execrable" and applauded the extermination of "that despicable and infected herd"; quoted in Fernández-Armesto, *Ferdinand*, 164.

64. Quoted in Lewis Hanke, *The First Social Experiments in America: A Study in the Development of Spanish Indian Policy in the Sixteenth Century* (Cambridge: Harvard University Press, 1935) xi.

65. Quoted in Borges, "Sentido," 154.

66. The first quoted passage is from Tambs, "Expulsion," 51; and the second is from Parry, *Spanish Theory*, 37.

67. See F. E. Peters, *Jerusalem: The Holy City in the Eyes of Chroniclers, Visitors, Pilgrims, and Prophets from the Days of Abraham to the Beginnings of Modern Times* (Princeton University Press, 1985) 505–506: "The Holy Sepulcher complex—actually the rotunda-shrine over the tomb of Jesus, which was named the *Anastasis*, or resurrection; the shrine at Calvary; and the immense

basilica, the 'Martyrium,' as Eusebius had already begun to call it—rapidly became the center and focus of Christian Jerusalem" (139). In 1343 the pope gave the Franciscans "the Custody of the Holy Land."

68. The quoted passages are from Cristóbal Colón, *Textos y documentos completos: relaciones de viajes, cartas y memorias*, ed. Consuelo Varela (Madrid: Alianza, 1984) 101. See also Columbus, *Libro*, 101.

69. See Columbus, *Libro*, 61–62. Following an alum stone discovery in 1462, Pope Pius II announced that the resources for liberation of Jerusalem would come from the earth; see John Boyd Thacher, *Christopher Columbus: His Life, His Work, His Remains* (New York: G. P. Putnam's Sons, 1904) 1/367.

70. The pertinent item in the will reiterated, before assigning the funds, that Columbus had made his first voyage "with the intention of supplicating the King and Queen, our Lords, that the revenue which their Highnesses might have from the Indies, they should determine to spend in the conquest of Jerusalem"; see Thacher, *Christopher Columbus*, 180. According to John Leddy Phelan, *The Millennial Kingdom of the Franciscans in the New World* (Berkeley and Los Angeles: University of California Press, 1970) 19, Columbus removed this clause from his final will of August 25, 1505. Leonard I. Sweet argues quite to the contrary that the final will underscored the item's importance; see "Christopher Columbus and the Millennial Vision of the New World," *Catholic Historical Review*, 72/3 (July 1986) 381, n. 47.

71. Quoted in Margarita Zamora, "Christopher Columbus's 'Letter to the Sovereigns,' " in Stephen Greenblatt, ed., *New World Encounters* (Berkeley and Los Angeles: University of California Press, 1993) 7. Variations of this ideal endured at least until the early nineteenth century, when backlanders in the Rodeador Mountains of Brazil planned a nonviolent religious crusade to free Jerusalem and witness the arrival of the millennial kingdom; see Robert M. Levine, *Vale of Tears: Revisting the Canudos Massacre in Northeastern Brazil, 1893–1897* (Berkeley and Los Angeles: University of California Press, 1992) 218.

72. Colón, *Textos*, 202.

73. Columbus, *Libro*, 105 and 111. See Bartolomé de Las Casas, *Historia de las Indias*, ed. André Saint-Lu (Caracas: Biblioteca Ayacucho, 1986) 1/510, where a similar prophesy is attributed to Isaiah. Columbus makes the same point in *Textos*, 203; see also Consuelo Varela's note to the same.

74. Colón, *Textos*, 323 and 263, respectively. For discussion see Milhou, *Colón*, 272–286. The second quoted passage follows Mark 6:50 and John 6:20.

75. The quoted passages are from Colón, *Textos*, 322–323. See also Isaiah 22:22, and Revelation 3:7.

76. Colón, *Textos*, 264.

77. Kenelm Burridge, *New Heaven, New Earth: A Study of Millenarian Activities* (New York: Schocken Books, 1969) 165.

78. Milhou, *Colón*, 404.

79. Kadir, *Columbus*, 150.

80. Thacher, *Christopher Columbus*, 2/369.

81. Hernán Pérez de Oliva, *Historia de la invención de las Yndias*, ed. José Juan Arrom (Bogotá: Publicaciones del Instituto Caro y Cuervo, 1965) 41. For a similar statement from Columbus's son, see Milhou, *Colón*, 196.

82. Charles L. Sanford, *The Quest for Paradise: Europe and the American Moral Imagination* (Urbana: University of Illinois Press, 1961) 60–61.

83. Gerónimo de Mendieta, *Historia eclesiástica indiana* (Mexico City: Editorial Porrúa, 1980) 15. Sahagún likewise viewed Cortés as a divine instrument "opening the door so that the preachers of the Holy Gospel could preach the Catholic faith"; see Villoro, "Grandes momentos," 41–42. Las Casas held a dissenting view: Cortés was "a pure tyrant and usurper of foreign kingdoms"; see Brading, *First America*, 76.

84. Mendieta, *Historia*, 174–175. See also Phelan, *Millennial Kingdom*, 29–38; and Borges, "Sentido," 147 ("Our Lord wanted to restore to the Church what the devil had stolen from it in England, Germany and France") and 149 ("We won from the devil more lands in the Indies than he stole from us with his Turks in Europe").

85. See Las Casas, *Historia*, 1/28. See also Fernando Colón, *The Life of the Admiral Christopher Columbus by His Son Ferdinand*, trans. Benjamin Keen (New Brunswick, N.J.: Rutgers University Press, 1959) 3–4. For discussion see Milhou, *Colón*, 59–63. Much was also made of Columbus's last name—Colón in Spanish—which, among other readings, evoked the verb *colonizar* (to colonize).

86. The quoted passages are from Las Casas, *Historia*, 1/342.

87. Quoted in Peter J. Bakewell, *Silver Mining and Society in Colonial Mexico: Zacatecas, 1546–1700* (Cambridge: Cambridge University Press, 1971) 1.

88. Lewis Hanke, *The Imperial City of Potosí* (The Hague: Martinus Nijhoff, 1956) 1.

89. See Felipe Guaman Poma de Ayala, *Nueva crónica y buen gobierno*, ed. Franklin Pease (Caracas: Biblioteca Ayacucho, 1980) 2/400 and 2/402.

90. Quoted in Hanke, *Imperial City*, 30.

91. Quoted in Milhou, *Colón*, 142 and 144; and Brading, *First America*, 400. See also Milhou, *Colón*, 125–144; and Borges, "Sentido," 148.

92. Quoted in Fernando Ainsa, *De la edad de oro a El Dorado: génesis del discurso utópico americano* (Mexico City: Fondo de Cultura Económica, 1992) 108.

93. Quoted in Constantino Bayle, *El Dorado fantasma* (Madrid: Consejo de la Hispanidad, 1943) 385. See also José de Acosta, *Historia natural y moral de las Indias* (Mexico City: Fondo de Cultura Económica, 1962) 142.

94. Quoted in Brading, *First America*, 144 (see also 417). As Africans frequently put it to the colonizers among them, "Now we have the Bible but you, the white people, possess the land"; see George Balandier, *Teoría de la descolonización*, trans. Rafael Di Muro (Buenos Aires: Editorial Tiempo Contemporáneo, 1973) 19.

95. The first quoted phrase is from Anthony Pagden, "*Ius et Factum*: Text and Experience in the Writings of Bartolomé de Las Casas," in Greenblatt, *New World Encounters*, 86. The second quoted phrase is in Milhou, *Colón*, 130; on the spiritualization of gold, see 125–132.

96. Arthur Edward Waite, *Alchemists through the Ages* (Blauvelt, N.Y.: Rudolf Steiner Publications, 1970) 11. See also Mircea Eliade, *The Forge and the Crucible*, trans. Stephen Corrin (London: Rider and Rider, 1962) 43–57, 68, 149–151, and 156.

97. The quoted passages are in José María Enguita Utrilla, "El oro de las Indias," in Francisco Solano and Fermín del Pino, *América y la España del siglo XVI* (Madrid: Instituto Gonzalo Fernández de Oviedo, 1982) 1/277.

98. The first quoted passage is in Teresa Gisbert, *Iconografía y mitos indígenas en el arte* (La Paz: Gisbert, 1980) 19; the second is in Teresa Gisbert, "The Artistic World of Felipe Guaman Poma," in Rolena Adorno et al., *Guaman Poma de Ayala: The Colonial Art of an Andean Author* (New York: Americas Society, 1992) 80. See also Daniel 2:31–35; and Milhou, *Colón*, 125–133 and 139–145.

99. Colón, *Textos*, 327.

100. See Bernard McGinn, *Visions of the End: Apocalyptic Traditions in the Middle Ages* (New York: Columbia University Press, 1979) 33; and Collins, *Apocalyptic Imagination*, 93–100. The quoted passage is from Norman Cohn, "Medieval Millenarism," in Sylvia L. Thrupp, ed., *Millennial Dreams in Action* (New York: Schocken Books, 1970) 34.

101. The quoted passages are in John J. Collins, *The Scepter and the Star: The Messiahs of the Dead Sea Scrolls and Other Ancient Literature* (New York: Doubleday, 1995) 24. See also Daniel 2:44.

102. Markus, "From Rome," 70. For an image of Constantine being crowned by the hand of God reaching down from a cloud, see 71.

103. The first quoted passage is from McGinn, "Symbolism," 150–151; the second is from Revelation 2:26–27; and the third from Reeves, *Influence*, 299–300. In some versions the emperor then dies, but in others he takes the Franciscan habit; see Milhou, *Colón*, 385. See also Maravall, *Utopía*, 319; Ernst H. Kantorowicz, "The Problem of World Unity," in Stanley Pargellis, ed., *The Quest for Political Unity in World History* (Washington, D.C.: American Historical Association, 1944) 31–37; and Mario Góngora, *Studies in the Colonial History of Spanish America*, trans. Richard Southern (Cambridge: Cambridge University Press, 1975) 208 and 214–215.

104. See the bull "Inter Caetera" in Frances Gardiner Davenport, ed., *European Treaties Bearing on the History of the United States and Its Dependencies to 1648* (Washington, D.C.: Carnegie Institution, 1974) 1/61–63. For discussion see Paulino Castañeda Delgado, *La teocracia pontificial y la conquista de América* (Vitoria, Spain: Editorial Eset, 1968) 245–301.

105. See Castañeda Delgado, *Teocracia*, 298 and 319–332. See also Weckmann, *Herencia*, 2/406–407; Parry, *Spanish Theory*, 1–8; Góngora, *Studies*, 33–43; and Lewis Hanke, "The 'Requirement' and Its Interpretors," *Revista de historia de América* 1 (1938) 25–34. For statements on the universal vicariate, see Columbus, *Libro*, 157; and Kadir, *Columbus*, 82.

106. Quoted in Patricia Seed, *Ceremonies of Possession In Europe's Conquest of the New World 1492–1640* (New York: Cambridge University Press, 1995) 92; see 69–99 for Islamic precedents. For the Las Casas view of the Requirement as "unjust and absurd," see his *Historia*, 3/617.

107. See Castañeda Delgado, *Teocracia*, 403.

108. Quoted in C. R. Boxer, *A Great Luso-Brazilian Figure: Padre António Vieira, S. J., 1680–1697* (London: Hispanic and Luso-Brazilian Councils, 1957) 12.

109. Phelan, *Millennial Kingdom*, 22–23. See also Weckmann, *Herencia*, 1/270.

110. Columbus, *Libro*, 110; See also Colón, *Textos*, 327. On Ferdinand as Last World Emperor, see Milhou, *Colón*, 389–400. In 2 Samuel 7:16, God tells David that his throne "will be established forever."

111. Quoted in Liss, *Isabel*, 138 and 140.

112. See Carmelo Lisón Tolosana, *La imagen del rey: monarquía, realeza y poder ritual en la Casa de los Austrias* (Madrid: Espasa-Calpe, 1992) 22; and Marie Tanner, *The Last Descendant of Aeneas: The Hapsburgs and the Mythic Image of the Emperor* (New Haven: Yale University Press, 1993) 126.

113. Quoted in Anthony Pagden, *Lords of All the World: Ideologies of Empire in Spain, Britain and France, c. 1500–c. 1800* (New Haven: Yale University Press, 1995) 42. See also Weckmann, *Herencia*, 1/265; and Revelation 2:26–27.

114. Regarding Cortés, see Lisón, *Imagen*, 23–23. Regarding Atahualpa, see Castañeda Delgado, *Teocracia*, 298. For Atahualpa's argument as adapted by an 1809 political tract, see Bernardo Monteagudo, *Diálogo entre Atawallpa y Fernando VII en los Campos Eliseos*, ed. Carlos Castañón Barrientos (La Paz: n.p., 1973) 8.

115. Quoted in Kadir, *Columbus*, 134. For other examples see Weckmann, *Herencia*, 2/398. More practical imperialists anticipated a certain facility of enterprise from world unity: "As everyone would be subject to a single Prince, one might travel everywhere with a single language and a single currency" (quoted

in Pagden, *Lords*, 40). Another practical imperialist later envisioned from Mexico "a whole world in disciplined commerce"; quoted in J. H. Elliott, "A World United," in Jay A. Levenson, ed., *Circa 1492: Art in the Age of Exploration* (Washington, D.C.: National Gallery of Art; and New Haven: Yale University Press, 1991) 649.

116. The first quoted passage is from John Lynch, *Spain Under the Hapsburgs* (New York: New York University Press, 1964) 1/278; for the complicated relation between Philip II and the papacy, see 273–286. The second quoted passage is in Bataillon, *Erasmo*, 227; see also Lisón, *Imagen*, 23. Byzantine soldiers were referred to as "champions of the whole world," and Barbarossa's motto was "One Church, one pope, one emperor"; see Kantorowicz, "Problem," 31–37, for these and other examples of the globalization of Christendom. The third quoted passage is from Phelan, *Millennial Kingdom*, 13. See also Columbus, *Libro*, 35.

117. See Geoffrey Parker, "David or Goliath? Philip II and His World in the 1580s," in Richard L. Kagan and Geoffrey Parker, eds., *Spain, Europe and the Atlantic World: Essays in Honor of John H. Elliott* (New York: Cambridge University Press, 1995) 248, 253, 254, and 259; and Geoffrey Parker, *Philip II* (Boston: Little, Brown, 1978) 111.

118. Tanner, *Last Descendant*, 135 and 145.

119. Quoted in Anthony Pagden, *Spanish Imperialism and the Political Imagination: Studies in European and Spanish-American Social and Political Theory, 1513–1830* (New Haven: Yale University Press, 1990) 50. See also Tanner, *Last Descendant*, 145; and John M. Headley, *Tommaso Campanella and the Transformation of the World* (Princeton: Princeton University Press, 1997) 197–228.

120. Quoted in Phelan, *Millennial Kingdom*, 14 (see also 106).

121. Quoted in Parker, "David," 181.

122. Richard L. Kagan, "Politics, Prophecy, and the Inquisition in Late Sixteenth-Century Spain," in Mary Elizabeth Perry and Anne J. Cruz, eds., *Cultural Encounters: The Impact of the Inquisition in Spain and the New World* (Berkeley and Los Angeles: University of California Press, 1991) 108.

123. John H. Elliott, *Imperial Spain, 1469–1716* (London: Edward Arnold Publishers, 1963) 293.

124. Parker, "David," 190.

125. On Motolinía see B. Salazar, *Los doce* (Mexico City: Imprenta Mexicana, 1943) 107–120.

126. Fernando Operé, "Indios, Moros y Cristianos en el México colonial," in Encuentro Internacional Quinto Centenario, *Impacto y futuro de la civilización española en el Nuevo Mundo* (San Juan, P.R.: n.p., 1991). See also Ricard, *Spiritual Conquest*, 196–198; Delno C. West, "Medieval Ideas of Apocalyptic Mission and the Early Franciscans in Mexico," *The Americas* 45/3 (January 1989) 293; and Marilyn Ekdahl Ravicz, *Early Colonial Religious Drama in Mexico: From Tzompantli to Golgotha* (Washington, D.C.: Catholic University of America Press, 1970) 54–55. Among the Tlaxcalans the mock battles may have evoked the preconquest flower wars against the Aztecs. For the Spaniards *The Conquest of Jerusalem* commemorated the 1538 Truce of Nice, which was mediated by the Vatican in the hope that the unencumbered Charles V would attack the Turks and capture Jerusalem; see West, "Medieval Ideas," 293. Another drama, entitled *The Last Judgment*, or *Representation of the End of the World*, was staged in Mexico (see Ravicz, *Early Colonial Religious Drama*, 49), as was *The Fall of Adam and Eve* (see Weckmann, *Herencia*, 1/366–367).

127. The first quoted passage is from Matthew 28:19 (see also 24:14), and the second is from 2 Peter 3:13.

128. Quoted in Borges, "Sentido," 173. For a similar statement, see West,

"Medieval Ideas," 313. In a modern Yucatec Maya narrative, Christ responds to the astonishing rapidity with which technology disseminates his word: "When you see that the telegraph wires above are in use and when you hear the railroad running along your roads, you shall know that My second coming is near"; quoted in M. Gutiérrez, "Christian Era," 275.

129. Quoted in Weckmann, *Herencia*, 1/269.

130. Phelan, *Millennial Kingdom*, 24. The quoted phrase is from Matthew 10:6. See Mendieta, *Historia*, 540 and 558; Isaiah 11:12 (the "outcasts of Israel" and the "dispersed of Judah"); L. Sprague de Camp, *Lost Continents* (New York: Dover Publications, 1970) 28–29; Hanke, *First Social Experiments*, 72–73; and Gershon Greenberg, "American Indians, Ten Lost Tribes and Christian Eschatology" in Le Beau and Mor, *Religion*, 127–148.

131. See Greenberg, "American Indians," 142.

132. Quoted in Kadir, *Columbus*, 182. For the chroniclers on Indian-Jews, see Franklin Pease G. Y., *Las crónicas y los Andes* (Lima: Pontificia Universidad Católica del Perú et al., 1995) 311–347, particularly 320.

133. Brading, *First America*, 198. See also Gregorio García, *Origen de los Indios del Nuevo Mundo* (Mexico City: Fondo de Cultura Económica, 1981).

134. Servando Teresa de Mier, *Ideario político* (Caracas: Biblioteca Ayacucho, 1978) 8. For another example of etymological pyrotechnics, see Augustín de Vetancurt, *Teatro mexicano* (Mexico City: Autores Clásicos Mexicanos, 1900) 1/145.

135. García, *Origen*, 86–100; the quoted passage is on 87.

136. Menasseh Ben Israel, *Origen de los Americanos: esperanza de Israel* (Madrid: Librería de Santiago Pérez Junquera, 1881) 114. See also Diego Andrés de Rocha, *Tratado único y singular del origen de los indios occidentales del Perú, México, Santa Fé y Chile* (Lima: Imprenta de Manuel de Olivos, 1681). For the equation of Jews and Indians in the late nineteenth century, see Silvia Ortiz Echánz, "Origen, desarrollo y características del espiritualismo en México," *América indígena* 39/1 (January–March 1979) 154.

137. Fernando Montesinos, *Memorias antiguas historiales del Perú*, ed. and trans. Philip Ainsworth Means (London: Hakluyt Society, 1920) 2.

138. Américo Vespucci, *Cartas de viaje*, ed. Luciano Fomisano (Madrid: Alianza, 1986) 76.

139. The quoted phrase is from ibid., 108. See also John H. Elliott, *The Old World and the New, 1492–1650* (Cambridge: Cambridge University Press, 1970) 25.

140. López de Gómara, *Historia*, 1/7. Sahagún, among others, made the same assertion; see Villoro, *Grandes momentos*, 40.

141. The first quoted phrase is from Phelan, *Millennial Kingdom*, 110; see Jacques Lafaye, *Mesías, cruzadas, utopías: el judeo-cristianismo en las sociedades ibéricas*, trans. Juan José Utrilla (Mexico City: Fondo de Cultura Económica, 1984) 158. The second quoted phrase is in Anthony Pagden, *The Fall of Natural Man: The American Indian and the Origins of Comparative Ethnology* (Cambridge: Cambridge University Press, 1982) 193.

142. Garcilaso de la Vega, El Inca, *Royal Commentaries of the Incas and General History of Peru*, trans. Harold V. Livermore (Austin: University of Texas Press, 1987) 40. See also Sabine MacCormack, *Religion in the Andes: Vision and Imagination in Early Colonial Peru* (Princeton: Princeton University Press, 1991) 334.

143. Garcilaso de la Vega, *Royal Commentaries*, 40.

144. Margarita Zamora, *Language, Authority, and Indigenous History in the* Comentarios reales de los Incas (Cambridge: Cambridge University Press, 1988) 128; see also 97–101, 111–114, and 160.

145. The quoted phrase is from 2 Corinthians 5:17. The Christian calendar was tardily instituted in the sixth century.

146. Collins, *Scepter*, 104.

147. See Kenelm Burridge, "Millennialisms and the Recreation of History," in Bruce Lincoln, ed., *Religion, Rebellion, Revolution: An Interdisciplinary and Cross-Cultural Collection of Essays* (London: Macmillan, 1985) 228.

148. Eva Perón, *Escribe Eva Perón* (Buenos Aires: n.p., 1950) 50. See also Juan Perón, *Habla Perón* (Buenos Aires: Editorial Freeland, 1973) 65 and 84.

149. Quoted in Brian Loveman and Thomas M. Davies Jr., *The Politics of Antipolitics: The Military in Latin America* (Lincoln: University of Nebraska Press, 1989) 194–195.

150. The quoted passages are in Graziano, *Divine Violence*, 26, 120, and 141.

151. The quoted passage is in Frederick Pike, *The Politics of the Miraculous in Peru: Haya de la Torre and the Spiritualist Tradition* (Lincoln: University of Nebraska Press, 1986) 121.

152. Lawrence E. Sullivan, *Icanchu's Drum: An Orientation to Meaning in South American Religions* (New York: Macmillan, 1988) 51.

153. See Roger N. Lancaster, *Life Is Hard: Machismo, Danger, and the Intimacy of Power in Nicaragua* (Berkeley and Los Angeles: University of California Press, 1992) 6–7.

154. Luis Arce Borja, ed., *Guerra popular en el Perú: el pensamiento gonzalo* (Brussels: n.p. 1989) 177 and 173–174 (see also 201); and Gustavo Gorriti Ellenbogen, *Sendero: historia de la guerra milenaria en el Perú* (Lima: Apoyo, 1990) 66–67 and 167. See also 1 Corinthians 15:52.

155. Quoted in Gustavo Benavides, "Millennial Politics in Contemporary Peru," in Gustavo Benavides and M. W. Daly, eds., *Religion and Political Power* (Albany: State University of New York Press, 1989) 232.

156. Second General Conference of Latin American Bishops, "The Church in the Present-Day Transformation of Latin America in the Light of the Council," in Alfred T. Hennelly, ed. and trans., *Liberation Theology: A Documentary History* (Maryknoll, N.Y.: Orbis Books, 1990) 91.

157. To avoid unnecessary repetition of *Catholic*, the word *Church* with a capital initial is used throughout this study in reference to the Catholic Church as an institution. When *church* appears with a lowercase initial, it refers to a particular building.

158. Quoted in David Lehmann, *Democracy and Development in Latin America: Economics, Politics, and Religion in the Post-War Period* (Philadelphia: Temple University Press, 1990) 188.

159. Agüero, *Millennium*, 51 and 74.

160. The first quoted phrase is from Mircea Eliade, *The Myth of the Eternal Return: Or, Cosmos and History*, trans. Willard R. Trask (Princeton: Princeton University Press, 1965) 75.

161. Barabas, *Utopías*, 169. The Greeks, following Heraclitus, also developed concepts of cyclical creation and destruction, from which the Stoic doctrine of eternal return was partially derived.

162. See Eliade, *Myth*, 73.

163. See Wachtel, *Sociedad*, 222; and Alberto Flores Galindo, *Europa y el país de los incas: la utopía andina* (Lima: Instituto de Apoyo Agrario, 1986) 42. Note the inversion's visual conformity with cyclicity.

164. Wachtel, *Sociedad*, 50.

165. Quoted in Jan Szemiński, *La utopía tupamarista* (Lima: Pontificia Universidad Católica del Perú, 1983) 99. See also Pierre Duviols, "Las cinco edades primitivas del Perú según Guaman Poma de Ayala," in Mariusz S. Ziólkowski

and Robert M. Sadowski, eds., *Time and Calendars in the Inca Empire* (Oxford: B.A.R. International, 1989) 8.

166. See Sabine MacCormack, "The Heart Has Its Reasons," *Hispanic American Historical Review* 65/3 (1985) 462. See also Luis E. Valcárcel, *Historia del Perú antiguo* (Lima: Editorial Juan Mejía Baca, 1964) 2/396–403.

167. Marzal, *Caminos*, 354–358. For Israelite time as cyclical, see Harald O. Skar, "Quest for a New Covenant: The Israelita Movement in Peru," in Harald O. Skar and Frank Salomon, eds., *Natives and Neighbors in South America* (Göteborg; Sweden: Ethnological Studies 38, 1987) 248.

168. Quoted in Marzal, *Caminos*, 357.

169. Quoted in Alfredo López Austin, *The Human Body and Ideology Concepts of the Ancient Nahuas*, trans. Thelma Ortiz de Montellano and Bernard Ortiz de Montellano (Salt Lake City: University of Utah Press, 1988) 1/65. For Aztec gods who "interchanged positions of predominance in a regular, cyclical order," see J. Jorge Klor de Alva, "Religious Rationalization and the Conversion of the Nahuas," in Davíd Carrasco, ed., *To Change Place: Aztec Ceremonial Landscapes* (Boulder: University of Colorado Press, 1991) 241.

170. López Austin, *Human Body*, 1/240. For similar indigenous periodizations, see Sullivan, *Icanchu's Drum*, 52. On the Aztec ages, see Gordon Brotherston, *Book of the Fourth World: Reading the Native Americans Through Their Literature* (New York: Cambridge University Press, 1992) 238–245.

171. M. Gutiérrez, "Christian Era," 252.

172. Quoted in Nathan Wachtel, *The Vision of the Vanquished: The Spanish Conquest of Peru Through Indian Eyes, 1530–1570*, trans. Ben Reynolds and Siân Reynolds (New York: Barnes and Noble, 1977) 31–32.

173. Ibid., 15.

174. See Franklin Pease, *El dios creador andino* (Lima: Mosca Azul Editores, 1973) 14–15 and 35. For Andean flood myths, see Frank Salomon and George L. Urioste, trans., *The Huarochirí Manuscript: A Testament of Ancient and Colonial Andean Religion* (Austin: University of Texas Press, 1991) 51–2; and Valcárcel, *Historia*, 2/392–396.

175. Johannes Wilbert and Karin Simoneau, eds., *Folk Literature of the Yanomami Indians* (Los Angeles: UCLA Latin American Center Publications, 1990) 35 and 48 (see also 67–75). See also Sullivan, *Icanchu's Drum*, 562–563; and Brotherston, *Book*, 256–265. On floods in the Judeo-Christian divine arsenal, see, for example, Exodus 15:5; and Psalms 78:13 and 106:11.

176. Johannes Wilbert and Karin Simoneau, eds., *Folk Literature of the Sikuani Indians* (Los Angeles: UCLA Latin American Center Publications, 1992) 128–129 and 172.

177. Johannes Wilbert and Karin Simoneau, eds., *Folk Literature of the Mataco Indians* (Los Angeles: UCLA Latin American Center Publications, 1982) 126. See also Johannes Wilbert and Karin Simoneau, eds., *Folk Literature of the Toba Indians* (Los Angeles: UCLA Latin American Center Publications, 1989), where, likewise, "Rainbow does not like women to enter water when they are menstruating" (1/88–89).

178. Wilbert and Simoneau, *Toba*, 2/94–99.

179. Ibid., 1/68–69.

180. Wilbert and Simoneau, *Sikuani*, 133. For additional examples, see Regan, *Hacia la tierra*, 130–139; Enrique Margery Peña, *El mito del diluvio en la tradición indoamericana* (Quito: Abya-Yala, 1997); and Sullivan, *Icanchu's Drum*, 57–73.

181. See Miguel León-Portilla, "Those Made Worthy by Divine Sacrifice," in Gossen, *Native Spirituality*, 42–44 and 49.

182. Geoffrey W. Conrad and Arthur A. Demarest, *Religion and Empire:*

The Dynamics of Aztec and Incan Expansionism (Cambridge: Cambridge University Press, 1984) 1.

183. Ibid., 41 and 182.

184. The quoted passage is from Reeves, *Influence*, vii.

185. Phelan, *Millennial Kingdom*, 23. See also West, "Medieval Ideas," 294–301; and Luis Weckmann, "Las esperanzas milenaristas de los franciscanos de la Nueva España," *Historia mexicana* 32/1 (1982) 89–105. For Spanish antecedents, see José Sala Catala and Jaime Vilchis Reyes, "Apocalíptica española y empresa misional en los primeros franciscanos de México," *Revista de Indias* 45/176 (1985) 421–427. For a Joachite model of sacred sites, see Richard M. Morse, "Crosscurrents in New World History," in Joseph Maier and Richard W. Weatherhead, eds., *Politics of Change in Latin America* (New York: Praeger, 1964) 46.

186. Hernán Cortés, *Letters from México*, ed. and trans. Anthony Pagden (New Haven: Yale University Press, 1986) 442–443.

187. Henrique-Osvaldo Urbano, "Dios Yaya, Dios Churi y Dios Espíritu Santo," *Journal of Latin American Lore* 6/1 (1980) 120. See also Juan M. Ossio, *Los indios del Perú* (Quito: Abya-Yala, 1995) 271–273; and Pease, *Crónicas*, 94. In some versions each Andean age is a millennium.

188. Flores Galindo, *Europa*, 45.

189. The quoted passages are in José María Arguedas, *Formación de una cultura nacional indoamericana*, ed. Angel Rama (Mexico City: Siglo Veintiuno, 1975) 181.

190. Juan M. Ossio, "El Mito de Inkarrí narrado por segunda vez diez años después," *Anthropológica* 2/2 (1984) 193. For an example of non-Joachite tripartition in indigenous discourse, see Guillermo Bonfil Batalla, ed., *Utopía y revolución: el pensamiento político contemporáneo de los indios en América Latina* (Mexico City: Editorial Nueva Imagen, 1981) 83–84.

191. Manuel Marzal, *La transformación religiosa peruana* (Lima: Pontificia Universidad Católica del Perú, 1983) 48–49. Similar myths have been collected elsewhere in Peru as well as in Bolivia and Ecuador. See Duviols, "Cinco edades," 7.

192. Quoted in Urbano, "Dios Yaya," 113. See also Thomas Muller and Helga Muller, "Mito de Inkarri-Qollari," *Allpanchis* 23 (1984) 133.

193. See Manuel M. Marzal, "La religión quechua surandina peruana," in Manuel M. Marzal, *El rostro indio de Dios* (Lima: Pontificia Universidad Católica del Perú, 1991) 261.

194. See Ortiz Echánz, "Origen," 151–155. For a quasi-Joachite succession among Tepehuans in colonial Mexico, see Huerta and Palacios, *Rebeliones*, 282.

195. Laënnec Hurbon, "New Religious Movements in the Caribbean," in James A. Beckford, ed., *New Religious Movements and Rapid Social Change* (Beverly Hills: Sage Publications, 1986) 164–165. For a quasi-Joachite periodization in highland Guatemala, see Kay B. Warren, *The Symbolism of Subordination: Indian Identity in a Guatemalan Town* (Austin: University of Texas Press, 1978) 34–41.

196. Cohn, "Medieval Millenarism," 35.

197. Alberto Flores Galindo, *Buscando un inca: identidad y utopía en los Andes* (Lima: Editorial Horizonte, 1988) 108.

198. Quoted in ibid., 57.

199. The quoted passage is from Eliade, *Myth*, 104.

200. Susan Harding, "Imagining the Last Days," in Martin E. Marty and R. Scott Appleby, eds., *Accounting for Fundamentalisms: The Dynamic Character of Movements* (Chicago: University of Chicago Press, 1994) 67.

201. Quoted in Alejandro Ortiz Rescaniere, *De Adaneva a Inkarrí: una vi-*

sión indígena del Perú (Lima: Ediciones Retablo de Papel, 1973) 33. See also Rosalind C. Gow, "Inkarrí and Revolutionary Leadership in the Southern Andes," *Journal of Latin American Lore* 8/2 (1982) 209, where a 1950 earthquake was God's punishment for cruelty and greed.

202. Wilfredo Kapsoli, *Guerreros de la oración: las nuevas iglesias en el Perú* (Lima: Sepec, 1994) 324–325. On earthquakes as signs in Mexico, see Enrique Marroquín, "Un signo apocalíptico del milenio," in Barabas, *Utopías*, 220; and Kurt Bowen, *Evangelism and Apostasy: The Evolution and Impact of Evangelicals in Modern Mexico* (Montreal: McGill-Queen's University Press, 1996) 117. For an example regarding drought, see Ricardo Falla, *Quiché rebelde: estudio de un movimiento de conversión religiosa, rebelde a las creencias tradicionales, en San Antonio Ilotenango, Quiché (1948–1970s)* (Guatemala City: Editorial Universitaria, 1980) 445.

203. Beatriz Pastor, *Discurso narrativo de la conquista de América* (Havana: Ediciones Casa de las Américas, 1983) 51.

204. The quoted phrase is in Leandro Tormo Sanz, "La cristianización de las Indias en la historia de Fernández de Oviedo," in Solano and del Pino, *América*, 94. See also Borges, "Sentido," 163.

205. See Jerry M. Williams and Robert E. Lewis, eds., *Early Images of the Americas: Transfer and Invention* (Tucson: University of Arizona Press, 1993) xxiv; and Borges, "Sentido," 145.

206. The quoted phrase is in Villoro, *Grandes momentos*, 39–40; See also Brading, *First America*, 122.

207. See Fernando Cervantes, *The Devil in the New World: The Impact of Diabolism in New Spain* (New Haven: Yale University Press, 1994) 44.

208. E. Bradford Burns, "Folk Caudillos," in Hugh M. Hamill ed., *Caudillos: Dictators in Spanish America* (Norman: University of Oklahoma Press, 1992) 123.

209. Bartolomé de Las Casas, *Brevísima relación de la destrucción de las Indias*, ed. André Saint-Lu (Madrid: Cátedra, 1984) 170 (see also 24). The second quoted passage is in Lewis Hanke, *The Spanish Struggle for Justice in the Conquest of America* (Philadelphia: University of Pennsylvania Press, 1949) 77.

210. See André Saint-Lu, introduction to Las Casas, *Brevísima relación*, 30–31. The trope is from Matthew 10:16 (see also 7:15); and Luke 10:3. See also Stelio Cro, *The American Foundations of the Hispanic Utopia (1492–1793)* (Tallahasee: DeSoto Press, 1994) 2/150.

211. Mendieta, *Historia*, 518. On the warlike Chichimeca as a divine scourge for the Spaniards' mistreatment of the Aztecs, see Philip Wayne Powell, *Soldiers, Indians, and Silver: The Northward Advance of New Spain, 1550–1600* (Berkeley and Los Angeles: University of California Press, 1952) 107.

212. See Burkhart, *Slippery Earth*, 58–59.

213. Valcárcel, *Historia*, 2/489–490.

214. Alejandro Ortiz Rescaniere, *Huarochirí: 400 años después* (Lima: Pontificia Universidad Católica del Peru, 1980) 120.

215. Wilbert and Simoneau, *Toba*, 1/332. The visit of Pope John Paul II to South America was interpreted by many Toba as a sign of the end of the world; see Sullivan, *Icanchu's Drum*, 868.

216. Tom Cummins, "A Tale of Two Cities," in Diana Fane, ed., *Converging Cultures: Art and Identity in Spanish America* (New York: Brooklyn Museum and Harry N. Abrams, 1996) 167–168.

217. The quoted phrase is from Horacio Cerutti Guldberg, "Sueño utópico, hontanar de ética política," *Cuadernos americanos* 259/2 (March–April 1985) 152.

218. See Daniel Florencio O'Leary, *Bolivar and the War of Independence*,

ed. and trans. Robert F. McNerney Jr. (Austin: University of Texas Press, 1970) 29–30.

219. Indalecio Liévano Aguirre, *Bolívar* (Madrid: Instituto de Cooperación Iberoamericana, 1983) 69.

220. See Michael Dodson and T. S. Montgomery, "The Churches in the Nicaraguan Revolution," in Thomas W. Walker, ed., *Nicaragua in Revolution* (New York: Praeger, 1982) 165–168.

221. Wilton M. Nelson, *Protestantism in Central America* (Grand Rapids: William B. Eerdmans Publishing, 1982) 73. For another Guatemalan example, see Sheldon Annis, *God and Production in a Guatemalan Town* (Austin: University of Texas Press, 1987) 1–2 and 79.

222. Quoted in Rafael Mondragón, *De indios y cristianos en Guatemala* (Mexico City: COPEC/CECOPE, 1983) 165. For a similar Argentine example, see Juan Perón *Yo, Juan Domingo Perón: relato autobiográfico*, ed. Torcuato Luca de Tena et al., (Barcelona: Editorial Planeta, 1976) 50–51 and 56.

223. See Simón Bolívar, *Selected Writings of Bolívar*, ed. Vicente Lecuna and Harold A. Bierck Jr., and trans. Lewis Bertrand (New York: Colonial Press, 1951) 1/173; Arce, *Guerra*, 181–182 (see also 169 and 201); and Leonardo Boff, *Faith on the Edge: Religion and Marginalized Existence*, trans. Robert R. Barr (San Francisco: Harper and Row, 1989) 81.

224. Quoted in Barabas, *Utopías*, 131.

225. Flores Galindo, *Buscando*, 57 and 109. On the use of the same tactics by Yahweh's heavenly army, see Miller, *Divine Warrior*, 158–159.

226. José L. Franco, "Maroons and Slave Rebellions in the Spanish Territories," in Richard Price, ed., *Maroon Societies: Rebel Slave Communities in the Americas* (Garden City, N.Y.: Anchor/Doubleday, 1973) 37. On other popular uprisings catalyzed by earthquakes, see Oswaldo Albornoz P., *Las luchas indígenas en el Ecuador* (Guayaquil, Ecuador: Editorial Claridad, 1971) 32 and 39.

227. Quoted in Gustavo Gutiérrez, *A Theology of Liberation: History, Politics and Salvation*, trans. Caridad Inda and John Eagleson (Maryknoll, N.Y.: Orbis Books, 1973) 175.

228. The first quoted passage is in ibid., 189. The second is from Gustavo Gutiérrez, *The God of Life*, trans. Matthew J. O'Connell (Maryknoll, N.Y.: Orbis Books, 1991) 104; see the milder wording of the same in G. Gutiérrez, *Theology*, 8–9.

229. See G. Gutiérrez, *Theology*, 168 and 232.

230. Ibid., 220 and 232.

231. Gustavo Gutiérrez, "Toward a Theology of Liberation," in Hennelly, *Liberation Theology*, 73.

232. For a tally of signs anticipating the Last Judgment in medieval Spain, see Milhou, *Colón*, 428.

233. Mary Elizabeth Brooks, *A King for Portugal: The Madrigal Conspiracy, 1594–95* (Madison: University of Wisconsin Press, 1964) 35–36. For comet interpretations, see Montesinos, *Memorias*, 36–37; Kapsoli, *Guerreros*, 305; Andrés Pérez de Ribas, *Historia de los triunfos de n.s. fe entre gentes las más bárbaras y fieras del nuevo orbe* (Mexico City: Editorial Layac, 1944) 3/273–274; and Santiago Sebastián, *El barroco iberoamericano: mensaje iconográfico* (Madrid: Ediciones Encuentro, 1990) 48.

234. Quoted in Manuel M. Marzal, "Transplanted Spanish Catholicism," in Gossen, *Native Spirituality*, 148.

235. The quoted passage is from Kermode, *Sense*, 95.

236. Wachtel, *Vision*, 15.

237. The last quoted phrase is from ibid. On the signs see Miguel León-Portilla, ed., *The Broken Spears: The Aztec Account of the Conquest of Mexico*

(Boston: Beacon Press, 1992) 4–6; and James Lockhart, ed. and trans., *We People Here: Nahuatl Accounts of the Conquest of Mexico* (Berkeley and Los Angeles: University of California Press, 1993) 50–56. On Inca prophesy of conquest, see MacCormack, *Religion*, 363.

238. Carlos Daniel Valcárcel, *Rebeliones coloniales sudamericanas* (Mexico City: Fondo de Cultura Económica, 1982) 95–96.

239. Kermode, *Sense*, 14.

240. The first quoted passage is from ibid., 97; and the second is from 1 Corinthians 10:11.

241. M. J. Sallnow, "A Trinity of Christs," *American Ethnologist* 9/4 (1982) 736. See also Manuel M. Marzal, *El mundo religioso de Urcos* (Cuzco: Instituto de Pastoral Andina, 1971) 225–231.

242. Kermode, "Sense," 8.

243. McGinn, *Visions*, 36.

244. Bernard McGinn, introduction to Richard K. Emmerson and Bernard McGinn, eds., *The Apocalypse in the Middle Ages* (Ithaca: Cornell University Press, 1992) 9.

245. Translation modified from Bolívar, *Selected Writings*, 1/197.

246. Ibid. The parenthetical quotation is from Américo Castro, *Aspectos del vivir hispánico* (Madrid: Alianza 1987) 128.

247. Robert C. Tucker, ed., *The Marx-Engels Reader* (New York: W. W. Norton, 1978) 597.

248. Kermode, *Sense*, 8.

249. Ibid., 17.

250. E. J. Hobsbawm, "Peasants and Politics," *Journal of Peasant Studies* 1/1 (October 1973) 13.

251. The quoted phrase is from Ernst Bloch, *The Principle of Hope*, trans. Neville Plaice et al. (Cambridge: MIT Press, 1986) 509.

252. Sullivan, *Icanchu's Drum*, 584.

253. The quoted passage is from Adela Yarbro Collins, *The Combat Myth in the Book of Revelation* (Missoula, Mont.: Scholars Press, 1976) 234.

254. The quoted phrase is from Isaiah 53:7.

255. Boff, *Faith*, 151. The quoted phrase "to die is to gain" is from Philippians 1:21; see also Romans 12:1–2.

256. Jon Sobrino, "Martyrdom of Maura, Ita, Dorothy, and Jean," in Hennelley, *Liberation Theology*, 315.

257. Quoted in Bernard McGinn, "The Meanings of the Millennium," lecture at the Inter-American Development Bank, Washington, D.C., January 1996.

258. The quoted phrase is from Regan, *Hacia la tierra*, 2/149.

259. Ibid., 2/153–154; see also 2/148.

260. Johannes Wilbert and Karin Simoneau, eds., *Folk Literature of the Chamacoco Indians* (Los Angeles: UCLA Latin American Center Publications, 1987) 114 and 129.

261. Wilbert and Simoneau, *Toba*, 1/26 (see also 1/102–103).

262. Quoted in René Ribeiro, "The Millennium That Never Came," in Ronald H. Chilcote, ed., *Protest and Resistance in Angola and Brazil: Comparative Studies* (Berkeley and Los Angeles: University of California Press, 1972) 173.

263. Bryan R. Wilson, *Magic and the Millennium: A Sociological Study of Religious Movements of Protest Among Tribal and Third-World Peoples* (London: Heinemann, 1973) 211. See also Sullivan, *Icanchu's Drum*, 575 where the tired earth says, "I have already devoured too many cadavers."

264. Quoted in Borges, "Sentido," 153.

265. See Sullivan, *Icanchu's Drum*, 577.

266. The quoted phrase is from Robert L. Spitzer et al., *DSM-III-R Case-*

book: A Learning Companion to the Diagnotic and Statistical Manual of Mental Disorders (Washington, D.C.: American Psychiatric Press, 1989) 377–378.

267. Quoted in Juan Friede, "Aportación documental al estudio de la demografía precolombina," *Revista colombiana de antropología* (1962) 311.

268. Quoted in Benno M. Biermann, "Bartolomé de Las Casas and Verapaz," in Juan Friede and Benjamin Keen, eds., *Bartolomé de Las Casas in History: Toward an Understanding of the Man and His Work* (De Kalb: Northern Illinois University Press, 1971) 475. See also Hanke, *First Social Experiments*, 68, where an Indian couple rescued their daughter from an experimental colonization project in Cuba and then hanged her and themselves.

269. Quoted in Barabas, *Utopías*, 144 and 147, respectively. For another example see Tzvetan Todorov, *The Conquest of America: The Question of the Other*, trans. Richard Howard (New York: Harper and Row, 1987) 116–117.

270. Quoted in Francisco Guerra, *The Pre-Columbian Mind* (London: Seminar Press, 1971) 253 and 876 (see also 108).

271. Quoted in Josefina Oliva de Coll, *La resistencia indígena ante la conquista* (Mexico City: Siglo Veintiuno, 1974) 38. See also Albornoz, *Luchas*, 145; and Todorov, *Conquest*, 116–117.

272. A. Alvarez, *The Savage God: A Study of Suicide* (New York: W. W. Norton, 1990) 75.

273. Oliva de Coll, *Resistencia*, 41. The cacique was burned alive. A Pueblo man encouraged to surrender in peace responded that he preferred to die and go to hell, and the obliging Spaniards killed him; see Charles Wilson Hackett, ed., *Revolt of the Pueblo Indians of New Mexico and Otermín's Attempted Reconquest, 1680–1682* (Albuquerque: University of New Mexico Press, 1970) 1/lviii.

274. See Germán Carrera Damas, "Huida y enfrentamiento," in Manuel Moreno Fraginals, ed., *Africa en América Latina* (Mexico City: Siglo Veintiuno, 1977) 42–43; and Solange Alberro, *Inquisición y sociedad en México* (Mexico City: Fondo de Cultura Económica, 1988) 263–264. On suicide as return to Africa, see Esteban Montejo, *The Autobiography of a Runaway Slave*, ed. Miguel Barnet (New York: Pantheon Books, 1968) 43–44; and Carlos Federico Guillot, *Negros rebeldes y negros cimarrones* (Buenos Aires: Fariña Editores, 1961) 36.

275. Quoted in Huerta and Palacios, *Rebeliones*, 39. Yucatec Maya "hanged themselves in the bush and uninhabited sites and hidden places" rather than abandon their religion; see Irwin Press, "Historical Dimensions of Orientation to Change in a Yucatec Peasant Community," in Grant D. Jones, ed., *Anthropology and History in Yucatán* (Austin: University of Texas Press, 1977) 280.

276. See Leopoldo Lugones, *El imperio jesuítico* (Buenos Aires: Comisión Argentina de Fomento Interamericano, 1945) 154; Wachtel, *Vision*, 27–29; and Ward Alan Minge, *Acoma: Pueblo in the Sky* (Albuquerque: University of New Mexico Press, 1991) 12.

277. Quoted in Wachtel, *Vision*, 27.

278. Quoted in Clendinnen, *Ambivalent Conquests*, 191 and 139. See also Brotherston, *Book*, 149.

279. The first quoted passage is in Steve Stern, *Populism in Peru: The Emergence of the Masses and the Politics of Social Control* (Madison: University of Wisconsin Press, 1980) 143; and the second is in Arturo Warman, *"We Come to Object": The Peasants of Morelos and the National State,* trans. Stephen K. Ault (Baltimore: Johns Hopkins University Press, 1980) 113–114. On fatalism in a messianic Mexican uprising ("we will lose and die"), see Paul J. Vanderwood, *The Power of God Against the Guns of the Government* (Stanford: Stanford University Press, 1998) 285 and 276.

280. Quoted in Herbert Braun, *The Assassination of Gaitán: Public Life and Urban Violence in Colombia* (Madison: University of Wisconsin Press, 1985) 45.

281. Osmán Morote, "A Frightening Thirst for Vengeance," in Orin Starn et al., eds., *The Peru Reader: History, Culture, Politics* (Durham: Duke University Press, 1995) 309.

282. Braun, *Assassination*, 159–160.

Chapter 2

1. William H. Crocker and Jean Crocker, *The Canela: Bonding Through Kinship, Ritual, and Sex* (New York: Harcourt Brace College Publishers, 1994) 22–23 and 42–43. Dry Woman turned out to be a deformed, stillborn male. For a similar myth of weapon distribution from the Brazilian jungle, see Johannes Wilbert and Karen Simoneau, eds., *Folk Literature of the Gê Indians* (Los Angeles: UCLA Latin American Center Publications, 1978) 126–134.

2. See James C. Scott, *Weapons of the Weak: Everyday forms of Peasant Resistance* (New Haven: Yale University Press, 1985) 331. For a nineteenth-century Spanish illustration of the *mundo al revés*, see Marion Oettinger Jr., ed., *Folk Art of Spain and the Americas: El Alma del Pueblo* (New York: San Antonio Museum of Art and Abbeville Press, 1997) 48.

3. The quoted passage is from Luis Arce Borja, ed., *Guerra popular en el Perú: el pensamiento gonzalo* (Brussels: n.p. 1989) 255.

4. Barbara G. Myerhoff, "Return to Wirikuta," in Barbara A. Babcock, *The Reversible World: Symbolic Inversion in Art and Society* (Ithaca: Cornell University Press, 1978) 222–223 and 236–237. Ritual redefinition likewise remakes the Huichol world: eyes are tomatoes, a burro is a cow, a piglet is an armadillo, a deer is a cat, and so on.

5. Quoted in Charles R. Hale, *Resistance and Contradiction: Miskitu Indians and the Nicaraguan State, 1894–1987* (Stanford: Stanford University Press, 1994) 64.

6. Quoted in María Teresa Huerta and Patricia Palacios, *Rebeliones indígenas de la época colonial* (Mexico City: Instituto Nacional de Antropología e Historia, 1976) 112.

7. Quoted in José María Arguedas, *Formación de una cultura nacional indoamericana*, Angel Rama, ed. (Mexico City: Siglo Veintiuno, 1975) 177. See also Alejandro Ortiz Rescaniere, *De Adaneva a Inkarrí: una visión indígena del Perú* (Lima: Ediciones Retablo de Papel, 1973) 14: "We make the *mistis* and *señores* work under the threat of our whips."

8. See Alberto Flores Galindo, *Buscando un inca: identidad y utopía en los Andes* (Lima: Editorial Horizonte, 1988) 23–24 and 419. José María Arguedas's "The Pongo's Dream" is translated in Orin Starn et al., eds., *The Peru Reader: History Culture, Politics* (Durham: Duke University Press, 1995) 258–263. Something of the same degradation is actualized in torture by immersion in excrement, which was common during Alfredo Stroessner's 1954–89 dictatorship in Paraguay.

9. Anatilde Idoyaga Molina, "Una esperanza milenarista entre los Pilagá (Chaco Central)," in Alicia Barabas, ed., *Religiosidad y resistencia indígenas hacia el fin del milenio* (Quito: Abya-Yala, 1994) 68.

10. Leopoldo J. Bartolomé, "Movimientos milenaristas de los aborígenes chaqueños entre 1905 y 1933," *Suplemento antropológico* 7/1–2 (1972) 110. For Andean examples, see Jan Szemiński, "El único español bueno es el español muerto," in Juan Ansión, ed., *Pishtacos: de verdugos a sacaojos* (Lima: Tarea, 1989) 24–28.

11. Quoted in Serge Gruzinski, *Man-Gods in the Mexican Highlands*, trans. Eileen Corrigan (Stanford: Stanford University Press, 1989) 163.

12. Ramón A. Gutiérrez, *When Jesus Came, the Corn Mothers Went Away: Marriage, Sexuality, and Power in New Mexico: 1500–1846* (Stanford: Stanford University Press, 1991) 195.

13. Quoted in Boleslao Lewin, *La rebelión de Túpac Amaru y los orígenes de la emancipación americana* (Buenos Aires: Librería Hachette, 1957) 724.

14. See Victoria Bricker, *The Indian Christ, the Indian King: The Historical Substrate of Maya Myth and Ritual* (Austin: University of Texas Press, 1986) 62; and Kevin Gosner, *Soldiers of the Virgin: The Moral Economy of a Colonial Maya Rebellion* (Tucson: University of Arizona Press, 1992) 143. Converted Tarahumaras also referred to the unbaptized Indians among them as Jews; see William L. Merrill, "Conversion and Colonialism in Northern Mexico," in Robert W. Hefner, ed., *Conversion to Christianity: Historical and Anthropological Perspectives on a Great Transformation* (Berkeley and Los Angeles: University of California Press, 1993) 155.

15. See Robert Wasserstrom, *Class and Society in Central Chiapas* (Berkeley and Los Angeles: University of California Press, 1983) 81–82.

16. Alicia M. Barabas, *Utopías indias: movimientos sociorreligiosos en México* (Mexico City: Grijalbo, 1987) 180; and Bricker, *Indian Christ*, 63.

17. June Nash, "The Passion Play in Maya Indian Communities," *Comparative Studies in Society and History* 10 (1967–68) 320.

18. Flores Galindo, *Buscando*, 42.

19. See Szemiński, "Unico español," 22–24.

20. Barabas, *Utopías*, 180; and Bricker, *Indian Christ*, 63.

21. Lewin, *Rebelión*, 574; and E. J. Hobsbawm, "Peasants and Politics," *Journal of Peasant Studies* 1/1 (October 1973) 6.

22. See Felipe Fernández-Armesto, *Columbus and the Conquest of the Impossible* (New York: Saturday Review Press, 1974) 109.

23. Francisco López de Gómara, *Historia general de las Indias y vida de Hernán Cortés* (Caracas: Biblioteca Ayacucho, 1979) 15–16.

24. John Mandeville, *The Travels of Sir John Mandeville*, trans. and intro. C. W. R. D. Moseley (Harmondsworth, England: Penguin Books, 1983) 129.

25. See Rudolf Wittkower, *Allegory and the Migration of Symbols* (London: Thames and Hudson, 1977); regarding the feet turned backward, see 60–61. In modern times Sendero Luminoso followed an Andean tactic of ritual defense by amputating hands and feet of some victims and then sewing them to their corpses backward. For a "schema of inversions" concerning the Amazonas, see Frank Lestringant, *Mapping the Renaissance World: The Geographical Imagination in the Age of Discovery*, trans. David Fausett (Cambridge: Polity Press, 1994) 79.

26. The first quoted passage is in Anthony Pagden, "*Ius et Factum*," in Stephen Greenblatt, ed., *New World Encounters* (Berkeley and Los Angeles: University of California Press, 1993) 87; and the second is in Barbara A. Babcock, introduction to Babcock, *Reversible World*, 13. Evidence from the field, such as the inversion of seasons south of the equator, contributed to these perceptions; see Fernando Ainsa, *De la edad de oro a El Dorado: génesis del discurso utópico americano* (Mexico City: Fondo de Cultura Económica, 1992) 64. See also Paulo Suess, *La nueva evangelización: desafíos históricos y pautas culturales*, trans. María Victoria C. de Vela (Abya-Yala, 1991) 220: "Here everything is different" but "the difference is in ourselves; we need to modify our concepts."

27. The quoted phrase is from Cristóbal Colón, *Textos y documentos completos: relaciones de viajes, cartas y memorias*, ed. Consuelo Varela (Madrid: Alianza, 1984) 141.

28. López de Gómara, *Historia*, 45. For Bernardino de Sahagún, the Aztec

deities were "not gods, but all devils"; see Luis Villoro, *Los grandes momentos del indigenismo en México* (Mexico City: Colegio de México, 1950) 30–31; and Elsa Cecilia Frost, "Indians and Theologians," in Gary H. Gossen, ed., *South and Meso-American Native Spirituality: From the Cult of the Feathered Serpent to the Theology of Liberation* (New York: Crossroad, 1993) 135. On "abominable ministers of the devil" in the Andes, see Pierre Duviols, *Cultura andina y represión: procesos y visitas de idolatrías y hechicerías en Cajatambo, siglo XVII* (Cuzco: Centro de Estudios Rurales Andinos Bartolomé de Las Casas, 1986) xxix.

29. Quoted in Rafael Villamar, "El liberalismo teórico y práctico," in Arturo Andrés Roig, ed., *La utopía en el Ecuador* (Quito: Banco Central del Ecuador and Corporación Editora Nacional, 1987) 354.

30. Quoted in Jeffrey Klaiber, *The Catholic Church in Peru, 1821–1985* (Washington: Catholic University of America Press, 1992) 60. See also Robert C. Tucker, ed., *The Marx-Engels Reader* (New York: W. W. Norton, 1978) 133–134. For an example of liberal-conservative polarization, see Florencia E. Mallon, *Peasant and Nation: The Making of Postcolonial Mexico and Peru* (Berkeley and Los Angeles: University of California Press, 1995) 23–62. In 1948 rampaging Colombian liberals decapitated conservatives and played soccer with the heads. See David Bushnell, *The Making of Modern Colombia: A Nation in Spite of Itself* (Berkeley and Los Angeles: University of California Press, 1993) 202.

31. Quoted in Carlos Malamud, *Juan Manuel de Rosas* (Madrid: Historia 16, 1987) 137.

32. See Ponciano del Pino, "Peasants at War," in Starn et al., *Peru Reader*, 380; and Carlos Iván Degregori, "Cosechando tempestades," in Carlos Iván Degregori, ed., *Las rondas campesinas y la derrota de Sendero Luminoso* (Lima: Instituto de Estudios Peruanos, 1996) 212.

33. The quoted phrases are in Barabas, *Utopías*, 257.

34. Judith Kimerling, "Dislocation, Evangelization, and Contamination," in Working Papers Series 215, *Ethnic Conflict and Governance in Comparative Perspective* (Washington, D.C.: Latin American Program, Woodrow Wilson International Center for Scholars, 1995) 71 and 75.

35. Alicia M. Barabas, "Identidad y cultura en nuevas iglesias milenaristas en México," in Barabas, *Religiosidad*, 262.

36. See William L. Merrill, *Rarámuri Souls: Knowledge and Social Process in Northern Mexico* (Washington, D.C.: Smithsonian Institution Press, 1988) 78 and 93–94.

37. Quoted in William W. Stein, "Myth and Ideology in a Nineteenth Century Peruvian Peasant Uprising," *Ethnohistory* 29/1–4 (1982) 252. In the historical account, Charles V was, in his own words, "displeased by the death of Atahualpa, since he was a monarch"; see John Hemming, *The Conquest of the Incas* (New York: Harvest/Harcourt Brace Jovanovich, 1970) 81. Charles III was horrified by the gruesome execution of Túpac Amaru II; see Lillian Estelle Fisher, *The Last Inca Revolt, 1780–1783* (Norman: University of Oklahoma Press, 1966) 239 and 384–386.

38. Quoted in Flores Galindo, *Buscando*, 59. Unification is also registered in the composite term Inkarrí (Inca-king) and in reference to the king as "Inca of the Spaniards" and "the Catholic Inca"; see Franklin Pease, *El dios creador andino* (Lima: Mosca Azul Editores, 1973) 88; and D. A. Brading, *The First America: The Spanish Monarchy, Creole Patriots, and the Liberal State, 1492–1867* (Cambridge: Cambridge University Press, 1991) 395.

39. See Mario Castro Arenas, *La rebelión de Juan Santos* (Lima: Carlos Milla Batres, 1973) 82.

40. Alonso Zarzar, *Apo Capac Huayna, Jesús Sacramentado: Mito, utopía*

y milenarismo (Lima: Centro Amazónico de Antropología y Aplicación Práctica, 1989) 43.

41. See Anthony F. C. Wallace, "Revitalization Movements," *American Anthropologist* 58 (1956) 277.

42. Quoted in Maria Helena Moreira Alves, "Grassroots Organizations, Trade Unions, and the Church," in Jorge I. Domínguez, ed., *The Roman Catholic Church in Latin America* (New York: Garland Publishing, 1994) 279.

43. Both quoted passages are in Enrique Dussel, "Religiosidad popular latinoamericana," in Frans Damen and Esteban Judd Zanon, eds., *Cristo crucificado en los pueblos de América Latina: antología de la religión popular* (Cuzco: Instituto de Pastoral Andina; and Quito: Abya-Yala, 1992) 44–45. For another example, see Christián Parker, *Popular Religion and Modernization in Latin America*, trans. Robert R. Barr (Maryknoll, N.Y.: Orbis Books, 1996) 161. One is reminded of the earlier soldiers' slogan: Praise the Lord and pass the ammo.

44. Quoted in Betsy Cohn and Patricia Hynds, "The Manipulation of the Religion Issue," in Thomas W. Walker, ed., *Reagan Versus the Sandinistas: The Undeclared War on Nicaragua* (Boulder: Westview Press, 1987) 106.

45. Quoted in Kurt Glaser, "Nineteenth-Century Messianism and Twentieth-Century Interventionism," *Modern Age* (Winter 1973) 20.

46. Quoted in Ernest Lee Tuveson, *The Redeemer Nation: America's Millennial Role* (Chicago: University of Chicago Press, 1968) vii.

47. See Exodus 19:3–6 and Charles Augustus Briggs, *Messianic Prophesy* (New York: Charles Scribner's Sons, 1886) 102–103.

48. Quoted in Kurt Ritter and David Henry, *Ronald Reagan: The Great Communicator* (New York: Greenwood Press, 1992) 16–19; see also 130, where Reagan is "toe to toe with this enemy—this evil force."

49. Deborah Poole and Gerard Rénique, *Peru: Time of Fear* (London: Latin America Bureau, 1992) 48 and 50. See also Arce *Guerra*, 199; and Gustavo Gorriti Ellenbogen, *Sendero: historia de la guerra milenaria en el Perú* (Lima: Apoyo, 1990) 351.

50. Gordon H. McCormick, "The Shining Path and Peruvian Terrorism," in David C. Rapoport, *Inside Terrorist Organizations* (New York: Columbia University Press, 1988) 121.

51. Quoted in Poole and Rénique, *Peru*, 2. See also Arce, *Guerra*, 191 and 199.

52. Abimael Guzmán, quoted in "Entrevista al Presidente Gonzalo," 17. Gonzalo was Guzmán's nom de guerre.

53. Arce, *Guerra*, 165.

54. Quoted in Gorriti, *Sendero*, 372; and in José Coronel, "Violencia política y respuestas campesinas en Huanta," in Degregori, *Rondas*, 81.

55. Degregori, "Cosechando," 203. The villagers were forbidden to bury the body.

56. Quoted in Carlos Iván Degregori, "Return to the Past," in David Scott Palmer, ed., *The Shining Path of Peru* (New York: St. Martin's Press, 1992) 38.

57. The quoted phrase is from Arce, *Guerra*, 233.

58. Quoted in Robin Kirk, *Grabado en piedra: las mujeres de Sendero Luminoso* (Lima: Instituto de Estudios Peruanos, 1993) 39–40.

59. Quoted in Americas Watch, *Human Rights in Guatemala: No Neutrals Allowed* (New York: Americas Watch, 1982) 14.

60. Quoted in ibid., 18. For testimony see Americas Watch, *Creating a Desolation and Calling It Peace* (New York: Americas Watch, 1983) 15–21.

61. Quoted in Americas Watch, *Human Rights*, 10.

62. Quoted in Argentine Commission for Human Rights, *Argentina: proceso al genocidio* (Madrid: Elías Querejeta Ediciones, 1977) 13.

63. See Frank Graziano, *Divine Violence: Spectacle, Psychosexuality, and Radical Christianity in the Argentine "Dirty War"* (Boulder: Westview Press, 1992) 128.

64. See Barabas, "Identidad," 257–259; see also 255–256 on the New Jerusalem sect.

65. The Spanish passage is in Rubén Bareiro-Saguier, "Reinterpretación de los mitos fundacionales guaraníes," in Manuel Gutiérrez Estévez, ed., *Mito y ritual en América* (Madrid: Editorial Alhambra, 1988) 324. The same is true of such shorthand signifiers as *black, white, mestizo,* and *mulatto,* which collapse diversity into easily exploited stereotypes.

66. Edison Carneiro, *Guerras de los Palmares,* trans. Tomás Muñoz Molina (Mexico City: Fondo de Cultura Económica, 1946) 9.

67. João José Reis, *Slave Rebellion in Brazil* (Ann Arbor, Mich.: University Microfilms International, 1984) 103, 161, and 281.

68. The quoted passage is from Alberto Flores Galindo, "Los sueños de Gabriel Aguilar," *Debates en sociología* 11 (1985) 173.

69. See Guillermo Bonfil Batalla, ed., *Utopía y revolución: el pensamiento político contemporáneo de los indios en América Latina* (Mexico City: Editorial Nueva Imagen, 1981) 37, 44, 46, and 97.

70. José María Morelos, "Banda de abolición de las castas y la esclavitud," in Albelardo Villegas, ed. *Antología del pensamiento social y político de América Latina* (Washington, D.C.: Unión Panamericana, 1964) 108.

71. Eric Van Young, "Millennium on the Northern Marches," *Comparative Studies in Society and History* 28 (July 1986) 404.

72. Daniel Florencio O'Leary, *Bolivar and the War of Independence,* ed. and trans. Robert F. McNerney Jr. (Austin: University of Texas Press, 1970) 61.

73. Ibid., 50.

74. All quoted passages are from Simón Bolívar, *Doctrina del Libertador,* ed. Manuel Pérez Vila (Caracas: Biblioteca Ayacucho, 1979) 22. See also Francisco de Miranda, "Proclamación a los pueblos del continente colombiano," in Villegas, *Antología,* 77–94. For war to the death in the rebellion of Túpac Catari, see Carlos Daniel Valcárcel, *Rebeliones coloniales sudamericanas* (Mexico City: Fondo de Cultura Económica, 1982) 95.

75. On Noah see Genesis 7–8; and on the millennial kingdom, see Revelation 20–21. See also Isaiah 1:9, 10:20, and 37:31–32.

76. The first quoted phrase is from Hebrews 10:10; and the second is from I Peter 1:3. On the new Noah, see Mircea Eliade, *The Sacred and the Profane: The Nature of Religion,* trans. Willard R. Trask (New York: Harper Torchbooks, 1961) 132–133.

77. Quoted in Abelino Martínez, *Las sectas en Nicaragua: oferta y demanda de salvación* (Managua: Editorial Departamento Ecuménico de Investigaciones, 1989) 93. See also Wilfredo Kapsoli, *Guerreros de la oración: las nuevas iglesias en el Perú* (Lima: Sepec, 1994) 305. For antecedents in Judeo-Christian apocalypses, see Jean Delumeau, *History of Paradise: The Garden of Eden in Myth and Tradition,* trans. Matthew O'Connell (New York: Continuum, 1995) 23–29.

78. René Ribeiro, "The Millennium That Never Came," in Ronald H. Chilcote, ed., *Protest and Resistance in Angola and Brazil: Comparative Studies* (Berkeley and Los Angeles: University of California Press, 1972) 170–172.

79. Dino Kraspedon, *My Contact with Flying Saucers,* trans. J. B. Wood (Hackensack, N.J.: Neville Spearman/Wehman Brothers, 1959) 55 (see also 25–26).

80. Eduardo Viveiros de Castro, *From the Enemy's Point of View: Hu-*

manity and Divinity in an Amazonian Society, trans. Catherine V. Howard (Chicago: University of Chicago Press, 1992) 59.

81. Jaime Regan, *Hacia la tierra sin mal: estudio sobre la religiosidad del pueblo en la Amazonía* (Iquitos, Peru: CETA, 1983) 2/153.

82. Quoted in Gonzalo Castillo-Cárdenas, *Liberation Theology from Below: The Life and Thought of Manuel Quintín Lame* (Maryknoll, N.Y.: Orbis Books, 1987) 151.

83. Barabas, *Utopías*, 232–252.

84. Sebastian Balfour, *Castro* (London: Longman, 1995) 80. For a religious example, see David J. Hess, *Spirits and Scientists: Ideology, Spiritism, and Brazilian Culture* (University Park: Pennsylvania State University Press, 1991) 77.

85. The quoted passages are from Jay Mallin, ed., *"Che" Guevara on Revolution: A Documentary Overview* (Coral Gables: University of Miami Press, 1969) 133.

86. Donald C. Hodges, *The Latin American Revolution* (New York: William Morrow, 1974) 134

87. John Gerassi, ed., *Venceremos! The Speeches and Writings of Ernesto Che Guevara* (New York: Macmillan, 1968) 398.

88. Ibid., 392.

89. Mallin, *"Che" Guevara*, 139.

90. Gerassi, *Venceremos!* 394.

91. Mallin, *"Che" Guevara*, 84, 131–132, 136, 140, and 143. See also Gerassi, *Venceremos!* 390.

92. Quoted in Fernando Nadra, *Conversaciones con Perón* (Buenos Aires: Editorial Anteo, 1985) 126.

93. Eva Perón, *Escribe Eva Perón* (Buenos Aires: n.p., 1950) 14–15.

94. Quoted in Richard H. Immerman, *The CIA in Guatemala* (Austin: University of Texas Press, 1982) 48; and Donald Hodges, *Sandino's Communism: Spiritual Politics for the Twenty-first Century* (Austin: University of Texas Press, 1992) 112. For Abimael Guzmán on violence as purifying, see, for example, Arce, *Guerra*, 201.

95. Teófilo Cabestrero, *Ministers of God, Ministers of the People: Testimonies of Faith from Nicaragua*, trans. Robert R. Barr (Maryknoll, N.Y.: Orbis Books, 1983) 32. For other examples, see Edward A. Lynch, *Religion and Politics in Latin America: Liberation Theology and Christian Democracy* (New York: Praeger, 1991) 25; and John Joseph Marsden, *Marxian and Christian Utopianism: Toward a Socialist Political Theory* (New York: Monthly Review Press, 1991) 93 and 100–101.

96. Quoted in Lynch, *Religion*, 92.

97. Leonardo Boff, *Faith on the Edge: Religion and Marginalized Existence* (San Francisco: Harper and Row, 1989) 22.

98. See Manuel Marzal, *Los caminos religiosos de los inmigrantes en la gran Lima: el caso de El Agustino* (Lima: Pontificia Universidad Católica del Perú, 1989) 209. Paul's quoted passage is from 2 Corinthians 5:17. See also Galatians 6:15.

99. Gustavo Gutiérrez M., "Notes for a Theology of Liberation," in Domínguez, *Roman Catholic Church*, 31; and Gustavo Gutiérrez, *A Theology of Liberation: History, Politics and Salvation*, ed. and trans. Caridad Inda and John Eagleson (Maryknoll, N.Y.: Orbis Books, 1973) 231.

100. Quoted in Michael A. Burdick, *For God and the Fatherland: Religion and Politics in Argentina* (Albany: State University of New York Press, 1995) 190.

101. Rafael Mondragón, *De indios y cristianos en Guatemala* (Mexico City: COPEC/CECOPE, 1983) 22 (see also 224).

102. The quoted phrases are in Leonardo Boff, *Liberating Grace*, trans. John Drury (Maryknoll, N.Y.: Orbis Books, 1981) 166.

103. Quoted in Mondragón, *De indios*, 69.

104. See Kenneth P. Langton, "The Church, Social Consciousness, and Protest," in Domínguez, *Roman Catholic Church*, 329. The Protestant Declaration of Jarabacoa of 1983 also held that sin had "acquired a social dimension"; see Pablo Alberto Deiros, ed., *Los evangélicos y el poder político en América Latina* (Grand Rapids: Nueva Creación and William B. Eerdmans Publishing, 1986) 348.

105. Mondragón, *De indios*, 61–62.

106. Paulo Freire, "Conscientizing as a Way of Liberating," in Alfred T. Hennelly, ed. and trans., *Liberation Theology: A Documentary History* (Maryknoll, N.Y.: Orbis Books, 1990) 11.

107. Quoted in José Luis González, "Cristo: el centro de la fe popular," in Damen and Judd Zanon, eds., *Cristo*, 89.

108. Luke 23:14 (see also 23:2 and 23:5); and Matthew 10:38 (see also 10: 16–39 and 24:5).

109. José Luis González Martínez, *La religión popular en el Perú* (Cuzco: Instituto de Pastoral Andina, 1987) 74, 187, 198, 199, and 202. The greatest consensus—64 percent—believed that God endorsed and supported the struggle, because "God inspires what is just."

110. Quoted in Yvon Le Bot, *La guerra en las tierras mayas: comunidad, violencia y modernidad en Guatemala (1970–1992)* (Mexico City: Fondo de Cultura Económica, 1995) 268.

111. Quoted in John Burdick, *Looking for God in Brazil: The Progressive Catholic Church in Brazil's Religious Arena* (Berkeley and Los Angeles: University of California Press, 1993) 184.

112. Quoted in Le Bot, *Guerra*, 147.

113. Camilo Torres, *Cristianismo y revolución*, ed. Oscar Madonado et al. (Mexico City: Ediciones Era, 1970) 526.

114. Quoted in Mondragón, *De indios*, 65–66.

115. Quoted in Le Bot, *Guerra*, 144.

116. Quoted in Fernando Mires, *La rebelión permanente: las revoluciones sociales en América Latina* (Mexico City: Siglo Veintiuno, 1988) 413. Clergy have taken up arms on occasion throughout Latin American history. For a colonial example, see Alberto Armani, *Ciudad de Dios y Ciudad del Sol: el "estado" jesuita de los guaraníes, 1609–1768* (Mexico City: Fondo de Cultura Económica, 1982) 84.

117. Quoted in Burdick, *Looking*, 1.

118. Quoted in Marzal, *Caminos*, 206.

119. The first quoted phrase is from Gustavo Gutiérrez, *The God of Life*, trans. Matthew J. O'Connell (Maryknoll, N.Y.: Orbis Books, 1991) 104. See Psalms 37:11; Isaiah 14:12–15; Ezekiel 28:12–19; and Luke 6:20.

120. G. Gutiérrez, *God*, 117.

121. Gustavo Gutiérrez, *The Truth Shall Make You Free: Confrontations*, trans. Matthew J. O'Connell (Maryknoll, N.Y.: Orbis Books, 1990) 152.

122. Sheldon H. Davis, "Guatemala: The Evangelical Holy War in El Quiché," *Global Reporter* 1/1 (1983) 7–8; and Minor Sinclair, "Faith, Community, and Resistance in the Guatemalan Highlands," in Minor Sinclair, ed., *The New Politics of Survival: Grassroots Movements in Central America* (New York: Monthly Review Press, 1995) 90.

123. See Sinclair, "Faith," 91–'92.

124. The quoted phrase is from Rigoberta Menchú, *I, Rigoberta Menchú: An Indian Woman in Guatemala*, ed. Elisabeth Burgos-Debray, trans. Ann

Wright (London: Verso, 1984) 134 (see also 131–140). Many Catholics buried their hymnals; see Mondragón, *De indios*, 67.

125. Fernando Bermúdez, *Death and Resurrection in Guatemala*, trans. Robert R. Barr (Maryknoll, N.Y.: Orbis Books, 1986) 28–29.

126. Sinclair, "Faith," 76–77.

127. See Linda Green, "Shifting Affiliations: Mayan Widows and *Evangélicos* in Guatemala," in Virginia Garrard-Burnett and David Stoll, eds., *Rethinking Protestantism in Latin America* (Philadelphia: Temple University Press, 1993) 161.

128. Sheldon Annis, *God and Production in a Guatemalan Town* (Austin: University of Texas Press, 1987) 79.

129. Quoted in Kapsoli, *Guerreros*, 219. Some two-thirds to three-quarters of Latin American Protestants are Pentecostals; see David Stoll, introduction to Garrard-Burnett and Stoll, *Rethinking*, 2–3. For a secular complement in rebirth of revolutionary cadres, see Kirk, *Grabado*, 41; and Arce, *Guerra*, 155.

130. See Eliade, *Sacred*, 132–133. See also René Ribeiro, "Relations of the Negro with Christianity in Portuguese America," *The Americas* 14/4 (1958) 481, where through gifts of the Holy Spirit, "a person becomes like a child, the world seems to a person like a cemetery."

131. See Romans 6:5–11; and 2 Corinthians 5:17, respectively.

132. On gifts of the Holy Spirit, see also Mark 16:17–18 (here they seem gifts of Jesus); Acts 2:38, 10:46–47, and 19:6; and John 20:22–23. In 1 Corinthians 14, prophesy is preferred to speaking in tongues because "unless you speak intelligible words with your tongue, how will anyone know what you are saying?"

133. Israelites of the New Covenant hold that "airplanes will be coming to take us to all the countries of the world" where "we will have no problems with language, because God will give us the gift of speech in all the 1664 languages of the world"; see Harald O. Skar, "Quest for a New Covenant: The Israelita Movement in Peru," in Harald O. Skar and Frank Salomon, eds., *Natives and Neighbors in South America* (Göteborg, Sweden: Ethnological Studies 38, 1987) 241–242.

134. Felicitas D. Goodman, "Apostolics of Yucatán: A Case Study of a Religious Movement," in Erika Bourguignon, ed., *Religion, Altered States of Consciousness, and Social Change* (Columbus: Ohio State University Press, 1973) 185–186.

135. 2 Corinthians 5:13. See also Acts 26:24.

136. Quoted in Alvaro Huerga, *Historia de los alumbrados*, vol. 3, *Los alumbrados de Hispanoamérica* (Madrid: Fundación Universitaria Española, Seminario Cisneros, 1986) 418. Fray Francisco also suggested that "the Pope lives more like a king than like St. Peter" and that the viceroyalty should tend to the needs of its subjects rather than to "making money for the king" (420–421).

137. The quoted phrase is from Inga Clendinnen, "Fierce and Unnatural Cruelty," in Greenblatt, *New World Encounters*, 12. For examples from Spanish chronicles, see Pedro Borges, "El sentido trascendente del descubrimiento y conversión de Indias," *Missionalia Hispánica* 13/37 (1956) 158–160.

138. Quoted in B. Salazar, *Los doce: primeros apóstoles franciscanos en México* (Mexico City: Imprenta Mexicana, 1943) 25–26. See also Hebrews 4:12, where the word of God is likened to a sword.

139. Quoted in Burdick, *For God*, 46.

140. Quoted in Kapsoli, *Guerreros*, 14 and 403. See also 2 Corinthians 10:3–4.

141. Quoted in ibid., 326 (see also 189).

142. Quoted in del Pino, "Peasants," 379. Sendero often attacked during

religious services and festivals, combining the practical benefit of surprising congregated enemies with an opportunity to violate the sacrosanct; see Coronel, "Violencia," 50.

143. See Kapsoli, *Guerreros*, 334. The quoted passages are from Revelation 6:8.

144. Quoted in del Pino, "Peasants," 380. See also Kapsoli, *Guerreros*, 318 and 329–330.

145. See Arce, *Guerra*, 141–143; Poole and Rénique, *Peru*, 41 and 43; and Gorriti, *Sendero*, 58. "Holy family" was used in reference to Guzmán's coterie of close associates in Ayacucho.

146. Quoted in Gorriti, *Sendero*, 356.

147. Quoted in Flores Galindo, *Buscando*, 329; and in William Rowe and Vivian Schelling, *Memory and Modernity: Popular Culture in Latin America* (London: Verso, 1991) 155. Mariátegui evidenced an early, strong religious conviction; see Jeffrey L. Klaiber, *Religion and Revolution in Peru, 1824–1976* (Notre Dame, Ind.: University of Notre Dame Press, 1977) 94–96.

148. Quoted in Flores Galindo, *Buscando*, 375.

149. Quoted in ibid., 374.

150. Quoted in Orin Starn, "Senderos," in Degregori, *Rondas*, 235.

151. Sergio Ramírez and Robert Edgar Conrad, eds., *Sandino: The Testimony of a Nicaraguan Patriot, 1921–1934*, trans. Robert Edgar Conrad (Princeton: Princeton University Press, 1990) 361–362.

152. See Alfredo Silletta, *Las sectas invaden la Argentina* (Buenos Aires: Puntosur, 1991) 97–107.

153. Quoted in María Albán Estrada and Juan Pablo Muñoz, *Con Dios todo se puede: la invasión de las sectas al Ecuador* (Quito: Editorial Planeta, 1987) 129 (see also 128–133).

154. Quoted in ibid., 125.

155. Quoted in Frederick M. Nunn, *The Time of the Generals: Latin American Professional Militarism in World Perspective* (Lincoln: University of Nebraska Press, 1992) 117.

156. Ibid., 120 and 124.

157. Ibid., 183.

158. See, for example, Diana Fane, ed., *Converging Cultures: Art and Identity in Spanish America* (New York: Brooklyn Museum and Harry N. Abrams, 1996) 227 and 228; and Fernando Silva Santisteban, "El pensamiento mágico-religioso en el Perú contemporáneo," in *Historia del Perú* (Lima: Editorial Juan Mejía Baca, 1980) 12/53.

159. Brian Loveman and Thomas M. Davies Jr., *The Politics of Antipolitics: The Military in Latin America* (Lincoln: University of Nebraska Press, 1989) 195.

160. See Burdick, *For God*, 128.

161. See Graziano, *Divine Violence*, 13.

162. See Kenneth Aman, "Fighting for God: The Military and Religion in Chile," *Cross Currents* 36 (November 1987) 459–460; and Humberto Lagos Schuffeneger and Arturo Chacón Herrera, *La religión en las fuerzas armadas y de orden* (Santiago: Presor, 1987) 45–48.

163. Aman, "Fighting," 460.

164. Quoted in ibid., 461–462 (see also 465).

165. See Lagos and Chacón, *Religión*, 15, 16, 19, 24, 26, 29, and 30. See also Brian H. Smith, *The Church and Politics in Chile* (Princeton: Princeton University Press, 1982) 300.

166. Le Bot, *Guerra*, 227. For perceptions of Ríos Montt's abuse of religion to political ends, see Mondragón, *De indios*, 171.

167. See Robert Lawrence, "Bucks for Butchers," *Covert Action* 18 (1983)

34–37. Ríos Montt had extensive counterinsurgency training in the United States.

168. Quoted in Gerald Colby with Charlotte Dennett, *Thy Will Be Done: The Conquest of the Amazon* (New York: HarperCollins, 1995) 816–817; and in Davis, "Guatemala," 10.

169. Mondragón, *De indios*, 173.

170. Quoted in Silleta, *Sectas*, 51.

171. Quoted in Davis, "Guatemala," 10; and Jane Bussey, "Guatemalan Makes Comeback," *Christian Science Monitor* (July 11, 1990) 2.

172. Quoted in Silleta, *Sectas*, 51. See Mondragón, *De indios*, 150–151 on the anointment.

173. Quoted in Annis, *God*, 4.

174. For examples see Americas Watch, *Human Rights*, 42; and Colby with Dennett, *Thy Will*, 816–817. See also Mark 12:17; and Hebrews 13:7.

175. Quoted in Davis, "Guatemala," 9.

176. Quoted in Mary Westropp, "Christian Counterinsurgency," *Cultural Survival Quarterly* 7/3 (1983) 28.

177. The quoted passages are in Joseph Anfuso and David Sczepanski, *Efraín Ríos Montt* (Barcelona: CLIE, 1984) 188.

178. Sara Castro-Klarén, "Discurso y transformación de los dioses en los Andes," in Luis Millones, ed., *El retorno de las huacas: estudios y documentos sobre el Taki Ongoy, siglo XVI* (Lima: Instituto de Estudios Peruanos and Sociedad Peruana de Psicoanálisis, 1990) 419.

179. Kay B. Warren, *The Symbolism of Subordination: Indian Identity in a Guatemala Town* (Austin: University of Texas Press, 1978) 40.

180. See Maria Isaura Pereira de Queiroz, *Historia y etnología de los movimientos mesiánicos: reforma y revolución en las sociedades tradicionales*, trans. Florentino M. Torner (Mexico City: Siglo Veintiuno, 1969) 113. In the Brazilian Caldeirão community of the 1930s, all dressed in black as a sign of mourning, the women covering their faces with veils; Robert M. Levine, *Vale of Tears: Revisiting the Canudos Massacre in Northeastern Brazil, 1893–1897* (Berkeley and Los Angeles: University of California Press, 1992) 224.

181. Oscar Alfredo Agüero, *The Millennium Among the Tupí-Cocama: A Case of Religious Ethno-Dynamism in the Peruvian Amazon* (Uppsala, Sweden: Uppsala Research Reports in Cultural Anthropology, 1992) 53.

182. See Jean-Pierre Chaumeil, *Historia y migraciones de los yagua: de finales del siglo XVII hasta nuestros días*, trans. María del Carmen Urbano (Lima: Centro Amazónico de Antropología y Aplicación Práctica, 1981) 113–114.

183. Agüero, *Millennium*, 46. For statutes of the Brotherhood of the Cross, see Regan, *Hacia la tierra*, 2/235–246.

184. See Numbers 2–5; and Marzal, *Caminos*, 349–350.

185. Marco Curatola, "Mesías andinos," *Historia y cultura* 21 (1991–92) 313.

186. The quoted passages are in Martínez, *Sectas*, 108; and Kirk, *Grabado*, 14, respectively.

187. Norman Cohn, *Cosmos, Chaos and the World to Come: The Ancient Roots of Apocalyptic Faith* (New Haven: Yale University Press, 1993) 209.

188. For an example see Kurt Bowen, *Evangelism and Apostasy: The Evolution and Impact of Evangelicals in Modern Mexico* (Montreal: McGill-Queen's University Press, 1996) 118.

189. Goodman, "Apostolics," 194.

190. Manuel García Rendueles, "Sectas cristianas en la selva del Perú," *Colección Shupihui* 6 (1975) 25.

191. See Emilio Willems, *Followers of the New Faith* (Nashville: Vanderbilt University Press, 1967) 52–54.

192. Manuel Jesús Granados, "Los Israelitas," *Socialismo y participación* 41 (1988) 99.

193. García Rendueles, "Sectas," 39.

194. Roger S. Greenway, "The 'Luz del Mundo' Movement in Mexico,"*Missiology: An International Review* 1/2 (April 1973) 118.

195. Blanca Muraturia, "Protestantism and Capitalism Revisited, in the Rural Highlands of Ecuador," in Domínguez, *Roman Catholic Church*, 261.

196. Elisabeth Rohr, *La destrucción de los símbolos culturales indígenas* (Quito: Abya-Yala, 1997) 164.

197. Ibid., 171 and 162.

198. Virginia Garrard-Burnetts, conclusion to Garrard-Burnett and Stoll, *Rethinking*, 207.

199. See Enrique Marroquín, "Un signo apocalíptico del milenio: persecusión a los protestantes indígenas de Oaxaca," in Barabas, *Religiosidad*, 224–225.

200. The quoted passage is from Galatians 3:28. See also Romans 8:14.

201. Catholicism earlier prohibited lay access even to the Bible; see Rohr, *Destrucción*, 120.

202. Frederick Pike, *The Politics of the Miraculous in Peru: Haya de la Torre and the Spiritualist Tradition* (Lincoln: University of Nebraska Press, 1986) 135.

203. Quoted in Klaiber, *Religion*, 149. Translation modified.

204. Coronel, "Violencia," 47 and 79.

205. Bushnell, *Making*, 264.

206. On Páez see John Lynch, *Caudillos in Spanish America, 1800–1850* (Oxford: Clarendon Press, 1992) 308.

207. Quoted in ibid., 324, 335, and 362.

208. See Stephen Haliczer, *Sexuality in the Confessional* (New York: Oxford University Press, 1996).

209. Juan Pablo Viqueira, "¿Qué había detrás del petate de la ermita de Cancuc?" in Gabriela Ramos and Henrique Urbano, eds., *Catolicismo y extirpación de idolatrías, siglos XVI–XVIII: Charcas, Chile, México, Perú*, (Cuzco: Centro de Estudios Regionales Andinos Bartolomé de Las Casas, 1993) 410.

210. Gruzinski, *Man-Gods*, 167.

211. Silletta, *Sectas*, 76.

212. See Silletta, *Sectas*, 75–93; and Albán and Muñoz, *Con Dios*, 136–140.

213. Albán and Muñoz, *Con Dios*, 141.

214. Roy Wallis, "Charisma, Commitment and Control in a New Religious Movement," in Roy Wallis, ed., *Millennialism and Charisma* (Belfast: Queen's University, 1982) 80. For an antecedent of free love in early Christianity, see Peter Brown, *The Body and Society: Men, Women, and Sexual Renunciation in Early Christianity* (New York: Columbia University Press, 1988) 147.

215. See Silletta, *Sectas*, 184–186.

216. See Juan Rossi, "Un episodio de amor en la colonia socialista Cecilia," in Carlos M. Rama, ed., *Utopismo socialista, 1830–1893* (Caracas: Biblioteca Ayacucho, 1987) 255. Charles Fourier called for "a new society founded on the emancipation of the passions and proclaiming the triumph of sexual pleasure"; See Frank E. Manuel, foreword to Charles Fourier, *Design for Utopia*, ed. Charles Gide (New York: Schocken Books, 1976) 3.

217. Quoted in Nadra, *Conversaciones*, 107.

218. See Lynch, *Caudillos*, 374–375.

219. The quoted phrase is from David C. Bailey, *¡Viva Cristo Rey! The Cristero Rebellion and the Church-State Conflict in Mexico* (Austin: University of Texas Press, 1974) 25.

220. See Michael C. Meyer and William L. Sherman, *The Course of Mexican*

History (New York: Oxford University Press, 1983) 588–589; and Josefa Vega and Pedro A. Vives, *Lázaro Cárdenas* (Madrid: Historia 16, 1987) 39.

221. Cornelia Butler Flora, *Pentecostalism in Colombia* (Rutherford; N.J.: Fairleigh Dickinson University Press, 1976) 40.

222. Levine, *Vale*, 225.

223. Silletta, *Sectas*, 49.

224. Ibid., 48–49.

225. Quoted in Fernando Giobellina Brumana, "Hechicería, antihechicería y cura de la aflicción en el campo religioso brasileño," in M. Gutiérrez, *Mito*, 373. For a Mexican example, see H. Russell Bernard and Jesús Salinas Pedraza, *Native Ethnography: A Mexican Indian Describes His Culture* (Newbury Park, Calif.: Sage Publications, 1989) 489. For a colonial precedent, see Sabine MacCormack, "The Heart Has Its Reasons," *Hispanic American Historical Review* 65/3 (1985) 462.

226. Susanna Rostas and André Droogers, introduction to Susanna Rostas and André Droogers, eds., *The Popular Use of Popular Religion in Latin America* (Amsterdam: CEDLA Publications, 1993) 11.

227. Barabas, *Utopías*, 111–112.

228. Quoted in Diego Irarrazaval, "Ingredientes y retos en la teología aymara," *Iglesia, pueblos y culturas* 13 (April–June 1989) 45. In parts of Perú, Pachamama is also called Santa María Mama Pacha; see Silva, "Pensamiento," 12/37.

229. Quoted in Michael Taussig, "Folk Healing and the Structure of Conquest in Southwest Colombia," *Journal of Latin American Lore* 6/2 (1980) 252–253. For other examples see Fernando Cervantes, *The Devil in the New World: The Impact of Diabolism in Spain* (New Haven: Yale University Press, 1994) 60; and Gonzalo Aguirre Beltrán, *Medicina y magia: el proceso de aculturación en la estructura colonial* (Mexico City: Instituto Nacional Indigenista, 1963) 147–148.

230. Quoted in Paul Jeffrey, "Market Sets the Mood for Churches," *Latinamerica Press* 28/35 (September 26, 1996) 6–7. For examples of Pentecostal faith healing elsewhere, see Christian Lalive D'epinay, *Haven of the Masses: A Study of the Pentecostal Movement in Chile*, trans. Marjorie Sandle (London: Lutterworth Press, 1969) 204–207.

231. William Cook, "Interview with Chilean Pentecostals," *International Review of Missions* 72 (October 1983) 592–593 and 595.

232. See Pereira de Queiroz, *Historia*, 119; and 2 Corinthians 8:9.

233. Quoted in Rohr, *Destrucción*, 137.

234. Quoted in Warren, *Symbolism*, 45.

235. Bartolomé, "Movimientos," 113–115.

236. Ibid., 115–116. See also Edgardo Jorge Cordeu and Alejandra Siffredi, *De la algarroba al algodón: movimiento mesiánico de los guaycurú* (Buenos Aires: Juárez Editor, 1971) 110 and 114.

237. Regarding Catholicism, expenditure, and sin, see William P. Mitchell, *Peasants on the Edge: Crop, Cult, and Crisis in the Andes* (Austin: University of Texas Press, 1991) 171–177. See also Tod D. Swanson, "Refusing to Drink with the Mountains," in Martin E. Marty and R. Scott Appleby, eds., *Accounting for Fundamentalisms: The Dynamic Character of Movements* (Chicago: University of Chicago Press, 1994) 79–98. Some fundamentalist churches, such as Príncipe de Paz in El Salvador, found their identity in reaction to upwardly mobile urban Pentecostalism; see Everett A. Wilson, "Sanguine Saints," *Church History* 52/2 (1983) 196.

238. See Annis, *God*, 86–87.

239. Elmer S. Miller, "The Argentine Toba Evangelical Religious Service," *Ethnology* 10 (1971) 157.

240. Jonathan D. Hill, *Keepers of the Sacred Chants: The Poetics of Ritual Power in Amazonian Society* (Tucson: University of Arizona Press, 1993) 48.

241. Quoted in Martínez, *Sectas*, 94.

242. Brian K. Goonan, "The New Look of the Churches," *Latinamerica Press* 28/35 (September 26, 1996) 3. For illiteracy as a factor in conversion, see Burdick, *Looking*, 79; and John Burdick, "Rethinking the Study of Social Movements," in Arturo Escobar and Sonia E. Alvarez, eds., *The Making of Social Movements in Latin America* (Boulder: Westview Press, 1992) 173–174.

Chapter 3

1. Inga Clendinnen, *Ambivalent Conquests: Maya and Spaniard in Yucatan, 1517–1570* (Cambridge: Cambridge University Press, 1987) 41. See also Alicia M. Barabas, *Utopías indias: movimientos sociorreligiosos en México* (Mexico City: Grijalbo, 1989) 109–110. The literal extirpation is particularly suggestive where "transplantation" of the Old World was comprehensive; see J. H. Parry et al., *A Short History of the West Indies* (New York: St. Martin's Press, 1968) v.

2. Alberto Flores Galindo, *Buscando un inca: identidad y utopía en los Andes* (Lima: Editorial Horizonte, 1988), 418.

3. Quoted in Leandro Tormo Sanz, "La cristianización de las Indias en la historia de Fernández de Oviedo," in Francisco Solano and Fermín del Pino, *América y la España del siglo XVI* (Madrid: Instituto Gonzalo Fernández de Oviedo, 1982) 99.

4. Barabas, *Utopías*, 194.

5. Quoted in Barabas, *Utopías*, 153.

6. Andrés Pérez de Ribas, *Historia de los triunfos de n.s. fe entre gentes las más bárbaras y fieras del nuevo orbe* (Mexico City: Editorial Layac, 1944) 3/67.

7. Andrés Pérez de Ribas, *My Life Among the Savage Nations of New Spain*, ed. and trans. Tomás Antonio Robertson (Los Angeles: Ward Ritchie Press, 1968) 97.

8. The quoted passages are from María Teresa Huerta y Patricia Palacios, *Rebeliones indígenas de la época colonial* (Mexico City: Instituto Nacional de Antropología e Historia, 1976) 288–289. See also Pérez de Ribas, *My Life*, 186 and 190–192; and Peter Masten Dunne, *Pioneer Jesuits in Northern Mexico* (Berkeley and Los Angeles: University of California Press, 1944) 128.

9. Pérez de Ribas, *Historia*, 3/179; and Pérez de Ribas, *My Life*, 190. Some of the natives dressed in the robes and hats of the dead priests.

10. See Segundo E. Moreno Yánez, *Sublevaciones indígenas en la audiencia de Quito: desde comienzos del siglo XVII hasta finales de la colonia* (Quito: Ediciones de la Universidad Católica, 1985) 193–194; and Oswaldo Albornoz P., *Las luchas indígenas en el Ecuador* (Guayaquil, Ecuador: Editorial Claridad, 1971) 27.

11. Moreno Yánez, *Sublevacieones indígenas*, 310. The eyes of victims were eaten or saved as talismans; see 305–306. The dismemberment and display of body parts is reminiscent of the Spanish practice. Procession of the eucharist was effective on some occasions; see 50–54.

12. Pérez de Ribas, *My Life*, 30.

13. Thomas H. Naylor and Charles W. Polzer, eds., *The Presidio and Militia on the Northern Frontier of New Spain* (Tucson: University of Arizona Press, 1986) 160, 387, 391.

14. See Michel Foucault, *Discipline and Punish: The Birth of the Prison*, trans. Alan Sheridan (New York: Vintage Books, 1979) 13.

15. The quoted phrase is in Julio César Cháves, *Túpac Amaru* (Buenos

Aires: Editorial Asunción, 1973) 131. On the Cochabamba incident, see Lillian Estelle Fisher, *The Last Inca Revolt 1780–1783* (Norman: University of Oklahoma Press, 1966) 160–161.

16. Fisher, *Last Inca Revolt*, 162.

17. Jan Szemiński, *La utopía tupamarista* (Lima: Pontificia Universidad Católica del Perú, 1983) 175. Apostate Europeans similarly argued that the host was "no more than some flour and water mixed together, and Christ never formed part of it"; see John Edwards, *Religion and Society in Spain* (Aldershot, England: Variorum, 1996) essay 3, 22.

18. Jan Szemiński, "The Last Time the Inca Came Back," in Gary H. Gossen, ed., *South and Meso-American Native Spirituality: From the Cult of the Feathered Serpent to the Theology of Liberation* (New York: Crossroad, 1993) 288.

19. Quoted in Fisher, *Last Inca Revolt*, 246.

20. See Huerta and Palacios, *Rebeliones*, 288.

21. Quoted in William L. Merrill, "Conversion and Colonialism in Northern Mexico," in Robert W. Hefner, ed., *Conversion to Christianity: Historical and Anthropological Perspectives on a Great Transformation* (Berkeley and Los Angeles: University of California Press, 1993) 140.

22. For examples from sixteenth-century Peru, see Nathan Wachtel, *The Vision of the Vanquished: The Spanish Conquest of Peru Through Indian Eyes, 1530–1570*, trans. Ben Reynolds and Siân Reynolds (New York: Barnes and Noble, 1977) 155.

23. Merrill, "Conversion," 138. See also Susan M. Deeds, "First-Generation Rebellions in Seventeenth-Century Nueva Vizcaya," in Susan Schroeder, ed., *Native Resistance and the Pax Colonial in New Spain* (Lincoln: University of Nebraska Press, 1998) 5–8, 11, and 24. On baptism as death, see Daniel T. Reff, "The 'Predicament of Culture' and Spanish Missionary Accounts of the Tepehuan and Pueblo Revolts," *Ethnohistory* 42/1 (Winter 1995) 73.

24. Pérez de Ribas, *Historia*, 3/85.

25. Fernando Cervantes, *The Devil in the New World: The Impact of Diabolism in New Spain* (New Haven: Yale University Press, 1994) 44.

26. Quoted in Manuel M. Marzal, "Las reducciones indígenas en la amazonía del virreinato peruano," *Amazonía peruana* 10 (March 1984) 35.

27. Quoted in Moreno *Sublevaciones*, 94.

28. See, for example, ibid., 97. For a modern example, see José María Arguedas, *Formación de una cultura nacional indoamericana*, ed. Angel Rama (Mexico City: Siglo Veintiuno, 1975) 193.

29. Moreno *Sublevaciones*, 157–159 (see also 39). Earlier, natives ran from Christians as though screaming, "Thieves, thieves; pirates, pirates; enemies, enemies"; see Gerónimo de Mendieta, *Historia eclesiástica indiana* (Mexico City: Editorial Porrúa, 1980) 506.

30. Felipe Guaman Poma de Ayala, *Nueva crónica y buen gobierno*, ed. Franklin Pease (Caracas: Biblioteca Ayacucho, 1980), 1/371 (see also 2/305–309). For illustrations of the corregidores' abuse, punishment, and torture of Indians, see 1/370, 1/373, 1/391, and 2/307.

31. Quoted in Boleslao Lewin, *La rebelión de Túpac Amaru y los orígenes de la emancipación americana* (Buenos Aires: Librería Hachette, 1957) 474; and in D. A. Brading, *The First America: The Spanish Monarchy, Creole Patriots, and the Liberal State, 1492–1867* (Cambridge: Cambridge University Press, 1991) 399 and 470.

32. Fisher, *Last Inca Revolt*, 10. *Repartimiento*, used here in reference to merchandise, is not to be confused with the same term used in reference to the allocation of Indian labor.

33. See Mark A. Burkholder and Lyman L. Johnson, *Colonial Latin Amer-*

ica (New York: Oxford University Press, 1990) 115–116. For parallel Mexican examples, see William B. Taylor, "Conflict and Balance in District Politics," in Arij Ouweneel and Simon Miller, eds., *The Indian Community of Colonial Mexico* (Amsterdam: CEDLA Publications, 1990) 270–294.

34. Quoted in Szemiński, "Last Time," 290.

35. These two examples and the quoted passage are from Oscar Cornblit, "Levantamientos de masas en Perú y Bolivia durante el siglo dieciocho," *Revista latinoamericana de sociología* 6/1 (1972) 101 and 105.

36. Erick D. Langer, "Andean Rituals of Revolt," *Ethnohistory* 37/3 (Summer 1990) 230; see also 240, where the body parts of fallen soldiers are eaten "with undefinable pleasure."

37. For an example of dismemberment and cannibalism as rituals of empowerment, see Deeds, "First-Generation Rebellions," 50.

38. Barabas, *Utopías*, 94.

39. Ibid., 169; and Vittorio Lanternari, "Nativistic and Socio-Religious Movements: A Reconsideration," *Comparative Studies in Society and History* 16 (1974) 489.

40. Lanternari, "Nativistic Movements," 489.

41. Barabas, *Utopías*, 44.

42. Wachtel, *Vision*, 187.

43. George Kubler, "A Peruvian Chief of State," *Hispanic American Historical Review* 24 (May 1944) 268; and Alberto Flores Galindo, *Europa y el país de los incas: la utopía andina* (Lima: Instituto de Apoyo Agrario, 1986) 50.

44. See Aquiles Escalante, "*Palenques* in Colombia," in Richard Price, ed., *Maroon Societies* (New York: Anchor, 1973) 77–79.

45. Quoted in Barabas, *Utopías*, 149.

46. Pérez de Ribas, *My Life*, 187.

47. The quoted phrase is from Barabas, *Utopías*, 170.

48. The quoted passage is in Carmen Bernand and Serge Gruzinski, *De la idolatría*, trans. Diana Sánchez F. (Mexico City: Fondo de Cultura Económica, 1992) 144.

49. Quoted in Richard Nebel, "El rostro mexicano de Cristo," in Frans Damen and Esteban Judd Zanon, eds., *Cristo crucificado en los pueblos de América Latina: antología de la religión popular* (Cuzco: Instituto de Pastoral Andina; and Quito: Abya-Yala, 1992) 65–66.

50. See Manuel Marzal, "La cristianización del indígena peruano," *Allpanchis Phuturinqa* 1 (1969) 95.

51. Teresa Gisbert, "The Artistic World of Felipe Guaman Poma," in Rolena Adorno et al., *Guaman Poma de Ayala: The Colonial Art of an Andean Author* (New York: Americas Society, 1992) 75.

52. Luis Weckmann, *La herencia medieval de México* (Mexico City: Colegio de México, 1984) 1/235–236. For other examples and for European precedents, see 1/234–237.

53. Sabine MacCormack, "The Heart Has Its Reasons," *Hispanic American Historical Review* 65/3 (1985) 443.

54. See Weckmann, *Herencia*, 1/234–235.

55. See Louise M. Burkhart, *The Slippery Earth: Nahua-Christian Moral Dialogue in Sixteenth-Century Mexico* (Tucson: University of Arizona Press, 1989) 181–183.

56. Quoted in Nebel, "Rostro," 66. See also Solange Alberro, "Acerca de la primera evangelización en México," in Gabriela Ramos, ed., *La venida del reino: religión, evangelización y cultura en América, siglos XVI–XX* (Cuzco: Centro de Estudios Regionales Andinos Bartolomé de Las Casas, 1994) 24.

57. Pablo Joseph Arriaga, *The Extirpation of Idolatry in Peru*, trans. L.

Clark Keating (Lexington: University of Kentucky Press, 1968) 70. See also Juan Carlos Estenssoro Fuchs, "Descubriendo los poderes de la palabra," in Ramos, *Venida*, 85.

58. The quoted phrase is in Henrique Urbano, "Idolos, figuras, imágenes," in Gabriela Ramos and Henrique Urbano, eds., *Catolicismo y extirpación de idolatrías, siglos XVI–XVIII: Charcas, Chile, México, Perú*, (Cuzco: Centro de Estudios Regionales Andinos Bartolomé de Las Casas, 1993) 24. See also Luis Fernando Botero, "La fiesta andina," in Luis Fernando Botero, ed., *Compadres y priostes: la fiesta andina como espacio de memoria y resitencia cultural* (Abya-Yala, 1991) 19; and Marzal, "Cristianización," 99.

59. Arriaga, *Extirpation*, 70. By the revolutionary 1780s, Andeans participated in the procession by carrying images of the sun or the Inca. See Jan Szemiński, "El único español bueno es el español muerto," in Juan Ansión, ed., *Pishtacos: de verdugos a sacaojos* (Lima: Tarea, 1989) 38.

60. Quoted in Bernand and Gruzinski, *De la idolatría*, 151.

61. Quoted in Suzanne Campbell-Jones, "Ritual in Performance and Interpretation," in M. F. C. Bourdillon and Meyer Fortes, eds., *Sacrifice* (London: Academic Press, 1980) 95.

62. Quoted in Robert Ricard, *The Spiritual Conquest of Mexico: An Essay on the Apostolate and the Evangelical Methods of the Mendicant Orders in New Spain, 1523–1572*, trans. Lesley Byrd Simpson (Berkeley and Los Angeles: University of California Press, 1966) 84.

63. Stephen Greenblatt, *Marvelous Possessions: The Wonder of the New World* (Chicago: University of Chicago Press, 1991) 9.

64. Quoted in Nebel, "Rostro," 69–70. For a Brazilian example see Riolando Azzi, "Del 'Bom Jesus' sufriente al Cristo liberador," in Damen and Judd Zanon, *Cristo*, 51.

65. Miles Richardson et al., "La imagen de Cristo en Hispanoamerica como modelo de sufrimiento," in Damen and Judd Zanon, *Cristo*, 99. The sheep trope is from Psalms 44: 22 and Romans 8: 36. See Sabine Speiser, "Pasión y muerte de Jesucristo en Esmeraldas," in Damen and Judd Zanon, *Cristo*, 165, where Christ staged his death "to teach us how to die."

66. Quoted in Nathan Wachtel, *Gods and Vampires: Return to Chipaya*, trans. Carol Volk (Chicago: University of Chicago Press, 1996) 61 and 62 (see also 99).

67. Quoted in Rafael Mondragón, *De indios y cristianos en Guatemala* (Mexico City: COPEC/CECOPE, 1983) 84. For additional examples see Fernando Bermúdez, *Death and Resurrection in Guatemala*, trans. Robert R. Barr (Maryknoll, N.Y.: Orbis Books, 1986) 27 and 62.

68. Scott Wright, *Promised Land: Death and Life in El Salvador* (Maryknoll, N.Y.: Orbis Books, 1994) 37–38 and 120.

69. Quoted in Mondragón, *De indios*, 63. For others, identification with Christ brought the accusation that expansionist Christianity was the cause rather than the consolation of indigenous suffering: "On this Cross that they brought to America they exchanged the Christ of Judea for the indigenous Christ"; see "Mensaje de los indígenas al Papa en Salta," *Iglesia, pueblos y culturas* 5 (1987) 158.

70. For an explicit modern example of syncretic iconography, see the illustrations by A. Huillca Huallpa in Damen and Judd Zanon, *Cristo*.

71. Quoted in Diego Irarrazaval, "El pueblo Mapuche en la evangelización," *Iglesia, pueblos y culturas* 12 (1989) 44.

72. D. A. Brading, "Images and Prophets," in Ouweneel and Miller, *Indian Community*, 191–192.

73. June Nash, "The Passion Play in Maya Indian Communities," *Comparative Studies in Society and History* 10 (1967–68) 323.

74. Victoria Bricker, *The Indian Christ, the Indian King: The Historical*

Substrate of Maya Myth and Ritual (Austin: University of Texas Press, 1986) 19. See also Clendinnen, *Ambivalent Conquests*, 91 and 187.

75. Ths quoted passage is in Huerta and Palacios, *Rebeliones*, 56–57.

76. See ibid., 83; and Barabas, *Utopías*, 111.

77. Bricker, *Indian Christ*, 20; and Clendinnen, *Ambivalent Conquests*, 90–91 and 204–207. The word *sacrifice* is rooted in the Latin *sacer* (sacred) and *facere* (to make), thereby connoting "to make sacred."

78. See Bricker, *Indian Christ*, 120–121; Barabas, *Utopías*, 214; Nelson Reed, *The Caste War of the Yucatan* (Stanford: Stanford University Press, 1964) 135; and Leticia Reina, *Las rebeliones campesinas en México, 1819–1906*, (Mexico City: Siglo Veintiuno, 1980) 45–47.

79. Martha Few, "Women, Religion and Power," *Ethnohistory* 42/4 (1995) 628–629.

80. Gonzalo Castillo-Cárdenas, *Liberation Theology from Below: The Life and Thought of Manuel Quintín Lame* (Maryknoll, N.Y.: Orbis Books, 1987) 29.

81. Cervantes, *Devil*, 54.

82. See Brading, "Images," 190; Fernando de Armas Medina, *Cristianización del Perú* (Seville: Escuela de Estudios Hispano-Americanos, 1953) 427–428; and Carolyn Dean, "The Renewal of Old World Images and the Creation of Colonial Peruvian Visual Culture," in Diana Fane, ed., *Converging Cultures: Art and Identity in Spanish America* (New York: Brooklyn Museum and Harry N. Abrams, 1996) 175–177.

83. Weckmann, *Herencia*, 1/237–239.

84. Richard Nebel, *Santa María Tonantzin, Virgen de Guadalupe: continuidad y transformación religiosa en México*, trans. Carlos Warnholtz Bustillos, et al. (Mexico City: Fondo de Cultura Económica, 1995) 90.

85. René Ribeiro, "Relations of the Negro with Christianity in Portuguese America," *The Americas* 14/4 (1958) 475–476.

86. See, for example, Melville J. Herskovits, "African Gods and Catholic Saints in New World Religious Belief," in William A. Lessa and Evon Z. Vogt, eds., *Reader in Comparative Religion: An Anthropological Approach* (Evanston, Ill.: Row, Peterson, 1958) 492–498; and Roger Bastide, *El prójimo y el extraño: el encuentro de las civilizaciones* (Buenos Aires: Amorrortu Editores, 1973) 252–254.

87. Herskovits, "African Gods," 497.

88. See Alberto Flores Galindo, "Los sueños de Gabriel Aguilar," *Debates en Sociología* 11 (1986) 142; and Karen Spalding, *Huarochirí: An Andean Society Under Inca and Spanish Rule* (Stanford: Stanford University Press, 1984) 273.

89. Jorge Hidalgo, "Amarus y Cataris," *Chungara* 10 (March 1983) 120–121.

90. Szemiński, "Last Time," 291–292.

91. Hidalgo, "Amarus," 122.

92. For a Christian parallel to the association of Illapa and firearms, see Justiniano Beltrán, *Los santos de las fuerzas armadas* (Bogotá: Ediciones Paulinas, 1991) 9–10.

93. Guaman Poma, *Nueva crónica*, 1/296 (see also 2/77).

94. Tom Cummins, "A Tale of Two Cities," in Fane, *Converging Cultures*, 163.

95. See Fernando Silva Santisteban, "El pensamiento mágico-religioso en el Perú contemporáneo," in *Historia del Perú* (Lima: Editorial Juan Mejía Baca, 1980) 12/43. See also Emilio Choy, *Antropología e historia* (Lima: Universidad Nacional Mayor de San Marcos, 1979) 1/433 and 1/435. In modern Chichicastenango, Guatemala, Santiago is identified with storm winds and seen as the

destroyer of cornfields; see Tony Pasinski, *The Santos of Guatemala* (Guatemala City: Didacsa, 1990) 1/113.

96. Américo Castro, *Santiago de España* (Buenos Aires; Emecé Editores, 1958) 135 (see also 100–103).

97. See Jack Autrey Dabbs, "A Messiah Among the Chiriguanos," *Southwestern Journal of Anthropology* 9 (1953) 48–51; Liliana Regalado de Hurtado, "Santiago entre los Chiriguanas," *Amazonía peruana* 22 (October 1992) 151–161; and Juan Gil, *Mitos y utopías del descubrimiento* (Madrid: Alianza, 1989) 3/309.

98. The quoted passage is cited in Cummins, "Tale," 163. See also David D. Gow, "The Roles of Christ and Inkarrí in Andean Religion," *Journal of Latin American Lore* 6/2 (1980) 281; and Choy, *Antropología*, 1/436. On the magical power of gunfire in a separate context, see William H. Crocker and Jean Crocker, *The Canela: Bonding Through Kinship, Ritual, and Sex* (New York: Harcourt Brace College Publishers, 1994) 22.

99. See Luis Millones Santa Gadea, "La 'Idolatría de Santiago,' " *Cuadernos del Seminario de la Historia* 7 (1964) 31; and Luis Millones, *Historia y poder en los Andes centrales (desde los orígenes al siglo XVII)* (Madrid: Alianza, 1987) 120–121.

100. Franklin Pease G. Y., "Un movimiento mesiánico en Lircay, Huancavelica (1811)," *Revista del Museo Nacional* 40 (1974) 222–223, 230, 234. See also Franklin Pease G. Y., *El dios creador andino* (Lima: Mosca Azul Editores, 1973) 83.

101. Pease, "Movimiento," 235 and 238. See also David D. Gow, "Símbolo y protesta," *América indígena* 39/1 (1979) 60–62.

102. Weckmann, *Herencia*, 1/152.

103. Arturo Warman Gryj, *La danza de moros y cristianos* (Mexico City: Secretaría de Educación Pública, 1972) 98–99. See also William B. Taylor, "Santiago's Horse," in William B. Taylor and Franklin Pease G. Y., eds., *Violence, Resistance, and Survival in the Americas: Native Americans and the Legacy of Conquest* (Washington, D.C.: Smithsonian Institution Press, 1994) 159.

104. Taylor, "Santiago's Horse," 161.

105. Olga Nájera-Ramírez, *La Fiesta de los Tastoanes: Critical Encounters in Mexican Festival Performance* (Albuquerque: University of New Mexico Press, 1997) 24 (see also 22–27 and 92).

106. Frances Gillmor, "Symbolic Representation in Mexican Combat Plays," in N. Ross Crumrine and Marjorie Halpin, eds., *The Power of Symbols: Masks and Masquerade in the Americas* (Vancouver: University of British Columbia Press, 1983) 106–108. See also Weckmann, *Herencia*, 2/655. In 1624 a curandera claimed that her powers resulted from intercourse with "an invisible Spaniard who came, like Santiago, on a white horse"; see Taylor, "Santiago's Horse," 159.

107. Gow, "Roles," 285; see also 283 for Inkarrí-like dismemberment and recorporalization.

108. Cervantes, *Devil*, 53.

109. Antonio M. Stevens-Arroyo, *Cave of the Jagua: The Mythological World of the Taínos* (Albuquerque: University of New Mexico Press, 1988) 60.

110. Quoted in Philip Caraman, *The Lost Paradise: The Jesuit Republic in South America* (New York: Seabury Press, 1976) 37–38.

111. Frances V. Scholes, *Troublous Times in New Mexico, 1659–1670* (Albuquerque: University of New Mexico Press, 1942) 13–14.

112. See Weckmann, *Herencia*, 1/259–261; and Cervantes, *Devil*, 67.

113. Lucía Gálvez, *Guaraníes y jesuitas: de la tierra sin mal al paraíso* (Buenos Aires: Editorial Sudamericana, 1995) 153–154.

114. Reed, *Caste War*, 134.

115. Barabas, *Utopías*, 118; and Bricker, *Indian Christ*, 20–21.

116. Merrill, "Conversion," 144. For another Mexican example see Barabas, *Utopías*, 155.

117. María Isaura Pereira de Queiroz, *Historia y etnología de los movimientos mesiánicos: reforma y revolución en las sociedades tradicionales*, trans. Florentino M. Torner (Mexico City: Siglo Veintiuno, 1969), 199–200.

118. Josefina Oliva de Coll, *La resistencia indígena ante la conquista* (Mexico City: Siglo Veintiuno, 1974) 144. For another example, see Deeds, "First-Generation Rebellions," 8.

119. Quoted in Cervantes, *Devil*, 35.

120. See Pérez de Ribas, *Historia*, 3/34; and Naylor and Polzer, *Presidio*, 175 and 180.

121. Barabas, *Utopías*, 143. For an eighteenth-century example see William B. Taylor, *Drinking, Homicide and Rebellion in Colonial Mexican Villages* (Stanford: Stanford University Press, 1979) 124.

122. Pereira de Queiroz, *Historia*, 201–202.

123. Pérez de Ribas, *Historia*, 2/119. See also Fernando Medina Ruiz, *El paraíso demolido: las reducciones jesuíticas del Paraguay* (Mexico City: Tradición, 1987) 70–71.

124. J. Jorge Klor de Alva, "Aztec Spirituality and Nahuatized Christianity," in Gossen, *Native Spirituality*, 187. On baptism as positive transformation, see Pérez de Ribas, *Historia*, 2/232.

125. John Hemming, *Amazon Frontier: The Defeat of the Brazilian Indians* (Cambridge: Harvard University Press, 1987) 321–325. See also Robin Wright, "Catastrophe and Regeneration," in Alicia Barabas, ed., *Religiosidad y resistencia indígenas hacia el fin del milenio* (Quito: Abya-Yala, 1994) 85.

126. See Michael F. Brown, "Beyond Resistance," *Ethnohistory* 38/4 (1991) 396; Jonathan D. Hill and Robin M. Wright, "Time, Narrative, and Ritual," in Jonathan D. Hill, ed., *Rethinking History and Myth* (Urbana: University of Illinois Press, 1988) 94–96 and 99; and Jonathan D. Hill, *Keepers of the Sacred Chants* (Tucson: University of Arizona Press, 1993) 49.

127. Quoted in Hemming, *Amazon Frontier*, 325. See also Pereira de Quieroz, *Historia*, 205.

128. See, for example, Heinrich Berlin et al., *Idolatría y superstición entre los indios de Oaxaca* (Mexico City: Ediciones Toledo, 1988) 38–40.

129. Quoted in Rafael Eladio Velázquez, *La rebelión de los indios de Arecayá: reacción indígena contra los excesos de la encomienda en el Paraguay* (Asunción: Centro Paraguayo de Estudios Sociológicos, 1965) 34.

130. See Serge Gruzinski, *Man-Gods in the Mexican Highlands: Indian Power and Colonial Society, 1520–1800*, trans. Eileen Corrigan (Stanford: Stanford University Press, 1989) 116–117, 122, 138, 150, 153, 156, 160, and 165. Note this schema's semblance to the last days as described by Joachim of Fiore.

131. Elmer S. Miller, "The Argentine Toba Evangelical Religious Service," *Ethnology* 10 (1971) 150 (see also 157 and 158). In regard to the ritual, see Matthew 24:35.

132. See Barabas, *Utopías*, 141–142.

133. Quoted in Ricard, *Spiritual Conquest*, 265.

134. *The quoted passages are in ibid.*

135. *See ibid.*, 265–266; and Juan M. Ossio A., ed., *Ideología mesiánica del mundo andino* (Lima: Ignacio Prado Pastor, 1973) 125–127.

136. Wachtel, *Vision*, 186; and Barabas, *Utopías*, 142. See also J. H. Parry, *The Audiencia of New Galicia in the Sixteenth Century: A Study in Spanish*

Colonial Government (Cambridge: Cambridge University Press, 1948) 27–28.

137. Steve J. Stern, *Peru's Indian Peoples and the Challenge of Spanish Conquest: Huamanga to 1640* (Madison: University of Wisconsin Press, 1982) 56. For an alternative estimate of the movement's range, see Rafael Varón Gabai, "El Taki Onqoy," in Luis Millones, ed., *El retorno de las huacas: estudios y documentos sobre el Taki Onqoy, siglo XVI* (Lima: Instituto de Estudios Peruanos and Sociedad Peruana de Psicoanálisis, 1990) 426; the work as a whole (331–405) provides an analytical overview. For a discussion of Taqui Onqoy as a historical construct, see Gabriela Ramos, "Política eclesiástica y extirpación de la idolatría," *Revista andina* 10/1 (1992) 147–169.

138. Quoted in Sabine MacCormack, "*Pachacuti*: Miracles, Punishments, and Last Judgment," *American Historical Review* 93 (October 1988) 983; specified were "Titicaca and Tiaguanaco, Chimboraco, Pachacamac, Tambotoco, Caruauilca, Caruaraco, and another sixty or seventy *huacas*." See also Millones, *Historia*, 167; and Wachtel, *Vision*, 180.

139. Quoted in Millones, *Historia*, 169. The Inca Titu Cusi may have attempted to organize and politicize Taqui Onqoy as an extension of the resistance from Vilcabamba.

140. Quoted in Luis Millones, *Mesianismo e idolatría en los Andes centrales* (Buenos Aires: Editorial Biblos, 1989) 15. On possible Christian influence, see Sabine MacCormack, *Religion in the Andes: Vision and Imagination in Early Colonial Peru* (Princeton: Princeton University Press, 1991) 184.

141. Quoted in Millones, *Historia*, 169; and Millones, *Mesianismo*, 18.

142. Marco Curatola, "Mito y milenarismo en los Andes," *Allpanchis* 10 (1977) 67.

143. Quoted in Millones, *Mesianismo*, 7 and 15.

144. These abstinences conformed to traditional rituals. See Stern, *Peru's Indian Peoples*, 58; Millones, *Mesianismo*, 5; and Arriaga, *Extirpation*, 37.

145. Curatola, "Mito," 68.

146. Quoted in Millones, *Mesianismo*, 19. Other Indians disloyal to nativist restoration would be transformed into animals.

147. See Wachtel, *Vision*, 181.

148. The quoted passage is from MacCormack, "*Pachacuti*," 984. See also Curatola, "Mito," 67. A penitential ritual of Taqui Onqoy was reminiscent of one practiced by the Incas during the Situa festival, "which was celebrated to expel sickness"; see Wachtel, *Gods*, 77.

149. See Billie Jean Isbell, "Shining Path and Peasant Responses in Rural Ayacucho," in David Scott Palmer, ed., *The Shining Path of Peru* (New York: St. Martin's Press, 1992) 74–76; and Curatola, "Mito," 68. On the pishtaco, see Wachtel, *Gods*, 74–89; Alejandro Ortiz Rescaniere, *De Adaneva a Inkarrí: una visión indígena del Perú* (Lima: Ediciones Retablo de Papel, 1973) 164–167; Wilfredo Kapsoli, *Guerreros de la oración: las nuevas iglesias en el Perú* (Lima: Sepec, 1994) 25–26 and 33–70; Jan Szemiński and Juan Ansión, "Dioses y hombres de Huamanga," *Allpanchis* 19 (1982) 210–216; and Ansión, *Pishtacos*.

150. See Bernal Díaz del Castillo, *The Discovery and Conquest of Mexico*, ed. Genaro García, trans. A. P. Maudslay (New York: Farrar, Strauss and Cudahy, 1956) 59. On friars described as devouring demons in Mexico, see J. Jorge Klor de Alva, "Martín Ocelotl: Clandestine Cult Leader," in David G. Sweet and Gary B. Nash, eds., *Struggle and Survival in Colonial America* (Berkeley and Los Angeles: University of California Press, 1981) 135 and 138.

151. The Cortés passage is in Francisco López de Gómara, *Cortés: The Life of the Conqueror by His Secretary*, ed. and trans. Lesley Byrd Simpson (Berkeley and Los Angeles: University of California Press, 1964) 58.

152. Quoted in Millones, *Mesianismo*, 15.

153. See Jack D. Forbes, *Apache, Navaho and Spaniard* (Norman: University of Oklahoma Press, 1960) 202–203.

154. On apparitions in which the Inca explains that he has sent the epidemics to induce return to ancestral ways, see MacCormack, "*Pachacuti*," 987.

155. See Curatola, "Mito," 70.

156. John J. Collins, *The Apocalyptic Imagination: An Introduction to the Jewish Matrix of Christianity* (New York: Crossroad, 1984) 162. For further discussion, see Adela Yarbro Collins, *The Combat Myth in the Book of Revelation* (Missoula, Mont.: Scholars Press, 1976).

157. Christopher Columbus, *The* Libro de las profecías *of Christopher Columbus*, trans. Delno C. West and August Kling (Gainesville: University of Florida Press, 1991) 141.

158. Norman Cohn, *Cosmos, Chaos and the World to Come: The Ancient Roots of Apocalyptic Faith* (New Haven: Yale University Press, 1993) 135 and 141. See also Psalms 82:1 and 95:3; and MacCormack, *Religion*, 184, where "the proponents of the revolt had learned to present the huacas as warlike and jealous."

159. Quoted in MacCormack, *Religion*, 182. See also Millones, *Historia*, 167; Millones, *Mesianismo*, 6; and Juan M. Ossio, *Los indios del Perú* (Quito: Abya-Yala, 1995) 185.

160. Quoted in Millones, *Mesianismo*, 17.

161. See Stern, *Peru's Indian Peoples*, 57 and 66.

162. Ramón A. Gutiérrez, *When Jesus Came, the Corn Mothers Went Away: Marriage, Sexuality, and Power in New Mexico, 1500–1846* (Stanford: Stanford University Press, 1991) 46–47. For a succinct historical overview, see J. Manuel Espinosa, ed., trans., and intro., *The Pueblo Indian Revolt of 1696 and the Franciscan Missions in New Mexico: Letters of the Missionaries and Related Documents* (Norman: University of Oklahoma Press, 1988) 3–27.

163. Andrew L. Knaut, *The Pueblo Revolt of 1680: Conquest and Resistance in Seventeenth-Century New Mexico* (Norman: University of Oklahoma Press, 1995) 76–77.

164. Quoted in ibid., 166–167.

165. Gutiérrez, *When Jesus Came*, 130.

166. Charles Wilson Hackett, ed., *Revolt of the Pueblo Indians of New Mexico and Otermín's Attempted Reconquest, 1680–1682* (Albuquerque: University of New Mexico Press, 1970) 1/xlv.

167. Quoted in ibid., 1/xix.

168. Scholes, *Troublous Times*, 17 and 253–254.

169. Ibid., 16.

170. Henry Warner Bowden, *American Indians and Christian Missions* (Chicago: University of Chicago Press, 1981) 5; and Scholes, *Troublous Times*, 16. On a similar occurrence among Zapotecs, see Jean E. F. Starr, "The Custodians of the Costumbres," in Susanna Rostas and André Droogers, eds., *The Popular Use of Popular Religion in Latin America* (Amsterdam: CEDLA Publications, 1993) 197.

171. Hackett, *Revolt*, 1/xxiv and 1/295–296. For examples of coercion in other contexts, see Barabas, *Utopías*, 146; and Pérez de Ribas, *Historia*, 3/165.

172. Gutiérrez, *When Jesus Came*, 131.

173. Quoted in Hackett, *Revolt*, 2/295.

174. Quoted in ibid., 2/361.

175. Quoted in ibid., 1/112–113.

176. Quoted in ibid., 1/102.

177. Quoted in ibid., 2/240 (see also 1/13).

178. Quoted in ibid., 1/13.

179. Quoted in Naylor and Polzer, *Presidio*, 532; see 598 for a similar incident among the Pimas.

180. Quoted in Hackett, *Revolt*, 1/clxxix.

181. See Gutiérrez, *When Jesus Came*, 136.

182. Quoted in Hackett, *Revolt*, 1/194–195; see also 2/287, where churches are used to house livestock.

183. Quoted in ibid., 1/177–178. See also 1/liii for the original text in Spanish.

184. Quoted in ibid., 2/225.

185. Ibid., 2/371 (see also 2/310).

186. Quoted in ibid., 1/25 and 2/345.

187. See David J. Weber, *The Spanish Frontier in North America* (New Haven: Yale University Press, 1992) 134–136; and Hackett, 2/382.

188. See Gutiérrez, *When Jesus Came*, 65.

189. Francisco Atanasio Domínguez, *The Missions of New Mexico*, trans. and annot. Eleanor B. Adams and Angélico Chávez (Albuquerque: University of New Mexico Press, 1956) 254–255.

190. Ibid., 258.

191. Quoted in Knaut, *Pueblo Revolt*, 115.

192. Bricker, *Indian Christ*, 56; and Barabas, *Utopías*, 172–174.

193. Barabas, *Utopías*, 176. La Candelaria is a popular Virgin in Latin American iconography.

194. Francisco Ximénez, *Historia de la provincia de San Vicente de Chiapa y Guatemala* (Guatemala City: Biblioteca Goathemala, 1931) 3/261.

195. See ibid., 257–258.

196. See Barabas, *Utopías*, 177; and Juan Pablo Viqueira, "¿Qué había detrás del petate de la ermita de Cancuc?" in Ramos and Urbano, *Catolicismo*, 411.

197. Quoted in Barabas, *Utopías*, 177.

198. Quoted in ibid.

199. Quoted in ibid., 178.

200. Quoted in Kevin Gosner, *Soldiers of the Virgin: The Moral Economy of a Colonial Maya Rebellion* (Tucson: University of Arizona Press, 1992) 122.

201. See Viqueira, "¿Qué?" 410 and 422, where death during first childbirth has religious meaning in Mesoamerica (see also 399). See also Gosner, *Soldiers*, 141; Barabas, *Utopías*, 178; and Robert Wasserstrom, *Class and Society in Central Chiapas* (Berkeley and Los Angeles: University of California Press, 1983) 82–85.

202. Barabas, *Utopías*, 181.

203. See ibid., 182–184.

204. See Bricker, *Indian Christ*, 73–75; Barabas, *Utopías*, 184–187; and Robert W. Patch, "Culture, Community, and 'Rebellion' in the Yucatec Maya Uprising of 1761," in Susan Schroeder, ed., *Native Resistance and the Pax Colonial in New Spain* (Lincoln: University of Nebraska Press, 1998) 67–83.

205. Barabas, *Utopías*, 204–210.

206. Quoted in Reina, *Rebeliones*, 374.

207. Quoted in ibid., 369; beginning in 1849, captured Maya rebels were sold into slave labor in Cuba (383).

208. Reed, *Caste War*, 136.

209. Nancy M. Farriss, *Maya Society Under Colonial Rule: The Collective Enterprise of Survival* (Princeton: Princeton University Press, 1984) 315. Oracles were prevalent in the nativist revolts of many cultures. See, for example, Edward H. Spicer, *Cycles of Conquest: The Impact of Spain, Mexico, and the United States on the Indians of the Southwest, 1533–1960* (Tucson: University of Arizona Press, 1976) 527.

210. Quoted in Reina, *Rebeliones*, 374; see 96–97 for an image of Jesus as patron of an 1843 rebellion in Guerrero.

211. Quoted in Reed, *Caste War*, 137.

212. Quoted in ibid., 137. See also Barabas, *Utopías*, 221.

213. Reed, *Caste War*, 139.

214. Ibid., 161. On Chiapas natives as the Holy Trinity in 1677, see Viqueira, "¿Qué?" 397.

215. Barabas, *Utopías*, 222.

216. Farriss, *Maya Society*, 315. The same is true in the modern Brotherhood of the Cross. In Maya Virgin cults, the transcendental Virgin, an image of her, and the Maya girl to whom these communicated also tended to fuse.

217. For the complete texts, see Reina, *Rebeliones*, 406–410.

218. See Barabas, *Utopías*, 204–210.

219. Reed, *Caste War*, 156.

220. See Barabas, *Utopías*, 222.

221. See ibid., 204–210.

222. Allan F. Burns, "The Caste War in the 1970s," in Grant D. Jones, ed., *Anthropology and History in Yucatán* (Austin: University of Texas Press, 1977) 267.

223. Reed, *Caste War*, 275.

224. The quoted phrase is in Fisher, *Last Inca Revolt*, 39.

225. The quoted passage is in Lewin, *Rebelión*, 475 (see also 299).

226. The first quoted passage is in Lewis Hanke, *The Imperial City of Potosí* (The Hague: Martinus Nijhoff, 1956) 25; and the second is from Flores Galindo, *Europa*, 49.

227. See Joseph Pérez, *Los movimientos precursores de la emancipación en Hispanoamérica* (Madrid: Editorial Alhambra, 1977) 111–112.

228. See Fisher, *Last Inca Revolt*, 8.

229. Quoted in Cháves, *Túpac Amaru*, 74. An estimated eight million Indians died in colonial Spanish mines.

230. Quoted in ibid., 34.

231. For the letter, see ibid., 125–126.

232. Quoted in Lewin, *Rebelión*, 452.

233. Quoted in Cháves, *Túpac Amaru*, 119.

234. Quoted in ibid., 131.

235. Quoted in Lewin, *Rebelión*, 473. See also Szemiński, "Last Time," 293–294.

236. Quoted in Lewin, *Rebelión*, 422 and 459; see 460–461 for Túpac Amaru's response.

237. Quoted in Pérez, *Movimientos*, 124.

238. Quoted in Cháves, *Túpac Amaru*, 129. See also Szemiński, "Unico español," 21.

239. Szemiński, *Utopía*, 245. In 1780 Túpac Amaru II declared the emancipation of slaves; see Cháves, *Túpac Amaru*, 121.

240. Quoted in Lewin, *Rebelión*, 423.

241. See Szemiński, *Utopía*, 198; and Szemiński, "Last Time," 293.

242. The quoted passage is in Cháves, *Túpac Amaru*, 120.

243. Szemiński, *Utopía*, 69.

244. See Szemiński, "Last Time," 286–287.

245. See ibid. See also Lewin, *Rebelión*, 465; and Hidalgo, "Amarus," 128. The apparition of the Christ of Qoyllur Rit'i is suggestive in this context; see Ana Gisbert-Sauch Colls, "La fiesta del Señor Qoyllur Rit'i," in Damen and Judd Zanon, *Cristo*, 297.

246. Quoted in Szemiński, "Unico español," 37.

247. Quoted in John H. Rowe, "El movimiento nacional inca del siglo

XVII," *Revista universitaria* 107 (1954) 30. On the arrests, see Fisher, *Last Inca Revolt*, 377. For a 1667 example of an Inca who based his entitlement on a genealogical painting, see MacCormack, "*Pachacuti*," 1003. See also Moreno, *Sublevaciones*, 137.

248. Quoted in Pérez, *Movimientos*, 114.

249. Quoted in Rowe, "Movimiento," 28.

250. Fisher, *Last Inca Revolt*, 279 (see also 242).

251. Quoted in Víctor Angles Vargas, *El Paititi no existe* (Cuzco: Imprenta Amauta, 1992) 28–29. For another use of Túpac Amaru's immortality, see John Leddy Phelan, *The People and the King: The Comunero Revolution in Colombia, 1781* (Madison: University of Wisconsin Press, 1978) 67 and 106.

252. Fisher, *Last Inca Revolt*, 377–378.

253. Quoted in Hidalgo, "Amarus," 123.

254. Quoted in Cháves, *Túpac Amaru*, 41.

255. Quoted in Cháves, *Túpac Amaru*, 188. See also Hidalgo, "Amarus," 126; and Lewin, *Rebelión* 549.

256. The quoted phrases are from Carlos Daniel Valcárcel, *Rebeliones coloniales sudamericanas* (Mexico City: Fondo de Cultura Económica, 1982) 96; and Szemiński, "Unico español," 55.

257. In the 1885 nativist rebellion in Huaraz, Pedro Pablo Atusparia obliged the Indians to attend Semana Santa (Holy Week) celebrations, presiding over the ceremonies himself; see Jeffrey Klaiber, *Religión y revolución en el Perú, 1824–1988* (Lima: Universidad del Pacífico, 1988) 79.

258. See Szemiński, "Unico español," 25–27; the blood drinking provided a figurative complement to the corregidores' "drinking the blood" of the native tributaries (31).

259. Lewin, *Rebelión*, 546. See also Cháves, *Túpac Amaru*, 194–198.

260. Quoted in Lewin, *Rebelión*, 528. Much the same occurred in 1745, when Jesuits sent by the viceroy met with Juan Santos Atahualpa to negotiate peace; see Jaime Regan, "En torno a la entrevista de los Jesuitas con Juan Santos Atahualpa," *Amazonía peruana* 22 (October 1992) 82.

261. Quoted in Lewin, *Rebelión*, 535.

262. See Flores Galindo, "Les sueños," 125–186. The quoted passages are from 140, 127, and 172. For a Mexican example see Eligio Ancona, *Historia de Yucatán desde la época más remota hasta nuestros días* (Mérida, Mexico: Imprenta de M. Heredia Argüelles, 1879) 3/20–26.

263. See Ossio, *Indios*, 232–233. For Hugo Blanco's ideology, see his *Land or Death* (New York: Pathfinder Press, 1972).

264. See Rosalind C. Gow, "Inkarrí and Revolutionary Leadership in the Southern Andes," *Journal of Latin American Lore* 8/2 (1982) 207; and Augusto Ramos Zambrano, *Rumi Maqui* (Puno, Peru: Centro de Publicaciones IIDSA-UNA, 1985) 52–53. For another example, the "Inca" Pablo Zárate Willca, see Gow, "Inkarrí," 203–204; and Fernando Mires, *La rebelión permanente: las revoluciones sociales en América Latina* (Mexico City: Siglo Veintiuno, 1988) 229.

Chapter 4

1. See Jean Baudrillard, *Simulations*, trans. Paul Foss et al. (New York: Semiotext[e], 1983) 2.

2. Henri Baudet, *Paradise on Earth: Some Thoughts on European Images of Non-European Man*, trans. Elizabeth Wentholt (New Haven: Yale University Press, 1965) 34.

3. See Louis-Andre Vigneras, *La búsqueda del paraíso y las legendarias islas del Atlántico* (Valladolid, Spain: Casa-Museo de Colón, 1976) 14.

4. For an overview of insular and other utopias, see Jean Delumeau, *History of Paradise: The Garden of Eden in Myth and Tradition*, trans. Matthew O'Connell (New York: Continuum, 1995) 6–10 and 97–109. More's fictional traveler was named Hythloday, meaning "a distributor of nonsense"; see Krishan Kumar, *Utopianism* (Minneapolis: University of Minnesota Press, 1991) 2. On Cuba as More's Utopia, see Fernando Ainsa, *Necesidad de la utopía* (Buenos Aires: Túpac Ediciones; and Montevideo: Nordan-Comunidad, 1990) 41.

5. See Enrique de Gandía, *Historia crítica de los mitos de la conquista americana* (Madrid: Sociedad General Española de Librería, 1929) 7; Ernst Bloch, *The Principle of Hope*, trans. Neville Plaice et al. (Cambridge: MIT Press, 1986) 764; and Luis Weckmann, *La herencia medieval de México* (Mexico City: Colegio de México, 1984) 1/42–43.

6. See Weckmann, *Herencia*, 1/44–45.

7. Francis Bacon, *New Atlantis*, ed. Alfred B. Gough (Oxford: Clarendon Press, 1924) xxiv–xxv.

8. See Fernando Ainsa, "Argirópolis, raíces históricas de una utopía," *Cuadernos americanos* 13 (January–February 1989) 119–134.

9. Quoted in George H. T. Kimble, *Geography in the Middle Ages* (New York: Russell and Russell, 1968) 185. This is illustrated on the Hereford mappamundi; see A. Bartlett Giamatti, *The Earthly Paradise and the Renaissance Epic* (Princeton: Princeton University Press, 1966) 14–15.

10. John Mandeville, *The Travels of John Mandeville*, trans. C. W. R. D. Moseley (New York: Penguin Books, 1983) 184–185.

11. The quoted phrase is from 1 Corinthians 2: 7. See also Matthew 11: 25; Mark 4: 11; and Luke 9: 45, 18: 34, 19: 42. "God returned this domain to Spain after so many centuries" of being "forgotten in the Universe"; see Djelal Kadir, *Columbus and the Ends of the Earth: Europe's Prophetic Rhetoric as Conquering Ideology* (Berkeley and Los Angeles: University of California Press, 1992) 132.

12. The quoted passage is in Alain Milhou, *Colón y su mentalidad mesiánica en el ambiente franciscanista medieval* (Valladolid, Spain: Casa-Museo de Colón, 1983) 133.

13. See Weckmann, *Herencia* 1/66

14. See ibid., 1/59.

15. Cleve Hallenbeck, *The Journeys of Fray Marcos de Niza* (Westport, Conn.: Greenwood Press, 1973) 34.

16. For the instructions given to and the report by Fray Marcos de Niza, see George P. Hammond and Agapito Rey, eds., and trans., *Narratives of the Coronado Expedition, 1540–1542*, (Albuquerque: University of New Mexico Press, 1940) 58–82.

17. Ramón A. Gutiérrez, *When Jesus Came, the Corn Mothers Went Away: Marriage, Sexuality, and Power in New Mexico, 1500–1846* (Stanford: Stanford University Press, 1991) 41–43.

18. Quoted in George P. Hammond, "The Search for the Fabulous in the Settlement of the Southwest," in David J. Weber, ed., *New Spain's Far Northern Frontier: Essays on Spain in the American West, 1540–1821* (Albuquerque: University of New Mexico Press, 1979) 26.

19. Quoted in Alberto Flores Galindo, *Europa y el país de los Incas: la utopía andina* (Lima: Instituto de Apoyo Agrario, 1986) 61. The name Paitití is also spelled without the accent.

20. Juan de Velasco, "Historia del Inca Bohorques y de la corte del Paitití," in Arturo Andrés Roig, ed., *La utopía en el Ecuador* (Quito: Banco Central del Ecuador, and Corporación Editora Nacional, 1987) 112–113. A Mataco myth has friars punished by God for searching for gold; see Pablo G. Wright, "Perspectivas teóricas en la antropología de los movimientos sociorreligiosos del

Chaco Argentino," in Alicia Barabas, ed., *Religiosidad y resistencia indígenas hacia el fin del milenio* (Quito: Abya-Yala, 1994) 36–37.

21. Henrique-Osvaldo Urbano, "Del sexo, incesto y los ancestros de Inkarrí," *Allpanchis* 15/17–18 (1981) 82–83.

22. Manuel Jesús Granados, "Los Israelitas," *Socialismo y Participación* 41 (1988) 103.

23. Marco Curatola, "Mesías andinos," *Historia y cultura* 21 (1991–92) 316. In 2 Kings 2: 11, Elijah is transported to heaven in a chariot of fire.

24. Velasco, "Historia," 109–112; and Manuel Burga, *Nacimiento de una utopía: muerte y resurrección de los incas* (Lima: Instituto de Apoyo Agrario, 1988) 395–396.

25. Quoted in Enrique de Gandía, *La ciudad encantada de los Césares* (Buenos Aires: Librería de A. García Santos, 1933) 29. For a Mexican complement to the White King, see Serge Gruzinski, "Las repercusiones de la conquista," in Carmen Bernand, ed., *Descubrimiento, conquista y colonización de América a quinientos años* (Mexico City: Fondo de Cultura Económica, 1994) 152.

26. Fernando Ainsa, *De la edad de oro a El Dorado* (Mexico City: Fondo de Cultura Económica, 1992) 162–163.

27. Quoted in Gandía, *Ciudad*, 30.

28. Ibid., 9 and 34–41.

29. Ibid., 11–13. See also Ernesto Morales, *La ciudad encantada de la Patagonia* (Buenos Aires: Emecé Editores, 1944) 51–53.

30. Fidel Sepúlveda Llanos, "Lectura estética de la literatura oral chilena," in Manuel Gutiérrez Estévez, ed., *Mito y ritual en América* (Madrid: Editorial Alhambra, 1988) 349 (see also 346–347). See also Gandía, *Ciudad*, 49.

31. See Gandía, *Ciudad*, 49; and Morales, *Ciudad*, 51–53.

32. See Elizabeth Hill Boone, "Migration Histories as Ritual Performance," in Davíd Carrasco, ed., *To Change Place: Aztec Ceremonial Landscapes* (Boulder: University of Colorado Press, 1991) 140 and 148; and Alfredo López Austin, *Hombre-dios: religión y política en el mundo náhuatl* (Mexico City: Universidad Nacional Autónoma de México, 1973) 86–87. On the creation of a sacred homeland by "singing of the boundary" in Yaqui Christianity, see Edward H. Spicer, *Cycles of Conquest: The Impact of Spain, Mexico, and the United States on the Indians of the Southwest, 1533–1960* (Tucson: University of Arizona Press, 1976) 400.

33. See Luis Leal, "In Search of Aztlán," in Rudolfo A. Anaya and Francisco A. Lomelí, *Aztlán: Essays on the Chicano Homeland* (Albuquerque: Academia/El Norte Press, 1989) 1 and 8; and Michael Pina, "The Archaic, Historical and Mythicized Dimensions of Aztlán," in Anaya and Lomelí, *Aztlán*, 15 and 35–36.

34. See Mircea Eliade, *The Sacred and the Profane: The Nature of Religion*, trans. Willard R. Trask (New York: Harper Torchbooks, 1961) 23.

35. Davíd Carrasco, *Quetzalcóatl and the Irony of Empire: Myths and Prophecies in the Aztec Tradition* (Chicago: University of Chicago Press, 1992) 170.

36. Ibid., 162.

37. Alejandro Ortiz Rescaniere, *De Adaneva a Inkarrí: una visión indígena del Perú* (Lima: Ediciones Retablo de Papel, 1973) 168. On Cuzco, see Garcilaso de la Vega, El Inca, *Royal Commentaries of the Incas and General History of Peru*, trans. Harold V. Livermore (Austin: University of Texas Press, 1987) 42–43. On a "navel of the world" in nonimperial culture, see Jonathan D. Hill and Robin M. Wright, "Time, Narrative, and Ritual," in Jonathan D. Hill, ed., *Rethinking History and Myth: Indigenous South American Perspectives on the Past* (Urbana: University of Illinois Press, 1988) 85.

38. Norman Cohn, *Cosmos, Chaos and the World to Come: The Ancient Roots of Apocalyptic Faith* (New Haven: Yale University Press, 1993) 137.

39. F. E. Peters, *Jerusalem: The Holy City in the Eyes of Chroniclers, Visitors, Pilgrims, and Prophets from the Days of Abraham to the Beginnings of Modern Times* (Princeton: Princeton University Press, 1985) 281–282.

40. See Norman Cohn, *The Pursuit of the Millennium* (New York: Oxford University Press, 1970) 64; Peters, *Jerusalem*, 281–282; and Milhou, *Colón*, 404. On ethnic centers of the world in Europe and the Americas, see Walter D. Mignolo, *The Darker Side of the Renaissance: Literacy, Territoriality, and Colonization* (Ann Arbor: University of Michigan Press, 1995) 219–258.

41. Quoted in D. A. Brading, *The First America: The Spanish Monarchy, Creole Patriots, and the Liberal State, 1492–1867* (Cambridge: Cambridge University Press, 1991) 109 (see also 110).

42. Quoted in ibid., 375.

43. See John F. Moffitt and Santiago Sebastián, *O Brave New People: The European Invention of the American Indian* (Albuquerque: University of New Mexico Press, 1996) 109–110.

44. Dolores Aramoni Calderón, "Iglesia, cultura y represión entre los zoques de Chiapas en el siglo XVII," in Gabriela Ramos and Henrique Urbano, eds., *Catolicismo y extirpación de idolatrías, siglos XVI–XVII: Charcas, Chile, México, Perú* (Cuzco: Centro de Estudios Regionales Andinos Bartolomé de Las Casas, 1993) 381.

45. Maria Isaura Pereira de Queiroz, *Historia y etnología de los movimientos mesiánicos: reforma y revolución en las sociedades tradicionales*, trans. Florentino M. Torner (Mexico City: Siglo Veintiuno, 1969).

46. Ralph Della Cava, *Miracle at Joaseiro* (New York: Columbia University Press, 1970) 84.

47. Quoted in René Ribeiro, "The Millennium That Never Came," in Ronald H. Chilcote, ed., *Protest and Resistance in Angola and Brazil: Comparative Studies* (Berkeley and Los Angeles: University of California Press, 1972) 176.

48. Alicia M. Barabas, "Identidad y cultura en nuevas iglesias milenaristas en México," in Barabas, *Religiosidad*, 255–256.

49. See David Stoll, "Evangelicals, Guerillas, and the Army," in Robert M. Carmack, ed., *Harvest of Violence: The Maya Indians and the Guatemalan Crisis* (Norman: University of Oklahoma Press, 1988) 90–91, 98, and 116; and Sheldon Annis, *God and Production in a Guatemalan Town* (Austin: University of Texas Press, 1987) 4.

50. See Oscar Agüero, "Milenarismo y utopía entre los Tupí-Cocama de la Amazonía peruana," in Barabas, *Religiosidad*, 132 and 139. For a Pentecostal New Jerusalem in the Amazon, see Jaime Regan, *Hacia la tierra sin mal: estudio sobre la religiosidad del pueblo en la Amazonía* (Iquitos, Peru: CETA, 1983) 2/132.

51. Clodomir Monteiro, "La cuestión de la realidad en la amazonía," *Amazonía peruana* 11 (February 1985) 93 and 99.

52. See Alberto Groisman, "Messias, milenio e salvação," in Barabas, *Religiosidad*, 269–287; Alicia Barabas, introduction to *Religiosidad*, 12–13; and Alberto Groisman, "Muerte y renacimiento," in M. S. Cipolletti and E. J. Langdon, eds., *La muerte y el más allá en las culturas indígenas latinoamericanas* (Quito: Abya-Yala, 1992) 91–111.

53. Curatola, "Mesías," 313–314.

54. See Robert C. Tucker, ed., *The Marx-Engels Reader* (New York: W. W. Norton, 1978) 54.

55. See Jan Szemiński, "El único español bueno es el español muerto," in Juan Ansión, ed., *Pishtacos: de verdugos a sacaojos* (Lima: Tarea, 1989) 36; and

Jeffrey Klaiber, "Religión y justicia en Túpac Amaru," *Allpanchis* 19 (1982) 179.

56. Quoted in Boleslao Lewin, *La rebelión de Túpac Amaru y los orígenes de la emancipación americana* (Buenos Aires: Librería Hachette, 1957) 474. See 1 Samuel 17.

57. John Leddy Phelan, *The People and the King: The Comunero Revolution in Colombia, 1781* (Madison: University of Wisconsin Press, 1978) 74.

58. Donald Hodges, *Sandino's Communism: Spiritual Politics for the Twenty-first Century* (Austin: University of Texas Press, 1992) 95.

59. Quoted in Daniel H. Levine, *Popular Voices in Latin American Catholicism* (Princeton: Princeton University Press, 1992) 38.

60. Quoted in Edward A. Lynch, *Religion and Politics in Latin America: Liberation Theology and Christian Democracy* (New York: Praeger, 1991) 93. For similar comparisons in Guatemala, see Yvon Le Bot, *La guerra en tierras mayas: comunidad, violencia y modernidad en Guatemala (1970–1992)* (Mexico City: Fondo de Cultura Económica, 1995) 123 and 273.

61. Quoted in Alvaro Huerga, *Historia de los alumbrados*, vol. 3, *Los alumbrados de Hispanoamérica* (Madrid: Fundación Universitaria Española, Seminario Cisneros, 1986) 418–419. On indigenous cities as Rome and Jerusalem, see, for example, Luis Villoro, *Los grandes momentos del indigenismo en México* (Mexico City: Colegio de México, 1950) 51; and Diego de Córdova y Salinas, *Crónica franciscana de las provincias del Perú*, ed. Lino G. Canedo (Washington, D.C.: Academy of American Franciscan History, 1957) 141.

62. See Huerga, *Historia*, 148; and Paulino Castañeda Delgado and Pilar Hernández Aparicio, *La Inquisición de Lima, 1570–1635* (Madrid: Editorial Deimos, 1989) 306.

63. Quoted in Huerga, *Historia*, 428.

64. Frederick B. Pike, "Latin America," in John McManners, ed., *The Oxford Illustrated History of Christianity* (Oxford: Oxford University Press, 1990) 425–426.

65. Brian R. Hamnett, *Roots of Insurgency: Mexican Regions, 1750–1824* (Cambridge: Cambridge University Press, 1986) 14.

66. Leonardo Boff, *Faith on the Edge: Religion and Marginalized Existence*, trans. Robert R. Barr (San Francisco: Harper and Row, 1989) 8.

67. José Vasconcelos, *La raza cósmica* (Mexico City: Espasa-Calpe, 1948) 47.

68. Quoted in Arturo Andrés Roig, "Estudio introductorio," in Roig, *Utopía*, 75.

69. The quoted passages are in Ainsa, *De la edad*, 11.

70. Pedro Henríquez Ureña, *La utopía de América*, ed. Angel Rama and Rafael Gutiérrez Girardot (Caracas: Biblioteca Ayacucho, 1989) 6–7. The first passage is quoted in Roig, "Estudio," 86.

71. On the place names, see Fernando Ainsa, "Tensión utópico e imaginario subversivo en Hispanoamérica," *Anales de literatura hispanoamericana* 13 (1984) 34.

72. See Giamatti, *Earthly Paradise*, 17; and Moffitt and Sebastián, *Brave New People*, 77. In Homer's *Odyssey*, the elysian fields are "at the world's end, where all existence is a dream of ease."

73. Ovid, *Metamorphoses*, trans. Mary M. Innes (New York: Penguin Books, 1986) 31–32. For Virgil on the golden age, see Giamatti, *Earthly Paradise*, 23–25.

74. The first two quoted passages are from Moffitt and Sebastián, *Brave New People*, 79; and the third quoted passage is from Genesis 2:9. See also Robert Hughes, *Heaven and Hell in Western Art* (New York: Stein and Day Publishers, 1968) 87.

75. Quoted in Jeanette Favrot Peterson, *The Paradise Garden Murals of Malinalco: Utopia and Empire in Sixteenth-Century Mexico* (Austin: University of Texas Press, 1993) 138.

76. Quoted in Brading, *First America*, 16.

77. Quoted in Moffitt and Sebastián, *Brave New People*, 150. The passage suggests a modern variation: *because* they have no government.

78. See Weckmann, *Herencia*, 67; and José Antonio Maravall, *Utopía y reformismo en la España de los Austrias* (Mexico City: Siglo Veintiuno, 1982) 146. The Indians "have a lot of gold but do not know how to take advantage of it"; see Francisco López de Gómara, *Historia general de las Indias y vida de Hernán Cortés* (Caracas: Biblioteca Ayacucho, 1979) 329.

79. Quoted in John H. Elliott, *Imperial Spain, 1469–1716* (London: Edward Arnold Publishers, 1963) 294.

80. Quoted in Anthony Pagden, "*Ius et Factum*," in Stephen Greenblatt, ed., *New World Encounters* (Berkeley and Los Angeles: University of California Press, 1993) 85.

81. Quoted in Sepúlveda, "Lectura," 348.

82. Dennis Tedlock, trans., *Popol Vuh: The Definitive Edition of the Mayan Book of the Dawn of Life and the Glories of Gods and Kings* (New York: Simon and Schuster, 1985) 124–125.

83. The Mexican case is from Susan M. Deeds, "Indigenous Responses to Mission Settlement in Nueva Vizcaya," in Erick Langer and Robert H. Jackson, eds., *The New Latin American Mission History* (Lincoln: University of Nebraska Press, 1995) 87.

84. Quoted in Isaac J. Pardo, *Fuegos bajo el agua: la invención de utopía* (Caracas: Biblioteca Ayacucho, 1990) 791. The same tendency brings "rejection of immediate responsibilities."

85. Quoted in John Joseph Marsden, *Marxian and Christian Utopianism: Toward a Socialist Political Theory* (New York: Monthly Review Press, 1991) 13 and 132.

86. The quoted phrase is in Melvin J. Lasky, *Utopia and Revolution: On the Origins of a Metaphor* (Chicago: University of Chicago Press, 1976) 15.

87. Hélène Clastres, *The Land-without-Evil: Tupí-Guaraní Prophetism*, trans. Jacqueline Grenez Brovender (Urbana: University of Illinois Press, 1995) 56.

88. See Gustavo Gutiérrez, *A Theology of Liberation: History, Politics and Salvation*, trans. Caridad Inda and John Eagleson (Maryknoll, N.Y.: Orbis Books, 1973) 232–236 and 255.

89. Leonardo Boff, *Liberating Grace*, trans. John Drury (Maryknoll, N.Y.: Orbis Books, 1981) 165.

90. G. Gutiérrez, *Theology*, 237.

91. Boff, *Faith*, 16.

92. Ibid., 104.

93. See Roig, "Estudio," 56–57.

94. See Acts 2: 44–45.

95. See Jacques Le Goff, *Medieval Civilization*, trans. Julia Barrow (New York: Basil Blackwell, 1989) 192–193.

96. Quoted in Delno C. West and Sandra Zimdars-Swartz, *Joachim of Fiore: A Study in Spiritual Perception and History* (Bloomington: Indiana University Press, 1983) 61.

97. See Edgardo Lander, "Democracia liberal, modernización y utopía en América Latina," in Oscar Agüero and Horacio Cerutti Guldberg, eds. *Utopía y nuestra América* (Quito: Abya-Yala, 1996) 227.

98. Horacio Cerutti Guldberg, "¿Teoría de la utopía?" in Agüero and Cerutti, *Utopía*, 99.

99. The quoted passages are from Kumar, *Utopianism*, 29.

100. Quoted in ibid., 74.

101. Vicente Rocafuerte, "Rocafuerte y el proyecto de Roberto Owen," in Roig, *Utopía*, 295–296.

102. Robert Owen, "Petición a la República Mexicana," in Roig, *Utopía*, 297–303.

103. See Carlos M. Rama, ed., *Utopismo socialista, 1830–1893* (Caracas: Biblioteca Ayacucho, 1987) lxi–lxii; and Albert Kinsey Owen, "El sueño de una ciudad ideal," in Rama, *Utopismo*, 244. See also Ainsa, *Necesidad*, 104, where a revolutionary movement proclaimed Baja California a socialist republic.

104. Rama, *Utopismo*, xix.

105. Rudolph Binion, *Frau Lou: Nietzsche's Wayward Disciple* (Princeton: Princeton University Press, 1968) 164.

106. Rama, *Utopismo*, lxiv–lxvii; Juan Rossi, "El por qué se fundió la colonia socialista Cecilia," in Rama, *Utopismo*, 273; and Ainsa, *Necesidad*, 104–105.

107. Angel J. Cappelletti, "Anarquismo latinoamericano," in Carlos M. Rama and Angel Cappelletti, *El anarquismo en América Latina* (Caracas: Biblioteca Ayacucho, 1990) clxxvi.

108. José Ignacio Abreu e Lima, "El socialismo," in Rama, *Utopismo*, 165 (see also xlix).

109. Plotino C. Rhodakanaty, "Cartilla Socialista," in Rama, *Utopismo*, 189–190.

110. Rama, *Utopismo*, lx. See also Cappelletti, "Anarquismo," clxxvii–clxxxii.

111. Tucker, *Marx-Engels Reader*, 145.

112. See ibid., 497–499.

113. See Lasky, *Utopia*, 38; and Krishan Kumar, *Utopia and Anti-Utopia in Modern Times* (Oxford: Basil Blackwell, 1987) 53. The utopianism of Fourier and Owen was thus "the anticipation and imaginative expression of a new world"; in Marsden, *Utopianism*, 21.

114. See Ainsa, "Tensión," 16, and 26.

115. Mircea Eliade, "Paradise and Utopia," in Frank E. Manuel, ed. *Utopias and Utopian Thought* (Boston: Houghton Mifflin, 1966) 274.

116. Virgil anticipated this maneuver by forecasting the return of the golden age; see Giamatti, *Earthly Paradise*, 23–25. For Mary as the new Eve, see Anne Baring and Jules Cashford, *The Myth of the Goddess: Evolution of an Image* (New York: Arkana/Penguin Books, 1991) 537–539 and 572–574.

117. The quoted phrases are from J. H. Plumb, *The Death of the Past* (Boston: Houghton Mifflin, 1970) 17; and Alicia M. Barabas, *Utopías indias: movimientos sociorreligiosos en México* (Mexico City: Grijalbo, 1989) 273, (see also 47). See also Michael Adas, *Prophets of Rebellion: Millenarian Protest Movements Against the European Colonial Order* (Chapel Hill: University of North Carolina Press, 1979) 42; Anthony F. C. Wallace, "Revitalization Movements," *American Anthropologist* 58 (1956) 268–272; and Cohn, *Cosmos*, 166 and 171.

118. The quoted passages are in Guillermo Bonfil Batalla, ed., *Utopía y revolución: el pensamiento político contemporáneo de los indios en América Latina* (Mexico City: Editorial Nueva Imagen, 1981) 128 and 135. For a survey of temporal ideas in Western culture, see Rudolph Binion, *After Christianity: Christian Survivals in Post-Christian Culture* (Durango, Colorado: Logbridge-Rhodes, 1986) 21–68.

119. Quoted in Wilfredo Kapsoli, *Guerreros de la oración: las nuevas iglesias en el Perú* (Lima: Sepec, 1994) 63. See also Alberto Flores Galindo, *Buscando un inca: identidad y utopía en los Andes* (Lima: Editorial Horizonte, 1988) 315.

120. Kapsoli, *Guerreros*, 70.

121. Ibid., 76.

122. Víctor Raúl Haya de la Torre, *Política aprista* (Lima: Editorial Amauta, 1967) 194.

123. Quoted in Rosalind C. Gow, "Inkarrí and Revolutionary Leadership in the Southern Andes," *Journal of Latin American Lore* 8/2 (1982) 199.

124. See Marie-Chantal Barre, *Ideologías indigenistas y movimientos indios*, trans. Luisa Salomone (Mexico City: Siglo Veintiuno, 1983) 114–115; and Bonfil, *Utopia*, 265–274.

125. The quoted phrase is from Mircea Eliade, *The Myth of the Eternal Return: Or, Cosmos and History*, trans. Willard R. Trask (Princeton: Princeton University Press, 1965) 129.

126. Bacon, *New Atlantis*, xxx.

127. Quoted in Joseph A. Page, *Perón: A Biography* (New York: Random House, 1983) 400.

128. Quoted in Moffitt and Sebastián, *Brave New People*, 42. See also Leonardo Olschki, "Ponce de Leon's Fountain of Youth: History of a Geographical Myth," *Hispanic American Historical Review* 21/3 (August 1941) 370.

129. Mandeville, *Travels*, 123.

130. Jean Delumeau, *Sin and Fear: The Emergence of a Western Guilt Culture, Thirteenth–Eighteenth Centuries*, trans. Eric Nicholson (New York: St. Martin's Press, 1990) 125.

131. Quoted in Olschki, "Fountain of Youth," 363.

132. See Bloch, *Principle*, 760; and Eliade, *Sacred*, 149–150.

133. Rutherford H. Platt Jr., *The Forgotten Books of Eden: Lost Books of the Old Testament* (New York: Gramercy Books, 1980) 5.

134. The quoted passages are from Jeremiah 2:13; and John 7:37–38, respectively. See also Donald R. Dickson, *The Fountain of Living Waters* (Columbia: University of Missouri Press, 1987) 55–71.

135. See Robert Hughes, *Heaven and Hell in Western Art* (New York: Stein and Day Publishers, 1968) 88 and 95–96.

136. See Weckmann, *Herencia*, 1/57.

137. Gandía, *Historia*, 54–56.

138. Andrés Pérez de Ribas, *Historia de los triunfos de n.s. fe entre gentes las más bárbaras y fieras del nuevo orbe* (Mexico City: Editorial Layac, 1944) 2/119.

139. See Bloch, *Principle*, 768 (see also 766–767).

140. Quoted in Delumeau, *History*, 96; see also 71–96.

141. Anthony Pagden, *Lords of All the World: Ideologies of Empire in Spain, Britain and France, c. 1500–c. 1800* (New Haven: Yale University Press, 1995) 39. The royal historian Gonzalo Fernández de Oviedo argued that the Indians were the descendants of a Visigothic diaspora.

142. For an example see Cristóbal Colón, *Textos y documentos completos: relaciones de viajes, cartas y memorias*, ed. Consuelo Varela (Madrid: Alianza, 1984) 311.

143. Hernán Pérez de Oliva, *Historia de la invención de las Yndias*, ed. José Juan Arrom (Bogotá: Publicaciones del Instituto Caro y Cuervo, 1965) 54–55. Indigenous perspective suggests a variation: to give to those lands the strange shape of our own.

144. Johannes Wilbert and Karin Simoneau, eds., *Folk Literature of the Mataco Indians* (Los Angeles: UCLA Latin American Center Publications, 1982) 60–61.

145. Kay B. Warren, *The Symbolism of Subordination: Indian Identity in a Guatemalan Town* (Austin: University of Texas Press, 1978) 33 and 36.

146. See Hughes, *Heaven*, 74–75.

147. Peters, *Jerusalem*, 155. In other versions Adam is associated with Bethlehem and the Holy Sepulchre; see 155–156.

148. Antonio de León Pinelo, *El paraíso en el nuevo mundo*, ed. Raúl Porras Barrenechea (Lima: Comité del IV Centenario del Descubrimiento del Amazonas, 1943) 1/119.

149. Juan Pablo II, *Viaje apostólico a Centroamérica* (Vatican City: Librería Editrice Vaticana; and Madrid: Biblioteca de Autores Cristianos, 1983) 181.

150. Paulo Suess, *La nueva evangelización: desafíos históricos y pautas culturales*, trans. María Victoria C. de Vela (Abya-Yala, 1991) 99 and 216. For Peruvian bishops in 1971, "the unity of humankind will be possible only through a justice effective for all"; Bishops of Peru, "Justice in the World," in Alfred T. Hennelly, ed. and trans., *Liberation Theology: A Documentary History* (Maryknoll, N.Y.: Orbis Books, 1990) 132.

151. Pope John Paul II, "Address to the Indians of Oaxaca and Chiapas," in Hennelly, *Liberation Theology*, 260. See also 1 Corinthians 10:17.

152. Pope John Paul II, "Address," 329–333 (see also 323–328). The quoted scriptures are from Ephesians 4:5–6. For the pope's Spanish text in context, see Juan Pablo II, *Viaje*, 59–66. For other examples of "Calls to the Unity of Catholics," see Michael A. Burdick, *For God and the Fatherland: Religion and Politics in Argentina* (Albany: State University of New York Press, 1995) 99 and 185.

153. Vasconcelos, *Raza*, 16, 32 and 54.

154. Simón Bolívar, *Selected Writings of Bolívar*, ed. Vicente Lecuna and Harold A. Bierck, Jr., trans. Lewis Bertrand (New York: Colonial Press, 1951) 191. See also Indalecio Liévano Aguirre, *Bolívar* (Madrid: Instituto de Cooperación Iberoamericana, 1983) 237, where Bolívar hoped to "recast the human race in one whole." For José Martí, "there can be no racial animosity, because there are no races"; see his *Our America: Writings on Latin America and the Struggle for Cuban Independence*, ed. Philip S. Foner (New York: Monthly Review Press, 1977) 93–94.

155. Henríquez, *Utopía*, 8.

156. George Kubler, "A Peruvian Chief of State," *Hispanic American Historical Review* 24 (May 1944) 261–262. See also George Kubler, "The Neo-Inca State," *Hispanic American Historical Review* 27/2 (May 1947) 189–203.

157. Flores Galindo, *Europa*, 50–51.

158. Anthony Pagden, *Spanish Imperialism and the Political Imagination: Studies in European and Spanish-American Social and Political Theory, 1513–1830* (New Haven: Yale University Press, 1990) 11 (see also 129).

159. Miguel Hidalgo, "Manifiesto," in Albelardo Villegas, ed., *Antología del pensamiento social y político de América Latina* (Washington, D.C.: Unión Panamericana, 1964) 104.

160. For a "Unified God" of the Maya, see Munro S. Edmonson, "The Mayan Faith," in Gary H. Gossen, ed., *South and Meso-American Native Spirituality: From the Cult of the Feathered Serpent to the Theology of Liberation* (New York: Crossroad, 1993) 67.

161. Fernando Ainsa, "Hostos y la unidad de América Latina," *Cuadernos americanos* 16 (July–August 1989) 67.

162. Liévano *Bolívar*, 237. José de San Martín argued to the contrary that traditional class structure must be preserved to avoid social chaos.

163. Bolívar, *Selected Writings*, 160–61.

164. Ibid., 191.

165. Quoted in Liévano, *Bolívar*, 414; and Daniel Florencio O'Leary, *Bolivar and the War of Independence*, ed. and trans. Robert F. McNerney Jr. (Austin: University of Texas Press, 1970) 172. See also Bolívar, *Selected Writings*, 765.

166. See Roig, "Estudio," 79–80.

167. Benigno Malo, "El nuevo mapa de América," in Roig, *Utopía*, 307–312.

168. See Leopoldo Zea, *¿ Por qué América Latina?* (Mexico City: Universidad Nacional Autónoma de México, 1988) 148–149. For a utopian contribution from Plotino C. Rhodakanaty, see his "Cartilla," 189–190.

169. Karl Marx and Friedrich Engels, *The Communist Manifesto*, ed. A. J. P. Taylor (New York: Penguin Books, 1967) 120–121.

170. Donald C. Hodges, *The Latin American Revolution: Politics and Strategy from Apro-Marxism to Guevarism* (New York: William Morrow, 1974) 134.

171. Jay Mallin, ed., *"Che" Guevara on Revolution: A Documentary Overview* (Coral Gables: University of Miami Press, 1969) 79, 100, 161, and 162.

172. Sergio Ramírez and Robert Edgar Conrad, eds., *Sandino: The Testimony of a Nicaraguan Patriot, 1921–1934*, trans. Robert Edgar Conrad (Princeton: Princeton University Press, 1990) 253.

173. Hodges, *Sandino's Communism*, 94.

174. Darcy Ribeiro, *The Americas and Civilization*, trans. Linton Lomas Barrett and Marie McDavid Barrett (New York: E. P. Dutton, 1971) 154.

175. Quoted in Frederick Pike, *The Politics of the Miraculous in Peru: Haya de la Torre and the Spiritualist Tradition* (Lincoln: University of Nebraska Press, 1986) 283.

176. See Haya de la Torre, *Política*, 123 and 61. See also Milda Rivarola and Pedro Planas, eds., *Víctor Raúl Haya de la Torre* (Madrid: Ediciones de Cultura Hispánica, 1988) 31.

177. Haya de la Torre, *Política*, 39.

178. Quoted in Pike, *Politics*, 139.

179. See ibid., 88–89.

180. Quoted in ibid., 91.

181. A. Métraux, "Messiahs of South America," *Inter-American Quarterly* 3/2 (1941) 54.

182. Quoted in Regan, *Hacia la tierra*, 1/140; see also 2/153. On ritual fitness among the Ticuna, see Jean Pierre Chaumeil, "La vida larga," in Cipolletti and Langdon, *Muerte*, 115.

183. Clastres, *Land-without-Evil*, 56. See also Curt Nimuendajú-Unkel, *Los mitos de creación y de destrucción del mundo como fundamento de la religión de los apapokúva-guaraní*, ed. Juergen Riester G. (Lima: Centro Amazónico de Antropología y Aplicación Práctica, 1978) 117.

184. Clastres, *Land-without-Evil*, 55–56 and 80.

185. Rubén Bareiro-Saguier, "Reinterpretación de los mitos fundacionales guaraníes," in M. Gutiérrez, *Mito*, 333. The terrestrial location was also troublesome, although it compared favorably to Eden and the millennial kingdom.

186. Clastres, *Land-without-Evil*, 77.

187. Quoted in Métraux, 56; and Clastres, *Land-without-Evil*, 53.

188. See Clastres, *Land-without-Evil*, 67; and Lawrence E. Sullivan, *Icanchu's Drum: An Orientation to Meaning in South American Religions* (New York: Macmillan, 1988) 577. The Guaraní referred to the Jesuits as paí rather than karaí.

189. See Oscar Alfredo Agüero, *The Millennium Among the Tupí-Cocama: A Case of Religious Ethno-Dynamism in the Peruvian Amazon* (Uppsala, Sweden: Uppsala Research Reports in Cultural Anthropology, 1992) 6, 23, and 90. See also Regan, *Hacia la tierra*, 1/139.

190. See Agüero, *Millennium*, 94, and Oscar Agüero, "El pensamiento indígena en América Latina," in Agüero and Cerutti, *Utopía*, 61.

191. Agüero, *Millennium*, 77. The migrations sometimes lack a utopian destination (see 53).

192. Ibid., 116–117.

193. Quoted in Ibid., 109.

194. See Jonathan D. Hill, foreword to Clastres, *Land-without-Evil*, viii; Sullivan, *Icanchu's Drum*, 576; and Nimuendajú-Unkel, *Mitos*, 31 and 117.

195. Quoted in Emiliano Jos, *La expedición de Ursúa al Dorado, la rebelión de Lope de Aguirre, y el itinerario de los "Marañones"* (Huesca, Spain: Imprenta V. Campo, 1927) 59–60; and in Clastres, *Land-without-Evil*, 50.

196. Marco Polo, *The Travels of Marco Polo*, trans. Ronald Latham (New York: Penguin Books, 1958) 243–244. For a similar description of legendary riches, see Mandeville, *Travels*, 170. For legends of colonial Mexican streets paved in silver, see Diana Fane, ed., *Converging Cultures: Art and Identity in Spanish America* (New York: Brooklyn Museum and Harry N. Abrams, 1996) 258.

197. James Lockhart, ed. and trans., *We People Here: Nahuatl Accounts of the Conquest of Mexico* (Berkeley and Los Angeles: University of California Press, 1993) 98. For images of this "appetite" for gold, see Felipe Guaman Poma de Ayala, *Nueva crónica y buen gobierno*, ed. Franklin Pease (Caracas: Biblioteca Ayacucho, 1980) 1/267 (where a Spaniard eats gold served by an Inca); and Michael Alexander, *Discovering the New World: Based on the Works of Theodore De Bry* (New York: Harper and Row, 1976) 146 (where rebelling Indians pour molten gold into the mouths of Spaniards).

198. John Hemming, *The Conquest of the Incas* (New York: Harvest/Harcourt Brace Jovanovich, 1970) 73. Atahualpa was executed afterward.

199. Pedro Cieza de León, *The War of Quito*, ed. and trans. Clements R. Markham (Nendeln, Liechtenstein: Hakluyt Society/Kraus Reprint, 1967) 11. Translation modified.

200. Quoted in Lewis Hanke, *The Spanish Struggle for Justice in the Conquest of America* (Philadelphia: University of Pennsylvania Press, 1949) 51. Translation modified.

201. See Ainsa, *De la edad*, 113.

202. Ibid., 107.

203. Quoted in Delumeau, *Sin*, 127.

204. Roig, "Estudio," 50 (see also 59–61).

205. See, for example, Manuel Ballesteros, *Gonzalo Jiménez de Quesada* (Madrid: Historia 16, 1987) 52–53; and Constantino Bayle, *El Dorado fantasma* (Madrid: Consejo de la Hispanidad, 1943) 19–20.

206. Quoted in Juan Gil, *Mitos y utopías del descubrimiento* (Madrid: Alianza, 1989) 2/153.

207. Quoted in José Alcina Franch, *Bartolomé de Las Casas* (Madrid: Historia 16, 1987) 76.

208. Córdova y Salinas, *Crónica*, 15.

209. Amérigo Vespucci, *Cartas de viaje*, ed. Luciano Fomisano (Madrid: Alianza, 1986) 76 (see also 53). For additional examples, see Delumeau, *History*, 109–115.

210. León Pinelo, *Paraíso*, 1/286 (see also 1/356–357).

211. See Brading, *First America*, 200–202.

212. I. Hunt, "Garden of Eden," in *New Catholic Encyclopedia* (New York: McGraw Hill, 1967) 5/102.

213. Quoted in J. A. Zahm, *The Quest for El Dorado* (New York: D. Appleton, 1977) 199.

214. See León Pinelo, *Paraíso*, 1/286. The original location of El Dorado was precisely inland, to the southwest, from the location where Columbus "discovered" Eden. See Bayle, *El Dorado*, plate 6.

215. The quoted passage is in Brading, *First America*, 394. See also Juan Gil, "De los mitos de las Indias," in Bernand, *Descubrimiento*, 272–273. For an

example see Colón, *Textos*, 311. On gold and Eden, see Genesis 2:11. For ancient and biblical antecedents, see Delumeau, *History*, 4–5.

216. See Bartolomé de Las Casas, *Historia de las Indias*, ed. André Saint-Lu (Caracas: Biblioteca Ayacucho, 1986) 1/529.

217. Ibid. 1/526–527.

218. Christopher Columbus, *The Four Voyages of Columbus*, ed. and trans. Cecil Jane (New York: Dover Publications, 1988) 2/32–33. Translations from this volume are sometimes modified; Spanish originals are on odd-numbered facing pages. The passages cited from Columbus's narrative of the third voyage are also in Colón, *Textos*, 202–219.

219. Columbus, *Four Voyages*, 2/26–27.

220. Ibid., 2/28–29.

221. Mircea Eliade, "The Yearning for Paradise in Primitive Tradition," in Henry A. Murray, ed., *Myth and Mythmaking* (Boston: Beacon Press, 1960) 69. See also Tzvetan Todorov, *The Conquest of America: The Question of the Other*, trans. Richard Howard (New York: Harper and Row, 1987) 28. Elsewhere Columbus quoted Isaiah: "Let the islands keep silence before me"; see Christopher Columbus, *The* Libro de las profecías *of Christopher Columbus*, trans. Delno C. West and August Kling (Gainesville: University of Florida Press, 1991) 169.

222. Columbus, *Four Voyages*, 2/18–19 and 2/24–25.

223. Las Casa, *Historia*, 1/530 and 1/539.

224. Columbus, *Four Voyages*, 2/14–15.

225. Las Casas, *Historia*, 1/539. See also Pedro Martyr D'Anghera, *De Orbe Novo*, trans. Francis Augustus MacNutt (New York: Burt Franklin, 1970) 1/137, where these natives have "bodies as white as ours."

226. Columbus, *Four Voyages*, 2/22–23 and 2/32–33.

227. See Las Casas, *Historia*, 1/536; and Genesis 2:25.

228. Columbus, *Four Voyages*, 2/16–17.

229. See Las Casas, *Historia*, 1/531 and 1/534.

230. Ibid., 1/552; and Columbus, *Four Voyages*, 2/26–27. Note that the poetics of two waters extend into the description of pitched roofs as *a dos aguas*; see Columbus, *Four Voyages*, 2/20–21.

231. See Las Casas, *Historia*, 1/566.

232. See Felipe Fernández-Armesto, *Before Columbus: Exploration and Colonization from the Mediterranean to the Atlantic, 1229–1492* (Philadelphia: University of Pennsylvania Press, 1987) 249. Amérigo Vespucci more soberly observed that "practice is worth more than theory"; see Vespucci, *Cartas*, 56.

233. Columbus, *Four Voyages*, 2/38–39 and 2/34–35.

234. Mandeville, *Travels*, 185.

235. Columbus, *Four Voyages*, 2/38–39.

236. Las Casas, *Historia*, 1/552.

237. Columbus, *Four Voyages*, 2/42–43. On the rivers of Eden, see Genesis 2:10. It was generally believed that the four rivers were the Nile, Ganges, Tigris, and Euphrates. After consideration of the same evidence interpreted by Columbus, Vespucci asserted, "We arrived at the conclusion that this was a mainland"; see Vespucci, *Cartas*, 59. Vespucci's 1503 *Mundus Novus* was the first published description of a major land mass absent from Ptolemy's geography, although it was mistakenly related to Asia.

238. Columbus, *Four Voyages*, 2/50–51 (see 2/48–49). See also Las Casas, *Historia*, 1/554.

239. Las Casas, *Historia*, 1/581. Columbus found further evidence in the Book of Esdras; see Las Casas, *Historia*, 1/554. See also Paolo Emilio Taviani, *Christopher Columbus: The Grand Design* (London: Orbis Books, 1985) 453.

240. Edmundo O'Gorman, *The Invention of America: An Inquiry into the Historical Nature of the New World and the Meaning of Its History* (Bloomington: Indiana University Press, 1961) 99 (see also 94–99).

241. See Columbus, *Four Voyages*, 2/30–31.

242. Quoted in Platt, *Forgotten Books*, 4. The eastern location of Eden was also supported by the interpretation of "in the beginning" (*bereschith; a principio*) as "in the east." See Columbus, *Four Voyages*, 2/37 n. 10; and Bloch, *Principle*, 760.

243. The first example is from Vigneras, *Búsqueda*, 13. The other examples are from Moffitt and Sebastián, *Brave New People*, 39–40. See also Delumeau, *History*, 15–21 and 39–70.

244. Quoted in Columbus, *Libro*, 18.

245. Mandeville, *Travels*, 184.

246. Ibid. See also Milhou, *Colón*, 407.

247. See Las Casas, *Historia*, 1/566 and 1/570. See also Mandeville, *Travels*, 184.

248. The quoted phrase is from Northrop Frye, *Anatomy of Criticism* (Princeton: Princeton University Press, 1957) 203; see 203–204 for examples.

249. Columbus, *Four Voyages*, 2/30–31 and 2/38–39.

250. Ibid., 2/32–33. See also Las Casas, *Historia*, 1/562.

251. Columbus, *Four Voyages*, 2/30–31 (see also 2/38–39).

252. Ibid., 2/30–31.

253. Las Casas, *Historia*, 1/562.

254. In the Museo del Prado see, for example, Pedro Machuca's *La virgen y las animas del purgatorio*. Related images also in the museum include Peter Paul Ruben's *La via lactea*, Alonso Cano's *San Bernardo y la Virgen*, and Bartolomé Estéban Murillo's *Aparición de la Virgen a San Bernardo*.

255. The quoted passage is from Joel 3:18. Exodus 3:8 is the first of many such images.

256. See Caroline Walker Bynum, *Jesus as Mother: Studies in Spirituality of the High Middle Ages* (Berkeley and Los Angeles: University of California Press, 1982) 110–169. For images see Caroline Walker Bynum, *Fragmentation and Redemption: Essays on Gender and the Human Body in Medieval Religion* (New York: Zone Books, 1992) 110–111. In Isaiah 60:16, people "suck the breast of kings." A nineteenth-century Mexican painting featured Christ's wounded, all powerful hand bleeding into a chalice-fountain that served as trough for the seven lambs of Revelation, while the surplus blood spilled out into creation; see Fane, *Converging Cultures*, 114 and 116.

257. See Leo Bagrow, *History of Cartography* (Chicago: Precedent Publishing, 1985) plate xviii.

258. Isaiah 66:11 (see also 49:23 and 66:12).

259. Todorov, *Conquest*, 9.

260. Columbus, *Four Voyages*, 2/44–45 and 2/46–47.

261. Quoted in Brading, *First America*, 203.

262. The Quoted in Maravall, "Utopía," 205 (see also 206 and 224); and Ainsa, *De la edad*, 154.

263. Alberto Armani, *Ciudad de Dios y Ciudad del Sol: el "estado" jesuita de los guaraníes, 1609–1768* (Mexico City: Fondo de Cultura Económica, 1982) 151.

264. See Ainsa, *De la edad*, 155.

265. Quoted in Stelio Cro, *Realidad y utopía en el descubrimiento y conquista de la América Hispana, 1492–1682* (Troy, Mich.: International Book Publishers, 1983), 69 (see also 65 and 73). See also Sabine MacCormack, *Religion in the Andes: Vision and Imagination in Early Colonial Peru* (Princeton:

Princeton University Press, 1991) 323; and Demetrio Ramos Pérez, *Las variaciones ideológicas en torno al descubrimiento de América* (Valladolid, Spain: Casa-Museo de Colón, 1982) 69–70.

266. The last quoted passage is from Gerónimo de Mendieta, *Historia eclesiástica indiana* (Mexico City: Editorial Porrúa, 1980) 451 (see also 437–442). The other quoted passages are in Maravall, "Utopía," 210–211, and Ainsa, *De la edad*, 110. For an example of the Dominican perspectives see Pedro Borges, "El sentido trascendente del descubrimiento y conversión de Indias," *Missionalia Hispánica* 13/37 (1956) 143.

267. Quoted in John Leddy Phelan, *The Millennial Kingdom of the Franciscans in the New World* (Berkeley and Los Angeles: University of California Press, 1970) 82.

268. Quoted in Elsa Cecilia Frost, "Indians and Theologians," in Gossen, *Native Spirituality*, 135.

269. The first quoted passage is in Ainsa, *De la edad*, 150; the second is in Maravall, "Utopía," 221–222.

270. Quoted in Ainsa, *De la edad*, 153. Soliciting the obedience of Pueblos in 1660, a friar preached "that the commandment which taught children to honor their parents also applied to the clergy as spiritual fathers of the faithful"; see Frances V. Scholes, *Troublous Times in New Mexico, 1659–1670* (Albuquerque: University of New Mexico Press, 1942) 56.

271. Quoted in Ainsa, *De la edad*, 75.

272. See Phelan, *Millennial Kingdom*, 52.

273. Quoted in Marcel Bataillon, *Erasmo y España: estudios sobre la historia espiritual del siglo XVI* (Mexico City: Fondo de Cultura Económica, 1950) 821.

274. Quoted in Felipe Tena Ramírez, *Vasco de Quiroga y sus pueblos de Santa Fe en los siglos XVIII y XIX* (Mexico City: Editorial Porrúa, 1990) 85. See also José Aparecido Gomes Moreira, *Conquista y conciencia cristiana: el pensamiento indigenista y jurídico teológico de Don Vasco de Quiroga* (Quito: Abya-Yala, 1992) 195.

275. Quoted in Phelan, *Millennial Kingdom*, 74.

276. Quoted in ibid., 69.

277. Lewis Hanke, "El despertar de la conciencia en América," *Cuadernos Americanos* 14 (1963) 187.

278. See MacCormack, *Religion*, 452.

279. C. R. Boxer, *The Church Militant and Iberian Expansion* (Baltimore: Johns Hopkins University Press, 1978) 73–74.

280. Quoted in Silvio Zavala, *Ideario de Vasco de Quiroga* (Mexico City: Colegio de México, 1995) 21; see also Paulino Castañeda Delgado, *Don Vasco de Quiroga y su "Información en derecho"* (Madrid: Ediciones José Porrúa Turanzas, 1974) 100.

281. Quoted in Castañeda, *Vasco de Quiroga*, 64. See also Marcel Bataillon and André Saint-Lu, *El Padre Las Casas y la defensa de los indios*, trans. Javier Alfaya y Bárbara McShane (Barcelona: Editorial Ariel, 1976) 181; and Lewis Hanke, *The First Social Experiments in America: A Study in the Development of Spanish Indian Policy in the Sixteenth Century* (Cambridge: Harvard University Press, 1935) 44.

282. Sir Thomas More, *Utopia*, ed. and trans. Robert M. Adams (New York: W. W. Norton, 1975) 79.

283. Quoted in Alcina, *Las Casas*, 52.

284. See Bataillon and Saint-Lu, *Padre*, 171.

285. Quoted in Hanke, *Spanish Struggle*, 74–75.

286. Bartolomé de Las Casas, *Del único modo de traer a todos los pueblos*

a la verdadera religión (Mexico City: Fondo de Cultura Económica, 1942) 315–316 (see also 475).

287. Quoted in Benno M. Biermann, "Bartolomé de Las Casas and Verapaz," in Juan Friede and Benjamin Keen, eds., *Bartolomé de Las Casas in History: Toward an Understanding of the Man and His Work* (De Kalb: Northern Illinois University Press, 1971) 475. A 1537 papal bull similarly argued that the Indians, "truly men," should be "called to the faith of Jesus Christ through preaching of the divine Word and by example of the virtuous and holy life." See Bataillon and Saint-Lu, *Padre*, 183; and Hanke, *Spanish Struggle*, 73.

288. The quoted passage is in Stelio Cro, *The American Foundations of the Hispanic Utopia (1492–1793)* (Tallahassee: DeSoto Press, 1994) 2/31.

289. See Hanke, *Spanish Struggle*, 54–55 (see also 63–70); and Pedro Borges Morán, *Misión y civilización en América* (Madrid: Editorial Alhambra, 1987) 88–97.

290. Armani, *Ciudad*, 50. The quoted phrase is from Hanke, *Spanish Struggle*, 54.

291. Biermann, "Las Casas," 474.

292. See ibid., 458.

293. Armani, *Ciudad*, 52.

294. On Vera Paz, see Hanke, *Spanish Struggle*, 77–80.

295. The quoted passages are in Castañeda, *Vasco de Quiroga*, 272 (see also 24 and 95).

296. Quoted in ibid., 24 (see also 269).

297. Quoted in Ainsa, *De la edad*, 150.

298. Quoted in Castañeda, *Vasco de Quiroga*, 269.

299. The first two quoted passages are in ibid., 112 and 23, respectively; and the third is in Gomes *Conquista*, 206.

300. Quoted in Cro, *Realidad*, 58.

301. Quoted in Castañeda, *Vasco de Quiroga*, 109.

302. The quoted phrase is in Cro, *Realidad*, 59.

303. The quoted passage is in Gomes, *Conquista* 192; on Vasco de Quiroga's *policía mixta* see 91–103.

304. See Tena, *Vasco de Quiroga*, 20–22; and Fintan B. Warren, *Vasco de Quiroga and His Pueblo-Hospitals of Santa Fe* (Washington, D.C.: Academy of American Franciscan History, 1963) 7.

305. Quoted in Cro, *Realidad*, 66. See also Bataillon and Saint-Lu, *Padre*, 126–127.

306. Quoted in Castañeda, *Vasco de Quiroga*, 110. See also Nicolás León, ed., *Documentos ineditos referentes al ilustrísimo señor Don Vasco de Quiroga* (Mexico City: Antigua Librería Robredo, 1940) 5–7 and 31–35.

307. Quoted in Zavala, *Ideario*, 45.

308. Quoted in Claudia Agostoni, "La utopía en el Nuevo Mundo," in Agüero and Cerutti, *Utopía*, 44–45. Zumárraga owned a heavily annotated copy of *Utopia*.

309. Silvio Zavala, *La "Utopia" de Tomás Moro en la Nueva España y otros estudios* (Mexico City: Biblioteca Histórica Mexicana, 1937) 4 and 6 (see also 2–29). See also the texts collected in Guillermo Tovar de Teresa, *La utopía mexicana del siglo XVI: lo bello, lo verdadero y lo bueno* (Mexico City: Grupo Azabache, 1992).

310. Quoted in Bataillon, *Erasmo*, 821. See also Gomes, *Conquista*, 76; and Castañeda, *Vasco de Quiroga*, 263.

311. Quoted in Ainsa, *De la edad*, 110. On Quiroga's reading of Lucian, see Zavala, *Ideario*, 63–64.

312. Quoted in Cro, *American Foundations*, 2/89; see also Armani, *Ciudad*,

69. In the discussion below I follow Brading, *First America*, 172–176. The periodization is from Magnus Morner, "Experiencia jesuita en el Paraguay," *Revista paraguaya de sociología* 22/62 (1985) 128–129.

313. On the execution of Jesuits in a 1628 revolt, see Lucía Gálvez, *Guaraníes y jesuitas: de la tierra sin mal al paraíso* (Buenos Aires: Editorial Sudamericana, 1995) 149–153.

314. Quoted in Cro, *American Foundations*, 2/152.

315. Quoted in ibid., 2/112; see 2/120 for the converts' echo of this discourse.

316. Armani, *Ciudad*, 154.

317. The secular clergy also felt shortchanged because Guaranís in reductions were exempt from tithes; see ibid., 87–88.

318. See Philip Caraman, *The Lost Paradise: The Jesuit Republic in South America* (New York: Seabury Press, 1976) 246–249.

319. Quoted in Cro, *American Foundations*, 2/161.

Chapter 5

1. See Norman Cohn, *The Pursuit of the Millennium* (New York: Oxford University Press, 1970) 72. For Charles V as a "new Charlemagne," see Alain Milhou, *Colón y su mentalidad mesiánica en el ambiente franciscanista medieval* (Valladolid, Spain: Casa-Museo de Colón, 1983) 331. In Iberia, Charlemagne was associated with Santiago. For an example of his twentieth-century presence in Latin American messianism, see Robert M. Levine, *Vale of Tears: Revisiting the Canudos Massacre in Northeastern Brazil, 1893–1897* (Berkeley and Los Angeles: University of California Press, 1992) 222.

2. Cohn, *Pursuit*, 91–92. See also 90–93 and the pseudo-Frederick on 113–15.

3. Milhou, *Colón* 347–348, and Maria Isaura Pereira de Queiroz, *Historia y etnología de los movimientos mesiánicos: reforma y revolución en las sociedades tradicionales*, trans. Florentino M. Torner (Mexico City: Siglo Veintiuno, 1969) 50–51. For an example from Spanish Iberia, see Richard L. Kagan, "Politics, Prophecy, and the Inquisition in Late Sixteenth-Century Spain," in Mary Elizabeth Perry and Anne J. Cruz, eds., *Cultural Encounters: The Impact of the Inquisition in Spain and the New World* (Berkeley and Los Angeles: University of California Press, 1991) 107.

4. Mary Elizabeth Brooks, *A King for Portugal: The Madrigal Conspiracy, 1594–95* (Madison: University of Wisconsin Press, 1964) 34 and 41.

5. Pereira de Queiroz, *Historia*, 98.

6. For access to another enchanted kingdom through a secret stone door, see René Ribeiro, "The Millennium That Never Came," in Ronald H. Chilcote, ed., *Protest and Resistance in Angola and Brazil: Comparative Studies* (Berkeley and Los Angeles: University of California Press, 1972) 174.

7. Pereira de Queiroz, *Historia*, 99; and Levine, *Vale*, 219.

8. See Ernst Bloch, *The Principle of Hope*, trans. Neville Plaice (Cambridge: MIT Press, 1986) 1132. For examples of returns from the dead to perform miracles, see Luis Weckmann, *La herencia medieval de México* (Mexico City: Colegio de México, 1984) 333–335.

9. Sabastian Balfour, *Castro* (London: Longman, 1995) 3.

10. Both examples are from Marco Curatola, "Mesías andinos," *Historia y cultura* 21 (1991–92) 319–320.

11. Eric Van Young, "Millennium on the Northern Marches," *Comparative Studies in Society and History* 28 (July 1986) 400.

12. "El 'Jesus de los pobres' de Nicaragua dice que cura el SIDA," *Nueva Imagen* (May 18, 1992) 18.

13. Eric Van Young, "Who Was That Masked Man, Anyway?" *Proceedings of the 32nd Annual Meeting of the Rocky Mountain Council on Latin American Studies* (1984) 20. See also Eric Van Young, "Quetzalcóatl, King Ferdinand, and Ignacio Allende Go to the Seashore," in Jaime E. Rodríguez O., *The Independence of Mexico and the Creation of the New Nation* (Los Angeles: UCLA Latin American Center Publications, 1989) 109–127.

14. Oscar Alfredo Agüero, *The Millennium Among the Tupí-Cocama: A Case of Religious Ethno-Dynamism in the Peruvian Amazon* (Uppsala, Sweden: Uppsala Research Reports in Cultural Anthropology, 1992) 78–79 and 52. See also Jaime Regan, *Hacia la tierra sin mal: estudio sobre la religiosidad del pueblo en la Amazonía* (Iquitos, Peru: CETA, 1983) 2/151.

15. Che Guevara, *Guerrilla Warfare*, trans. J. P. Morray (New York: Vintage Books, 1968) xiv.

16. See Esteban Montejo, *The Autobiography of a Runaway Slave*, ed. Miguel Barnet (New York: Pantheon Books, 1968) 128, 201, and 222.

17. Quoted in Margarita de Orellana, *Villa y Zapata: la revolución mexicana* (Madrid: Ediciones Anaya, 1988) 112; and Serge Gruzinski, *Man-Gods in the Mexican Highlands: Indian Power and Colonial Society, 1520–1800*, trans. Eileen Corrigan (Stanford: Stanford University Press, 1989) 187–188. See also Pedro A. Vives, *Pancho Villa* (Madrid: Historia 16, 1987) 5 and 148, where an effort to demythologize Villa results in exhumation and decapitation.

18. Mary Dillom and Thomas Abercrombie, "The Destroying Christ," in Jonathan D. Hill, ed., *Rethinking History and Myth: Indigenous South American Perspectives on the Past* (Urbana: University of Illinois Press, 1988) 50.

19. Alberto Flores Galindo, *Europa y el país de los incas* (Lima: Instituto de Apoyo Agrario, 1986) 47. Rumors on the coast held that Pachacámac's resurrection was imminent; see David D. Gow, "Símbolo y protesta," *América indígena* 39/1 (1979) 57.

20. Diane Kitchen, *Before We Knew Nothing*, 1989, videocassette. For other cases with parallels to Inkarrí motifs, see Leopoldo J. Bartolomé, "Movimientos milenaristas de los aborígenes chaqueños entre 1905 y 1933," *Suplemento antropológico* 7/1–2 (1972) 116; and Juan Andrés Ramírez E., "La novena del Señor de Qoyllur Rit'i," *Allpanchis Phuturinqa* 1 (1969) 61–67.

21. Nathan Wachtel, *The Vision of the Vanquished: The Spanish Conquest of Peru Through Indian Eyes, 1530–1570*, trans. Ben Reynolds and Siân Reynolds (New York: Barnes and Noble, 1977) 50. In the historical account, Cuauhtémoc is later executed by Cortés. For similar examples, see Sylvia Rodríguez, *The Matachines Dance: Ritual Symbolism and Interethnic Relations in the Upper Río Grande Valley* (Albuquerque: University of New Mexico Press, 1996) 1–2; Sabine MacCormack, "*Pachacuti*: Miracles, Punishments, and Last Judgment," *American Historical Review* 93 (October, 1988) 1003; and Florencia E. Mallon, *Peasant and Nation: The Making of Postcolonial Mexico and Peru* (Berkeley and Los Angeles: University of California Press, 1995) 203–204.

22. See Weckmann, *Herencia*, 2/652–667; Robert Ricard, *The Spiritual Conquest of Mexico: An Essay on the Apostolate and the Evangelical Methods of the Mendicant Orders in New Spain, 1523–1572*, trans. Lesley Byrd Simpson (Berkeley and Los Angeles: University of California Press, 1966) 186; Angel López Cantos, *Juegos, fiestas, y diversiones en la América española* (Madrid: Editorial MAPFRE, 1992) 183–188; and Arturo Warman Gryj, *La danza de moros y cristianos* (Mexico City: Sep/Setentas, 1972) 148. For a nineteenth-century example, see Flora Tristán, "Peregrinaciones de una paria," in Carlos M. Rama, ed., *Utopismo socialista, 1830–1893* (Caracas: Biblioteca Ayacucho, 1987) 15–16.

23. Ramón A. Gutiérrez, *When Jesus Came, the Corn Mothers Went Away: Marriage, Sexuality, and Power in New Mexico, 1500–1846* (Stanford: Stanford

University Press, 1991) 47–49. According to Marx, historical personages appear twice, "the first time as tragedy, the second as farce"; see Robert C. Tucker, ed., *The Marx-Engels Reader* (New York: W. W. Norton, 1978) 594.

24. Gabriela Cerruti, *El jefe: vida y obra de Carlos Saúl Menem* (Buenos Aires: Editorial Planeta, 1993) 15–16.

25. See Joseph A. Page, *Perón: A Biography* (New York: Random House, 1983) 227; and Tad Szulc, *Twilight of the Tyrants* (New York: Henry Holt, 1959) 210. See also Pedro A. Vives, *Augusto César Sandino* (Madrid: Historia 16, 1987) 77, where Sandino is the son of Bolívar.

26. See Brian Loveman and Thomas M. Davies Jr., *The Politics of Antipolitics: The Military in Latin America* (Lincoln: University of Nebraska Press, 1989) 26–27; and Richard H. Immerman, *The CIA in Guatemala* (Austin: University of Texas Press, 1982) 32.

27. See J. M. Taylor, *Eva Perón: The Myths of a Woman* (Chicago: University of Chicago Press, 1979) 65, 69, 70, 82, and 83; and Page, *Perón*, 343–344. Evita's mortician published a memoir: Pedro Ara, *El caso Eva Perón* (Buenos Aires: CVS Ediciones, 1974). On the spirit transfer, see Page, *Perón*, 425; and José Pablo Feinmann, *López Rega, la cara oscura de Perón* (Buenos Aires: Editorial Lagasa, 1987) 59–60.

28. Eva Perón, *La última voluntad de Eva Perón* (Buenos Aires: Presidencia de la Nación, Subsecretaría de Informaciones, 1952) n.p.

29. Michael C. Meyer and William L. Sherman, *The Course of Mexican History* (New York: Oxford University Press, 1983) 332; and John Lynch, *Caudillos in Spanish America* (Oxford: Clarendon Press, 1992) 345. Santa Anna retaliated, "I bore with pride the loss of an important member of my body" (346).

30. Stephen Clissold, *The Saints of South America* (London: Charles Knight, 1972) 6. In 1987 Juan Perón's hands were amputated from his corpse for purposes that remain a mystery.

31. See Liza Gross, *Handbook of Leftist Guerilla Groups in Latin America and the Caribbean* (Boulder: Westview Press, 1995) 55 and 72.

32. On Túpac Catari as the resurrection of Tomás Catari, see Jorge Hidalgo, "Amarus y Cataris," *Chungara* 10 (March 1983) 128.

33. Quoted in Rosalind C. Gow, "Inkarrí and Revolutionary Leadership in the Southern Andes," *Journal of Latin American Lore* 8/2 (1982) 199.

34. See ibid., 199; and Marie-Chantal Barre, *Ideologías indigenistas y movimientos indios*, trans. Luisa Salomone (Mexico City: Siglo Veintiuno, 1983) 114. For a similar example—concerning Salvadoran archbishop Oscar Arnulfo Romero, who asserted, "If I am killed, I shall rise again in the struggle of the Salvadoran people"—see Jon Sobrino, "Messiahs and Messianisms," in Wim Beuken et al., *Messianism in History* (London: SCM Press, 1993) 122.

35. Alicia M. Barabas, *Utopías indias: movimientos sociorreligiosos en México* (Mexico City: Grijalbo, 1989) 187.

36. Nancy M. Farriss, *Maya Society Under Colonial Rule: The Collective Enterprise of Survival* (Princeton: Princeton University Press, 1984) 314.

37. Victoria Bricker, *The Indian Christ, the Indian King: The Historical Substrate of Maya Myth and Ritual* (Austin: University of Texas Press, 1986) 60.

38. In 1599 the Jesuits of Lima used the "cadavers of Indians, whole and dried," to represent the resurrection of the dead in a staged allegory of the Last Judgment. See José Juan Arrom, *Historia del teatro hispanoamericano: época colonial* (Mexico City: Ediciones de Andrea, 1967) 32.

39. Miguel León-Portilla, *The Aztec Image of Self and Society: An Introduction to Nahua Culture*, ed. J. Jorge Klor de Alva (Salt Lake City: University of Utah Press, 1992) 22.

40. The quoted phrase is from Inga Clendinnen, *Aztecs: An Interpretation* (Cambridge: Cambridge University Press, 1991) 57. After conquest Tezcatlipoca was associated with Lucifer.

41. León-Portilla, *Aztec Image*, 25.

42. Quoted in Georges Baudot, "Quetzalcóatl o la 'Serpiente Emplumada' en la fundación de las sociedades precolombinas postclásicas de Mesoamérica," in Manuel Gutiérrez Estévez, ed., *Mito y ritual en América* (Madrid: Editorial Alhambra, 1988) 51.

43. Quoted in León-Portilla, *Aztec Image*, 27. In other versions, Quetzalcóatl sacrifices himself by fire and rises to become Venus; see Gordon Brotherston, *Book of the Fourth World: Reading the Native Americans Through Their Literature* (New York: Cambridge University Press, 1992) 270–272.

44. See Davíd Carrasco, *Quetzalcóatl and the Irony of Empire: Myths and Prophecies in the Aztec Tradition* (Chicago: University of Chicago Press, 1992) 35; Nigel Davies, *The Aztec Empire: The Toltec Resurgence* (Norman: University of Oklahoma Press, 1987) 250; Nigel Davies, *The Toltecs: Until the Fall of Tula* (Norman: University of Oklahoma Press, 1977) 23; Alfredo López Austin, *The Human Body and Ideology Concepts of the Ancient Nahuas*, trans. Thelma Ortiz de Montellano and Bernard Ortiz de Montellano (Salt Lake City: University of Utah Press, 1988) 1/84; and Jacques Lafaye, *Quetzalcóatl y Guadalupe: la formación de la conciencia nacional en México*, trans. Ida Vitale (Mexico City: Fondo de Cultura Económica, 1977) 212.

45. Carrasco, *Quetzalcóatl*, 150 and 162.

46. See Alfredo López Austin, *Hombre-dios: religión y política en el mundo náhuatl* (Mexico City: Universidad Nacional Autónoma de México, 1973) 27. The entire work treats Quetzalcóatl in depth.

47. The first quoted passage is from Francisco López de Gómara, *Cortés: The Life of the Conqueror by His Secretary*, ed. and trans. Lesley Byrd Simpson (Berkeley and Los Angeles: University of California Press, 1964) 58. On Quetzalcóatl and the wind see Baudot, "Quetzalcóatl," 49.

48. James Lockhart, ed. and trans., *We People Here: Nahuatl Accounts of the Conquest of Mexico* (Berkeley and Los Angeles: University of California Press, 1993) 62 (see also 58). For similar expectations in Peru, see Sabine MacCormack, *Religion in the Andes: Vision and Imagination in Early Colonial Peru* (Princeton: Princeton University Press, 1991) 309.

49. See Lockhart, *We*, 64–68.

50. See ibid., 78, 82, 84, and 116.

51. Quoted in Maureen Ahern, "The Cross and the Gourd," in Jerry M. Williams and Robert E. Lewis, eds., *Early Images of the Americas: Transfer and Invention* (Tucson: University of Arizona Press, 1993) 225.

52. See Carrasco, *Quetzalcóatl*, 187–191.

53. Wachtel, *Vision*, 15.

54. See Hernán Cortés, *Letters from Mexico*, ed. and trans. Anthony Pagden (New Haven: Yale University Press, 1986) 85–86.

55. Ibid., 85.

56. Ibid., 85–86 (see also 98–99). For discussion see John H. Elliott, *Spain and Its World* (New Haven: Yale University Press, 1989) 27–41.

57. Cortés, *Letters*, 86–87.

58. Some mestizo chroniclers cautiously followed suit; see Fernando Cervantes, *The Devil in the New World: The Impact of Diabolism in New Spain* (New Haven: Yale University Press, 1994) 75–76. For an overview of the literature on Queztalcóatl-Thomas, see López Austin, *Hombre-dios*, 14–25.

59. See Enrique Florescano, *El mito de Quetzalcóatl* (Mexico City: Fondo de Cultura Económica, 1993) 67–69; and López Austin, *Hombre-dios*, 148.

60. See Carrasco, *Quetzalcóatl*, 30 and 157; Lafaye, *Quetzalcóatl*, 226; and López Austin, *Hombre-dios*, 13–25.

61. Matthew 24:27. On Quezalcóatl and his Maya version, Kukulcán, as Christ, see López Austin, *Hombre-dios*, 24; and Farriss, *Maya Society*, 303 and 306.

62. Lafaye, *Quetzalcóatl*, 227; and López Austin, *Hombre-dios*, 21. See also John 20:24.

63. Servando Teresa de Mier, *Ideario político* (Caracas: Biblioteca Ayacucho, 1978) 11. See also López Austin, *Hombre-dios*, 25; Anthony Pagden, *Spanish Imperialism and the Political Imagination: Studies in European and Spanish-American Social and Political Theory, 1513–1830* (New Haven: Yale University Press, 1990) 96; and D. A. Brading, "La historia natural y la civilización amerindia," in Carmen Bernand, ed., *Descubrimiento, conquista y colonización de América a quinientos años* (Mexico City: Fondo de Cultura Económica, 1994) 26–27.

64. D. A. Brading, *The First America: The Spanish Monarchy, Creole Patriots, and the Liberal State, 1492–1867* (Cambridge: Cambridge University Press, 1991) 583. Following the 1712 Tzeltal Rebellion, Dominicans explained to the natives that they (the indigenous population) were Jews who rejected two centuries of preaching, as their ancestors had earlier rejected Saint Thomas. See Murdo J. MacLeod, "Dominican Explanations for Revolts and Their Suppression in Colonial Chiapas," in Susan Ramírez, ed., *Indian-Religious Relations in Colonial Spanish America* (Syracuse: Maxwell School of Citizenship and Public Affairs, Syracuse University, 1989) 46.

65. Lafaye, *Quetzalcóatl*, 228. For an example of Thomas in India, see Milhou, *Colón*, 186.

66. The map is reproduced in Luis Revenga, ed., *Los Beatos* (Madrid: Biblioteca Nacional, 1986) 38.

67. Quoted in Bloch, *Principle*, 768. John Mandeville concurs; see John Mandeville, *The Travels of John Mandeville*, trans. C. W. R. D. Moseley (New York: Penguin Books, 1983) 182.

68. Bartolomé de Las Casas, *Historia de las Indias*, ed. André Saint-Lu, (Caracas: Biblioteca Ayacucho, 1986) 3/26–27.

69. Quoted in Baudot, "Quetzalcóatl," 42.

70. Quoted in Lafaye, *Quetzalcóatl*, 224.

71. See Enrique de Gandía, *Historia crítica de los mitos y leyendas de la conquista americana* (Buenos Aires: Centro Difusor del Libro, 1946) 153–154; and Leonardo Olschki, "Ponce de Leon's Fountain of Youth," *Hispanic American Historical Review* 21/3 (August 1941) 382. For a similar episode in Madeira, see Sergio Buarque de Holanda, *Visión del paraíso: motivos edénicos en el descubrimiento y colonización del Brasil*, trans. Estela Dos Santos (Caracas: Biblioteca Ayacucho, 1987) 152.

72. See Stelio Cro, *The American Foundations of the Hispanic Utopia (1792–1793)* (Tallahassee: DeSoto Press, 1994) 58–61.

73. Leopold Lugones, *El imperio jesuítico* (Buenos Aires: Comisión Argentina de Fomento Interamericano, 1945) 155. Paí Zumé, cultural hero of the Guaraní, was also called Abaré (Man Different from Others Because He Is Chaste), and the Jesuits themselves were referred to by these names; see Lucía Gálvez, *Guaraníes y Jesuitas: de la tierra sin mal al paraíso* (Buenos Aires: Editorial Sudamericana, 1995) 172.

74. Franklin Pease G. Y., "Estudio preliminar," in Gregorio García, *Origen de los indios del Nuevo Mundo* (Mexico City: Fondo de Cultura Económica, 1981) xxi. See also Brading, *First America*, 326; Luis E. Valcárcel, *Historia del Perú antiguo* (Lima: Editorial Juan Mejía Baca, 1964) 2/437–450; Emilio Choy, *Antropología e historia* (Lima: Universidad Nacional Mayor de San Marcos,

1979) 416; and Jan Szemiński, *Un kuraca, un dios, y una historia* (Jujuy, Argentina: Instituto de Ciencias Antropológicas, 1987) 47–59.

75. MacCormack, *Religion*, 320–321. See also Frank Salomon, "Chronicles of the Impossible," in Rolena Adorno, ed., *From Oral to Written Expression: Native Andean Chronicles of the Early Colonial Period* (Syracuse: Maxwell School of Citizenship and Public Affairs, Syracuse University, Latin American Series, 1982) 18.

76. Quoted in MacCormack, *Religion*, 331.

77. The quoted passage is in Rolena Adorno, *Guaman Poma: Writing and Resistance in Colonial Peru* (Austin: University of Texas Press, 1986) 26–27. See Felipe Guaman Poma de Ayala, *Nueva crónica y buen gobierno*, ed. Franklin Pease (Caracas: Biblioteca Ayacucho, 1980), 1/65–70, and 2/75–76.

78. These examples are from Valcárcel, *Historia*, 2/439–448.

79. MacCormack, *Religion*, 313. See also Garcilaso de la Vega, El Inca, *Royal Commentaries of the Incas and General History of Peru*, trans. Harold V. Livermore (Austin: University of Texas Press, 1987) 291.

80. The quoted passage is from Lafaye, *Quetzalcóatl*, 222.

81. Quoted in Barabas, *Utopías*, 133.

82. Ibid., 133–137 and 139–140.

83. Ibid., 158.

84. Quoted in ibid., 206. Regarding the Maya Kukulcán, see Florescano, *Mito*, 58–61. For a female messiah assimilated to Quetzalcóatl and to the mother of Moctezuma, see Paul J. Vanderwood, *The Power of God Against the Guns of Government* (Stanford: Stanford University Press, 1998) 303. For Quetzalcóatl returning for the "Harmonic Convergence" in 1987, see Damian Thompson, *The End of Time: Faith and Fear in the Shadow of the Millennium* (Hanover, N.H.: University Press of New England, 1997) 208–209.

85. Quoted in Miguel León-Portilla, ed., *The Broken Spears: The Aztec Account of the Conquest of Mexico* (Boston: Beacon Press, 1992) 171–172.

86. The quoted phrase is from Alonso Zarzar, *Apo Capac Huayna, Jesús Sacramentado: mito, utopía y milenarismo* (Lima: Centro Amazónico de Antropología y Aplicación Práctica, 1989) 54.

87. The quoted phrases are from Flores Galindo, *Europa*, 20.

88. Alejando Vivanco G., "Una nueva versión del mito de Inkarrí," *Anthropológica* 2/2 (1984) 198. On the capture and ransom of Atahualpa, see John Hemming, *The Conquest of the Incas* (New York: Harcourt Brace Jovanovich, 1970) 47–49.

89. The quoted passage is from Nathan Wachtel, *Sociedad e ideología: ensayos de historia y antropología andinas* (Lima: Instituto de Estudios Peruanos, 1973) 159. A 1614 Quechua-Spanish dictionary defines *Atahualpa* as "inga rey"; see Mercedes López-Baralt, *El retorno del inca rey: mito y profecía en el mundo andino* (La Paz: Hisbol, 1989) 45. The word *"inca"* in its broadest sense connotes "a model or prototype of man and Andean society"; D. Gow, "Símbolo," 71. In the modern Amazon, Inca refers to a deity with no association to the former emperors of Tahuantinsuyo; see Gerald Weiss, "Elements of Inkarrí East of the Andes," in Edmundo Magaña and Peter Mason, eds, *Myth and the Imaginary in the New World* (Dordrecht, Holland: Foris Publications, 1986) 307. For an Amazonian myth derived from Inkarrí, see Michael F. Brown and Eduardo Fernández, *War of Shadows: The Struggle for Utopia in the Peruvian Amazon* (Berkeley and Los Angeles: University of California Press, 1991) 55.

90. See Hemming, *Conquest*, 448–450.

91. See, for example, Alejandro Ortiz Rescaniere, *De Adaneva a Inkarrí: una visión indígena del Perú* (Lima: Ediciones Retablo de Papel, 1973) 151. On other myths of living heads in South America, see López-Baralt, *Retorno*, 85.

92. Quoted in Jan Szemiński, *La utopía tupamarista* (Lima: Pontificia Universidad Católica del Perú, 1983) 145–146.

93. Quoted in Franklin Pease, *El dios creador andino* (Lima: Mosca Azul Editores, 1973) 90. On Pachacuti Yamqui, see MacCormack, *Religion*, 284.

94. Henrique-Osvaldo Urbano, "Dios Yaya, Dios Churi y Dios Espíritu Santo," *Journal of Latin American Lore* 6/1 (1980) 121. On the huacas, see Pablo Joseph Arriaga, *The Extirpation of Idolatry in Peru*, trans. L. Clark Keating (Lexington: University of Kentucky Press, 1968) 81, 82, and 131.

95. See López-Baralt, *Retorno*, 47–49.

96. Flores Galindo, *Europa*, 72.

97. For an example, see Diana Fane, ed., *Converging Cultures: Art and Identity in Spanish America* (New York: Brooklyn Museum and Harry N. Abrams, 1996) 243. See also Teresa Gisbert, "Los Incas en la pintura virreinal del siglo XVIII," *América indígena* 39/4 (1979) 749–772.

98. Quoted in Ramón Mujica Pinilla, "El ancla de Rosa de Lima," in José Flores Araoz et al., eds., *Santa Rosa de Lima y su tiempo* (Lima: Colección Arte y Tesoros del Perú, 1995) 192–193. On Bolívar as agent of the new pachacuti in an 1825 painting, see MacCormack, "*Pachacuti*," 1003.

99. Quoted in Indalecio Liévano Aguirre, *Bolívar* (Madrid: Instituto de Cooperación Iberoamericana, 1983) 303–305. For Bolívar "on the rock of creation in the American heaven" with the Inca beside him, see José Martí, *Our America: Writings on Latin America and the Struggle for Cuban Independence*, ed. Philip S. Foner (New York: Monthly Review Press, 1977) 101–102. For a parallel myth from Mexico, see Raúl Vidales, *Utopía y liberación: el amanecer del indio* (San José, Costa Rica: DEI, 1988) 81.

100. Quoted in Juan M. Ossio, "El Mito de Inkarrí narrado por segunda vez diez años después," *Antropológica* 2/2 (1984) 194.

101. For an example, see Jack Autry Dabbs, "A Messiah Among the Chiriguanos," *Southwestern Journal of Anthropology* 9 (1953) 51. The Penitente confraternities in New Mexico refer to themselves as the Brothers of Our Father Jesus.

102. In Ephesians 4:12, the body of Christ is similarly constructed by the faithful. The Christ of Chalhuanca was probably a fertility amulet. Andeans sometimes buried carvings of Santiago in pastures to protect livestock.

103. See Alberto Flores Galindo, *Buscando un inca: identidad y utopía en los Andes* (Lima: Editorial Horizonte, 1988) 45.

104. 1 Corinthians 10:17. On the Last Supper see Mark 14:22; Matthew 25: 26; Luke 22.19; and 1 Corinthians 11:24.

105. Joan Myers et al., *Santiago: Saint of Two Worlds* (Albuquerque: University of New Mexico Press, 1991) 6 and 9. See also Acts 12:1–12. After he was decapitated, the third-century Saint Denis picked up his head and walked two miles to his grave. In medieval imagery, the body parts lost to beasts and swords were returned to corpses resurrected for the Last Judgment; see Caroline Walker Bynum, *The Resurrection of the Body in Western Christianity, 200–1336* (New York: Columbia University Press, 1995).

106. Weiss, "Elements," 311 and 315.

107. Quoted in D. Gow, "Símbolo," 73. See also Efraín Morote Best, "Cabezas voladoras," *Perú indígena* 4/9 (April 1953) 107–124. For a parallel in Nicaragua, see Milagros Palma, "El padre sin cabeza," in Pablo Richard, ed., *Raíces de la teología latinoamericana* (San José, Costa Rica: DEI/CEHILA, 1985) 389–391. For a separate Andean conception of the soul, see MacCormack, *Religion*, 410.

108. Henrique-Osvaldo Urbano, "Del sexo, incesto y los ancestros de Inkarrí," *Allpanchis* 15/17–18 (1981) 82.

109. Quoted in José María Arguedas, *Formación de una cultura nacional*

indoamericana (Mexico City: Siglo Veintiuno, 1975) 175. For more on the sun and wind motifs, see Gregorio Condori Mamani and Asunta Quispe Huamán, *Andean Lives*, ed. Ricardo Valderrama Fernández and Carmen Escalante Gutiérrez, trans. Paul H. Gelles et al. (Austin: University of Texas Press, 1996) 22. Some Aztec myths of the birth of the sun similarly have a celestial father and terrestrial mother; see López Austin, *Human Body*, 1/56.

110. Quoted in Arguedas, *Formación*, 178.

111. Weiss, "Elements," 310.

112. See Agustín de Zárate, *The Discovery and Conquest of Peru*, trans. J. M. Cohn (Baltimore: Penguin Books, 1968) 102–103.

113. Quoted in Ortiz, *De Adaneva*, 134.

114. Pease, *Dios*, 90 and 138.

115. Ortiz, *De Adaneva*, 132.

116. See, for example, Szemiński, *Kuraca*, 151.

117. Quoted in Caroline Bynum, *Holy Feast and Holy Fast: The Religious Significance of Food to Medieval Women* (Berkeley and Los Angeles: University of California Press, 1987) 62. For emphasis on Paul's epistles in the American mission, see Silvio Zavala, *The Colonial Period in the History of the New World*, ed. Max Savelle (Mexico City: Instituto Panamericano de Geografía e Historia, 1962) 232. Paradise on some mappamundi was depicted as the head of the earth's body; see Milhou, *Colón*, 407. For Christ as head of the body-church, see, for example, Ephesians 5:23; and Colossians 1:18 and 2:19.

118. Quoted in Ernst H. Kantorowicz, *The King's Two Bodies: A Study in Medieval Political Theology* (Princeton: Princeton University Press, 1957) 200.

119. Quoted in ibid., 194.

120. Attributed to José de Acosta, *Doctrina christiana y catecismo para instrucción de los indios* (Lima: Antonio Ricardo, 1584) 17.

121. See Northrop Frye, *Anatomy of Criticism* (Princeton: Princeton University Press, 1957) 142–143. For an image of the king displacing Christ, see Henry Mayr-Harting, "The West: The Age of Conversion," in John McManners, ed., *The Oxford Illustrated History of Christianity* (Oxford: Oxford University Press, 1990) 107.

122. Quoted in José Rabasa, "Writing and Evangelization in Sixteenth-Century Mexico," in Williams and Lewis, *Early Images*, 83. See Romans 12:4–5; and 1 Corinthians 12:20–27. Medieval Spanish imagery also likened the relation of the king and his realm to the mystical marriage of Christ and his church. See Américo Castro, *Aspectos del vivir hispánico* (Madrid: Alianza, 1970) 24.

123. Kantorowicz, *King's Two Bodies*, 130. See also Carmelo Lisón Tolosana, *La imagen del rey: monarquía, realeza y poder ritual en la Casa de los Austrias* (Madrid: Espasa-Calpe, 1992) 96–103 and 184.

124. See MacCormack, "*Pachacuti*," 962 and 965–966; López-Baralt, *Retorno*, 82–83; and Luis Millones, *Actores de altura: ensayos sobre el teatro popular andino* (Lima: Editorial Horizonte, 1992) 42–43. For a modern theatrical example, see Urbano, "Del sexo," 99.

125. The quoted phrase is from Marco Curatola, "Mito y milenarismo en los Andes," *Allpanchis* 10 (1977) 89.

126. Szemiński, *Utopía*, 75 and 78–79; Túpac Catari also referred to himself as Inca Rey and Rey Inca (75).

127. The quoted phrase is in ibid., 192.

128. The quoted passages are in Boleslao Lewin, *La rebelión de Túpac Amaru y los orígenes de la emancipación americana* (Buenos Aires: Liberería Hachette, 1957) 497–498.

129. Quoted in ibid., 498.

130. For the same intent in an execution by Incas, see Hemming, *Conquest*, 419.

131. See J. H. Parry, *The Discovery of South America* (New York: Taplinger Publishing, 1979) 37. The first and second quoted passages are in John F. Moffitt and Santiago Sebastián, *O Brave New People: The European Invention of the American Indian* (Albuquerque: University of New Mexico Press, 1996) 72 (see also 126–127). The third quoted passage is in Michael Palencia-Roth, "The Cannibal Law of 1503," in Williams and Lewis, *Early Images*, 53. On America as the consolidation of the four quarters and their four races, see José Vasconcelos, *La raza cósmica* (Mexico City: Espasa-Calpe, 1948) 53. On indigenous configurations of space, see Brotherston, *Book*, 82–102.

132. See Wilfredo Kapsoli, *Guerreros de la oración: las nuevas iglesias en el Perú* (Lima: Sepec, 1994) 24.

133. For diagrams of the "four corners of the sky" in Aztec cosmology, see Florescano, *Mito*, 140. Quetzalcóatl is "the god of the four winds"; see Lafaye, *Quetzalcóatl*, 211.

134. See Ronald Sanders, *Lost Tribes and Promised Lands* (Boston: Little Brown, 1978) 10–11; and Milhou, *Colón*, 406–407. Jerusalem is coterminous with Christ's navel. The crucifix also served as a model for Romanesque and Gothic cathedrals.

135. See López Austin, *Human Body*, 1/348. For comparative examples of calendars and zodiacs, see Serge Gruzinski, *Painting the Conquest: The Mexican Indians and the European Renaissance,* trans. Deke Dusinberre (Paris: UNESCO/Flammarion, 1992) 91.

136. Quoted in Oliver LaFarge, *Santa Eulalia: The Religion of a Cuchumatán Town* (Chicago: University of Chicago Press, 1947) 57. Earlier in Mexico, the man-god Martín Ocelotl—cut to pieces by Moctezuma—spontaneously reintegrated his body; see J. Jorge Klor de Alva, "Martín Ocelotl," in David G. Sweet and Gary B. Nash, eds. *Struggle and Survival in Colonial America* (Berkeley and Los Angeles: University of California Press, 1981) 135 and 138. On the underground reconstitution of a cultural hero of the Mixes in Mexico, see Vidales, *Utopía*, 81.

137. See Luis Millones, *Historia y poder en los Andes centrales (desde los orígenes al siglo XVII)* (Madrid: Alianza, 1987) 108–109 and 119; Geoffrey W. Conrad and Arthur A. Demarest, *Religion and Empire: The Dynamics of Aztec and Incan Expansionism* (Cambridge: Cambridge University Press, 1984) 111 and 182; Sabine G. MacCormack, "Children of the Sun and Reasons of State," Working Paper 6, University of Maryland, Department of Spanish and Portuguese, 1990, 12; MacCormack, *Religion*, 120–122; Szemiński, *Utopía*, 103; and Brotherston, *Book*, 206.

138. See Wachtel, *Vision*, 172; and George Kubler, "The Neo-Inca State (1537–1572)," *Hispanic American Historical Review* 27/2 (May 1947) 202. Each royal mummy coexisted on earth and "in the sky with his father the Sun"; see MacCormack, *Religion*, 131. On Quetzalcóatl as the sun, see López Austin, *Hombre-dios*, 134; and Antonio de León Pinelo, *El paraíso en el nuevo mundo*, ed. Raúl Porras Barrenechea (Lima: Comité del IV Centenario del Descubrimiento del Amazonas, 1943) 1/293–294.

139. Rafael Díaz Maderuelo, *Francisco de Orellana* (Madrid: Historia 16, 1987) 54.

140. Alvar Núñez Cabeza de Vaca, *Naufragios y comentarios* (Madrid: Espasa-Calpe, 1985) 73.

141. See George P. Hammond and Agapito Rey, eds. and trans., *Narratives of the Coronado Expedition, 1540–1542* (Albuquerque: University of New Mexico Press, 1940) 132–134 and 144; and R. Gutiérrez, *When Jesus Came*, 43–44. On Pedro de Alvarado as "the Sun," see Gerónimo de Mendieta, *Historia eclesiástica indiana* (Mexico City: Editorial Porrúa, 1980) 388.

142. R. Gutiérrez, *When Jesus Came*, 88.

143. See John J. Collins, *The Scepter and the Star: The Messiahs of the Dead Sea Scrolls and Other Ancient Literature* (New York: Doubleday, 1995) 39; and John J. Collins, *The Apocalyptic Imagination: Introduction to the Jewish Matrix of Christianity* (New York: Crossroad, 1984) 96. The sun-emperor link common to Inca and Japanese cultures led one investigation to conclude that "Manco Capac, founder of the Empire of the Incas, was Japanese"; see Luis Jochamowitz, *Ciudadano Fujimori: la construcción de un político* (Lima: Peisa, 1993) 315–316.

144. Barbara Von Barghahn, "A Crucible of Gold," in Barbara Von Barghahn et al., eds., *Temples of Gold, Crowns of Silver: Reflections of Majesty in the Viceregal Americas* (Washington, D.C.: Art Museum of the Americas, 1991) 35.

145. Regarding the solar cult, see Mircea Eliade, *A History of Religious Ideas*, trans. William R. Trask (Chicago: University of Chicago Press, 1982) 2/411.

146. The quoted passages are from John 8:12; Matthew 17:2; and Revelation 21:23, respectively. See also Psalms 84:11; Matthew 17:2; John 1:4–5 and 9:5; and Revelation 1:16, 22:5, and 22:16. For ancient precedents and early Christian interpretations of Christ as sun, see Von Barghahn, "Crucible," 34–38; Weckmann, *Herencia*, 1/148; and André Grabar, *Early Christian Art*, trans. Stuart Gilbert and James Emmons (New York: Odyssey Press, 1968) 80. For Christ as the church fathers' "sun of justice," see Santiago Sebastián, *El barroco iberoamericano: mensaje iconográfico* (Madrid: Ediciones Encuentro, 1990) 16 (see also 41–43).

147. See Fane, *Converging Cultures*, 120 and 122; and Larry Frank, *New Kingdom of the Saints* (Santa Fe: Red Crane Books, 1992) 82, 119, 120, 160, 161, and 174.

148. See LaFarge, *Santa Eulalia*, 104; Xavier Albo, "La experiencia religiosa aymara," in Manuel M. Marzal, ed., *El rostro indio de Dios* (Lima: Pontificia Universidad Católica del Perú, 1991) 295–296; and Tod Swanson, "Cristo y el sentido del tiempo en las tradiciones andinas y amazónicas," *Allpanchis* 33 (1989) 289 and 292. For Christ as Inti in the Amazon, see Regan, *Hacia la tierra*, 1/129.

149. See, for example, Hidalgo, "Amarus," 127; Marie Howes, "Priests, People and Power: A North Peruvian Case Study," in Susanna Rostas and André Droogers, eds., *The Popular Use of Popular Religion in Latin America* (Amsterdam: CEDLA Publications, 1993) 152; and Jan Szemiński, "El único español bueno es el español muerto," in Juan Ansión, ed., *Pishtacos: de verdugos a sacaojos* (Lima: Tarea, 1989) 41. For an iconographic example of the sunlike monstrance, see Sebastián, *Barroco*, fig. 48.

150. See MacCormack, *Religion*, 195 and 368–369. For an overview of Corpus Christi celebrations, see Angel López, *Juegos*, 82–92; and Manuel Burga, *Nacimiento de una utopía: muerte y resurrección de los Incas* (Lima: Instituto de Apoyo Agrario, 1989) 377.

151. Quoted in Sebastián, *Barroco*, 52. The neo-Joachite age of Dios Churi is associated with Christ and characterized by the sun; see Urbano, "Dios Yaya," 121.

152. See Brown and Fernández, *War*, 62–65 and 120–121.

153. Ibid., 121.

154. See ibid., 75–76 and 167. See also Charles Teel Jr., "Las raíces radicales del adventismo en el altiplano peruano," *Allpanchis* 33 (1989) 211. In Mexican Spiritualism the supreme leader is referred to as The Great Son of the Sun; see Silvia Ortiz Echániz, "Origen, desarrollo y características del espiritualismo en México," *América indígena* 39/1 (January–March 1979) 155.

155. Harald O. Skar, "Quest for a New Covenant," in Harald O. Skar and

Frank Salomon, eds., *Natives and Neighbors in South America* (Göteborg, Sweden: Ethnological Studies 38, 1987) 239. See also Manuel Jesús Granados, "Los Israelitas," *Socialismo y participación* 41 (1988) 103.

156. Frederick Pike, *The Politics of the Miraculous in Peru: Haya de la Torre and the Spiritualist Tradition* (Lincoln: University of Nebraska Press, 1986) 112, 114, and 134. General Ignacio Luque responded officially to the death of Simón Bolívar by proclaiming "the Sun of Colombia has died"; see José Luis Busaniche, *Bolívar visto por sus contemporáneos* (Mexico City: Fondo de Cultura Económica, 1960) 328.

157. See R. Gow, "Inkarrí," 218–219.

158. See Simon Strong, *Shining Path: Terror and Revolution in Peru* (New York: Times Books, 1992) 61–62 and 75. On Sendero Luminoso as "light become steel," see Luis Arce Borja, ed., *Guerra popular en el Perú: el pensamiento gonzalo* (Brussels: n.p., 1989) 147; see also 177: "We will populate the Earth with light and joy."

159. Strong, *Shining Path*, 31.

160. Corinne Schmidt, "Capture Seen in Peru as Major Blow to Shining Path," *Washington Post*, September 14, 1992, A1 and A18. Guzmán informed his comrades, "Our obligation is to put ourselves at the head" of the people's war. See Arce, *Guerra*, 154, and 155 for Peru depicted in corporal imagery.

161. See William W. Stein, "Myth and Ideology in a Nineteenth Century Peruvian Peasant Uprising," *Ethnohistory* 29/1–4 (1982) 252.

162. Quoted in Zarzar, *Apo Capac Huayna*, 44. See also Mario Castro Arenas, *La rebelión de Juan Santos Atahualpa* (Lima: Carlos Milla Batres, 1973) 80; Juan M. Ossio, *Los indios del Perú* (Quito: Abya-Yala, 1995) 189 (Santos Atahualpa as "the first expression of the myth of Inkarrí carried to action"); and B. Sara Mateos Fernández-Maquieira, "Juan Santos Atahualpa," *Amazonía peruana* 22 (October 1992) 57.

163. Brown and Fernández, *War*, 32.

164. Zarzar, *Apo Capac Huayna*, 50.

165. Quoted in Flores Galindo, *Buscando*, 106.

166. M. Castro, *Rebelión*, 31.

167. Stefano Varese, *La sal de los cerros: una aproximación al mundo Campa* (Lima: Ediciones Retablo de Papel, 1973) 140; and Zarzar, *Apo Capac Huayna*, 38.

168. Zarzar, *Apo Capac Huayna*, 39 (see also 56).

169. See ibid., 47; and Varese, *Sal*, 68. See also Jaime Regan, "En torno a la entrevista de los Jesuitas con Juan Santos Atahualpa," *Amazonía peruana* 22 (October 1992) 61–92.

170. Zarzar, *Apo Capac Huayna*, 15, 45, 56, and 62.

171. See Varese, *Sal*, 71; and Brown and Fernández, *War*, 41.

172. The quoted phrase is in MacCormack, "Children," 15.

173. Quoted in Varese, *Sal*, 85.

174. Francisco A. Loayza, ed., *Juan Santos, el invencible: manuscritos del año de 1742 al año de 1755* (Lima: Pequeños Grandes Libros de Historia Americana, 1942) xii–xiii. In a Church account, the smoke was given off as Santos Atahualpa entered hell.

175. Regan, *Hacia la tierra*, 2/132. In some versions, Inkarrí also disappears into the jungle; see Zarzar, *Apo Capac Huayna*, 54.

176. Brown and Fernández, *War*, 46.

177. Quoted in Zarzar, *Apo Capac Huayna*, 36 (see also 37).

Chapter 6

1. Rutherford H. Platt Jr., *The Forgotten Books of Eden: Lost Books of the Old Testament* (New York: Gramercy Books, 1980) 8. See also Genesis 2:22 and 3:5.

2. See Mark 10:47; and Matthew 21:9.

3. See John J. Collins, *The Scepter and the Star: The Messiahs of the Dead Sea Scrolls and Other Ancient Literature* (New York: Doubleday, 1995) 141–142. See also Matthew 19:28; and Luke 22:30, where the apostles will sit on thrones to judge the tribes of Israel.

4. Leonardo Boff, *Faith at the Edge: Religion and Marginalized Existence*, trans., Robert R. Barr (San Francisco: Harper and Row, 1989) 153. See also Norman Cohn, *Cosmos, Chaos and the World to Come: The Ancient Roots of Apocalyptic Faith* (New Haven: Yale University Press, 1993) 204; and Marjorie Reeves, *Joachim of Fiore and the Prophetic Future* (London: SPCK, 1976) 295.

5. Colin M. MacLachlan, *Spain's Empire in the New World: The Role of Ideas in Institutional and Social Change* (Berkeley and Los Angeles: University of California Press, 1988) 2.

6. Carmelo Lisón Tolosana, *La imagen del rey: monarquía, realeza y poder ritual en la Casa de los Austrias* (Madrid: Espasa-Calpe, 1992) 96–98.

7. Ibid., 100–101.

8. Quoted in MacLachlan, *Spain's Empire*, 6; and in Geoffrey Parker, "David or Goliath?" in Richard L. Kagan and Geoffrey Parker, eds., *Spain, Europe and the Atlantic World: Essays in Honor of John H. Elliott* (New York: Cambridge University Press, 1995) 258–259. For a similar view from colonial Mexico, see D. A. Brading, *The First America: The Spanish Monarchy, Creole Patriots, and the Liberal State, 1492–1867* (Cambridge: Cambridge University Press, 1991) 363.

9. Quoted in Brading, *First America*, 226.

10. Quoted in Robert Ricard, *The Spiritual Conquest of Mexico: An Essay on the Apostolate and the Evangelical Methods of the Mendicant Orders in New Spain, 1523–1572*, trans. Lesley Byrd Simpson (Berkeley and Los Angeles: University of California Press, 1966) 86. Moctezuma gave the same assurance to Cortés; see David Carrasco, *Quetzalcóatl and the Irony of Empire: Myths and Prophecies in the Aztec Tradition* (Chicago: University of Chicago Press, 1992) 202.

11. Nathan Wachtel, *The Vision of the Vanquished: The Spanish Conquest of Peru Through Indian Eyes, 1530–1570*, trans. Ben Reynolds and Siân Reynolds (New York: Barnes and Noble, 1977) 22.

12. See Sabine MacCormack, *Religion in the Andes: Vision and Imagination in Early Colonial Peru* (Princeton: Princeton University Press, 1991) 308–309 and 363–364.

13. Lewis Hanke, *The First Social Experiments in America: A Study in the Development of Spanish Indian Policy in the Sixteenth Century* (Cambridge: Harvard University Press, 1935) 68–69. For another example, see George P. Hammond and Agapito Rey, eds. and trans., *Narratives of the Coronado Expedition, 1540–1542* (Albuquerque: University of New Mexico Press, 1940) 160.

14. Robert M. Levine, *Vale of Tears: Revisiting the Canudos Massacre in Northeastern Brazil, 1893–1897* (Berkeley and Los Angeles: University of California Press, 1992) 185.

15. Marco Curatola, "Mesías andinos" *Historia y cultura* 21 (1991–92) 308.

16. On Moctezuma as Huitzilopochtli, see Hernán Cortés, *Letters from*

Mexico, ed. and trans. Anthony Pagden (New Haven: Yale University Press, 1986) 467, n. 42.

17. Alfredo López Austin, *Hombre-dios: religión y política en el mundo náhuatl* (Mexico City: Universidad Nacional Autónoma de México, 1973) 127; see 122 on Maya man-gods.

18. Serge Gruzinski, *Man-Gods in the Mexican Highlands: Indian Power and Colonial Society, 1520–1800*, trans. Eileen Corrigan (Stanford: Stanford University Press, 1989) 22. See López Austin, *Hombre-dios*, 125 for a modern adaptation.

19. Quoted in Elsa Cecilia Frost, "Indians and Theologians," in Gary H. Gossen, ed., *South and Meso-American Native Spirituality: From the Cult of the Feathered Serpent to the Theology of Liberation* (New York: Crossroad, 1993) 135.

20. Gruzinski, *Man-Gods*, 36–37.

21. The first quoted passage is from ibid., 42; and the others are from Serge Gruzinski, *The Conquest of Mexico: The Incorporation of Indian Societies into the Western World, Sixteenth–Eighteenth Centuries*, trans. Eileen Corrigan (Cambridge, U.K.: Polity Press, 1993) 222–223.

22. See Gruzinski, *Man-Gods*, 72–73 and 76; and Gruzinski, *Conquest*, 224.

23. Quoted in A. Métraux, "Messiahs of South America," *Inter-American Quarterly* 3/2 (1941) 57.

24. See Métraux, "Messiahs," 57; Maria Isaura Pereira de Queiroz, *Historia y etnología de los movimientos mesiánicos: reforma y revolución en las sociedades tradicionales* trans. Florentino M. Torner (Mexico City: Siglo Veintiuno, 1969) 203; Alicia M. Barabas, *Utopías indias: movimientos sociorreligiosos en México* (Mexico City: Grijalbo, 1989) 7; and Hélène Clastres, *The Land-without-Evil: Tupí-Guaraní Prophetism*, trans. Jacqueline Grenez Brovender (Urbana: University of Illinois Press, 1995) 59–64. Clastres's stress of the event as a "supratribal war incited for a political purpose by a village prophet-chief" does not, in my estimation, undermine its messianic content (64).

25. See Silvia Ortiz Echánz, "Origen, desarrollo y características del espiritualismo en México," *América indígena* 39/1 (January–March 1979) 151–155.

26. Mircea Eliade, *The Sacred and the Profane: The Nature of Religion*, trans. Willard R. Trask (New York: Harper Torchbooks, 1961) 13. As a hymn from Nicaragua has it, "You are the God of the poor, / the human, unassuming God,/the God who sweats in the street"; see Victorio Araya G., "The God of the Strategic Covenant," in Pablo Richard et al., eds., *The Idols of Death and the God of Life*, trans. Barbara E. Campbell and Bonnie Shepard (Maryknoll, N.Y.: Orbis Books, 1983) 104.

27. On the apocalypses, see Collins, *Scepter*, 140–141.

28. See John Edwards, *Religion and Society in Spain* (Aldershot, England: Variorum, 1996) essay 8, 82–83.

29. For a Pentecostal example, see Abelino Martínez, *Las sectas en Nicaragua: oferta y demanda de salvación* (Managua: Editorial Departamento Ecuménico de Investigaciones, 1989) 86.

30. Quoted in Barabas, *Utopías*, 114.

31. Ibid., 116; and Fernando Medina Ruiz, *El paraíso demolido: las reducciones jesuíticas del Paraguay* (Mexico City: Tradición, 1987) 71.

32. The quoted passages are in Alvaro Huerga, *Historia de los alumbrados*, vol. 3, *Los alumbrados de Hispanoamérica* (Madrid: Fundación Universitaria Española, Seminario Cisneros, 1986) 417–418. See also Vidal Abril Castelló, "Francisco de la Cruz," *Cuadernos para la historia de la evangelización en América Latina* 3 (1988) 14–67.

33. Roger Bastide, *El prójimo y el extraño: el encuentro de las civilizaciones* (Buenos Aires: Amorrortu Editores, 1973) 284.

34. See René Ribeiro, "The Millennium That Never Came," in Ronald H. Chilcote, ed., *Protest and Resistance in Angola and Brazil: Comparative Studies* (Berkeley and Los Angeles: University of California Press, 1972) 166–167; and René Ribeiro, "Brazilian Messianic Movements," in Sylvia L. Thrupp, ed., *Millennial Dreams in Action* (New York: Schocken Books, 1970) 69.

35. Bastide, *Prójimo*, 286–287.

36. See Roger S. Greenway, "The 'Luz del Mundo' Movement in Mexico," *Missiology: An International Review* 1/2 (April 1973) 114. See also Alicia M. Barabas, "Identidad y cultura en nuevas iglesias milenaristas en México," in Alicia Barabas, ed., *Religiosidad y resistencia indígenas hacia el fin del milenio* (Quito: Abya-Yala, 1994) 257–259.

37. For an example, see Barabas, *Utopías*, 261. For iconographic examples, see Alfredo Moreno Cebrián, *Túpac Amaru: el cacique inca que rebeló los Andes* (Mexico City: Biblioteca Iberoamericana, 1988) 116–117.

38. Gonzalo Castillo-Cárdenas, *Liberation Theology from Below: The Life and Thought of Manuel Quintín Lame* (Maryknoll, N.Y.: Orbis Books, 1987) 41.

39. Quoted in ibid., 110 and 147.

40. John Hemming, *Amazon Frontier: The Defeat of the Brazilian Indians* (Cambridge: Harvard University Press, 1987) 321.

41. Quoted in Gonzalo Aguirre Beltrán, *Medicina y magia: el proceso de aculturación en la estructura colonial* (Mexico City: Instituto Nacional Indigenista, 1963) 65–66.

42. Fernando Cervantes, *The Devil in the New World: The Impact of Diabolism in New Spain* (New Haven: Yale University Press, 1994) 38.

43. Curt Nimuendajú, *The Tukuna* (Berkeley and Los Angeles: University of California Press, 1957) 138–139.

44. Andrés Pérez de Ribas, *My Life Among the Savage Nations of New Spain*, ed. and trans. Tomás Antonio Robertson (Los Angeles: Ward Ritchie Press, 1968) 194.

45. Ibid., 30.

46. Barabas, *Utopias*, 161.

47. Quoted in Clastres, *Land-without Evil*, 37.

48. William H. Crocker and Jean Crocker, *The Canela: Bonding Through Kinship, Ritual, and Sex* (New York: Harcourt Brace College Publishers, 1994) 43–45.

49. Nelson Reed, *The Caste War of Yucatan* (Stanford: Stanford University Press, 1964) 134; and Barabas, *Utopías*, 117–118 and 126.

50. See Victoria Bricker, *The Indian Christ, the Indian King: The Historical Substrate of Maya Myth and Ritual* (Austin: University of Texas Press, 1986) 104–105 and 115; and Reed, *Caste War*, 216.

51. The quoted phrase is from Geoffrey W. Conrad and Arthur A. Demarest, *Religion and Empire: The Dynamics of Aztec and Incan Expansionism* (Cambridge: Cambridge University Press, 1984) 1 (see also 114, 125, and 221). See also MacCormack, *Religion*, 425–430; Luis Millones, *Historia y poder en los Andes centrales (desde los orígenes al siglo XVII)* (Madrid: Alianza, 1987) 123; and Catherine J. Allen, "Body and Soul in Quechua Thought," *Journal of Latin American Lore* 8/2 (1982) 183.

52. See Luis Millones, *Mesianismo e idolatría en los Andes centrales* (Buenos Aires: Editorial Biblos, 1989) 6 and 20; and Millones, *Historia*, 168.

53. See Norman Cohn, *The Pursuit of the Millennium* (New York: Oxford University Press, 1970) 43, 62, 94, and 134.

54. For examples of heavenly letters, see Susan M. Deeds, "First-Generation Rebellions in Seventeenth-Century Nueva Vizcaya," in Susan Schroeder, ed., *Na-*

tive Resistance and the Pax Colonial in New Spain (Lincoln: University of Nebraska Press, 1998) 8; and Paul J. Vanderwood, *The Power of God Against the Guns of Government* (Stanford: Stanford University Press, 1998) 161–162.

55. Segundo E. Moreno Yánez, *Sublevaciones indígenas en la audiencia de Quito: desde comienzos del siglo XVII hasta finales de la colonia* (Quito: Ediciones de la Universidad Católica, 1985) 329–330.

56. Carlos Felice Cardot, *Rebeliones, motines y movimientos de masas en el siglo XVIII venezolano (1730–1781)* (Caracas: Academia Nacional de la Historia, 1977) 72–73; Federico Brito Figueroa, *Las insurrecciones de los esclavos negros en la sociedad colonial venezolana* (Caracas: Editorial Cantaclaro, 1961) 39, 49, and 59; and Pedro M. Arcaya, *Insurrección de los negros de la serranía de Coro* (Caracas: Instituto Panamericano de Geografía e Historia, 1949) 28.

57. MacLachlan, *Spain's Empire*, 21.

58. Eric Van Young, "Quetzalcóatl, King Ferdinand, and Ignacio Allende Go to the Seashore," in Jaime E. Rodríguez O., *The Independence of Mexico and the Creation of the New Nation* (Los Angeles: UCLA Latin American Center Publications, 1989) 110–111.

59. See Joseph Pérez, *Los movimientos precursores de la emancipación en Hispanoamérica* (Madrid: Editorial Alhambra, 1977) 117; Boleslao Lewin, *La rebelión de Túpac Amaru y los orígenes de la emancipación americana* (Buenos Aires: Liberería Hachette, 1957) 421; and Jan Szemiński, "El único español bueno es el español muerto," in Juan Ansión, ed., *Pishtacos: de verdugos a sacaojos* (Lima: Tarea, 1989) 30.

60. Quoted in Lewin, *Rebelión*, 408.

61. Quoted in John Lynch, *Caudillos in Spanish America, 1800–1850* (Oxford: Clarendon Press, 1992) 49.

62. Pérez, *Movimientos*, 70 and 106–107.

63. Moreno, *Sublevaciones*, 70–72.

64. For examples see López Austin, *Hombre-dios*, 130–131; Millones, *Historia*, 108; Leopoldo J. Bartolomé, "Movimientos milenaristas de los aborígenes chaqueños entre 1905 y 1933," *Suplemento antropológico* 7/1–2 (1972) 115; Marco Curatola, "Mito y milenarismo en los andes," *Allpanchis* 10 (1977) 70; María Teresa Huerta y Patricia Palacios, *Rebeliones indígenas de la época colonial* (Mexico City: Instituto Nacional de Antropología e Historia, 1976) 74; and E. Jean Langdon, "Mueren en realidad los shamanes," in M. S. Cipolletti and E. J. Langdon, eds., *La muerte y el más allá en las culturas indígenas latinoamericanas* (Quito: Abya-Yala, 1992) 142–143.

65. For examples see Luis Weckmann, *La herencia medieval de México* (Mexico City: Colegio de México, 1984) 1/320–339. See also Matthew 8: 26–27.

66. Pedro Lozano, *Historia de la Compañía de Jesús de la provincia del Paraguay* (Westmead, England: Gregg International Publishers, 1970) 192 and 204.

67. B. Salazar, *Los doce: primeros apóstoles franciscanos en México* (Mexico City: Imprenta Mexicana, 1943) 53–54.

68. Curatola, "Mesías," 310; and Oscar Alfredo Agüero, *The Millennium Among the Tupí-Cocama: A Case of Religious Ethno-Dynamism in the Peruvian Amazon* (Uppsala, Sweden: Uppsala Research Reports in Cultural Anthropology, 1992) 52.

69. See Rosalind C. Gow, "Inkarrí and Revolutionary Leadership in the Southern Andes," *Journal of Latin American Lore* 8/2 (1982) 216. See also Angelina Pollak-Eltz, *María Lionza: mito y culto venezolano* (Caracas: Universidad Católica Andrés Bello, 1985) 35 and 39, where a Venezuelan religious and healing cult includes among its deities Simón Bolívar and Pedro Camejo, "The First Negro," who was one of Bolívar's generals.

70. The quoted passage is from Matthew 11:5. See also Isaiah 35: 4–6.

71. Elmer S. Miller, "The Argentine Toba Evangelical Religious Service," *Ethnology* 10 (1971) 153. See also Bryan R. Wilson, *Magic and the Millennium: A Sociological Study of Religious Movements of Protest Among Tribal and Third-World Peoples* (London: Heinemann, 1973) 123.

72. William L. Merrill, "Conversion and Colonialism in Northern Mexico," in Robert W. Hefner, ed., *Conversion to Christianity: Historical and Anthropological Perspectives on a Great Transformation* (Berkeley and Los Angeles: University of California Press, 1993) 138. For a syncretic case, see Gruzinski, *Conquest*, 202–203.

73. Quoted in Frans Kamsteeg, "The Message and the People," in Susanna Rostas and André Droogers, eds., *The Popular Use of Popular Religion in Latin America* (Amsterdam: CEDLA Publications, 1993) 130–131.

74. See, for example, Miller, "Religious Service," 150–151.

75. Quoted in "El 'Jesus de los pobres' de Nicaragua dice que cura el SIDA," *Nueva Imagen* (May 18, 1992) 18.

76. See David J. Hess, *Spirits and Scientists: Ideology, Spiritism, and Brazilian Culture* (University Park: Pennsylvania State University Press, 1991) 2.

77. Pollak-Eltz, *María Lionza*, 57 and 69.

78. Quoted in Cervantes, *Devil*, 61.

79. See Dore Gardner, ed., *Niño Fidencio: A Heart Thrown Open* (Santa Fe: Muesum of New Mexico Press, 1992) 64–65, 91, and 126. For a similar example, see Octavio Ignacio Romano V., "Charismatic Medicine, Folk-Healing, and Folk-Sainthood," *American Anthropologist* 67 (1965) 1158–1164.

80. See Michael Taussig, "Folk Healing and the Structure of Conquest in Southwest Colombia," *Journal of Latin American Lore* 6/2 (1980) 235 and 254.

81. See Levine, *Vale*, 194; and Euclides da Cunha, *Los sertones*, trans. Estela Dos Santos (Caracas: Biblioteca Ayacucho, 1980) 116.

82. See Michael F. Brown and Eduardo Fernández, *War of Shadows: The Struggle for Utopia in the Peruvian Amazon* (Berkeley and Los Angeles: University of California Press, 1991) 75; and Miller, "Religious Service," 150.

83. Agüero, *Millennium*, 79; and Jaime Regan, *Hacia la tierra sin mal: estudio sobre la religiosidad del pueblo en la Amazonía* (Iquitos, Peru: CETA, 1983) 2/135.

84. The quoted passages are in, respectively, Stephen Clissold, *The Saints of South America* (London: Charles Knight, 1972) 5; Arturo Andrés Roig, "Estudio introductorio," in Arturo Andrés Roig, ed., *La utopía en el Ecuador* (Quito: Banco Central del Ecuador and Corporación Editora Nacional, 1987) 78; Lynch, *Caudillos*, 78; Marjorie Becker, *Setting the Virgin on Fire: Lázaro Cárdenas, Michoacán Peasants, and the Redemption of the Mexican Revolution* (Berkeley and Los Angeles: University of California Press, 1995) 1; and Frederick Pike, *The Politics of the Miraculous in Peru: Haya de la Torre and the Spiritualist Tradition* (Lincoln: University of Nebraska Press, 1986) 112.

85. See Lynch, *Caudillos*, 402–411.

86. Quoted in ibid., 256.

87. Ibid., 372, 381–382, and 384.

88. François Chevalier, "The Roots of Caudillismo," in Hugh M. Hamill, ed., *Caudillos: Dictators in Spanish America* (Norman: University of Oklahoma Press, 1992) 38.

89. Michael C. Meyer and William L. Sherman, *The Course of Mexican History* (New York: Oxford University Press, 1983) 331–332.

90. The quoted phrases are in Melvin J. Lasky, *Utopia and Revolution: On the Origins of a Metaphor* (Chicago: University of Chicago Press, 1976) 15. See also Eliade, *Sacred*, 206–207; and Fernando Ainsa, "Bases para una nueva fun-

ción de la utopía en América Latina," in Oscar Agüero and Horacio Cerutti Guldberg, eds., *Utopía y nuestra América* (Quito: Abya-Yala, 1996) 10.

91. Quoted in Alberto Flores Galindo, *Buscando un inca: identidad y utopía en los Andes* (Lima: Editorial Horizonte, 1988) 327.

92. Che Guevara, *Guerrilla Warfare*, trans. J. P. Morray (New York: Vintage Books, 1968) 33.

93. Luis Arce Borja, "Prólogo a la edición extranjera," in Luis Arce Borja, ed., *Guerra popular en el Perú: el pensamiento gonzalo* (Brussels, n.p.: 1989) 28.

94. Quoted in José Coronel, "Violencia política y respuestas campesinas en Huanta," in Carlos Iván Degregori, ed., *Las rondas campesinas y la derrota de Sendero Luminoso* (Lima: Instituto de Estudios Peruanos, 1996) 81.

95. See Gustavo Gorriti, "Shining Path's Stalin and Trotsky," in David Scott Palmer, ed., *The Shining Path of Peru* (New York: St. Martin's Press, 1992) 151; and Gordon H. McCormick, "The Shining Path and Peruvian Terrorism," in David C. Rapoport, *Inside Terrorist Organizations* (New York: Columbia University Press, 1988) 112 and 119.

96. Anonymous, "Oath of Loyalty, in Orin Starn et al., eds., *The Peru Reader: History, Culture, Politics* (Durham: Duke University Press, 1995) 336.

97. Quoted in Donald Hodges, *Sandino's Communism: Spiritual Politics for the Twenty-first Century* (Austin: University of Texas Press, 1992) 105.

98. Quoted in María Luisa Laviana Cuetos, *José Martí, la libertad de Cuba* (Madrid: Ediciones Anaya, 1988) 100. Martí was also a "saint" and "apostle."

99. Quoted in ibid., 97. Eva Perón similarly referred to "the very essence of Jesus: man"; see her *La palabra, el pensamiento, y la acción de Eva Perón* (Buenos Aires: Editorial Freeland, 1973) 63.

100. Quoted in Clissold, *Saints*, 5.

101. Joshua Hammer, "The Local Deity," *Newsweek* (July 21, 1997), 16.

102. Quoted in Clissold, *Saints*, 6.

103. Max Weber, *The Theory of Social and Economic Organization*, ed. Talcott Parsons, trans. A. M. Henderson and Talcott Parsons (New York: Free Press, 1947) 358–359.

104. See Michael F. Brown, "Beyond Resistance," *Ethnohistory* 38/4 (1991) 392.

105. The quoted phrase is in Steve Stern, *Populism in Peru: The Emergence of the Masses and the Politics of Social Control* (Madison: University of Wisconsin Press, 1980) 102–103.

106. Pereira de Queiroz, *Historia*, 111 and 113.

107. Carlos Federico Guillot, *Negros rebeldes y negros cimarrones* (Buenos Aires: Fariña Editores, 1961) 111.

108. See Timothy P. Wickham-Crowley, *Guerrillas and Revolution in Latin America* (Princeton: Princeton University Press, 1992) 327–339. In E. J. Hobsbawm, "Peasants and Politics," *Journal of Peasant Studies* 1/1 (October 1973) 11, outside agency is a necessary condition of general campesino movements.

109. Nelson Manrique, "Political Violence, Ethnicity and Racism in Peru in the Time of War," *Journal of Latin American Cultural Studies* 4/1 (June 1995) 16.

110. See Ronald H. Berg, "Peasant Responses to Shining Path in Andahuaylas," in Palmer, *Shining Path*, 98.

111. The quoted phrase is from Levine, *Vale*, 40. See also Pereira de Queiroz, *Historia*, 131–132.

112. The quoted passage is from Pereira de Queiroz, *Historia*, 121.

113. Wilfredo Kapsoli E., *Los movimientos campesinos en el Perú* (Lima: Ediciones Atusparia, 1982) 28–29.

114. Laënnec Hurbon, "New Religious Movements in the Caribbean," in

James A. Beckford, ed., *New Religious Movements and Rapid Social Change* (Beverly Hills: Sage Publications, 1986) 167.

115. Vanderwood, *Power of God*, 15, 223, 226–227, and 270–277. See also Edward H. Spicer, *Cycles of Conquest: The Impact of Spain, Mexico, and the United States on the Indians of the Southwest, 1533–1960* (Tucson: University of Arizona Press, 1976) 529.

116. See John 10:9–18; and Psalms 78:52.

117. The quoted phrase is from John Gerassi, ed., *Venceremos! The Speeches and Writings of Ernesto Che Guevara* (New York: Macmillan, 1968) 389.

118. Ibid., 205.

119. The quoted phrase is from Cohn, *Pursuit*, 60. See also Michael Adas, *Prophets of Rebellion: Millenarian Protest Movements Against the European Colonial Order* (Chapel Hill: University of North Carolina Press, 1979) 112.

120. Clastres, *Land-without-Evil*, 103. Paul believed that he embodied "the mind of Christ" and "spirit of god," and that his utterances were divine: "It is Christ speaking in me." See 1 Corinthians 2:16 and 7:40; 2 Corinthians 13:3; and Romans 15:18.

121. Robert C. Tucker, ed., *The Marx-Engels Reader* (New York: W. W. Norton, 1978) 15.

122. See Weber, *Theory*, 361; Kenelm Burridge, *New Heaven, New Earth: A Study of Millenarian Activities* (New York: Schocken Books, 1969) 173; and James C. Scott, *Weapons of the Weak: Everyday Forms of Peasant Resistance* (New Haven: Yale University Press, 1985) 333.

123. See David Aberbach, *Charisma in Politics, Religion and the Media: Private Trauma, Public Ideals* (New York: New York University Press, 1996) 16.

124. Coronel Juan Perón, *El pueblo ya sabe de qué se trata* (Buenos Aires: Editorial Freeland, 1973) 205.

125. Quoted in Samuel Brunk, *Emiliano Zapata: Revolution and Betrayal in Mexico* (Albuquerque: University of New Mexico Press, 1995) 90.

126. Manuel González Prada, "El intelectual y el obrero," in Albelardo Villegas, ed., *Antología del pensamiento social y político de América Latina* (Washington, D.C.: Unión Panamericana, 1964) 594.

127. See Adas, *Prophets*, 112.

128. José Martí, *Our America: Writings on Latin America and the Struggle for Cuban Independence*, ed. Philip S. Foner (New York: Monthly Review Press, 1977) 98–99.

129. Víctor Raúl Haya de la Torre, *Política aprista* (Lima: Editorial Amauta, 1967) 158; Herbert Braun, *The Assassination of Gaitán: Public Life and Urban Violence in Colombia* (Madison: University of Wisconsin Press, 1985) 101–102; and E. Perón, *Palabra*, 103–104. On Sendero Luminoso as the "fury of the people," see Robin Kirk, *Grabado en piedra: las mujeres de Sendero Luminoso* (Lima: Instituto de Estudios Peruanos, 1993) 69.

130. Burridge, *New Heaven*, 155 (see also 98).

131. Juan Perón, *Habla Perón* (Buenos Aires: Editorial Freeland, 1973) 55 (see also 54 and 72); and in Lynch, *Caudillos*, 433. See also E. Perón, *Palabra*, 96; and Juan Perón, *Tres revoluciones militares* (Buenos Aires: Escorpión Ediciones, 1963) 98.

132. Quoted in Braun, *Assassination*, 83.

133. Quoted in Lynch, *Caudillos*, 415.

134. The first quoted passage is from Adas, *Prophets*, 112; the second is in Steve Bruce, *The Rise and Fall of the New Christian Right: Conservative Protestant Politics in America, 1978–1988* (Oxford: Clarendon Press, 1988) 21; and the third is from Aberbach, *Charisma*, 16.

135. Quoted in Braun, *Assassination*, 97 and 99.

136. The first quoted phrase is in Douglas Madsen and Peter G. Snow, *The*

Charismatic Bond: Political Behavior in Time of Crisis (Cambridge: Harvard University Press, 1991) 50; and the other quoted passages are in Joseph A. Page, *Perón: A Biography* (New York: Random House, 1983) 223. See Juan Perón, *Yo, Juan Domingo Perón: relato autobiográfico*, ed. Torcuato Luca de Tena et al. (Barcelona: Editorial Planeta, 1976) 66, where "it seems there is an exterior force that inspires one."

137. J. Perón, *Yo,* 66.

138. See Pike, *Politics,* 108–109, 170, and 269.

139. Quoted in Lee Lockwood, "Fidel Castro Speaks on Personal Power," in Hamill, *Caudillos,* 312.

140. Sebastian Balfour, *Castro* (London: Longman, 1995) 79–80.

141. Jay Mallin, ed., *"Che" Guevara on Revolution: A Documentary Overview* (Coral Gables: University of Miami Press, 1969) 130 and 143. For examples of oratory in nativist rebellion, see Barabas, *Utopías,* 148; Huerta and Palacios, *Rebeliones,* 282; and Thomas H. Naylor and Charles W. Polzer, eds., *The Presidio and Militia on the Northern Frontier of New Spain* (Tucson: University of Arizona Press, 1986) 389.

142. Paulo Suess, *La nueva evangelización: desafíos históricos y pautas culturales,* trans. María Victoria C. de Vela (Quito: Abya-Yala, 1991) 89.

143. Quoted in Levine, *Vale,* 127.

144. Da Cunha, *Sertones,* 111.

145. Ibid., 118.

146. Teniente General [Juan Domingo] Perón, *Conducción política* (Buenos Aires: Secretaría Política de la Presidencia de la Nación, 1974) 184 and 37 (see also 61 and 151–152).

147. Barabas, *Utopías,* 85.

148. Henri Desroche, *The Sociology of Hope,* trans. Carol Martin-Sperry (London: Routledge and Kegan Paul, 1979) 44.

149. Ramón A. Gutiérrez, *When Jesus Came, the Corn Mothers Went Away: Marriage, Sexuality, and Power in New Mexico, 1500–1846* (Stanford: Stanford University Press, 1991) 139.

150. The quoted passage is from J. Perón, *Conducción,* 222.

151. Aberbach, *Charisma,* 16.

152. On messianism as rescue and revenge, see Robert D. Stolorow and George E. Atwood, "Messianic Projects and Early Object-Relations," *American Journal of Psychoanalysis* 33 (1973) 213–215.

153. See Victor Turner, *Dramas, Fields, and Metaphors: Symbolic Action in Human Society* (Ithaca: Cornell University Press, 1974) 122–124.

154. Miller, "Religious Service," 149.

155. Greenway, "Luz del Mundo," 114–115. For another example, see Hemming, *Amazon Frontier,* 322.

156. J. Perón, *Conducción,* 149.

157. Ibid., 206 (see also 150–151).

158. See Page, *Perón,* 309; Eva Perón, *Escribe Eva Perón* (Buenos Aires: n.p., 1950) 44; and Marysa Navarro, "Is a Caudilla Possible?" in Hamill, *Caudillos,* 281.

159. Quoted in Balfour, *Castro,* 111.

160. Quoted in Robert M. Levine, *Father of the Poor? Vargas and His Era* (Cambridge: Cambridge University Press, 1998) 151.

161. Quoted in Deborah Poole and Gerard Rénique, *Peru: Time of Fear* (London: Latin America Bureau, 1992) 10.

162. Arce, *Guerra,* 293.

163. Quoted in Gustavo Gorriti Ellenbogen, *Sendero: historia de la guerra milenaria en el Perú* (Lima: Apoyo, 1990) 167.

164. Quoted in Ribeiro, "Millennium," 167.

165. Mark 8:34–35. See also Matthew 16:24–25.

166. Quoted in J. Manuel Espinosa, ed. and trans., *The Pueblo Indian Revolt of 1696 and the Franciscan Missions in New Mexico: Letters of the Missionaries and Related Documents* (Norman: University of Oklahoma Press, 1988) 242–243.

167. The first quoted passage is in Stelio Cro, *The American Foundations of the Hispanic Utopia (1492–1793)* (Tallahassee: DeSoto Press, 1994) 2/152. The second and third are in Rosario Romeo, "The Jesuit Sources and the Italian Political Utopia in the Second Half of the Sixteenth Century," in Fredi Chiappelli, ed., *The First Images of America: The Impact of the New World on the Old* (Berkeley and Los Angeles: University of California Press, 1976) 1/167.

168. The quoted passages are from Revelation 7:14–17.

169. The first quoted passage is from Galatians 2:20.

170. On Bahia, see João José Reis, *Slave Rebellion in Brazil* (Ann Arbor, Mich.: University Microfilms International, 1984) 143; on Chiapas, see Vicente Pineda, *Historia de las sublevaciones indígenas habidas en el estado de Chiapas* (Chiapas: Tipografía del Gobierno, 1888) 18–19; and on Oaxaca, see Barabas, *Utopías*, 238. For another modern Mexican example, see Vanderwood, *Power of God*, 4 and II.

171. Johannes Wilbert and Karin Simoneau, eds., *Folk Literature of the Mataco Indians* (Los Angeles: UCLA Latin American Center Publications, 1982) 229.

172. Promises of resurrection were also reported. See Barabas, *Utopías*, 181 and 186–187. On bulletproof Tarahumara, see Spicer, *Cycles*, 527.

173. Tony Pasinski, *The Santos of Guatemala* (Guatemala City: Didacsa, 1990) 1/113.

174. Anatilde Idoyaga Molina, "Una esperanza milenarista entre los Pilagá (Chaco Central)," in Barabas, *Religiosidad*, 54.

175. Quoted in Hobsbawm, "Peasants," 7; and Curatola, "Mesías," 322.

176. Harald O. Skar, "Quest for a New Covenant," in Harald O. Skar and Frank Salomon, eds., *Natives and Neighbors in South America* (Göteborg, Sweden: Ethnological Studies 38, 1987) 245. The same belief was held in a 1914 Brazilian revolt; see Ralph Della Cava, *Miracle at Joaseiro* (New York: Columbia University Press, 1970) 55.

177. See Huerta and Palacios, *Rebeliones*, 288–289; and Barabas, *Utopías*, 151–152.

178. Barabas, *Utopías*, 154.

179. See Jan Szemiński, "The Last Time the Inca Came Back," in Gossen, *Native Spirituality*, 287. See also Jorge Hidalgo, "Amarus y Cataris," *Chungara* 10 (March 1983) 128.

180. Quoted in Hidalgo, "Amarus," 129.

181. Quoted in Juan B. Lastres, *Lope de Aguirre, el rebelde* (Lima: Ministerio de Relaciones Exteriores del Perú, 1942) 99.

182. Métraux, "Messiahs," 59–60.

183. Bartolomé, "Movimientos," 110–111.

184. See ibid., 111–113. See also Edgardo Jorge Cordeu and Alejandra Siffredi, *De la algarroba al algodón: movimiento mesiánico de los guaycurú* (Buenos Aires: Juárez Editor, 1971) 67–71.

185. J. H. Parry and Robert G. Keith, eds., *New Iberian World: A Documentary History of the Discovery and Settlement of Latin America to the Early Seventeenth Century* (New York: Times Books, 1983) 4/197. The "young and idle persons" who "had nothing to do but eat and loaf" were similarly dispatched in Mexico; see Gutiérrez, *When Jesus Came*, 43.

186. The quoted phrase is from Parry and Keith, *New Iberian World*, 4/142.

For biographical data on Aguirre's novelesque career, see Francisco Vázquez, *Relación de todo lo que sucedió en la jornada de Omagua y Dorado* (Madrid: Sociedad de Bibliófilos Españoles, 1881) vii–x; and Anthony Smith, *Explorers of the Amazon* (New York: Viking, 1990) 95–96.

187. In a deceitful ploy, Ursúa poisoned the rebel leaders who had come to negotiate and celebrate a treaty; see Guillot, *Negros*, 116.

188. The quoted phrase is in Emiliano Jos, *La expedición de Ursúa al Dorado, la rebelión de Lope de Aguirre, y el itinerario de los "Marañones"* (Huesca, Spain: Imprenta V. Campo, 1927) 87.

189. Quoted in Parry and Keith, *New Iberian World*, 143.

190. Quoted in Lastres, *Lope de Aguirre*, 49.

191. See Vázquez, *Relación* 46–47; and Jos, *Expedición*, 234.

192. See Jos, *Expedición*, 75 and 79.

193. Quoted in ibid., 237.

194. Quoted in ibid.

195. Quoted in ibid., 213.

196. Quoted in Lastres, *Lope de Aguirre*, 55.

197. These and all subsequent quotations from Lope de Aguirre's October 1561 letter to Philip II are from the appendix to Jos, *Expedición*, 196–200.

198. See Lastres, *Lope de Aguirre*, 55. See also Juan Gil, *Mitos y utopías del descubrimiento* (Madrid: Alianza, 1989) 3/216, where Aguirre would be remembered because "God had sent him as His wrath and punishment." See also Romans 12:19; and Deuteronomy 32:35.

199. Jos, *Expedición*, 246. During his 1541–42 Amazon expedition, Francisco de Orellana likewise named one of his brigatines Victoria; see Rafael Díaz Maderuelo, *Francisco de Orellana* (Madrid: Historia 16, 1987) 58.

200. Jos, *Expedición*, 238.

201. See ibid., 92.

202. Gil, *Mitos*, 215.

203. See Lastres, *Lope de Aguirre*, 23.

204. The quoted phrase is in ibid.

205. Quoted in Jos, *Expedición*, 250 (see also 116 and 241).

206. Narration of these Lope de Aguirre episodes follows Parry and Keith, *New Iberian World*, 141–144; and John Hemming, *The Search for El Dorado* (London: Michael Joseph, 1978) 142–144.

207. See Beatriz Pastor, *Discurso narrativo de la conquista de América* (Havana: Ediciones Casa de las Américas, 1983) 445.

208. See ibid., 415 and 438.

209. The quoted passages are in Miguel Otero Silva, *Casa muertas; Lope de Aguirre, príncipe de la libertad* (Caracas: Biblioteca Ayacucho, 1985) 259. See also Jos, *Expedición*, 119; and Lastres, *Lope de Aguirre*, 9.

210. Quoted in Jos, *Expedición*, 250; and in Constantino Bayle, *El Dorado fantasma* (Madrid: Consejo de la Hispanidad, 1943) 281.

211. The quoted passages are in H. J. Mozans, *Along the Andes and Down the Amazon* (New York: D. Appleton, 1912) 475; and Vázquez, *Relación*, 187.

212. Quoted in Lastres, *Lope de Aguirre*, 52.

213. See Flores Galindo, *Buscando*, 36.

214. See Gil, *Mitos*, 215.

215. Quoted in Lastres, *Lope de Aguirre*, 44.

216. Quoted in Indalecio Liévano Aguirre, *Bolívar* (Madrid: Instituto de Cooperación Iberoamericana, 1983) 180.

217. See ibid., 69.

218. Quoted in Parry and Keith, *New Iberian World*, 144.

219. Martí, *Our America*, 100.

220. Matthew 8:27.

221. Daniel Florencio O'Leary, *Bolivar and the War of Independence*, ed. and trans. Robert F. McNerney Jr. (Austin: University of Texas Press, 1970) 54.

222. See ibid., 70; and Liévano, *Bolívar*, 106.

223. Quoted in Liévano, *Bolívar*, 200.

224. Quoted in ibid., 185.

225. Martí, *Our America*, 100.

226. Quoted in Liévano, *Bolívar*, 417.

227. Quoted in ibid., 147; and Simón Bolívar, *Doctrina del Libertador*, ed. Manuel Pérez Vila (Caracas: Biblioteca Ayacucho, 1979) 34.

228. The quoted phrase is from Horacio Cerutti Guldberg, "Sueño utópico, hontanar de ética política," *Cuadernos americanos* 259/2 (March–April 1985) 153.

229. See O'Leary, *Bolivar*, 62 and 274.

230. Quoted in Gerhard Masur, *Simon Bolivar* (Albuquerque: University of New Mexico Press, 1948) 692–693.

231. William Rowe and Vivian Schelling, *Memory and Modernity: Popular Culture in Latin America* (London: Verso, 1991) 26.

232. Bolívar, *Doctrina*, 245.

233. Miguel Angel Asturias, *Bolívar* (San Salvador: n.p., 1955). For similar adaptation of the creed for Peruvian heroes, see Stern, *Populism*, 108–109; and Pike, *Politics*, 132.

234. Luis Subieta Sagárnaga, *Bolívar en Potosí* (Potosí, Bolivia: Círculo de Bellas Artes, 1925) 1 and 69. The less-bemused Lewis Hanke observed that Potosí "outdid itself in preparing a flamboyant welcome of the type relished by the Liberator," including "a series of triumphal arches about which gaudily beplumed Indians performed a sort of ballet"; Lewis Hanke, *The Imperial City of Potosí* (The Hague: Martinus Nijhoff, 1956) 4.

235. Quoted in Masur, *Bolívar*, 687.

236. Quoted in Liévano, *Bolívar*, 399.

237. The quoted passage is from O'Leary, *Bolívar*, 30.

238. Quoted in Masur, *Bolívar* 35. See also Bolívar, *Doctrina*, 326.

239. Quoted in Stern, *Populism*, 176.

240. See Víctor Raúl Haya de la Torre, "Espacio-tiempo histórico," in Milda Rivarola and Pedro Planas, eds., *Víctor Raúl Haya de la Torre* (Madrid: Ediciones de Cultura Hispánica, 1988) 121.

241. Haya de la Torre, *Política*, 110 (see also 205).

242. Pike, *Politics*, 131; and Jeffrey L. Klaiber, *Religion and Revolution in Peru, 1824–1976* (Notre Dame, Ind.: University of Notre Dame Press, 1977) 154.

243. Stern, *Populism*, 175.

244. See ibid., 131.

245. Quoted in ibid.

246. Quoted in Stern, *Populism*, 167 (see also 114). See also Haya de la Torre, *Política*, 185–186.

247. Klaiber, *Religion*, 143.

248. Quoted in ibid., 122; and Haya de la Torre, *Política*, 102.

249. Quoted in Klaiber, *Religion*, 143.

250. Quoted in Stern, *Populism*, 145.

251. Quoted in ibid., 147–148.

252. Haya de la Torre, *Política*, 54.

253. Quoted in Stern, *Populism*, 178.

254. Haya de la Torre, *Política*, 200 and 204. See also Klaiber, *Religion*, 142–145.

255. Quoted in Klaiber, *Religion*, 150–151. Translation modified.

256. Quoted in Pike, *Politics*, 271.

257. Quoted in Klaiber, *Religion*, 149.

258. Quoted in Pike, *Politics*, 135.

259. Klaiber, *Religion*, 146,

260. Haya de la Torre, *Política*, 97.

261. Quoted in Klaiber, *Religion*, 150; and Haya de la Torre, *Política*, 194.

262. The quoted phrase is in Imelda Vega Centeno, *Aprismo popular: mito, cultura e historia* (Lima: Tarea, 1985) 75.

263. Haya de la Torre, *Política*, 201.

264. Quoted in Klaiber, *Religion*, 155.

265. The first two quoted passages are in Nelson Martínez, *Juan Domingo Perón* (Madrid: Historia 16, 1987) 55; and the last quoted passage is from E. Perón, *Escribe*, 52. Following common usage, in this discussion Juan Perón will be referred to as "Perón" and Eva Perón as "Eva" or "Evita."

266. E. Perón, *Escribe*, 5.

267. The first quoted passage is from J. Perón, *Pueblo*, 13; the second is from J. Perón, *Conducción*, 149; and the third and fourth are from J. Perón, *Habla*, 141.

268. J. Perón, *Habla*, 78–79.

269. See Michael A. Burdick, *For God and the Fatherland: Religion and Politics in Argentina* (Albany: State University of New York Press, 1995) 56; and Austen Ivereigh, *Catholicism and Politics in Argentina, 1810–1960* (New York: St. Martin's Press, 1995) 159–160.

270. J. Perón, *Yo*, 175.

271. See Burdick, *For God*, 66.

272. Quoted in 100.

273. See ibid., 52; and Eva Perón, *La última voluntad de Eva Perón* (Buenos Aires: Presidencia de la Nación, Subsecretaría de Informaciones, 1952) n.p.

274. Quoted in Ivereigh, *Catholicism*, 167.

275. Ibid., 171.

276. Quoted in Madsen and Snow, *Charismatic Bond*, 49.

277. J. Perón, *Yo*, 219.

278. J. Perón, *Pueblo*, 188.

279. Quoted in J. M. Taylor, *Eva Perón: The Myths of a Woman* (Chicago: University of Chicago Press, 1979) 55.

280. Ibid., 42 and 47.

281. J. Perón, *Yo*, 198.

282. The quoted word is from Ivereigh, *Catholicism*, 160.

283. See Taylor, *Eva Perón*, 62–65; for dissenting opinions see 80–82 and 97. An earlier "cult of the fatherland" delivered pedagogical ideas like "Let us make every child of school age a fanatical idolater of the Argentine Republic"; see Ivereigh, *Catholicism*, 71.

284. Taylor, *Eva Perón*, 95.

285. See Taylor, *Eva Perón*, 141. The quoted phrase is from E. Perón, *Palabra*, 32 (see also 50–51).

286. Quoted in Taylor, *Eva Perón*, 108.

287. Ibid., 88 and 107; and Ivereigh, *Catholicism*, 160.

288. See Taylor, *Eva Perón*, 108 and 82–83.

289. The slogan defies translation, but it conveys the idea that Perón delivers on his promises and Evita dignifies these accomplishments.

290. Quoted in Taylor, *Eva Perón*, 11.

291. J. Perón, *Conducción*, 225 (see also 156).

292. Quoted in Taylor, 128. See also Page, *Perón*, 422 and 425.

293. The quoted phrase is in Taylor, *Eva Perón*, 91.

294. E. Perón, *Escribe*, 37.

295. See Taylor, *Eva Perón*, 55; and Martínez, *Juan Domingo Perón*, 97.

296. See E. Perón, *Palabra*, 87; and J. Perón, *Habla*, 152.
297. E. Perón, *Última voluntad*, n.p.
298. See Page, *Perón*, 252.
299. Quoted in Taylor, *Eva Perón*, 91.
300. See Perón, *Pueblo*, 185–187.
301. See J. Perón, *Yo*, 195.
302. E. Perón, *Palabra*, 34 and 40.
303. Ibid., 62–63.
304. Quoted in Levine, *Vale*, 224.
305. See ibid., 42.
306. On beatos as a lay auxiliary assisting the clergy in the understaffed backlands, see ibid., 34 and 125. The rather exclusive title Conselheiro signified status as a wise counselor; see ibid., 124.
307. Pereira de Queiroz, *Historia*, 100.
308. Levine, *Vale*, 129.
309. Pereira de Queiroz, *Historia*, 114.
310. Levine, *Vale*, 34.
311. Ibid., 122. His mother died when he was six.
312. Quoted in ibid., 140.
313. Quoted in da Cunha, *Sertones*, 139.
314. See Levine, *Vale*, 185 and 194. On a miracle attesting to his sanctity, see da Cunha, *Sertones*, 117–118.
315. Pereira de Queiroz, *Historia*, 101.
316. Da Cunha, *Sertones*, 136.
317. Ibid. 137.
318. Ibid., 115–116.
319. Ibid., 117.
320. See Levine, *Vale*, 132 and 198; the quoted phrase is on 2.
321. Ibid., 61.
322. Da Cunha, *Sertones*, 125–126.
323. Ibid., 112.
324. Quoted in ibid., 113.
325. In Levine, *Vale*, 64 and 140. See also da Cunha, *Sertones*, 132.
326. See Levine, *Vale*, 142; and Pereira de Queiroz, *Historia*, 102.
327. The quoted word is in Levine, *Vale*, 2.
328. Ibid., 184.
329. Ibid.,
330. Ibid., 206–207.
331. Pereira de Queiroz, *Historia*, 112.
332. Ibid., 100.
333. Bernard J. Siegel, "The Contestado Rebellion," *Journal of Anthropological Research* 33 (1977) 207.
334. Pereira de Queiroz, *Historia*, 109–110; and Levine, *Vale*, 222.
335. Levine, *Vale*, 223. See also Todd A. Diacon, *Millenarian Vision, Capitalist Reality* (Durham: Duke University Press, 1991) 1–4 and 115–129.
336. Della Cava, *Miracle*, 10–11.
337. Pereira de Queiroz, *Historia*, 100–101 and 104.
338. Quoted in Della Cava, *Miracle*, 35.
339. Ibid., 55.
340. Ralph Della Cava, "The Entry of Padre Cícero into Partisan Politics," in Chilcote, *Protest*, 135.
341. Quoted in ibid., 148.
342. Della Cava, *Miracle*, 129.
343. Della Cava, "Entry," 133–134.
344. Pereira de Queiroz, *Historia*, 106.

345. See ibid., 106–107.
346. Ibid., 107; Levine, *Vale*, 222; and Bastide, *Prójimo*, 285.
347. Ribeiro, "Millennium," 159.
348. Ibid., 160–161.
349. Ibid., 161.
350. Ibid., 162.
351. Ribeiro, "Millennium," 171.
352. Ibid., 163,
353. Ibid., 164–165.
354. Ibid., 175 (see also 166 and 177).
355. Ribeiro, "Millennium," 179 and 168.
356. Quoted in ibid., 169.
357. See Manuel M. Marzal, *Los caminos religiosos de los inmigrantes en la gran Lima: el caso de El Agustino* (Lima: Pontificia Universidad Católica del Perú, 1989) 342–348.
358. Ibid., 342–351. See also Manuel M. Marzal, "La religión quechua sur-andina peruana," in Manuel M. Marzal, *El rostro indio de Dios* (Lima: Pontificia Universidad Católica del Perú, 1991) 261; Manuel Jesús Granados, "Los Israelitas," *Socialismo y Participación* 41 (1988) 95; and Skar, "Quest," 235. The "third heaven" appears in 2 Corinthians 12:2–5.
359. See Curatola, "Mesías," 313; Skar, "Quest," 247; and Granados, "Israelitas," 95.
360. Quoted in Marzal, *Caminos*, 352; see also 359, where East and West are united in the sect's logo. In the sixteenth-century, Motolinía observed that "since at the beginning the Church flourished in the East, which is at the start of the world, now at the end of the centuries, it has to flower in the West, which is at the end of the world"; quoted in Brading, *First America*, 109.
361. Marzal, *Caminos*, 52–53.
362. Quoted in ibid., 357.
363. Ibid., 359 and 360.
364. Granados, "Israelitas," 101.
365. Curatola, "Mesías," 317.
366. See Marzal, *Caminos*, 359–360; Marzal, "Religión," 265; and Granados, "Israelitas," 102.
367. Quoted in Granados, "Israelitas," 103. Elementary school texts used throughout Peru as late as the 1980s (and perhaps into the present) represent Peru as a Promised Land populated by New Men; María E. Heise and Teresa Valiente, "El mundo maravilloso que nos rodea," *Amazonía peruana* 18 (December 1989) 149.
368. Quoted in Granados, "Israelitas," 98.
369. Marzal, *Caminos*, 369; and Granados, "Israelitas," 102.
370. Celio Moreno Mendoza, "La secta del fin del mundo," *Vistazo* 622 (July 15, 1993) 62–66. The accusations are inflated but not ungrounded. In the Israelite community at Puerto Sira, for example, at least three people were killed in 1991–92 for impiety and for breaking the divine law; Curatola, "Mesías," 322.
371. Granados, "Israelitas," 96.
372. Skar, "Quest," 262.
373. Matthew 14:17–21 and 13:47.
374. The quoted phrase is from Matthew 4:19.
375. M. A. Cubas, "Playa de peces" and "Sétima profecía," *Caretas* 1101 (March 26, 1990) 80–81. On the manipulation of religious issues by supporters of Mario Vargas Llosa in the same campaign, see Carlos Iván Degregori and Romeo Grompone, *Demonios y redentores en el nuevo Perú* (Lima: Instituto de Estudios Peruanos, 1991) 92.

376. Skar, "Quest," 235.

377. See Marzal, *Caminos*, 360; Marzal, "Religión," 262–264; and Curatola, "Mesías," 313. On circumcision of the heart, see Romans 2.29, which follows Deuteronomy 10.16 and Jeremiah 4.4; see also Mark 7.5.

378. Skar, "Quest," 249.

379. Granados, "Israelitas," 103; and Marzal, "Religión," 263–264.

380. Curatola, "Mesías," 314.

381. Ibid., 313.

382. Marzal, "Religión," 263–264. See also Skar, "Quest," 233.

383. Marzal, *Caminos*, 372. Establishment of the communities was facilitated by federal programs to colonize the eastern frontier. On religious dogma and migrations as disruption of economic stability, see Skar, "Quest," 242–243.

384. Curatola, "Mesías," 315.

385. Granados, "Israelitas," 100; and Curatola, "Mesías," 316.

Bibliography

Aberbach, David. *Charisma in Politics, Religion and the Media: Private Trauma, Public Ideals*. New York: New York University Press, 1996.

Abril Castelló, Vidal. *Francisco de la Cruz—Inquisición (actas)*. Madrid: Consejo Superior de Investigaciones Científicas, 1992.

Acosta, José de. *Historia natural y moral de las Indias*. Mexico City: Fondo de Cultura Económica, 1962.

———. *Doctrina christiana y catecismo para instrucción de los indios*. Lima: Antonio Ricardo, 1584.

Adas, Michael. *Prophets of Rebellion: Millenarian Protest Movements Against the European Colonial Order*. Chapel Hill: University of North Carolina Press, 1979.

Adorno, Rolena. *Guaman Poma: Writing and Resistance in Colonial Peru*. Austin: University of Texas Press, 1986.

———, ed. *From Oral to Written Expression: Native Andean Chronicles of the Early Colonial Period*. Syracuse: Maxwell School of Citizenship and Public Affairs, Syracuse University, Latin American Series, 1982.

Adorno, Rolena, et al. *Guaman Poma de Ayala: The Colonial Art of an Andean Author*. New York: Americas Society, 1992.

Agüero, Oscar Alfredo. *The Millennium Among the Tupí-Cocama: A Case of Religious Ethno-Dynamism in the Peruvian Amazon*. Uppsala, Sweden: Uppsala Research Reports in Cultural Anthropology, 1992.

Agüero, Oscar, and Horacio Cerutti Guldberg, eds. *Utopía y nuestra América*. Quito: Abya-Yala, 1996.

Aguirre Beltrán, Gonzalo. *Medicina y magia: el proceso de aculturación en la estructura colonial*. Mexico City: Instituto Nacional Indigenista, 1963.

Ainsa, Fernando. *De la edad de oro a El Dorado: génesis del discurso utópico americano*. Mexico City: Fondo de Cultura Económica, 1992.

———. *Necesidad de la utopía*. Buenos Aires: Túpac Ediciones; and Montevideo: Nordan-Comunidad, 1990.

331

Albán Estrada, María, and Juan Pablo Muñoz. *Con Dios todo se puede: la invasión de las sectas al Ecuador*. Quito: Editorial Planeta, 1987.

Alberro, Solange. *Inquisición y sociedad en México*. Mexico City: Fondo de Cultura Económica, 1988.

Albornoz P., Oswaldo. *Las luchas indígenas en el Ecuador*. Guayaquil, Ecuador: Editorial Claridad, 1971.

Alcina Franch, José. *Bartolomé de Las Casas*. Madrid: Historia 16, 1987.

Alexander, Michael, ed. *Discovering the New World: Based on the Works of Theodore De Bry*. New York: Harper and Row, 1976.

Allen, Don Cameron. *The Legend of Noah*. Urbana: University of Illinois Press, 1963.

Alvarez, A. *The Savage God: A Study of Suicide*. New York: W. W. Norton, 1990.

Americas Watch. *Creating a Desolation and Calling It Peace*. New York: Americas Watch, 1983.

————. *Human Rights in Guatemala: No Neutrals Allowed*. New York: Americas Watch, 1982.

Anaya, Rudolfo A., and Francisco A. Lomelí. *Aztlán: Essays on the Chicano Homeland*. Albuquerque: Academia/El Norte Press, 1989.

Ancona, Eligio. *Historia de Yucatán desde la época más remota hasta nuestros días*. Mérida, Mexico: Imprenta de M. Heredia Argüelles, 1879.

Anfuso, Joseph, and David Sczepanski. *Efraín Ríos Montt*. Barcelona: CLIE, 1984.

Angles Vargas, Víctor. *El Paititi no existe*. Cuzco: Imprenta Amauta, 1992.

Annis, Sheldon. *God and Production in a Guatemalan Town*. Austin: University of Texas Press, 1987.

Ansión, Juan, ed. *Pishtacos: de verdugos a sacaojos*. Lima: Tarea, 1989.

Ara, Pedro. *El caso Eva Perón*. Buenos Aires: CVS Ediciones, 1974.

Arcaya, Pedro M. *Insurrección de los negros de la serranía de Coro*. Caracas: Instituto Panamericano de Geografía e Historia, 1949.

Arce Borja, Luis, ed. *Guerra popular en el Perú: el pensamiento gonzalo*. Brussels, n.p., 1989.

Argentine Commission for Human Rights. *Argentina: proceso al genocidio*. Madrid: Elías Querejeta Ediciones, 1977.

Arguedas, José María. *Formación de una cultura nacional indoamericana*. Edited by Angel Rama. Mexico City: Siglo Veintiuno, 1975.

Ariés, Philippe. *Western Attitudes Toward Death: From the Middle Ages to the Present*. Baltimore: Johns Hopkins University Press, 1974.

Armani, Alberto. *Ciudad de Dios y Ciudad del Sol: el "estado" jesuita de los guaraníes, 1609–1768*. Mexico City: Fondo de Cultura Económica, 1982.

Armas Medina, Fernando de. *Cristianización del Perú*. Seville: Escuela de Estudios Hispano-Americanos, 1953.

Arriaga, Pablo Joseph. *The Extirpation of Idolatry in Peru*. Translated by L. Clark Keating. Lexington: University of Kentucky Press, 1968.

Arrom, José Juan. *Historia del teatro hispanoamericano: época colonial*. Mexico City: Ediciones de Andrea, 1967.

Asturias, Miguel Angel. *Bolívar*. San Salvador: n.p., 1955.

Babcock, Barbara A. *The Reversible World: Symbolic Inversion in Art and Society*. Ithaca: Cornell University Press, 1978.

Bacon, Francis. *New Atlantis*. Edited by Alfred B. Gough. Oxford: Clarendon Press, 1924.

Bagrow, Leo. *History of Cartography*. Chicago: Precedent Publishing, 1985.

Bailey, David C. *¡Viva Cristo Rey! The Cristero Rebellion and the Church-State Conflict in Mexico*. Austin: University of Texas Press, 1974.

Bakewell, Peter J. *Silver Mining and Society in Colonial Mexico: Zacatecas, 1546–1700.* Cambridge: Cambridge University Press, 1971.

Balandier, Georges. *Teoría de la descolonización.* Translated by Rafael Di Muro. Buenos Aires: Editorial Tiempo Contemporáneo, 1973.

Balfour, Sebastian. *Castro.* London: Longman, 1995.

Ballesteros, Manuel. *Gonzalo Jiménez de Quesada.* Madrid: Historia 16, 1987.

Bamat, Tomás. *¿Salvación o dominación? Las sectas religiosas en el Ecuador.* Quito: Editorial El Conejo, 1986.

Barabas, Alicia M. *Utopías indias: movimientos sociorreligiosos en México.* Mexico City: Grijalbo, 1989.

———, ed. *Religiosidad y resistencia indígenas hacia el fin del milenio.* Quito: Abya-Yala, 1994.

Baring, Anne, and Jules Cashford. *The Myth of the Goddess: Evolution of an Image.* New York: Arkana/Penguin Books, 1991.

Barnes, Robin Bruce. *Prophecy and Gnosis: Apocalypticism in the Wake of the Lutheran Reformation.* Stanford: Stanford University Press, 1988.

Barre, Marie-Chantal. *Ideologías indigenistas y movimientos indios.* Translated by Luisa Salomone. Mexico City: Siglo Veintiuno, 1983.

Barton, Allen H. *Communities in Disaster: A Sociological Analysis of Collective Stress Situations.* Garden City, N.Y.: Doubleday, 1969.

Bastide, Roger. *El prójimo y el extraño: el encuentro de las civilizaciones.* Buenos Aires: Amorrortu Editores, 1973.

Bataillon, Marcel. *Erasmo y España: estudios sobre la historia espiritual del siglo XVI.* Mexico City: Fondo de Cultura Económica, 1950.

Bataillon, Marcel, and André Saint-Lu. *El Padre Las Casas y la defensa de los indios.* Translated by Javier Alfaya and Bárbara McShane. Barcelona: Editorial Ariel, 1976.

Baudet, Henri. *Paradise on Earth: Some Thoughts on European Images of Non-European Man.* Translated by Elizabeth Wentholt. New Haven: Yale University Press, 1965.

Baudrillard, Jean. *Simulations.* Translated by Paul Foss et al. New York: Semiotext(e), 1983.

Bayle, Constantino. *El Dorado fantasma.* Madrid: Consejo de la Hispanidad, 1943.

Becker, Marjorie. *Setting the Virgin on Fire: Lázaro Cárdenas, Michoacán Peasants, and the Redemption of the Mexican Revolution.* Berkeley and Los Angeles: University of California Press, 1995.

Beckford, James A., ed. *New Religious Movements and Rapid Social Change.* Beverly Hills: Sage Publications, 1986.

Beltrán, Justiniano. *Los santos de las fuerzas armadas.* Bogotá: Ediciones Paulinas, 1991.

Benavides, Gustavo, and M. W. Daly, eds. *Religion and Political Power.* Albany: State University of New York Press, 1989.

Ben Israel, Menasseh. *Origen de los americanos: esperanza de Israel.* Madrid: Librería de Santiago Pérez Junquera, 1881.

Berlin, Heinrich, et al. *Idolatría y superstición entre los indios de Oaxaca.* Mexico City: Ediciones Toledo, 1988.

Bermúdez, Fernando. *Death and Resurrection in Guatemala.* Translated by Robert R. Barr. Maryknoll, N.Y.: Orbis Books, 1986.

Bernand, Carmen, ed. *Descubrimiento, conquista y colonización de América a quinientos años.* Mexico City: Fondo de Cultura Económica, 1994.

Bernand, Carmen, and Serge Gruzinski. *De la idolatría: una arqueología de las ciencias religiosas..* Trans. Diana Sánchez F. (Mexico City: Fondo de Cultura Económica, 1992).

Bernard, H. Russell, and Jesús Salinas Pedraza. *Native Ethnography: A Mexican*

Indian Describes His Culture. Newbury Park, Calif.: Sage Publications, 1989.

Bernstein, Michael André. *Foregone Conclusions: Against Apocalyptic History*. Berkeley and Los Angeles: University of California Press, 1994.

Beuken, Wim, et al. *Messianism in History*. London: SCM Press, 1993.

Bierhorst, John. *The Mythology of South America*. New York: William Morrow, 1988.

Binion, Rudolph. *After Christianity: Christian Survivals in Post-Christian Culture*. Durango, Colorado: Logbridge-Rhodes, 1986.

———. *Frau Lou: Nietzsche's Wayward Disciple*. Princeton: Princeton University Press, 1968.

Bloch, Ernst. *The Principle of Hope*. Translated by Neville Plaice et al. Cambridge: MIT Press, 1986.

Boff, Leonardo. *Faith on the Edge: Religion and Marginalized Existence*. Translated by Robert R. Barr. San Francisco: Harper and Row, 1989.

———. *Liberating Grace*. Translated by John Drury. Maryknoll, N.Y.: Orbis Books, 1981.

Bolívar, Simón. *Doctrina del Libertador*. Edited by Manuel Pérez Vila. Caracas: Biblioteca Ayacucho, 1979.

———. *Selected Writings of Bolívar*. Edited by Vicente Lecuna and Harold A. Bierck Jr. Translated by Lewis Bertrand. New York: Colonial Press, 1951.

Bonfil Batalla, Guillermo, ed. *Utopía y revolución: el pensamiento político contemporáneo de los indios en América Latina*. Mexico City: Editorial Nueva Imagen, 1981.

Bonilla, Luis. *Mitos y creencias sobre el fin del mundo*. Madrid: Escelicer, 1967.

Borges Morán, Pedro. *Misión y civilización en América*. Madrid: Editorial Alhambra, 1987.

Botero, Luis Fernando, ed. *Compadres y priostes: la fiesta andina como espacio de memoria y resistencia cultural*. Quito: Abya-Yala, 1991.

Bourdillon, M. F. C., and Meyer Fortes, eds. *Sacrifice*. London: Academic Press, 1980.

Bourguignon, Erika, ed. *Religion, Altered States of Consciousness, and Social Change*. Columbus: Ohio State University Press, 1973.

Bowden, Henry Warner. *American Indians and Christian Missions*. Chicago: University of Chicago Press, 1981.

Bowen, Kurt. *Evangelism and Apostasy: The Evolution and Impact of Evangelicals in Modern Mexico*. Montreal: McGill-Queen's University Press, 1996.

Bowser, Frederick P. *El esclavo africano en el Perú colonial, 1524–1650*. Mexico City: Siglo Veintiuno, 1977.

Boxer, C. R. *The Church Militant and Iberian Expansion*. Baltimore: Johns Hopkins University Press, 1978.

———. *A Great Luso-Brazilian Figure: Padre António Vieira, S. J., 1680–1697*. London: Hispanic and Luso-Brazilian Councils, 1963.

Boyer, Paul. *When Time Shall Be No More: Prophecy Belief in Modern American Culture*. Cambridge: Harvard University Press, 1992.

Brading, D. A. *The First America: The Spanish Monarchy, Creole Patriots, and the Liberal State, 1492–1867*. Cambridge: Cambridge University Press, 1991.

Braun, Herbert. *The Assassination of Gaitán: Public Life and Urban Violence in Colombia*. Madison: University of Wisconsin Press, 1985.

Bricker, Victoria. *The Indian Christ, the Indian King: The Historical Substrate of Maya Myth and Ritual*. Austin: University of Texas Press, 1986.

Brito Figueroa, Federico. *Las insurrecciones de los esclavos negros en la sociedad colonial venezolana*. Caracas: Editorial Cantaclaro, 1961.

Brooks, Mary Elizabeth. *A King for Portugal: The Madrigal Conspiracy, 1594–95.* Madison: University of Wisconsin Press, 1964.

Brotherston, Gordon. *Book of the Fourth World: Reading the Native Americans Through Their Literature.* New York: Cambridge University Press, 1992.

Brown, Michael F., and Eduardo Fernández. *War of Shadows: The Struggle for Utopia in the Peruvian Amazon.* Berkeley and Los Angeles: University of California Press, 1991.

Brown, Peter. *The Body and Society: Men, Women, and Sexual Renunciation in Early Christianity.* New York: Columbia University Press, 1988.

Bruce, Steve. *The Rise and Fall of the New Christian Right: Conservative Protestant Politics in America, 1978–1988.* Oxford: Clarendon Press, 1988.

Brunk, Samuel. *Emiliano Zapata: Revolution and Betrayal in Mexico.* Albuquerque: University of New Mexico Press, 1995.

Buarque de Holanda, Sergio. *Visión del paraíso: motivos edénicos en el descubrimiento y colonización del Brasil.* Translated by Estela Dos Santos. Caracas: Biblioteca Ayacucho, 1987.

Burdick, John. *Looking for God in Brazil: The Progressive Catholic Church in Brazil's Religious Arena.* Berkeley and Los Angeles: University of California Press, 1993.

Burdick, Michael A. *For God and the Fatherland: Religion and Politics in Argentina.* Albany: State University of New York Press, 1995.

Burga, Manuel. *Nacimiento de una utopía: muerte y resurrección de los incas.* Lima: Instituto de Apoyo Agrario, 1988.

Burkhart, Louise M. *The Slippery Earth: Nahua-Christian Moral Dialogue in Sixteenth-Century Mexico.* Tucson: University of Arizona Press, 1989.

Burkholder, Mark A., and Lyman L. Johnson. *Colonial Latin America.* New York: Oxford University Press, 1990.

Burridge, Kenelm. *Mambu: A Melanesian Millennium.* London: Methuen, 1960.

———. *New Heaven, New Earth: A Study of Millenarian Activities.* New York: Schocken Books, 1969.

Busaniche, José Luis. *Bolívar visto por sus contemporáneos.* Mexico City: Fondo de Cultura Económica, 1960.

Bushnell, David. *The Making of Modern Colombia: A Nation in Spite of Itself.* Berkeley and Los Angeles: University of California Press, 1993.

Bynum, Caroline Walker. *The Resurrection of the Body in Western Christianity, 200–1336.* New York: Columbia University Press, 1995.

———. *Fragmentation and Redemption: Essays on Gender and the Human Body in Medieval Religion.* New York: Zone Books, 1992.

———. *Holy Feast and Holy Fast: The Religious Significance of Food to Medieval Women.* Berkeley and Los Angeles: University of California Press, 1987.

———. *Jesus as Mother: Studies in Spirituality of the High Middle Ages.* Berkeley and Los Angeles: University of California Press, 1982.

Cabestrero, Teofilo. *Ministers of God, Ministers of the People: Testimonies of Faith from Nicaragua.* Translated by Robert R. Barr. Maryknoll, N.Y.: Orbis Books, 1983.

Caraman, Philip. *The Lost Paradise: The Jesuit Republic in South America.* New York: Seabury Press, 1976.

Carmack, Robert M. ed. *Harvest of Violence: The Maya Indians and the Guatemalan Crisis.* Norman: University of Oklahoma Press, 1988.

Carneiro, Edison. *Guerras de los Palmares.* Translated by Tomás Muñoz Molina. Mexico City: Fondo de Cultura Económica, 1946.

Carrasco, Davíd. *Quetzalcóatl and the Irony of Empire: Myths and Prophecies in the Aztec Tradition.* Chicago: University of Chicago Press, 1992.

————, ed. *To Change Place: Aztec Ceremonial Landscapes*. Boulder: University of Colorado Press, 1991.

Castañeda Delgado, Paulino. *Don Vasco de Quiroga y su "Información en derecho."* Madrid: Ediciones José Porrúa Turanzas, 1974.

————. *La teocracia pontifical y la conquista de América*. Vitoria, Spain: Editorial Eset, 1968.

Castañeda Delgado, Paulino, and Pilar Hernández Aparicio. *La Inquisición de Lima, 1570–1635*. Madrid: Editorial Deimos, 1989.

Castillo-Cárdenas, Gonzalo. *Liberation Theology from Below: The Life and Thought of Manuel Quintín Lame*. Maryknoll, N.Y.: Orbis Books, 1987.

Castro, Américo. *Aspectos del vivir hispánico*. Madrid: Alianza, 1987.

————. *Santiago de España*. Buenos Aires: Emecé Editores, 1958.

Castro Arenas, Mario. *La rebelión de Juan Santos Atahualpa*. Lima: Carlos Milla Batres, 1973.

Cerruti, Gabriela. *El jefe: vida y obra de Carlos Saúl Menem*. Buenos Aires: Editorial Planeta, 1993.

Cervantes, Fernando. *The Devil in the New World: The Impact of Diabolism in New Spain*. New Haven: Yale University Press, 1994.

Chaumeil, Jean-Pierre. *Historia y migraciones de los yagua de finales del siglo XVII hasta nuestros días*. Translated by María del Carmen Urbano. Lima: Centro Amazónico de Antropología y Aplicación Práctica, 1981.

Chaves, Julio César. *Tupac Amaru*. Buenos Aires: Editorial Asunción, 1973.

Chávez, Angélico. *Our Lady of the Conquest*. Santa Fe: The Historical Society of New Mexico, 1948.

Chiappelli, Fredi, ed. *The First Images of America: The Impact of the New World on the Old*. Berkeley and Los Angeles: University of California Press, 1976.

Chilcote, Ronald H. ed., *Protest and Resistance in Angola and Brazil: Comparative Studies*. Berkeley and Los Angeles: University of California Press, 1972.

Choy, Emilio. *Antropología e historia*. 3 vols. Lima: Universidad Nacional Mayor de San Marcos, 1979.

Cieza de León, Pedro. *The War of Quito*. Edited and translated by Clements R. Markham. Nendeln, Liechtenstein: Hakluyt Society/Kraus Reprint, 1967.

Cipolletti, M. S., and E. J. Langdon, eds. *La muerte y el más allá en las culturas indígenas latinoamericanas*. Quito: Abya-Yala, 1992.

Clastres, Hélène. *The Land-without-Evil: Tupí-Guaraní Prophetism*. Translated by Jacqueline Grenez Brovender. Urbana: University of Illinois Press, 1995.

Clastres, Pierre. *Society Against the State: Essays in Political Anthropology*. New York: Zone Books, 1987.

Clendinnen, Inga. *Aztecs: An Interpretation*. Cambridge: Cambridge University Press, 1991.

————. *Ambivalent Conquests: Maya and Spaniard in Yucatan, 1517–1570*. Cambridge: Cambridge University Press, 1987.

Clissold, Stephen. *The Saints of South America*. London: Charles Knight, 1972.

Cohn, Norman. *Cosmos, Chaos and the World to Come: The Ancient Roots of Apocalyptic Faith*. New Haven: Yale University Press, 1993.

————. *The Pursuit of the Millennium*. New York: Oxford University Press, 1970.

Colby, Gerald, with Charlotte Dennett. *Thy Will Be Done: The Conquest of the Amazon*. New York: HarperCollins, 1995.

Collier, David. *The New Authoritarianism in Latin America*. Princeton: Princeton University Press, 1979.

Collingwood, R. G. *The Idea of History*. Oxford: Clarendon Press, 1946.

Collins, Adela Yarbro. *The Combat Myth in the Book of Revelation*. Missoula, Mont.: Scholars Press, 1976.

Collins, John J. *The Scepter and the Star: The Messiahs of the Dead Sea Scrolls and Other Ancient Literature*. New York: Doubleday, 1995.

———. *The Apocalyptic Imagination: An Introduction to the Jewish Matrix of Christianity*. New York: Crossroad, 1984.

Colón, Cristóbal. *Textos y documentos completos: relaciones de viajes, cartas y memorias*. Edited by Consuelo Varela. Madrid: Alianza, 1984.

Colón, Fernando. *The Life of the Admiral Christopher Columbus by His Son Ferdinand*. Translated by Benjamin Keen. New Brunswick, N.J.: Rutgers University Press, 1959.

Columbus, Christopher. *The* Libro de las profecías *of Christopher Columbus*. Translated by Delno C. West and August Kling. Gainesville: University of Florida Press, 1991.

———. *The Four Voyages of Columbus*. Edited and translated by Cecil Jane. New York: Dover Publications, 1988.

Condori Mamani, Gregorio, and Asunta Quispe Huamán. *Andean Lives*. Edited by Ricardo Valderrama Fernández and Carmen Escalante Gutiérrez. Translated by Paul H. Gelles et al. Austin: University of Texas Press, 1996.

Conrad, Geoffrey W., and Arthur A. Demarest. *Religion and Empire: The Dynamics of Aztec and Incan Expansionism*. Cambridge: Cambridge University Press, 1984.

Cordeu, Edgardo Jorge, and Alejandra Siffredi. *De la algarroba al algodón: movimiento mesiánico de los guaycurú*. Buenos Aires: Juárez Editor, 1971.

Córdova y Salinas, Diego de. *Crónica franciscana de las provincias del Perú*. Edited by Lino G. Canedo. Washington, D.C.: Academy of American Franciscan History, 1957.

Cortés, Hernán. *Letters from Mexico*. Edited and translated by Anthony Pagden. New Haven: Yale University Press, 1986.

Cro, Stelio. *The American Foundations of the Hispanic Utopia (1492–1793)*. 2 vols. Tallahassee: DeSoto Press, 1994.

———. *Realidad y utopía en el descubrimiento y conquista de la América Hispana, 1492–1682*. Troy, Mich.: International Book Publishers, 1983.

Crocker, William H., and Jean Crocker. *The Canela: Bonding Through Kinship, Ritual, and Sex*. New York: Harcourt Brace College Publishers, 1994.

Crumrine, N. Ross, and Marjorie Halpin, eds. *The Power of Symbols: Masks and Masquerade in the Americas*. Vancouver: University of British Columbia Press, 1983.

Da Cunha, Euclides. *Los sertones*. Translated by Estela Dos Santos. Caracas: Biblioteca Ayacucho, 1980.

Damen, Frans, and Esteban Judd Zanon, eds. *Cristo crucificado en los pueblos de América Latina: antología de la religión popular*. Cuzco: Instituto de Pastoral Andina; and Quito: Abya-Yala, 1992.

Davenport, Frances Gardiner, ed. *European Treaties Bearing on the History of the United States and Its Dependencies to 1648*. Washington, D.C.: Carnegie Institution, 1974.

Davidson, James West. *The Logic of Millennial Thought*. New Haven: Yale University Press, 1977.

Davies, Nigel. *The Aztec Empire: The Toltec Resurgence*. Norman: University of Oklahoma Press, 1987.

———. *The Toltecs: Until the Fall of Tula*. Norman: University of Oklahoma Press, 1977.

De Certeau, Michel. *The Writing of History*. Translated by Tom Conley. New York: Columbia University Press, 1988.

————. *Heterologies: Discourse on the Other.* Translated by Brian Massumi. Minneapolis: University of Minnesota Press, 1986.

De Chartreux, Denis. *Este es un compendio breve que tracta d'la manera de como se han de hazer processiones.* Mexico City: Juan Cromberger, 1544.

Degregori, Carlos Iván. *Qué difícil es ser Dios: ideología y violencia política en Sendero Luminoso.* Lima: Zorro de Abajo Ediciones, 1990.

————. *El surgimiento de Sendero Luminoso: Ayacucho 1969–1979.* Lima: Instituto de Estudios Peruanos, 1990.

————. *Sendero Luminoso: los hondos y mortales desencuentros.* Lima: Instituto de Estudios Peruanos, 1986.

————. ed. *Las rondas campesinas y la derrota de Sendero Luminoso.* Lima: Instituto de Esudios Peruanos, 1996.

Degregori, Carlos Iván, and Romeo Grompone. *Demonios y redentores en el nuevo Perú.* Lima: Instituto de Estudios Peruanos, 1991.

Deiros, Pablo Alberto, ed. *Los evangélicos y el poder político en América Latina.* Grand Rapids: Nueva Creación and William B. Eerdmans Publishing, 1986.

Della Cava, Ralph. *Miracle at Joaseiro.* New York: Columbia University Press, 1970.

Delumeau, Jean. *History of Paradise: The Garden of Eden in Myth and Tradition.* Translated by Matthew O'Connell. New York: Continuum, 1995.

————. *Sin and Fear: The Emergence of a Western Guilt Culture, Thirteenth–Eighteenth Centuries.* Translated by Eric Nicholson. New York: St. Martin's Press, 1990.

D'epinay, Christian Lalive. *Haven of the Masses: A Study of the Pentecostal Movement in Chile.* Translated by Marjorie Sandle. London: Lutterworth Press, 1969.

Desroche, Henri. *The Sociology of Hope.* Translated by Carol Martin-Sperry. London: Routledge and Kegan Paul, 1979.

Diacon, Todd A. *Millenarian Vision, Capitalist Reality.* Durham: Duke University Press, 1991.

Díaz del Castillo, Bernal. *The Discovery and Conquest of Mexico.* Edited by Genaro García. Translated by A. P. Maudslay. New York: Farrar, Strauss, and Cudahy, 1956.

Díaz Maderuelo, Rafael. *Francisco de Orellana.* Madrid: Historia 16, 1987.

Dickson, Donald R. *The Fountain of Living Waters.* Columbia: University of Missouri Press, 1987.

Domínguez, Francisco Atanasio. *The Missions of New Mexico.* Translated and annotated by Eleanor B. Adams and Angélico Chávez. Albuquerque: University of New Mexico Press, 1956.

Domínguez, Jorge I., ed. *The Roman Catholic Church in Latin America.* New York: Garland Publishing, 1994.

Dunne, Peter Masten. *Pioneer Jesuits in Northern Mexico.* Berkeley and Los Angeles: University of California Press, 1944.

Duviols, Pierre. *Cultura andina y represión: procesos y visitas de idolatrías y hechicerías en Cajatambo, siglo XVII.* Cuzco: Centro de Estudios Rurales Andinos Bartolomé de Las Casas, 1986.

Edwards, John. *Religion and Society in Spain.* Aldershot, England: Variorum, 1996.

Eliade, Mircea. *Symbolism, the Sacred, and the Arts.* Edited by Diane Apostolos-Cappadona. New York: Crossroad, 1985.

————. *A History of Religious Ideas.* Translated by Willard R. Trask. Chicago: University of Chicago Press, 1982.

————. *The Quest: History and Meaning in Religion.* Chicago: University of Chicago Press, 1969.

———. *The Myth of the Eternal Return: Or, Cosmos and History*. Translated by Willard R. Trask. Princeton: Princeton University Press, 1965.

———. *The Forge and the Crucible*. Translated by Stephen Corrin. London: Rider and Rider, 1962.

———. *The Sacred and the Profane: The Nature of Religion*. Translated by Willard R. Trask. New York: Harper Torchbooks, 1961.

Eliav-Feldon, Miriam. *Realistic Utopias: The Ideal Imaginary Societies of the Renaissance*. Oxford: Clarendon Press, 1982.

Elliott, John H. *Spain and Its World, 1500–1700*. New Haven: Yale University Press, 1989.

———. *The Old World and the New, 1492–1650*. Cambridge: Cambridge University Press, 1970.

———. *Imperial Spain, 1469–1716*. London: Edward Arnold Publishers, 1963.

Emmerson, Richard K., and Bernard McGinn, eds. *The Apocalypse in the Middle Ages*. Ithaca: Cornell University Press, 1992.

Encuentro Internacional Quinto Centenario. *Impacto y futuro de la civilización española en el Nuevo Mundo*. San Juan, P.R.: n.p., 1991.

Escobar, Arturo, and Sonia E. Alvarez, eds. *The Making of Social Movements in Latin America*. Boulder: Westview Press, 1992.

Espinosa, J. Manuel, ed. and trans. *The Pueblo Indian Revolt of 1696 and the Franciscan Missions in New Mexico: Letters of the Missionaries and Related Documents*. Norman: University of Oklahoma Press, 1988.

Falla, Ricardo. *Quiché rebelde: estudio de un movimiento de conversión religiosa, rebelde a las creencias tradicionales, en San Antonio Ilotenango, Quiché (1948–1970s)*. Guatemala City: Editorial Universitaria, 1980.

Fane, Diana, ed. *Converging Cultures: Art and Identity in Spanish America*. New York: Brooklyn Museum and Harry N. Abrams, 1996.

Farriss, Nancy M. *Maya Society Under Colonial Rule: The Collective Enterprise of Survival*. Princeton: Princeton University Press, 1984.

Feinmann, José Pablo. *López Rega, la cara oscura de Perón*. Buenos Aires: Editorial Legasa, 1987.

Felice Cardot, Carlos. *Rebeliones, motines y movimientos de masas en el siglo XVIII venezolano (1730–1781)*. Caracas: Academia Nacional de la Historia, 1977.

Fernández-Armesto, Felipe. *Before Columbus: Exploration and Colonization from the Mediterranean to the Atlantic, 1229–1492*. Philadelphia: University of Pennsylvania Press, 1987.

———. *Ferdinand and Isabella*. New York: Taplinger Publishing, 1975.

———. *Columbus and the Conquest of the Impossible*. New York: Saturday Review Press, 1974.

Fisher, Lillian Estelle. *The Last Inca Revolt, 1780–1783*. Norman: University of Oklahoma Press, 1966.

Flora, Cornelia Butler. *Pentecostalism in Colombia*. Rutherford, N.J.: Fairleigh Dickinson University Press, 1976.

Flores Araoz, José, et al., eds. *Santa Rosa de Lima y su tiempo*. Lima: Colección Arte y Tesoros del Perú, 1995.

Florescano, Enrique. *El mito de Quetzalcóatl*. Mexico City: Fondo de Cultura Económica, 1993.

Flores Galindo, Alberto. *Buscando un inca: identidad y utopía en los Andes*. Lima: Editorial Horizonte, 1988.

———. *Europa y el país de los incas: la utopía andina*. Lima: Instituto de Apoyo Agrario, 1986.

Forbes, Jack D. *Apache, Navaho and Spaniard*. Norman: University of Oklahoma Press, 1960.

Foucault, Michel. *Discipline and Punish: The Birth of the Prison.* Translated by Alan Sheridan. New York: Vintage Books, 1979.

Fourier, Charles. *Design for Utopia.* Edited by Charles Gide. New York: Schocken Books, 1976.

Frank, Larry. *New Kingdom of the Saints.* Santa Fe: Red Crane Books, 1992.

Freyre, Gilberto. *The Masters and the Slaves.* Translated by Samuel Putnam. New York: Alfred A. Knopf, 1963.

Friede, Juan, and Benjamin Keen, eds. *Bartolomé de Las Casas in History: Toward an Understanding of the Man and His Work.* De Kalb: Northern Illinois University Press, 1971.

Friedrich, Paul. *Agrarian Revolt in a Mexican Village.* Englewood Cliffs, N.J.: Prentice-Hall, 1970.

Frye, Northrop. *Anatomy of Criticism.* Princeton: Princeton University Press, 1957.

Galanter, Marc, ed. *Cults and New Religious Movements.* Washington, D.C.: American Psychiatric Association, 1989.

Gálvez, Lucía. *Guaraníes y jesuitas: de la tierra sin mal al paraíso.* Buenos Aires: Editorial Sudamericana, 1995.

Gandía, Enrique de. *Historia crítica de los mitos y leyendas de la conquista americana.* Buenos Aires: Centro Difusor del Libro, 1946.

————. *La ciudad encantada de los Césares.* Buenos Aires: Librería de A. García Santos, 1933.

García, Gregorio. *Origen de los indios del Nuevo Mundo.* Mexico City: Fondo de Cultura Económica, 1981.

García Cantú, Gastón. *Utopías mexicanas.* Mexico City: Fondo de Cultura Económica, 1978.

Garcilaso de la Vega, El Inca. *Royal Commentaries of the Incas and General History of Peru.* Translated by Harold V. Livermore. Austin: University of Texas Press, 1987.

Gardner, Dore, ed. *Niño Fidencio: A Heart Thrown Open.* Santa Fe: Museum of New Mexico Press, 1992.

Garrard-Burnett, Virginia, and David Stoll, eds. *Rethinking Protestantism in Latin America.* Philadelphia: Temple University Press, 1993.

Gerassi, John, ed. *Venceremos! The Speeches and Writings of Ernesto Che Guevara.* New York: Macmillan, 1968.

Gettleman, Marvin E., et al., eds. *El Salvador: Central America in the Cold War.* New York: Grove Press, 1981.

Giamatti, A. Bartlett. *The Earthly Paradise and the Renaissance Epic.* Princeton: Princeton University Press, 1966.

Gil, Juan. *Mitos y utopías del descubrimiento.* 3 vols. Madrid: Alianza, 1989.

Girard, René. *Violence and the Sacred.* Translated by Patrick Gregory. Baltimore: Johns Hopkins University Press, 1977.

Gisbert, Teresa. *Iconografía y mitos indígenas en el arte.* La Paz: Gisbert, 1980.

Glazier, Stephen P. *Perspectives on Pentecostalism: Case Studies from the Caribbean and Latin America.* Washington, D.C.: University Press of America, 1980.

Gómara, Francisco López de. *Historia general de las Indias y vida de Hernán Cortés.* Caracas: Biblioteca Ayacucho, 1979.

————. *Cortés: The Life of the Conqueror by His Secretary.* Edited and translated by Lesley Byrd Simpson. Berkeley and Los Angeles: University of California Press, 1964.

Gomes Moreira, José Aparecido. *Conquista y conciencia cristiana: el pensamiento indigenista y jurídico teológico de Don Vasco de Quiroga.* Quito: Abya-Yala, 1992.

Góngora, Mario. *Studies in the Colonial History of Spanish America.* Translated by Richard Southern. Cambridge: Cambridge University Press, 1975.

González Martínez, José Luis. *La religión popular en el Perú.* Cuzco: Instituto de Pastoral Andina, 1987.

Gorriti Ellenbogen, Gustavo. *Sendero: historia de la guerra milenaria en el Perú.* Lima: Apoyo, 1990.

Gosner, Kevin. *Soldiers of the Virgin: The Moral Economy of a Colonial Maya Rebellion.* Tucson: University of Arizona Press, 1992.

Gossen, Gary H., ed. *South and Meso-American Native Spirituality: From the Cult of the Feathered Serpent to the Theology of Liberation.* New York: Crossroad, 1993.

Grabar, André. *Early Christian Art.* Translated by Stuart Gilbert and James Emmons. New York: Odyssey Press, 1968.

Graziano, Frank. *Divine Violence: Spectacle, Psychosexuality, and Radical Christianity in the Argentine "Dirty War."* Boulder: Westview Press, 1992.

Greenblatt, Stephen. *Marvelous Possessions: The Wonder of the New World.* Chicago: University of Chicago Press, 1991.

———, ed. *New World Encounters.* Berkeley and Los Angeles: University of California Press, 1993.

Gross, Liza. *Handbook of Leftist Guerilla Groups in Latin America and the Caribbean.* Boulder: Westview Press, 1995.

Gruzinski, Serge. *The Conquest of Mexico: The Incorporation of Indian Societies into the Western World, Sixteenth–Eighteenth Centuries.* Translated by Eileen Corrigan. Cambridge, U.K.: Polity Press, 1993.

———. *Painting the Conquest: The Mexican Indians and the European Renaissance.* Translated by Deke Dusinberre. Paris: UNESCO/Flammarion, 1992.

———. *Man-Gods in the Mexican Highlands: Indian Power and Colonial Society, 1520–1800.* Translated by Eileen Corrigan. Stanford: Stanford University Press, 1989.

Guaman Poma de Ayala, Felipe. *Nueva crónica y buen gobierno.* Edited by Franklin Pease. Caracas: Biblioteca Ayacucho, 1980.

Guerra, Francisco. *The Pre-Columbian Mind.* London: Seminar Press, 1971.

Guevara, Che. *Guerrilla Warfare.* Translated by J. P. Morray. New York: Vintage Books, 1968.

Guillot, Carlos Federico. *Negros rebeldes y negros cimarrones.* Buenos Aires: Fariña Editores, 1961.

Gutiérrez, Gustavo. *The God of Life.* Translated by Matthew J. O'Connell. Maryknoll, N.Y.: Orbis Books, 1991.

———. *The Truth Shall Make You Free: Confrontations.* Translated by Matthew J. O'Connell. Maryknoll, N.Y.: Orbis Books, 1990.

———. *A Theology of Liberation: History, Politics and Salvation.* Translated by Caridad Inda and John Eagleson. Maryknoll, N.Y.: Orbis Books, 1973.

Gutiérrez, Ramón A. *When Jesus Came, the Corn Mothers Went Away: Marriage, Sexuality, and Power in New Mexico, 1500–1846.* Stanford: Stanford University Press, 1991.

Gutiérrez Estévez, Manuel, ed. *Mito y ritual en América.* Madrid: Editorial Alhambra, 1988.

Hackett, Charles Wilson, ed. *Revolt of the Pueblo Indians of New Mexico and Otermín's Attempted Reconquest, 1680–1682.* Albuquerque: University of New Mexico Press, 1970.

Hale, Charles R. *Resistance and Contradiction: Miskitu Indians and the Nicaraguan State, 1894–1987.* Stanford: Stanford University Press, 1994.

Haliczer, Stephen. *Sexuality in the Confessional.* New York: Oxford University Press, 1996.

Hallenbeck, Cleve. *The Journeys of Fray Marcos de Niza*. Westport, Conn.: Greenwood Press, 1973.

Hamerton-Kelly, Robert G., ed. *Violent Origins: Walter Burkert, René Girard, and Jonathan Z. Smith on Ritual Killing and Cultural Formation*. Stanford: Stanford University Press, 1987.

Hamill, Hugh M., ed. *Caudillos: Dictators in Spanish America*. Norman: University of Oklahoma Press, 1992.

Hammond, George P., and Agapito Rey, eds. and trans. *Narratives of the Coronado Expedition, 1540–1542*. Albuquerque: University of New Mexico Press, 1940.

Hamnett, Brian R. *Roots of Insurgency: Mexican Regions, 1750–1824*. Cambridge: Cambridge University Press, 1986.

Hanke, Lewis. *Aristotle and the American Indians*. Bloomington: Indiana University Press, 1975.

———. *The Imperial City of Potosí*. The Hague: Martinus Nijhoff, 1956.

———. *The Spanish Struggle for Justice in the Conquest of America*. Philadelphia: University of Pennsylvania Press, 1949.

———. *The First Social Experiments in America: A Study in the Development of Spanish Indian Policy in the Sixteenth Century*. Cambridge: Harvard University Press, 1935.

Hanke, Lewis, et al., eds. *Cuerpo de documentos del siglo XVI: sobre los derechos de España en las Indias y Filipinas*. Mexico City: Fondo de Cultura Económica, 1977.

Haya de la Torre, Víctor Raúl. *Política aprista*. Lima: Editorial Amauta, 1967.

Headley, John M. *Tommaso Campanella and the Transformation of the World*. Princeton: Princeton University Press, 1997.

Hefner, Robert W., ed. *Conversion to Christianity: Historical and Anthropological Perspectives on a Great Transformation*. Berkeley and Los Angeles: University of California Press, 1993.

Hemming, John. *Amazon Frontier: The Defeat of the Brazilian Indians*. Cambridge: Harvard University Press, 1987.

———. *The Search for El Dorado*. London: Michael Joseph, 1978.

———. *The Conquest of the Incas*. New York: Harvest/Harcourt Brace Jovanovich, 1970.

Hennelly, Alfred T., ed. and trans. *Liberation Theology: A Documentary History*. Maryknoll, N.Y.: Orbis Books, 1990.

Henríquez Ureña, Pedro. *La utopía de América*. Edited by Angel Rama and Rafael Gutiérrez Girardot. Caracas: Biblioteca Ayacucho, 1989.

Hess, David J. *Spirits and Scientists: Ideology, Spiritism, and Brazilian Culture*. University Park: Pennsylvania State University Press, 1991.

Hill, Jonathan D. *Keepers of the Sacred Chants: The Poetics of Ritual Power in Amazonian Society*. Tucson: University of Arizona Press, 1993.

———, ed. *Rethinking History and Myth: Indigenous South American Perspectives on the Past*. Urbana: University of Illinois Press, 1988.

Hobsbawm, Eric J. *Primitive Rebels: Studies in Archaic Forms of Social Movement in the Nineteenth and Twentieth Centuries*. New York: W. W. Norton, 1959.

Hodges, Donald. *Sandino's Communism: Spiritual Politics for the Twenty-first Century*. Austin: University of Texas Press, 1992.

———. *The Latin American Revolution: Politics and Strategy from Apro-Marxism to Guevarism*. New York: William Morrow, 1974.

Huerga, Alvaro. *Historia de los alumbrados*. Vol. 3, *Los alumbrados de Hispanoamérica, 1570–1630*. Madrid: Fundación Universitaria Española, Seminario Cisneros, 1986.

Huerta, María Teresa, and Patricia Palacios. *Rebeliones indígenas de la época colonial*. Mexico City: Instituto Nacional de Antropología e Historia, 1976.

Hughes, Robert. *Heaven and Hell in Western Art*. New York: Stein and Day Publishers, 1968.

Immerman, Richard H. *The CIA in Guatemala*. Austin: University of Texas Press, 1982.

Ivereigh, Austen. *Catholicism and Politics in Argentina, 1810–1960*. New York: St. Martin's Press, 1995.

Jochamowitz, Luis. *Ciudadano Fujimori: la construcción de un político*. Lima: Peisa, 1993.

Jones, Grant D., ed. *Anthropology and History in Yucatán*. Austin: University of Texas Press, 1977.

Jos, Emiliano. *La expedición de Ursúa al Dorado, la rebelión de Lope de Aguirre, y el itinerario de los "Marañones."* Huesca, Spain: Imprenta V. Campo, 1927.

Juan Pablo II. *Viaje apostólico a Centroamérica*. Vatican City: Librería Editrice Vaticana; and Madrid: Biblioteca de Autores Cristianos, 1983.

Kadir, Djelal. *Columbus and the Ends of the Earth: Europe's Prophetic Rhetoric as Conquering Ideology*. Berkeley and Los Angeles: University of California Press, 1992.

Kagan, Richard L., and Geoffrey Parker, eds. *Spain, Europe and the Atlantic World: Essays in Honor of John H. Elliott*. New York: Cambridge University Press, 1995.

Kantorowicz, Ernst H. *The King's Two Bodies: A Study in Medieval Political Theology*. Princeton: Princeton University Press, 1957.

Kapsoli, Wilfredo. *Guerreros de la oración: las nuevas iglesias en el Perú*. Lima: Sepec, 1996.

———. *Los movimientos campesinos en el Perú*. Lima: Ediciones Atusparia, 1982.

Kermode, Frank. *The Sense of an Ending: Studies in the Theory of Fiction*. New York: Oxford University Press, 1967.

Kimble, George H. T. *Geography in the Middle Ages*. New York: Russell and Russell, 1968.

Kirk, Robin. *Grabado en piedra: las mujeres de Sendero Luminoso*. Lima: Instituto de Estudios Peruanos, 1993.

Klaiber, Jeffrey. *The Catholic Church in Peru, 1821–1985*. Washington, D.C.: Catholic University of America Press, 1992.

———. *Religión y revolución en el Perú, 1824–1988*. Lima: Universidad del Pacífico, 1988.

———. *Religion and Revolution in Peru, 1824–1976*. Notre Dame, Ind.: University of Notre Dame Press, 1977.

Knaut, Andrew L. *The Pueblo Revolt of 1680: Conquest and Resistance in Seventeenth-Century New Mexico*. Norman: University of Oklahoma Press, 1995.

Kohlenberger, John R., II, ed. *The Precise Parallel New Testament*. New York: Oxford University Press, 1995.

Kraspedon, Dino. *My Contact with Flying Saucers*. Translated by J. B. Wood. Hackensack, N.J.: Neville Spearman/Wehman Brothers, 1959.

Krauze, Enrique. *Porfirio Díaz: místico de la autoridad*. Mexico City: Fondo de Cultura Económica, 1987.

Kumar, Krishan. *Utopianism*. Minneapolis: University of Minnesota Press, 1991.

———. *Utopia and Anti-Utopia in Modern Times*. Oxford: Basil Blackwell, 1987.

Kumar, Krishan, and Stephen Bann. *Utopias and the Millennium*. London: Reaktion Books, 1993.

LaFarge, Oliver. *Santa Eulalia: The Religion of a Cuchumatán Town*. Chicago: University of Chicago Press, 1947.

Lafaye, Jacques. *Mesías, cruzadas, utopías: el judeo-cristianismo en las sociedades ibéricas*. Translated by Juan José Utrilla. Mexico City: Fondo de Cultura Económica, 1984.

———. *Quetzalcóatl y Guadalupe: la formación de la conciencia nacional en México*. Translated by Ida Vitale. Mexico City: Fondo de Cultura Económica, 1977.

Lagos Schuffeneger, Humberto, and Arturo Chacón Herrera. *La religión en las fuerzas armadas y de orden*. Santiago: Presor, 1987.

Lancaster, Roger N. *Life Is Hard: Machismo, Danger, and the Intimacy of Power in Nicaragua*. Berkeley and Los Angeles: University of California Press, 1992.

Landes, Richard. *Relics, Apocalypse, and the Deceits of History*. Cambridge: Harvard University Press, 1995.

Langer, Erick, and Robert H. Jackson, eds. *The New Latin American Mission History*. Lincoln: University of Nebraska Press, 1995.

Lanternari, Vittorio. *The Religions of the Oppressed: A Study of Modern Messianic Cults*. Translated by Lisa Sergio. New York: Alfred A. Knopf, 1963.

Las Casas, Bartolomé de. *Historia de las Indias*. Edited by André Saint-Lu. Caracas: Biblioteca Ayacucho, 1986.

———. *Brevísima relación de la destrucción de las Indias*. Edited by André Saint-Lu. Madrid: Cátedra, 1984.

———. *Del Único modo de traer a todos los pueblos a la verdadera religión*. Mexico City: Fondo de Cultura Económica, 1942.

Lasky, Melvin J. *Utopia and Revolution: On the Origins of a Metaphor*. Chicago: University of Chicago Press, 1976.

Lastres, Juan B. *Lope de Aguirre, el rebelde*. Lima: Ministerio de Relaciones Exteriores del Perú, 1942.

Laviana Cuetos, María Luisa. *José Martí: la libertad de Cuba*. Madrid: Ediciones Anaya, 1988.

LeBeau, Bryan F., and Menachem Mor, eds. *Religion in the Age of Exploration: The Case of Spain and New Spain*. Omaha: Creighton University Press, 1996.

Le Bot, Yvon. *La guerra en tierras mayas: comunidad, violencia y modernidad en Guatemala (1970–1992)*. Mexico City: Fondo de Cultura Económica, 1995.

Le Goff, Jacques. *Medieval Civilization*. Translated by Julia Barrow. New York: Basil Blackwell, 1989.

Lehmann, David. *Democracy and Development in Latin America: Economics, Politics, and Religion in the Post-War Period*. Philadelphia: Temple University Press, 1990.

León, Nicolás, ed. *Documentos ineditos referentes al ilustrísimo señor Don Vasco de Quiroga*. Mexico City: Antigua Librería Robredo, 1940.

León Pinelo, Antonio de. *El paraíso en el nuevo mundo*. 2 vols. Edited by Raúl Porras Barrenechea. Lima: Comité del IV Centenario del Descubrimiento del Amazonas, 1943.

León-Portilla, Miguel. *The Aztec Image of Self and Society: An Introduction to Nahua Culture*. Edited by J. Jorge Klor de Alva. Salt Lake City: University of Utah Press, 1992.

———, ed. *The Broken Spears: The Aztec Account of the Conquest of Mexico*. Boston: Beacon Press, 1992.

Lessa, William A., and Evon Z. Vogt, eds. *Reader in Comparative Religion: An Anthropological Approach.* Evanston, Ill: Row, Peterson, 1958.

Lestringant, Frank. *Mapping the Renaissance World: The Geographical Imagination in the Age of Discovery.* Translated by David Fausett. Cambridge, U.K.: Polity Press, 1994.

Levenson, Jay A., ed. *Circa 1492: Art in the Age of Exploration.* Washington, D.C.: National Gallery of Art; and New Haven: Yale University Press, 1991.

Levine, Daniel H. *Popular Voices in Latin American Catholicism.* Princeton: Princeton University Press, 1992.

Levine, Robert M. *Father of the Poor? Vargas and His Era.* Cambridge: Cambridge University Press, 1998.

———. *Vale of Tears: Revisiting the Canudos Massacre in Northeastern Brazil, 1893–1897.* Berkeley and Los Angeles: University of California Press, 1992.

Lewin, Boleslao. *La rebelión de Túpac Amaru y los orígenes de la emancipación americana.* Buenos Aires: Librería Hachette, 1957.

Liévano Aguirre, Indalecio. *Bolívar.* Madrid: Instituto de Cooperación Iberoamericana, 1983.

Lincoln, Bruce, ed. *Religion, Rebellion, Revolution: An Interdisciplinary and Cross-Cultural Collection of Essays.* London: Macmillan, 1985.

Lisón Tolosana, Carmelo. *La imagen del rey: monarquía, realeza y poder ritual en la Casa de los Austrias.* Madrid: Espasa-Calpe, 1992.

Liss, Peggy K. *Isabel the Queen: Life and Times.* New York: Oxford University Press, 1992.

Loayza, Francisco A., ed. *Juan Santos, el invencible: manuscritos del año de 1742 al año de 1755.* Lima: Pequeños Grandes Libros de Historia Americana, 1942.

Lockhart, James, ed. and trans. *We People Here: Nahuatl Accounts of the Conquest of Mexico.* Berkeley and Los Angeles: University of California Press, 1993.

López Austin, Alfredo. *The Human Body and Ideology Concepts of the Ancient Nahuas.* 2 vols. Translated by Thelma Ortiz de Montellano and Bernard Ortiz de Montellano. Salt Lake City: University of Utah Press, 1988.

———. *Hombre-dios: religión y política en el mundo náhuatl.* Mexico City: Universidad Nacional Autónoma de México, 1973.

López-Baralt, Mercedes. *El retorno del inca rey: mito y profecía en el mundo andino.* La Paz: Hisbol, 1989.

López Cantos, Angel. *Juegos, fiestas, y diversiones en la América española.* Madrid: Editorial MAPFRE, 1992.

Loveman, Brian, and Thomas M. Davies Jr. *The Politics of Antipolitics: The Military in Latin America.* Lincoln: University of Nebraska Press, 1989.

Lowenthal, Abraham F. *Partners in Conflict: The United States and Latin America.* Baltimore: Johns Hopkins University Press, 1987.

Lozano, Pedro. *Historia de la Compañía de Jesús de la provincia del Paraguay.* Westmead, England: Gregg International Publishers, 1970.

Lugones, Leopoldo. *El imperio jesuítico.* Buenos Aires: Comisión Argentina de Fomento Interamericano, 1945.

Lynch, Edward A. *Religion and Politics in Latin America: Liberation Theology and Christian Democracy.* New York: Praeger, 1991.

Lynch, John. *Caudillos in Spanish America, 1800–1850.* Oxford: Clarendon Press, 1992.

———. *The Spanish American Revolutions.* New York: W. W. Norton, 1973.

———. *Spain Under the Habsburgs.* New York: New York University Press, 1964.

MacCormack, Sabine. *Religion in the Andes: Vision and Imagination in Early Colonial Peru.* Princeton: Princeton University Press, 1991.

MacLachlan, Colin M. *Spain's Empire in the New World: The Role of Ideas in Institutional and Social Change.* Berkeley and Los Angeles: University of California Press, 1988.

Madsen, Douglas, and Peter G. Snow. *The Charismatic Bond: Political Behavior in Time of Crisis.* Cambridge: Harvard University Press, 1991.

Magaña, Edmundo, and Peter Mason, eds. *Myth and the Imaginary in the New World.* Dordrecht, Holland: Foris Publications, 1986.

Maier, Joseph, and Richard W. Weatherhead, eds. *Politics of Change in Latin America.* New York: Praeger, 1964.

Malamud, Carlos. *Juan Manuel de Rosas.* Madrid: Historia 16, 1987.

Mallin, Jay, ed. *"Che" Guevara on Revolution: A Documentary Overview.* Coral Gables: University of Miami Press, 1969.

Mallon, Florencia E. *Peasant and Nation: The Making of Postcolonial Mexico and Peru.* Berkeley and Los Angeles: University of Californial Press, 1995.

Mandeville, John. *The Travels of John Mandeville.* Translated by C. W. R. D. Moseley. New York: Penguin Books, 1983.

Mannheim, Karl. *Ideology and Utopia.* New York: Harvest, 1936.

Manuel, Frank E., ed. *Utopias and Utopian Thought.* Boston: Houghton Mifflin, 1966.

Maravall, José Antonio. *Utopía y reformismo en la España de los Austrias.* Mexico City: Siglo Veintiuno, 1982.

Margery Peña, Enrique. *El mito del diluvio en la tradición indoamericana.* Quito: Abya-Yala, 1997.

Mariátegui, José Carlos. *Siete ensayos de interpretación de la realidad peruana.* Lima: Editora Amauta, 1989.

Marin, Louis. *Utopics: Spatial Play.* Translated by Robert A. Vollrath. Atlantic Highlands, N.J.: Humanities Press, 1984.

Marsden, John Joseph. *Marxian and Christian Utopianism: Toward a Socialist Political Theory.* New York: Monthly Review Press, 1991.

Martí, José. *Our America: Writings on Latin America and the Struggle for Cuban Independence.* Edited by Philip S. Foner. New York: Monthly Review Press, 1977.

Martínez, Abelino. *Las sectas en Nicaragua: oferta y demanda de salvación.* Managua: Editorial Departamento Ecuménico de Investigaciones, 1989.

Martínez, Nelson. *Juan Domingo Perón.* Madrid: Historia 16, 1987.

Marty, Martin E., and R. Scott Appleby, eds., *Accounting for Fundamentalisms: The Dynamic Character of Movements.* Chicago: University of Chicago Press, 1994.

Martyr D'Anghera, Pedro. *De Orbe Novo.* Translated by Francis Augustus MacNutt. New York: Burt Franklin, 1970.

Marx, Karl, and Friedrich Engels. *The Communist Manifesto.* Edited by A. J. P. Taylor. New York: Penguin Books, 1967.

Marzal, Manuel M. *Los caminos religiosos de los inmigrantes en la gran Lima: el caso de El Agustino.* Lima: Pontificia Universidad Católica del Perú, 1989.

———. *La transformación religiosa peruana.* Lima: Pontificia Universidad Católica del Perú, 1983.

———. *El mundo religioso de Urcos.* Cuzco: Instituto de Pastoral Andina, 1971.

———, ed. *El rostro indio de Dios.* Lima: Pontificia Universidad Católica del Perú, 1991.

Masur, Gerhard. *Simon Bolivar.* Albuquerque: University of New Mexico Press, 1948.

McAlister, Lyle N. *Spain and Portugal in the New World, 1492–1700.* Minneapolis: University of Minnesota Press, 1984.

McGinn, Bernard. *Visions of the End: Apocalyptic Traditions in the Middle Ages.* New York: Columbia University Press, 1979.

McManners, John, ed. *The Oxford Illustrated History of Christianity.* Oxford: Oxford University Press, 1990.

Medina Ruiz, Fernando. *El paraíso demolido: las reducciones jesuíticas del Paraguay.* Mexico City: Tradición, 1987.

Mellafe, Rolando. *Negro Slavery in Latin America.* Translated by J. W. S. Judge. Berkeley and Los Angeles: University of California Press, 1975.

Menchú, Rigoberta. *I, Rigoberta Menchú: An Indian Woman in Guatemala.* Edited by Elisabeth Burgos-Debray. Translated by Ann Wright. London: Verso, 1984.

Mendieta, Gerónimo de. *Historia eclesiástica indiana.* Mexico City: Editorial Porrúa, 1980.

Merrill, William L. *Rarámuri Souls: Knowledge and Social Process in Northern Mexico.* Washington, D.C.: Smithsonian Institution Press, 1988.

Meyer, Michael C., and William L. Sherman. *The Course of Mexican History.* New York: Oxford University Press, 1983.

Mier, Servando Teresa de. *Ideario político.* Caracas: Biblioteca Ayacucho, 1978.

Mignolo, Walter D. *The Darker Side of the Renaissance: Literacy, Territoriality, and Colonization.* Ann Arbor: University of Michigan Press, 1995.

Milhou, Alain. *Colón y su mentalidad mesiánica en el ambiente franciscanista medieval.* Valladolid, Spain: Casa-Museo de Colón, 1983.

Miller, Patrick D., Jr. *The Divine Warrior in Early Israel.* Cambridge: Harvard University Press, 1973.

Millones, Luis. *Actores de altura: ensayos sobre el teatro popular andino.* Lima: Editorial Horizonte, 1992.

————. *Mesianismo e idolatría en los Andes centrales.* Buenos Aires: Editorial Biblos, 1989.

————. *Historia y poder en los Andes centrales (desde los orígenes al siglo XVII).* Madrid: Alianza, 1987.

————, ed. *El retorno de las huacas: estudios y documentos sobre el Taki Onqoy, siglo XVI.* Lima: Instituto de Estudios Peruanos and Sociedad Peruana de Psicoanálisis, 1990.

Mills, Kenneth. *An Evil Lost to View? An Investigation of Post-Evangelisation Andean Religion in Mid-Colonial Peru.* Liverpool: Institute of Latin American Studies, University of Liverpool, 1994.

Minge, Ward Alan. *Acoma: Pueblo in the Sky.* Albuquerque: University of New Mexico Press, 1991.

Mires, Fernando. *La rebelión permanente: las revoluciones sociales en América Latina.* Mexico City: Siglo Veintiuno, 1988.

Mitchell, William P. *Peasants on the Edge: Crop, Cult, and Crisis in the Andes.* Austin: University of Texas Press, 1991.

Moffitt, John F., and Santiago Sebastián. *O Brave New People: The European Invention of the American Indian.* Albuquerque: University of New Mexico Press, 1996.

Mondragón, Rafael. *De indios y cristianos en Guatemala.* Mexico City: COPEC/CECOPE, 1983.

Monteagudo, Bernardo. *Diálogo entre Atawallpa y Fernando VII en los Campos Elíseos.* Edited by Carlos Castañón Barrientos. La Paz: n.p., 1973.

Montejo, Esteban. *The Autobiography of a Runaway Slave.* Edited by Miguel Barnet. New York: Pantheon Books, 1968.

Montesinos, Fernando. *Memorias antiguas historiales del Perú.* Edited and translated by Philip Ainsworth Means. London: Hakluyt Society, 1920.

Morales, Ernesto. *La ciudad encantada de la Patagonia.* Buenos Aires: Emecé Editores, 1944.

More, Sir Thomas. *Utopia*. Edited and translated by Robert M. Adams. New York: W. W. Norton, 1975.

Moreno Cebrián, Alfredo. *Túpac Amaru: el cacique inca que rebeló los Andes.* Mexico City: Biblioteca Iberoamericana, 1988.

Moreno Fraginals, Manuel, ed. *Africa en América Latina.* Mexico City: Siglo Veintiuno, 1977.

Moreno Yánez, Segundo E. *Sublevaciones indígenas en la audiencia de Quito: desde comienzos del siglo XVII hasta finales de la colonia.* Quito: Ediciones de la Universidad Católica, 1985.

Morote Best, Efraín. *Aldeas sumergidas: cultura popular y sociedad en los Andes.* Cuzco: Centro de Estudios Rurales Andinos Bartolomé de Las Casas, 1988.

Mozans, H. J. *Along the Andes and Down the Amazon.* New York: D. Appleton, 1912.

Murray, Henry A., ed. *Myths and Mythmaking.* Boston: Beacon Press, 1960.

Myers, Joan, et al. *Santiago: Saint of Two Worlds.* Albuquerque: University of New Mexico Press, 1991.

Nadra, Fernando. *Conversaciones con Perón.* Buenos Aires: Editorial Anteo, 1985.

Nájera-Ramírez, Olga. *La Fiesta de los Tastoanes: Critical Encounters in Mexican Festival Performance.* Albuquerque: University of New Mexico Press, 1997.

Naylor, Thomas H., and Charles W. Polzer, eds. *The Presidio and Militia on the Northern Frontier of New Spain.* Tucson: University of Arizona Press, 1986.

Nebel, Richard. *Santa María Tonantzin, Virgen de Guadalupe: continuidad y transformación religiosa en México.* Translated by Carlos Warnholtz Bustillos et al. Mexico City: Fondo de Cultura Económica, 1995.

Nelson, Wilton M. *Protestantism in Central America.* Grand Rapids: William B. Eerdmans Publishing, 1982.

Nimuendajú-Unkel, Curt. *Los mitos de creación y de destrucción del mundo como fundamento de la religión de los Apapokúva-Guaraní.* Edited by Juergen Riester G. Lima: Centro Amazónico de Antropología y Aplicación Práctica, 1978.

———. *The Tukuna.* Berkeley and Los Angeles: University of California Press, 1957.

Núñez Cabeza de Vaca, Alvar. *Naufragios y comentarios.* Madrid: Espasa-Calpe, 1985.

Nunn, Frederick M. *The Time of the Generals: Latin American Professional Militarism in World Perspective.* Lincoln: University of Nebraska Press, 1992.

Nutini, Hugo G. *Todos Santos in Rural Tlaxcala: A Syncretic, Expressive, and Symbolic Analysis of the Cult of the Dead.* Princeton: Princeton University Press, 1988.

O'Donnell, Guillermo. *Modernization and Bureaucratic-Authoritarian Regimes: Studies in South American Politics.* Berkeley: Institute of International Studies, 1973.

Oettinger, Marion, Jr., ed. *Folk Art of Spain and the Americas: El Alma del Pueblo.* New York: San Antonio Museum of Art and Abbeville Press, 1997.

O'Gorman, Edmundo. *The Invention of America: An Inquiry into the Historical Nature of the New World and the Meaning of Its History.* Bloomington: Indiana University Press, 1961.

O'Leary, Daniel Florencio. *Bolívar and the War of Independence.* Edited and translated by Robert F. McNerney Jr. Austin: University of Texas Press, 1970.

O'Leary, Stephen D. *Arguing the Apocalypse: A Theory of Millennial Rhetoric.* New York: Oxford University Press, 1993.

Oliva de Coll, Josefina. *La resistencia indígena ante la conquista.* Mexico City: Siglo Veintiuno, 1974.

Olson, Theodore. *Millennialism, Utopianism, and Progress.* Toronto: University of Toronto Press, 1982.

Orellana, Margarita de. *Villa y Zapata: la revolución mexicana.* Madrid: Ediciones Anaya, 1988.

Ortiz Rescaniere, Alejandro. *Huarochirí: 400 años después.* Lima: Pontificia Universidad Católica del Perú, 1980.

———. *De Adaneva a Inkarrí: una visión indígena del Perú.* Lima: Ediciones Retablo de Papel, 1973.

Ossio, Juan M. *Los indios del Perú.* Quito: Abya-Yala, 1995.

———, ed. *Ideología mesiánica del mundo andino.* Lima: Ignacio Prado Pastor, 1973.

Otero Silva, Miguel. *Casas muertas; Lope de Aguirre, príncipe de la libertad.* Caracas: Biblioteca Ayacucho, 1985.

Ouweneel, Arij, and Simon Miller, eds. *The Indian Community of Colonial Mexico.* Amsterdam: CEDLA Publications, 1990.

Ovid, *Metamorphoses.* Translated by Mary M. Innes. New York: Penguin Books, 1986.

Pagden, Anthony. *Lords of All the World: Ideologies of Empire in Spain, Britain and France, c. 1500–c. 1800.* New Haven: Yale University Press, 1995.

———. *Spanish Imperialism and the Political Imagination: Studies in European and Spanish-American Social and Political Theory, 1513–1830.* New Haven: Yale University Press, 1990.

———. *The Fall of Natural Man: The American Indian and the Origins of Comparative Ethnology.* Cambridge: Cambridge University Press, 1982.

Page, Joseph A. *Perón: A Biography.* New York: Random House, 1983.

Palmer, David Scott, ed. *The Shining Path of Peru.* New York: St. Martin's Press, 1992.

Pardo, Isaac J. *Fuegos bajo el agua: la invención de utopía.* Caracas: Biblioteca Ayacucho, 1990.

Pargellis, Stanley, ed. *The Quest for Political Unity in World History.* Washington, D.C.: American Historical Association, 1944.

Parker, Christián. *Popular Religion and Modernization in Latin America.* Translated by Robert R. Barr. Maryknoll, N.Y.: Orbis Books, 1996.

Parker, Geoffrey. *Philip II.* Boston: Little, Brown, 1978.

Parry, J. H. *The Discovery of South America.* New York: Taplinger Publishing, 1979.

———. *The Spanish Theory of Empire in the Sixteenth Century.* New York: Octagon Books, 1974.

Parry, J. H., et al. *A Short History of the West Indies.* New York: St. Martin's Press, 1968.

———. *The Audiencia of New Galicia in the Sixteenth Century: A Study in Spanish Colonial Government.* Cambridge: Cambridge University Press, 1948.

Parry, J. H. and Robert G. Keith, eds. *New Iberian World: A Documentary History of the Discovery and Settlement of Latin America to the Early Seventeenth Century.* New York: Times Books, 1983.

Pasinski, Tony. *The Santos of Guatemala.* Guatemala City: Didacsa, 1990.

Pastor, Beatriz. *Discurso narrativo de la conquista de América.* Havana: Ediciones Casa de las Américas, 1983.

Pease G. Y., Franklin. *Las crónicas y los Andes.* Lima: Pontificia Universidad Católica del Perú et al., 1995.

——. *El dios creador andino*. Lima: Mosca Azul Editores, 1973.

Pereira de Queiroz, Maria Isaura. *Historia y etnología de los movimientos mesiánicos: reforma y revolución en las sociedades tradicionales*. Translated by Florentino M. Torner. Mexico City: Siglo Veintiuno, 1969.

Pérez, Joseph. *Los movimientos precursores de la emancipación en Hispanoamérica*. Madrid: Editorial Alhambra, 1977.

Pérez de Oliva, Hernán. *Historia de la invención de las Yndias*. Edited by José Juan Arrom. Bogotá: Publicaciones del Instituto Caro y Cuervo, 1965.

Pérez de Ribas, Andrés. *My Life Among the Savage Nations of New Spain*. Edited and translated by Tomás Antonio Robertson. Los Angeles: Ward Ritchie Press, 1968.

——. *Historia de los triunfos de n.s. fe entre gentes las más bárbaras y fieras del nuevo orbe*. Mexico City: Editorial Layac, 1944.

Perón, Eva. *La palabra, el pensamiento, y la acción de Eva Perón*. Buenos Aires: Editorial Freeland, 1973.

——. *La última voluntad de Eva Perón*. Buenos Aires: Presidencia de la Nación, Subsecretaría de Informaciones, 1952.

——. *Escribe Eva Perón*. Buenos Aires: n.p., 1950.

Perón, Juan. *Yo, Juan Domingo Perón: relato autobiográfico*. Edited by Torcuato Luca de Tena et al. Barcelona: Editorial Planeta, 1976.

——. *Conducción política*. Buenos Aires: Secretaría Política de la Presidencia de la Nación, 1974.

——. *Habla Perón*. Buenos Aires: Editorial Freeland, 1973.

——. *El pueblo ya sabe de qué se trata*. Buenos Aires: Editorial Freeland, 1973.

——. *Tres revoluciones militares*. Buenos Aires: Escorpión Ediciones, 1963.

Perry, Mary Elizabeth, and Anne J. Cruz, eds. *Cultural Encounters: The Impact of the Inquisition in Spain and the New World*. Berkeley and Los Angeles: University of California Press, 1991.

Peters, F. E. *Jerusalem: The Holy City in the Eyes of Chroniclers, Visitors, Pilgrims, and Prophets from the Days of Abraham to the Beginnings of Modern Times*. Princeton: Princeton University Press, 1985.

Peterson, Jeanette Favrot. *The Paradise Garden Murals of Malinalco: Utopia and Empire in Sixteenth-Century Mexico*. Austin: University of Texas Press, 1993.

Phelan, John Leddy. *The People and the King: The Comunero Revolution in Colombia, 1781*. Madison: University of Wisconsin Press, 1978.

——. *The Millennial Kingdom of the Franciscans in the New World*. Berkeley and Los Angeles: University of California Press, 1970.

Pike, Frederick. *The Politics of the Miraculous in Peru: Haya de la Torre and the Spiritualist Tradition*. Lincoln: University of Nebraska Press, 1986.

Pineda, Vicente. *Historia de las sublevaciones indígenas habidas en el estado de Chiapas*. Chiapas: Tipografía del Gobierno, 1888.

Platt, Rutherford H., Jr. *The Forgotten Books of Eden: Lost Books of the Old Testament*. New York: Gramercy Books, 1980.

Plumb, J. H. *The Death of the Past*. Boston: Houghton Mifflin, 1970.

Pollak-Eltz, Angelina. *María Lionza: mito y culto venezolano*. Caracas: Universidad Católica Andrés Bello, 1985.

Polo, Marco. *The Travels of Marco Polo*. Translated by Ronald Latham. New York: Penguin Books, 1958.

Poole, Deborah, and Gerard Rénique. *Peru: Time of Fear*. London: Latin America Bureau, 1992.

Powell, Philip Wayne. *Soldiers, Indians, and Silver: The Northward Advance of*

New Spain, 1550–1600. Berkeley and Los Angeles: University of California Press, 1952.

Price, Richard, ed. *Maroon Societies: Rebel Slave Communities in the Americas*. Garden City: Anchor/Doubleday, 1973.

Rama, Carlos M., ed. *Utopismo socialista, 1830–1893*. Caracas: Biblioteca Ayacucho, 1987.

Rama, Carlos M., and Angel Cappelletti. *El anarquismo en América Latina*. Caracas: Biblioteca Ayacucho, 1990.

Ramírez, Sergio, and Robert Edgar Conrad, eds. *Sandino: The Testimony of a Nicaraguan Patriot, 1921–1934*. Translated by Robert Edgar Conrad. Princeton: Princeton University Press, 1990.

Ramírez, Susan, ed. *Indian-Religious Relations in Colonial Spanish America*. Syracuse: Maxwell School of Citizenship and Public Affairs, Syracuse University, 1989.

Ramos, Gabriela, ed. *La venida del reino: religión, evangelización y cultura en América, siglos XVI–XX*. Cuzco: Centro de Estudios Regionales Andinos Bartolomé de Las Casas, 1994.

Ramos, Gabriela, and Henrique Urbano, eds. *Catolicismo y extirpación de idolatrías, siglos XVI–XVIII: Charcas, Chile, México, Perú*. Cuzco: Centro de Estudios Regionales Andinos Bartolomé de Las Casas, 1993.

Ramos Pérez, Demetrio. *Las variaciones ideológicas en torno al descubrimiento de América*. Valladolid, Spain: Casa-Museo de Colón, 1982.

Rapoport, David C. *Inside Terrorist Organizations*. New York: Columbia University Press, 1988.

Ravicz, Marilyn Ekdahl. *Early Colonial Religious Drama in Mexico: From Tzompantli to Golgotha*. Washington, D.C.: Catholic University Press of America, 1970.

Reed, Nelson. *The Caste War of Yucatan*. Stanford: Stanford University Press, 1964.

Reeves, Marjorie. *Joachim of Fiore and the Prophetic Future*. London: SPCK, 1976.

———. *The Influence of Prophecy in the Later Middle Ages: A Study in Joachimism*. Oxford: Clarendon Press, 1969.

Regan, Jaime. *Hacia la tierra sin mal: estudio sobre la religiosidad del pueblo en la Amazonía*. 2 vols. Iquitos, Peru: CETA, 1983.

Reina, Leticia. *Las rebeliones campesinas en México, 1819–1906*. Mexico City: Siglo Veintiuno, 1980.

Revenga, Luis, ed. *Los Beatos*. Madrid: Biblioteca Nacional, 1986.

Ribeiro, Darcy. *The Americas and Civilization*. Translated by Linton Lomas Barrett and Marie McDavid Barrett. New York: E. P. Dutton, 1971.

Ricard, Robert. *The Spiritual Conquest of Mexico: An Essay on the Apostolate and the Evangelical Methods of the Mendicant Orders in New Spain, 1523–1572*. Translated by Lesley Byrd Simpson. Berkeley and Los Angeles: University of California Press, 1966.

Richard, Pablo, ed. *Raíces de la teología latinoamericana*. San José, Costa Rica: DEI/CEHILA, 1985.

Richard, Pablo, et al., eds. *The Idols of Death and the God of Life*. Translated by Barbara E. Campbell and Bonnie Shepard. Maryknoll, N.Y.: Orbis Books, 1983.

Riley-Smith, Jonathan. *The Crusades: A Short History*. New Haven: Yale University Press, 1987.

Ritter, Kurt, and David Henry. *Ronald Reagan: The Great Communicator*. New York: Greenwood Press, 1992.

Rivarola, Milda, and Pedro Planas, eds. *Víctor Raúl Haya de la Torre*. Madrid: Ediciones de Cultura Hispánica, 1988.

Rocha, Diego Andrés de. *Tratado único y singular del origen de los indios occidentales del Perú, México, Santa Fé, y Chile*. Lima: Imprenta de Manuel de Olivos, 1681.

Rodríguez, Sylvia. *The Matachines Dance: Ritual Symbolism and Interethnic Relations in the Upper Río Grande Valley*. Albuquerque: University of New Mexico Press, 1996.

Rodríguez O., Jaime E. *The Independence of Mexico and the Creation of the New Nation*. Los Angeles: UCLA Latin American Center Publications, 1989.

Rohr, Elisabeth. *La destrucción de los símbolos culturales indígenas*. Quito: Abya-Yala, 1997.

Roig, Arturo Andrés, ed. *La utopía en el Ecuador*. Quito: Banco Central del Ecuador and Corporación Editora Nacional, 1987.

Rostas, Susanna, and André Droogers, eds. *The Popular Use of Popular Religion in Latin America*. Amsterdam: CEDLA Publications, 1993.

Rout, Leslie B., Jr. *The African Experience in Spanish America: 1502 to the Present Day*. Cambridge: Cambridge University Press, 1976.

Rowe, William, and Vivian Schelling. *Memory and Modernity: Popular Culture in Latin America*. London: Verso, 1991.

Salazar, B. *Los doce: primeros apóstoles franciscanos en México*. Mexico City: Imprenta Mexicana, 1943.

Sallnow, Michael J. *Pilgrims of the Andes: Regional Cults in Cuzco*. Washington, D.C.: Smithsonian Institution Press, 1987.

Salomon, Frank, and George L. Urioste, trans. *The Huarochirí Manuscript: A Testament of Ancient and Colonial Andean Religion*. Austin: University of Texas Press, 1991.

Sánchez Albornoz, Claudio. *La edad media española y la empresa de América*. Madrid: Instituto de Cooperación Iberoamericana, 1983.

Sanders, Ronald. *Lost Tribes and Promised Lands*. Boston: Little Brown, 1978.

Sandoval Z., Godofredo, and M. Fernanda Sostres. *La ciudad prometida: pobladores y organizaciones sociales en El Alto*. La Paz: ILDIS-Systema, 1989.

Sanford, Charles L. *The Quest for Paradise: Europe and the American Moral Imagination*. Urbana: University of Illinois Press, 1961.

Scholes, Frances V. *Troublous Times in New Mexico, 1659–1670*. Albuquerque: University of New Mexico Press, 1942.

Schroeder, Susan, ed. *Native Resistance and the Pax Colonial in New Spain*. Lincoln: University of Nebraska Press, 1998.

Schwartz, Hillel. *Century's End: A Cultural History of the Fin de Siècle from the 990s through the 1990s*. New York: Doubleday, 1990.

Scott, James C. *Weapons of the Weak: Everyday Forms of Peasant Resistance*. New Haven: Yale University Press, 1985.

Sebastián, Santiago. *El barroco iberoamericano: mensaje iconográfico*. Madrid: Ediciones Encuentro, 1990.

Sebeok, Thomas A., ed. *Carnival*. New York: Mouton Publishers, 1984.

Seed, Patricia. *Ceremonies of Possession in Europe's Conquest of the New World, 1492–1640*. New York: Cambridge University Press, 1995.

Silleta, Alfredo. *Las sectas invaden la Argentina*. Buenos Aires: Puntosur, 1991.

Sinclair, Minor, ed. *The New Politics of Survival: Grassroots Movements in Central America*. New York: Monthly Review Press, 1995.

Skar, Harald O., and Frank Salomon, eds. *Natives and Neighbors in South America*. Göteborg, Sweden: Ethnological Studies 38, 1987.

Smith, Anthony. *Explorers of the Amazon*. New York: Viking, 1990.

Smith, Brian H. *The Church and Politics in Chile*. Princeton: Princeton University Press, 1982.

Solano, Francisco, and Fermín del Pino. *América y la España del siglo XVI.* Madrid: Instituto Gonzalo Fernández de Oviedo, 1982.

Spalding, Karen. *Huarochirí: An Andean Society Under Inca and Spanish Rule.* Stanford: Stanford University Press, 1984.

Spicer, Edward H. *Cycles of Conquest: The Impact of Spain, Mexico, and the United States on the Indians of the Southwest, 1533–1960.* Tucson: University of Arizona Press, 1976.

Spitzer, Robert L., et al. *DSM-III-R Casebook: A Learning Companion to the Diagnostic and Statistical Manual of Mental Disorders.* Washington, D.C.: American Psychiatric Press, 1989.

Sprague de Camp, L. *Lost Continents.* New York: Dover Publications, 1970.

Stallybrass, Peter, and Allon White. *The Politics and Poetics of Transgression.* Ithaca: Cornell University Press, 1986.

Starn, Orin, et al., eds. *The Peru Reader: History, Culture, Politics.* Durham: Duke University Press, 1995.

St. Clair, Michael. *Millenarian Movements in Historical Context.* New York: Garland Publishing, 1992.

Stern, Steve J. *Peru's Indian Peoples and the Challenge of Spanish Conquest: Huamanga to 1640.* Madison: University of Wisconsin Press, 1982,

———. *Populism in Peru: The Emergence of the Masses and the Politics of Social Control.* Madison: University of Wisconsin Press, 1980.

———, ed. *Resistance, Rebellion, and Consciousness in the Andean Peasant World, Eighteenth to Twentieth Centuries.* Madison: University of Wisconsin Press, 1987.

Stevens-Arroyo, Antonio M. *Cave of the Jagua: The Mythological World of the Taínos.* Albuquerque: University of New Mexico Press, 1988.

Stoll, David. *Is Latin America Turning Protestant? The Politics of Evangelical Growth.* Berkeley and Los Angeles: University of California Press, 1990.

Strong, Simon. *Shining Path: Terror and Revolution in Peru.* New York: Times Books, 1992.

Subieta Sagárnaga, Luis. *Bolívar en Potosí.* Potosí, Bolivia: Círculo de Bellas Artes, 1925.

Suess, Paulo. *La nueva evangelización: desafíos históricos y pautas culturales.* Translated by María Victoria C. de Vela. Quito: Abya-Yala, 1991.

Sullivan, Lawrence E. *Icanchu's Drum: An Orientation to Meaning in South American Religions.* New York: Macmillan, 1988.

Sweet, David G., and Gary B. Nash, eds. *Struggle and Survival in Colonial America.* Berkeley and Los Angeles: University of California Press, 1981.

Szemiński, Jan. *Un kuraca, un dios, y una historia.* Jujuy, Argentina: Instituto de Ciencias Antropológicas, 1987.

———. *La utopía tupamarista.* Lima: Pontificia Universidad Católica del Perú, 1983.

Szulc, Tad. *Twilight of the Tyrants.* New York: Henry Holt, 1959.

Tanner, Marie. *The Last Descendant of Aeneas: The Hapsburgs and the Mythic Image of the Emperor.* New Haven: Yale University Press, 1993.

Taviani, Paolo Emilio. *Christopher Columbus: The Grand Design.* London: Orbis Books, 1985.

Taylor, J. M. *Eva Perón: The Myths of a Woman.* Chicago: University of Chicago Press, 1979.

Taylor, William B. *Drinking, Homicide, and Rebellion in Colonial Mexican Villages.* Stanford: Stanford University Press, 1979.

Taylor, William B., and Franklin Pease G. Y., eds. *Violence, Resistance, and Survival in the Americas: Native Americans and the Legacy of Conquest.* Washington, D.C.: Smithsonian Institution Press, 1994.

Tedlock, Dennis, trans. *Popol Vuh: The Definitive Edition of the Mayan Book of the Dawn of Life and the Glories of Gods and Kings*. New York: Simon and Schuster, 1985.

Tena Ramírez, Felipe. *Vasco de Quiroga y sus pueblos de Santa Fe en los siglos XVIII y XIX*. Mexico City: Editorial Porrúa, 1990.

Thacher, John Boyd. *Christopher Columbus: His Life, His Work, His Remains*. New York: G. P. Putnam's Sons, 1904.

Thompson, Damian. *The End of Time: Faith and Fear in the Shadow of the Millennium*. Hanover, N.H.: University Press of New England, 1997.

Thrupp, Sylvia L., ed. *Millennial Dreams in Action*. New York: Schocken Books, 1970.

Tibesar, Antonine. *Franciscan Beginnings in Colonial Peru*. Washington, D.C.: Academy of American Franciscan History, 1953.

Todorov, Tzvetan. *The Conquest of America: The Question of the Other*. Translated by Richard Howard. New York: Harper and Row, 1987.

Torres, Camilo. *Cristianismo y revolución*. Edited by Oscar Maldonado et al. Mexico City: Ediciones Era, 1970.

Tovar de Teresa, Guillermo. *La utopía mexicana del siglo XVI: lo bello, lo verdadero y lo bueno*. Mexico City: Grupo Azabache, 1992.

Tucker, Robert C., ed. *The Marx-Engels Reader*. New York: W. W. Norton, 1978.

Turner, Victor. *Dramas, Fields, and Metaphors: Symbolic Action in Human Society*. Ithaca: Cornell University Press, 1974.

Tuveson, Ernest Lee. *The Redeemer Nation: America's Millennial Role*. Chicago: University of Chicago Press, 1968.

Urbano, Henrique, ed. *Poder y violencia en los Andes*. Cuzco: Centro de Estudios Regionales Andinos Bartolomé de Las Casas, 1991.

Valcárcel, Carlos Daniel. *Rebeliones coloniales sudamericanas*. Mexico City: Fondo de Cultura Económica, 1982.

Valcárcel, Luis E. *Historia del Perú antiguo*. Lima: Editorial Juan Mejía Baca, 1964.

Varese, Stefano. *La sal de los cerros: una aproximación al mundo Campa*. Lima: Ediciones Retablo de Papel, 1973.

Vanderwood, Paul J. *The Power of God Against the Guns of Government*. Stanford: Stanford University Press, 1998.

Vasconcelos, José. *La raza cósmica*. Mexico City: Espasa-Calpe, 1948.

Vázquez, Francisco. *Relación de todo lo que sucedió en la jornada de Omagua y Dorado*. Madrid: Sociedad de Bibliófilos Españoles, 1881.

Vega, Josefa, and Pedro A. Vives. *Lázaro Cárdenas*. Madrid: Historia 16, 1987.

Vega Centeno, Imelda. *Aprismo popular: mito, cultura e historia*. Lima: Tarea, 1985.

Velázquez, Rafael Eladio. *La rebelión de los indios de Arecayá: reacción indígena contra los excesos de la encomienda en el Paraguay*. Asunción: Centro Paraguayo de Estudios Sociológicos, 1965.

Verbeke, Werner, et al., eds. *The Use and Abuse of Eschatology in the Middle Ages*. Louvain, Belgium: Louvain University Press, 1988.

Vespucci, Amérigo. *Cartas de viaje*. Edited by Luciano Fomisano. Madrid: Alianza, 1986.

Vetancurt, Augustín de. *Teatro mexicano*. Mexico City: Autores Clásicos Mexicanos, 1900.

Vidales, Raúl. *Utopía y liberación: el amanecer del indio*. San José, Costa Rica: DEI, 1988.

Vigneras, Louis-Andre. *La búsqueda del paraíso y las legendarias islas del Atlántico*. Valladolid, Spain: Casa-Museo de Colón, 1976.

Villegas, Albelardo, ed. *Antología del pensamiento social y político de América Latina*. Washington, D.C.: Unión Panamericana, 1964.

Villoro, Luis. *Los grandes momentos del indigenismo en México*. Mexico City: Colegio de México, 1950.

Viveiros de Castro, Eduardo. *From the Enemy's Point of View: Humanity and Divinity in an Amazonian Society*. Translated by Catherine V. Howard. Chicago: University of Chicago Press, 1992.

Vives, Pedro A. *Augusto César Sandino*. Madrid: Historia 16, 1987.

———. *Pancho Villa*. Madrid: Historia 16, 1987.

Von Barghahn, Barbara, et al., eds., *Temples of Gold, Crowns of Silver: Reflections of Majesty in the Viceregal Americas*. Washington, D.C.: Art Museum of the Americas, 1991.

Wachtel, Nathan. *Gods and Vampires: Return to Chipaya*. Translated by Carol Volk. Chicago: University of Chicago Press, 1996.

———. *The Vision of the Vanquished: The Spanish Conquest of Peru Through Indian Eyes, 1530–1570*. Translated by Ben Reynolds and Siân Reynolds. New York: Barnes and Noble, 1977.

———. *Sociedad e ideología: ensayos de historia y antropología andinas*. Lima: Instituto de Estudios Peruanos, 1973.

Waite, Arthur Edward. *Alchemists through the Ages*. Blauvelt, N.Y.: Rudolf Steiner Publications, 1970.

Walker, Thomas W., ed. *Reagan Versus the Sandinistas: The Undeclared War on Nicaragua*. Boulder: Westview Press, 1987.

———. *Nicaragua in Revolution*. New York: Praeger, 1982.

Wallis, Roy, ed. *Millennialism and Charisma*. Belfast: Queen's University, 1982.

Walsh, Michael, ed. *Butler's Lives of the Patron Saints*. San Francisco: Harper and Row, 1987.

Warman Gryj, Arturo. *"We Come to Object": The Peasants of Morelos and the National State*. Translated by Stephen K. Ault. Baltimore: Johns Hopkins University Press, 1980.

———. *La danza de moros y cristianos*. Mexico City: Sep/Setentas, 1972.

Warren, Fintan B. *Vasco de Quiroga and His Pueblo-Hospitals of Santa Fe*. Washington, D.C.: Academy of American Franciscan History, 1963.

Warren, Kay B. *The Symbolism of Subordination: Indian Identity in a Guatemalan Town*. Austin: University of Texas Press, 1978.

Wasserstrom, Robert. *Class and Society in Central Chiapas*. Berkeley and Los Angeles: University of California Press, 1983.

Weber, David J., *The Spanish Frontier in North America*. New Haven: Yale University Press, 1992.

———, ed. *New Spain's Far Northern Frontier: Essays on Spain in the American West, 1540–1821*. Albuquerque: University of New Mexico Press, 1979.

Weber, Max. *The Theory of Social and Economic Organization*. Edited by Talcott Parsons. Translated by A. M. Henderson and Talcott Parsons. New York: Free Press, 1947.

Weber, Timothy P. *Living in the Shadow of the Second Coming*. New York: Oxford University Press, 1979.

Weckmann, Luis. *La herencia medieval de México*. 2 vols. Mexico City: Colegio de México, 1984.

West, Delno C., and Sandra Zimdars-Swartz. *Joachim of Fiore: A Study in Spiritual Perception and History*. Bloomington: Indiana University Press, 1983.

Wickham-Crowley, Timothy P. *Guerrillas and Revolution in Latin America*. Princeton: Princeton University Press, 1992.

Wilbert, Johannes, and Karin Simoneau, eds. *Folk Literature of the Sikuani Indians*. Los Angeles: UCLA Latin American Center Publications, 1992.

————, eds. *Folk Literature of the Yanomami Indians*. Los Angeles: UCLA Latin American Center Publications, 1990.

————, eds. *Folk Literature of the Toba Indians*. 2 vols. Los Angeles: UCLA Latin American Center Publications, 1989.

————, eds. *Folk Literature of the Chamacoco Indians*. Los Angeles: UCLA Latin American Center Publications, 1987.

————, eds. *Folk Literature of the Mataco Indians*. Los Angeles: UCLA Latin American Center Publications, 1982.

————, eds. *Folk Literature of the Gê Indians*. Los Angeles: UCLA Latin American Center Publications, 1978.

Willems, Emilio. *Followers of the New Faith*. Nashville: Vanderbilt University Press, 1967.

Williams, Ann, ed. *Prophesy and Millenarianism: Essays in Honor of Marjorie Reeves*. Essex, England: Longman, 1980.

Williams, Jerry M., and Robert E. Lewis, eds. *Early Images of the Americas: Transfer and Invention*. Tucson: University of Arizona Press, 1993.

Wilson, Bryan R. *The Noble Savage: The Primitive Origins of Charisma and Its Contemporary Survivals*. Berkeley and Los Angeles: University of California Press, 1975.

————. *Magic and the Millennium: A Sociological Study of Religious Movements of Protest Among Tribal and Third-World Peoples*. London: Heinemann, 1973.

Wittkower, Rudolf. *Allegory and the Migration of Symbols*. London: Thames and Hudson, 1977.

Wright, Scott. *Promised Land: Death and Life in El Salvador*. Maryknoll, N.Y.: Orbis Books, 1994.

Ximénez, Francsico. *Historia de la provincia de San Vicente de Chiapa y Guatemala*. Guatemala City: Biblioteca Goathemala, 1931.

Zahm, J. A. *The Quest for El Dorado*. New York: D. Appleton, 1977.

Zamora, Margarita. *Language, Authority, and Indigenous History in the Comentarios reales de los incas*. Cambridge: Cambridge University Press, 1988.

Zárate, Agustín de. *The Discovery and Conquest of Peru*. Trans. J. M. Cohn. Baltimore: Penguin Books, 1968.

Zarzar, Alonso. *Apo Capac Huayna, Jesús Sacramentado: mito, utopía y milenarismo*. Lima: Centro Amazónico de Antropología y Aplicación Práctica, 1989.

Zavala, Silvio. *Idearío de Vasco de Quiroga*. Mexico City: Colegio de México, 1995.

————. *The Colonial Period in the History of the New World*. Edited by Max Savelle. Mexico City: Instituto Panamericano de Geografía e Historia, 1962.

————. *Filosofía de la conquista*. Mexico City: Fondo de Cultura Económica, 1947.

————. *La "Utopía" de Tomás Moro en la Nueva España y otros estudios*. Mexico City: Biblioteca Histórica Mexicana, 1937.

Zea, Leopoldo. *¿Por qué América Latina?* Mexico City: Universidad Nacional Autónoma de México, 1988.

Ziólkowski, Mariusz S., and Robert M. Sadowski, eds., *Time and Calendars in the Inca Empire*. Oxford: B.A.R. International, 1989.

Index